St. John the Evangelist Catholic Church

Baptisms
1882-1915

Edward Patrick Arthur

Colonial Roots
17296 Coastal Highway
Lewes, Delaware 19958
800-576-8608
FAX 302-644-0484

Genealogical and Local History Resources for the Mid-Atlantic Region

Visit us on the web at www.colonialroots.com

Visit our store in Lewes, Delaware
Store hours: Monday through Saturday from 10 am to 5 pm
Wednesday from 12 noon to 5 pm

Catalog available upon request

Other Baltimore record books include:

➢ St. John the Evangelist Catholic Church Baptisms 1853-1882
➢ St. Peter the Apostle Church Marriage Records, 1842-1918
➢ St. Paul's Protestant Episcopal Church Records, 1826-1935
➢ First Presbyterian Church Records, 1840-1879
➢ Methodist Records of Baltimore City (3 volumes)
➢ Index of Obituaries and Marriages in the Baltimore Sun (6 volumes covering from 1861-1865, 1866-1870, 1871-1875, 1876-1880, 1881-1885, and 1891-1894)
➢ Baltimore County Deed Abstracts, 1659-1750
➢ Orphans and Indentured Children of Baltimore County, 1777-1797

Visit our website for the most current catalog listings. We also feature a Surname Listing.
Check to see if we have published any books on your family lines

CONTENTS

Dedication

This book is dedicated to all who were born, baptized and raised in old St John's Church, of the Irish 10th Ward of Baltimore City, and for all of those who descended from them.

Introduction

St. John the Evangelist Catholic Church
Valley and Eager Streets, Baltimore MD
Baptisms 1882-1915

This manuscript is the second volume of Baptism transcripts completed for this Catholic Church in Baltimore City. The first volume published in May 2010 covered the period from1853 to 1882. Baltimore City births were not recorded until 1875 so these records are significant to genealogy research. While the St. John's Church Register of Baptisms was preserved on microfilm, the film contains only a snapshot of the Register by date and is a sequential record. I recorded each entry by name and date and did an alphabetical sort so that a researcher can find individual records by name without knowing the date of Baptism. The priests, who recorded this data in the Register, varied in their use of spelling of names either because of a literacy problem or carelessness. In 1870 the Archdiocese of Baltimore required priests to record names in Latin and that caused more problems in understanding what was hand-written into the Register. The actual record, subject to much interpretation by the compiler, was completed by looking at the microfilm images over and over for clarity, reviewing descriptions of "Old Handwriting" and checking unfamiliar names in the Baltimore City Directories. The reader may notice problems with some entries because of what looks like obvious errors such as misspellings. Although an attempt was made to correct these differences it was only done in clear cases of errors in the original record and with great care so as to not create a new record. There are many ways to spell "Flanagan," "Finnegan," "Casey," "Kavanaugh," etc. with changes made as the years went by. I had a patron at the Maryland Historical Society once argue with me that his ancestors were Kane's and not Cain to give you an example of a common problem. The priest and the parents provided these entries in the Register. People looking at these records today can get concerned by a misspelling of a name they have used for years and I hope that they will understand that there are reasons for the differences. Finally, I did my best to include as much information from the original record as I could but notes showing extraordinary circumstances such as births at home (in Dormo), children who were stillborn, and baptisms of "colored" persons or orphans were not included. Any questions over the author's interpretations can be easily resolved by searching the original record that is preserved on microfilm.

When I finished the first volume of St. John's Baptisms (1853-1882), Francis O'Neill, the librarian at the Maryland Historical Society's H. Furlong Baldwin Library, suggested that I compile a second book covering the Baptisms through 1915, which is the last date captured on microfilm. He reasoned that many people who come to the library looking for a connection to their "Irish Roots" are inclined to look for information in the last part of the 19th century and the beginning of the 20th. This period in Baltimore's history was noted for a heavy influx of Irish immigrants. St. John the Evangelist was the center of the Irish "Tenth Ward", one of twenty-four political wards in the City that produced numerous elected officials. The annual St. Patrick's parade features hundreds of marchers proudly displaying their Irish "Tenth Ward" heritage. Many of them with German, Polish and Lithuanian surnames as a result of marriage can now find that unique name in their family background to prove their Irish heritage.

St. John the Evangelist began as a small neighborhood church in a little house on Valley Street near Eager. St James was the closest church but the parishioners were largely German. In the 19th century immigrants tended to gather in specific ethnic areas. Irish Catholics were flooding the churches on the east side of Baltimore City moving from St. Patrick's in Fells Point to St. Vincent de Paul located on North Front Street. The Archdiocese opened St. John's to accommodate the Irish moving from those areas.

The original record of St John the Evangelist's Baptism Register can be found on microfilm at the Maryland Historical Society's H. Furlong Baldwin Library, The Maryland State Archives in Annapolis, MD, and the Archdiocesan of Baltimore Archives at St Mary's Seminary on Roland Avenue in Baltimore City.

<u>Acknowledgements</u>

I received assistance in finishing this manuscript from a number of persons worthy of special mention. Adrianne Mary Arthur, Megan Mary Arthur Madden, Mary Elizabeth Zorzi, Mary Warfield and my wife Betty Mae Cashen Arthur were very helpful in proofing the thousands of entries and making suggestions on presentation, etc. Finally, my thanks go to the genealogical professionals of the Maryland Historical Society and the Maryland Genealogical Society such as Francis O'Neill and Allender Sybert who encouraged me along the way.

Edward P. Arthur 2011

LAST NAME	FIRST NAME	MIDDLE	BAPTISM	BIRTH	Father	Mother	SPONSORS
Abbot	George	Francis	16-Jan-1887	13-Jan-1887	George Abbot	Booth, Margaret	William Booth
Abbott	Milton	Taylor	24-Jan-1897	07-Oct-1876	John Abbott	Merrican, Isabelle	George H. Hoen
Acker	Margaret	Catherine	12-Aug-1883	30-Jul-1883	Peter Acker	Joyce, Mary	Catherine O'Neill
Ackerman	Julia	M.	4-Apr-1904	23-Jun-1859	John Ackerman	[Blank]	George W. Hoen
Adam	Josephine		17-Oct-1885	28-Jul-1885	Frederick Adam	Hupthman, Margaret	Catherine McCann
Adam	William		27-Aug-1899	25-Aug-1899	George Adam	Murrary, Catherine	Mary Adam
Adam	Catherine	Ann	13-Oct-1895	12-Oct-1895	William Adam	Doyle, Margaret	Catherine McIntyre
Adam	Elizabeth		20-May-1888	17-May-1888	William Adam	Doyle, Margaret	Mary Finnessy
Adam	Charles		14-Feb-1886	13-Feb-1886	William C. Adam	Doyle, Margaret	Edward A. Finnessy
Adam	John	Aloysius	02-Mar-1884	29-Feb-1884	William C. Adam	Doyle, Margaret	George Bereis
Adam	Clara	Josephine	12-Feb-1882	07-Feb-1882	William Charles Adam	Doyle, Margaret	James Finnessy
Adam	Francis	William	12-Oct-1890	08-Oct-1890	William Charles Adam	Doyle, Margaret	George Benes
Adam	Francis	Aloysius	8-Apr-1906	29-Mar-1906	William Joseph Adam	O'Connor, Mary	Francis P. Lacy
Adams	Murray	Joseph	4-Dec-1904	25-Nov-1904	George E. Adams	Murrary, Catherine	Linus Duerling
Adams	Clara	Margaret	13-Sep-1908	29-Aug-1908	George Edward Adams	Murray, Catherine Regina	Henry Wigart
Adams	Genevieve	Mary	31-Aug-1902	28-Aug-1902	Joseph Adams	Blum, Mary E.	Albert Adams
Adams	Joseph	H.E.	4-Nov-1906	28-Oct-1906	Joseph M. Adams	Blum, Mary E.	Henry C. Codel
Adams	Leoba	Regina	7-May-1905	30-Apr-1905	Joseph M. Adams	Blum, Mary Elizabeth	John Edelman
Adams	Mary	Agnes	10-Feb-1901	25-Jan-1901	William Adams	Thomas, Mary	William Joseph
Adams	Mildred	Josephine	04-May-1902	19-Apr-1902	William Adams	O'Connor, Mary A.	William Adams
Adams	Laurence	Vincent	24-Apr-1910	10-Apr-1910	William J. Adams	O'Conner, Mary A.	Laurence O'Connor
Adams	Margaret	Catherine	16-Mar-1913	9-Mar-1913	William J. Adams	O'Conner, Mary A.	Catherine O'Connor
Adams	William	C.	25-Dec-1904	10-Dec-1904	William J. Adams	O'Conner, Mary A.	Sara E. O'Connor
Adamson (Colored)	Martin		25-Jul-1892	About 1822	[Blank]	[Blank]	
Ader	Catherine	Veronica	6-Dec-1908	18-Nov-1908	Henry Ader	O'Brien, Catherine	John Lynch
Ader	Julia	Rosalie	28-Jun-1914	14-Jun-1914	Henry Ader	O'Brien, Catherine	William J. Albright
Ader	Mary	Regina	21-May-1905	3-May-1905	Henry Ader	O'Brien, Catherine	Thomas Smart
Ader	William	Leon	16-Mar-1902	26-Feb-1902	Henry Ader	O'Brien, Catherine	William McLaughlin
Adolphus	Ann	Christian	5-Nov-1911	17-Oct-1911	John Adolphus	Ahart, Genevieve	George Adolphus
Affayroux	Helen	Elizabeth	26-Feb-1888	15-Feb-1888	James Affayroux	Hatton, Mary	Daniel V.I. O'Sullivan
Affayroux	John	Edward	12-Aug-1883	08-Sep-1883	James Affayroux	Hatton, Mary	Catherine McMahon
Affayroux	Francis	Peter	26-Feb-1882	16-Feb-1882	James Henry Affayroux	Hatton, Mary Joan	Elizabeth Affayroux
Affayroux	John	Francis	04-Feb-1883	21-Jan-1883	John Francis Affayroux	McCarron, Mary Catherine	Mary Teresa Affayroux
Affayroux	Mary	Irene	17-Aug-1884	04-Aug-1884	John Francis Affayroux	McCarron, Mary Catherine	Thelma Brannam
Affayroux	Agnes	Elizabeth	12-Aug-1894	26-Jul-1894	William Affayroux	Connolly, Mary	Ann McShane
Affayroux	Ann	Elizabeth	29-Mar-1885	14-Mar-1885	William Affayroux	Connolly, Mary	Ann R. Connolly
Affayroux	Genevieve		26-Sep-1886	07-Sep-1886	William Affayroux	Connolly, Mary	Roae Connolly
Affayroux	Gertrude		26-Oct-1890	17-Sep-1890	William Affayroux	Connolly, Mary	Ann McShane
Affayroux	Mary	Teresa	02-Sep-1883	23-Aug-1883	William Affayroux	Connolly, Mary	Sara Affayroux
Affayroux	Mary	Rose	21-Mar-1897	05-Mar-1897	William Affayroux	Connolly, Mary Teresa	Francis Dolan
Affayroux	Thomas		11-Jun-1893	25-May-1893	William Affayroux	Connolly, Mary	John McShane
Affayroux	William	Charles	11-Aug-1889	31-Jul-1889	William Affayroux	Connolly, Mary	Timothy McShane
Affayroux	Francis	Peter	29-Nov-1891	18-Nov-1891	William Moore Affayroux	Connolly, Mary Teresa	Edward John Connelly
Affreux	Agnes		26-Apr-1885	07-Apr-1885	John Affreux	Ward, Mary	Bernard Ward
Ahearn	Jerome		15-Oct-1893	11-Oct-1893	Jerome Ahearn	Welsh, Mary	James Thorton
Ahern	Alice		10-Jun-1888	21-May-1888	Lawrence Ahern	Kelly, Catherine	Charles L. Ahern
Ahern	Lawrence		19-Jan-1890	28-Dec-1890	Lawrence Jerome Ahern	Kelly, Catherine	William O'Brien
Albers	Edward	George	26-Jul-1903	10-Jul-1903	Howard Albers	Gallagher, Mary	John Murray
Albers	Jeanette	Catherine	26-Jul-1903	10-Jul-1903	Howard Albers	Gallagher, Mary	Thomas O'Neill
Albright	Richard	A.	13-May-1906	18-Mar-1906	Penny Albright	Kinstle, Agnes	
Albright	Paul	G.	22-Jun-1905	23-Feb-1905	Perry Albright	Kinstle, Agnes	
Alexander	William		28-Aug-1910	23-Jul-1910	William Alexander	Murphy, Dora F.	Mary Elwood
Allen	Joseph	Marvin	26-Aug-1900	05-Jun-1900	Francis Allen	Scruffer, Barbara	Catherine Edelman
Allen	August	Phillip	15-Oct-1905	6-Oct-1905	Nicolas Allen	Burrier, Mary S.	Margaret B. Burrier
Allen	John		14-Feb-1886	13-Feb-1886	Thomas Allen	Byrnes, Margaret	Mary Adele Byrnes
Allender/Wilson	Mary		03-Apr-1897	About 1816	William Allender	Allender, Sarah	Catherine McCluskey
Allison	Rose	Mary	17-Apr-1911	25-Nov-1891	Francis Allison	Robinson, Alice	Margaret Farrell
Alluisi	Thomas	Stanley	14-Sep-1890	28-Aug-1890	John V. Alluisi	Fitzpatrick, Mary	Bernard J. Fitzpatrick
Alluisi	Eleanor		06-Apr-1890	23-Mar-1890	Thomas F. Alluisi	Farrell, Margaret A.	Salvatore Alluisi
Alluisi	Mary	Margaret	25-Nov-1888	09-Nov-1888	Thomas F. Alluisi	Alluisi, Margaret A.	Andrew Alluisi
Alluisi	Thomas	Talbot	10-Oct-1887	10-Oct-1887	Thomas F. Alluisi	Farrell, Margaret A.	Ann Farrell
Alsruhe	Pauline	Olga	22-Aug-1915	8-Aug-1915	Henry Alsruhe	Kirchner, Helen C.	Pauline Kirchner
Amelong	Nicholas		25-Dec-1898	10-Sep-1898	Frederick Amelong	Schuster, Mary	Edward Kirchner

1

LAST NAME	FIRST NAME	MIDDLE	BAPTISM	BIRTH	Father	Mother	SPONSORS	
Amnen	George		04-Jan-1891	24-Dec-1890	Francis L. Amnen	Moffitt, Ella V.	George H. Litz	Isabelle M. Litz
Amos	Catherine	Ann	25-Dec-1892	09-Oct-1878	George Amos	Hanson, Agnes	James McDevitt	Mary Amelia Amos
Anderson	Elizabeth	Eugenia	28-Mar-1909	8-Mar-1909	Andrew Anderson	O'Connor, Elizabeth Frances	John Vogel	Anderson, Elizabeth
Anderson	Mary		26-May-1915	22-Apr-1915	August Anderson	Kavanaugh, Ann		Julia Bouchet
Anderson	James		17-Feb-1882	11-Feb-1882	Daniel Anderson	Connolly, Bridget		
Anderson	James		02-Apr-1882	11-Feb-1882	Daniel Anderson	Connolly, Bridget		Murphy, Margaret
Anderson	Ann	Loretta	29-Oct-1893	17-Oct-1893	E. Anderson	Miller, Elizabeth	Michael Ford	Catherine Fanin
Anderson	Evelyn	Mary	9-Jun-1912	20-May-1912	Gustaf Anderson	Kavanaugh, Ann	Adam John Trageser	Julia Bouchet
Anderson	Helen		17-Oct-1909	23-Sep-1909	Gustaf Anderson	Kavanaugh, Ann	John Connolly	Julia Bouchett
Anderson	Catherine		11-Feb-1906	2-Feb-1906	John J. Anderson	Trier, Catherine	Frederick Haskell	Sarah E. Yeakle
Anderson	Margaret		28-Sep-1902	20-Sep-1902	John P. Anderson	Etzel, Catherine	John E. Etzel	Mary Nislein
Anderson	Joseph	Elwood	9-Jun-1913	24-Oct-1862	Maurice Anderson	[Blank], Mary		
Anderson	Mary	Catherine	11-Apr-1909	19-Mar-1909	Thomas D. Anderson	Soulant, Catherine	William Leipold	Sarah Leipold
Anderson	Elizabeth		18-Jan-1891	02-Jan-1891	Wilbert Anderson	Miller, Elizabeth	Daniel Keleher	Julia M. Carr
Anderson	Albert	John	17-May-1896	13-May-1896	William Anderson	Fannon, Mary	John Wright	Frances Fannon
Anderson	Edna	Mary	11-Dec-1898	29-Nov-1898	William Anderson	Fannon, Mary Elizabeth	John McLaughlin	Genevieve Wright
Anderson	Mary	Margaret	29-Jul-1888	17-Jul-1888	William E. Anderson	Fannon, Mary E.	William P. Klinefelter	Jame T. Klinefelter
Anderson	James		01-May-1892	24-Apr-1892	William Edward Anderson	Fannon, Mary Elizabeth	William Joseph Klinefelter	Margaret Klinefelter
Anderson	Rose	Agatha	11-Feb-1894	05-Feb-1894	William Edward Anderson	Fannon, Mary Elizabeth	James Fannon	Ann Meers
Anderson	William	Edward	23-Mar-1890	08-Mar-1890	Wm E. Anderson	Fallon, Mary E.	J. Daily	Ellen Daily
Anderton	Marshall	Hopkins	15-Jan-1899	01-Jan-1899	Francis Anderton	Hopkins, Rosalie	Walter Anderton	Ann Hopkins
Andrathy	John		09-Apr-1882	31-Mar-1882	August Francis Andrathy	Griffin, Ann	William Phillip Westcamp	Mayhilda Westcamp
Andrathy	A.		19-Jun-1904	4-Jun-1904	John Andrathy	Trier, Catherine	Jerome Murphy	Hannah Murphy
Andrathy	Mary	Edna	19-Sep-1915	8-Sep-1915	John Andrathy	Trier, Catherine	Thomas Trier	Mary Fenton
Andrathy	Bernard	Louis	21-Aug-1910	11-Aug-1910	John J. Andrathy	Trier, Catherine M.	Hugh O'Connor	Mary O'Connor
Andrathy	John		15-Dec-1907	2-Dec-1907	John J. Andrathy	Trier, Catherine M.	Louis Trier	Ann Trier
Andrathy	Charles	Joseph	12-Jan-1913	27-Dec-1912	John Joseph Andrathy	Trier, Catherine	Charles E. Artz	Catherine Artz
Andrews	Alphonse		19-Aug-1908	5-Aug-1908	[Blank]	[Blank]		Veronica Hoch
Andrews	Robert		29-Apr-1888	09-Apr-1888	Robert Andrews	McClennahan, Mary	Luke Quirk	Ann Kelly
Annen	John	Henry	19-May-1889	13-May-1889	Francis Louis Annen	Moffitt, Helen	Henry Annen	Eva Annen
Annesley	Isabelle		27-Mar-1904	17-Dec-1866	Robert Annesley	Howard, Ann		Margaret Flanagan
Appel	Mary	Teresa	09-Aug-1893	26-Jul-1893	John Appel	Kane, Mary Helen		Margaret Mackin
Ardison	Cecelia	Emily	23-Aug-1908	23-Jul-1908	Henry Ardison	Proctor, Lillian		Mary Atec
Ardison	Mary	Riva	23-Aug-1908	3-Jul-1908	Henry Ardison	Proctor, Lillie		Sylvia Ridinger
Armiger	Edith	Mary	31-May-1891	18-May-1891	Joseph Armiger	Lannan, Elizabeth	James Joseph Lannan	Helen Lannan
Armiger	Thomas	Edwin	23-Feb-1885	01-Aug-1852	Joseph Armiger	Armiger, Sarah E.	Michael J. Kuper	Catherine Stoffel
Armiger	Lillian	de Sales	01-Jul-1894	18-Jun-1894	Joseph L. Armiger	Lannan, Elizabeth G.	Terence Lannan	Catherine Wiedefeld
Armiger	Joseph	Leon	19-Feb-1888	14-Feb-1888	Joseph Lee Armiger	Lannon, Elizabeth	Edward Francis Lannon	Mary Lannon
Armstrong	Margaret	Gertrude	19-Jan-1902	09-Jan-1902	William Armstrong	Shaugnessey, Mary Elizabeth	John Shaugnessey	Mary Shaugnessey
Arnold	Martin		15-Mar-1882	Jan 1811	Nathan Benjamin	Harvey, Martha		
Arthur	Ann	Grace	21-Jan-1906	11-Jan-1906	George W. Arthur	Kelly, Margaret R.	Robert P. Arthur	Mary G. Kelly
Arthur	George	William	31-Jul-1897	31-Jul-1897	George W. Arthur	Kelly, Margaret R.	James Kelly	Mary Arthur
Arthur	James	Thomas	13-May-1900	29-Apr-1900	George W. Arthur	Kelly, Margaret	Joseph Rock	Agnes Holden
Arthur	John	Francis	13-Apr-1902	04-Apr-1902	George W. Arthur	Kelly, Margaret	James Holden	Jeanette Ward
Arthur	Margaret	Pierce	13-Oct-1907	3-Oct-1907	George W. Arthur	Kelly, Margaret R.	Charles V. Kelly	Hannah Kelly
Arthur	Mary	Regina	20-Mar-1904	12-Mar-1904	George W. Arthur	Kelly, Margaret R.	Thomas Kelly	Mary Kelly
Arthur	Ann	Elizabeth	13-Nov-1898	02-Nov-1898	John Arthur	Kelly, Margaret R.	James E. Arthur	Mary Skelton
Artman	Mary	Agnes	23-Dec-1900	12-Dec-1900	Constantine Artman	Skelton, Margaret	Patrick O'Neill	Barbara Stump
Aumen	Helen	Grace	13-Apr-1884	30-Mar-1884	Francis Aumen	McCormick, Mary Agnes	William McCormick	Mary Landers
Aumen	Mary	Elizabeth	7-Jan-1906	29-Dec-1905	Francis Aumen	Landers, Julia	Joseph Rock	Mary Donohue
Aumen	William	Sylvester	29-Sep-1901	20-Sep-1901	Francis Aumen	Landers, Julia	William Aumen	Lucinda Aumen
Ayers	Thomas	Leonard	10-Apr-1898	28-Mar-1898	James Alfred Ayers	Yates, Margaret	Francis McDermott	Margaret Burkhard
Ayres	William	Glenn	14-Sep-1913	3-Sep-1913	Valandium Ayres	Manning, Mary	Thomas Leonard	Helen Manning
B utler	Catherine	D.	27-Dec-1914	2-Dec-1914	Arthur Butler	Swayne, Eleanor	Francis Manning	Elizabeth Brown
Baader	Margaret		13-Aug-1902	19-Jan-1897	John Baader	Guckert, Mary	John J. O'Brien	
Bach	Helen		12-Aug-1901	13-Jan-1901	Isidore Bach	Bick, Mary	Joseph Whelan	Rose Fowler
Bacon	Daniel		11-Jun-1900	11-Apr-1900	William Bacon	Bacon, Ida	James Bacon	Margaret Bacon
Bader	Charles	William	29-Sep-1901	10-Aug-1901	John Bader	Guckert, Francis	Charles Wheelen	Josephin Guckert
Bader	John		29-Apr-1904	25-Mar-1904	John H. Bader	Guckert, Frances		Margaret Cook
Bader	Joseph	Leroy	6-Jun-1915	15-May-1915	Joseph Bader	Clemons, Ellen	Daniel Crummnis	Margaret Crummnis
Bader	Mary	Margaret	24-May-1914	11-May-1914	Joseph Bader	Clemens, Ellen	William Bader	Helen Manning
Baer	John		01-Dec-1896	01-Nov-1875	John Baer	Kemps, Edith		Mary Ricker

LAST NAME	FIRST NAME	MIDDLE	BAPTISM	BIRTH	Father	Mother	SPONSORS
Baier/Simmel	Katherine	Margaret	11-Dec-1914	14-Dec-1886	George Baier	Dilger, Elizabeth	Francis J. Nossel / Eleanor Agnes Nossel
Bailey	Edward		25-Dec-1883	09-Dec-1883	Henry Bailey	Ratrey, Helen	Rachel Ratrey
Bailey	Rachell		13-Sep-1885	18-Aug-1885	Henry N. Bailey	Ratrey, Helen	Rachel Ratrey
Bailey	Henry	Nordyke	04-May-1890	23-Apr-1890	Henry Nordyke Bailey	Ratrey, Helen	Thomas Donohoe / Ann Donohue
Bailey	Rose	Mary	30-Nov-1912	8-Sep-1900	William H. Bailey	Bambers, Estelle F.	Catherine Loughran
Bailey	Edna		30-Nov-1912	19-Feb-1903	William Hayes	Bambers, Estelle F.	Cecelia Dolan
Bain/Hagnet	Catherine	Joan	23-Aug-1883	25-Feb-1820	George Hagnet	Foy, Florence	
Baird	James		12-Nov-1904	22-May-1880	James Baird	Baird, Ann	Margaret Mitchell
Baker	Victoria	E.	01-Sep-1885	04-Apr-1885	Elijah Baker	McGee, Helen	Sarah Baker
Baker	Charles	Theodore	24-Jul-1883	09-May-1883	Elisha Baker	McGee, Helen	Elizabeth Gough
Baker	Bernard	Edward	20-Aug-1905	7-Aug-1905	Francis Alfred Baker	Burke, Ann F.	Henry E. Burke / Carolina F. Burke
Baker	George	Ivan	25-Oct-1883	17-Oct-1883	Greenbury Baker	Falkahan, Mary	Elizabeth M. Baker
Baker	John	Wilson	28-Oct-1883	29-Jun-1878	Greenbury Baker	Falkahan, Mary	Caroline A. Sadler
Baker	Jerome		17-Sep-1911	1-Sep-1911	Jerome Baker	Dolby, Clara	Mary A. Cunningham
Baker	George	Thomas	06-Sep-1896	August 1896	John Baker	Kelley, Mary	Thomas Baker / Delia Kelly
Baker	Mary	Elizabeth	27-Aug-1899	14-Aug-1899	John Baker	Kelly, Mary A.	Eugene Kelly / Margaret Kelly
Baker	Robert	Joseph	17-Mar-1901	19-Feb-1901	John Baker	Kelly, Mary	Thomas Walsh / Catherine Walsh
Baker	Mary		18-May-1896	About 1830	John McGuigan	March, Joan	Joan Lanaghan
Baker	Catherine	Helen	22-Jul-1894	09-Jul-1894	John Oliver Baker	Kelly, Mary, Ann	Joseph Glenn / Mary Glenn
Baker	Charles	F.	4-Nov-1906	28-Oct-1906	John Oliver Baker	Kelly, Mary A.	William H. Kelly / Mary Kelly
Baker	Margaret	Alice	31-May-1903	19-May-1903	John Oliver Baker	Kelly, Mary A.	Joseph H. Baker / Mary A. Kelly
Baker	Ann	Mary	24-May-1896	11-May-1896	Robert Baker	Kehm, Estelle	Catherine Lanahan
Baley	Vernon		11-Jul-1897	09-Jul-1897	Benjamin Baley	Taylor, Cora	Joseph Rich
Ball	Mary	Grace	12-Jan-1913	10-Jan-1913	Ephraim J. Ball	Toher, Sara	Percy J. McConnell / Mary F. Toher
Ballard	Richard	Waters	29-Mar-1908	7-Mar-1908	Richard Waters Ballard	Kelley, Catherine	William J. O'Brien / Julia Kelley
Bamberger	Joseph		09-Aug-1896	31-Jul-1895	John Bamberger	Regan, Mary	John Mee / Mary Peat
Bamberger	Margaret		22-Jun-1902	08-Jun-1902	John Bamberger	Regan, Mary	Mary Ann Walter
Bamberger	Bernard	A.	11-Feb-1906	3-Feb-1906	John F. Bamberger	Regan, Mary	Ann Bamberger
Bamberger	Charles	Frank	05-Jul-1903	22-Jun-1903	John Franklin Bamberger	Regan, Mary	Annegan Finn
Bamberger	John	Franklin	07-Jul-1895	28-Jun-1895	John Franklin Bamberger	Regan, Mary	Thomas Bamberger / Julia Regan
Bamberger	Catherine		08-Oct-1895	08-Oct-1895	Joseph Bamberger	Poole, Virginia	Catherine Delavigne
Bamberger	George	Edward	05-Apr-1885	17-Feb-1885	Joseph Bamberger	Poole, Virginia	Catherine Carmody
Bamberger	Hannah	S.	30-Apr-1905	24-Feb-1905	Joseph Bamberger	Poole, Virginia	Mary Bamberger
Bamberger	Herbert	Vincent	13-Apr-1890	13-Feb-1890	Joseph Bamberger	Poole, Virginia Clark	Emma Conroy
Bamberger	Joseph	Thomas	14-Oct-1883	15-Aug-1883	Joseph Bamberger	Poole, Virginia	Mary Bryan
Bamberger	Margaret		25-Jun-1899	23-Dec-1898	Joseph Bamberger	Poole, Virginia	Agnes Crawford
Bamberger	William	Albert	18-Mar-1888	29-Jan-1888	Joseph W. Bamberger	Poole, Virginia Clark	Ann Kelly
Bamberger	John	Poole	30-May-1894	11-Jul-1894	Joseph Wenceslas Bamberger	Poole, Virginia Clark	John Henry Leach / Virginia Clark Leach
Bamberger	George	William	11-Feb-1909	23-Nov-1884	Robert Turner Bamberger	Smith, Christina	Joseph Carroll / Bridget Kavanaugh
Bamberger	Joseph	Carroll	12-Dec-1909	1-Dec-1909	William Turner Bamberger	Guffey, Ann V.	Edward Hayden Gentry / Bridget Kavanaugh
Bamburger	Francis		8-Jun-1905	26-Dec-1904	John Bamburger	Regan, Mary	Josephine Brown
Bamburger	Julia	Regan	08-Apr-1900	04-Mar-1900	John Bamburger	Regan, Mary	Phillip Jeney / Clara Sillery
Bamburger	Teresa		11-Sep-1898	25-Aug-1898	John Bamburger	Regan, Mary	John Bamburger / Elizabeth Bamburger
Bamburger	Helen	Virginia	26-Feb-1893	10-Oct-1892	Joseph Bamburger	Poole, Virginia	Mary McDermott
Bamburger	Elizabeth		17-Sep-1882	19-Jul-1882	Joseph W. Bamburger	Poole, Virginia Clark	Mary Porter
Bangs	George	Edward	27-Sep-1908	4-Sep-1908	William Bangs	Bangs, Lizzie	
Bangs	William	B.	9-Sep-1906	10-Mar-1906	William Bangs	Wess, Elizabeth	Mary L. Wess
Banke	Edward	Josephiah	29-May-1902	03-May-1902	F.J. Banke	Briggeman, B.C.	Joseph Kelly / Barbara [Blank]
Banke	Raymond	Milton	29-May-1902	03-Nov-1892	F.J.Banke	Briggeman, B.C.	J. Kelly / Barbara [Blank]
Banke	Justin	Laurence	08-Feb-1903	08-Jan-1903	Frederick John Banke	Grob, Lillian	Patrick O'Neill / Margaret Weinick
Banke	Mary	Dorman	29-May-1902	22-Nov-1890	Frederick John Banke	Briggeman, Bertha C.	Joseph Kelly / Barbara [Blank]
Banke	John	F.	22-Aug-1902	26-Jan-1859	Herman Banke	Sherman, Louise	Mr. Hamlin
Bankert	William	F.	22-Aug-1902	22-Jun-1888	John F. Burke	Briggeman, Bertha C.	Mary Romana
Bankert	John	Arthur	23-Mar-1915	14-Nov-1911	Charles Henry Bankert	Frasch, Ann	Edward Cusick / Mary Mooney
Bankert	Joseph	Leonard	23-Mar-1915	15-Apr-1907	Charles Henry Bankert	Frasch, Ann	Patrick O'Neill / Mary Mooney
Bannan	Ann	Margaret	21-Dec-1902	17-Dec-1902	Hugh Bannan	O'Neil, Catherine	James McNulty / Ann Bannan
Bannan	Hugo		13-Oct-1895	08-Oct-1895	Hugh Bannan	O'Neill, Catherine	Patrick O'Neill / Ann O'Neill
Bannan	James		15-May-1898	10-May-1898	Hugh Bannan	O'Neill, Catherine	Terence Cusick / Ann Bannon
Bannon	Catherine	Margaret	20-Sep-1891	15-Sep-1891	Eugene Bannon	O'Neill, Catherine	John Bannon / Mary Bannon
Bannon	Catherine	Theresa	04-Jun-1899	01-Jun-1899	Hugh Bannon	O'Neill, Catherine	Philip Bannon / Ann O'Neill
Bannon	John		16-Sep-1894	14-Sep-1894	Hugh Bannon	O'Neill, Catherine	Thomas Bannon / Rose O'Neill
Bannon	John	Phillip	28-Jan-1906	25-Jan-1906	Hugh Bannon	O'Neill, Catherine	Rose McNulty
Bannon	Mary	Helen	08-Sep-1889	04-Sep-1889	Hugh Bannon	O'Neill, Catherine	Mary O'Neill

LAST NAME	FIRST NAME	MIDDLE	BAPTISM	BIRTH	Father	Mother	SPONSORS
Bannon	Rose	Ann	18-Dec-1892	08-Dec-1892	Hugh Bannon	O'Neill, Catherine	Ann O'Neill
Bantz	Alice	Cecelia	24-Apr-1892	13-Apr-1892	Michael Bantz	Touhy, Hannah	Ann Hand
Bantz	Catherine		21-Aug-1904	10-Aug-1904	Michael L. Bantz	McCormick, Mary A.	Joseph M. McCormick
Barber	Eugene	Bernard	1-Sep-1912	12-Jun-1912	Walter Barber	Henry, Genevieve	John Henry
Barker	Ralph	Caldwell	05-Jul-1886	22-May-1886	Enoch Barker	Caldwell, Cora L.	William Surratt
Barker	Cora	Loretta	13-Apr-1883	20-Feb-1883	Enoch M. Barker	Caldwell, Cora Loretta	Henry McShane
Barking	John	Thomas	26-May-1889	11-May-1889	Francis Barking	O'Neill, Catherine	Dennis Carroll
Barlow	George		1-Jul-1914	30-Jun-1914	George Barlow	Margaret Marie [Blank]	Mary Leddy
Barnitz	Frances	Margaret	21-Jun-1910	20-Jun-1911	Francis H. Barnitz	Barry, Blanche	Mrs. Slaysman
Barrett	Leonard	Samuel	23-Sep-1915	10-Sep-1915	[Blank]	Barrett, Frances	Agnes Griffin
Barrett	Margaret		07-Jan-1894	26-Dec-1893	Edward Barrett	Patterson, Mary A.	Palmer, Margaret
Barrett	Mary	Helen	21-Aug-1892	04-Aug-1892	Edward Barrett	Patterson, Mary A.	William Barrett
Barrett	James	Stephen	08-Nov-1891	24-Oct-1891	James Barrett	Shanahan, Ann	John Barrett
Barrett	James		1-Oct-1911	16-Sep-1911	James Barrett	Price, Adelina	Dennis Driscoll
Barrett	John	Redding	5-Jul-1907	28-Jun-1907	John G. Barrett	Redding, Nora S.	William Barrett
Barrett	Margaret	D.	22-Oct-1905	5-Oct-1905	Nicholas Barrett	Lally, Margaret	Michael Redding
Barrett	Bridget	T.	30-Oct-1904	6-Oct-1904	Nicholo Barrett	Lally, Margaret	Thomas Barrett
Barrett	Catherine		23-Nov-1902	10-Nov-1902	William Barrett	Timment, Bridget	John A. O'Dea
Barry	Benjamin	Leon	15-Sep-1907	28-Aug-1907	Benjamin Barry	Creaney, Carolina	James Daley
Barry	William	Gustavus	14-May-1905	30-Apr-1905	Benjamin Barry	Creaney, Carolina	John Bunch
Barry	Regina		07-Feb-1886	28-Jan-1886	George W. Barry	LeBrun, Petit	Gustavus Creaney
Barry	Francis		25-Mar-1883	18-Mar-1883	Henry Barry	Adams, Emma	Regina Barry
Barry	Irma	Elizabeth	21-Mar-1897	07-Mar-1897	Henry Barry	Adams, Emma	Christina Reed
Barry	Raymond	Leroy	17-Feb-1895	01-Feb-1895	Henry Francis Barry	Adams, Emma Mary	Lizzie Nehran
Barry	Mary	Bridget	13-Dec-1908	30-Nov-1908	James Barry	Murphy, Mary Margaret	Elizabeth Barry
Barry	David	Edward	15-Dec-1889	07-Dec-1889	John Barry	Cronin, Honora Elizabeth	Josephine Barry
Barry	Mary		19-Feb-1888	14-Feb-1888	John Barry	Cronin, Honora Elizabeth	Eva Haneplipe
Barry	Michael	Nicholas	10-Jan-1904	11-Dec-1903	John Barry	Gray, Bridget	Mary Ann Cronin
Barry	Patrick	Francis	19-Jun-1901	16-Jun-1901	John Barry	Gray, Bridget	Josephine O'Leary
Barry	John	Edgar	15-Feb-1891	18-Jan-1891	John R. Barry	Smith, Mary D.	Patrick Early
Barry	Charles	Edward	02-Aug-1896	23-Jul-1896	Samuel Barry	LeBrun, Blanche Petit	Mary Quigley
Barry	George	Mullen Waidner	07-Jan-1894	28-Dec-1893	Samuel H. Barry	LeBrun, Blanche M. Petit	Genevieve C. Cassidy
Barry	Cecelia	Mary	25-Nov-1906	4-Nov-1906	Samuel H.Barry	LeBrun, Blanche Petite	Mary McNamara
Barry	Alphonse	Peter Lebrum	14-Apr-1895	04-Apr-1895	Samuel Harden Barry	LeBrun, Blanche Mary Petit	Rachel A. Barry
Barry	Benjamin		23-Aug-1896	28-Jul-1896	William Barry	Timmins, Bridget	Rachelle Erline
Barry	Bridget	Alice	24-Feb-1898	14-Feb-1898	William Barry	Timmins, Bridget	Nadine Alexandra Prevast
Barry	Eleanor		24-Nov-1888	24-Nov-1888	William Barry	Barrett, Mary	Thomas Ring
Barry	Elizabeth		18-Oct-1900	15-Oct-1900	William Barry	Timmons, Bridget	Joan Hickey
Barry	Margaret	Mary	01-May-1887	25-Apr-1887	William Barry	Barrett, Mary	Alice Reddy
Barry	Mary	Helen	23-Feb-1885	19-Feb-1885	William Barry	Barrett, Mary	Julia Lucey
Barry	Mary	Loretta	04-Aug-1895	23-Jul-1895	William Barry	Timmins, Bridget	Alice Reddy
Barry	Phillip	Patrick	04-Mar-1883	26-Feb-1883	William Barry	Barrett, Mary	Mary Lucey
Barry	William	John	10-Jun-1894	24-May-1894	William David Barry	Timmins, Bridget	Ann McSweeney
Barsotti	Ann	Estelle	4-Apr-1915	10-Mar-1915	James Barsotti	Hollar, Ada	Ann Hickey
Barsotti	Vincent		01-Jan-1891	13-Dec-1890	James Barsotti	Fareschi, Mary Angela	Ann O'Sullivan
Barton	Henry	Lee	13-Jun-1915	01-Jun-1815	Kennedy Barsotti	Leoni, Elizabeth	Helen Stevenson
Barton	Henry	A.	03-Mar-1901	08-Dec-1900	Henry Barton	Kendall, Amelia	Mary Murphy
Barton	Mary		9-Dec-1904	30-Nov-1906	Henry Barton	Kennedy, Emelia	Ann Angelier
Barton	Paul	Samuel	15-Jun-1902	02-Jun-1902	Henry G. Barton	Kendall, Amelia	Christina Barsotti
Barton	Charles	F.	13-Oct-1908	20-Sep-1908	Howard Barton	Kendall, Amelia	Gertrude Kendall
Barton	William		18-Sep-1904	2-Sep-1904	Joseph Barton	Cardwell, Margaret	Helen Halloran
Bass	John	Raymond	27-Jun-1892	24-Feb-1866	Charles Bass	Greenwell, Gertrude	Mary Kendall
Bass	William	Eppinger	15-Apr-1894	16-Mar-1894	Robert Parrott Bass	Lox, Mary	Ann McCart
Batchett	Margaret		12-Feb-1884	10-Feb-1884	Peter Batchett	Batchett, Margaret	Alice Kendall
Bateman	Leo		19-Mar-1904	12-Dec-1856	George Bateman	Fallon, Katherine	Catherine Connolly
Bateman	Constance	Stuart Teresae	23-Oct-1898	12-Oct-1898	Samuel Bateman	Robinson, Elizabeth Genevieve	Mary Henry
Batterden	Agnes		23-Apr-1882	13-Apr-1882	John Thomas Batterden	Thompson, Catherine	Mary Bukel
Batterden	Mary	Catherine	5-Jan-1913	27-Dec-1912	John Thomas Batterden	Thompson, Catherine J.	Margaret Batemen
Batterden	Mary	Rosalie	1-Aug-1909	19-Jul-1909	Joseph Baterden	Eagan, Ann	Susan A. Koop
Batterden	Ann	Veronica	06-Mar-1893	20-Feb-1893	Joseph Batterden	Eagan, Ann	Agnes Fitzpatrick
Batterden	Bridget	Agnes	26-Nov-1899	07-Nov-1899	Joseph Batterden	Eagan, Ann	Margaret Jamison
Batterden	Catherine		7-Aug-1904	21-Jul-1904	Joseph Batterden	Eagan, Ann	Margaret Batterden
			28-Sep-1902	12-Sep-1902	Joseph Batterden	Eagan, Ann	Michael Wood

4

LAST NAME	FIRST NAME	MIDDLE	BAPTISM	BIRTH	Father	Mother	SPONSORS
Batterden	Francis		10-Oct-1897	29-Sep-1897	Joseph Batterden	Eagan, Ann	Catherine Kennedy
Batterden	William		13-Oct-1895	05-Oct-1895	Joseph Batterden	Eagan, Ann	John Kennedy
Batterden	Margaret	Mildred	13-Mar-1910	28-Feb-1910	Joseph P. Batterden	Eagan, Ann	John Ward
Batterden	Joseph	Patrick	30-Aug-1891	23-Aug-1891	Joseph Patrick Batterden	Eagan, Ann	Henry Sadtler
Batterden	Mary		08-Jul-1883	26-Jun-1883	Patrick Batterden	Williams, Mary	Ann Richards
Batzer	George	Henry	12-Nov-1905	3-Nov-1905	Joseph Batzer	Wilson, Ann	Catherine Reardon
Batzer	Joseph	John	17-Apr-1904	11-Apr-1904	Joseph Batzer	Wilson, Ann	Parr, Maryish
Bauer	William	Winfield	01-May-1887	20-Apr-1887	Robert Joseph Bauer	Gerben, Mary Caroline	Dora Christ
Baum	Josephine	Sophia	23-Jan-1910	28-Dec-1909	Valentine Baum	Wagner, Ann	Nellie A. Simmons
Bausch	Margaret	Ann	27-Jul-1890	25-Jul-1890	Michael Bausch	Turpey, Hannah	Clara Kupp
Baustead	Jessie	Mary	05-Jul-1882	01-Mar-1882	Clarence Baustead	Murphy, Helen	Josephine Sophia Logue
Bautz	Laurence	Joseph	30-Nov-1884	14-Nov-1884	John Bautz	Devlin, Sarah J.	Maggie Turpey
Bautz	Bernard	James	03-Feb-1889	24-Jan-1889	Michael Bautz	Turpey, Hannah	Elizabeth Glenn Dempster
Bautz	John	Raymond	13-Sep-1908	31-Aug-1908	Michael Bautz	McCormick, Mary A.	Ann O'Donnell
Bautz	Thomas	B.	18-Nov-1906	26-Oct-1906	Michael L. Bautz	McCormick, Mary A.	Hannah Turpey
Bavis	John		29-Apr-1900	17-Apr-1900	Charles Bavis	Wood, Caroline	Jennie Gisrael
Bavis	Mary	L.	30-Sep-1906	25-Sep-1906	Francis J. Bavis	Murphy, Ellen	Lillian E. Flack
Bavis	Alice	Florence	9-Nov-1902	7-Nov-1902	James Bavis	Walters, Sophia	Ann Wood
Bavis	Charles	Leon	26-Feb-1888	16-Feb-1888	James Bavis	Dunn, Mary	Carrie Bavis
Bavis	Edward		27-Aug-1899	14-Aug-1899	James Bavis	Kirby, Edith	Ellen Bavis
Bavis	Francis		14-Jul-1909	14-Jul-1909	James Bavis	Walters, Mary	Margaret E. Cullen
Bavis	Mary	Anthony	06-Jan-1901	24-Dec-1900	James Bavis	Walters, Sophia	Alice Bavis
Bavis	Helen	Monica	28-May-1905	14-May-1905	James M. Bavis	Walters, Sophia	Ellen Doyle
Bavis	James		18-Aug-1907	14-Aug-1907	James M. Bavis	Walters, Sophia	Alice Bavis
Bavis	Francis		27-Sep-1885	22-Sep-1885	William Bavis	Byrnes, Helen	Helen M. Bavis
Bavis	Mary	Bernardine	16-May-1897	10-May-1897	William Bavis	Fullerton, Emma	Helen Dowd
Bavis	Myrtle	Mary	18-Nov-1900	30-Oct-1900	William Bavis	Fullerton, Emma	Alice Bavis
Bavis	Robert	Joseph	17-Jun-1900	06-Jun-1900	William Bavis	Stevenson, Alana	Quinn, Ella
Bavis	Mildred	F.	1-Jan-1905	29-Dec-1904	William F. Bavis	Fullerton, Emma Elizabeth	Ellen Doyle
Bavis	William		9-Dec-1906	1-Dec-1906	William F. Bavis	Fullerton, E.	Lettie Bavis
Beard	Charles	Edward	6-Aug-1905	1-Jul-1905	Charles Beard	Kelly, E.	Mary Hausmann
Beard	Francis	Joseph	30-Oct-1898	08-Oct-1898	Charles Beard	Kelly, Helen	Margaret Kelly
Beard	James	Henry	20-Jun-1897	06-Jun-1897	Charles Beard	Kelly, Helen	Ann Mariott
Beard	Margaret	Elizabeth	15-Jul-1900	20-Jun-1900	Charles Beard	Kelly, Eleanor	Ann McMahon
Beard	Bernard	Ignatius	24-Aug-1902	14-Jul-1902	Charles H. Beard	Kelly, Ella	Kelly, Margaret
Beck	Ann	Rebecca	29-Oct-1912	13-Dec-1893	Joseph Beck	Engle, Ann	Mary E. [Blank]
Beck	John	Francis	28-Jul-1912	10-Jul-1912	Louis Beck	Hauser, Olympia E.	Elizabeth Hoeckel
Becker	Dorothy	Frances	7-Apr-1912	24-Dec-1911	[Blank]	Becker, Margaret E.	Mary Shaughnessy
Becker	Mary	F.	19-Nov-1911	6-Nov-1911	Leon Becker	Yeakle, Mary	Mary O'Connor
Becker	William	Franklin	21-Jul-1912	12-Jun-1912	William C. Becker	Siebold, Louise	Rose Virginia Becker
Beckhold	George	Hunter	16-Mar-1891	21-Feb-1891	Christopher George Beckhold	Hunter, Mary M.	Marya Cloeff Albert
Beckman	Mary	Loretta	08-Dec-1901	24-Nov-1901	Charles Beckman	Curran, Mary	Frances Stuart
Beckum	William	Joseph	11-Apr-1892	29-Nov-1866	Charles Beckum	McFadden, Mary	Josephine Beckman
Beckwith	Charles	LeRoy	24-Aug-1902	05-Aug-1902	Charles Beckwith	Johnson, Ella	Samuel Beckwith
Bees	Edward	Flavien	08-Jan-1899	22-Dec-1898	Martin Bees	Hanly, Joan	Terence Lannon
Bees	James	Carroll	01-Nov-1896	14-Oct-1896	Martin Bees	Hanly, Joan	William Kennedy
Bees	Joseph	Leonard	24-Mar-1901	07-Mar-1901	Martin Bees	Hanly, Joan	Thomas Hagerty
Bees	Thomas		6-Jan-1907	22-Dec-1906	Martin Bees	Hanley, Janeta	Margaret O'Neil
Bees	John	Henry	29-Jul-1894	15-Jul-1894	Martin L. Bees	Hanly, Jane	Alma Phillips
Beideman	Francis	Louis	6-Nov-1904	24-Oct-1904	Martin Louis Bees	Hanly, Joan	Mary Finnernan
Beilser	Emma	Frances	08-Apr-1886	29-Jun-1874	Samuel Beideman	Chamberlain, Hannah	Helen M. O'Neill
Bein	John	Henry	06-Oct-1901	22-Sep-1901	Edward Beilser	Rudolph, Catherine	Elizabeth Smitz
Beirne	Catherine	Ann	23-Dec-1906	13-Dec-1906	George Bein	Freidel, Catherine	Catherine A. Potts
Beirne	Henry		18-Jul-1897	09-Jul-1897	John Beirne	White, Bridget	Ann Neary
Beirne	Elizabeth	Ann	18-Feb-1906	6-Feb-1906	Patrick Beirne	Toulan, Catherine C.	Helen Dover
Bell	William		09-Jan-1898	12-Sep-1868	Henry Bell	Clements, Marsha	Helen A. Beirne
Bell	Martha	Ellen	28-Oct-1907	9-Sep-1907	Joseph Bell	Byrne, Cecelia	
Bell	Elizabeth	Annette	09-Jan-1887	28-Dec-1886	Thomas Bell	Kilduff, Joan	Mary Wales
Bell	Thomas	Raymond	06-Dec-1891	29-Nov-1891	Thomas Bell	Lanham, Mary	Joan Kilduff
Bell	Mary	Joan	7-Feb-1904	22-Jan-1904	Thomas H. Bell	Murphy, Catherine	Ann Lanham
Bell	Stephen	Clarence	12-Jan-1902	26-Dec-1901	Thomas H. Bell	Murphy, Catherine	Mary Moran
Bell	Ann		27-Jul-1884	18-Jul-1884	Thomas Louis Bell	Kilduff, Virginia Ignatius	Maryelly Farr
Bell	Thomas	Stephen	18-Aug-1889	05-Aug-1889	Thomas Louis Bell	Kilduff, Virginia Ignatius	Sophia Schweikert
							Stephen Joseph Kilduff
							Ann Elizabeth Thompson

5

LAST NAME	FIRST NAME	MIDDLE	BAPTISM	BIRTH	Father	Mother	SPONSORS	
Bell	Joseph	Gerald	10-Nov-1889	21-Oct-1889	William C. Bell	Heffner, Margaret N.	John W. Lemmon	Agnes Hannafin
Bell	James	William	03-Mar-1895	20-Feb-1895	William Francis Bell	Wehr, Mary Catherine	James Francis Kelly	Philomena Kelly
Belt	Margaret		5-Jul-1914	7-Jun-1914	Charles Belt	Kenny, Margaret		Ann McCormickl
Belt	John	Edgar	24-Nov-1889	01-Nov-1889	Joseph Belt	Carroll, Elizabeth	John Caspar	Emma McCormick
Belt	Charles	Edward	29-Aug-1909	8-Jul-1909	William Joseph Belt	Byrne, Cecelia		Blanche Von Holtem
Beltz	Eugene	Graher	26-Jul-1903	21-Jul-1903	Peter Eugene Beltz	Graher, Mary R.	Charles H. Graher	Teresa W. Graher
Belz	Elizabeth	Mary	31-Jul-1898	20-Jul-1898	Ferdinand Belz	Doyle, Catherine	James A. Doyle	Margaret Belz
Belz	Leon	Edward	23-Jul-1905	21-Jul-1905	Peter Eugene Belz	Graher, Regina Mary	Charles Leo Belz	Catherine Agnes Belz
Bennett	Bartholomew	Joseph	07-Jun-1896	04-Jun-1896	Edward Bennett	McKenna, Sarah	Patrick Vaughan	Catherine Curtin
Bennett	Edward	M.	05-Sep-1897	29-Aug-1897	Edward Bennett	McKenna, Sarah	John Donnolly	Margaret Maynor
Bennett	Helen	Nora	22-Sep-1907	15-Sep-1907	Edward Bennett	McKenna, Sarah	Charles Elwood	Mary Elwood
Bennett	James	Patrick	30-Jun-1901	10-Jun-1901	Edward Bennett	McKenna, Sarah	Bartley Bennett	Ellen Leahy
Bennett	John	Leon	02-Aug-1903	20-Jul-1903	Edward Bennett	McKenna, Sarah	Peter McKenna	Catherine McKenna
Bennett	Katherine		11-Dec-1898	29-Nov-1898	Edward Bennett	McKenna, Sarah	Peter Brodman	Honora Bennett
Bennett	Margaret	Mary	4-Jun-1905	3-Apr-1905	Edward Bennett	McKenna, Sarah	James Bennett	Catherine McNeal
Bennett	Thomas		22-Apr-1900	09-Apr-1900	Edward Bennett	McKenna, Sarah	Andrew O'Brien	Mary McCann
Bennett	William		23-May-1909	11-May-1909	Edward Bennett	McKenna, Sarah	William	Elizabeth McCaffrey
Bennett	Julia		19-Jun-1899	14-Jan-1899	John Bennett	Hooker, Clara		
Benoit	Edward	John	09-May-1886	26-Apr-1886	Arthur Benoit	Glenn, Ada	H.A. Brady	Mary G. Brady
Benoit	Horace	Otto	24-Jun-1888	01-Jun-1888	Arthur Benoit	Glenn, Adeline	Francis Joseph Anderson	Ann Dawson
Benson	Rosalia		12-May-1907	27-Apr-1904	Robert Benson	Affayroux, Elizabeth	James J. McNancy	Mary C. Affayroux
Berentine	George	Leonard	18-Nov-1894	10-Nov-1894	George Berentine	McCluskey, Ella	Edward McElroy	Ella Rigney
Berger	Charles	Joseph	24-Sep-1900	09-Sep-1900	Harry Berger	Carter, Mary Margaret	Joseph Carter	Elizabeth Metzger
Berkholder	Alice		15-Sep-1895	29-Aug-1895	William Berkholder	Lynch, Margaret		Catherine Frazier
Bernard	Sara	Ann	13-Jan-1889	14-Mar-1814	James Bernard	Rigby, Margaret		Sr. Mary, Little Sisters/Poor
Berntina	John	Elmer	29-Nov-1908	8-Nov-1908	George Berntina	McCluskey, Eleanor		Catherine Farrell
Berrier	Mary	Ellen	13-Jan-1884	06-Jan-1884	John Berrier	Zinnineweich, Elizabeth	Hugh Willis	Ann Finn
Bertrand	James	John Julius	25-Jun-1882	13-Jun-1882	George Silvester Bertrand	Collins, Mary Francis	Michael Torpey	Catherine Bertrand
Bertrand	James	Michael	14-Feb-1886	23-Jan-1886	John J. Bertrand	Moree, Mary	Andrew J. Wetherstine	Eleanor Wetherstine
Betz	Mary	Amelia	20-Dec-1908	18-Feb-1891	James Betz	Hildebrand, Elizabeth		Mary Blake
Betz	Mary	Agnes	12-Jan-1891	22-Dec-1890	John L. Betz	Westervelt, Emma Cecelia		Susan Volkman
Beynon	Grace	Mary	14-Mar-1897	25-Feb-1897	William Beynon	Welch, Bridget		Ann March
Biddison	James	Louis	28-Oct-1894	24-Jul-1846	James Albert Biddison	Mantle, Martha Jane	Joseph L. Dunn	
Biddison	Mary	Regina	13-Jan-1888	12-Nov-1887	William G. Biddison	Warmaling, Frances		Mary Regina Oldham
Biddle	Ellen	Elizabeth	11-Dec-1889	27-Nov-1889	Charles Biddle	Phar, Ann	Thomas Kelley	Mary Phar
Biemiller	John	Lloyd	3-Apr-1910	26-Mar-1910	Francis Ferdinand Biemiller	Mooney, Sarah Alice	Timothy Leonard	Agnes Mooney
Biettger	Mary	Katherine	12-Oct-1902	14-Oct-1902	George Boettzer	Bracken, Ann		Katherine Summers
Bigsley	Catherine		21-Jan-1894	03-Jan-1894	William Bigsley	Gunning, Ellen	Charles Satterfield	Catherine Brown
Billingmeyer	John	Edward	24-Sep-1893	30-Aug-1893	John Edward Billingmeyer	Gill, Virginia	Edward Jefferson Davis	Mary Ann Rogers
Bilzer	Edward	Emil	23-Jul-1905	30-Jun-1905	Edward Bilzer	Rudolph, Carolina	James Clarke	Julia Parr
Bilzer	Helen		26-Feb-1899	13-Feb-1899	Edward Bilzer	Rudolph, Caroline	John Gorman	Caroline Silverson
Binbicchi	Mary		4-Oct-1914	26-Jul-1914	Egisto Binbicchi	Boni, Zelindo	Anthony Prevosto	Teresa Prevosto
Bingley	Margaret	McLean	21-Feb-1909	8-Feb-1908	Thomas A. Bingley	Curley, Mary	William Curly	Mary Clarke
Bingley	Thomas	A.	19-Feb-1905	6-Feb-1905	Thomas Anderson Bingley	Curley, Mary E.	Michael Curley	Margaret Curley
Binstead	Eliza	Ann	26-Jul-1891	23-Jul-1891	George Binstead	O'Neill, Margaret	Patrick O'Neill	Ann O'Neill
Binstead	Mary	Joan	18-Aug-1889	11-Aug-1889	George Binstead	O'Neill, Margaret	John Enniget	Ann Kennedy
Binsteed	Margaret	Mary	15-Jan-1888	09-Jan-1888	George Binsteed	O'Neill, Margaret	Michael O'Neill	Mary Lally
Birdgel	Samuel			About 1812	[Blank]	[Blank]		
Birney	Francis		30-Mar-1891	04-Sep-1871	Charles Birney	Youngman, Elizabeth		
Bishop	Ann	Loretta	10-Dec-1893	01-Dec-1893	George Bishop	Hagerty, Susan	John Woods	Sara McCourt
Bishop	Catherine		25-Oct-1896	18-Oct-1896	George Bishop	Hagerty, Susann	Hugh Hagerty	Ann Wilkins
Bishop	George	Franklin	22-May-1887	12-May-1887	George Bishop	Hagerty, Susan	James Courtney	Elizabeth Hagerty
Bishop	Helen		18-Jun-1892	10-Jun-1892	George Bishop	Hagerty, Susan	Charles Jerome Coyle	Lillian Goonan
Bishop	Hugo		15-Jan-1899	05-Jan-1899	George Bishop	Hagerty, Susanna	Christian Wilkening	Catherine Weber
Bishop	John	Joseph	11-Jan-1903	31-Dec-1902	George Bishop	Hagerty, Susanna	John P. Gibson	Mary Hagerty
Bishop	William		04-Oct-1883	02-Oct-1883	George Bishop	Hagerty, Susan	Michael Farran	Catherine Duffy
Bishop	Catherine		24-May-1885	23-May-1885	George W. Bishop	Hagerty, Susan		Elizabeth Hagerty
Bishop	Madeline		13-Jan-1907	4-Jan-1907	John W. Bishop	Bruder, Catherine Teresa	John J. Gessner	Madeline Bruder
Bishop	Henry	William	18-May-1884	22-Feb-1884	William Bishop	Seiter, Catherine		Mary Felzman
Bishop	John	Owen	7-Mar-1915	22-Feb-1915	William Bishop	Friedel, Margaret	John M. Polhaus	Agnes Schutte
Bisker	Agnes	R.	02-Jan-1898	27-Dec-1898	John Bisker	Keane, Margaret		C. McDonnell
Bisker	Andrew		19-Nov-1899	14-Nov-1899	John Bisker	Keane, Margaret	John Wright	Ella O'Donnell
Bisker	Margaret	Rita	01-Sep-1901	27-Aug-1901	John Bisker	Keane, Mary	Jerome Bisker	Mary Langmead

6

LAST NAME	FIRST NAME	MIDDLE	BAPTISM	BIRTH	Father	Mother	SPONSORS	
Bitter	Mary	G. Caldwell	03-May-1891	25-Apr-1891	Christian Bitter	Duffy, Mary	Robert Vincent Cassidy	Elizabeth Edward
Bittner	Thomas	Henry	20-Dec-1888	28-Jun-1888	Christian Bittner	MacCubbin, Agnes		Mary MacCubbin
Bittner	Richard	James	31-Aug-1890	23-Aug-1890	William Bittner	Coughlin, Elizabeth	Caspar Bittner	Bridget Coughlin
Bivens	Wilber	Oscar	30-Apr-1896	05-Jan-1896	William Leonard Bivens	Cushing, Wilhelmina		Catherine Cushing
Blake	John	William	3-Sep-1905	26-Aug-1905	Henry A. Blake	Batterden, Catherine	John Batterden	Mary Batterden
Blake	Mary	Alice	15-Oct-1905	6-Oct-1905	James B. Blake	Monaghan, Ann	Arthur B. Blake	Mary A. Monaghan
Blake	Alan	Joseph	08-Sep-1889	04-Sep-1889	James Blake	Mullen, Ann	John Blake	Mary Elizabeth Drean
Blake	Alan	Joseph	20-Aug-1911	9-Aug-1911	James Blake	Monaghan, Ann	Martin J. Monaghan	Mary E. Blake
Blake	Ann	Elizabeth	10-Oct-1886	06-Oct-1886	James Blake	Mullen, Ann	John J. Cassidy	Genevieve Spence
Blake	Arthur		17-Aug-1884	10-Aug-1884	James Blake	Mullen, Ann	Thomas Jones	Elizabeth Jones
Blake	James	Brooke	15-Feb-1914	4-Feb-1914	James Blake	Monaghan, Ann Theresa	Albert J. Murphy	Elinor Dunn
Blake	Joseph		27-Mar-1898	21-Mar-1898	James Blake	Mullen, Ann	William Blake	Ann Drean
Blake	Mary	Ann	03-Jan-1892	23-Dec-1891	James Blake	Mullen, Ann	James Blake	Catherine Blake
Blake	William	Joseph	09-Apr-1882	01-Apr-1882	James Blake	Mullen, Ann		Mary Maguire
Blake	John	Walter	30-May-1909	20-May-1909	James Brooke Blake	Monaghan, Ann	William J. Blake	Sarah J. Monaghan
Blake	James	Brook	17-Feb-1907	10-Feb-1907	James J. Blake	Monaghan, Ann	John Monaghan	Ann B. Blake
Blake	Catherine	Elizabeth	19-Aug-1883	09-Aug-1883	Laurence Blake	McGraw, Catherine	William J. Flynn	Mary Ann Flynn
Blakeney	Francis		10-May-1898	20-Apr-1898	Thomas Blakeney	Steiner, Mary	Francis Steiner	Ann Steiner
Blakeney	William		10-May-1898	20-Apr-1898	Thomas Blakeney	Steiner, Mary	William Blakeney	Frances Blakeney
Blakeney	Francis	Mary	21-Dec-1890	08-Dec-1890	William Blakeney	Crosby, Frances	William Melin	Mary Byrne
Blakney	William	Maurice	23-Jul-1882	13-Jul-1882	William Blakney	Crosby, Frances	William Charles Mason	Eva Senft
Blanche	Joseph		01-Apr-1883	04-Mar-1883	Charles Blanche	Johnson, Blanche		Selina Johnson
Blaney	Samuel	Thomas	25-Jan-1888	19-Apr-1857	John Thomas Blaney	Mumma, Amanda Melvina	James McDevitt	Mary Mulligan
Blaney	Howard	Francis	29-Nov-1891	08-Nov-1891	Samuel Blaney	Ryan, Margaret	Patrick George Dyer	Mary Butler
Blaney	John	James	21-Sep-1884	17-Sep-1884	Samuel Blaney	Ryan, Margaret	John Ryan	Catherine Ryan
Blaney	Edward	Francis	26-Feb-1888	05-Feb-1888	Samuel Thomas Blaney	Ryan, Margaret Theresa	Michael James Scully	Mary Ann Scully
Blessing	Daniel		31-Dec-1882	[Blank]	[Blank]	[Blank]		
Blessing	Mabel	Loretta	23-Sep-1883	17-Sep-1883	Daniel Blessing	Peters, Mary Helen	Joseph W. Dale	Mary Blessing
Blessing	Mary	Josephine Edna	11-Mar-1888	25-Feb-1888	Edwin Francis Blessing	O'Donnell, Ann	Callistus Morgan Daily	Margaret Gillerlain
Blessing	William	Raymond	21-Nov-1914	21-Aug-1885	Ferdinand Blessing	North, Katherine	Margaret Moylan	
Bletsch	Julia	Edna	20-Oct-1889	04-Oct-1889	L. Bletsch	Wadom, Catherine		Mary Parrish
Blizzard	James	Leslie	8-Nov-1914	17-Oct-1914	Leslie Blizzard	Parlett, Matilda		Margaret Farley
Blizzard/Thompson	Virginia	Rebecca	04-May-1884	16-Mar-1851	Stephen Blizzard	Weinberger, Elizabeth		Alma Werrett
Bloysom	Raymond		28-Mar-1897	21-Mar-1897	Thomas Bloysom	Judan, Susannah		Sophia [Blank]
Blummer	Lillian		9-Oct-1914	14-Sep-1886	John Blummer	Bonsoff, Ludonia		Catherine Agnes Foley
Boegline	Catherine	Lydia	16-Sep-1888	10-Sep-1888	Charles Boegline	Fussell, Mary P.	Michael B. Fitzpatrick	Mrs. Kesterson
Boen	William		18-Mar-1891	04-Jan-1891	William Boen	O'Hare, Margaret		Joan Elizabeth Bracken
Boettger	Joan	Elizabeth	12-Apr-1896	02-Apr-1896	George M. Boettger	Bracken, Ann Elizabeth	Edward Peter	Florence Claus
Boettinger	Rosalie		25-Nov-1900	13-Nov-1900	George Boettinger	[N], Mary Louise	Louis Krummel	Ann Mary Krummel
Boettzer	Ann		27-Mar-1898	23-Mar-1898	George Boettzer	Krause, Louise	George F. Cain	Maggie Baker
Boettzer	George	Otto	07-Oct-1894	23-Sep-1894	George M. Boettzer	Bracken, Ann	William Stevenson	Margaret Stevenson
Bogy	Ann	Elizabeth	28-Jul-1889	18-Jul-1889	George L. Bogy	Stevenson, Ann E.		
Boland	John		15-Aug-1897	12-Aug-1897	John Boland	Conroy, Susan	James Newton Smith	Helen Hunter
Boland	Thomas	Charles	17-Sep-1882	01-Sep-1882	John Boland	Conroy, Susan	John Robinson Boland	Sarah Neary
Boland	Mary	Dolores	19-Apr-1914	10-Apr-1914	Thomas Carroll Boland	Neary, Mary	John Boland	Margaret Neary
Boland	John	Charles	25-Feb-1906	8-Feb-1906	Thomas Charles Boland	Neary, Mary		Mary Cunningham
Boland	Ann		30-Jul-1906	22-Jun-1906	John Bolger	Malone, Ann		Margaret Egan
Bolger	Frances	L.	4-Feb-1906	15-Jan-1906	Joseph Bolger	Fullen, Julia	John Dyer	Mary Shields
Bolgiano	Gertrude	Esther	01-Apr-1883	24-Mar-1883	William G. Bolgiano	Shields, Martha J.	Rev. M.F. Foley	Mary McGary
Bollinger	Elmer	Edward	22-Aug-1897	28-Jul-1897	George Bollinger	Quigley, Catherine		Mary Bolst
Bolst	Joseph	Patrick	21-Feb-1882	01-Feb-1882	Frederick Bolst	Peri, Velia		Diodata Dauda
Bona	William	Joseph	7-Feb-1915	31-Dec-1914	Joseph Bona			
Bond	Emma	Elizabeth	23-Oct-1885	About 1877	George W. Bond	Pryor, Francis A.	Simon Scarletta	Emma Pryor
Bond	Charles		12-Sep-1893	About 1850	Henry Bond	John, Susanna		
Bond	Ida	May Cecelia	03-May-1898	15-Oct-1867	Lorenza Dow Bond	Zergable, Mary		
Bond/Byrnes	Jeanette		13-Jul-1914	24-Aug-1879	George Bond	Bond, Elizabeth		Mrs. Byrnes
Bonner	Ida	Virginia	07-Feb-1897	31-Oct-1896	David Bonner	Lusby, Sophia	Andrew O'Day	Mary O'Day
Bonner	John	Francis	16-Mar-1913	1-Mar-1913	John Bonner	Deitz, Mary	Francis Dietz	Helen Kernan
Boone	Mary	Elizabeth	02-May-1913	24-Apr-1886	Davage Boone	Martz, Mary E.		Mary Martz
Boone	Elizabeth	Adele	09-Jul-1886	26-May-1886	John Boone	Smiley, Elizabeth		Jennie Smiley
Boone	Mary		03-Aug-1888	23-Jul-1888	John Boone	Smiley, Lizzie	J. McGrane	
Boone	Catherine	Eleanor	19-Jun-1887	17-Jun-1887	John H.D. Boone	Mantz, Mary		Mary Virginia Boone
Boone	Mary	Catherine	05-Aug-1888	30-Jul-1888	John H.D. Boone	Mantz, Mary E.		Catherine Kunkle

7

LAST NAME	FIRST NAME	MIDDLE	BAPTISM	BIRTH	Father	Mother	SPONSORS
Boone	Joseph	Monroe	02-Apr-1882	22-Mar-1882	Robert Charles Boone	McGregor, Catherine Agnes	Joan Maglone
Born	Francis		21-Mar-1897	23-Feb-1897	Francis Born	Dempsey, Lizzie	Ann Murray
Borsella	Teresa		15-Jun-1913	19-Mar-1913	Francis Borsella	Lantine, Mary	Rose Patti
Bortas	William	George	8-May-1910	7-Apr-1910	Louis Bortas	Orban, Margaret	Theresa Bogar
Bosley	Charles	Leon	13-Sep-1903	20-Jul-1903	Charles Bosley	Williams, Ida	James Conlan
Bosley	William	Henry	25-Feb-1906	21-Nov-1905	Charles L. Bosley	Williams, Ida Mary	Francis M. Chipman
Bosley	C.		20-Sep-1887	04-Sep-1831	N. Tracey	Bosley, Diana	Henrietta Glenn
Bosson	Ann	Helen	19-Oct-1884	21-Aug-1884	James Bosson	Delaney, Mary	Lily Bosson
Bosson	Edith	Winchell	04-Sep-1892	13-Aug-1892	James Bosson	Delaney, Mary	Edith Brady
Bosson	Eugene	H.	19-Dec-1886	25-Nov-1886	James Bosson	Delaney, Mary Ann	Ann Donahue
Bosson	Gertrude	De Sales	12-Aug-1888	20-Jul-1888	James Bosson	Delaney, Mary	William Dugan
Bosson	Lillian	Merceda	18-Nov-1894	29-Oct-1894	James Bosson	Delaney, Mary	James W. Dugan
Bosson	Henry	Edgar	25-Jun-1882	08-Jun-1882	James Winsell Bosson	Delaney, Mary	James Grady
Bosson	Margaret		24-Sep-1902	24-Sep-1902	William Bosson	Rusk, Margaret	Helen Bosson
Boston	Charles		24-Sep-1884	20-Sep-1884	George Boston	Kilner, Mary J.	Catherine Kelly
Botsch	Andrew	William	22-Mar-1914	10-Mar-1914	William C. Botsch	Berger, Josephine M.	Rose Reilly
Botta	Martin	Peter	14-Dec-1913	18-Nov-1913	Frederick Botta	Vincent, Louise	Urlig Bora
Botta	Robert	Leon	15-Nov-1914	28-Oct-1914	Frederick Botta	Vincent, Louise	Amelia Vincent
Boubon	John	Francis	06-Jun-1898	30-May-1898	August Bourbon	McGinnis, Catherine	Mary Bourbon
Bouchet	Catherine		26-Mar-1911	21-Mar-1911	Samuel Bouchet	Kavanaugh, Catherine	Ann Anderson
Bouchet	Ellen	Elizabeth	23-Aug-1903	04-Aug-1903	Samuel Bouchet	Sullivan, Julia	Ann Cavanaugh
Bouchett	William		8-Oct-1905	24-Sep-1905	S. Bouchette	Sullivan, Julia	Mary Byrnes
Bouchier	Charles	Adele	15-Mar-1885	10-Feb-1885	Francis Bouchier	Creney, Margaret	Delia Burke
Bourbon	Ann	Elizabeth	07-Mar-1900	27-Feb-1900	August Bourbon	McGuiness, Catherine	Rose Bourbon
Bourbon	Arthur	Basil	26-Oct-1902	19-Oct-1902	August Bourbon	McGuiness, Catherine	Mary Bourbon
Bourbon	Catherine	Cecelia	05-Jan-1896	30-Dec-1895	August Bourbon	McGuiness, Catherine	Rose Bourbon
Bourbon	Jerome		18-Aug-1889	20-Jul-1889	August Claude Bourbon	McGuiness, Catherine	Ann Bautz
Bourbon	Augustus	James	05-Nov-1893	19-Oct-1893	Augustus Bourbon	McGuiness, Catherine	James Cain
Bourdon	Mary		06-Sep-1891	01-Sep-1891	August Bourdon	McGuiness, Catherine	Mary Roder
Bourke	Samuel	Thomas	31-Jul-1904	17-Jul-1904	Samuel Bourke	Owens, Elizabeth A.	Ann Owens
Bovello	Vincent		06-Dec-1896	29-Nov-1896	Angelo Bovello	Bananes, Conserta	Felice Zido
Bovello	Concetta		12-Jun-1898	29-May-1898	John Baptist Bovello	Seres, Vincentia	Joseph Serio
Bowen	Helen	Mary	26-Jan-1890	13-Jan-1890	Godfried Bowen	Heim, Ann	Joseph Bovello
Bowen	Laurence	Cornelius	09-Jul-1893	22-Jun-1893	Henry Bowen	Cornelius, Mary	Helen Moore
Bower	Helen	Joan (Janet)	06-Jun-1886	28-Apr-1886	Thomas C. Bower	Strible, Jeanette S.	Charles Jendrick
Bower	Charles	Alfred	26-Feb-1888	17-Dec-1887	Thomas Clifford Bower	Strible, Jeanette S.	
Bower	Clarence	Wilcox	25-Nov-1883	01-Nov-1883	Thomas Clifford Bower	Strible, John Sophia	William Wilcox
Bower	Ferdinand	Clifford	07-Dec-1884	08-Nov-1884	Thomas Clifford Bower	Strible, Joan	Mary Helen Strible
Bowers	Mary	Lydia	14-Jul-1895	04-Jul-1895	Henry M. Bowers	Cornelius, Mary	Bridget Cornelius
Bowers/Long	Ann	Catherine	22-May-1886	27-Apr-1854	Nicolas Bowers	Foegelsohn, Margaret S.	Julia Quirk
Bowes	A.	Maskell	05-Jun-1898	24-May-1898	Joseph Bowes	Kelly, Mary	Ella Kelly McGraw
Bowes	Leo		15-Jan-1893	08-Jan-1893	Patrick A. Bowes	Manning, Mary	Francis Maskell
Bowes	William	Joseph	23-Nov-1890	15-Nov-1890	Patrick A. Bowes	Manning, Mary	Joseph Bowes
Bowes	Thomas		19-Apr-1896	About 1896	Patrick Bowes	Manning, Mary	William Bowes
Bowes	Urban	James	04-Feb-1900	28-Jan-1900	Patrick Bowes	Manning, Mary	James Brown
Bowes	Catherine	Elizabeth	20-Jan-1895	09-Jan-1895	William Bowes	McDonald, Mary	Matthew Lynch
Bowes	Joseph	Patrick	20-Oct-1889	07-Oct-1889	William Bowes	McDonald, Mary	Michael James Sheehy
Bowes	Mary	Elizabeth	21-Nov-1886	08-Nov-1886	William J. Bowes	[Blank]	Joseph Bowes
Bowes	Isabelle		24-Sep-1893	19-Sep-1893	William Joseph Bowes	McDonnell, Mary Ann	McDonald, Mary
Bowes	Margaret	Joseph	17-Jul-1892	14-Jun-1892	William Joseph Bowes	McDonnell, Mary Ann	Patrick Laurie
Bowman	Joseph	James	21-Apr-1907	30-Mar-1907	Joseph F. Bowman	Napfel, Elizabeth	Peter McCormick
Boylan	Ann	Elizabeth	6-Jun-1915	31-May-1915	William Boylan	O'Hara, Ann	Joseph James Kube
Boylan	Margaret		8-Mar-1908	26-Feb-1908	William Guy Boylan	O'Hara, Ann	Joseph Hagerty
Boylan	Thomas	William	3-Mar-1912	28-Feb-1912	William Guy J. Boylan	O'Hara, Ann	James O'Hara
Boylan	Catherine		06-Aug-1882	18-Jul-1882	William Henry Boylan	Todd, Mary Ann	Thomas Sheeler
Boylan	William	Henry	23-Mar-1884	02-Mar-1884	William Henry Boylan	Todd, Mary Ann	John Duff
Boylan	Charles	Joseph	18-Feb-1914	2-Feb-1914	William J. Boylan	O'Hara, Ann E.	Charles R. O'Hara
Boylan	Mary		30-Jan-1910	26-Jan-1910	William J. Boylan	O'Hara, Ann E.	James Garrity
Boyle	Mary	Elizabeth	21-Sep-1890	15-Aug-1890	Edward Francis Boyle	Danks, Caroline Virginia	James Francis Boyle
Boyle	Ann	Gertrude	25-Oct-1885	16-Oct-1885	John Boyle	Brooks, Ann E.	Charles J. Brooks
Boyle	James		14-Oct-1888	28-Sep-1888	John Boyle	Brooks, Ann E.	Samuel Boyle
Boyle	John	Brooke	12-Dec-1886	22-Nov-1886	John Boyle	Brooks, Ann E.	John Brooks
Boyle	William		01-Jun-1884	11-May-1884	Patrick Boyle	Sprigg, Mary Ann	James Boyle

Additional sponsor column entries (right-most):
Lillian Campbell; Ann Anderson; Joseph Cavanaugh; Patrick J. Brady; Jerome Bourbon; Claude Bourbon; Michael Bautz; William Roder; Polonia Bovello; Augusta Wilcox; Iola Wilson; Ann Wilcox; John Gormley; McDonald, Mary; Mary Bowes; Bridget Lynch; Ann Lynch; Elizabeth McCormick; Mary Corrigan; Patrick Bowes; Mary Ann Teresa Hughes; Ann Manning; Mary Elizabeth Bowes; Mary L. Kube; Hazel Donahue; Alma G. Boylan; Ann O'Hara; Mary Dugan; Elizabeth Dugan; Mildred O'Hara; Margaret O'Hara; Mary Shea; Catherine Brooks; Elizabeth Boyle; Susan Brooks; Mary Kelly

LAST NAME	FIRST NAME	MIDDLE	BAPTISM	BIRTH	Father	Mother	SPONSORS	
Boyle	Robert	Jerome	01-Sep-1889	11-Aug-1889	Robert J. Boyle	Hagerty, Mary	Patrick Hagerty	Maru A. Hagerty
Bracken	William		11-Mar-1888	27-Feb-1888	John Bracken	Flaherty, Ann	Matthew Louis Dauger	Helen Orr
Bracken	William		15-Mar-1896	24-Feb-1896	Joseph Bracken	Corcoran, Margaret	William Wilcox	Margaret Kirwan
Bracken	Ann	Cecelia	30-Jul-1893	19-Jul-1893	Joseph Daniel Bracken	Cochran, Margaret Cecelia	Robert Ambrose Reed	Ann Elizabeth Bracken
Bracken	Mary	Helen	02-Jun-1901	08-May-1901	Samuel Bracken	Coughlen, Elizabeth	Hugh Shea	Susanna Coughlen
Braden	Catherine	Henrietta	23-Sep-1894	25-Aug-1894	George Washington Brady	Garrity, Ann Elizabeth	Edward August Roberts	Catherine Garrity
Braden	John	Joseph	29-Aug-1915	16-Aug-1915	John Braden	Cohan, Mary	John Cox	Mary Kelly
Braden	Mary	Bridget	14-Jun-1914	6-Jun-1914	John Braden	Cohen, Mary	Joseph Muldoon	Bridget Muldoon
Braden	Frankford	Leonard	03-Jul-1887	15-Jun-1887	Lemuel Braden	Glenn, Mary	George Wash. Braden	Ann Elizabeth Braden
Braden	Grover	Raymond	24-Aug-1884	31-Jul-1884	Lemuel T. Braden	Dempster, Mary Glenn	Francis M. King	Margaret Fitzpatrick
Bradford	Mary	Regina	15-Feb-1914	3-Feb-1914	James Bradford	Hubbard, Catherine	James H. Hubbard	Margaret Hubbard
Bradley	Mary		04-May-1884	24-Apr-1884	Andrew Joseph Bradley	Driscoll, Margaret	James Carr	Mary Carr
Bradley	Joseph		6-May-1913	31-Mar-1836	Elijah Bradley	Collier, Elizabeth	Robert Tray	
Bradley	James	Michael	29-May-1887	16-May-1887	James Bradley	Nertney, Mary	John Nertney	Cecelia Brown
Bradley	John	George	22-May-1892	10-May-1892	James Bradley	Nertney, Mary		Clara Trainor
Bradley	Rebecca	Laura	17-Jun-1888	03-Jun-1888	James Bradley	Nertney, Mary		Mary McNamee
Bradley	Michael	Francis	12-Sep-1887	08-Sep-1887	John Bradley	McCarron, Ann	Francis McCarron	Mary C. Affayroux
Brady	Alexander	William	04-Jul-1886	19-Jun-1886	Andrew Brady	Driscoe, Margaret	William T. Murphy	Elizabeth McKenna
Brady	Agnes		20-Nov-1910	6-Nov-1910	Edward Brady	Banahan, Agnes	Raymond Flaherty	Mary A. Lavery
Brady	Winfred		5-Apr-1914	21-Mar-1814	Edward Brady	Banahan, Agnes	Joseph McEvoy	Joan Mooney
Brady	Mary	Frances	13-Sep-1908	3-Sep-1908	Edward J. Brady	[Blank], Agnes Mary	John [Blank]	Agnes Mooney
Brady	Alma	Alice Marr	08-Jan-1888	28-Dec-1887	Hugh A. Brady	Donohue, Mary G.	Rev. J.D. Marr	Alice McMahon
Brady	Hugh	Alexander	28-May-1885	16-May-1885	Hugh A. Brady	Donohue, Mary	John W. Sullivan	Mary Foley
Brady	Helen	Ann	12-Nov-1882	28-Oct-1882	Hugh Alexander Brady	Donohue, Mary Gertrude	Charles Edwin Dudrow	Helen Virginia Gosden
Brady	Henry	Delaney	25-Nov-1883	17-Nov-1883	James Henry Brady	Delaney, Elizabeth	John Vincent Delaney	Mary Gertrude Brady
Brady	Robert		25-Apr-1885	03-Apr-1885	John O'Connell	Daly, Helen	John Smith	Catherine Smith
Brady	Albert		18-Mar-1888	06-Feb-1888	Joseph Brady	Snyder, Lotta	Edward Boyle	Ann Carey
Brady	Margaret		07-Aug-1887	01-Aug-1887	Thomas Brady	Roddy, Mary	Michael Roddy	Bridget Roddy
Brady	Patrick	Roddy	23-Sep-1894	10-Sep-1894	Thomas Brady	Roddy, Mary	Patrick Roddy	Catherine West
Brady	Thomas		12-Jan-1890	04-Jan-1890	Thomas Brady	Roddy, Mary	Thomas Roddy	Margaret Roddy
Brady	Emma	Theresa	29-Jun-1890	05-Apr-1890	William J. Brady	Hinton, Ann B.		Sara Dean
Braguglio	Anthony		2-Aug-1908	5-Dec-1907	Anthony Braguglio	Venitiano, Rose	Vincent Piraino	Antoinette Venitiano
Brandan	Francis	Xavier	1-Jun-1913	12-May-1913	Howard E. Brandan	Whittie, Agnes R.		Catherine Loller
Brandt	Henry	Albert	17-May-1891	08-May-1891	Charles Brandt	Geotz, John [sic]	Henry Hucht	Sophia Hucht
Brandt	Robert	L.	27-Dec-1903	11-Nov-1903	William Edward Brandt	Taylor, Rebecca	Robert Oliver Hooper	Margaret Brandt
Brannan	Catherine	Genevieve	2-Aug-1908	23-Jul-1908	Hugh Edward Brannan	Snyder, Ada Frances	Michael Thomas Brannan	Genevieve Snyder
Brannan	John	Patrick	28-Mar-1909	18-Mar-1909	Jerome Joseph Brannan	Booker, Mary		Mary Brannan
Brannan	John		29-Apr-1883	22-Apr-1883	John Brannan	Hennings, Mary Elizabeth	Owen Murphy	Sara Brannan
Brannan	Ann	Mary	3-Sep-1911	26-Aug-1911	John J. Brannan	Booker, Ann M.	Patrick Stafford	Mary G. Brannan
Brannan	Bernard	Joseph	14-Sep-1913	2-Sep-1913	John J. Brannan	Booker, Ann M.	Bernard McNally	Mary Haire
Brannan	Margaret	C.	26-Oct-1907	26-Oct-1907	John Joseph Brannan	Booker, Ann Mary		
Brannan	Mary		9-Dec-1906	30-N0v-1906	John Joseph Brannan	Booker, Ann M.	James Jenkins	Margaret McEnder
Brannan	Mary		14-May-1899	02-May-1899	John P. Brannan	Jennings, Mary	Frederick Lang	Caroline Lang
Bratton	Joseph	Henry	14-Jul-1912	02-Jan-1870	Abel Bratton	Eubanks, Mary	Francis Irwin	Mary Irwin
Brawner	Francis	Pearl	22-Jul-1883	22-Jul-1883	Daniel Walter Brawner	Phillips, Francis McClellan	Daniel A. Conners	Ida M. Phillips
Brawner	John	David	29-Jul-1894	30-May-1894	George L. Brawner	Brown, Maud	Henry McDevitt	Isabelle Dawson
Brazier	Catherine	Ellen	13-Jul-1902	23-Jun-1902	Thomas Brazier	Long, Catherine	Thomas Davey	Catherine Brazier
Brazier	Helen	Mary	21-Aug-1892	05-Aug-1892	Thomas Brazier	Long, Catherine	Thomas Finn	Mary Finn
Brazier	James		23-Sep-1894	08-Sep-1894	Thomas Brazier	Long, Catherine		Martha Croghan
Breen	Elizabeth		28-Jun-1895	26-Jun-1895	James Breen	McGinnity, Catherine		Mary McGinnity
Breen	John	Albert	23-Dec-1888	10-Dec-1888	James Breen	McGinnity, Catherine	John Hand	Elizabeth Hand
Breen	Francis		21-Jun-1891	17-Jun-1891	James M. Breen	McGinnity, Catherine	Robert C. Brown	Francis R. Brown
Breighner	Mary	Estelle	11-Dec-1892	04-Dec-1892	Francis Breighner	Stoter, Laura Catherine		Agnes Willet
Bremer	Catherine		27-Mar-1887	15-Mar-1887	Charles Bremmer	Lynch, Mary		Mary Riordan
Bremmer	Honora	Theresa	13-Jan-1885	10-Dec-1884	Charles Bremmer	Lynch, Mary Agnes		Ann Murphy
Bremmer	Mary	Agnes	13-May-1883	01-May-1883	Charles Bremmer	Lynch, Mary Agnes	Edward Lynch	Mary Carey
Brennan	George	Joseph	7-Aug-1904	29-Apr-1887	George W. Brennan	Nugent, Alice	Patrick J. Brennan	Letitia Murphy
Brentine	Helen		7-Aug-1904	25-Jul-1904	George Brentine	McCluskey, Helen	Joseph Welsh	Catherine Murphy
Brentine	Mary	Elizabeth	09-Jun-1889	20-May-1889	George Brentine	McCluskey, Ella	Charles L. McPoland	Elizabeth McCluskey
Brentine	William	Edward	28-Aug-1892	25-Aug-1892	George Brentine	McCluskey, Helen	Aquila Brentine	Mary Brentine
Brere	Martin	Floyd	15-Jan-1911	10-Dec-1910	Martin Laurence Brere	Weber, Mary	Floyd Smith	Ann Mary Leonard
Bresnan	Helen	Gertrude	12-Nov-1893	04-Nov-1893	Peter Bresnan	Smith, Ann	John Joseph Rea	Ida Mary Burke
Breuning	Dolores	Cecelia	20-Nov-1904	13-Oct-1904	Joseph Breuning	Mitchell, Mary		Sadie May

9

LAST NAME	FIRST NAME	MIDDLE	BAPTISM	BIRTH	Father	Mother	SPONSORS
Brewer	Francis	Joseph	22-Nov-1914	6-Oct-1914	Henry Brewer	Bloomer, Stella	Lillian Kavanaugh
Brewer	Isabelle	Dorothy	10-Mar-1912	31-Dec-1911	John Brewer	Buttner, Mary E.	Ellenor Walters
Brewster	Francis	Edmund	10-Jun-1883	25-Apr-1883	John Brewster	Ahearn, Catherine	Catherine Walsh
Brewster	James	Joseph	09-Oct-1885	27-Aug-1885	John Brewster	Ahearn, Catherine	Grace Mary Lyons
Brewster	Rose	Viola	14-Feb-1892	31-Jan-1892	John Brewster	Ahearn, Catherine	Bernard Byrnes / Ann De Vaughn
Brewster	Carmelita		12-Apr-1908	2-Apr-1908	John J. Brewster	Culleton, Mary C.	James Callahan / Elizabeth McGonigle
Brewster	Charles	Leonard	4-Mar-1906	15-Feb-1906	John Joseph Brewster	Ahern, Catherine	James Colleton / Blanche O'Brien
Brian	Elizabeth	Mary	13-Jul-1882	22-Jun-1882	George Brian	Berry, Elizabeth	Catherine Murphy
Brian	Helen	Mary	30-Jun-1885	23-May-1885	George Brian	Barry, Elizabeth	Catherine Eason
Brickham	Arthur	O.	21-Sep-1890	12-Aug-1890	John Emmanuel Brickham	Keller, Elizabeth Barbara	George Alphonsus Keller / Elizabeth Agnes Keller
Briggs	Ann	Clara	5-Oct-1913	19-Sep-1913	Raymiond Briggs	Saunders, Stella	Allen Saunders / Clara Saunders
Brignardello	Edith	Mary	26-Aug-1888	26-Jun-1888	Louis Brignardello	Lentz, Elizabeth	Edith Lentz
Brink	Margaret	Elizabeth	26-Sep-1897	12-Aug-1897	William Brink	Ryan, Mary Agnes	John P. Lacey / Helen O'Keefe
Brinsteed	Agnes	Aloysius	10-Jun-1894	03-Jun-1894	George Brinsteed	O'Neill, Margaret	William Bray / Mary O'Keefe
Broad	Ferdenand		22-Aug-1897	05-Aug-1897	George Broad	Fitzpatrick, Alice	Ann Mochstein
Broderick	Mary	Magdalene	22-Jul-1883	05-Jul-1883	Thomas M. Broderick	Kilchenstein, Mary Elizabeth	Michael Kilchenstein / Mary Magdelene Krener
Brogan	Ann	M.	30-Aug-1914	22-Aug-1914	Patrick Brogan	Burke, Mary	James Nolan / Bridget Burke
Bronisky	Joseph	Vincent	22-Apr-1900	13-Apr-1900	Theodore Bronisky	White, Laura C.	Elizabeth White
Brooks	Flora	Isabelle	17-Nov-1898	About 1898	Joseph Brooks	Crouch, Florence	Joan Boone
Brooks	Flora	Isabelle	05-Mar-1899	17-Nov-1898	Joseph Brooks	Crouch, Flora	Francis Crouch / Joan Boone
Brooks	Joseph	Rodney	17-Mar-1895	04-Mar-1895	Joseph Brooks	Crouch, Flora	Albanus Brinton Crouch / Laura Crouch
Brooks	William	Crouch	21-Feb-1892	12-Feb-1892	Joseph Brooks	Crouch, Flora	Hugh A. Brady / Virginia Boone
Brooks	Mary	Elizabeth	10-Jun-1883	02-Feb-1861	Louis Brooks	Morris, Elizabeth	Frances J. Bevan
Brooks	Peter	Murray	11-Apr-1886	26-Mar-1886	Peter Brooks	Meehan, Catherine	James Vincent Brooks / Elizabeth Getz
Brooks	Catherine	Meehan	11-Nov-1888	26-Oct-1888	Peter Murray Brooks	Meehan, Catherine	Edward Meehan / Susanna Brooks
Brooks	Mary	Irene	10-Aug-1893	11-Sep-1892	Samuel Brooks	Brooks, Ann	Mary Garity
Brooks	Thomas	Catherine	11-Aug-1889	07-Aug-1889	Thomas Brooks	Foley, Eleanor	Daniel Geary / Eleanor Condlan
Brooks	Agnes	Joseph	25-Oct-1891	13-Oct-1891	Thomas Brooks	Foley, Helen	Frederick Blackison / Mary Foley
Brosnan	Ann		15-Sep-1887	05-Sep-1887	Peter Brosnan	Smith, Ann	Rose Toner
Brosnan	Elizabeth		23-Aug-1891	11-Aug-1891	Peter Brosnan	Smith, Ann	John Roddy / Helen Dockry
Brosnan	Elizabeth	Carlos	29-Mar-1896	15-Mar-1896	Peter Brosnann	Murphy, Ann	John Murphy / Margaret Carlos
Brosnan	Margaret		14-Jun-1885	04-Jun-1885	Peter Brosnann	Smith, Ann	Andrew O'Brien / Susan Roddy
Broughtin	Margaret	Mary	31-Aug-1913	14-Aug-1913	Henry Broughtin	McLaughlin, Catherine	Leo Smith / Agnes Willis
Browing	Joseph	Edward	26-Mar-1882	12-Mar-1882	Edward Browing	Smith, Mary	James Reilly / Mary Reilly
Brown	Francis	Joseph	07-Nov-1886	31-Oct-1886	Charles Brown	Hill, Mary	Francis J. Osterman / Ann Koenig
Brown	George	Byron	16-Nov-1911	8-Sep-1911	George B. Brown	Wills, Ann E.	E.A. Hannan / Hannah Lambreck
Brown	John		02-Mar-1886	14-Feb-1858	Henry Brown	Patterson, Mary Ann	Margaret McDonald
Brown	Wilmer	Valentine	27-Aug-1910	13-Aug-1910	Henry Brown	Nelson, Ellen	[Blank] Schofield / Rose A. Klug
Brown	Ann	Elizabeth	01-Aug-1897	21-Jul-1897	James Brown	Rosensteel, Victoria E.	Edward Stewart / Mary Donelly
Brown	Grace		08-Sep-1901	01-Jul-1901	James Brown	Rosensteel, Victoria	Ann M. Farren
Brown	Walter	Scott	11-Apr-1908	24-Aug-1851	James Brown	Gillen, Sarah	Josephine Brown
Brown	Francis	Louis	19-Dec-1909	15-Dec-1909	James Ignatius Brown	Rosensteel, Victoria	Albert Brown / Josephine Brown
Brown	Ignatius		16-Nov-1890	08-Nov-1890	James Ignatius Brown	Rosensteel, Victoria Elizabeth	Edward C. Bamberger / Mary Louis Rosensteel
Brown	Joseph	Bartlett	18-Nov-1888	09-Nov-1888	James Ignatius Brown	Rosensteel, Victoria Elizabeth	Louis Charles Brown / Gertrude Rosensteel
Brown	Theodore	Rosensteel	17-Mar-1895	08-Mar-1895	James Ignatius Brown	Rosensteel, Victoria Elizabeth	John McIntyre / Catherine Lewis
Brown	Victor		18-Sep-1892	08-Sep-1892	James Ignatius Brown	Rosensteel, Victoria Elizabeth	Thomas Patrick Shehan / Harriet Kearney
Brown	Mary		30-Jun-1886	29-Apr-1886	James W. Brown	McGreevey, Hannah	Mary O'Dea
Brown	William		18-Jul-1886	10-Jun-1886	Joseph Brown	McFarland, Frances (Hattie)	Rose Brown
Brown	Elizabeth	Eleanor	28-Mar-1909	13-Mar-1909	Michael J. Brown	Cox, Sarah	Thomas O'Dea / Joan McGraw
Brown	Edward	Benedict	04-Apr-1886	21-Mar-1886	Patrick Brown	McCormick, Mary	Michael Brown / Rose McCormick
Brown	John		12-Sep-1887	05-Sep-1887	Patrick Brown	McCormick, Mary	William Long / Lenora Seager
Brown	Mary	Ann	03-Aug-1884	24-Jul-1884	Patrick Brown	McCormick, Mary	John E. McCormick / Catherine Brown
Brown	Blanche	Catherine	1-Dec-1914	30-Jul-1903	Richard Brown	Baugher, Mary	Mary Cassidy
Brown	Mary		07-Oct-1888	15-Sep-1888	Richard Brown	Barton, Emma	William Brown / Delia Moran
Brown	Wilson	John	9-May-1915	3-Jul-1907	Richard Brown	Baugher, Mary	Maurice King / Mary Kelly
Brown	Margaret	L.	7-Aug-1904	26-Jul-1904	Richard P. Brown	Baugher, Maud	Margaret Genoy
Brown	Emma	Catherine	06-Feb-1887	28-Jan-1887	Robert Brown	Grady, Ann	Martin Holmes / Catherine Breen
Brown	Helen		08-Jun-1884	01-Jun-1884	Robert Brown	Grady, Ann	Dennis Riordan / Mary McGinnity
Brown	Robert		06-Aug-1882	31-Jul-1882	Robert Brown	Grady, Ann	Patrick Elwood / Helen McGinnity
Brown	Mary	Teresa	08-Sep-1889	01-Sep-1889	Robert C. Brown	McGinnity, Francis	James Breen / Mary Ellen Hurd
Brown	Agnes		22-Feb-1891	13-Feb-1891	Robert Charles Brown	McGinnity, Francis Regina	Andrew Linhard
Brown	Catherine		25-Dec-1892	17-Dec-1892	Robert Charles Brown	McGinnity, Francis Regina	Joseph Bernard Mitchel
Brown	Robert	Charles	21-Oct-1894	14-Oct-1894	Robert Charles Brown	McGinity, Ann	Joseph Stoltmeir

LAST NAME	FIRST NAME	MIDDLE	BAPTISM	BIRTH	Father	Mother	SPONSORS
Brown	Rebecca		21-Mar-1890	About 1820	Stephen Brown	Murray, Phoebe	Elizah Milburne
Brown	Blanche	Mary	22-Feb-1891	05-Feb-1891	Thomas Brown	Ruff, Isabelle	Robert Brown	Virginia Ruff
Brown	Charles	Thomas	15-Dec-1889	27-Nov-1889	Thomas Brown	Ruff, Isabelle	William R. Ruff	Clara Curran
Brown	Herbert		29-Sep-1895	08-Sep-1895	Thomas Brown	Ruff, Isabelle	William Curran	Joan Ruff
Brown	Edna	Mary	10-Jul-1892	24-Jun-1892	Thomas J. Brown	Ruff, Isabelle	William Curran	Isabelle Ruff
Brown	Thomas	James	27-Jun-1897	18-Jun-1897	Thomas J. Brown	Ruff, Isabelle	Walter Curran	Elizabeth Clifford
Brown	Edward		17-Apr-1910	3-Apr-1910	Timothy Brown	Brown, Nellie	William McCardell	Ann Brown
Brown	Elmer	Joseph	9-Aug-1908	20-Jul-1908	Timothy Brown	Brown, Nellie	Robert Sheehan	Mrs. Gorsuch
Brown	Helen	Regina	15-Aug-1915	31-Jul-1915	Timothy Brown	Brown, Helen Regina	Joseph Sheehan	Ann Sheehan
Brown	Robert	Timothy	17-Nov-1912	6-Nov-1912	Timothy Brown	Brown, Helen	John Sheridan	Sarah McNamee
Brown	Catherine	Rita	22-Jun-1913	3-Jun-1913	W. J. Brown	Moylan, Catherine		Margaret Tarr
Brown	Charles	Hopkins	17-Apr-1908	17-Apr-1900	Walter Brown	Kirk, Mary		Elizabeth McGonigle
Brown	Edward	Wallace	17-Apr-1908	15-Mar-1895	Walter Brown	Kirk, Mary		Ann Farren
Brown	James	Oliver	17-Apr-1908	30-Nov-1897	Walter Brown	Kirk, Mary		Ann Farren
Brown	Joseph	Leon	19-Apr-1908	24-Mar-1908	Walter Brown	Kirk, Mary	George Leo McCart	Mary Hawkins
Brown	Joseph	Walter	3-Mar-1915	21-Jan-1915	Walter Brown	Moylan, Catherine		Roger Wooden
Brown	Ida	Isabelle	19-May-1890	18-Nov-1889	Walter S. Brown	Kirk, Mary		Helen King
Brown	Mary	Eliza	18-Sep-1885	18-Aug-1885	Walter S. Brown	Kirk, Mary		Julia McLaughlin
Brown	Sara	Jacob	10-Apr-1887	24-Mar-1887	Walter Scot Brown	Kirk, Mary		Mary Carroll
Brown	Walter	Hugo	08-Jul-1894	29-Jun-1894	Walter Scott Brown			Olivia Dunn
Brown	Charles		18-Feb-1883	[Blank]	William Brown	Campbell, Sara	Alfred Wooley	Elizabeth Reardon
Brown	James	Joseph	11-Dec-1898	05-Dec-1898	William Brown	Gunning, Catherine	James Gunning	Mary Gunning
Brown	Mary	Helen	13-Mar-1887	10-Mar-1887	William Brown	Campbell, Sara	Charles Lindevall	Mary Lindevall
Brown	William	Hugh	17-Oct-1889	10-Oct-1889	William Brown	Gunning, Catherine	Thomas Gunning	Ann Fenerty
Brown	William	Salesium	28-Sep-1890	17-Sep-1890	William Brown	Campbell, Sara	Patrick Brown	Elizabeth Riordan
Brown	John		05-Feb-1888	31-Jan-1888	William H. Brown	Campbell, Sara H.	John E. McCormick	Bridget Harvey
Brown	Mary		13-Sep-1903	25-Aug-1903	William J. Brown	Skelton, Mary	James J. Connelly	Hanna Brown
Browne	Catherine	Mary	22-Oct-1911	5-Oct-1911	Michael Browne	Cox, Sara A.	Terence Cox	Ann Skelton
Browne	John	Joseph	22-May-1910	5-May-1910	Michael J. Browne	Cox, Sarah	John Cox	Ellen Cox
Browning	Francis	Albert	02-Nov-1893	09-Feb-1893	[Blank]	Browning, Laura Cecelia		Genevieve Nessler
Bruce	Mary	Louise	22-Nov-1903	11-Nov-1903	Henry Bruce	O'Keefe, Josephine	Joseph Moylan	Mary Donohye
Bruce	Emma	D.	22-Oct-1905	8-Oct-1905	Howard Bruce	O'Keefe, Joan	John Welby	Catherine Sigwuld
Bruce	Howard	Josephine	3-Dec-1904	27-Oct-1877	William Bruce	Leith, Emma		Mary O'Keefe
Bruck	Frederick	Edward	26-Aug-1883	20-Aug-1883	George Bruck	Lyons, Eleonora	Frederick Bitler	Catherine Bitler
Brunner	Esther	Ann	25-Jun-1911	15-Jun-1911	Joseph Brunner	Hayden, Margaret	James Hayden	Ann Brunner
Brunning	Catherine	Mary	3-Nov-1901	30-Oct-1901	Henry Brunning	Lyons, Mary	Henry Rosendale	Catherine Lyons
Bryd	William	Edward	29-Feb-1890	05-Jan-1890	William Byrd	Kelley, Sarah		
Buberl	Ann	Beatrice	17-Oct-1897	02-Oct-1897	Bernard Buberl	Singer, Genevieve	A.S. Papka	Ann Luntz
Buberl	Bernard		21-Jun-1891	11-Jun-1891	Bernard Buberl	Singer, Virginia		Catherine Simper
Buberl	Theresa	Loretta	09-Sep-1894	28-Aug-1894	Bernard Buberl	Singer, Joan	Henry Singer	Theresa Brink
Buberl	Joseph	Leroy	31-Mar-1901	14-Mar-1901	Bernard Buberl	Singer, Genevieve	Joseph Gumbert	Rebecca Wooden
Bucannan	Mary	Ethel	04-Feb-1900	24-Jan-1900	William Bucannan	Murray, Mary	William Buccanan	Catherine Murray
Buchanan	Robert		20-Nov-1904	31-Oct-1904	William Buchanan	Murray, Mary	Henry O'Connell	Helen Buchanan
Buchanan	Catherine		18-Jan-1887	17-Jan-1887	William Buchanon	Murray, Mary		Susan Murphy
Buchanan	William		08-May-1883	07-May-1883	William James Buchanan	Murray, Mary Theresa	Rev. M.F. Foley	Elizabeth Agnes Murray
Buchanon	Helen		16-Mar-1890	04-Mar-1890	William Buchanon	Murray, Mary	John O'Connell	Ann Campbell
Buchanon	James	Bernard	19-Feb-1888	14-Feb-1888	William Buchanon	Murray, Mary	Michael Murray	Elizabeth Wilson
Buchanon	James	Henry	01-May-1892	20-Apr-1892	William Buchanon	Murray, Mary	Edward John Burke	Elizabeth McKee
Bucher	George	Heller	15-Jan-1889	06-Mar-1888	Pierce Fink Bucher	Shortel, Margaret	Francis Burgan	Mary Shanks
Buckmyer	Mary	Gertrude	09-Nov-1884	31-Oct-1884	William Buchman	Murphy, Mary	William Burke	Catherine Manning
Buckmyer	Miller		12-Nov-1904	26-Aug-1876	Hennry Buckmyer	Buckmyer, Ann	Joseph Haupt	
Buffington	Henry	Stephen	09-Apr-1901	26-Jan-1901	Henry Buffington	Whelan, Laura		Gertrude Whelan
Bulger	John		30-Oct-1904	29-Sep-1904	John L. Bulger	Malone, Mary		Loretta Hand
Bull	Gertrude	Frances	01-Aug-1883	27-May-1883	Michael Bull	Kane, Helen	Henry Byrne	Ann Shannon
Bullock	Mary	Helen	19-Jul-1914	7-Jul-1914	Joseph E. Bullock	Donovan, Helen	Albert R. Bullock	Amelia Donovan
Bunce	Sara	Mary	16-May-1892	02-May-1838	Edward Bunce	West, Joan	G.W. Devine	
Burch	Lillian		22-Mar-1914	2-Mar-1914	Victor E. Burch	Gately, Mary E.		Lillian Krause
Burgan	Philip		10-Jun-1891	About 1811	Joseph Burgan	Parlett, Debora		
Burger	Edward	Joseph	17-Nov-1912	19-Oct-1912	Henry Burger	Kelly, Margaret	Thomas Kelly	Ann Boylan
Burger	Mary	Christina	08-Jun-1902	25-May-1902	Henry Burger	Carter, Mary		Mary Carter
Burk	Elizabeth	Ann	20-Jul-1890	15-Jul-1890	Ed Burk	Tulley, Ellen	John Tulles	Mary Gisriel
Burk	James		15-Aug-1886	28-Jul-1886	Edward Burk	Tulley, Ellena	George Kline	Ann Rooney

LAST NAME	FIRST NAME	MIDDLE	BAPTISM	BIRTH	Father	Mother	SPONSORS	
Burke	Ann	Florence	22-Jun-1884	07-Jun-1884	Edward Burke	Boone, Barbara	Bernard J. Ash	Ann Hamilton
Burke	Charles	Joan	18-Sep-1887	08-Sep-1887	Edward Burke	Tully, Eleanor	James Reilly	Joan Baker
Burke	Edward	James	14-Jan-1883	29-Dec-1882	Edward Burke	Tully, Helen	John Tully	Catherine Casby
Burke	Edward	John	15-Mar-1914	2-Mar-1914	Edward Burke	Monaghan, Mary	Michael Dean	Emma Dean
Burke	Helen	Elizabeth	18-Nov-1888	13-Nov-1888	Edward Burke	Tully, Helen	Edward James Brannan	Mary Ann Hall
Burke	John	Jacob	21-May-1882	06-May-1882	Edward Burke	Boone, Barbara	John T. O'Connor	Helen O'Connor
Burke	John		25-Jun-1893	06-Jun-1893	Edward Burke	Tully, Helen	Charles Gordon	Catherine McCusker
Burke	Margaret		21-Mar-1886	07-Mar-1886	Edward Burke	Boone, Barbara	Francis W. Whitney	Margaret Whitney
Burke	Walter	John	25-Sep-1898	10-Sep-1898	Edward Burke	Tully, Ellen	Peter Tully	Ann Tully
Burke	William		03-Feb-1884	21-Jan-1884	Edward Burke	Kelly, Ellena	James Kehoe	Catherine Kehoe
Burke	Leon		6-Jun-1909	26-May-1909	Edward J. Burke	Monaghan, Mary Alice	Thomas Fallon	Helen Brooks
Burke	James	Stehenson	02-Mar-1882	[Blank]	James Burke	O'Donovan, Catherine	Francis Xavier Lipp	Caroline Ann Lipp
Burke	John		28-Oct-1888	16-Oct-1888	James Burke	Dougherty, Mary Catherine	Michael Burke	Catherine Dougherty
Burke	Laura		15-Jan-1893	01-Jan-1893	James Burke	Dougherty, Mary Catherine	Thomas J. Dougherty	Agnes Joyce
Burke	Catherine		01-Apr-1894	16-Mar-1894	James J. Burke	Dougherty, Mary C.	James Finn	Joan Fallon
Burke	Mary	Teresa	08-May-1891	22-Feb-1891	James Joseph Burke	Dougherty, Mary Catherine	Thomas Edward Burke	Bridget Curley
Burke	Catherine		09-Aug-1896	13-Jul-1896	John Burke	Flaherty, Lilia	Michael Redding	Catherine Redding
Burke	Gertrude	Mary	30-Jun-1895	11-Jun-1895	John Burke	Flaherty, Lilly	George Cook	Laura Cook
Burke	James	Patrick	29-Mar-1896	14-Mar-1896	John Burke	Caveny, Margaret	James Burke	Susanna McDonough
Burke	Julia	Mary	09-Sep-1894	28-Aug-1894	John Burke	Keaveney, Margaret	Patrick Cunningham	Mary Casey
Burke	Helen		09-Nov-1890	28-Oct-1890	John F. Burke	Flaherty, Lillian F.	Joseph B. Lemley	Emma J. Phillips
Burke	Ann		03-Dec-1893	16-Nov-1893	John Thomas Burke	Flaherty, Lily Bernardine	John Flaherty	Ann Flaherty
Burke	Lillian		13-Dec-1891	30-Nov-1891	John Thomas Burke	Flaherty, Lillian Bernardine	William Burke	Mary Teresa Burke
Burke	Mary	Catherine	14-Jul-1889	02-Jul-1889	John Thomas Burke	Flaherty, Lilio Bernardine	Michael J. Redding	Ann Teresa Burke
Burke	Mary		05-Jul-1885	19-Mar-1885	Michael Burke	Mullen, Ann C.		Mary Hubbard
Burke	Margaret	Matilda	14-Feb-1912	4-Jan-1912	Patrick Burke	Mullen, Ruth		Ella Hall
Burke	Mary	Agaths	27-Dec-1914	17-Nov-1914	Patrick Burke	Mullen, Ruth		Catherine Kelly
Burke	Robert		15-Sep-1889	03-Sep-1889	Patrick Burke	Mullen, Ruth		Ruth Cotter
Burke	Joseph	John	07-Dec-1884	24-Nov-1884	Stephen Burke	Killilea, Sabina	Joseph Snyder	Sabina Morris
Burke	Stephen	William	31-Oct-1886	21-Oct-1886	Stephen Burke	Killilea, Sabina	Michael Burke	Honora Nolan
Burke	Walter	Francis	13-Feb-1885	17-Jan-1885	Stephen Burke	Killilea, Sabina	James Fay	Ann Morris
Burke	Jane		24-Oct-1909	14-Oct-1909	Thomas Burke	McGlynn, Margaret		Mary Reilly
Burke	John	Thomas	28-Jun-1887	18-Jun-1887	Thomas Burke	Mehling, Theresa	Peter J. Dignan	Ella Dignan
Burke	Patrick		7-May-1911	28-Apr-1911	Thomas Burke	McGlynn, Margaret		Mary Clark
Burke	Vincent	Eugene	24-Oct-1915	14-Oct-1915	Thomas Burke	Mehling, Theresa	J. Vincent Burke	Mary Alma Burke
Burke	Mary	Teresa	29-Mar-1914	19-Mar-1914	Thomas N. Burke	Mehling, Teresa M.	Bernard J. Burke	Mary Josephine Mehling
Burke	Mary	Josephine	10-Aug-1902	27-Jul-1902	Walter F. Burke	Mullen, Mary Alice	Joseph Burke	Sarah Agnes Burke
Burke	Ann	Lillian	27-Oct-1901	17-Oct-1901	William Burke	Schultheis, Edith M.	Edward Mesler	Ann Burke
Burke	Edward		26-Nov-1905	10-Nov-1905	William Burke	Cheney, Mary	Bernard Burke	Catherine Burke
Burke	Edward	Henry	16-Apr-1899	25-Mar-1899	William Burke	Schulteis, Edith	Henry Burke	Ann Baker
Burke	Mary		9-Nov-1913	31-Oct-1913	William Burke	Chaney, Mary	Edward Burke	Mary Goode
Burke	Francis	Aloysius	18-Dec-1904	4-Dec-1904	William J. Burke	Schultheis, Edith M.	Francis G. Burke	Cora. Muth
Burke	Mary	F.	24-Mar-1907	9-Mar-1907	William J. Burke	Schultheis, Edith Moore	Francis G. Baker	Mary C. Burke
Burke	John	William	16-Jan-1898	08-Jan-1898	William Joseph Burke	Schultheis, Edith M.	John Dillen	Myrtle Habnicht
Burke	William	Joseph	04-Dec-1892	22-Nov-1892	William T. Burke	[N], Mary	John P. Burns	Gertrude Buchanan
Burke	Thomas	Fallon	03-Jan-1886	17-Dec-1885	William Thomas Burke	Chaney, Mary	William B. Fallon	Elle G. Chaney
Burkhardt	Elizabeth	Dora	26-Feb-1882	16-Feb-1882	William C. Burkhardt	Kelly, Ann		Eleanor Rigney
Burkhart	Margaret		22-Jul-1883	11-Jul-1883	William Burkhart	Kelly, Ann		Elizabeth Hinners
Burkhart	Mary	Ann	6-Jan-1907	24-Dec-1906	William Burkhart	Kelly, Ann		Dora Carter
Burkins	Mary	Margaret	7-Apr-1912	28-Mar-1912	Howard Burkins	Maloney, Mary	Michael Driscoll	Elizabeth Collins
Burlage	Catherine	Mary	20-Dec-1908	10-Dec-1908	Charles Burlage	Ogden, Susanna Oliver	Henry Burlage	Mary Burlage
Burlage	John	Leon	3-Mar-1907	20-Feb-1907	Charles Thomas Burlage	Ogden, Susie	Leo Burlage	Catherine Burlage
Burlage	John	Edward	28-Apr-1889	15-Apr-1889	George Edward Burlage	Kelly, Margaret	Edward Dempsey	Elizabeth Kelly
Burlage	Catherine		21-Dec-1890	14-Dec-1890	John Burlage	Coleman, Catherine	Patrick Coleman	Mary McNamee
Burlage	Joseph	Leo	28-Nov-1882	13-Nov-1882	John Burlage	Coleman, Catherine	John J. Rock	Ella McNamee
Burlage	Mary		22-Jun-1884	08-Jun-1884	John Burlage	Coleman, Catherine		Mary Madgalene White
Burlege	Charles		12-Sep-1886	28-Aug-1886	Charles Burlege	Burlege, Catherine	Lucas Kearney	Margaret Callan
Burns	Catherine		30-Nov-1913	18-Nov-1913	Charles Burns	Touhy, Mary	John A. Casseyet	Margaret Cain
Burns	Mary	Ellen	08-Jun-1890	24-May-1890	Daniel Burns	Muligan, Mary	John Touhy	Ann Hammell
Burns	Bernard		22-Mar-1908	25-Feb-1908	Edward Burns	Murphy, Ann	William Curley	Bridget Mangan
Burns	James	E.	11-Jul-1897	02-Jul-1896	Edward Burns	Murphy, Ann	Laurence Conlon	Mary Byrne
Burns	James		27-Sep-1914	13-Sep-1914	Edward Burns	[N], Catherine	Cornelius Dinan	Margaret Burns

ST JOHN'S BAPTISMS 1882-1912

LAST NAME	FIRST NAME	MIDDLE	BAPTISM	BIRTH	Father	Mother	SPONSORS
Burns	Katherine		14-Aug-1910	12-Jul-1910	Edward Burns	Murphy, Ann	Ann Krouger
Burns	Margaret	Rosalie	14-Oct-1900	03-Oct-1900	Edward Burns	Murphy, Ann	Ann Krauger
Burns	William		26-May-1895	15-May-1895	Edward Burns	Murphy, Ann	Bridget Murphy
Burns	John	Francis	28-Jul-1912	16-Jul-1912	Henry J. Burns	Mills, Sarah V.	William Burns
Burns	Edward		29-Sep-1895	20-Sep-1895	James Burns	Connaughton, Mary	J.F. Mills
Burns	Mary	Laura	26-Oct-1884	25-Oct-1884	James Burns	Connaughton, Mary	Edward Healy	Elizabeth Reilly
Burns	Mary	Helen	30-Jan-1887	17-Jan-1887	James Burns	Croghan, Mary	Frederick Nestor	Mary Feely
Burns	William		14-Jan-1883	08-Jan-1883	James Burns	Connaughton, Mary	Michael Connaughton	Elizabeth Burn
Burns	George		13-Aug-1893	07-Aug-1893	James F. Burns	Connaughton, Mary	Andrew G. Schaub	Mary M. Burns
Burns	Joseph	Carroll	15-Dec-1889	12-Nov-1889	James Francis Burns	Connaughton, Mary Elizabeth	William Connaughton	Catherine L. Dunn
Burns	Edward	Patrick	18-Nov-1888	09-Nov-1888	James Joseph Burns	Quirk, Margaret Elizabeth	Luke Burns	Ann Quirk
Burns	Henry		23-Feb-1890	15-Feb-1890	John Burns	Ward, Ann	John Logan	Mary Wiss
Burns	John	Patrick	16-Jan-1887	13-Jan-1887	John Burns	Ward, Ann	William Burke	Catherine Ward
Burns	Margaret		26-Aug-1888	24-Aug-1888	John Burns	Ward, Ann	Patrick Burns	Margaret Burns
Burns	Mary		4-Jun-1905	20-May-1905	John Burns	Ward, Ann	John Kenny	Mary Hulton
Burns	John		09-Aug-1903	26-Jul-1903	John H. Burns	Murphy, Mary	James Dudley	Margaret Burns
Burns	Josephine		21-Mar-1897	17-Mar-1897	John P. Burns	Ward, Ann	John Furlong	Ann Furlong
Burns	Mary	Madeline	15-Sep-1901	10-Sep-1901	John P. Burns	Ward, Ann	Bernard Wiss	Colette Wiss
Burns	Catherine	Eleanor	29-Nov-1891	23-Nov-1891	John Patrick Burns	Ward, Ann	John Michael Meers	Mary Ward
Burns	Patrick		22-Jul-1894	14-Jul-1894	John Patrick Burns	Ward, Ann	Julius George Wess	Margaret Donohue
Burns	Alice	Margaret	05-Jul-1903	04-Jun-1903	Joseph Burns	Kilroy, Katherine	Michae O'Leary	Sara Kilroy
Burns	Mary		03-Jun-1892	25-May-1892	Luke Burns	McDonnell, Bridget		
Burns	Catherine	Louise	8-May-1910	26-Apr-1910	Martin Burns	Grannon, Mary	Timothy Sexton	Catherine Engle
Burns	Edward		26-Mar-1899	11-Mar-1899	Patrick Burns	Ahern, Agnes	Patrick Leach	Mary Kelly
Burns	James	Aloysius	30-Sep-1900	17-Sep-1900	Patrick Burns	Ahern, Agnes	Edward Healey	Mary Burns
Burns	John		26-Jan-1902	22-Dec-1901	Patrick Burns	Toulan, Catherine	Michael Toulan	Elizabeth Toulan
Burns	Margaret	Mary	14-Jun-1903	03-Jun-1903	Patrick Burns	Ahern, Agnes	John B. Mullen	Helen O'Brien
Burns	Patrick	Leon	21-Feb-1904	7-Feb-1904	Patrick Burns	Toulan, Catherine	Francis Holtman	Mary Toulan
Burns	Catherine	Dolores	9-Jul-1911	1-Jul-1911	Patrick J. Burns	Toulan, Catherine	James St. Leger	Elizabeth Mary Toulan
Burns	Jerome	Patrick	20-Dec-1908	8-Dec-1908	Patrick J. Burns	Ahern, Agnes	Martin Healey	Mary E. Middleton
Burns	William Ignatius		27-Dec-1914	17-Dec-1914	Patrick J. Burns	Toulan, Catherine	William Evans	Ann Evans
Burns	Mary	Ellen	13-Sep-1909	29-Aug-1908	Patrick Joseph Burns	Toulan, Catherine Theresa	Thomas Joseph Toulan	Mary Margaret Evans
Burns	Peter		29-Dec-1901	17-Dec-1901	Peter Joseph Burns	Roach, Catherine	Batholomew Shea	Catherine Shea
Burns	Catherine	Helen	02-Aug-1901	28-Jul-1901	Robert Burns	McGovern, Helen		Catherine Gallagher
Burns	John	James	18-Nov-1894	08-Nov-1894	Robert Burns	McGovern, Ella	William Glorius	Mary O'Connor
Burns	Mary		29-Apr-1906	23-Mar-1906	Robert Burns	McGovern, Helen		Bridget O'Connor
Burns	Joseph		31-Jul-1897	30-Jul-1897	Thomas Burns	Dempsey, Ann		
Burns	Elsie	Mary	25-Aug-1895	07-Aug-1895	Thomas J. Burns	Lederer, Hannah	Hugh McElroy	Alice McElroy
Burns	Mary	Theresa	16-Aug-1903	03-Aug-1903	Thomas J. O'Brien	Nestry, Elizabeth S.		Rose Clayton
Burrier	Ann		26-Jun-1908	14-Jul-1908	James L. Burrier	Herzing, Margaret	Nicholas J. Herzing	Ann Amand
Burrier	Catherine	Elizabeth	10-Jun-1906	3-Jun-1906	James Louis Burrier	Herzing, Margaret	Julius Etzel	Catherine Elizabeth Potts
Burrier	Elizabeth		15-Jun-1890	02-Jun-1890	John Burrier	[N], Eliza		
Burrier	Mary	Agnes	14-Mar-1886	07-Mar-1886	John Burrier	Cenowitch, Elizabeth	Henry Heck	Margaret Murley
Burrier	John	William	20-May-1888	16-May-1888	John R. Burrier	Zenowitch, Elizabeth	John Moore	Margaret Hoeck
Burrier	Maria	Ann	12-Feb-1882	03-Feb-1882	John Richard Burrier	Zinninewick, Elizabeth	William J. Burke	Helen Zinninewick
Burrier	Ellen		25-Feb-1912	1-Feb-1912	John W. Burrier	Dietz, Mary C.	Philip Bitner	Ellen Kernan
Burrier	Margaret	Elizabeth	11-Dec-1910	26-Nov-1910	John W. Burrier	Deitz, Mary	John Busterman	Elizabeth Burrier
Burroughs	Clarence	Gerald	30-Sep-1899	26-Aug-1899	John Burroughs	Reynolds, Ann	Thomas Reynolds	Sarah Burroughs
Burroughs	Sarah	Atta	15-Jan-1905	9-Jan-1905	John H.C. Burroughs	Reynolds, Ann	John Stone	Mary C. Reynolds
Bursella	Nicolaum		11-Dec-1910	26-Nov-1910	Francis Bursella	Landina, Mary	Emory J. Mullen	Mary Curran
Busch	Florence	Elizabeth	18-Oct-1903	04-Oct-1903	Henry B. Busch	Bennett, Margaret		Elizabeth McNeal
Busch	Henry	Richard	05-Mar-1899	22-Feb-1899	Henry Busch	Bennett, Margaret	Henry Brescham	Henry Page
Busch	Margaret		12-Aug-1900	30-Jul-1900	Henry Busch	Bennett, Margaret		Elizabeth Henderson
Busch	William	Bernard	30-Dec-1894	23-Dec-1894	Henry Busch	Bennett, Margaret	William Schellenberger	Mary Schellenberger
Busch	John		06-Oct-1889	11-Sep-1889	John Busch	Peters, Catherine E.		Eleanor Busch
Busch	William	Edward	10-Jun-1892	12-Feb-1892	William Busch	NeidHammer, Lydia		Harriet NeidHammer
Bush	Esther		17-Apr-1892	31-Mar-1892	William Henry Busch	Peters, Caroline	Joseph Jerome Peters	Esther Fay
Bush	Elizabeth		17-Sep-1899	27-Aug-1899	James Bush	Dietzway, Margaret		Elizabeth Murphy
Bush	James		30-May-1897	06-May-1897	James Bush	Dietzway, Margaret		Ann Maloney Amrhein
Bush	Margaret	Emma	26-Apr-1891	03-Apr-1891	James Bush	Dietzway, Margaret		Margaret Dietzway
Bush	Margaret	Mary	22-Jan-1893	01-Jan-1893	James Bush	Dietzway, Margaret		Ann Maloney Emerine
Bush	Mary	Margaret	04-Sep-1887	26-Aug-1887	James Ward Bush	Dieway, Margaret		Mary Dietzway
Bushe	James	Bernard	3-Aug-1913	25-Jul-1913	Thomas Bushe	Mehling, Teresa M.	Henry Hartley	Julia Hartley

ST JOHN'S BAPTISMS 1882-1912

LAST NAME	FIRST NAME	MIDDLE	BAPTISM	BIRTH	Father	Mother	SPONSORS	
Bushmiller	George	Bernard	02-Jun-1889	14-May-1889	George Bernard Bushmiller	Kelly, Mary	John Joseph Firzpatrick	Matilda Fitzpatrick
Bushmiller	Margaret		20-Nov-1887	28-Oct-1887	George Bushmiller	Kelly, Mary	Thomas Brown	Margaret Dollard
Bushmiller	Mary	Elizabeth	30-Nov-1884	17-Nov-1884	George Bushmiller	Kelly, Mary	Peter McAdams	Elizabeth Bushmiller
Bushmiller	William		18-Feb-1883	13-Feb-1883	George Bushmiller	Kelly, Mary	Joseph Bushmiller	Magdalena Bushmiller
Busick	Mary	M.	05-Apr-1896	23-Mar-1896	Robert Busick	Shipley, Minnie		Elizabeth Busick
Busick	Robert	Hall	29-Jun-1890	15-May-1890	Robert Busick	Shipley, Minnie		Mary J. Sullivan
Busick	James	Henry	18-Oct-1885	22-Sep-1885	Roberta H. Busick	Shipley, Minnie		Emma Busick
Bussey	Ann		30-Sep-1888	23-Sep-1888	Thomas Bussey	Stonebraker, Octavia Amelia	James Francis Rock	Helen Elizabeth Kelly
Butcher	George	James	02-Dec-1883	14-Nov-1883	John F. Butcher	Donohoe, Elizabeth	Patricia Norton	Mary Kelly
Butler	Eugene		05-Feb-1893	21-Jan-1893	Eugene Butler	Kilduff, Mary R.	Stephen J. Kilduff	Mary Caroline Kilduff
Butler	William	Samuel	02-Oct-1887	15-Sep-1887	Eugene Butler	Kilduff, Mary A.	William S. Callahan	Bridget Ryan
Butler	S.	Mary	06-May-1888	04-Apr-1888	Francis Butler	Eskridge, Martha (Busick)	John Butler	Mary Dixon
Butler	Ann		26-Feb-1888	03-Dec-1887	Joseph Butler	Gepp, Susanna		Mary Butler
Byrne	Ann	Charlotte	3-Jul-1904	17-Jun-1904	Edward Byrne	Murphy, Ann	Henry Byrne	Joan Byrne
Byrne	Catherine		31-Dec-1905	10-Dec-1905	Edward Byrne	Murphy, Ann	John Byrne	Rose Byrne
Byrne	Edward	Joseph	16-Mar-1890	01-Mar-1890	James Byrne	Hawkins, Catherine	Miles Byrne	Eliza Hawkins
Byrne	Mary		28-Feb-1897	22-Feb-1897	James Byrne	Roche, Mary	Michael Kehoe	Catherine Byrne
Byrne	Mary	Helen	05-Mar-1899	19-Feb-1899	John Byrne	Murphy, Mary	Henry Byrne	Ann Brown
Byrne	Teresa		20-Jan-1897	06-Jan-1897	John Byrne	Gilder, Bridget	Patrick Byrne	Catherine Byrne
Byrne	John	Thomas	25-Jan-1914	9-Jan-1914	John Thomas Byrne	Colbert, Catherine	Thomas Colbert	Catherine Byrnes
Byrne	Mary	Margaret	21-Feb-1915	7-Feb-1915	Laurence Byrne	Dillon, Margaret Ann	Matthew Noctor	Mary Ellen Keys
Byrne	Ann	Mary	14-Dec-1913	4-Dec-1913	Laurence Joseph Byrne	Dillon, Mary A.	James Keyes	Catherine Roche
Byrne	Laura		26-May-1882	26-May-1882	Martin G. Byrne	McCabe, Catherine	Rev M.F. Foley	Catherine Byrne
Byrne	Helen	Agnes	01-Feb-1891	20-Jan-1891	Michael Byrne	Conners, Magdalene	Edward Byrne	Mabel Conners
Byrne	Lucy		30-Oct-1910	19-Oct-1910	Miles Byrne	Byrne, Catherine	Edward J. McEvoy	Delia Byrnes
Byrne	Hugh	Michael	9-Feb-1908	1-Feb-1908	Thomas Byrne	McNally, Mary	Thomas Byrne	Mary Kernan
Byrne	Julian		3-Nov-1901	19-Oct-1901	Thomas Byrne	McNally, Mary	Frederick Mullen	Catherine McNally
Byrne	Margaret	Mary	05-Jul-1896	14-Jun-1896	Thomas Byrne	McNally, Mary	Michael Byrne	Nellie Whittle
Byrne	Thomas		26-Apr-1888	16-Apr-1888	Thomas J. Byrne	Mulloy, Nora	Joseph Rock	Katherine McNally
Byrne	Margaret		20-Nov-1887	14-Nov-1887	Christopher Byrnes	McClellan, Martha	John Nolan	Mary Clarke
Byrnes	George	Murray	10-Jul-1910	1-Jan-1909	Christopher Byrnes	Bower, Daisy	Patrick Lambert	Mary Lambert
Byrnes	Josephine	James	17-Jul-1887	09-Jul-1887	Daniel Byrnes	Mulligan, Mary	Peter McCabe	Theresa M. Byrnes
Byrnes	John		11-Nov-1888	07-Nov-1888	Daniel Byrnes	Mulligan, Mary	Daniel O'Sullivan	Ann King
Byrnes	Joseph	Rowland	17-Jan-1909	7-Jan-1909	Dennis James Byrnes	Katzenberger, Mary Catherine	Michael F. Byrne	Mary O'Sullivan
Byrnes	Ann		13-Nov-1898	30-Oct-1898	Edward Byrnes	Murphy, Ann	Thomas Byrnes	Mary Katzenberger
Byrnes	Mary	Bartow	04-Dec-1892	24-Nov-1892	Edward Byrnes	Murphy, Ann	Robert Byrnes	Elizabeth Hanley
Byrnes	James		14-Jun-1914	3-Jun-1914	James B. Byrnes	Byrnes, Florence	Michael Byrnes	Bridget Bray
Byrnes	Frances		8-Jan-1905	24-Dec-1904	James Byrnes	Hawkins, Katherine	Johnston McCarthy	Ellan M. Connor
Byrnes	Josephine	Ann	15-Sep-1902	23-Aug-1902	James Byrnes	McGovern, Ella		Kathrina Satterfield
Byrnes	Mary		03-Jan-1897	24-Dec-1896	James Byrnes	Hawkins, Catherine	John Dalrymple	Abigail Roche
Byrnes	Mary	Catherine	19-May-1907	4-May-1907	James P. Byrnes	Hawkins, Catherine	Bernard J. Lee	Anne Byrne
Byrnes	Margaret		25-Dec-1903	11-Dec-1903	John B. Byrnes	Gutberlet, Mary E.	Joseph Kelly	Elizabeth Gutberlet
Byrnes	Elizabeth		02-Jun-1901	17-May-1901	John Byrne	Murphy, Mary	Thomas Flaherty	Margaret Conroy
Byrnes	Ann	Mary	12-Nov-1911	28-Oct-1911	John Byrnes	Colbert, Catherine	William Colbert	Agnes Colbert
Byrnes	John	Edward	21-Jan-1900	10-Jan-1900	John Byrnes	Byrnes, Delia	Francis Johnson	Marcella Johnson
Byrnes	Martin		04-Dec-1898	29-Nov-1898	John Byrnes	Ward, Ann	Daniel Hyland	Mary Mercer
Byrnes	Mary	Elizabeth	9-Sep-1907	25-Jul-1901	John Byrnes	Samsel, Elizabeth	Eugene Samsel	Margaret Samsel
Byrnes	Robert	Joseph	13-Apr-1902	03-Apr-1902	John Byrnes	Gilder, Delia	Edward Fahey	Katherine Meritt
Byrnes	Helen	Elizabeth	1-Sep-1907	20-Aug-1907	John C. Byrnes	Gildey, Bridget Delia	John Garrity	Helen Garrity
Byrnes	James	Clare	17-Oct-1909	1-Oct-1909	John Clarence Byrnes	Gilda, Delia	Charles Murphy	L.M. Lafferty
Byrnes	William	Henry	12-Feb-1882	27-Dec-1881	John F. Byrnes	Dunn, Mary M.	B.J. Mullen	Rose Goodman
Byrnes	Ann	Catherine	10-May-1891	11-Apr-1891	Joseph Byrnes	Miller, Ellen	Joseph Byrnes	Katie Wooden
Byrnes	Elizabeth		12-Feb-1888	07-Feb-1888	M. Byrnes	Byrnes, Catherine	Hugh Byrnes	Margaret Hagerty
Byrnes	Helen	Mary	30-Sep-1888	25-Sep-1888	Michael Byrnes	O'Keefe, Elizabeth	Patrick Joseph Sullivan	Mary Helen White
Byrnes	Vincent		12-Aug-1883	04-Aug-1883	Michael J. Byrnes	O'Keefe, Elizabeth	Joseph Neville	Mary Downey
Byrnes	Leon	Michael	07-Mar-1886	04-Mar-1886	Michael Joseph Byrnes	O'Keefe, Elizabeth	J. W. O'Keefe	Delia Teresa O'Keefe
Byrnes	Mary	Ann	04-Oct-1885	24-Sep-1885	Miles Byrnes	Byrnes, Catherine	James J. Connelly	Lucy Byrnes
Byrnes	Michael	Francis	23-Sep-1900	14-Sep-1900	Patrick Byrnes	Toulan, Catherine	John Boyd	Hanna Byrnes
Byrnes	Lillian	May	16-Apr-1899	05-Apr-1899	Peter Byrnes	Roach, Catherine	Bernard Byrnes	Lillian M. Byrnes
Byrnes	Margaret	Patrick	20-Dec-1896	12-Dec-1896	Peter Byrnes	Roach, Catherine	Michael Redding	Michael Roach
Byrnes	Bernard		28-Oct-1894	14-Oct-1894	Peter Joseph Byrnes	Roach, Catherine	Bernard Joseph McKenna	Rose Byrnes
Byrnes	Margaret	Mary	30-Jun-1889	25-Jun-1889	Robert Byrnes	McGovern, Helen	Arthur McMahon	Ann McGovern

14

LAST NAME	FIRST NAME	MIDDLE	BAPTISM	BIRTH	Father	Mother	SPONSORS
Byrnes	Mary	Veronica	12-Jun-1892	02-Jun-1892	Robert Byrnes	McGovern, Helen	Joseph Walter Byrnes
Byrnes	Robert		07-May-1897	21-Feb-1897	Robert Byrnes	McGovern, Helen	Catherine Farley
Byrnes	Catherine		18-Nov-1906	29-Oct-1906	Thomas B. Byrnes	McNally, Mary A.	John F. Riordan
Byrnes	James		25-Mar-1894	12-Mar-1894	Thomas Byrnes	Dempsey, Ann	James Dempsey
Byrnes	James	V.	21-Nov-1897	03-Nov-1897	Thomas Byrnes	Short, Margaret	James Short
Byrnes	Joan		24-Apr-1898	15-Apr-1894	Thomas Byrnes	[N], Joan	William Byrnes
Byrnes	John		13-Jun-1886	01-Jun-1886	Thomas Byrnes	Dempsey, Ann	William Dempsey
Byrnes	John	Bernard	03-Sep-1899	20-Aug-1899	Thomas Byrnes	McNally, Mary	Peter Short
Byrnes	Mary	Mercedes	10-Jan-1904	14-Dec-1903	Thomas Byrnes	McNally, Mary	
Byrnes	Thomas		27-May-1888	18-May-1888	Thomas Byrnes	Dempsey, Ann	Patrick McKewen
Cadden	John	O'Carroll	31-Dec-1911	12-Dec-1911	John T. Cadden	Cannon, Mary	William Lannon
Caffrey	Joseph	Richard	02-Apr-1893	23-Mar-1893	Thomas Caffrey	Daily, Mary E.	Matthew Connolly
Caffrey	Thomas		09-Nov-1890	26-Oct-1890	Thomas Caffrey	Dailey, Mary E.	Patrick Hart
Cahill	John	Edward	30-Jan-1887	09-Jan-1887	Joseph Cahill	Smith, Mary	Helen Coyne
Cain	John	Andrew	14-Feb-1886	04-Feb-1886	James Cain	Dowd, Ann	Patrick Hepburn
Cain	Rosalie		12-Mar-1882	22-Feb-1882	James Cain	Dowd, Ann	John Hepburn
Cain	Charles	Warren	16-Sep-1906	2-Sep-1906	John Cain	Colgan, Margaret	Edward Cain
Cain	John	Paul	02-Feb-1890	25-Jan-1890	John Cain	Morwood, Agnes	George Morwood
Cain	John	Edward	19-Feb-1905	10-Feb-1905	John Cain	Colgan, Margaret	Edward Healy
Cain	William		13-Oct-1901	05-Oct-1901	John Cain	Colgan, Margaret	William Cain
Cain	James		27-Nov-1887	20-Nov-1887	John Thomas Cain	Morwood, Agnes	Joseph Henry McNally
Cain	Ann	Regina	21-Dec-1884	18-Dec-1884	William Cain	O'Brien, Catherine	Catherine A. Golden
Cain	Francis		30-Sep-1883	26-Sep-1883	William Cain	O'Brien, Catherine	John O'Brien
Cain	Genevieve		19-Jun-1887	16-Jun-1887	William Cain	O'Brien, Catherine	John Golden
Calahan	Ann		30-Oct-1910	14-Oct-1910	Michael Callahan	McDonald, Cecelia	W.B. McCardell
Caldwell	Jesse	Homar	25-Sep-1892	08-Sep-1892	Hesse Homar Caldwell	Plunkett, Alice Maud	Michael McDonald
Caldwell	William	Herbert	07-May-1882	10-Feb-1882	William Hugh Caldwell	Phillips, Isabelle	Francis J. Plunkett
Calender	Emma		09-Aug-1885	07-Jul-1885	William E. Callender	Martin, Laura	Joseph O'Donnell
Callaghan	James Edward	Francis	28-Oct-1906	14-Oct-1906	John Callaghan	McCormick, Mary	Patrick J. Davey
Callaghan	Mary	Virginia	03-Feb-1884	10-Jan-1881	John Henry Callaghan	Braden, Joan Lee	David Warnick
Callaghan	Catherine	Bernardine	3-Mar-1912	16-Feb-1912	Thomas Callaghan	McDonald, Ann	James McDonald
Callahan	Loretta		15-May-1887	09-May-1887	John Callaghan	Manly, Mary	Edward Cunningham
Callahan	Ann		02-Aug-1885	26-Jul-1885	John Callaghan	Manley, Mary	Thomas Sexton
Callahan	Elizabeth		8-Nov-1903	21-Oct-1903	John Callahan	McCormack, Mary	Michael Callahan
Callahan	Helen	Genevieve	21-Dec-1913	8-Dec-1913	John Callahan	McCormick, Mary	John Callahan
Callahan	John		05-Oct-1900	05-Oct-1900	John Callahan	McCormick, Mary	
Callahan	John		25-Nov-1900	05-Oct-1900	John Callahan	McCormick, Mary	P.J. Carlos
Callahan	Mary		16-May-1909	5-May-1909	John Callahan	McCormick, Mary	Ann McCormick
Callahan	Thomas	Francis	24-Mar-1912	7-Mar-1912	John J. Callahan	McCormick, Mary	James McCormick
Callahan	Leroy	John Holmes	06-Dec-1891	29-Nov-1891	John J. Callahan	Manley, Mary	Henry Prine
Callahan	Mary	Helen	9-May-1909	24-Apr-1909	Joseph Callahan	Burns, Margaret	Richard A. Callahan
Callahan	Cecelia	Frances	22-Nov-1908	2-Nov-1908	Michael Callahan	McDonald, Cecelia	Patrick Dorsey
Callahan	Michael	James	27-Oct-1907	11-Oct-1907	Michael James Callahan	McDonnell, Cecelia	Martin Callahan
Callahan	Ann	Mary	9-Sep-1906	25-Aug-1906	Thomas Callahan	McDonald, Ann	John Coogan
Callahan	Cecelia	T.	9-Sep-1906	25-Aug-1906	Thomas Callahan	McDonald, Ann	John J. Butler
Callahan	Francis	Bernard	23-Nov-1913	10-Nov-1913	Thomas Callahan	McDonald, Ann	John McDonold
Callahan	John	Andrew	22-May-1910	8-May-1910	Thomas Callahan	McDonald, Ann	Patrick McDonald
Callahan	Thomas		16-Aug-1908	24-Jul-1908	Thomas Callahan	McDonald, Ann	Andrew Gohan
Callan	Margaret		05-Jul-1885	21-Jun-1885	James Callan	Poole, Mary	Thomas Reiley
Callander	Henry	Eugene	31-Jul-1883	06-Jul-1887	William E. Callander	Martin, Laura	John F. Byrne
Callender	Charles	Leo	16-Oct-1898	27-Sep-1898	William Callender	Martin, Laura	U.F. Hamill
Callender	Laura	Frances	22-Nov-1891	24-Oct-1891	William Callender	Martin, Laura	
Callender	Sophia	M.	21-Jun-1896	30-May-1896	William Callender	Martin, Laura E.	Sophia Yeager
Callender	Helen	Grace	01-Sep-1901	13-Aug-1901	William E. Callender	Martin, Laura E.	John McCabe
Callender	Mary	Amanda	01-Sep-1889	03-Aug-1889	William E. Callender	Martin, Laura E.	
Callender	Thomas		18-Apr-1905	1-Apr-1905	William E. Callender	Davey, Margaret	Thomas Davey
Callender	Catherine	Thelma	31-Dec-1911	9-Dec-1911	William Edward Callender	Davey, Margaret	John Davey
Callender	Edward	Raymond	21-Apr-1907	13-Apr-1907	William Edward Callender	Davey, Margaret	Henry Callender
Callender	William	Edward	17-Jun-1883	29-May-1883	William Edward Callender	Martin, Laura	Richard Edward Higgins
Calwell	Ann		15-Apr-1883	24-Mar-1883	George W. Calwell	Ryan, Margaret	Ann Josephine Bryson
Campbell	Francis	Edith	6-Apr-1913	31-Mar-1913	Edward Campbell	Lundy, Mary	Thomas Lundy
Campbell	Hettie	Ann	29-Jul-1883	19-Jul-1883	Felice Campbell	Pryor, Mary	Stephen Campbell
Campbell	Francis	Earl	05-Jul-1903	15-May-1903	Henry W. Campbell	Jones, Susanna	Edward Campbell

SPONSORS (continued)
Mary O'Dea
Catherine Farley
Sara Byrnes
Catherine Dempsey
Mary McNally
Mary Chase
Catherine Dempsey
Mary Short
Catherine Short
Mary Murphy
Cecelia Fahey
Bridget Dudley
Ann Isabelle Dudley
Helen Coyne
Rose Nugent
Rose Maynes
Genevieve Cain
Agnes Kuhan
Elizabeth Lucy
Margaret Cain
Helen McNally
Catherine A. Golden
Mary Cavan
Mary Gaynor
Mary Rafferty
Joan Meskell
Helen Frederick
Mary Lynch
Ann Bresnan
Catherine Cullen
Sarah Manning
Ann Sexton
Julia Manley
Della McCormack
Joan Fitzgerald
Mary Bresnahan
Mary Brennan
Ann McCormick
Elizabeth McConnell
Virginia Buberl
Catherine M. Callahan
Mary Whelan
Mary McDonnell
Elizabeth A. Blondell
Cecelia McDonald
Mary [Blank]
Mary [Blank]
Mary Baker
Rose Gray
Mary M. Byrnes
Mary Hinkle
Mary Finn
Mary Amanda Brady
Florence Henning
Catherine Madden
Laura Callender
Ann Colligan
Ann O'Connor
Mary Ann Campbell
Frances Campbell

LAST NAME	FIRST NAME	MIDDLE	BAPTISM	BIRTH	Father	Mother	SPONSORS	
Campbell	Charles		15-May-1898	15-Feb-1870	James Campbell	Eichelberger, Mary	August Dellone	Genevieve Dellone
Campbell	Edward		9-Mar-1912	13-May-1891	John Campbell	Ramble, Edith		Winifred Geidt
Campbell	James		08-Mar-1885	20-Feb-1885	John Campbell	Pince, Mary	Henry Meaney	Mary Meaney
Campbell	Bennett	B.	04-Feb-1900	16-Jan-1900	Peter Campbell	Kelly, Francis	William Reinhardt	Philomena Rein
Campbell	Catherine	B.	18-Nov-1906	9-Nov-1906	Peter J. Campbell	Campbell, Frances L.	Wilbur Mullin	Nellie Mullen
Campbell	James	Edward	28-Nov-1897	07-Nov-1897	Robert Campbell	Kennedy, Mary	Charles Givener	Margaret Donnelly
Campbell	John	Daniel	21-Dec-1890	09-Dec-1890	Robert Campbell	Kennedy, Mary	Patrick J. Murphy	Margaret McGill
Campbell	Thomas	Joseph	24-Jun-1888	14-Jun-1888	Stephen Campbell	Kennedy, Mary	John Francis Coghlan	Margaret Magraw
Campbell	Bernard	Matthew	18-May-1884	09-May-1884	Stephen Campbell	Kane, Mary Ann	Hugh Gribbin	Ann Gribbin
Campbell	Carl	Henry	08-Aug-1886	27-Jul-1886	Stephen Campbell	Kane, Mary	James Connolly	Ann Connolly
Campbell	Ann		05-Apr-1885	21-Mar-1885	Thomas Campbell	Craven, Bridget	Dennis Hogan	Jennie Hogan
Campbell	Margaret	Adele	17-Dec-1902	14-Dec-1902	Thomas Campbell	Cain, Elizabeth		Mrs. Cain
Campbell	Vincent		28-Jul-1901	18-Jul-1901	Thomas Campbell	Cain, Elizabeth	Thomas Kelly	Mary Cain
Campbell	James	Thomas	24-Jun-1906	17-Jun-1906	Thomas H. Campbell	Cain, Elizabeth G.	James A. Cain	Margaret Campbell
Campbell	Mary	Regina	22-May-1904	19-May-1904	Thomas H. Campbell	Cain, Elizabeth	Thomas Campbell	Bridget Campbell
Campbell	Laura	Ethel	13-Sep-1891	29-Aug-1891	William Campbell	Fisher, Elizabeth	William Buchnon	Mary Genoy
Campbell	Louise		19-Jan-1896	21-Nov-1895	William Campbell	Fisher, Elizabeth		Hanah Conway
Campbell	Genevieve	Cora	24-Oct-1886	11-Oct-1886	William H. Campbell	Fisher, Elizabeth	James Holden	Margaret Magraw
Campbell	Ida	Agnes	27-Jan-1884	13-Jan-1884	William H. Campbell	Fisher, Elizabeth	James Dunn	Mary Burns
Campbell	Florence	Mary	16-Jun-1889	19-May-1889	William Henry Campbell	Fisher, Elizabeth	John Joseph McGarvey	Mary Virginia Pasco
Campbell	Mary	C.	22-Oct-1882	15-Oct-1882	William Henry Campbell	Fisher, Elizabeth	John Joseph McGarvey	Agnes Burke
Campbell/Gilroy	Mary	Elizabeth	19-Nov-1899	12-Nov-1899	Joseoh Campbell	Mayison, Mary	Thomas Lyons	Ella Campbell
Canavan	Henry	Alfred	06-Mar-1898	22-Feb-1898	Philip J. Canavan	Peare, Euphrasia		Alicia Lane
Canby	Ann		6-Feb-1910	28-Jan-1910	Joseph Canby	Manning, Lillian	Henry Manning	Irene Canby
Canby	Genevieve	Catherine	19-Sep-1915	7-Sep-1915	Joseph E. Canby	Manning, Elizabeth Lillian	William P. Sullivan	Katherine M. Campbell
Canby	Joseph	Edward	1-Sep-1912	20-Aug-1912	Joseph Edward Canby	Manning, Elizabeth		Josephine Conabaugh
Canby	Margaret	Ann	16-Aug-1908	5-Aug-1908	Joseph Edward Canby	Manning, Elizabeth	W. Canby	Jennie Manning
Canby	Thomas	Winfield	17-Oct-1909	5-Oct-1909	Joseph Winfield Scott Canby	Dailey, Pasqualina Mary	Thomas Lanahan	Ann Canby
Canby	Bernard	Lloyd	6-Jun-1915	22-May-1915	Winfield Canby	Bailey, Mary	Bernard Byrnes	Blanche Canby
Canby	Mary	Rose	14-Jan-1912	1-Jan-1912	Winfield Canby	Bailey, Mary		Irene Canby
Canby	Ann	Elizabeth	27-Feb-1892	26-Feb-1892	Winfield Scott Canby	Affayroux, Ann		Ann McShane
Canby	Joseph	Edward	04-Oct-1885	18-Sep-1885	Winfield Scott Canby	Affayroux, Ann	John J. Boland	Sarah Affayroux
Canby	Mary	Irene	16-Oct-1887	27-Sep-1887	Winfield Scott Canby	Affayroux, Ann	Michael Jos. Dougherty	Mary Magraw
Canby	Mary	Blanche	20-Feb-1896	25-Nov-1895	Winfield Scott Canby	Affayroux, Ann E.	Charles Boland	Helen Boland
Canby	Thomas	Winfield Scott	02-Feb-1890	15-Jan-1890	Winfield Scott Canby	Affayroux, Ann	Thomas J. Brown	Susan Boland
Canfield	Helen		29-Aug-1882	16-Aug-1882	Hugh M. Canfield	Quinn, Sara		Mary Fahey
Cannon	Henrietta	Mary	9-Jun-1912	07-Dec-1887	Herbert M. Cannon	Schardt, Helen		Mary Kuhn
Cannon	Thomas	James	15-Mar-1885	11-Feb-1885	Michael Cannon	Downs, Mary Ann	Peter McKenna	Julia McKenna
Canoles	William		24-May-1896	19-Apr-1872	John Canoles	Dash, Rebecca	William Adam	
Canoles	Genevieve		13-Oct-1895	05-Oct-1895	William Canoles	Loretz, Cecelia	John Brenning	Genevieve Miller
Canton	Charles		25-Jul-1882	25-Jul-1882	Michael Canton	McGraw, Susan Leonora		Helen Hogan
Cantwell	Elenore	Frances	25-Apr-1886	[Blank]	[Blank]	[Blank]		
Cape/Everest	Sarah	Ann	05-Apr-1898	25-Aug-1855	John Cape	Cape, Sarah	Catherine Mooney	Mary Dolan
Carberry	John	Randall	03-Sep-1882	17-Aug-1882	Richard Carberry	Randall, Mary	John Carberry	Mary Folley
Carbery	Richard	Henry	29-Nov-1885	09-Nov-1885	Richard H. Carbery	Randall, Mary E.		Martha Durning
Carbery	Thomas	Fiore	21-Dec-1904	18-Nov-1904	Richard H. Carbery	Patrilli, Angella	Thomas Manilla	Pasqualina Rossi
Cardellini	William		23-Jan-1912	22-Mar-1883	Leandro Cardellini	Measell, Martha	Michael [Blank]	Margaret Miller
Cardwell	William				William Cardwell	Brown, Lucia		
Carette	Stephenie	Mary	14-Jan-1912	October 3, 1911	Louis Carette		John Carette	Louise Carrete
Carey	Edward	P.	5-Jul-1914	25-Jun-1914	Charles Carey	Flynn, Matilda		Ann Ridenour
Carey	Gertrude		18-Aug-1889	02-Aug-1889	Cornelius Carey	Crosby, Emma	Samuel Kane	Caroline Achenback
Carey	Agnes	Francis	27-Nov-1887	11-Nov-1887	Cornelius Jerome Carey	Crosby, Emma	Edward Fields	Caroline Achenback
Carey	Charles		31-May-1897	11-May-1892	Edward Carey	Mills, Amanda	Mary Cassidy	P.K. Lanahan
Carey	Edward	Leo	04-Sep-1898	19-Aug-1898	Edward Carey	Mills, Amanda	Francis Lynch	Ann Daily
Carey	Francis	Joseph	11-Nov-1900	27-Oct-1900	Edward Carey	Mills, Amanda	Michael King	Ann King
Carey	Ignatius	Florence	31-May-1897	17-Oct-1894	James C. Carey	Crosby, Emma	Ann Cassidy	P.K. Lanahan
Carey	Catherine	Gertrude	02-May-1897	18-Apr-1897	James F. Carey	Crosby, Emma	Thomas Fitzpatrick	Gertrude Blakeney
Carey	James		19-May-1895	10-May-1895	Laurence Matthew Carey	Fitzgerald, Ann Catherine	Thomas Sexton	Mary Carey
Carey	Charles	Christopher	7-Aug-1910	25-Jul-1910	Laurence Matthew Carey	Fitzgerald, Ann Catherine	Charles Joseph Carey	Hanna Fitzgerald
Carey	Michele	Allison	29-Jul-1886	16-Jul-1886	Michael J. Carey	Boylan, Mary T.		Mary A. Boylan
Carey	Irene	Elizabeth	12-Feb-1893	29-Jan-1893	William Carrico	Kyle, Emma G.	James Dooley	Mary Finn
Carico/Kyle	Emma	Genevieve	13-Jan-1898	31-Mar-1868	William Kyle	Luna, Sara		Mary O'Dea
Carlon	Helen		30-Aug-1891	21-Aug-1891	Edward Carlon	McGovern, Ann	Thomas Barrett	Margaret Beuzel
Carns	Teresa	Gertrude	17-Nov-1895	06-Nov-1895	William Carns	Yakel, Philomena	John Braker	Theresa Owens

LAST NAME	FIRST NAME	MIDDLE	BAPTISM	BIRTH	Father	Mother	SPONSORS
Carolan	John		25-Sep-1898	19-Aug-1898	Edward Carolan	McGovern, Ann	Mary Farley
Carolan	Margaret		05-Mar-1893	07-Feb-1893	Edward Carolan	McGovern, Ann	Mary Clancy
Carpenter	William	Clark	8-May-1910	22-Apr-1910	Herbert Carpenter	Clark, Elizabeth	Elizabeth Schwartzkopf
Carr	Joan		01-May-1885	31-Oct-1872	Alexander A. Carr	Melroy, Ann	Dennis Maher
Carr	Joseph		27-Dec-1896	16-Dec-1896	Charles Carr	Boylan, Catherine	Joseph Carey
Carr	Charles	Edward	30-Nov-1890	10-Nov-1890	Charles Edwin Forrest Carr	Boylan, Catherine Agnes	Allen James Cavey
Carr	John	Chambers	08-Jan-1889	27-Dec-1888	Charles Edwin Forrest Carr	Boylan, Catherine Agnes	William Henry Boylan
Carr	John		25-Mar-1889	08-Jan-1889	Charles Edwin Forrest Carr	Boylan, Catherine Agnes	William Henry Boylan
Carr	James	Leon	20-Dec-1908	9-Dec-1908	Jesse William Carr	Flynn, Ellen M.	Mary Catherine Manfield
Carr	Agnes	Margaret	13-May-1900	03-May-1900	John Carr	Holden, Agnes	Kilian Volk
Carr	Charles	Edward	07-May-1893	28-Apr-1893	John Carr	Holden, Agnes	William J. Holden
Carr	Francis	Cyril	21-Jul-1895	10-Jul-1895	John Carr	Holden, Agnes	Alice Halpin
Carr	John	Joseph	28-Jul-1889	18-Jul-1889	John Carr	Holden, Agnes M.	Thomas L. McGinn
Carr	Julia	Anita	05-Jul-1896	19-Jun-1896	John Carr	McGrann, Mary	William McGrann
Carr	Mary		29-May-1898	16-May-1898	John Carr	Holden, Agnes	John McGinn
Carr	Thomas	Gregory	22-Mar-1903	12-Mar-1903	John Carr	Holden, Agnes M.	John McCabe
Carr	John	Joseph	13-Jun-1915	23-May-1915	John Joseph Carr	Kennedy, Mary	Charles Johnson
Carr	Catherine		15-May-1887	12-Apr-1887	John T. Carr	Magraw, Mary	Mortimer Magraw
Carr	Elizabeth		10-Jan-1892	02-Jan-1892	John Thomas Carr	Holden, Agnes Mary	John Radden
Carr	Francis	Patrick	26-Aug-1888	15-Aug-1888	John Thomas Carr	McGrann, Mary	George Peter Carr
Carr	John	Royal	30-Mar-1890	17-Mar-1890	John Thomas Carr	McGrann, Mary Aloysius	Thomas J. Quillen
Carrigan	Mary		12-Mar-1882	04-Mar-1882	Jeremia Carrigan	Wilson, Elizabeth Theresa	Catherine Elizabeth Malloy
Carrigan	John	Joseph	03-Jun-1883	21-May-1883	Michael Corrigan	Dolan, Catherine	Sara Dolan
Carrigan	Michael	James	03-Aug-1884	14-Jul-1884	Patrick Carrigan	Brady, Bridget	Elizabeth Brady
Carroll	William	Paul	31-Aug-1884	16-Aug-1884	Aloysius Carroll	Meek, Ellen	Hamilton S. Hoggsol
Carroll	Henry	Lee	22-May-1892	13-May-1892	Charles Carroll	Easten, Florence	Margaret Upton
Carroll	Ann	Lillian	24-Nov-1882	22-Nov-1882	Charles M. Carroll	Wales, Jane	Francesca Halton
Carroll	Margaret	Ann	27-Apr-1884	25-Apr-1884	Daniel Carroll	Kelly, Fannie	Mary Ellen McCaffrey
Carroll	Edward	Thomas	21-Mar-1886	25-Feb-1886	Edward T. Carroll	Gittings, Mary Belle	Mary E. Carroll
Carroll	William	Lee	13-Aug-1888	12-Jun-1888	Edward Thomas Carroll	Gittings, Mary Isabelle	Ann Isabelle Dudley
Carroll	John	Catherine	15-Apr-1883	07-Apr-1883	Gregory Carroll	Donohoe, Mary Helen	John Donohoe
Carroll	Mary	Regina	30-Oct-1898	11-Oct-1898	John B. Carroll	McCaffrey, Mary Helen	
Carroll	John		11-May-1902	26-Apr-1902	John Carroll	Braun, Francis	Joseph Carroll
Carroll	Mary	Elizabeth	07-Oct-1883	26-Sep-1883	John Carroll	McCaffrey, Mary	William McGivney
Carroll	Rosie		29-Mar-1885	17-Mar-1885	John Carroll	McCaffrey, Mary	John McGuire
Carroll	William		23-Jun-1894	29-Nov-1893	John Carroll	McCaffrey, Mary Francis	Ann Isabelle Dudley
Carroll	Francis	Collins	07-May-1893	23-Apr-1893	Joseph F. Carroll	Collins, Catherine C.	Jennie Waterhouse
Carrs	Robert	Francis	14-Nov-1909	28-Oct-1909	Robert F. Carrs	Gibson, Blanche	George J. Krug
Carter	Amelia	Dolores	24-Aug-1913	9-Aug-1913	[Blank] S. Carter	Bilzer, Mary	John Riordan
Carter	Charles	William	01-Jan-1882	03-Dec-1881	James Carter	Spellman, Maria	George V. Slack
Carter	John	Mitchell	03-Jan-1886	17-Dec-1885	James Carter	Spellman, Mary	James Mulligan
Carter	John	Joseph	30-Mar-1890	14-Mar-1890	James Carter	Spellman, Mary	John Steadman
Carter	Mary		22-May-1892	07-May-1892	James Carter	Spellman, Mary	James McKeever
Carter	Patrick	Maura	08-Jan-1888	18-Dec-1887	James Carter	Spellman, Mary	Edward Mulligan
Carter	Sara	Norris	26-Nov-1883	01-Nov-1883	James Carter	Spellman, Mary	Patrick Joseph Donahue
Case	Albert		06-Jun-1895	About 1816	Robert Case	Barber, Ann	
Casey	John	Vincent	29-Jul-1888	19-Jul-1888	John A. Casey	Glenn, Margaret	John Glenn
Casey	Margaret		06-Sep-1896	August 1896	John A. Casey	Glenn, Margaret	Bartley Gereghty
Casey	Catherine		03-Dec-1893	24-Nov-1893	John Andrew Casey	Glenn, Margaret Helen	Francis Joseph Casey
Casey	Francis	Joseph	31-Aug-1890	16-Aug-1890	John Andrew Casey	Glenn, Margaret Helen	Edward E. McNamara
Casey	Mary	Edith	24-Jul-1892	09-Jul-1892	John Casey	Glenn, Margaret	Charles McShane
Casey	Margaret	Mary	16-Apr-1893	01-Apr-1893	Joseph B. Casey	Mullen, Catherine V.	Michael Mullen
Casey	Francis	Aloysius	21-May-1893	08-May-1893	William B. Casey	Schaefer, Mary C.	Francis A. Casey
Cash	Agnes	Mary	28-Aug-1892	27-Aug-1892	Patrick Cash	Callaghan, Delia	William Callaghan
Cash	Edward		14-Aug-1898	05-Aug-1898	Peter Cash	Callahan, Delia	Michael Hoban
Cashman	Jane	Mary	21-Jul-1907	15-Jul-1907	William Cashman	Moore, Jane	Edmund Moore
Cashman	Mary	Margaret	15-Sep-1912	4-Sep-1912	William Cashman	Moore, Joan	Joan Moore
Cashman	Mildred		7-Feb-1904	24-Jan-1904	William Cashman	Moore, Jennie	Joseph Cashman
Cashman	William	J.	27-Sep-1908	15-Sep-1908	William J. Cashman	Moore, Genevieve	J. Thomas Moore
Caskey	Joseph		13-Jan-1907	7-Jan-1907	Joseph Caskey	Byrne, Mary	Thomas Dougherty
Casserly	Ann		17-Oct-1886	27-Sep-1886	James Casserly	Flately, Mary	Hubert Caufield
Casserly	Catherine		08-Jul-1900	24-Jun-1900	James Casserly	Flattery, Mary	Thomas Casserly
Casserly	James	Joseph	10-May-1891	23-Apr-1891	James Casserly	Flatly, Mary Ellen	John Casserly

17

LAST NAME	FIRST NAME	MIDDLE	BAPTISM	BIRTH	Father	Mother	SPONSORS
Casserly	John	Michael	30-Oct-1898	16-Oct-1898	James Casserly	Flatley, Mary Helen	Michael McDermott / Ann Casserly
Casserly	Margaret		06-Jan-1889	29-Dec-1888	James Casserly	Flatly, Mary	John Feely / Catherine Ward
Casserly	Thomas		10-Sep-1893	29-Aug-1893	James Casserly	Flatly, Mary Helen	Letitia Sullivan
Cassidy	Florence	Elizabeth	10-Nov-1907	8-Nov-1907	Eugene Cassidy	Wright, Florence Olivia	Elizabeth Clarke
Cassidy	Elizabeth	Stewart	29-Mar-1896	03-Mar-1896	Francis Cassidy	Stewart, Estelle	Henry Cassidy / Margaret Griffith
Cassidy	George	Walter	14-Nov-1886	08-Nov-1886	James Bartholomew Cassidy	Davis, Clara Rebecca	George W. Couch / Mary Silverson
Cassidy	Florence		03-Jul-1892	10-Jun-1892	James Cassidy	Carlin, Florence	Margaret Cassidy
Cassidy	Francis		25-Aug-1889	30-Jul-1889	James Cassidy	Cassidy, Florence	Joseph Cassidy / Florence Cassidy
Cassidy	Helen	Mary	31-May-1896	11-May-1896	James Cassidy	Flatley, Mary Helen	Michael Gahan / Mary Conroy
Cassidy	John	Leon	26-Aug-1888	19-Aug-1888	James Cassidy	Davis, Clara	Teresa Cassidy
Cassidy	Dorothy		13-Feb-1898	21-Jan-1898	James J. Cassidy	Carlin, Florence	A.S. Papka / Mary Cassidy
Cassidy	Jerome		03-Dec-1899	20-Nov-1899	John Cassidy	Spence, Mary	George Evans / Mary Connor
Cassidy	Loretta		14-Feb-1897	28-Jan-1897	John Cassidy	Spence, Genevieve	George Evans / Mary Spence
Cassidy	Isabelle		07-Jan-1894	21-Dec-1893	Michael Cassidy	Gallagher, Elizabeth	James Gallagher / Kernan, Catherine
Cassidy	Mary		29-Dec-1895	12-Dec-1895	Michael Cassidy	Gallagher, Elizabeth	Danile Whelan / Mary McAnally
Cassidy	Samuel	James	06-Sep-1891	20-Aug-1891	Michael Cassidy	Gallagher, Elizabeth	John Gallagher / Elizabeth Hagerty
Cassidy	William	John	31-Jul-1904	11-Jul-1904	Michael Cassidy	Gallagher, Elizabeth	William F. Noonan / Mary Whalen
Cassidy	Susanna		14-Jul-1889	07-Jul-1889	Michael Francis Cassidy	Gallagher, Elizabeth	Thomas Whelan / Margaret Gallagher
Cassidy	Eugene	James	04-Jul-1889	20-Jul-1889	Patrick Cassidy	Duffy, Helen Elizabeth	Hamilton S. Hoggdon / Mary Cassidy
Cassidy	George	Jerome	06-Dec-1885	22-Nov-1885	Patrick Cassidy	Duffy, Helen	Bernard Finnegan / Mary Kernan
Cassidy	Helen	Laura	18-Dec-1887	07-Dec-1887	Patrick Cassidy	Duffy, Helen Elizabeth	James Aloysius Duffy / Margaret Lynch
Cassidy	Mary	Winifred	12-Feb-1882	01-Feb-1882	Patrick Cassidy	Duffy, Helen	Patrick F. Finnegan / Helen Finnegan
Cassidy	William	Bradley	30-Dec-1883	22-Dec-1883	Patrick Cassidy	Duffy, Helen E.	John Carr / Joan Frances Mahoney
Castley	Elizabeth		4-Oct-1908	4-Oct-1908	Thomas Castley	Feeley, Elizabeth	Thomas Feeley / Norah C. Norton
Caton	Joseph	Leo	20-Mar-1892	08-Mar-1892	Michael Henry Caton	O'Brien, Mary Francis	Thomas Martin / Alice O'Brien
Caton	Julia	Isabelle	12-Nov-1893	04-Nov-1893	Michael Henry Caton	O'Brien, Mary Francis	Henry Davis / Helen O'Brien
Caulfield	Agnes		01-Oct-1893	24-Sep-1893	Michael Caulfield	Byrne, Catherine	Hugh Caulfield / Mary Caulfield
Caulfield	Helen	Theresa	09-Oct-1892	26-Sep-1892	Michael Caulfield	Burns, Catherine	Samuel J. Eppelr / Catherine Cunningham
Caulfield	Mary	Catherine	15-Sep-1889	07-Sep-1889	Michael Caulfield	Burke, Catherine	Thomas Nolan / Bridget Caulfield
Cavanaugh	Joseph	Benedict	15-Mar-1897	14-Mar-1897	Benedict Cavanaugh	McCormick, Elizabeth	Ann McCormick
Cavanaugh	Mary		14-Mar-1892	12-Mar-1892	Benedict Cavanaugh	McCormick, Elizabeth	Mary McCormick
Cavanaugh	Adele	Isabelle	04-Apr-1890	27-Mar-1890	George Cavanaugh	Griffin, Ann	Eleanor Connolly
Cavanaugh	Joseph		08-Jun-1890	25-May-1890	Roger Cavanaugh	Sullivan, Julia	M. Sullivan / Ellen Sullivan
Cavey	Charles	Kenneth	19-Jun-1911	27-May-1911	Charles Cavey	McIntyre, Margaret	Mary Goldrick
Cavey	Edward	Keys	4-May-1913	11-Apr-1913	Charles Key Cavey	Clemson, Lillian V.	William R. Blessing / Elizabeth E. Clemson
Cawley	Mary	Catherine	23-Jul-1893	17-Jul-1893	James Cawley	Mitchell, Joan	John Cryan / Margaret Cryan
Chailon	George	August	16-Apr-1894	03-Oct-1892	George W. Chailon	Zulauf, Catherine C.	Eliza Chailon
Chambers	Sara	Genevieve	2-May-1909	23-Apr-1909	Lee Chambers	Padden, Sarah	John Monaghan / Ellen Carey
Chambers	Leon	Clarence	06-Dec-1903	25-Nov-1903	Leon Chambers	Padden, Sara	Thomas Conroy / Rose M. Dougherty
Chambers	Mary		28-May-1899	19-May-1899	Richard Lee Chambers	Padden, Elizabeth Martina	John Conroy / Mary Chambers
Chanee	James	Leo	8-Aug-1915	17-Jul-1915	Charles Chanee	Garey, Bertha M.	Thomas Slowery / Madeline Chanee
Chapman	John	James	16-Feb-1913	12-Feb-1913	Michael Chapman	Bannon, Mary	James Chapman / Mary Byrnes
Chapman	Mary	Margaret	18-Sep-1907	14-Sep-1907	Michael Chapman	Bannon, Mary	John Cox / Margaret Bannon
Chase	Arthur	Elmer	17-Aug-1890	27-Jul-1890	George Chase	O'Neill, Elizabeth	John Arthur McGreevey / Isabelle O'Neill
Chase	Isabelle		17-Dec-1882	30-Nov-1882	George W. Chase	O'Neill, Elizabeth Martha	James J. O'Neill / Isabelle O'Neill
Chase	Ethel	Elizabeth	28-Feb-1886	11-Feb-1886	George Warren Chase	O'Neill, Elizabeth Martina	James Byrne / Ann O'Neill
Chase	George	Warren	19-Oct-1884	22-Sep-1884	George Warren Chase	O'Neill, Elizabeth	James O'Neil / Margaret O'Neil
Chase	James		15-Apr-1888	18-Mar-1888	George Warren Chase	O'Neill, Elizabeth Martin	Henry John McClannon / Matilda O'Neill
Chilcote	William		25-Jul-1915	20-Mar-1915	William J. Chilcote	Wilson, Mary E.	Sarah Chilcote
Chilcote	Catherine	Helen	05-Jan-1902	18-Dec-1901	William M. Chilcote	Dillehunt, Sarah C.	Regina Ross / Carroll Moore
Chopper	Thomas	James	02-Mar-1902	14-Feb-1902	Joseph Chopper	Clancy, Mary	Daniel Quinn / Margaret Clancy
Chrisall	George	Washington	30-Oct-1887	24-Jan-1861	George W. Chridall	Chridall, Eleanor	John O'Callahan
Chrismer	Margaret (Pearl)	Gertrude	01-Apr-1888	07-Mar-1888	William A. Chrismer	Hoffman, Margaret Cecelia	Elizabeth Joan Bradyhouse
Christle	Helen	Mary	30-Apr-1893	25-Mar-1893	George Christle	Kenny, Ann	Mary McMahon
Christle	Helen	Mary	31-Mar-1893	25-Mar-1893	George M. Christle	Kenny, Ann	
Christmer	Ann	Rebecca	03-May-1883	08-Apr-1883	Samuel Edward Christmer	Jennings, Bridget	Mary Kelly
Christopher	Joseph		17-Jan-1886	23-Dec-1885	Charles Christopher	McGraw, Catherine	Michael McGraw / Bridget Hannan
Christopher	Thomas	Franklin	16-Apr-1882	27-Mar-1882	Thomas Andrew Christopher	McGraw, Catherine Theresa	Charles A. Eichelberger / Henriett M. Eichelberger
Christopher	William	Clarence	29-Jun-1884	07-Jun-1884	Thomas Andrew Christopher	McGrath, Catherine Theresa	Ida Christopher
Christopher/Hillman	Julia		16-Mar-1898	12-Mar-1817	Charles Christopher	Tyler, Zeppin	Mary Sullivan
Chunnult	Lucille		8-Apr-1906	29-Oct-1902	William Chunnelt	Connor, Elizabeth	Catherine Stephenson
Cinningham	George	William	02-Mar-1884	02-Feb-1884	Francis Cunningham	Welsh, Virginia	William Baumann / Bridget Donovan
Cloeff	Susan		20-Jul-1902	11-Jun-1902	Valentine Cloeff	Arch, James [sic]	William Arch / Susan Arch

ST JOHN'S BAPTISMS 1882-1912

LAST NAME	FIRST NAME	MIDDLE	BAPTISM	BIRTH	Father	Mother	SPONSORS
Cioeff	Agnes	L.	28-Jul-1912	19-Jul-1912	Valentino Cioeff	Arch, Bene	Ann Gorman
Cioeff	Ferdinand	William	17-May-1896	20-Apr-1896	Valentino Cioeff	Arch, Elberta	Helen Cioeff
Cioeff	George	Richard	9-Mar-1904	22-Feb-1904	Valentino Cioeff	Arch, Jacobina Alberta	William Arch
Cioeff	James		30-Jan-1897	13-Apr-1874	William Arch Cioeff	Sommers, Susanna	E.J. Healy
Ciorff	Josephine	Casper	31-Jan-1915	19-Jan-1915	Valentino Cioeff	Arch, J. Alberta	Julia Giralla
City	Ann	Dolores	29-Jul-1906	11-Jul-1906	Francis D. City	Hughes, Ann	Katherine Wagner
City	Marshall	Jerome	02-Oct-1890	22-Oct-1886	John Washington City	Reynolds, Ann Foreman	Joseph Wagner
Clancey	James		10-Oct-1897	24-Sep-1897	James Clancy	Duggan, Bridget	Joseph H. Nelson
Clancey	John	Stephen	07-Jan-1894	24-Dec-1893	James Clancy	Duggan, Bridget	Helen Silberson
Clancy	Agnes		03-Sep-1882	14-Aug-1882	James Clancy	Malloy, Catherine	Bridget Goodman
Clancy	Edward		25-Aug-1901	14-Aug-1901	James Clancy	Dugan, Bridget	[Blank] Welsh
Clancy	Helen		26-Feb-1905	13-Feb-1905	James Clancy	Dugan, Bridget	James Ryan
Clancy	Joseph		01-Jan-1900	27-Dec-1899	James Clancy	Duggan, Bridget	John Clancy
Clancy	Margaret		08-Dec-1895	24-Nov-1895	James Clancy	Dugan, Bridget	Dennis Lardner
Clancy	Mary	Leo	12-Jul-1903	25-Jun-1903	James Clancy	Dugan, Bridget	Thomas Clancy
Clancy	Patrick		27-Mar-1892	17-Mar-1892	James Clancy	Dugan, Bridget	John McTighe
Clancy	Thomas		21-Dec-1890	09-Dec-1890	James Clancy	Duggan, Delia	James Maguire
Clancy	Catherine		23-Jul-1893	03-Jul-1893	John Clancy	Fay, Joan	George Passano
Clancy	Julia		16-Feb-1908	7-Feb-1908	John Clancy	Dugan, Bridget	Daniel Donovan
Clancy	Margaret		25-Jun-1882	19-Jun-1882	Thomas Clancy	Connolly, Mary	Michael Hessian
Clarity	Catherine	Bernardine	27-Sep-1903	6-Sep-1903	John Clarity	McNamee, Mary	Edward Herrington
Clark	Florence	Isabelle	02-Mar-1890	17-Feb-1890	Adam Clark	Kane, Mary	Joseph Myers
Clark	Mary	Lola	11-Aug-1900	31-Jul-1900	Edward Clark	Wentze, Mary	Thomas Barrett
Clark	Charles	S.	11-Feb-1900	24-Jan-1900	James Clark	Wynn, Mary	Rev. J.J. Dillon
Clark	Francis	Burke	15-Nov-1914	19-Oct-1914	James J. Clark	McNamera, Mary	
Clark	Mary	Joan	07-Jan-1895	26-Aug-1893	John Clark	Smith, Amelia	Edward Wynn
Clark	Mary	Bridget	8-Jul-1906	4-May-1906	John Clark	Winters, Ann	Thomas J. Burns
Clark	Bernard	Joseph	2-Nov-1902	24-Oct-1902	Patrick Clark	Gillen, Ann	Charls Mackin
Clark	Catherine	Mary	6-Nov-1904	19-Oct-1904	Patrick Clark	Gillen, Ann	James Logue
Clark	Margaret	Regina	04-Mar-1900	18-Feb-1900	William Clark	Duffy, Margaret	John Kerns
Clarke	William	Edward	04-Mar-1888	25-Feb-1888	Adam Clarke	Kane, Isabelle	Edwin Rosensteel
Clarke	Helen	Rosalie	03-Nov-1895	22-Oct-1895	Adam R. Clarke	Kane, Isabelle	James Hunter
Clarke	Ann	Josephine	09-Dec-1900	28-Nov-1900	Adam Ray Clarke	Kane, Mary	Frank O'Neill
Clarke	Francis	Ray	11-Oct-1891	04-Oct-1891	Adam Ray Clarke	Ward, Isabelle	August J. Borddeken
Clarke	John	Thomas	13-Jun-1886	18-May-1886	Adam Ray Clarke	Kane, Mary Elizabeth	Patrick McGuire
Clarke	Leo	Raymond	19-Jul-1896	23-Jun-1896	Charles E. Clarke	Craft, Louise	John O'Neil
Clarke	James	Ray	18-Jan-1914	28-Dec-1913	James R. Clarke	Constance, Mary	Charles E. Baldwin
Clarke	Francis	Elbridge	03-May-1903	28-Apr-1903	John E. Clarke	Winters, Ann	Ray Clarke
Clarke	Matthew		28-Feb-1892	25-Feb-1892	Luke Clarke	Davis, Cecelia	Clarence Thornberg
Clarke	Mary	Jane	27-Jan-1895	15-Jan-1895	Michael Clark	Hussy, Ann	Mary Clarke
Clarke	Bernard		06-Aug-1893	27-Jul-1893	Michael Clarke	Hussy, Ann	John Hussy
Clarke	Margaret		20-Nov-1898	10-Nov-1898	Michael Clarke	Hussy, Ann	Daniel Grady
Clarke	Michael		11-Oct-1896	02-Oct-1896	Michael Clarke	Hussy, Ann	Hugh Byrnes
Clarke	John		08-Mar-1893	23-Dec-1892	Peter Clarke	Bolden, Eliza	William Clarke
Clarke	Adam	Ray	3-Nov-1901	27-Oct-1901	Ray Clarke	Kane, Belle	James Clarke
Clarke	Thomas	Pierce	08-Jan-1893	23-Dec-1892	Ray Clarke	Kain, Mary Isabelle	Francis Kane
Clarke	William	Edward	10-Jan-1904	28-Dec-1903	Ray J. Clarke	Kain, Isabelle	William Bernard Dowd
Clarke	Irene		01-Mar-1901	10-Jun-1887	Robert Clarke	Shea, Elenora	Henry Burns
Clarke	Katherine		01-Mar-1901	15-Sep-1889	Robert Clarke	Shea, Elenora	
Clarke	C. Josephine		1-Nov-1908	21-Oct-1908	William Clarke	Duffey, Margaret Regina	John Brooks
Clarke	William	Hazel	07-Aug-1898	26-Jul-1898	William Clarke	Duffy, Margaret	Charles Duffy
Clarke	Mary	Jenette	15-Jan-1905	6-Jan-1905	William J. Clarke	Duffey, Margaret R.	Joseph Reilly
Clautice	Joseph	Ellen Lavinia	13-Nov-1892	08-Nov-1892	Francis Clautice	Purnell, Mary	James Clautice
Clautice	Mary	Leon	29-Aug-1886	04-Aug-1886	George W. Clautice	Brady, Ann	James Clautice
Clayton	Lillian	Blanche	02-Sep-1888	10-Aug-1888	George W. Clautice	Brady, Mary Ann	James Cavanaugh
Cleary	James		28-Aug-1898	28-Aug-1892	Elsworth Clayton	Rock, Rose	Mary Clarke
Cleary	Margaret		21-Dec-1894	22-Jul-1877	James Cleary	Meara, Ann	
Clements	Edith	Elizabeth	15-Dec-1894	18-Jan-1875	James Cleary	Meara, Ann	John Gagan
Clements	Mary	Agnes	17-Jun-1900	15-Feb-1900	Daniel Clements	McDermott, Margaret	Patrick Kelly
Clemsen	Lily	Viola	13-Mar-1890	06-Nov-1889	John Adam Clement	Arthur, Catherine	John Michael Corcoran
Clemsen	Mary	Agnes	30-Aug-1891	24-Aug-1891	Edward Clemsen	Wright, Mary	John Wright
Clew	Oliver		16-May-1915	27-Apr-1915	Edward Clemsen	Denn, Lillian	William Blessing
			29-Oct-1913	17-Jun-1875	John R. Clew	Mooney, Elizabeth	

19

LAST NAME	FIRST NAME	MIDDLE	BAPTISM	BIRTH	Father	Mother	SPONSORS
Clifford	Mary		03-Jan-1897	21-Dec-1896	James Clifford	Byrnes, Mary	John McCabe / Mary Mulligan
Clifford	Thomas		31-Mar-1895	16-Mar-1895	James Patrick Clifford	Byrnes, Mary Ann	William Byrnes / Mary Chase
Clifford	John		24-Mar-1907	4-Mar-1907	John Clifford	Clifford, Margaret	George Gammie / Mary Quirk
Clifford	Mary		12-Feb-1905	3-Feb-1905	John Joseph Clifford	Clifford, Margaret	Charles B. Lamana / Ann M. Myles
Clifford	Caherine	Elizabeth	21-Apr-1912	2-Apr-1912	Thomas Clifford	Bowen, Ann	Edward Clifford / Ann Bowen
Clifford	John	Joseph	23-Jun-1912	4-Jun-1912	Thomas Clifford	Kelly, Mary	Joseph Cloonan / Mary Kelly
Clifford	Katherine		20-Dec-1914	1-Dec-1914	Thomas Clifford	Kelly, Mary	John Kelly / Katherine Flannagan
Clifford	Mary	Cecelia	10-Sep-1882	31-Aug-1882	Thomas Clifford	[Blank]	/ Mary E. Griffin
Clifford	Thomas	Edward	5-Jun-1914	5-Jun-1914	Thomas D. Clifford	Bowen, Ann C.	Edward Clifford / Ann R. Clifford
Clifford	Thomas	Laurence	23-Jan-1910	30-Dec-1909	Thomas Joseph Clifford	Kelly, Mary Margaret	Patrick Kelly / Ann Kelly
Clifford	Agnes	Elizabeth	16-Jul-1905	18-Jun-1905	William Clifford	Roberts, Harriet	James McDonnell / Mary Margaret Smeykal
Clifford	Alice	Mary	26-Apr-1902	23-Mar-1902	William Clifford	Roberts, Harriet	Henry Wege / Mary Wege
Clifford	Ann		19-Feb-1893	09-Jan-1893	William Clifford	Roberts, Hattie	Thomas McBride / Mary McBride
Clifford	Elsie	Mary	19-May-1895	01-May-1895	William Clifford	Roberts, Hattie	Martin Roach / Margaret Bracken
Clifford	Mary	Slaughter	25-Feb-1900	22-Jan-1900	William Clifford	Roberts, Harriet	William McKenna / Honora Barrett
Clifford	John	Eugene	16-Aug-1908	22-Jul-1908	William H. Clifford	Roberts, Harriet A.	Eugene Manning / Mary Dennis
Clinefelter	Jerome		19-Apr-1896	About 1847	Jesse Clinefelter	Ellgenfretz, Rebecca	
Clinton	Ann	Delia	10-Jan-1904	25-Dec-1903	John Clinton	McDonald, Delia	Patrick Clinton / Elizabeth Clinton
Clinton	Catherine		17-Sep-1905	3-Sep-1905	John Clinton	McDonnell, Bridget	Joseph Muldoon / Catherine McDonnell
Clinton	Mary	Leon	28-Apr-1907	15-Apr-1907	John Clinton	McDonald, Bridget Delia	John Coogan / Sarah McDonald
Clottis	Sara	Catherine	11-Aug-1901	25-Jul-1901	Patrick Clinton	Wallace, Elizabeth	Joseph Muldoon / Delia Muldoon
Clubb	Henry	Jerome	16-Nov-1884	03-Aug-1884	George B. Clottis	Brady, Mary Ann	Michael Augustine Brady / Mary Ann Hart
Codd	Angela	Regina	11-Jan-1891	30-Dec-1890	Henry Clubb	Steinmeier, Josephine	Henry Rabe / Mary Rabe
Codd	Mary	Catherine	18-Jun-1911	8-Jun-1911	Joseph Codd	Griffin, Margaret	William Codd / Caherine Brooke
Codd	Margaret		23-May-1909	10-May-1909	Joseph R. Codd	Griffin, Ella Theresa	John P. Codd / Catherine Theresa Griffin
Codd	Michael	P.	23-Jul-1905	2-Jul-1905	Michael Codd	Savage, Mary Ann	James Byrne / Helen Wafer
Codd	Mary	Ann	9-Dec-1906	19-Nov-1906	Michael Codd	Savage, Mary A.	William Codd / Ann McKenna
Codd	Michael	William	16-Jul-1899	06-Jul-1899	William Codd	Cleary, Elizabeth	John Somers / Ann Hagerty
Codd	Joseph	Benedict	01-Sep-1901	25-Apr-1901	William Codd	Cleary, Elizabeth	Hugh Toner / Mary Savage
Codd	Laurence	Edward	3-Oct-1915	20-Sep-1915	William J. Codd	Cleary, Elizabeth	Francis P. Harris / Nora Barrett
Codd	William	Joseph	6-Aug-1905	17-Jul-1905	William J. Codd	Cleary, Elizabeth	Charles J. Gray / Bridget Gray
Codd	Eleanor	Elizabeth	17-May-1903	04-May-1903	William J. Codd	Cleary, Elizabeth	Michael F. Conway / Mary E. Kennedy
Codd	John	James	10-Oct-1909	20-Sep-1909	William Joseph Codd	Cleary, Elizabeth	Michael J. Hanlon / Ann Donnelly
Coffay	William	LeRoy	6-Oct-1907	18-Sep-1907	William Joseph Codd	Cleary, Elizabeth	James W. Hart / Jennie Sweeny
Coffey	Catherine	Loretta	10-Mar-1912	3-Dec-1911	Joseph Coffay	[N], Emma	/ Agnes Coffay
Coffey	Ignatius		24-Jan-1897	14-Jan-1897	John Coffey	Tiernan, Mary	William McKnight / Catherine Coffey
Cohen	Mary		06-Aug-1882	31-Jul-1882	John Coffey	Croghan, Elizabeth	Timothy Croghan / Elizabeth O'Keefe
Colbert	Ellen	Cecelia	16-Jan-1909	16-Jan-1909	[Blank]	[Blank]	
Colbert	Patrick	Leon	3-May-1914	16-Apr-1914	Robert Colbert	Molloy, Mary	Luke Molloy / Agnes Colbert
Colbert	William	Joseph	26-Jul-1903	11-Jul-1903	Robert Colbert	Molloy, Mary	Edward Curran / Catherine Colbert
Colbert	Mary	Agnes	17-Mar-1907	27-Feb-1907	Robert Colbert	Molloy, Mary	William Colbert / Helen Kenny
Colbert	Robert	Joseph	30-Apr-1905	15-Apr-1905	Robert J. Colbert	Molloy, Mary	Thomas Colbert / Mary Colbert
Colbert	Thomas	Michael	17-Jul-1910	1-Jul-1910	Robert Joseph Colbert	Molloy, Mary	William Coffay / Julia Coffay
Colbert	Agnes	Teresa	17-Mar-1912	2-Mar-1912	Robert Joseph Colbert	Molloy, Mary	Michael Vallee / Mary Kehoe
Colder	Thomas	Leroy	16-Dec-1894	04-Dec-1894	William Colbert	O'Keefe, Mary	Daniel Colbert / Ann Colbert
Cole	Agnes	Gertrude	07-Nov-1886	24-Oct-1886	Louis Colder	Davey, Mary	Thomas Davey / Margaret Callender
Cole	Genevieve	Josephine	05-Feb-1888	23-Jan-1888	John H. Cole	Finnegan, Mary A.	Patrick F. Finnegan / Agnes M. Holden
Cole	Mary	Bernard	01-Jun-1884	20-May-1884	John H. Cole	Finnegan, Mary Ann	Laurence Finnegan / Mary Finnegan
Cole	John	Mary	21-Jul-1889	09-Jul-1889	John H. Cole	Finnegan, Mary Ann	Bernard Finegan / Mary Finegan
Cole	Lillian	Helen	04-Feb-1883	24-Jan-1883	John Henry Cole	Phillips, Ida	Bernard Finegan / Bridget Finnegan
Colerin	Mary	Patrick	27-Aug-1893	13-Aug-1893	Robert Cole	Gaynor, Mary	Edmund Joseph Meskill / Mary Cole
Colleran	Josephine		21-Mar-1897	17-Mar-1897	John Colerin	Callahan, Sarah	Patrick Cash / Helen Smith
Colleran	Julian	Francis	29-Jul-1902	26-Jan-1902	Martin Colleran	Callahan, Sarah	Martin Brennan / Mary Williams
Colleran	Martin		14-Aug-1898	05-Aug-1898	Martin Colleran	Callahan, Sarah	William Williams / Delia Dunlevy
Colleran	Mary		22-May-1894	20-May-1894	Martin Colleran	Callahan, Sara	/ Margaret Hogan
Colleran	William	Leo	27-May-1894	20-May-1894	Martin Colleran	Callahan, Sara	William Callahan / Mary Colleran
Colleran	Joseph	Louis	21-Jul-1895	15-Jul-1895	Martin Colleran	Callahan, Sarah	Martin Jennings / Delia Cash
Colleran	Mary	Helen	24-Dec-1893	11-Dec-1893	Thomas Colleran	Madden, Mary	Michael Garman / Mary Guerin
Colleran	Thomas	Vincent	10-Mar-1889	18-Feb-1889	Thomas Colleran	Madden, Mary	Michael Jennings / Mary Mullaghey
Collier	Robert	Finlay	20-Nov-1891	14-Nov-1891	Thomas Colleran	Madden, Mary	
Collier	Thomas		12-Feb-1888	[Blank]	Abraham Collier	Golden, Emma E.	John Houchens / Mary Houchens
			15-Dec-1895	21-Apr-1855	Henry Collier	Peal, Martha	

LAST NAME	FIRST NAME	MIDDLE	BAPTISM	BIRTH	Father	Mother	SPONSORS
Collier	Hilda	Regina	29-Mar-1891	14-Mar-1891	Otis P. Collier	Ward, Mary V.	James Carey	Elizabeth O'Boy
Collier	Annabelle	Gertrude	10-Jun-1888	01-Jun-1888	Otis Perkins Collier	Ward, Mary	Peter Ward	Gertrude Ward
Collins	Helen	Mary	24-May-1908	13-May-1908	Henry Collins	Puhl, Mary	Claudius Gaskin	Mary Dowd
Collins	Earl	Joseph	28-Jan-1912	19-Jan-1912	Henry J. Collins	Puhl, Mary	James Hagan	Margaret Hagan
Collins	Joan	Josephine	21-Mar-1897	14-Mar-1897	John Collins	Gaynor, Mary	John Finan	Sarah Coughlin
Collins	Margaret		24-Feb-1884	09-Feb-1884	John Collins	Cash, Mary	Edward Daly	Catherine Ryan
Collins	Catherine	Loretta	20-Apr-1890	09-Mar-1890	Thomas Collins	Madden, Mary	Patrick Jennings	Catherine Ward
Collins	Howard	Leon	17-Aug-1886	14-Mar-1884	Thomas E. Collins	Gibbs, Helen		Elizabeth Connor
Collins	Martha	Myrtle	21-Dec-1891	17-Jun-1887	Thomas E. Collins	Gibbs, Ella		Ann R. Maguire
Collins	Joseph		21-Jun-1892	22-Jun-1892	William Collins	Geigan, Catherine		Mary Geigan
Collins	Catherine	Margaret	19-Nov-1893	05-Nov-1893	William P. Collins	Geigan, Catherine	Dennis Reardon	Margaret Geigan
Collison	Lola		28-Jan-1890	20-Dec-1889	George Collison	Sheehan, Ann		Mary Lafete
Collison	Florence	Rose	29-Sep-1895	04-Sep-1895	Thomas Collison	Rowland, Delia	John Donahoe	Helen Connor
Collison	Rowland	Edward	17-Dec-1893	08-Dec-1893	Thomas Collison	Rowland, Delia	William Rowland	Rose Toner
Colton	Mary		30-Jun-1882	02-May-1882	Alexander Colton	Duffy, Isabelle		Mary ames
Colvin	Samuel	Halbert	5-Apr-1908	16-Mar-1908	Samuel Newton Colvin	Phillips, Laura Ada	J.C. Anstine	Maud Brown
Colwell	Mary	Ruth	02-Dec-1902	21-Jul-1902	John F. Colwell	Emory, Rose		Geneva Sweeney
Comella	Thomas	August	11-Oct-1891	04-Oct-1891	Thomas Comella	McLaughlin, Ann	George Carroll	Catherine McLaughlin
Concannon	Mary	Ann	22-Nov-1908	4-Nov-1908	Thomas Concannon	Riley, Mary	James [Blank]	Bridget Feeney
Condon	Caroline	Mary	21-Jul-1889	16-Apr-1889	John Condon	Mitchell, Ida	Henry Francis Evans	Agnes Murphy
Condy	Martin		01-Sep-1889	18-Aug-1889	James Condy	McGarrity, Ann	James Breen	Catherine Breen
Conelius	John		24-Nov-1907	11-Nov-1907	John Conelius	Kelly, Winifred	Thomas Kelly	Mary Bowers
Coniff	Teresa		3-Jul-1910	14-Jun-1910	Patrick Conif	McEvoy, Teresa	William Moran	Nora Donlan
Coniff	Patrick	Joseph	5-Sep-1915	23-Aug-1915	Patrick Coniff	McEvoy, Teresa	Joseph P. Stafford	Ann Kelly
Coniff	W.		12-Sep-1915	7-Sep-1915	Elmer Conklin	Freshline, Helen M.	Henry Freshline	Margaret Wiedefeld
Conklin	Clarence	Vinton	28-Jan-1901	18-Jan-1901	W.H. Conklin	Genoy, Mary	William Foster	Margaret Foster
Conklin	Walter	Clarence	27-Oct-1904	26-Sep-1904	Walter Clarence Conklin	Genoy, Mary A.		Ann Richards
Conklin	Margaret		20-Nov-1902	03-Oct-1902	Walter Conklin	Genoy, Mary A.	Charles Foster	Mary Foster
Conklin	Elmer	Walter	31-May-1912	16-Jun-1889	Walter Hamilton Conklin	Brown, Barbara	Henry wiedefeld	Mary Irving
Conklin	Henry	Andrew	3-Aug-1913	27-Jul-1913	William Conklin	Freshline, Helen M.	Andrew Freshline	Catherine Clinton
Conley	Ann		08-Sep-1895	22-Aug-1895	Edward Conley	Ryan, Norah		Elizabeth Suholer
Conlon	Helen	Josephine	19-Jan-1890	13-Jan-1890	Joseph Conlon	Lardner, Mary	Joseph A. Conlon	Ann Leonard
Conlon	Mary	Ann	25-Jan-1885	19-Jan-1885	Laurence Conlon	Lardner, Mary	Owen Donegan	Winifred Lardner
Conlon	Laurence	Joseph	05-Aug-1888	04-Aug-1888	Laurence J. Conlon	Lardner, Mary	Dennis Lardner	Mary Dunn
Conlon	Margaret	Teresa	26-Sep-1886	25-Sep-1886	Laurence J. Conlon	Lardner, Mary	Jerome Carey	Margaret McCoulin
Conlon	Ann	Cecelia	29-Nov-1891	21-Nov-1891	Laurence Joseph Conlon	Lardner, Mary	Dennis Lardner	Mary Dunn
Conlon	James	Joseph	2-Nov-1913	28-Sep-1913	Patrick Conlon	[N], Emma		Elizabeth Kelly
Conn	Daniel		08-Jul-1900	02-May-1900	Edward Conn	Reinhardt, Mary	August Reinhardt	Philomena Reinhardt
Connabaugh	Howard	Jerome	06-Feb-1887	24-Jan-1887	Dennis Connabaugh	Cleary, Margaret	William Keeley	Catherine Connabaugh
Connally	Rose	Elizabeth	20-Jul-1890	09-Jul-1890	Charles W. Connally	Clarke, Catherine	George M. Riley	Elizabeth R. Magruder
Connelly	Isabelle		25-Jul-1897	24-Jul-1897	Edward Connelly	Ryan, Nora		Theresa Affayroux
Connelly	Joseph	James	22-Oct-1899	08-Oct-1899	Edward Connelly	Ryan, Nora	James Dooley	Mary Cronin
Connelly	Helen	Geraldine	26-Apr-1908	10-Apr-1908	John Joseph Connelly	Connelly, Helen Mary		Agnes Connelly
Connelly	John	Joseph	20-Aug-1911	5-Aug-1911	John Joseph Connelly	Richmond, Catherine	Michael J. Pell	Mary Catherine Miles
Connelly	Thomas		31-Jan-1892	22-Jan-1892	Peter Connelly	Quillan, Sara	James Conley	Catherine Carr
Connelly	John	Joseph	05-Jul-1883	02-Jul-1883	William Connelly	Kelly, Sara		Emma Keelan
Connelly	Sara	Joan	19-Aug-1888	09-Aug-1888	William Joseph Connelly	Kelly, Sara Catherine	Joseph Eugene Kelly	Eva Teresa Carey
Conner	John	Leon	01-Jul-1883	22-Jun-1883	Thomas Connor	Murphy, Catherine Ann	Ambrose Kennedy	Margaret Farrell
Conner	Thomas		07-Nov-1886	27-Oct-1886	Thomas Connor	Murphy, Catherine	Patrick O'Neill	Margaret Deveraux
Conners	Mary	Isabelle	11-Oct-1908	25-Sep-1908	William Samuel Conners	Dennert, Margaret Elizabeth	William F. Dennert	Ann Hubbard
Conniff	Edward		12-Aug-1884	11-Aug-1884	Daniel Connolly	Redding, Catherine	Thomas Connolly	Mary Monica Whittle
Conniff	Elizabeth	Catherine	3-Dec-1911	19-Nov-1911	Patrick Conniff	McAvoy, Theresa	Thomas Gillmartin	Hannah Riley
Conniff	Francis	Xavier	16-Nov-1913	27-Oct-1913	Patrick Conniff	McAvoy, Theresa	John McAvoy	Mary McGrady
Conniff	James	Patrick	8-Nov-1908	26-Oct-1908	Patrick Francis Conniff	Kelly, Sara	Patrick Joseph Moran	Mary Kelly
Connolly	Agnes		08-Aug-1886	09-Jul-1886	Andrew Connolly	Larkins, Bridget	John Connolly	Ann Jordan
Connolly	Catherine		22-Jan-1882	15-Jan-1882	Andrew Connolly	Larkins, Bridget	Edward Joseph Kanna	Mary Byrnes
Connolly	Thomas	Patrick	30-Mar-1884	13-Mar-1884	Andrew Connolly	Larkins, Bridget	Daniel Holden	Sara Ann Kelly
Connolly	Helen	Frances	09-Jul-1893	30-Jun-1893	Charles William Connolly	Clark, Catherine	James Joseph Leary	Catherine Kelly
Connolly	Mary	Florence	18-Nov-1888	08-Nov-1888	Charles William Connolly	Clark, Florence Catherine		Ann Catherine Leary
Connolly	Edward		12-Aug-1884	11-Aug-1884	Daniel Connolly	Redding, Catherine	Thomas Connolly	Mary Monica Whittle
Connolly	Ann		08-Feb-1891	27-Jan-1891	Edward Connolly	Ryan, Honora	Owen Kelly	Margaret Kelly
Connolly	Edward		20-Nov-1892	24-Oct-1892	Edward Connolly	Ryan, Honora	W.J. Kearney	Mary E. Dorsey
Connolly	Honora		01-Apr-1888	23-Mar-1888	Edward Connolly	Ryan, Honora	John O'Neil	Ann Connolly
Connolly	Mary		28-Jul-1889	04-Jul-1889	Edward Connolly	Ryan, Honora	Michael Dolly	Mary Helen Tobin

21

LAST NAME	FIRST NAME	MIDDLE	BIRTH	BAPTISM	Father	Mother	SPONSORS
Connolly	Ann		07-Feb-1887	09-Feb-1887	James Connolly	Campbell, Ann	Mary Dorsey
Connolly	Isabelle		18-Aug-1883	02-Sep-1883	James Connolly	Campbell, Ann	Isabelle Fopless
Connolly	Mary	Joan	14-Feb-1882	19-Feb-1882	James Connolly	Campbell, Ann	Edward Connolly
Connolly	James	Francis	17-Apr-1888	22-Apr-1888	James Frances Connolly	Campbell, Ann	William M. Affayroux
Connolly	James	Howard	4-Jan-1906	4-Feb-1906	James P. Connolly	Brown, Mary R.	Edward Connelly
Connolly	Daniel		01-Aug-1889	02-Aug-1889	John Connolly	Cusick, Rose Ann	Francis Connolly
Connolly	Mary	Loretta	11-Dec-1895	15-Dec-1895	John Connolly	Cusick, Rose	Honora Burger
Connolly	Catherine	Dorothy	3-Mar-1908	15-Mar-1908	John J. Connolly	Richmond, Catherine	Bridget Doyle
Connolly	Mildred	Frances	7-Jul-1909	25-Jul-1909	John J. Connolly	Richmond, Catherine	Ann Connolly
Connolly	Joseph		21-May-1890	01-Jun-1890	Michael Connolly	Donahue, Teresa	Ann Connolly
Connolly	Henry	Thomas	29-Dec-1887	15-Jan-1888	Michael H. Connolly	Donahue, Theresa	Catherine Connolly
Connolly	Mary	Catherine	30-Apr-1883	10-Jun-1883	Owen Connolly	Dugan, Rose	Eleanor Donohue
Connolly	John		18-Oct-1882	22-Oct-1882	Patrick Connolly	Devanny, Honora	Ann Rooney
Connolly	Ann		14-Jan-1902	02-Feb-1902	Peter Connolly	Quillen, Sarah	Mary Clancy
Connolly	Edward		21-Feb-1898	13-Mar-1898	Peter Connelly	Quillan, Sarah	Ann Brown
Connolly	James		13-Sep-1906	30-Sep-1906	Peter Connelly	Quillan, Sarah	Catherine Horan
Connolly	Michael		30-Nov-1893	10-Dec-1893	Peter Connelly	Quillan, Sarah	Margaret Clark
Connolly	Peter		07-May-1900	20-May-1900	Peter Connolly	Quillin, Sarah	Catherine Connolly
Connolly	Caroline		01-Dec-1889	12-Jan-1890	Terence Connolly	Smith, Caroline	Mary Ann Quillin
Connolly	Elizabeth		06-Jan-1891	07-Jun-1891	Terence Connolly	Siemon, Caroline	Ann Wilcox
Connolly	Margaret	Ann	07-Nov-1880	22-May-1897	Terence Michael Connolly	Guy, Medora	Alice Connolly
Connolly	George		25-Nov-1886	26-Dec-1886	Thomas Connolly	Dunn, Rose	Catherine D. Dougherty
Connolly	Thomas	John	21-Sep-1895	06-Oct-1895	Thomas Connolly	O'Connor, Elizabeth	Matilda Dunn
Connolly	Elizabeth		29-Sep-1882	29-Oct-1882	Thomas Henry Connolly	Dunn, Rose	Delia O'Connor
Connolly	Francis		05-Jan-1887	16-Jan-1887	William Connolly	Kelly, Sara	Bridget Connolly
Connolly	Agnes		27-Oct-1890	09-Nov-1890	William J. Connolly	Kelly, Sarah J.	Mary Fannon
Connolly	Eleanor		07-Jun-1885	21-Jun-1885	William J. Connolly	Kelly, Sarah Catherine	Mary E. Cain
Connor	John	Joseph	29-Dec-1888	18-Jan-1889	Frances Connor	Clurken, Catherine	Joan Daugherty
Connor	Francis	Joseph	12-Jul-1884	13-Jul-1884	Francis Connor	McAleer, Ann M.	Mary Brady
Connor	Joseph		20-Mar-1886	04-Apr-1886	Francis J. Connor	McAleer, Ann	Alice McMahon
Connor	Ann		9-Nov-1907	1-Dec-1907	John Connor	Lanahan, Bertha	Mary McGinnity
Connor	William		16-Jun-1911	13-Jul-1911	John Connor	Lanahan, Katherine	Cecelia Connor
Connor	Helen	Elizabeth	18-Feb-1890	02-Mar-1890	John Joseph Connor	Alluisi, Mary Elizabeth	Bridget Connor
Connor	Thomas J	Joseph	27-Nov-1888	09-Dec-1888	John Joseph Connor	Alluisi, Mary Elizabeth	Ann Alluisi
Connor	Mary		8-Sep-1905	24-Sep-1905	John M. Connor	Lanahan, Bertha	Helen Collins
Connor	Charles	L.	17-Oct-1903	25-Oct-1903	Laurence Connor	Ward, Mary	Bridget Connor
Connor	William	Edward	20-Mar-1887	10-Apr-1887	Maythias Connor	Grady, Mary Ann	Elizabeth Miller
Connor	Rose		24-Nov-1892	11-Oct-1892	Patrick Connor	McGovern, Mary	Francis Kelly
Connor	Margaret	Ann	20-Aug-1893	01-Oct-1893	Peter Connor	Donohue, Mary	Margaret Barrett
Connor	Agnes	Mary	20-Oct-1884	09-Nov-1884	Thomas Connor	Murphy, Catherine	Margaret Cook
Connor	Catherine		05-Feb-1882	19-Feb-1882	Thomas Connor	Murphy, Catherine	Catherine O'Neil
Connor	Edward		26-Aug-1888	09-Sep-1888	Thomas Connor	Murphy, Catherine	Mary Elizabeth Murphy
Connor	George		15-Nov-1889	01-Dec-1889	Thomas Connor	Murphy, Catherine	Rose Cassidy
Connor	Mary	Estelle	07-Jan-1892	17-Jan-1892	Thomas Connor	Murphy, Catherine	Rose McKeever
Connor	Margaret	Mary	2-Nov-1902	9-Nov-1902	Thomas J. Connor	Cullen , Lola	Catherine Connor
Connor	Thomas	Joseph	26-Jan-1904	7-Feb-1904	Thomas J. Connor	Cullen, Margaret	Delia Conner
Connor	Agnes	Bridget	12-Nov-1892	27-Nov-1892	Timothy Connor	Moran, Agnes	Catherine Williams
Connors	Helen		27-Apr-1893	07-May-1893	George Connors	Kearney, Catherine	Bridget O'Connor
Connors	Margaret	Mary	23-Nov-1890	30-Nov-1890	George Connors	Kearney, Catherine	Margaret Kearney
Connors	Charles	Edward	28-Aug-1903	18-Oct-1903	James Connors	Jacob, Christina	Martin Gerald Byrne
Connors	Thomas	Spurrier	09-Jul-1903	19-Jul-1903	Joseph Connors	Arata, Margaret	Charles E. Murphy
Connors	James		03-Sep-1902	28-Sep-1902	Laurence Connors	Ward, Mary	Nannie Connor
Connors	Lawrence	William	10-Jan-1896	08-Mar-1896	Laurence Connors	Ward, Mary	Catherine Connors
Connors	Helen		27-Dec-1891	22-Feb-1891	Peter Connors	Donahoe, Mary	Clara Brocmeyer
Conroy	Edward	Gibbons	26-Dec-1909	16-Jan-1910	Edward G. Conroy	Thomas, Mary	Sarah Brown
Conroy	Thomas	Melvin	1-Dec-1911	10-Dec-1911	Edward Gibbons Conroy	Thomas, Mary	Margaret Burns
Conroy	Agnes	Grace	23-Jul-1888	05-Aug-1888	James Conroy	Gereghty, Ann	S. Conroy
Conroy	Aloysius		17-Apr-1896	03-May-1896	James Conroy	Garrity, Ann	Ann Dietz
Conroy	Ann		03-Sep-1894	09-Sep-1894	James Conroy	Garrity, Ann	Margaret Holmes
Conroy	Honora		08-Apr-1892	17-Apr-1892	James Conroy	Garrity, Ann	Francis Slaughter
Conroy	James		24-Aug-1884	31-Aug-1884	James Conroy	Garrity, Ann	Julia Gallagher
Conroy	Joseph	Thomas	08-Apr-1892	17-Apr-1892	James Conroy	Garrity, Ann	Caroline Bowers
Conroy	Loretta		03-Sep-1894	09-Sep-1894	James Conroy	Garrity, Ann	Carrie Conroy

Note: additional sponsor column entries visible: James King, Thomas Carney, Michael Connolly, Peter Connelly, Thomas Connolly, Edward Quillin, Catherine D. Dougherty, Joan Daugherty, John Fannon, John Flaherty, Andrew Connolly, Joseph Kennedy, Joseph Fannon, Joseph Connor, M.A. Connor, Thomas Lanahan, Stephen Connor, William Cahil, Martin Connor, Charles Miller, Daniel Grady, Thomas Joseph Barrett, John Connor, Peter Murphy, William Rowley, John Murphy, Edward Connor, William L. Connor, John Mullen, John Kelly, George Nagan, Thomas McSweeney, James Brocmeyer, John Patrick Burns, William Mahoney, John Conroy, George Powitz, Joseph Fleishell, Joseph Gleason, Patrick Garrity, John Garrity, Joseph Garrity, John Riordon

LAST NAME	FIRST NAME	MIDDLE	BAPTISM	BIRTH	Father	Mother	SPONSORS	
Conroy	Mary		11-Mar-1883	06-Mar-1883	James Henry Conroy	Gereghty, Ann	Joseph Gereghty	Mary Gereghty
Conroy	Mary	Isabelle	31-Aug-1902	22-Aug-1902	John Conroy	Corcoran, Ann	James Conroy	Mary Conroy
Conroy	William	Walter	8-Jan-1905	24-Dec-1904	John Conroy	Corcoran, Ann	William Conroy	Mary Slattery
Conroy	Catherine	Edna	4-Feb-1912	14-Jan-1912	Martin Conroy	Lynch, Martina	Francis Lynch	Agnes Griffin
Conroy	Mary		27-May-1883	21-May-1883	Thomas Conroy	Sinclair, Caroline	William Holland	Margaret Giblin
Conroy	Howard	Irvin	03-Jun-1894	02-May-1894	William Edward Conroy	Dunn, Alice Rosina	Rudolph Wissman	Mary Garvey
Conry	Genevieve		24-Feb-1884	13-Feb-1884	John Conry	Masey, Ann	Edward Richards	Ann Conry
Considine	James		11-Dec-1887	06-Dec-1887	James F. Considine	Kelly, Ann F.	James Considine	Mary Krener
Considine	Mary	Agnes	03-Feb-1889	24-Jan-1889	James F. Considine	Kelly, Ann F.	George A. Krener	Bridget A. Coffay
Constance	Mary	Agnes	27-Oct-1889	11-Oct-1889	John Constance	Gordon, Nellie		
Constance	Margaret	Laura	10-Oct-1886	13-Sep-1886	John G. Constance	Gordon, Helen V.	Charles G. Kirk	Margareta Meyerhall
Constance	Eva	Isabelle	12-Jul-1891	14-Jun-1891	John George Constance	Gordon, Helen Virginia		Isabelle Kirk
Constance	Helen	Virginia	15-Jul-1888	28-Jun-1888	John George Constance	Gordon, Helen Virginia		Mary Elizabeth Litz
Constant	Julia		5-Apr-1914	23-Oct-1910	Leon Constant	[N], Clementa		
Conway	Mary		1-Jan-1905	27-Nov-1904	Bernard Conway	Miller, Pauline		Mary Miller
Conway	John	Joseph	18-Nov-1888	06-Nov-1888	Charles Conway	Dempsey, Margaret	John Dempsey	Mary Dempsey
Conway	Sarah	Catherine	12-Sep-1897	08-Aug-1897	Charles Conway	Dempsey, Margaret	Jerome Lynch	Mary Leonard
Conway	Elizabeth	Mary	06-Dec-1891	20-Sep-1891	William A. Conway	Kidd, Alice		Sarah Redd
Conway	John	Francis	30-Jan-1885	12-Dec-1884	William Conway	Toole, Mary	Francis Conway	Frances Conway
Coogan	Ann		24-Sep-1899	17-Sep-1899	John Coogan	McNally, Rose	Joseph Mullen	Margaret Coogan
Coogan	Florence	Valentine	18-Feb-1906	14-Feb-1906	John Coogan	McNally, Rose		Ann Mullin
Coogan	James		19-Aug-1888	13-Aug-1888	John Coogan	McNally, Rose	John Francis McNally	Mary Ann McNally
Coogan	John		30-Jun-1895	25-Jun-1895	John Coogan	McNally, Rose	Patrick Coogan	Mary Coogan
Coogan	Margaret		08-Feb-1903	04-Feb-1903	John Coogan	McNally, Rose	Bernard King	Margaret Coogan
Coogan	Mary		20-Jul-1890	17-Jul-1890	John Coogan	McNally, Rose	John Lemmon	Agnes Hannafin
Coogan	Rose		25-Dec-1892	19-Dec-1892	John Coogan	McNally, Rose	Patrick Coogan	Rose Kennedy
Cook	Henry		4-Jul-1906	About 1885	Charles Cook	Wortche, Florence		
Cook	Francis		9-Apr-1911	3-Feb-1911	Chauncey Cook	Miller, Mary		Lena Miller
Cook	Edward	Cleveland	04-Jan-1885	24-Dec-1884	Edward Cook	Rock, Margaret	Joseph Rock	Catherine Elliott
Cook	Teresa	Helen	15-Oct-1882	04-Oct-1882	Edward Cook	Rock, Margaret	Charles McShane	Joan Elliott
Cook	Cora	Elizabeth	03-Jan-1886	26-Nov-1885	George A. Cook	Thomas, Ginnetta		Elizabeth Cook
Cook	John		01-Jun-1884	25-Sep-1883	George A. Cook	Thomas, Nettie		Elizabeth Cook
Cook	Ann	Virginia	07-Sep-1884	10-May-1884	George Cook	Meade, Margaret	James Donovan	Virginia Maguire
Cook	Earle	Jerome	22-Oct-1899	04-Oct-1899	George Cook	Meade, Margaret	Edgar McGuire	Ann McGuire
Cook	George	Laura	31-Jul-1887	13-Jun-1887	George Cook	Meade, Margaret	James Meade	Catherine Fink
Cook	John		25-Sep-1883	25-Sep-1883	George H. Cook	Thomas, Nettie		Elizabeth Cook
Cook	Margaret	E.	21-Sep-1902	09-Sep-1902	George H. Cook	Meade, Margaret E.	James J. Heagan	Catherine Wright
Cook	Dorothy	Mary	22-Nov-1914	6-Nov-1914	George L. Cook	O'Connor, Addia	Gerald O'Connor	Mary Dowell
Cook	John		14-Nov-1886	29-Mar-1862	Henry E. Cook	Fitzsimmon, Sara		Elizabeth McShane
Cook	John	James	02-Dec-1883	16-Nov-1883	John Cook	Rogers, Julia	Michael Maloney	Mary Maloney
Cook	John	Scott	25-Jun-1908	15-May-1908	John Cook	Cannon, Elsie		Mary Anderson
Cook	Winfield		11-Feb-1898	01-Aug-1878	Winfield Scott Cook	McMecken, Emma		Thomas Leonard
Cooney	Margaret	Elizabeth	20-Mar-1892	03-Mar-1892	Michael Cooney	Tuder, Catherine	Charles Habnicht	Margaret Elizabeth Hugh
Cooney	Albert	Michael	17-Feb-1884	10-Feb-1884	Thomas Cooney	Harvey, Ann	John Egan	Honora Mee
Cooney	Ann		19-Jun-1887	17-Jun-1887	Thomas Cooney	Harvey, Hannah	Charles Donahue	Bridget Harvey
Cooney	Josephine		02-Aug-1885	26-Jul-1885	Thomas Cooney	Harvey, Hannah	Daniel Cronier	Margaret Downey
Cooney	Thomas	G.	21-Jan-1883	10-Jan-1883	Thomas Cooney	Harvey, Joan	Patrick Cooney	Elizabeth Godfrey
Cooper	Blanche	Mary	10-Sep-1911	17-Nov-1910	Laurence B. Cooper	Derr, Lillian Mary	Eugene E. Scharnagle	Ann Purcell
Cooper	Laurence		14-Nov-1915	20-Oct-1915	Laurence Burgan Cooper	Dorr, Lillian		Margaret Cook
Cooper	Albert		1-Mar-1914	22-Jul-1913	Laurence Cooper	Dorr, Lillian		Margaret Cook
Coppinger	Mary	Clare	24-Jan-1909	12-Jan-1909	John Coppinger	Brogan, Agnes	Peter Brogan	Mary Mullin
Coppinger	Jane		11-Jun-1911	4-Jun-1911	John J. Coppinger	Brogan, Agnes	Joseph Brogan	Jane Brogan
Corbett	Matilda	Catherine	23-Jul-1893	14-Jul-1893	Michael Corbett	McHale, Delia	William Sexton	Rose Sexton
Cordelino	Adam		20-Sep-1908	15-Mar-1908	Leandro Cordelino	Petrilli, A.		
Cordelino	Ann	G.	20-Sep-1908	22-Jan-1907	Leandro Cordelino	Petrilli, A.	M.E. Lynn	Harry Damico
Cordelino	Nicholas		30-Aug-1908	27-Nov-1905	Leandro Cordelino	Petrilli, A.	Henry Dames	Mary Lion
Cornelius	James	Patrick	6-May-1906	15-Mar-1909	Jerome Cornelius	Kelley, Winifred	Patrick Riley	Delia Conlon
Cornelius	Thomas		20-Jul-1884	25-Apr-1906	John Cornelius	Kelly, Winifred	Martin Shanahan	Mary Kelly
Cornelius	Grace	Mary	20-Jul-1884	03-Jul-1884	Nicholas Cornelius	Ewing, Hannah		Catherine Fitzgerald
Cornelius	Walter	Joseph	18-Jun-1882	25-May-1882	Nicolas Cornelius	Ewing, Hannah		Mary Conway
Coroner	Martin	Joseph	11-Dec-1887	28-Feb-1887	Thomas Coroner	Madden, Mary	Martin Coroner	Bridget Burke
Corrigan	Henry		19-Oct-1885	09-Oct-1885	Henry Corrigan	Fay, Mary, Catherine		Ann Gough
Corrigan	Elizabeth		6-Jul-1913	5-Jul-1913	James Corrigan	Gephardt, Carolina	Francis Casey	Mary Dowd

23

LAST NAME	FIRST NAME	MIDDLE	BAPTISM	BIRTH	Father	Mother	SPONSORS
Corrigan	James		12-Feb-1911	11-Feb-1911	James Corrigan	Gephardt, Mary	Samuel Gephardt
Corrigan	Margaret		5-Sep-1915	1-Sep-1915	James Corrigan	Gephardt, Caroline	Mary Dowd
Corrigan	Edward	Michael	01-May-1887	17-Apr-1887	Michael Corrigan	Dolan, Catherine	John Flynn	Mary Dolan
Corrigan	Thomas	Patrick	25-Aug-1889	10-Aug-1889	Michael Corrigan	Dolan, Catherine	Peter Gillen	Mary Dolan
Corrigan	Mary		11-Dec-1898	06-Dec-1898	Peter Corrigan	[N], Margaret	Joseph McKenna	Mary Price
Corrigan	Mary	Alice	05-Oct-1902	28-Sep-1902	Peter Corrigan	Migan, Mary Anita	Richard Migan	Helen Crowley
Costello	Henry	Francis	23-Aug-1885	13-Aug-1885	John Costello	Hannan, Margaret	Phillip McIntyre	Alice Murphy
Costello	Joseph	Leon	28-Apr-1882	07-Apr-1882	John Costello	Hannan, Margaret		Rose Fitzpatrick
Costello	Mary		05-May-1887	05-May-1887	John Costello	Hannan, Margaret		
Costello	Rose		28-Oct-1883	05-Oct-1883	John Costello	Hannan, Margaret	Francis Hannan	Ann Ratican
Costelo	Catherine	M.	02-Jan-1898	12-Dec-1897	James Costelo	Gadon, Ella	Edward Mooney	Catherine Philbin
Coster	Jennie	Frances	08-Oct-1883	04-Sep-1883	James T. Coster	Medley, Joan E.		
Coster	Dorothy	Mary	9-Feb-1908	1-Feb-1908	Joseph Coster	O'Brien, Mary	Joseph Schott	Dorothy O'Brien
Coster	Joseph	Henry	7-Oct-1906	29-Sep-1906	Joseph Coster	O'Brien, Mary Catherine	Henry Coster	Catherine Steadman
Cotton	Helen	Elizabeth	23-Nov-1899	22-Sep-1899	Louis Cotton	Sebrey, Helen		
Couch	Mary		16-Mar-1890	01-Mar-1890	George W. Couch	Batterden, Catherine E.	John W. Couch	Margaret Batterden
Couch	Gertrude		15-Nov-1891	10-Nov-1891	George Walter Couch	Batterden, Catherine Elizabeth	Edward Vincent Dunn	Mary Helen Couch
Coughlan	Thomas	Joseph	4-Dec-1910	12-Nov-1910	James Coughlan	Cavanaugh, Mary Ann	John Coughlan	Ida Ward
Coughlan	Joseph		24-Feb-1885	05-Mar-1884	Thomas Coughlan	Myers, Mary		Alice Coughlan
Coughlin	Catherine		10-Oct-1897	03-Oct-1897	James Coughlin	Cavanaugh, Mary	Patrick Barlow	Julia Barlow
Coughlin	John	Joseph	27-Nov-1898	13-Nov-1898	James Coughlin	Cavanaugh, Mary	John Barlow	Mary Helen Barlow
Coughlin	Mary	Ann Elizabeth	28-Apr-1907	17-Apr-1907	James Coughlin	Cavender, Mary Ann	George Koenig	Catherine Coughlin
Coughlin	Michael	Joseph	2-Jun-1912	3-May-1912	James Coughlin	Kavanaugh, Mary	John Coughlin	Katherine Coughlin
Coughlin	Peter	Joseph	8-Feb-1914	19-Jan-1914	James Coughlin	Cavanaugh, Mary	Patrick Coughlin	Mildred Pate
Coughlin	Winifred	Teresa	7-Feb-1909	20-Jan-1909	James Coughlin	Kavanaugh, Mary	John P. Coughlin	Elizabeth Koenig
Coughlin	C. Agnes		17-Oct-1915	28-Sep-1915	James J. Coughlin	Kavanaugh, Mary A.	Francis M. Coughlin	Catherine Donnelly
Coughlin	Francis	M.	26-Jun-1904	17-Jun-1904	James J. Coughlin	Cavenaugh, Mary A.	Frederick C. Blum	Elizabeth Blum
Coughlin	James	Joseph	22-Feb-1903	14-Feb-1903	James Joseph Coughlin	Cavenaugh, Mary A.	John Harrigan	Ella Harrigan
Coulahan	Catherine		09-Nov-1882	02-Nov-1882	Michael Coulahan	Doyle, Ann	Edward Coolahan	Elizabeth Foley
Coulter	Mary	Joan	23-Jun-1898	22-Jun-1898	Andrew Coulter	Maguire, Sarah		Sarah Colley
Coulter	Mary	Helen	03-Jul-1898	22-Jun-1898	Andrew Coulter	Maguire, Sarah	William Coulter	Sarah Colley
Coulter	Mary		09-Feb-1902	26-Jan-1902	William Coulter	Maguire, Mary	John Coulter	Mary McGuire
Coulter	Sara	Ellen	18-Nov-1894	07-Nov-1894	William Coulter	Maguire, Mary	Andrew Coulter	Sallie Coulter
Coulter	W.	Vincent	27-Feb-1898	18-Feb-1898	William Coulter	Maguire, Mary	James Forestall	Ann Forestall
Coulter	William	Thomas	23-May-1909	10-May-1909	William Thomas Coulter	Coulter, Mary Agnes	Francis Fivez	Mary Magnus
Coulter/Forrester	Lucretia	Cecelia	09-Dec-1892	About 1835	John H. Coulter	Millikin, Ann		Philomena Reinhardt
Courtney	Edward	Anthony	23-Dec-1906	6-Dec-1906	Edward Courtney	Tilman, Elizabeth		Christine Hufnagel
Courtney	John	Adam	09-Apr-1899	18-Mar-1899	Edward Courtney	Tilman, Elizabeth	John Adams Huber	Ann Frank
Courtney	Catherine	Ellennor	22-Aug-1887	18-Aug-1887	John Courtney	Tobin, Catherine		Eleanor Lanaghan
Courtney	Edward		12-Jul-1895	11-Jul-1895	John Courtney	Broderick, Catherine		Barbara Hennessy
Courtney	Francis	Andrew	23-Jun-1894	23-Jun-1894	John Courtney	Broderick, Catherine		Margaret Rechiell
Courtney	James		03-Jul-1899	03-Jul-1899	John Courtney	Broderick, Catherine	James Courtney	Helen Courtney
Courtney	Margaret		16-May-1897	07-May-1897	John Courtney	Broderick, Catherine	James Courtney	Catherine Courtney
Courtney	Mary		06-May-1884	02-May-1884	John Courtney	Tobin, Catherine		Mary Reilly
Courtney	Mary		18-Sep-1898	08-Sep-1898	John Courtney	Broderick, Catherine	Arthur McKevitt	Mary McKevitt
Courtney	Mary		23-Feb-1902	14-Feb-1902	John Courtney	Broderick, Catherine	Francis Broderick	Jennie Reule
Courtney	Catherine		31-May-1893	31-May-1893	John J. Courtney	Broderick, Catherine	James Courtney	Catherine Courtney
Coury	Helen		25-Oct-1885	06-Oct-1885	John Coury	Massy, Ann	John Fallow	Hannah Fallow
Cousins	Cora	Elizabeth	21-May-1883	02-Dec-1883	Edward Cousins	Cousins, Margaret Elizabeth		Mary McCardell
Cousins	Virginia	Elizabeth	25-Nov-1887	22-Oct-1887	Edward E. Cousins	Drane, Margaret		Mary Drane
Cowman	Gertrude	Elizabeth	3-Mar-1907	16-Feb-1907	William A. Cowman	Bersterman, Ann Eva	Edward G. Starkloff	Barbara Starkloff
Cox	Bernard	LeRois	07-Aug-1898	01-Jun-1898	John Cox	Morrow, Margaret	Andrew Morrow	Mary Bathon
Cox	Bernard		12-Nov-1882	03-Nov-1882	Luke Cox	Moran, Abby	Bernard Moran	Catherine Moran
Cox	Charles		22-Jan-1893	14-Jan-1893	Luke Cox	Moran, Abby	Peter Magee	Mary McDonough
Cox	Luck		08-Feb-1891	26-Jan-1891	Luke Cox	Moran, Abby	John Cox	Mary Moran
Cox	Luke		18-Jul-1886	10-Jul-1886	Luke Cox	Moran, Abby	Patrick Cox	Clara Wallace
Cox	Mary		23-Mar-1884	14-Mar-1884	Luke Cox	Moran, Abby	Patrick McGaret	Bridget Sweeny
Cox	Catherine		19-Feb-1886	05-Feb-1886	Michael Cox	Maguire, Mary		Catherine West
Cox	George		11-Mar-1885	01-Feb-1885	Michael Cox	Maguire, Ingrid		Catherine West
Cox	Ann	Elizabeth	03-Jul-1887	23-Jun-1887	Patrick Cox	Eagan, Helen	Bernard Moran	Bridget Eagan
Cox	Luke		23-Nov-1884	26-Oct-1884	Patrick Cox	Eagan, Ellen	John Eagan	Mary Ann Donegan
Cox	Margaret		24-Dec-1882	16-Dec-1882	Patrick Cox	Egan, Helen	Thomas Donegan	Catherine Donegan
Cox	William	Henry	20-Oct-1889	13-Oct-1889	Patrick Cox	Egan, Ellen	Timothy Burns	Katie Moran

LAST NAME	FIRST NAME	MIDDLE	BAPTISM	BIRTH	Father	Mother	SPONSORS	
Coyle	Charles	William	22-Sep-1901	07-Sep-1901	Charles Coyle	Schlaugh, Elizabeth	William Weber	Mary Ann Coyle
Coyle	Anthony	W.	15-Nov-1903	30-Oct-1903	Charles H. Coyle	Schlaugh, Elizabeth	Walter Coyle	Margaret Renner
Coyle	William	Francis	31-Jul-1887	14-Jul-1887	Henry Cole	Hagerty, Mary	Francis B. Gately	Mary Coyle
Coyle	Howard	Joseph	15-Jul-1883	24-Jun-1883	Patrick Cole	Hagerty, Mary Jane	Charles H. Coyle	Ann Wilkensing
Coyle	Henry	Slocum	21-Jul-1889	27-Jun-1889	Patrick Coyle	Hagerty, Mary	Hugh Hagerty	Ann Wilkensing
Coyle	James	Leo	14-Mar-1892	20-Feb-1892	Patrick Coyle	Hagerty, Mary J.	Hugh McLaughlin	Matilda O'Neill
Coyle	Walter	Hugh	28-Jun-1885	12-Jun-1885	Patrick Coyle	Hagerty, Mary	Joseph Cain	Helen Brosnan
Coyle	Charles	Russell	25-May-1913	16-May-1913	William Coyle	Gephardt, Ann	Joseph Holmes	Mary Gephardt
Coyle	Howard	William	17-Sep-1911	5-Sep-1911	William Coyle	Gephardt, Ann	Martin Murphy	Margaret Coyle
Coyle	Ann	Margaret	10-Jul-1910	7-Jul-1910	William G. Coyle	Gebhart, Ann	Henry Coyle	Margaret Coyle
Coyne	Catherine	Ann	2-Oct-1904	17-Sep-1904	Edward Coyne	Davere, Mary	Patrick Tool	Margaret Clancy
Coyne	Charles	Edward	05-Jan-1891	12-Dec-1890	John J. Coyne	Hitchcock, Laura J.		Mary E. Gieske
Coyne	Bernard	Ambrose	12-Mar-1893	06-Mar-1893	Patrick Coyne	Durkin, Catherine	Michael Cavey	Helen Monaghan
Coyne	Catherine		27-Dec-1891	20-Dec-1891	Patrick Coyne	Durkin, Catherine	Patrick Clinton	Catherine Coyne
Coyne	David		29-Aug-1886	18-Aug-1886	Patrick Coyne	Durkin, Catherine	William Wallace	Ellen Coulehan
Coyne	Edmund	Joseph	23-Sep-1889	12-Sep-1889	Patrick Coyne	Durkin, Catherine	William Wallace	Eleanor Durkin
Coyne	Edmund		20-Oct-1889	12-Sep-1889	Patrick Coyne	Durkin, Ellen	Wm Morris	Ellen Durkin
Coyne	Mary		31-Dec-1882	07-Dec-1882	Patrick Coyne	Durkin, Catherine	James Manion	Elizabeth Wallace
Coyne	Thomas	Stewart	6-Aug-1905	26-Jul-1905	Thomas F. Coyne	Finnerty, Mary	Edward Coyne	Julia Finnerty
Craig	Jerome	Edward	15-Aug-1909	26-Jul-1909	Edward Craig	Margaret Craig	John Craig	Ellen Craig
Cranbaugh	Catherine		20-Sep-1885	07-Sep-1885	Joseph J. Cranbaugh	Martin, Josephine	John Hoben	Elizabeth Martin
Crane	Orio	August	03-Oct-1883	17-Sep-1883	William Crane	Orioke, Esther		Susan Wilback
Cranston	Glenn	Paul	5-Dec-1909	06-Mar-1888	William A. Cranston	Amos, Ann B.	Alonzo Joseph Morris	Mary Joseph Morris
Crawley	Margaret	Mary	28-Apr-1907	21-Apr-1907	Edward B. Crawley	McKewen, Helen	Thomas McKewen	Mary Agnes McKewen
Crawley	Rose	Elizabeth	15-Mar-1897	12-Mar-1897	George Crawley	Kelly, Julia	John Kelly	Emma Mae Cubbins
Creaghan	Mary	Frances	05-Feb-1882	22-Jan-1882	Matthew Aloysius Creaghan	McCarthy, Joan Vincent	Peter Scully	Mary McCarthy
Creaghan	Joseph	Aloysius	27-Jul-1884	12-Jul-1884	Maythias A. Creaghan	McCarthy, Hanna V.	John McCarthy	Mary Coyne
Creamer	Margaret	Pauline	11-Dec-1889	01-Nov-1889	George E. Creamer	Pfiston, Catherine		Margaret Pfiston
Creamer	Joseph	Roland	30-Aug-1914	16-Aug-1914	Robert Creamer	Beam, Elizabeth M.	Edmund Creamer	Mary A. Creamer
Cremin	Thomas	Joseph	19-Jul-1908	2-Dec-1908	James Cremin	Linihan, Catherine	Jerome Regan	Mary Kelly
Crew	Rosalie	Mary	14-Jan-1894	16-Dec-1894	Charles Crew	Kehoe, Mary		Elizabeth Toal
Crew	Ellen		31-Oct-1914	28-May-1904	Oliver H. Crew	Collery, Susanne		Alice O'Neill
Crew/McLaughlin	Rebecca		25-Oct-1882	08-Aug-1822	William Crew	Wilson, Elizabeth		Helen Agnes Connolly
Crismer	George	William	08-Nov-1889	27-Oct-1889	William A. Chrismer	Hoffman, Margaret C.		Margaret Hoffman
Croghan	James	Ambrose	10-Jul-1885	08-Jul-1885	Luke Croghan	Fahey, Elizabeth	James Croghan	Caroline O'Connor
Croghan	John	Jerome	22-Aug-1886	14-Aug-1886	Luke J. Croghan	Fahey, Eliza	Richard Hanley	Mary Kearney
Croghan	Cecelia		22-Sep-1901	08-Sep-1901	Martin Croghan	Murray, Margaret	James Gosnell	Margaret Croghan
Croghan	Agnes		10-Jan-1886	29-Dec-1885	Patrick Croghan	Queeney, Catherine	John P. Timothy	Sarah Jennings
Croghan	Genevieve		30-Jun-1907	11-Jun-1907	Patrick Croghan	Murray, Catherine	Michael Jenny	Genevieve Rommel
Croghan	Ann	Theresa	15-Nov-1885	28-Oct-1885	Thomas Croghan	Difley, Theresa	Patrick Croghan	Margaret Coots
Croghan	John		08-Jan-1888	24-Dec-1887	Thomas Croghan	Difley, Teresa	Patrick Timothy	Catherine Maytison
Croghan	Thomas	Joseph	02-Sep-1883	20-Aug-1883	Thomas Croghan	Difley, Teresa	James McCart	Catherine Daley
Cromwell	Laurence		18-Mar-1906	9-Mar-1906	William Cromwell	Rice, Mary	John Healy	Carry Gephardt
Cromwell	William	Leon	29-Jul-1903	24-Jul-1903	William Cromwell	Rice, Mary		Elizabeth Anderson
Cronin	Catherine		04-Aug-1886	27-Jul-1886	[Blank]	Cronin, Mary		Mary Parrell
Cronin	Catherine	Mary	25-Apr-1915	10-Apr-1915	Bernard Cronin	Watson, Catherine	James Whalen	Ann Clark
Cronin	Helen		24-Jun-1888	10-Jun-1888	Dennis Cronin	Driscoll, Catherine	Daniel Connor	Catherine Driscoll
Cronin	Bernard		29-May-1892	18-May-1892	Jerome Cronin	Gillen, Mary	Patrick Clarke	Catherine Gillen
Cronin	Catherine		31-Oct-1886	25-Oct-1886	Jerome Cronin	Gillen, Mary	Patrick J. Duffy	Mary A. Kelly
Cronin	James	Thomas	19-Feb-1888	13-Feb-1888	Jerome Cronin	Gillen, Mary	John Barry	Mary McGough
Cronin	John	Thomas	17-Feb-1895	04-Feb-1895	Jerome Cronin	Gillen, Mary	James Duffy	Alice Duffy
Cronin	Joseph		29-Mar-1891	20-Mar-1891	Jerome Cronin	Gillen, Mary		Rose Duffy
Cronin	Mary	Ann	29-Sep-1889	22-Sep-1889	Jerome Cronin	Gillen, Mary	Peter Duffy	Ann Gillen
Cronin	Thomas		26-Feb-1899	02-Feb-1899	Jerome Cronin	Gillen, Mary	Patrick Giblin	Joan Gamble
Crook	Mary	Kirby	22-Feb-1883	June 1877	James Crook	Browning, Mary		Calestice Ann Kirby
Crosby	Catherine	Agnes	12-Sep-1897	03-Sep-1897	Francis Crosby	Auld, Rose	Edward Wilson	Catherine Blakeney
Crosby	Francis	Thomas	07-Sep-1902	29-Aug-1902	Francis Crosby	Auld, Rose	Francis McGrain	Ida M. Kelly
Crosby	Rose	Mary	18-Aug-1901	08-Aug-1901	Francis Crosby	Auld, Rose	J. McComb	Mary Kelly
Crosby	James	Louis	25-Aug-1889	05-Jul-1889	Hugh Crosby	Hunter, Margaret	James Hunter	Martha Hunter
Crosby	Virginia	Minerva	12-Jun-1887	30-Apr-1887	Hugh Crosby	Hunter, Margaret	James Hunter	Frances Stuart
Crosby	Marion	Crosby	22-May-1912	15-Aug-1889	John Crosby	Smith, Jeanetta		Mary C. Connors
Crosby	Ellen	Mary	9-Mar-1913	27-Feb-1913	Mary Crosby	Connor, Margaret	Patrick Murphy	Catherine Murphy
Crosby	John	Leo	18-Aug-1895	03-Aug-1895	Matthew Crosby	Ward, Margaret	John Devall	Catherine Devall

ST JOHN'S BAPTISMS 1882-1912

LAST NAME	FIRST NAME	MIDDLE	BAPTISM	BIRTH	Father	Mother	SPONSORS
Crosby	Mary	Laura	18-Nov-1883	06-Nov-1883	Matthew Crosby	Ward, Margaret	James Ward / Susan Finnegan
Cross	John	Henry Francis	21-Jul-1907	27-Jun-1907	George T. Cross	Gross, Elizabeth E.	John Henry Gross / Wilhilmena Gross
Crouse	Eugenia	Mary	13-Sep-1914	26-Aug-1914	Andrew Crouse	Byrnes, Lucia	Charles Evers / Ann Wilkens
Crouse	Mary	A.	15-May-1904	1-May-1904	Francis Crouse	Baily, Mary Elizabeth	Helen Baily
Crowley	Edward	Edward	17-Apr-1904	7-Apr-1904	Edward Crowley	McCuen, Ellen	Patrick McDermott / Margaret Crowley
Crowley	John	Edward	05-Aug-1900	28-Jul-1900	Edward Crowley	McKewen, Ella	John Crowley / Susannah McKewen
Crowley	Mary	Annabelle	16-Feb-1890	04-Feb-1890	James Crowley	Kreutzer, Magdalene	Ann Eckhart
Crowley	George	Bennet	15-Jul-1888	06-Jul-1888	James Simon Crowley	Kruetzer, Mary Magdalene	George Kruetzer / Mary Crowley
Crowley	William		14-Feb-1886	12-Feb-1886	Patrick Crowley	Wallace, Margaret	Michael Wallace / Catherine Stafford
Crowley	Thomas	Raymond	3-Dec-1907	8-Jun-1902	Thomas Crowley	Creuse, Ann	Jennie Crowley
Cuckerty	Charles	F.	19-Mar-1899	10-Mar-1899	Charles Cuckerty	Ward, Mary	Michael Shanahan / Catherine Burke
Cullen	John	Joseph	28-Jun-1885	20-Jun-1885	Charles Cullen	Montgomery, Christina	John Halpin / Bridget Halpin
Cullen	Christopher	Ignatius	17-Dec-1882	03-Dec-1882	Christopher Ignatius Cullen	Burton, Sara	Francis Patrick Kelly / Mary Helen Mulgrew
Cullen	Elizabeth		9-Nov-1902	2-Nov-1902	James Cullen	Fuller, Mary E.	Patrick Roddy / Margaret Cullen
Cullen	Katherine		07-Jul-1901	04-Jul-1901	James Cullen	Fuller, Mary	James Burke / Mary Shanahan
Cullen	Margaret	Mary	16-Dec-1906	13-Nov-1906	Patrick Cullen	Grey, Mary	Joseph Cavanaugh / Helen Lawler
Cullen	Margaret	Loretta	24-May-1914	17-May-1914	Patrick Cullen	Gray, Mary	James Doyle / Mary Freeman
Cullen	Mary	Katherine	29-May-1904	21-May-1904	Patrick Cullen	Grey, Mary	Martin Freeman / Mary Cullen
Cullen	Patrick	Laurence	2-Nov-1913	22-Oct-1913	Patrick Cullen	O'Connor, Esther	John O'Connor / Mary O'Connor
Cullen	James	Patrick	7-Apr-1912	29-Mar-1912	Patrick Joseph Cullen	Gray, Mary	John Donegan / Julia Donegan
Cullen	John	Theodore	02-Mar-1884	17-Feb-1884	William Cullen	Williams, Helen	Michael Breen / Ann Doyle
Cullen	William		25-Jun-1882	14-Jun-1882	William Cullen	Williams, Helen	Matthew Connor / Mary Ann Curran
Culleton	Mary	Rose	30-Aug-1908	16-Aug-1908	James R. Culleton	Lynch, Catherine	Charles Lynch / Helen Lee Smith
Culleton	Mary	Catherine	26-Feb-1911	19-Feb-1911	James R. Culleton	Lynch, Catherine Elizabeth	Matthew Lynch / Sarah G. Culleton
Cullin	Mary		21-Jan-1883	12-Jan-1883	Charles Cullin	Montgomery, Christine	Greenbury Wilson / Mary Cullin
Culling	Frederick	George	14-Oct-1883	01-Oct-1883	Isaac James Culling	O'Keefe, Elizabeth	James Leo Murphy / Sara McAlister
Cummings	Cecelia	Joan	19-Oct-1913	2-Oct-1913	James Cummings	O'Keefe, Joan	Anthony O'Keefe / Mary O'Keefe
Cummings	Edwin	Rusk	17-Aug-1884	12-Aug-1884	James Cummings	Rusk, Mary Frances	Edward A. Wiedefield / Barbara Rusk
Cummings	Francis	Joseph	27-Oct-1912	24-Apr-1912	James Cummings	Brady, Mary	Francis Russell / Frances Baker
Cummings	James	Elmer	12-Mar-1911	19-Feb-1911	James Cummings	Brady, Mary	John Cummings / Agnes Toomey
Cummings	Margaret	Eugene	19-Jul-1896	08-Jul-1896	James Cummings	Rusk, Mary F.	William Leonard / Delia Tully
Cummings	Robert	Victor	11-Oct-1914	25-Sep-1914	James Cummings	Brady, Mary	Francis Roach / Ellen Cummings
Cummings	Thomas	Irene	22-Jan-1899	10-Jan-1899	James Cummings	Rusk, Mary	Thomas Comeford / Mary Tully
Cummings	Barbara	Theresa	08-Jan-1888	30-Dec-1887	James E. Cummings	Rusk, Mary Frances	Joseph Rusk / Margaret Rusk
Cummings	Charlotte	Marr	26-Oct-1890	15-Oct-1890	James E. Cummings	Rusk, Mary F.	James P. Lyness / Barbara Rusk
Cummings	James	Patrick	19-Feb-1893	04-Feb-1893	James E. Cummings	Rusk, Mary Francis	Ann Barton
Cummings	Alfred		5-Jul-1908	26-Jun-1908	James Joseph Cummings	Brady, Mary T.	Alfred Joseph Cummings / Ann R.E. Hall
Cummings	Leon	Lillian	14-Mar-1886	10-Mar-1886	John Cummings	Heaphy, Joan	John Griffin / Catherine Murray
Cummings	Catherine	Veronica	12-Jun-1892	02-Jun-1892	Robert Cummings	Scott, Catherine	George Hagan / Margaret Scott
Cummings	Edna		22-Mar-1899	03-Mar-1899	Robert Cummings	Scott, Catherine Ann	Rose Cummings
Cummings	Margaret	Dolores	20-Dec-1896	02-Dec-1896	Robert Cummings	Scott, Catherine	James Kelly / Mary Scott
Cummings	Ethel	Joseph	22-Mar-1899	03-Mar-1899	Robert Joseph Cummings	Scott, Catherine Ann	Joan Scott
Cummings	Robert		05-Nov-1893	25-Oct-1893	Robert James Cummings	Scott, Ann	Robert Healey / Catherine Cummings
Cummins	Mary	Frederick	24-Jan-1886	14-Jan-1886	James Cummins	Rusk, Mary Francis	James T. Kelly / Emma E. Lyness
Cunnabaugh	Dennis	Howard	13-Feb-1887	22-Jan-1887	Jerome Joseph Cunnabaugh	Martin, Josephine	William Cunnabaugh / Mary Cunnabaugh
Cunningham	Catherine	Agnes	04-Nov-1883	28-Oct-1883	Christopher A. Cunningham	Parr, Lucy	Robert T. Alluisi / Catherine Hamilton
Cunningham	Ann	Elizabeth	21-Aug-1887	12-Aug-1887	Christopher Cunningham	Parr, Louise E.	George Hamilton / Ann Pealing
Cunningham	Mary	Theresa	21-Jun-1885	08-Jun-1885	Christopher Cunningham	Parr, Louise	James Gaffey / Mary O'Neill
Cunningham	Margaret		20-Nov-1887	18-Nov-1887	Edward J. Cunningham	Madden, Mary Agnes	Francis Hoban / Ann Sexton
Cunningham	Alice		23-Nov-1880	11-Nov-1890	Edward James Cunningham	Madden, Margaret A.	William J. Murray / Mary Murray
Cunningham	Charles	Frederick	20-May-1886	23-Mar-1886	Francis Cunningham	Welch, Agnes	Mary Clarke
Cunningham	John	C.	19-Jan-1908	5-Jan-1908	John M. Cunningham	Mack, Mary A.	Catherine Kelly
Cunningham	Mary		28-Mar-1909	11-Mar-1909	John M. Cunningham	Mack, Mary	F. Blackeney / Clara Mack
Cunningham	Charles	Rezon	07-Sep-1883	10-Jun-1883	Louis Vinton Cunningham	Robinson, Mary Louis	Stephen C. Elwood / Laura Frances Fay
Cunningham	Mary	Gammie	28-Jun-1893	03-Jul-1870	Samuel Cunningham	Arnold, Catherine E.	Emma B. Mead
Cunningham	John		12-Jun-1887	01-Jun-1887	Thomas Cunningham	Dugan, Mary	Thomas Hughes / Ann Hester
Cunningham	Thomas		12-Apr-1891	01-Apr-1891	Thomas Cunningham	Duggan, Mary	Patrick Duggan / Hannah Kennedy
Curley	Vincent	De Paul	7-May-1911	27-Apr-1911	Patrick Vincent Curley	Schwartz, Ann	Paul Schwartz / Margaret Olszewski
Curly	Richard	B.	17-Dec-1899	02-Dec-1899	K. Curly	Oursler, Florence	
Curran	William	Edward	23-Aug-1914	13-Aug-1914	Edward A. Curran	Noonan, Mary	Francis Jones / Ann Jones
Curran	Catherine	Teresa	13-Jul-1913	27-Jun-1913	Edward Curran	Kenny, Ellen	James Curran / Mary Snively
Curran	Mary		22-Sep-1912	10-Sep-1912	Edward Curran	Noonan, Mary Elizabeth	Edmund J. Noonan / Elizabeth McGlone
Curran	Elizabeth	Ellen	12-Mar-1911	24-Feb-1911	Edward M. Curran	Kenny, Ellen A.	Thomas J. Colbert / Mary Lovell

LAST NAME	FIRST NAME	MIDDLE	BAPTISM	BIRTH	Father	Mother	SPONSORS
Curran	Blanche		29-Jun-1890	10-Jun-1890	Peter Curran	Ruff, Clara	Isabelle Brown
Curran	Elizabeth	Isabelle	23-Dec-1883	11-Dec-1883	Peter Curran	Ruff, Clara	Elizabeth Isabelle Ruff
Curran	Howard	Thomas	14-Aug-1887	27-Jul-1887	Peter Curran	Ruff, Clara	Thomas James Brown
Curran	Edith	Virginia	06-Jan-1889	21-Dec-1888	Peter J. Curran	Ruff, Clara	William Ruff
Curran	Ethel	Mary	19-Mar-1894	18-Mar-1894	Peter J. Curran	Ruff, Clara	
Curran	Alberty	Joseph	03-Jul-1892	14-Jun-1892	Peter John Curran	Ruff, Clara	William Ruff
Curran	Walter	Carroll	31-Mar-1912	25-Mar-1912	Walter Curran	Martin, Rose	Albert Curran
Curran	William		30-Jun-1882	25-Mar-1881	William Curran	Sheridan, Ann	Stewart Ames
Currran	Clara	Margaret	25-Mar-1906	16-Mar-1906	Walter C. Curran	Martin, Roselina	Howard T. Curran
Curry	Alice	Veronica	3-May-1908	16-Apr-1908	Edward Curry	Wallace, Elizabeth	Thomas Handy
Cursey	George	Earl M.	10-Sep-1905	30-Aug-1905	George Webster Cursey	Emge, Catherine Elizabeth	Martin J. Emge
Curtain	John	William	2-May-1915	20-Apr-1915	John William Curtain	McLaughlin, Elizabeth	Francis Satterfield
Curtin	Mary	Adele	4-Feb-1912	18-Jan-1912	John Curtin	McLaughlin, Elizabeth	William Staples
Curtis	Margaret	Anastasia	01-Dec-1901	23-Nov-1901	Francis Curtis	Kelly, Maud F.	John Curtis
Curtis	Adalaide	M.	20-Sep-1908	6-Sep-1908	Francis P. Curtis	Kelly, M. Josephine	Josephine Curtis
Curtis	Josephine		24-Jan-1904	9-Jan-1904	Francis P. Curtis	Kelly, Maud Josephine	John S. Curtis
Cushman	Joseph		12-Jul-1896	10-Jun-1896	George Albert Cushman	Ray, Ada	Mary Sullivan
Cusick	Mary	Helen	27-Sep-1896	14-Sep-1896	Edward Cusick	Tobin, Mary	Ann Cusick
Cusick	Catherine		20-Dec-1896	12-Dec-1896	Terence Cusick	Bannon, Mary	Ella Cusick
Cusick	Edward	Joseph	10-Jun-1894	05-Jun-1894	Terence Cusick	Bannon, Mary	Patrick Norton
Cusick	Mary		28-Nov-1899	26-Nov-1899	Terence Cusick	Bannon, Mary	
Cuskey	James	L.	4-Sep-1904	25-Aug-1904	Joseph Cuskey	Byrne, Ann	Catherine Byrne
Dailey	Mary	A.	01-Feb-1898	28-Jan-1898	Jerome C. Daily	Reinfelder, Elizabeth	John Reinfelder
Dailey	Francis	F.	24-Jan-1903	15-Jan-1903	John Dailey	Anderson, Ellen	J. Carroll Dailey
Dailey	Margaret		10-Nov-1901	1-Nov-1901	Michael Dailey	Krein, Margaret	Mary Hagerty
Dailey	Helen		16-Nov-1890	30-Oct-1890	Patrick Daily	Kelly, Margaret	Thomas Donlon
Daily	Francis		22-Jul-1885	21-Jul-1885	Eugene Daily	Bolst, Mary	Catherine Baitler
Daily	Catherine		05-Feb-1888	16-Jan-1888	John Daily	Reynolds, Rose	Catherine Polet
Daily	Elizabeth		31-May-1885	25-May-1885	John Daily	Reynolds, Roseann	James O'Rourke
Daily	Joan	Laurence	26-Aug-1883	11-Aug-1883	John Daily	Reynolds, Rosanna	Cormick Finigan
Daily	Mary	Angela	19-Feb-1905	9-Feb-1905	John Daily	Anderson, Ella B.	Arthur Hogan
Daily	Robert	Jerome	19-Dec-1886	21-Nov-1886	John Daily	Reynolds, Rose	Margaret O'Rourke
Daily	Robert		05-Feb-1882	22-Jan-1882	John Laurence Daily	Reynolds, Rose Ann	Mary E. Anderson
Daily	John	Carroll Edward	19-Oct-1884	13-Oct-1884	John T. Daily	Anderson, Ellen B.	Mary Finnegan
Daily	Rose	Florence	11-Nov-1906	7-Nov-1906	John T. Daily	Anderson, Ella B.	Edward McNeal
Daily	William	Marc	29-Jul-1888	27-Jul-1888	John T. Daily	Anderson, Eleanor B.	Owen Daily
Daily	Charles	Henry	12-Jul-1905	25-Jun-1905	Joseph Daily	Moffett, Emma	Margaret J. Kerley
Daily	Patrick	Joseph	26-Nov-1893	05-Nov-1893	Patrick Daily	Welby, Margaret	Mary A. Kerley
Daily	Ann		24-Apr-1892	19-Apr-1892	Timothy Daily	Lanahan, Ann	Mary Daily
Daily	Catherine		17-Mar-1899	03-Mar-1899	Timothy Daily	Lenaghan, Ann	Alice Stelle
Daley	Margaret		28-Jan-1900	25-Jan-1900	Jerome Daley	Reinsfelder, Elizabeth	Mary Clancy
Daley	Francis		08-Dec-1889	23-Nov-1889	John Daley	Reynolds, Rose	Catherine Golden
Daley	Joseph	William	15-Mar-1903	01-Mar-1903	Joseph Daley	Morgan, Emily	Margaret Murphy
Daley	Anthony		24-Feb-1889	20-Feb-1889	Patrick Daley	Welby, Margaret	Ella V. Daley
Daley	John		24-Feb-1889	20-Feb-1889	Patrick Daley	Welby, Margaret	Kate Courtney
Daley	Margaret	Regina	20-Oct-1895	27-Sep-1895	Patrick Daley	Welby, Margaret	Bridget Daley
Daley	Mary	Ann	21-Aug-1892	05-Aug-1892	Patrick Daley	Welby, Margaret	Mary O'Keefe
Daley	George	Leroy	02-Jul-1888	25-Mar-1888	Phillip Francis T. Daley	Yorke, Francis	Catherine Welby
Daley	Mary		28-Aug-1887	19-Aug-1887	Timothy Daley	Lanahan, Ann	Mary O'Keefe
Daley	Timothy		15-Mar-1903	02-Mar-1903	Timothy Daley	Lanahan, Ann	David O'Keefe
Daley	James	Edward	15-Mar-1885	17-Nov-1884	William Daley	Waldgive, Georgia	Amanda Julia Hyde
Dalrymple	Gertrude		04-Oct-1896	15-Sep-1896	William Dalrymple	Kelly, Mary A.	Delia McIntyre
Dalrymple	Mary	Agnes	18-Nov-1894	24-Oct-1894	William Dalrymple	Kelly, Mary Agnes	Mary Sutton
Dalrymple	John		25-Jun-1893	16-Jun-1893	William Thomas Dalrymple	Kelly, Mary Agnes	Ann Daley
Dalton	Mary		21-Oct-1883	07-Oct-1883	Michael Dalton	Luney, Mary	Cecelia Clarke
Daly	Margaret	Alice	25-Aug-1894	19-Aug-1894	[Blank]	[Blank]	Margaret Noonan
Daly	Bernard		10-Apr-1897	About 1867	Bernard Daly	Singleton, Bridget	Mary Agnes Dalrymple
Daly	Margaret	Ann	29-Jun-1888	27-Jun-1888	Edward Daly	Ryan, May	Mary Brazer
Daly	Edward	Eugene	7-Jul-1907	30-Jun-1907	Henry Daly	Callender, Mary	
Daly	Catherine	Rose	04-Oct-1901	14-Sep-1901	Joseph Daly	Moffitt, Emma	Catherine Ryan
Daly	Patrick		18-Aug-1901	30-Jul-1901	Patrick Daly	Callaghan, Ann	Florence Hennings
Daly	Daniel	Vincent	13-Dec-1896	02-Dec-1896	Timothy Daly	Lanahan, Ann	Margaret McKenna
Daly	Elizabeth		19-May-1889	14-Mar-1884	Timothy Daly	Lanahan, Ann	Margaret Kimmett
							Ann Lehane
							Mary Moylan

27

LAST NAME	FIRST NAME	MIDDLE	BAPTISM	BIRTH	Father	Mother	SPONSORS
Dames	Lillian		5-Apr-1914	23-Mar-1914	George Dames	Lucas, Lillian M.	Margaret Cooke
Daniels	Mary	Gertrude	13-Mar-1887	22-Feb-1887	William Daniels	Jamison, Margaret	Mary Jamison
Dare	Ellen	Martha	1-May-1910	8-Apr-1910	Joseph Dare	Wetherstine, Caroline	Ellen Emmart
Dare	Robert	Ephram	26-Apr-1908	9-Apr-1908	Joseph W. Dare	Weatherstine, Carrie	Florence Weatherstine
Darrell	Helen	Carlotta	13-Jun-1915	30-May-1915	James Darrel	Tuttle, Katherine	Mary E. Rick
Darrell	Mary		22-May-1886	12-Aug-1874	William J. Darrell	O'Connor, Mary	Rev. P.J. Donahue
Daugherty	Joseph	Leon	7-Jun-1914	22-May-1914	Thomas Daugherty	Harris, Rose M.	Mary S. Hyde
Dauphline	Mary		19-Aug-1910	7-Apr-1910	A. Dauphine	O'Connor, Helen	Thomas Conway
Davern	Elizabeth		14-Dec-1884	07-Dec-1884	John Davern	Burns, Ann	Catherine Seltzer
Davern	John		29-Oct-1882	20-Oct-1882	John Davern	Byrne, Ann	Ann McGovern
Davey	Elizabeth		24-Jan-1886	09-Jan-1886	James Davey	Finn, Mary	Lucy Byrne
Davey	John	Morris	05-Nov-1893	18-Oct-1893	James Davey	Finn, Mary	Mary Brazier
Davey	Joseph	Hubert	08-Feb-1891	17-Jan-1891	James Davey	Finn, Mary	Margaret Trailor
Davey	Margaret		10-Feb-1884	16-Jan-1884	James Davey	Finn, Mary	Mary McGuire
Davey	Mary	Agnes	22-Jul-1888	10-Jul-1888	James Davey	Finn, Mary	Mary Ann Landers
Davey	Thomas		11-May-1882	11-May-1882	James Davey	Finn, Mary	Catherine McKenna
Davey	Hugo		22-May-1910	18-May-1910	Michael Davey	Cryan, Margaret	Helen Russell
Davey	James		29-Oct-1905	16-Oct-1905	Michael Davey	Cryan, Margaret	Katherine Donellan
Davey	John		08-Jul-1900	22-Jun-1900	Michael Davey	Cryan, Margaret	Catherine McDonald
Davey	John		18-Jul-1915	9-Jul-1915	Michael Davey	Cryan, Margaret	Mary [Blank]
Davey	Patrick	D.	06-Nov-1898	18-Oct-1898	Michael Davey	Cryan, Margaret	Mary Minton
Davey	Thomas	Michael	20-May-1903	15-May-1903	Michael Davey	Cryan, Margaret	Katherine O'Hara
Davey	Mary		18-Oct-1896	02-Oct-1896	Mike Davey	Egan, Margaret	Jane Hoolahan
Davey	Mary		28-Jan-1900	10-Jan-1900	Patrick Davey	Calahan, Ann	Mary Davey
Davey	Thomas	Gibbons	18-Sep-1898	29-Aug-1898	Patrick Davey	Calaghan, Ann	Sara Williams
Davey	Francis	Xavier	26-Apr-1903	08-Apr-1903	Patrick J. Davey	Gallagher, Mary	Thomas Calaghan
Davey	Elizabeth		5-Jun-1904	19-May-1904	Patrick Joseph Davey	Callaghan, Margaret	John Callaghan
Davey	John		2-Sep-1906	21-Aug-1906	Thomas Davey	Kelly, Ida	Margaret Davey
Davey	Joseph	Russell	18-Apr-1909	7-Apr-1909	Thomas Davey	Kelly, Ida	Mary Finny
Davey	Mary	Elizabeth	14-Aug-1904	3-Aug-1904	Thomas Davey	Kelly, Ida	John Byrne
Davidson	Francis	Eugene	29-Jan-1905	11-Jan-1905	Frederick Davidson	Kelly, Elizabeth	John Moore
Davidson	Helen	Amelia	21-Oct-1906	27-Sep-1906	Frederick Davidson	Kelly, Elizabeth	Andrew Gruhert
Davidson	William	James	23-Aug-1908	10-Aug-1908	Frederick Davidson	Kelly, Elizabeth	Eugene Kelly
Davidson	Catherine	Regina	6-Dec-1908	11-Nov-1908	James Davidson	Clancy, Margaret	James Kelly
Davidson	Mary	Honora	24-Nov-1907	10-Nov-1907	James Davidson	Clancy, Margaret	William Kelly
Davidson	Henry	Thomas	16-Jul-1911	29-Jun-1911	James E. Davidson	Frank, Mary Agnes	Bernard Galland
Davidson	Frederick	David	28-Apr-1912	14-Mar-1912	John Davidson	Frank, Mary	
Davidson	John		24-Jan-1915	18-Dec-1914	John Davidson	[Blank]	John Davidson
Davis	John	Francis	17-Mar-1896	[Blank]	[Blank]	McWilliams, Ann	
Davis	Daniel		23-Jun-1884	20-Jun-1884	Elisha Davis	Jones, Mary Elizabeth	Mary McCluskey
Davis	George	Charles	16-Sep-1894	30-Aug-1894	Elisha Jones	Davis, Josephine	Ann Carter
Davis	George	Daniel	6-Jun-1907	About 1877	John Davis	Coughlan, Elizabeth	Mary McGirr
Davis	Thomas	William	12-Dec-1886	07-Dec-1886	Thomas Davis	Kemp, Elizabeth	Margaret Considine
Davis	Hattie		20-Aug-1895	01-Aug-1847	Walter Davis	Hogekiss, Joan	
Davis/O'Brien	Susanne		7-May-1908	06-Oct-1845	William Davis	McGah, Therese	Isabelle Gillen
Dawson	Ann		18-Jan-1891	06-Jan-1891	John Dawson	McGah, Teresa	Catherine McGah
Dawson	Daniel	Joseph	08-Sep-1889	29-Aug-1889	John Dawson	Gormley, Mary	Mary Redinan
Dawson	Elizabeth		06-Apr-1884	23-Mar-1884	John Dawson	McGah, Theresa	Isabelle Dawson
Dawson	John	Leon	12-Jan-1888	01-Jan-1888	John Dawson	Gormley, Mary	George Dawson
Dawson	Mary	Adriann	02-Apr-1882	20-Mar-1882	John Dawson	McGah, Teresa	Margaret Gormly
Dawson	Thomas	Albert	14-Jun-1896	04-Jun-1896	John Dawson	McGah, Theresa	Delia Digleman
Dawson	William	Francis	10-Jul-1892	26-Jun-1892	John Dawson	Donegan, Susan	Bridget Burke
Dawson	Margaret	Aloysius	15-Jun-1884	04-Jun-1884	Owen Dawson	Hammell, Ann	Margaret Gunoy
Dawson	George	Thomas	16-Feb-1894	21-Nov-1893	Thomas B. Dawson	Hammell, Ann	Catherine Dawson
Dawson	Isabelle	Mary	10-Dec-1895	24-Oct-1895	Thomas Dawson	Mooney, Mary	Mary Dawson
Dawson	William	Albert	17-Oct-1897	14-Sep-1897	Thomas Dawson	Devlin, Elizabeth Josephine	Theresa Megalk
Dawson	Thomas	Gordon	09-Jul-1899	10-Jun-1899	Thomas Dawson	Devlin, Elizabeth	Catherine Gibson
De Pucy	Albert		17-Aug-1913	14-Apr-1913	Ernest Gordon De Pucy	Devlin, Elizabeth	Mary Finn
Dean	Ann		18-Dec-1887	29-Nov-1887	George Alexander Dean	George Dean	Virginia Bantz
Deane	Henry		06-Apr-1884	Mar 1884	George Deane	Deane	Mary Ann Gann
DeBarry	Charotte		17-Oct-1886	14-Oct-1886	Walter DeBarry	McKenna, Mary	Sarah Bautz
DeBarry	Robert	James	07-Jul-1900	20-Oct-1899	William DeBarry	McKenna, Mary	Charlotte DeBarry
			03-Jul-1898	22-Jun-1898			Margaret McKenna

28

LAST NAME	FIRST NAME	MIDDLE	BAPTISM	BIRTH	Father	Mother	SPONSORS	
Debring	Emma	Margaret	16-Nov-1884	08-Nov-1884	Alohonse Joseph Debring	Thalheimer, Elizabeth	Charles Jerome Braden	Emma Debring
Debring	Mary		21-Feb-1886	14-Feb-1886	Alphonse Debring	Thalheimer, Elizabeth		Ann Debring
Debring	Paul		05-Aug-1894	21-Jul-1894	Alphonse Debring	Thalheimer, Elizabeth Ann	Charles A. Thalheimer	Genevieve Thalheimer
Debring	Clyde	Joseph	17-Jan-1897	02-Jan-1897	Joseph L. Debring	Thalheimer, Elizabeth	Joseph F. Thalheimer	Mary Catherine Thalheimer
Deckwar	Joseph	Walter	27-Mar-1910	6-Mar-1910	Joseph Walter Deckwar	Erb, Helen	George Joseph Christ	Margaret Christ
Deets	Howard	Leroy	8-Aug-1915	23-Jul-1915	Charles L. Deets	Ormond, Teresa		Agnes Drimond
Deets	John	Joseph	1-Jun-1913	10-May-1913	Leroy Deets	Ormond, Teresa	John Ormond	Ellen Ormond
Deiscel	John	Michael	19-Jan-1908	12-Jan-1908	Michael Deiscel	Dorsey, Helen	James Brennan	Catherine Ingle
Deise	William	August	29-Jul-1888	09-Jul-1888	George Deise	Kirby, Mary	Richard Tierney	Elizabeth Tierney
DeKatow	Grace	Matilda	29-Nov-1911	20-May-1905	Albano DeKatow	Warnick, Mary		Mary E. Clark
Dekwar	Ann	Mary	10-May-1896	27-Mar-1896	John Dekwar	Krueger, Margaret	Charles Dekwar	Ann Dekwar
Delaney	Helen		26-Nov-1899	17-Nov-1899	John Delaney	Kelly, Ann	Thomas Quirk	Agnes McKenna
Delaney	Ann		01-Sep-1889	27-Aug-1889	John J. Delaney	Kelly, Ann	William Johnson	Hannah Connaughton
Delaney	Catherine		01-Sep-1895	25-Aug-1895	John J. Delaney	Kelly, Ann G.	Patrick Delaney	Ann Fannon
Delaney	John	Leo	18-Mar-1894	07-Mar-1894	John J. Delaney	Kelly, Ann	James J. Kelly	Honora Kern
Delaney	Mary	Agnes	11-Oct-1891	02-Oct-1891	John Joseph Delaney	Kelly, Ann	John Hussy	Catherine Kelly
Delaney	Joseph		26-Sep-1886	20-Sep-1886	Patrick Delaney	Morgan, Genevieve	Cornelius Kerhan	Mary Kernan
Delaney	William	Patrick	17-Feb-1884	12-Feb-1884	Patrick Delaney	Morwood, Virginia (Jennie)	John Delaney	Rose Delaney
Delaney/Renner	Josepha		20-Jul-1900	22-Dec-1871	William Delaney	Meek, Mary Ann		Ann McShane
Delanty	Rose	Ann	12-Dec-1883	10-Oct-1883	William Delanty	Saunders, Mary		Sara Agnes Saunders
Delauder	Mary	Margaret	27-Mar-1904	17-Mar-1904	Andrew Delauder	Dennegan, Mary	John Dennegan	Margaret Dennegan
DeLauder	Thomas	Andrew	01-Dec-1901	15-Nov-1901	Andrew DeLauder	Dunnigan, Mary	Edward DeLauder	Catherine Dunnigan
Delavingne	Theodore	Edward	29-Jun-1890	20-Jun-1890	Arthur C. Delavingne	Cairns, Catherine A.	Patrick Logue	Mary Neville
Delevingne	Charles	Gormley	27-Mar-1892	11-Mar-1892	Arthur C. Delevingne	Cairns, Catherine	John Gormley	Hannah Creaghan
Delevingne	Mary	C.	14-Feb-1897	29-Jan-1897	Arthur C. Delevingne	Kearns, Catherine	James Cullan	Catherine Mooney
Delevingne	Victoria		03-Sep-1893	20-Aug-1893	Arthur C. Delevingne	Curns, Catherine	James J. Touhy	Ellen Cluny
Delevingne	Joseph	Phillips	31-Mar-1895	19-Mar-1895	Arthur Cooley Delevingne	Curns, Catherine	James Patrick Phillips	Catherine Smick
Delia	John		13-Dec-1896	11-Dec-1896	John Delia	Ford, Helen	Patrick McGuire	Cecelia Braburn
Dellone	Edwin	Winfield Scott	03-Aug-1890	27-Jul-1890	August F. Dellone	Devine, Agnes	William Dellone	Margaret Flannigan
Delude	James	Joseph	15-Feb-1906	1-Dec-1905	George Delude	Dyer, Gennie	James J. Burke	Mary C. Burke
Demico	Lida	Margaret	18-May-1902	14-Feb-1902	Josephine Demico	Donetelli, Lida	Henry Rossi	Mary Cunningham
Dempsey	Mary		5-Apr-1914	29-Mar-1914	Edward Dempsey	Bateman, Constance	James Burke	Margaret Rosensteel
Dempsey	Bernard		13-Oct-1889	09-Oct-1889	James Dempsey	Dempsey, Elizabeth	Thomas Dempsey	Helen O'Brien
Dempsey	Ellen		08-Nov-1896	26-Oct-1896	James Dempsey	Dempsey, Elizabeth	John Dailey	
Dempsey	Francis		05-Feb-1893	26-Jan-1893	James Dempsey	Dempsey, Elizabeth	Willioam B. Dempsey	Catherine Dempsey
Dempsey	James	Robert	14-Jun-1891	10-Jun-1891	James Dempsey	Dempsey, Elizabeth	John Sheridan	Margaret Conaway
Dempsey	James		18-Jan-1898	08-Jan-1898	James Dempsey	Dempsey, Elizabeth		Mary Dempsey
Dempsey	Joseph		05-Mar-1899	09-Feb-1899	James Dempsey	Dempsey, Elizabeth	Edward Dempsey	Mary Dempsey
Dempsey	Mary	Regina	21-Oct-1894	07-Oct-1894	James Dempsey	Dempsey, Lizzie	Peter Dempsey	Catherine Sheridan
Dempsey	Mary	Margaret	27-Oct-1907	16-Oct-1907	James Dempsey	Carter, Myra		Mary Bitter
Dempsey	Paul		05-Jan-1902	13-Oct-1902	James Dempsey	Dempsey, Elizabeth	John Dempsey	Margaret Conway
Dempsey	William		27-May-1900	08-May-1900	James Dempsey	Dempsey, Elizabeth	John Casey	Mary Ward
Dempsey	Mary		26-Jun-1898	09-Jun-1898	Peter Dempsey	Sheridan, Catherine	Edward Dempsey	Mary Dempsey
Dempsey	Catherine		25-Nov-1888	22-Nov-1888	Thomas Dempsey	Fay, Mary H.	William Dempsey	Mary Dempsey
Dempsey	Mary		21-Sep-1884	07-Sep-1884	Thomas F. Dempsey	Fay, Mary	Michael Kearney	Mary Burns
Dempsey	Thomas	Francis	17-Oct-1886	11-Oct-1886	Thomas F. Dempsey	Fey, Mary H.	James F. Rock	Catherine Dempsey
Dempsey	William		25-Jan-1891	18-Jan-1891	Thomas F. Dempsey	Fay, Mary H.	Peter J. Dempsey	Mary A. Fallon
Dempsey	Edward	Townsend	12-Nov-1882	31-Oct-1882	Thomas Francis Dempsey	Holden, Margaret	William E. Broderick	Elizabeth Cecelia Dempsey
Dempsey	Margaret	L.	17-Sep-1886	17-Sep-1886	William B. Dempsey			
Dempsey	Mary		03-Jul-1890	28-Jun-1890	William Dempsey	Kane, Mary L.	Charles McShane	Catherine Kane
Dengler	George	Barbara	20-Dec-1891	08-Dec-1891	George Dengler	Hauth, Ann	Henry Anton	Barbara Rusk
Dengler	George	Henry	07-Sep-1890	02-Sep-1890	George H. Dengler	Hauth, Ann	Henry P. Dengler	Julia Doyle
Dengler	John	Joseph	20-May-1894	08-May-1894	George H. Dengler	Hauth, Ann	James Joseph Hauth	Mary Donegan
Denhardt	James	Laurence	2-Feb-1913	22-Jan-1913	Samrul H. Denhardt	Fisher, Ann	William Manning	Ann Lynch
Dennert	George	"May"	20-Nov-1887	09-Nov-1887	Andrew Dennert	Reinhardt, Cecelia B.	G.W. Hiskell	Catherine McNulty
Denning	William		09-Jul-1882	27-Jun-1882	Thomas Denning	Landrigan, Catherine	William Landrigan	Mary Keller
Denson	Emma	Catherine	16-Jun-1907	4-May-1907	Ambrose Denson	Macurek, Francis		Francis Lang
Denson	Francis	Ambrose	16-Jul-1911	21-Mar-1911	Ambrose Denson	Macurek, Frances		Frances Kutcher
Denson	Mary	Ann	29-Jun-1902	3-May-1902	Ambrose Denson	Marcurek, Frances		Mary Lang
Denson	Ellen		2-Jul-1911	14-Jun-1911	William J. Denson	Hanley, Ellen F.		Mary Gilhooly
Densor	Lena	Frances	5-Mar-1905	26-Dec-1905	Ambrose Densor	Macurek, Frances		Mary Lang
Depish	Francis	Walter	13-Apr-1884	24-Mar-1884	Francis Depish	Quigley, Helen	William McCluskey	Sara McCluskey
DePotiers	Edward		30-Aug-1896	13-Jan-1890	August W. DePotiers	Shy, Wally		Bertha Kaskatis

LAST NAME	FIRST NAME	MIDDLE	BAPTISM	BIRTH	Father	Mother	SPONSORS
DePoiters	Helen	Bertha	23-Aug-1896	13-Aug-1896	August W. DePotiers	Shy, Wally	Bertha Kaskatis
Deppish	Eleanora	Loretta	20-Feb-1887	28-Jan-1887	Francis Deppish	Quigley, Eleanora	Mary E. Sanders
Deppish	Pauline	Genevieve	20-Jul-1890	12-Jul-1890	Francis Deppish	Quigley, Ellen	Catherine Shaw
Deppish	William	Elmer	10-Sep-1893	26-Aug-1893	Francis Deppish	Quigley, Helen Mary	Emma Pryor
Dermody	James	Christopher	04-Apr-1902	30-Jan-1902	James Christopher Dermody	Bergmann, Augusta	William Caster
Devall	William	Eugene	16-Jan-1887	29-Dec-1886	John Devall	Ward, Ann	Margaret Ward
Devine	Raymond	Edward	2-Dec-1906	7-Nov-1906	Edward Devine	Steinmetz, Dora	George Devine
Devine	Ann		26-Jul-1885	06-Jul-1885	Michael Devine	Fitzpatrick, Catherine	William Dempsey
Devine	Charles		31-Aug-1890	15-Aug-1890	Michael Devine	Fitzpatrick, Catherine	Catherine Fitzpatrick
Devine	George		30-Dec-1888	11-Dec-1888	Michael Devine	Fitzpatrick, Catherine	Ann Hoyle
Devine	Julia		23-Oct-1892	03-Oct-1892	Michael Devine	Fitzpatrick, Catherine	Mary Fitzpatrick
Devine	Michael	John	22-May-1887	26-Apr-1887	Michael Devine	Fitzpatrick, Catherine	Catherine Fitzpatrick
Devine	Jerome		11-Apr-1897	28-Mar-1897	Michael E. Devine	Fitzpatrick, Catherine	Helen Heil
Devine	Catherine	Mary	11-Nov-1894	26-Oct-1894	Michael Edward Devine	Fitzpatrick, Catherine	Mary Fitzpatrick
Devouges	Eugene	P.	04-Jul-1886	02-Jul-1886	Alphonse Devouges	O'Farrell, Mary Theresa	Bridget O'Farrell
Devring	Wilmer	Alphonsus	01-May-1892	16-Apr-1892	Joseph Alphonse Debring	Thalheimer, Elizabeth Ann	Genevieve Thalheimer
Dewey	Ella		20-Mar-1898	25-Feb-1898	John Dewey	Proctor, Ann	Sarah Logan
Di Domenico	Rose	I.	18-Oct-1908	24-Mar-1908	Francis Di Domenico	Filicicchia, Michelle	Rose Di Domenico
Dice	Francis	Martin	10-Oct-1915	22-Sep-1915	William Dice	Busch, Mary	Margaret Heilman
Dickinson	Thomas	Julian	29-Sep-1912	22-Sep-1912	Harvey Dickinson	Loughran, Elizabeth M.	Frances O'Brien
Dickinson	Edward	Augustus	6-Jun-1909	20-May-1909	Harvey J. Dickinson	Loughran, Elizabeth M.	Ann Burroughs
Didsch	Catherine		8-Apr-1906	27-Oct-1906	Bernard Didsch	Connor, Margaret	Ida Frazer
Diehl	Mary	Joseph	03-Dec-1893	21-Sep-1893	John Henry Diehl	Pohlmann, Clara	Mary Garrett
Dienstbach	Edward		22-Mar-1914	5-Mar-1914	August Dienstbach	Connelly, Mary	Francis McGrann
Dienstbach	Mary		3-Sep-1911	15-Aug-1911	August Dienstbach	Connelly, Mary	John Fiddes
Dienstbach	Ann	Barbara	18-Oct-1908	6-Oct-1908	August A. Dientsbach	Connelly, Mary	Ezdward J. Connelly
Dietrick	Ethel	May	06-May-1888	14-Dec-1887	James B. Dietrick	Isenburg, Ida	Catherine Connelly
Dietz	G.	May	30-Nov-1912	06-Mar-1889	Y. Dietz	Foreman, Susanna	Mary Hart
Dietzway	Margaret	Bridget	16-Aug-1896	07-Jul-1896	Joseph Dietzway	Kirk, Emma	
Diggins	Joseph	Francis	18-Jul-1915	30-Jun-1915	Edward J. Diggins	Albert, Ann M.	Barbara Shaw
Dignan	Rita	Francis	20-Jun-1915	11-Jun-1915	Joseph M. Dignan	Bowley, Mary E.	Mary E. Kelly
Dignan	Michael	Joseph	1-Jan-1911	17-Dec-1910	Michael Joseph Dignan	Bowling, Mary	Lona McDonald
Dillon	Jarlette		01-Aug-1897	23-Jul-1897	Patrick Dillon	Collins, Ellen	Alice Kenny
Dinan	Helen	Agatha	24-Jan-1897	12-Jan-1897	John Thomas Dinan	Hanrahan, Honora	Julia Riordan
Dinan	Honora	Mary	20-Jan-1895	29-Dec-1894	John Thomas Dinan	Hanrahan, Honora	Cornelius Dinan
Dinan	Catherine	Agnes	24-Dec-1911	12-Dec-1911	William F. Dinan	Kernan, Catherine	Joseph Dinan
Dinan	John	Hall	26-Jul-1914	13-Jul-1914	William F. Dinan	Kernan, Maura C.	John Dinan
Dinan	William	Francis	9-May-1909	25-Apr-1909	William Francis Dinan	Kernan, Mary Catherine	Cornelius Francis Dinan
Dingle	Mary	Dorothy	19-Apr-1914	10-Feb-1914	Francis Dingle	Gibbons, Rose	Earl Dingle
Dimsback	Joseph	Augustus	13-Feb-1910	7-Jan-1910	Augustus Dimsback	Connolly, Mary	Edward Connolly
Disney/Kirsch	Helen	Elizabeth	05-Dec-1900	26-Nov-1855	John Kirsh	Kirsh, Katherine	Helen McDonald
Dixon	Thomas	Howard	10-May-1896	15-Apr-1896	Henry R. Dixon	Bierlein, Catherine	Howard Dixon
Dixon/McCafferty	Susannah		20-Jul-1891	About 1815	Thomas Dixon	Candia, Mary	Rachel Crouch
Doane	Ann	Cecelia	23-Jan-1910	3-Jan-1910	Richard Doane	Gallagher, Ann	Albert Doane
Dobbins	James		28-Oct-1898	16-Oct-1816	James Dobbins	McCaughlin, Ann	George Stemple
Dobbins	Catherine		06-May-1888	26-Apr-1888	John Dobbins	Ryan, Margaret	Margaret Dobbins
Dobbs	Claude	Eugene	2-Dec-1906	23-Oct-1906	Claude Dobbs	McAleer, Emma	Catherine McAleer
Dobbs	Edward		21-Dec-1894	16-Aug-1886	Claude Dobbs	Young, Ann	Rebecca Roundtree
Dobbs	Ruben	McClellan	25-May-1913	30-Apr-1913	Claude W. Dobbs	McAleer, Emma Gertrude	Catherine Hafele
Dobbs	John	Joseph	3-Sep-1915	8-May-1915	Claudio Dobbs	McAleer, Emma	Mary Quinn
Dobbs	William	Doory	18-Jul-1909	1-Jul-1909	James Dobson	Deare, Nattie	Ella Rudolph
Dobson	Edith	Irene	19-May-1895	06-Nov-1865			Ann Silverson
Dock	George		13-Jul-1897	02-Jan-1889	George Wendell Dock	Cosgrove, Mary Catherine	Thomas Radigan
Doggett/Wahn	Elizabeth		31-Jul-1897	10-Oct-1870	James Doggett	[Blank]	Thomas Shaughnessy
Doherty	Rose	Mary	21-Apr-1895	18-Apr-1895	Charles Doherty	Owens, Jane	Catherine Elizabeth Green
Dolan	Cecelia		03-Feb-1884	24-Jan-1884	Daniel Dolan	Lanahan, Ann	Edward Quigley
Dolan	Daniel	V.	05-Sep-1897	29-Aug-1897	Daniel Dolan	Lanahan, Ann	Thomas McGavin
Dolan	John		16-Jun-1889	09-Jun-1889	Daniel Dolan	Lanahan, Ann	Francis Patrick Cavanaugh
Dolan	Theresa	Loretta	29-May-1892	17-May-1892	Daniel Dolan	Taneyane, Ann	Mary Ryan
Dolan	Ann	Regina	29-Aug-1886	22-Aug-1886	David Dolan	Lanahan, Ann	Ellenora Cavanaugh
Dolan	Catherine	Mary	10-Jul-1904	22-Jun-1904	Hugh Dolan	Murphy, Catherine	Nellie Dolan
Dolan	Hugh	Leonard	9-Jul-1911	3-Jul-1911	Hugh Dolan	Murphy, Catherine	John Steadman
Dolan	Mary	B.	21-Jan-1906	10-Jan-1906	Hugh Dolan	Murphy, Catherine	Patrick J. Dolan

LAST NAME	FIRST NAME	MIDDLE	BAPTISM	BIRTH	Father	Mother	SPONSORS	
Dolan	Joseph	Jacob	02-Nov-1884	20-Oct-1884	Joseph Dolan	Gunnip, Ann	James McGinnis	Catherine Hanlon
Dolan	Margaret		25-Mar-1888	15-Mar-1888	Joseph Dolan	Gunnip, Catherine	Patrick Dolan	Margaret Henning
Dolan	Mary	Catherine	08-Aug-1886	29-Jul-1886	Joseph Dolan	Gunnip, Ann	Thomas Hance	Hanna Brannan
Dolan	Michael	Joseph	24-Sep-1882	18-Sep-1882	Joseph Dolan	Gunnip, Ann	Francis McQuillan	Mary Gunnip
Dolan	Catherine	Agnes	07-Jun-1885	28-May-1885	Patrick Dolan	Kimmett, Mary	John Kimmett	Catherine Cryan
Dolan	Charles	Vincent	18-Sep-1892	30-Aug-1892	Patrick Dolan	Kimmett, Mary	James Daniel Goldrick	Mary Cleophas Goldrick
Dolan	John	Joseph	13-May-1888	28-Apr-1888	Patrick Dolan	Kimmett, Mary	John Mitchell	Joan Mitchell
Dolan	Mary	Frances	26-Sep-1886	16-Sep-1886	Patrick Dolan	Kimmett, Mary	Michael Kimmett	Mary Kimmett
Dolan	Mary	Laura	23-Dec-1894	08-Dec-1894	Patrick Dolan	Kimmett, Mary	John Joseph Corrigan	Catherine Corrigan
Dolan	Thomas	Michael	04-Nov-1883	23-Oct-1883	Patrick Dolan	Kimmett, Mary	Dennis Kimmett	Mary Dolan
Dolan	William	Patrick	24-Aug-1890	04-Aug-1890	Patrick Dolan	Kimmett, Mary		Kate Gallagher
Dolan	Edward	Ignatius	25-Feb-1912	10-Feb-1912	Richard Dolan	Gallagher, Catherine	Edward Dolan	Loretta Farnan
Dolan	John	Edward	26-Aug-1906	3-Aug-1906	Richard Dolan	Gallagher, Catherine	John Dolan	Ann E. Gallagher
Dolan	Richard	Patrick	7-Feb-1909	28-Jan-1909	Richard Dolan	Gallagher, Catherine	Edward Dolan	Frances Fannon
Dolan	Richard	Patrick	14-Dec-1913	29-Nov-1913	Richard Dolan	Gallagher, Catherine	James Wright	Mary Clinton
Dollard	Elizabeth		17-Sep-1882	20-Aug-1882	John Dollard	Kane, Margaret	George Brushwiller	Mary Brushwiller
Dollard	Mary	Louise	31-Aug-1884	15-Aug-1884	John Dollard	Kane, Margaret		Magdalen Bushmiller
Dollard	William		25-Apr-1886	03-Apr-1886	John Dollard	Kane, Margaret	Charles Coyle	Mary Coyle
Dominicis	Amelia		16-Oct-1910	26-Sep-1909	Antonio Dominicis	Appugliese, Rose		Angela Rossi
Dominicis	Clornicam		16-Oct-1910	25-Aug-1907	Antonio Dominicis	Appugliese, Rose	Michael Bolognese	
Donahue	Elizabeth		30-Sep-1900	12-Sep-1900	John Donohue	O'Leary, Bridget	Thomas Donahue	Ann Doyle
Donaldson	Ann	Teresa	29-Jan-1886	05-Jan-1886	Samuel W. Donaldson	Krichton, Agnes Treacy	Francis Krichton	Louise Krichton
Donatelli	Donato		27-Sep-1908	9-Aug-1908	Anthony Donatelli	Rossi, Adeline	Venanzo Donatelli	Carmela Manella
Donatelli	Pasquale		26-May-1912	6-Jan-1912	Anthony Donatelli	Rossi, Adalina	Venantius Donatelli	Carmalla Manualla
Donatelli	Rose		24-Oct-1915	14-Dec-1914	Anthony Donatelli	Rossi, Adellina	Ralph Donatelli	Carmel Donatelli
Donatelli	Vincent		27-Nov-1910	20-Sep-1910	Anthony Donatelli	Rossi, Helen	Vincent Donatelli	
Donegan	Robert	Emmet	29-Oct-1905	21-Oct-1905	Eugene Donegan	Collins, Mary	Edward Milton Smith	Alice Donegan
Donegan	Sara	Catherine	22-Feb-1903	11-Feb-1903	John F. Donegan	Doyle, Julia	James P. Doyle	Mary Delauder
Donegan	Agnes	Catherine	06-Dec-1891	23-Nov-1891	Owen Donegan	Collins, Mary	Micharl Gereghty	Joan Casey
Donegan	Daniel	Albert	24-Oct-1897	12-Oct-1897	Owen Donegan	Collins, Mary	Patrick Donegan	Rose Houck
Donegan	Francis	Xavier	24-Apr-1910	17-Apr-1910	Owen Donegan	Collins, Mary E.	Albert Donegan	Agnes May
Donegan	Genevieve	Frances	24-Feb-1889	11-Feb-1889	Owen Donegan	Collins, Mary	James Phillips	Sara Collins
Donegan	Mary	Patrick	25-Aug-1901	19-Aug-1901	Owen Donegan	Collins, Mary	Owen Donegan	Bessie Donegan
Donegan	Owen		11-May-1890	29-Apr-1890	Owen Donegan	Collins, Mary	Thomas Lyons	Grace Lyons
Donegan	Margaret	R.	05-Jul-1903	24-Jun-1903	Owen F. Donegan	Collins, Mary Elizabeth	Francis Casey	Genevieve Donegan
Donegan	Mary	Elizabeth	11-Sep-1887	04-Sep-1887	Owen F. Donegan	Collins, Mary E.	Patrick Donegan	Catherine McMahon
Donegan	Joseph		28-Oct-1894	16-Oct-1894	Owen Francis Donegan	Collins, Mary Elizabeth	John Andrew Casey	Margaret Mary Conlon
Donegan	Alice	Gertrude	08-Jan-1893	28-Dec-1892	Owen Franklin Donegan	Collins, Mary Elizabeth	Patrick Joseph Donegan	Mary Ann Morsell
Donlin	Ann		27-Jun-1909	21-Jun-1909	Thomas Donlin	O'Hara, Catherine	Michael Davey	Mary Davey
Donlin	Margaret		27-Jun-1909	21-Jun-1909	Thomas Donlin	O'Hara, Catherine	Thomas Cawley	Mary Davey
Donnelly	Nathaniel	George	01-Mar-1894	01-Feb-1894	James Donnelly	Rhein, Mary		Mary Rhein
Donnelly	Ambrose		22-Sep-1907	6-Sep-1907	John Donnelly	Brazier, Mary	William Brown	Mary C. Merriman
Donnelly	Mary	Helen	14-Feb-1909	30-Jan-1909	John Joseph Donnelly	Brazier, Mary Ellen	Francis McGrieven	Margaret L. Finn
Donnelly	Joan	Mary	16-Feb-1896	06-Feb-1896	Martin Donnelly	McNally, Helen	John O'Keefe	Mary Donnelly
Donnelly	John	Joseph	25-Nov-1900	12-Nov-1900	Martin Donnelly	McNally, Ella	James Kenny	Ella Colbert
Donnelly	Mary	Helen	30-Jul-1899	16-Jul-1899	Martin Donnelly	McNally, Helen	Thomas O'Keefe	Margaret Donnelly
Donnelly	Arthur	Leon	02-Aug-1903	14-Jul-1903	Martin J. Donnelly	McNally, Ella	John McNally	Rose Griffin
Donnelly	Catherine	Joseph	03-Oct-1897	21-Sep-1897	Martin J. Donnelly	McNally, Helen	Thomas J. Colbert	Helen Colbert
Donnelly	Martin	Charles	17-Apr-1910	8-Apr-1910	Martin J. Donnelly	McNally, Helen	John Griffin	Mary Griffin
Donnelly	John		21-Jun-1885	11-Jun-1885	William Donnelly	McKenna, Mary	Joseph Haughey	Rose McNally
Donnelly	Mary	Helen	16-May-1886	08-May-1886	William James Donnelly	McKenna, Mary	William Farley	Rose K. Haughey
Donohoe	Mary	Ann	04-Aug-1885	31-Jul-1885	Thomas Donohoe	Tydings, Frances	Thomas Donohoe	Margaret Piqueth
Donohue	Leo	David	30-Jun-1895	12-Jun-1895	David Donohue	McGraw, Sarah	Fred Youngheim	Mary A. Donahue
Donohue	John	Martin	18-Oct-1896	11-Sep-1896	John Donohue	O'Leary, Bridget	John Curtis	Julia McGraw
Donohue	Anastasia		05-Oct-1902	19-Sep-1902	John Donohue	Leary, Bridget	Martin Doyle	Mary McCabe
Donohue	John		04-Dec-1898	07-Nov-1898	John Donohue	Leary, Bridget		
Donohue	Edward		1-Dec-1907	25-Nov-1907	Patrick Donohue	Quinn, Mary	Patrick J. Green	Cecelia O'Connor
Donohue	James	Joseph	14-Sep-1902	23-Aug-1902	Thomas Donohue	Powers, Mary	James Donohue	Catherine Donohue
Donovan	Agnes		8-Nov-1914	18-Dec-1907	Dennis Donovan	Weber, Mary		Mary Powers
Donovan	John	Walter	8-Nov-1914	21-Dec-1900	Dennis Donovan	Weber, Mary	Edward Hanrahan	
Donovan	Louis	Edward	8-Nov-1914	20-Aug-1898	Dennis Donovan	Weber, Mary		
Donovan	Mary	Elizabeth	01-May-1892	25-Mar-1892	Edward Donovan	Carr, Margaret		Mary Ann Collins
Donovan	Cecelia		14-Oct-1905	14-Oct-1905	Henry Donovan	Laughlin, Julia		Lily Donovan

LAST NAME	FIRST NAME	MIDDLE	BAPTISM	BIRTH	Father	Mother	SPONSORS
Donovan	Patrick	Joseph	14-Oct-1905	14-Oct-1905	Henry Donovan	Laughlin, Julia	Lilly Donovan
Donovan	Mary	Isabelle	21-Mar-1909	5-Mar-1909	John P. Donovan	Hassett, Elizabeth E.	Ann C. Lupton
Dooley	Alice	G.	09-Sep-1883	25-Aug-1883	James Dooley	Kerwick, Helen	Alice McMahon
Dooley	Martha	Estelle	23-Jan-1887	19-Oct-1886	John F. Dooley	Velliness, Martha F.	Ann Hogan
Dooley	Martha	Thomas	08-Feb-1891	19-Dec-1890	John Francis Dooley	Velliness, Margaret Thomas	Catherine Agnes Fay
Dooley	Mary	Louise	24-Jun-1888	25-Mar-1888	John Francis Dooley	Velliness, Margaret Thomas	Joan Teresa Sullivan
Dooley	Teresa		25-Aug-1889	22-Jun-1889	John Francis Dooley	Velliness, Martha Thomas	Joan Teresa Sullivan
Dooly	William	B.	15-Nov-1896	24-Oct-1896	John Dooly	Velliness, Martha	Agnes Deelone
Doory	Francis	Proctor	17-Nov-1895	23-Oct-1895	John Doory	Proctor, Ann	Catherine Doyle
Doory	John		15-Apr-1900	15-Mar-1900	John Doory	Proctor, Emma	Agnes Doory
Doory	Richard		09-Mar-1902	22-Feb-1902	John Doory	Proctor, Ann	Ann McLaughlin
Doran	George	Daniel	28-Aug-1910	16-Aug-1910	George Daniel Doran	McGirr, Mary	Mary Colton
Doran	George		9-Feb-1908	9-Feb-1908	George Doran	McGinn, Mary	
Doray	Elsie	Elizabeth	09-Apr-1882	19-Feb-1882	William Dorsey	Baker, Martha J.	Ann Leggett
Dore	Dennis		04-Mar-1896	02-Mar-1896	Dennis Dore	Maskell, Catherine	Mary Cunningham
Dore	Dennis		22-Mar-1896	02-Mar-1896	Dennis Dore	Maskell, Catherine	Mary Cunningham
Dore	M.	Margaret	20-Sep-1908	8-Sep-1908	Joseph A. Dore	Dore, Margaret Agnes	Annie Goodwin
Dorr	Edward	Leroy	22-Mar-1911	26-Sep-1910	Albert Caspar Dorr	Swinney, Elizabeth Parkins	Laurence J. Roach
Dorse	Francis	Newton	28-Jul-1884	09-Jun-1884	Francis Newton Dorse	Fisher, Frederick	Bridget Fahey
Dorsey	Mary	Helen	21-Aug-1892	06-Aug-1892	Dennis Dorsey	Welby, Helen	Margaret O'Day
Dorsey	James		14-Jan-1890	10-Jan-1890	Edward Dorsey	Coughlan, Mary Ann	John Dorsey
Dorsey	Edward	Joseph	16-Jan-1910	26-Oct-1909	Joseph Dorsey	Connelly, Nora	Elizabeth Sheerlin
Dorsey	Catherine		14-Jan-1900	26-Dec-1899	Peter Dorsey	Sheridan, Catherine	John L. O'Neill	Alma Connelly
Dorsey	Thomas		10-Apr-1892	04-Feb-1892	Thomas H. Dorsey	Kesterson, Alma	Charles Conway	Margaret Conroy
Dorsey	James	Francis	16-Apr-1911	3-Apr-1911	William H. Dorsey	Clarke, Mary	Edwin Kesterson	Ella Bullock
Dorsey/Smith	Sarah	Patrick	17-Mar-1896	About 1854	William Dorsey	Dorsey, Lucy		Mary Dorsey
Dotterick	Ann		29-Apr-1900	25-Nov-1899	Henry Dotterick	Walters, Mary	Thomas Wynn	Ann [Blank]
Doud	Helen		18-Aug-1900	05-Aug-1900	John Doud	Ryan, Ellen	Charles Dowd	Mary Agnes Clark
Doud	Edward	Raymond	26-Sep-1897	11-Sep-1897	John Dowd	Dolan, Ella	John Dolan	Margaret Dowd
Doud	John	Henry	19-Jul-1908	6-Jul-1908	John H. Doud	Dolan, Nellie	Samuel J. Kane	Mary Griffin
Doud	Charles	C.	06-Jul-1902	29-Jun-1902	John H. Dowd	Dolan, Mary E.	Thomas Quirk	Mary Anderson
Doud	John	Joseph	05-Mar-1899	28-Feb-1899	John H. Dowd	Dolan, Mary	Edward R. Dolan	Catherine Juagi
Doud	Thomas	Jefferson	06-Jul-1902	29-Jun-1902	John H. Dowd	Dolan, Mary E.	Thomas J. Dowd	Ann Fannon
Doud	Mary	Helen	16-Jul-1907	29-May-1907	John Henry Doud	Dolan, Mary Helen	William P. Fannin	Mary Fannin
Douglas	Laurence		16-Jul-1889	09-Jul-1889	Charles Dougherty	Owens, Joan		Delia Owens
Dougherty	Mary	Joan	18-Dec-1887	03-Dec-1887	Charles Dougherty	Owens, Joan	Patrick McEnroe	Bridget Owens
Dougherty	Francis	Anthony	17-Aug-1890	08-Aug-1890	Cornelius Dougherty	Dolan, Margaret	William A. Quinn	Ella M. Hook
Dougherty	Julius	William	15-Jul-1892	02-Jul-1892	Julius Dougherty	Ruppert, Margaret		Barbara Wisrt
Dougherty	Catherine	Theresa	19-Dec-1909	3-Dec-1909	Thomas Dougherty	Harris, Florence	John Young	Theresa Burke
Dougherty	Thomas	Francis	18-Jun-1911	1-Jun-1911	Thomas Dougherty	Harris, Rose	Francis Harris	Margaret Roesch
Dougherty	John	Wilson	10-Nov-1912	23-Oct-1912	Thomas J. Dougherty	Harris, Rose M.	John J. Burke	Mary O'Brien
Douglas	John		21-Oct-1888	06-Oct-1888	Joseph Doughlas	Gillece, Mary	John Brannan	Mary Brannan
Douglas	Margaret	Elizabeth	01-May-1887	18-Apr-1887	Joseph Douglas	Gillece, Mary	Joseph Douglas	Ann Douglas
Douglas	Thomas		07-Feb-1886	18-Jan-1886	Joseph Douglas	Gillece, Mary	Patrick Gillece	Mrs. Gillece
Douglas	William		22-May-1883	15-May-1883	Joseph Douglas	Gillece, Mary		Ida Gillece
Douglas	William	James	15-Jan-1893	22-Dec-1892	Joseph Polk Douglas	Gillese, Mary	Joseph Patrick Douglas	Ann Douglas
Douglass	Peter	Henry	22-Jun-1884	22-May-1884	Joseph P. Douglass	Gillese, Mary	Joseph Douglass	Clara Douglas
Douthet	Henry	Chester	25-Sep-1898	22-Sep-1898	Henry E. Douthet	Byrnes, Mary	Helen Blackney	James Byrnes
Dowd	Walter	Aloysius	04-Sep-1887	25-Aug-1887	Charles Dowd	Leach, Christine	Thomas Moore	Rebecca Leach
Dowd	William	Ignatius	10-Jun-1906	4-Jun-1906	John H. Dowd	Dolan, Helen	Edward Dolan	Ann Fogarty
Dowd	Mary	Helen	11-Jan-1885	05-Jan-1884	Thomas Dowd	Quinn, Mary	Thomas Toolen	Mary Toolen
Dowd	Thomas	Francis	09-May-1886	01-May-1886	Thomas Dowd	Quinn, Mary	John Reilly	Margaret Quinn
Dowd	Winifred		19-Feb-1888	31-Jan-1888	Thomas Dowd	Quinn, Mary	Patrick Kenny	Winifred Kenny
Dowling	Catherine		02-Jun-1901	15-May-1901	Samuel Dowling	Kelleher, Mary	James McCarthy	Mary McCarthy
Dowling	Honora	Marcella	06-Jun-1897	24-May-1897	Samuel Dowling	Kelleher, Mary Ann	Michael Droney	Joan Kelleher
Dowling	James		17-Dec-1899	29-Nov-1899	Simon Dowling	Kelleher, Mary	Thomas [Blank]	Margaret Burger
Dowling	John	Joseph	04-Feb-1894	30-Jan-1894	Simon Dowling	Kelleher, Mary Ann	John Murnane	Nora Berger
Dowling	Margaret		29-Jul-1906	20-Jul-1906	Simon Dowling	Kelleher, Mary	John Cooney	Mary McCarthy
Dowling	Mary	Bridget	03-Feb-1895	27-Jan-1895	Simon Dowling	Keleher, Mary	Humphrey Keleher	Margaret McCarthy
Downing	Margaret		19-Aug-1909	4-Aug-1909	Howell Downing	Lemaitre, Margaret		
Downs	James	Allen	16-Jun-1907	15-Mar-1907	James Clifton Downs	Emerich, Ann R.		Bertha Luber
Doyle	Anastasia		28-Jun-1903	21-Jun-1903	Eugene Doyle	Maloney, Anastasia	Andrew O'Dea	Catherine Gavin
Doyle	Joseph	Laurence	06-Sep-1891	01-Sep-1891	Gerald Doyle	McCreager, Ann		Mary Clancy

32

LAST NAME	FIRST NAME	MIDDLE	BAPTISM	BIRTH	Father	Mother	SPONSORS	
Doyle	Mary	Cecelia	06-Sep-1891	01-Sep-1891	Gerald Doyle	McCreager, Ann	John Dee	Catherine Dee
Doyle	Mary	Agnes	23-Jan-1898	21-Jan-1898	Gerald Doyle	McCreager, Ann	Martin A. Freeman	Mary A. Freeman
Doyle	James	Joseph	15-Mar-1896	07-Mar-1896	James Doyle	Lacey, Margaret	John McIntyre	Rose Grey
Doyle	John		28-Jul-1907	28-Jul-1907	James Doyle	Lacey, Margaret E.		Mary Freeman
Doyle	Margaret		4-Apr-1905	4-Apr-1905	James Doyle	Lacey, Margaret E.		
Doyle	Mary		26-Dec-1886	21-Dec-1886	James Doyle	Burns, Ann	James Conroy	Bridget Caufield
Doyle	Patrick		09-Aug-1898	09-Aug-1898	James Doyle	Lacey, Margaret		
Doyle	Sara		06-Aug-1893	27-Jul-1893	James Doyle	Lacey, Margaret	John Lacy	Julia Doyle
Doyle	William	Gerald	11-Nov-1894	04-Nov-1894	James Patrick Doyle	Lacy, Margaret Elizabeth	John Thomas Donegan	Ann Donegan
Doyle	Francis	Xavier	07-Oct-1888	01-Oct-1888	Jerome Doyle	Creager, Ann	Francis Williams	Mary Williams
Doyle	Francis	Patrick	28-Apr-1889	01-Apr-1889	John F. Doyle	Hughes, Mary E.	Michael F. Donohue	Elizabeth Doyle
Doyle	Mary	Catherine	20-Jul-1884	08-Jul-1884	John F. Doyle	Doory, Catherine	John J. Doyle	Margaret G. Doory
Doyle	Robert	James	11-Jul-1886	18-Jun-1886	John F. Doyle	Doory, Catherine	Dennis Reardon	Mary C. Doory
Doyle	Francis	George	17-Dec-1882	30-Nov-1882	John Francis Doyle	Doory, Catherine Agnes	Patrick Joseph Donohue	Mary Agnes Doyle
Doyle	Mary		25-Jan-1903	13-Jan-1903	Joseph Doyle	Connor, Julia	Joseph Mewshaw	Margaret Curley
Doyle	John	Joseph	13-Jul-1890	21-Jun-1890	Matthew Doyle	Connolly, Catherine	Patrik McDermott	Mary McDermott
Doyle	Anastasia		14-Dec-1902	11-Dec-1902	Michael Doyle	Curtis, Ann	John Curtis	Martha Doyle
Doyle	Catherine		20-Feb-1898	08-Feb-1898	Michael Doyle	Curtis, Ann	Thomas Lung	Catherine O'Leary
Doyle	John	Bartly	24-Nov-1895	09-Nov-1895	Michael Doyle	Curtis, Ann	Thomas Kehoe	Mary Leary
Doyle	Ellen	Mary	18-Oct-1896	09-Nov-1895	Michael Doyle	Curtis, Ann	Thomas Kehoe	Martha Doyle
Doyle	Margaret	M.	07-Jul-1901	28-Jun-1901	Owen Doyle	Malone, Anastasia	W.G. Doyle	Ella Norris
Doyle	Owen	Anthony	7-May-1905	22-Apr-1905	Owen H. Doyle	Maloney, Anastasia	Martin Doyle	Mary McGlone
Doyle	Catherine		15-Nov-1908	3-Nov-1908	Owen Henry Doyle	Maloney, Anastasia	Joseph McGlone	Margaret E. Hart
Doyle	Mary	Francis	14-Feb-1915	9-Feb-1915	Thomas E. Doyle	Roche, Catherine A.	Dennis Roche	Mary Donnelly
Doyle	James	Charles	01-Sep-1884	21-Aug-1884	William H. Doyle	Donnelly, Margaret		Ann Donnelly
Doyle	Helen	Mary	03-Nov-1889	25-Oct-1889	William Henry Doyle	Donnelly, Margaret	James Doyle	Mary Kilroy
Dreau	Ann		24-May-1896	15-Mar-1896	William J. Doyle	Layman, Ida	Henry Doyle	Ann Dreau
Dressel	Joseph	Henry	15-Jun-1897	14-Jun-1896	Joseph H. Dreau	Langemann, Mary		Mary McKevitt
Dressel	Joseph	Patrick	26-Oct-1913	22-Oct-1913	Henry Dressel	McEnroe, Ann	John McKenna	Mary McDevitt
Dressel	Francis		18-Apr-1915	13-Apr-1915	Henry Dressel	McEnroe, Ann	Arthur McDevitt	Margaret Jacobs
Driscol	Thomas	Cornelius	27-Sep-1891	03-Aug-1891	John Conrad Dressel	Sheffer, Emma	Francis Dressel	Margaret McEenery
Driscoll	Daniel	Fenton	6-May-1906	1-May-1906	Michael Driscol	Doray, Ellen	Thomas Jennings	Ann Driscoll
Driscoll	Thaddeus		8-Mar-1914	17-Feb-1914	Daneil E. Driscoll	Bradley, Margaret E.	Dennis J. Driscoll	Mary Farrell
Driscoll	Albert		09-Dec-1883	03-Dec-1883	Daniel Driscoll	Farrell, Bridget	Francis Patrick Byrne	Abby McAuliffe
Driscoll	Ann		16-Aug-1891	16-Aug-1891	Dennis Driscoll	Toulan, Catherine	Michael Kelly	Ann Driscoll
Driscoll	Ann		09-Sep-1883	20-Aug-1883	Dennis Driscoll	Fenton, Catherine	Patrick Driscoll	Mary Magner
Driscoll	Daniel		24-Sep-1893	12-Sep-1893	Dennis Driscoll	Fenton, Catherine	Patrick Driscoll	Catherine Driscoll
Driscoll	Dennis		29-Nov-1885	14-Nov-1885	Dennis Driscoll	Fenton, Catherine	Jerome Murphy	Joan Donohue
Driscoll	Francis		07-Feb-1897	23-Jan-1897	Dennis Driscoll	Fenton, Catherine	James Fenton	Mary Kemp
Driscoll	Helen		11-Dec-1889	29-Nov-1889	Dennis Driscoll	Fenton, Kate	Thomas Driscoll	Bridget Doyle
Driscoll	John	Timothy	26-Aug-1888	17-Aug-1888	Dennis Driscoll	Fenton, Catherine	Benjamin Horan	Hannah Fenton
Driscoll	Thomas		30-Nov-1884	18-Nov-1884	Dennis Driscoll	Fenton, Catherine	Daniel Driscoll	Ella Fenton
Driscoll	William	Dennis	02-Jan-1887	20-Dec-1886	Dennis Driscoll	Fenton, Catherine	Jerome Driscoll	Katherine Jennings
Driscoll	Thomas	Joseph	9-Oct-1904	29-Sep-1904	Michael Driscoll	Dorsey, Helen	Dennis Driscoll	Mary Jennings
Druery	John	James	4-May-1913	27-Apr-1913	Michael J. Driscoll	Dorsey, Helen	Thomas Jennings	Adalaide Sella
Drumgoole	Mary	Elizabeth	4-Sep-1910	8-Aug-1910	Otto Druery	Gould, Bertha	John J. Schroen	
Drumgoole	Ann	Margaret	31-Oct-1882	09-Sep-1864	Henry Danze	[Blank]		
Drumgoole	Christina		18-Jul-1883	27-Oct-1863	John Campbell	Gosnell, Ann	Thomas J. Gaule	Mary Lewis
Drumgoole	Martin		11-Apr-1886	29-Mar-1886	Martin Drumgoole	Hildwein, Ann	Martin McMorrow	Mary Drumgoole
Drumgoole	Mary	Helen	20-Sep-1891	26-Aug-1891	Martin Drumgoole	Hildwein, Ann		Agnes Clark
Drumgoole	Teresa		02-Sep-1883	24-Aug-1883	Martin Drumgoole	Hildwein, Ann	Thomas Driumgoole	Bridget Murphy
Drumgoole	Patrick	Henry	07-Dec-1884	28-Nov-1884	Martin Drumgoole	Hildwein, Ann	Wilton Brown Clarke	Mary Parrell
Drumgoole	Edward		30-Nov-1888	01-Sep-1888	Thomas Drumgoole	Hildwein, Ann		Mary Drumgoole
Drury	William	Clifton	11-Mar-1883	09-Feb-1883	Thomas James Drumgoole	Dantz, Mary	Patrick Drumgoole	Julia Dignan
Drury	Floyd	Alexander	25-May-1893	24-Apr-1893	Otto Druery	Danz, Mary		Mary M. Steer
Dubois	Rebecca		29-Apr-1906	6-Apr-1906	Otto Drury	Gould, Bertha		Alice Kendall
Dudley	Helen		15-Nov-1908	25-Oct-1908	Otto Keife Drury	Gould, Bertha Estelle	Floyd Smith	Mary Brady
Dudley	Catherine	Emma	16-Apr-1887	About 1824	Malone Dubois	Slaysman, Ann	Elizabeth Brady	Kate H. Dwyer
Dudley	Richard	Thomas C.	03-Jan-1886	08-Dec-1885	Rcihard Dudley	Norton, Catherine	James H. Dudley	Mary Norton
Dudley	Mary	Isabelle	30-Apr-1882	22-Apr-1882	Richard Henry Dudley	Norton, Catherine	Edward John Westervelt	Agnes Greely
Dudley	Joseph	Patrick Cleveland	07-Oct-1883	20-Sep-1883	Richard Henry Dudley	Norton, Catherine	Joseph Dudley	Mary E. Geisendopfer
Dudley			14-Mar-1886	28-Dec-1846	Robert C. Dudley	Caffrey, Bridget A.	John Gittings	Ann Isabelle Dudley
Dudley			16-Nov-1884	01-Nov-1884	Robert Clinton Dudley	Caffrey, Bridget	Thomas Joseph Caffrey	

LAST NAME	FIRST NAME	MIDDLE	BAPTISM	BIRTH	Father	Mother	SPONSORS
Dudrow	Charles	Edwin	26-Mar-1885	14-Feb-1885	John C. Dudrow	Egan, Agnes	Charles E. Dudrow
Dudrow	Helen	Victoria	10-Nov-1889	26-Sep-1889	John C. Dudrow	Eagan, Agnes	Charles E. Dougherty
Dudrow	Margaret	Elizabeth	02-Oct-1887	20-Jul-1887	John C. Dudrow	Eagan, Bridget A.	
Duering	Florence	Celeste	25-Apr-1885	25-Apr-1885	Joseph Duering	Gibbons, Florence	
Duffy	Mary	Agnes	22-Feb-1885	14-Feb-1885	Bernard J. Duffy	Duffy, Ellen	James Duffy
Duffy	Helen	Catherine	01-Apr-1883	21-Mar-1883	Bernard James Duffy	Duffy, Helen	James Hayden
Duffy	William	James	03-Mar-1901	1-Feb-1901	Charles Duffy	Mackin, Margaret	Joseph Mackin
Duffy	Alice	Elizabeth	10-Feb-1901	28-Jan-1901	James Duffy	McCall, Bridget	Daniel Quigley
Duffy	Catherine		2-Oct-1904	10-Sep-1904	James Duffy	McCall, Bridget	Patrick Finnegan
Duffy	Hugh	Joseph	10-Feb-1901	28-Jan-1901	James Duffy	McCall, Bridget	Thomas Monaghan
Duffy	James		05-Jan-1896	28-Dec-1895	James Duffy	McCall, Bridget	Peter Duffy
Duffy	Mary	V.	11-Sep-1898	05-Sep-1898	James Duffy	McCall, Bridget	Patrick Duffy
Duffy	John	Bernard	04-Mar-1900	06-Feb-1900	John Duffy	O'Brien, Rose	
Duffy	Rose	Regina	12-Jul-1903	01-Jul-1903	John Duffy	McCabe, Bridget	John Sherry
Duffy	Mary	Catherine	25-Sep-1892	27-Jul-1892	John T. Duffy	O'Brien, Rosaline	
Duffy	Mary	R.	07-Nov-1897	29-Sep-1897	John Thomas Duffy	O'Brien, Rose	Josephine Minnick
Duffy	Luke		07-Jul-1895	19-Jun-1895	Michael Duffy	Carr, Cassie	Michael McDermott
Duffy	Patrick		31-Dec-1893	22-Dec-1893	Michael Duffy	Carr, Cassandra	James Duffy
Duffy	Mary	Teresa	15-Oct-1882	07-Oct-1882	Patrick James Duffy	Clark, Bridget	Dennis Healy
Dugan	Mary	Regina	24-Jan-1904	15-Jan-1904	Thelma L. Dugan	Nester, Mary Elizabeth	Dominicus McCarthy
Dugan	Mary	Catherine	5-Sep-1909	14-Aug-1909	Thomas L. Dugan	Nester, Mary L.	Daniel Dugan
Dugan	Raymond	Francis	19-Jan-1908	1-Jan-1908	Thomas L. Dugan	Nester, Mary L.	Dominic Dugan
Dugan	Thomas	A.	3-Sep-1905	24-Aug-1905	Thomas L. Dugan	Nester, Mary	Andrew J. Kearney
Dugan	William	Cecelia	21-Jun-1914	12-Jun-1914	Thomas L. Dugan	Nester, Mary E.	Joseph L. Dugan
Dugan	Henry	Anthony	14-Apr-1907	3-Mar-1907	William Dugan	Montgomery, Lillian	James T. O'Hara
Duke	Agnes	Francis	31-Jan-1915	18-Jan-1915	John Duke	Price, Mary	Nelson Warren
Duke	James	Genevieve	19-Jan-1913	3-Jan-1913	John Duke	Price, Mary	Francis McGraw
Duke	Mildred	Josephine	19-Jan-1913	3-Jan-1913	John Duke	Price, Mary	James Price
Duke	Mary	Beatrice	25-Mar-1888	08-Feb-1888	Joseph Duke	Blessing, Ida	Frances Roundtree
Duke	Myrtle	August	21-Jan-1883	02-Jan-1883	Joseph Duke	Blessing, Ida	Louis Rosensteel
Duke	Raymond	W.	13-Jun-1886	28-May-1886	Joseph W. Duke	Blessing, Ida J.	Gustave Duke
Duke	Wilton		28-Sep-1884	14-Sep-1884	Joseph W. Duke	Blessing, Ida Joan	James W. Duke
Duley	John		22-Nov-1914	8-Nov-1914	John Duley	Callaghan, Catherine	Augustine Whitfield Duke
Dulude	Caroline	Cecelia	6-Feb-1910	16-Jan-1910	George Delude	Dill, Jennie	John Dunn
Dulude	George	Oral	14-Jun-1908	16-May-1908	George Oral Dulude	Deys, Gennie	James Healy
Dumay	Edward	Emil	16-Dec-1888	08-Nov-1888	Edward Dumay	Rowe, Sara	Emil Cage
Dumphy	[Blank]		24-Jan-1886	21-Dec-1885	John Dumphy	Durkin, Winifred	Bernard J. O'Boy
Dumphy	Agnes		1-Nov-1908	24-Oct-1908	John Dumphy	Banahan, Mary	John Mooney
Dundon	John	Joseph	11-Oct-1885	24-Sep-1885	John Dundon	Mulligan, Catherine	David O'Connell
Dunkirk	Henry	Lynne	15-Feb-1904	03-Jul-1884	William P. Dunkirk	Carson, Virginia C.	James P. Davner
Dunleavy	Ann		16-Sep-1883	24-Aug-1883	Francis Dunleavy	Waxmuth, Ann	James Dunleavy
Dunleavy	Rose	Eleanor	23-Sep-1888	03-Sep-1888	Francis Dunleavy	Waxmuth, Ann	John Sands
Dunlevy	William	Frederick	07-Feb-1897	01-Feb-1897	James Dunlevy	Saunders, Amelia	William Carey
Dunn	Bernard	Edmund	30-Sep-1900	26-Sep-1900	Bernard Dunn	Barry, Catherine	Daniel Murphy
Dunn	Ellen	Virginia	14-Sep-1913	2-Sep-1913	Bernard Dunn	Barry, Catherine	James McDonald
Dunn	Mary	Catherine	16-Jan-1899	30-Dec-1898	Bernard Dunn	Barry, Catherine	Michael Nester
Dunn	William	Walter	26-Sep-1897	03-Sep-1897	Bernard Dunn	Barry, Catherine	Charles Dunn
Dunn	Joseph	Chester	28-Jan-1906	13-Jan-1906	Bernard E. Dunn	Barry, Catherine	Hugh E. Toner
Dunn	Leon	H.	03-Aug-1902	20-Jul-1902	Bernard E. Dunn	Barry, Catherine M.	Elizabeth Dunn
Dunn	Sara		12-Jan-1883	19-Dec-1882	Edward Dunn	McKenna, Helen	
Dunn	Regina		23-Jan-1887	11-Jan-1887	F. M. Dunn	Mullen, Mary E.	James H. Dunn
Dunn	James	Wilmer	22-Mar-1885	12-Mar-1885	Franklin M. Dunn	Mullen, Mary Elizabeth	William Dunn
Dunn	John	Carroll	06-Sep-1891	21-Aug-1891	Franklin M. Dunn	Mullen, Mary E.	
Dunn	Mary	Cecelia	26-Nov-1882	15-Nov-1882	Franklin Mills Dunn	Mullen, Mary Elizabeth	Henry Dunn
Dunn	Agnes	Mary	15-Sep-1895	01-Sep-1895	Harry Dunn	Daley, Mary	Adam Dempert
Dunn	Catherine	Laura	29-Nov-1885	18-Nov-1885	James Dunn	Horgan, Catherine	Henry S. Dunn
Dunn	Elizabeth	G.	21-Nov-1897	15-Nov-1897	James Dunn	Owens, Catherine	John Owens
Dunn	Julia	Ann	29-Jul-1888	26-Jul-1888	James H. Dunn	Horrigan, Catherine	Dennes E. Reardon
Dunn	Herbert	Leo	25-Feb-1894	14-Feb-1894	James Thomas Dunn	Sheridan, Catherine	Joseph Charles Dunn
Dunn	Ann		04-Jun-1885	24-May-1885	John Dunn	McKenna, Olivia	
Dunn	Catherine		23-Apr-1882	20-Apr-1882	John Dunn	Leary, Catherine	Daniel Joseph Robinson
Dunn	Helen	Mary	18-Aug-1901	08-Aug-1901	John Dunn	Callaghan, Ellen	Francis Zellers
Dunn	John		09-Sep-1900	26-Aug-1900	John Dunn	Callaghan, Ella	Richard Callaghan

Column 9 (SPONSORS second column):

SPONSORS (2)
Catherine A. Dudrow
Victoria Dougherty
Julia Redmond
Adalaide Hutch
Margaret C. Duffy
Ann Jordan
Gertrude Duffy
Alice Duffy
Rose McCall
Mary McCourt
Mary Collins
Mary Duffy
Mary Ann O'Neill
Rose Duffy
Esther Brown
Josephine Minnick
Margaret Connolly
Elizabeth Carr
Mary Graham
Delia Dugan
Delia McCarthy
Mary Strobel
Mary Kearney
Gertrude McCarthy
Marsha Murphy
James Price
Elizabeth Kilroy
Catherine Roache
Frances Roundtree
Louis Rosensteel
Josephine Duke
Josephine Victoria Duke
Helen Dunn
Mary Thompson
Margaret McCabe
Emilia Rowe
Ann O'Boy
Murphy, Margaret
Mary O'Connell
Helen Dunleavy
Theresa Dunleavy
Catherine Murphy
Eleanor Menger
Arthur [Blank]
Sarah Dougherty
Mary E. Quinn
H.E. Dunn
Mary Martin Drane
Joan Dunn
Frances McGrane
Sara Mullen
Virginia Dunn
Sarah E. Daly
Julia Sexton
Mary Dunn
Josephine Dunn
Teresa Bridget Sheridan
Mary M. Drane
Mary Moylan
Ellen Dunn
Mary Dunn

LAST NAME	FIRST NAME	MIDDLE	BAPTISM	BIRTH	Father	Mother	SPONSORS	
Dunn	Miles	August	10-May-1885	07-May-1885	John Dunn	Leary, Catherine	Philip Ahearn	Mary Mulholland
Dunn	Catherine	Ann	4-Aug-1907	28-Jul-1907	John J. Dunn	Callahan, Catherine	Dennis Sexton	Mary C. Horrigan
Dunn	Francis	Xavier	3-Nov-1912	3-Nov-1912	John J. Dunn	Callahan, Helen B.	Joseph Callahan	Catherine Dunn
Dunn	Mary	Cecelia	12-Jan-1890	30-Dec-1889	John J. Dunn	McGlennan, Margaret A.	James Fullerton	Mary Fullerton
Dunn	Mary	Helen	26-Nov-1905	16-Nov-1905	John J. Dunn	Callahan, Helen V.	Edward J. Dunn	Catherine M. Callahan
Dunn	Mary	Helen	18-Dec-1887	11-Dec-1887	John Joseph Dunn	McGlennan, Margaret Ann	Christopher Joseph Dunn	Mary Ann Dunn
Dunn	Mary	Helen	25-Mar-1888	04-Mar-1888	Joseph B. Dunn	Dunn, Elizabeth	Francis Magrann	Julia Donahue
Dunn	Joseph	Thomas	09-Sep-1883	31-Aug-1883	Joseph Bernard Dunn	Kelly, Elizabeth	Thomas McNally	Helen Dunn
Dunn	James	Patrick	19-Mar-1882	16-Mar-1882	Joseph Dunn	Kelly, Elizabeth	Edward Dunn	Alice Coffey
Dunn	Michael	Francis	06-Jan-1885	30-Dec-1884	Joseph Dunn	Kelly, Elizabeth	Michael M. Kelly	Margaret McCann
Dunn	Raymond	Michael	23-Feb-1890	19-Feb-1890	Joseph Dunn	Keller, Elizabeth	Michael Keller	Bridget Ulan Connelly
Dunn	Norbert		13-Jun-1886	06-Jun-1886	Joseph Dunn	Kelly, Elizabeth	John Carr	Mary T. Carr
Dunn	Eleanor	Veronica	03-May-1889	01-Mar-1889	Joseph E. Dunn	Kehoe, Ann B.	Richard H. Troy	Mary J. Dougherty
Dunn	Mary	Elizabeth	23-Nov-1880	06-Nov-1890	Joseph L. Dunn	Kehoe, Ann B.		Catherine McGarrity
Dunn	Naomi		04-Apr-1886	20-Mar-1886	Joseph L. Dunn	Kehoe, Ann B.	John B. Burns	Ann R. Meehan
Dunn	Ruth	Genevieve	17-Jan-1897	04-Jan-1896	Joseph L. Dunn	Kehoe, Bridget	John Biddison	Ann Ruckle
Dunn	William	Joseph	02-Oct-1887	17-Sep-1887	Joseph L. Dunn	Kehoe, Ann B.	James G. McGarrity	Sarah G. Hanrahan
Dunn	Helen		26-Dec-1886	03-Dec-1886	Peter Dunn	Kelly, Catherine	Bernard Dunn	Amelia Dunn
Dunn	Dennis		05-Aug-1883	24-Jul-1883	Thomas Dunn	Connell, Helen	William Campbell	Catherine Breen
Dunn	Joseph	Latta	28-Nov-1882	01-Jul-1859	William Dunn	Latta, Mary	Thomas J. Gaule	
Dunne	William	Edward	03-May-1903	15-Apr-1903	William E. Dunne	Carnick, Mary		Margaret Gereghty
Dunnegan	Thomas	Anthony	25-Oct-1898	07-Oct-1898	Owen Donegan	Collins, Mary		Mary L. Shields
Dunphy	Helen		26-Jun-1887	14-Jun-1887	John Dunphy	Dolan, Mary		Ann Lavery
Dunphy	Margaret		25-Dec-1885	21-Dec-1885	John Dunphy	Durkin, Winifred	Bernard O'Boyle	Ann C. O'Boy
Dunworth	John	Robert	14-Nov-1915	24-Oct-1915	Robert Dunworth	Ellis, Elizabeth	Matthew O'Brien	Katherine Reynolds
Durham	Ellen		20-Dec-1893	16-Nov-1862	Parker Durham	Hooper, Margaret		Margaret Adams
Dushett	Catherine		05-Jan-1896	06-Dec-1895	Samuel Dushett	Sullivan, Julia		Catherine Dushett
Duvall	George	Washington	14-Aug-1898	06-Jul-1898	George Duvall	Christopher, Ida B.	James Hubbard	Mary Anita Hubbard
Duvall	M.	Cecil	05-Apr-1891	15-Mar-1891	George Duvall	Christopher, Ida		Mary McGraw
Duvall	William	Raymond	14-Jul-1889	29-Jun-1889	George Washington Duvall	Christopher, Ida Brittana		Mary Catherine Winsinger
Duvall	Helen	Gertrude	01-Oct-1882	08-Sep-1882	John Duvall	Ward, Ann	James Ward	Margaret Fitzpatrick
Dwyer	Ellen	Margaret	21-Jan-1900	25-Dec-1899	John Dwyer	Manion, Nora	Laurence Conniff	Delia Manion
Dwyer	Thomas	Edward	04-Jan-1885	12-Dec-1884	Thomas Dwyer	Meskill, Ann	Michael J. Meskill	Ann Rhodes
Dwyer	Helen		26-Jun-1887	28-May-1887	William Dwyer	Morrison, Bridget		Margaret Kelly
Dyas	William	Thomas	02-May-1897	22-Mar-1897	John Dyas	Coxson, Mary	James Dunn	
Dyer	John	Thomas	04-Sep-1884	21-Aug-1884	Patrick Dyer	Duffy, Mary Catherine	John Thomas Duffy	Mary Ann McDermott
Dyer	John	Edmund	26-May-1889	16-May-1889	Patrick G. Dyer	Duffy, Mary	James F. Smith	Mary Rodgers
Eagers	Henry		03-May-1891	26-Apr-1891	Henry Eagers	Kennedy, Mary	Dennis Kennedy	Agnes Kennedy
Eagers	Joseph	Albin	05-Nov-1893	17-Oct-1893	Henry Eagers	Kennedy, Mary	Albin Ryan	Catherine Ryan
Eastwood	Alice	Louise	29-May-1887	10-May-1887	Francis J. Eastwood	Douglas, Mary F.		Louise Hucht
Eastwood	Raymond	Joseph	24-Mar-1889	25-Feb-1889	James Francis Eastwood	Douglas, Mary Francis		Frances Agnes Douglas
Eaton	Rose		04-Jan-1903	04-Dec-1902	John Eaton	Rayner, Loretta	Mary Rayner	Mary Rayner
Ebaugh	Eugene		23-Sep-1906	10-Aug-1906	Earl Ebaugh	Donner, Margaret		Catherine Stevenson
Eberle	Georgia	Irene	26-Jun-1894	30-Apr-1894	George Eberle	Kennedy, Laura Virginia		Ann McDonald
Eberline	Vincent		4-Nov-1906	19-Oct-1906	Francis Eberline	Hall, Sophia	Douglas Hall	Ann Hall
Ebert	Mary	Lillian	26-Jun-1892	18-Jun-1892	Joseph Ebert	Zeigler, Emma		Mary Faulstich
Ebert	William		12-Feb-1887	19-Jun-1885	Joseph Ebert	Lescor, Louise		Catherine Rosensteel
Eccleston	Helen	Mary	17-Feb-1883	11-Feb-1883	Wallace Eccleston	Boylan, Margaret		Helen Boylan
Echart	Thomas	Irving	25-Sep-1887	31-Aug-1887	Henry A. Echart	Glenn, Ann	John T. Flannigan	Mary Glenn
Echman	Mary	Joan	22-Nov-1914	16-Nov-1914	John M. Echman	Murphy, Joan	Patrick McCarthy	Sarah E. Murphy
Eckert	Mary	Regina	15-Mar-1891	27-Feb-1891	Henry Eckert	Glenn, Ann	Leo Murphy	Wellzetta Larkin
Eckhardt	M.	Jerome	20-Jul-1899	17-Jun-1899	Walter Eckhardt	Manly, Gertrude M.	John Manley	Mary Brian
Eckhardt	M.		10-Aug-1899	17-Jun-1899	Walter Eckhardt	Manly, Gertrude M.	John Manly	Mary Brian
Edell	Joseph	Augustus	12-Nov-1893	28-Oct-1893	Augustus Edell	Holdfish, Ann	Joseph Edell	Agnes Edell
Edell	Agnes	Josephine	17-Apr-1887	31-Mar-1887	George Edell	Culver, Emma B.	Joseph Edell	Agnes Edell
Edell	Mary	Francis	28-Apr-1889	22-Mar-1889	George W. Edell	Culver, Emma	John T. Flannigan	Mary F. Flannigan
Edell	Patrick	Albert	15-Feb-1891	05-Feb-1891	Joseph Edell	Killmyer, Agnes	Patrick McCarthy	Ann Keener
Edwards	John	Patrick	30-Aug-1885	04-Aug-1885	John Edwards	Ryan, Julia	William F. Ryan	Mary M. Ryan
Effing	Henry		31-May-1889	23-Mar-1889	Henry Effing	Meehan, Catherine	Francis Malstrom	Mary McGinnis
Egan	James	Collins	30-Aug-1914	18-Aug-1914	James Egan	Collins, Ellen	Francis Egan	Margaret Kennedy
Egan	Margaret		12-Jan-1913	17-Dec-1912	James P. Egan	Collins, Ellen	Hugo Duffy	Ann Cashen
Egan	Martin	Raymond	30-Sep-1900	13-Sep-1900	Martin Aloysius Egan	Schley, Margaret	Samuel Andrew	Mary A. Hall
Ege/Maguire	Laura	Anastasia	14-Feb-1890	17-Jun-1862	Peter F. Ege	Johns, Eliza M.		Ann Mobley

35

LAST NAME	FIRST NAME	MIDDLE	BAPTISM	BIRTH	Father	Mother	SPONSORS
Eggleston	Mary Lillian		06-Sep-1885	24-Aug-1885	Wallace Eggleston	Boylan, Margaret	Catherine Boylan / William Boylan
Ehns	John		16-Feb-1898	About 1874	Charles Schmidy	Geelhaar, Amelia	Julia O'Connor
Ehns	James		10-Apr-1898	30-Mar-1898	Joseph Ehns	Logue, Sarah	Joan Logue / John Logue
Ehns	Joseph	Bernard	10-Apr-1898	01-Apr-1898	Peter Ehns	Schmitt, Joan	Caroline Schiermyer / Joseph Finnan
Eholein	George		21-Aug-1910	1-Aug-1910	Francis Eholein	Watson, Alberta	Margaret Sader
Ehrhart	Mary	Clara	13-Jun-1911	25-Oct-1891	Martin Ehrhart	Snyder, Mary Catherine	Lillian Anderson
Ehrlein	Elizabeth	Clare	12-Sep-1915	17-Aug-1915	Francis Ehrlein	Watson, Alberta	Elizabeth Connor / George Weiner
Ehrlein	Margaret		8-Feb-1914	4-Mar-1909	Francis Ehrlein	Watson, Alberta	Mildred Willis / William Ehrlein
Ehrlein	Edward	Joseph	9-Nov-1913	24-Oct-1912	Francis J. Ehrlein	Watson, Alberta	Ann G. Miller / Edward Willis
Ehrlein	Mary	Constance	4-Oct-1914	9-Sep-1914	William Aloysius Ehrlein	Barry, Rachel Mary	Constance Mary Barry / Samuel Barry
Ehrlich	Mary	Regina	22-Sep-1912	16-Jul-1893	Berthold Ehrlich	Pines, Sara	Mary Morris
Eick	Irene		03-May-1885	10-Apr-1885	Andrew Eick	Fowler, Mary Elizabeth	Elizabeth Fowler
Eick	Thomas	Hillen	26-Dec-1886	19-Dec-1886	Andrew Henry Eick	Fowler, Mary	Catherine Fowler / Thomas Hillen
Eisenhour	Frances	Ann Florence	19-Apr-1885	12-Apr-1885	Francis Eisenhour	Fletcher, Elizabeth	Wilhelmina Wooden
Eline	Helen	Eva	01-May-1892	22-Apr-1892	John Eline	Bisker, Ann	Helen Bisker / James Farron
Eline	Mary	Edna	10-Mar-1889	19-Feb-1889	John Eline	Bisker, Ann	Mary Brown / John Touhy
Eline	Mary	Edna	26-Feb-1889	19-Feb-1889	John F. Eline	Bisker, Ann	
Eline	Mary	Catherine	30-Sep-1894	24-Sep-1894	John Francis Eline	Bisker, Ann	Catherine Eline / Samuel Peton Eline
Eline	Teresa	Victoria	10-Mar-1895	25-Feb-1895	Thomas C. Eline	[Blank], Ann	Catherine Feehan / Bernard Wilkens
Eline	Frances		27-Mar-1898	10-Mar-1898	Thomas Eline	Veazey, Ann	Maybella Wilson / Peter McCabe
Eliot	Arthur	Stanislau	07-Jun-1884	08-Oct-1883	John A. Eliot	Cleary, Mary E.	Elizabeth Golden
Eliott	[Blank]		16-Mar-1882	16-Mar-1882	John Elliott	Cleary, Mary E.	
Ellender	George	Daily	24-Apr-1887	12-Apr-1887	George B. Ellender	Green, Mary	Catherine T. Bogy / James J. McDonald
Elliot	Clara	Virginia	29-Aug-1886	17-Jun-1862	Edward Elliot	Wright, Sara	Catherine Byrne / Martin Byrne
Elliott	Joseph	Howard	24-Mar-1889	10-Jul-1877	Jacob Elliott	Waljer, Corinne	John Henry Barlow
Elliott	William	Jennings Bryan	22-Aug-1897	24-May-1897	John Elliott	Magnus, Lydia	Ann Costello / Bernard Dunn
Ellis	Ann	Rosalie	27-Apr-1883	16-Jan-1860	George Ellis	Kohler, Quincy Ann	
Ellis	James	Allan	18-Sep-1898	04-Sep-1898	James Ellis	Adams, Catherine	Elizabeth [Blank] / John Ellis
Ellis	James	David	11-Nov-1900	23-Oct-1900	James Ellis	Furlong, Mary	Margaret O'Shea / Thomas O'Shea
Ellis	John	Joseph	08-Mar-1896	25-Feb-1896	James Ellis	Furlong, Mary	Mary Ellis / Nicolas McGraw
Ellis	Joseph		02-Apr-1899	17-Mar-1899	James Ellis	Furlong, Mary	Margaret McGraw / Thomas Luby
Ellis	Joseph	P.	30-Apr-1899	17-Apr-1899	James Ellis	Furlong, Mary	Margaret McGraw / Thomas Lusby
Ellis	Ann		11-Jul-1897	26-Jun-1897	John Ellis	Adams, Catherine	Ann Lane
Ellis	Charles	Henry	22-Oct-1900	04-Oct-1900	John Ellis	Adams, Catherine	Elizabeth Bayne / Charles Bayne
Ellis	Francis	A.	22-Oct-1899	08-Oct-1899	John Ellis	Adams, Catherine	Margaret Bayne
Ellis	Loretta	Mabel	07-Jun-1896	22-May-1896	John Ellis	Adams, Catherine	Mabel Agnes Adams
Ellis	Elizabeth	Teresa	10-Mar-1895	22-Feb-1895	John H. Ellis	Adams, Kate O.	Mary A. Bowen
Ellis	Robert	Newton	19-Nov-1893	05-Nov-1893	John H. Ellis	Adams, Catherine	Mary Connolly
Ellis	Stella	Catherine	24-May-1891	10-May-1891	John H. Ellis	Adams, Catherine	Catherine Curran
Ellis	Paul	Carroll	16-Oct-1892	04-Oct-1892	John Henry Ellis	Wilson, Mary	Mary Winifred Kesterson / Paul Edwin Kesterson
Elmore	Joseph	Patrick	23-Mar-1890	20-Mar-1890	[Blank] Elmore	Wilson, Mary	Ed. Braden
Elmore	Ann	Virginia	30-Apr-1893	25-Apr-1893	Upton Elmore	Wilson, Mary Margaret	Victoria Murphy / John Moore
Elmore	Francis	Upton	26-Jul-1891	14-Jul-1891	Upton Elmore	Wilson, Mary	Grace Murphy / James P. Kelly
Elwood	Ann	Francis	21-Jan-1883	08-Jan-1883	Harnez Elwood	Raymo, Mary	Mary Dames
Elwood	Thomas	Johan	16-Jun-1907	2-Jun-1907	Maurice Elwood	Kelly, Helen	Mary Fraunholz / Francis T. Elwood
Elwood	Leon	Kelly	25-Jun-1905	15-Jun-1905	Maurice H. Elwood	Kelly, Helen M.	Margaret Elwood / William Kelly
Elwood	Catherine		25-Jul-1909	15-Jul-1909	Stephen C. Elwood	Murphy, Elizabeth	Mary A. Elwood / Richard Murphy
Elwood	Elizabeth	Lauren	23-Jun-1907	8-Jun-1907	Stephen C. Elwood	Murphy, Elizabeth	Bridget Snyder / Richard Murphy
Elwood	Richard	Joseph	23-Jul-1905	11-Jul-1905	Stephen C. Elwood	Murphy, Elizabeth Catherine	Frances Ficher / John H. Ficher
Elwood	Stephen	Charles	22-Aug-1897	11-Aug-1897	Stephen C. Elwood	Murphy, Elizabeth	Smith, Margaret / Joseph Sheehan
Elwood	Elizabeth		20-Dec-1901	13-Dec-1901	Stephen E. Elwood	Murphy, Elizabeth	Mary Elwood
Elwood	Ellen		20-Sep-1903	09-Sep-1903	Stephen Elwood	Murphy, Elizabeth	Margaret McDermott / Richard Murphy
Elwood	John		17-Dec-1899	28-Nov-1899	Stephen Elwood	Murphy, Elizabeth	Margaret Slater / John Slater
Elwood	Mary	Ann	07-Jul-1895	28-Jun-1895	Stephen Elwood	Murphy, Elizabeth	Mary Elwood / Edward Lally
Elwood	Thomas	Patrick	14-Jan-1894	05-Jan-1894	Stephen Elwood	Murphy, Elizabeth	Bridget Murphy / Henry Hunter
Emery	Gertrude		11-Dec-1887	11-Nov-1887	Thomas Emery	Mugan, Mary Louise	Mary May / Francis Randall
Emge	Francis	M.	16-Apr-1905	10-Apr-1905	John Emge	Popp, Ann	Mary A. Emge / Martin J. Emge
Emge	Wilbur	Martin	22-Nov-1908	8-Nov-1908	Martin J. Emge	Popp, Ann	
Emmary	Robert		24-Aug-1890	11-Aug-1890	Thomas J. Emmary	Meehan, Mary L.	Mrs. A. Emmary
Emmett	Ann	M.	30-Jul-1905	15-Jul-1905	John E. Emmart	Weatherstone, Elizabeth	Genevieve Weatherstone / Thomas J. McClain
Emmett	Charles	H.	30-Sep-1906	12-Sep-1906	John Emmert	Westerstine, Elizabeth	Laura Wetherstine / Joseph Dare
Emory	Charles	Edward	01-Jul-1883	15-Jun-1883	F. Julian Emory	Meegan, Mary	Catherine Fogarty / Charles E. O'Donnell
Emory	Mary	Louise	23-Aug-1885	30-Jul-1885	Thomas Emory	Meegan, Mary	Joan Fitzpatrick / Francis Reese

ST JOHN'S BAPTISMS 1882-1912

LAST NAME	FIRST NAME	MIDDLE	BAPTISM	BIRTH	Father	Mother	SPONSORS	
Emory	Arthur	O'Donnell	26-Aug-1894	10-Aug-1894	Thomas J. Emory	Meehan, Mary L.	James Bachelor	Ann McShane
Emory	William	Julian	24-Jan-1893	22-Jan-1893	Thomas Julian Emory	Meegan, Mary Louise	Thomas Joseph Emory	
Engel	Helen	Mary	21-Jun-1914	10-Jun-1914	William Engel	Salasky, Mary	Francis Spooney	Helen Lavery
England	Rachel		13-May-1885	27-Dec-1873	Caspar England	Hutton, Elizabeth		Cassandra Lee Murphy
England	Francis	Joseph	13-Nov-1910	11-Jun-1907	Christian England	Zohmy, Sophia Ann		Emma Hofmeyer
England	Mary	Ann	13-Nov-1910	2-Jun-1909	Christian England	Zohmy, Sophia Ann		Emma Hofmeyer
Englemeyer	Mary		30-Apr-1905	25-Apr-1905	Charles M. Englemeyer	Giblin, Sara B.	John Giblin	Mary Englemeyer
Engles	William	Joseph	21-Jun-1904	6-Feb-1904	Samuel J. Engles	Ruckle, Mary S.	Joseph L. Dunne	Ann Ruckle
Engles	Edward	Bernard	5-Jan-1913	28-Dec-1912	Samuel James Engels	Ruckle, Mary L.	Joseph Quinnt	Naomi M. Dunn
Engles	Mary	Elizabeth	25-Jul-1897	06-Jul-1897	Samuel James Engles	Ruckle, Mary L.	William A. Ruckle	Agnes Ruckle
English	Beatrice		19-Jul-1914	13-Jul-1914	John English	Becker, Elsie		Clara Powell
Ennis	William	Joseph	12-May-1912	1-May-1912	William Ennis	Byron, Catherine	James Kendellan	Ann Kendellan
Enright	John	Edwin	18-Mar-1906	3-Mar-1906	Charles Henry Enright	Phillips, Mary Catherine	John Phillips	Genevieve Phillips
Enright	William	Francis	08-Sep-1895	23-Aug-1895	Philip Enright	Quinn, Mary	William Quinn	Katie Steckline
Eppel	Judith		30-Jan-1898	20-Jan-1898	Martin Eppel	Clark, Mary	John Dressell	Judith Eppell
Eppel	Martin		30-Jan-1898	20-Jan-1898	Martin Eppel	Clark, Mary	Anthony Eppel	Catherine Stack
Epple	Ann	Catherine	11-Dec-1892	10-Dec-1892	Martin Epple	Clarke, Mary	Anthony Epple	Honora Clarke
Epple	Mary	Elizabeth	04-Apr-1895	04-Apr-1895	Martin Epple	Clarke, Mary	Thomas Clarke	Kate Epple
Eppler	John	Charles	07-Jul-1882	Dec 1873	Charles Alfred Eppler	Troy, Margaret		Mary Manning
Eppler	Joseph	Edward	13-Jun-1909	8-Jun-1909	Samuel Eppler	Denn, Florence May	Joseph Denn	Margaret Denn
Eppler	William	Harold	21-May-1911	7-May-1911	Samuel J. Eppler	Denn, Florence M.	Edward W. Clemson	Lillian Denn
Eppler	James	Thomas	13-Oct-1907	30-Sep-1907	Samuel Joseph Eppler	Deen, Florence	Henry Hoeckel	Jeanette Ward
Eppley	Mary	Jeannete	26-Feb-1888	01-Feb-1888	John A. Eppley	Holland, Mary	Edward Satterfield	Mary Satterfield
Eppley	Royland	Raymond	6-Jan-1907	3-Dec-1906	John A. Eppley	Olfers, Sara E.	Walter Eppley	Helen Langmeade
Epply	Charles	Le Roy	2-Nov-1907	28-Oct-1907	John A. Epply	Olfus, Sara Emma		Mary J. Hubbard
Epps/Middleton	Sarah		15-Mar-1892	26-Dec-1809	Francis Epps	Williams, Sarah		
Erdman	Ellenore		05-Nov-1899	30-Sep-1899	James Erdman	Carlos, Mary		Mary Moran
Erdman	Gertrude		22-Oct-1893	16-Oct-1893	James Erdman	Carlos, Mary Joan		Helen Monaghan
Erdman	John	Carlos	12-Jun-1892	08-Jun-1892	James Erdman	Carlos, Mary Joan		Joan Godfrey
Erdman	Mary	L.	08-Sep-1895	26-Aug-1895	John Erdman	Collins, Mary Jane		Martina Mary Carlos
Erline	John		4-Apr-1915	21-Mar-1915	Francis Erline	Dauses, Dorothy	George Erline	Mary Erline
Erline	Mary		04-Nov-1886	22-Dec-1885	George Erline	Watson, Elberta	William Erline	Rachel Erline
Ernst	John	V.	3-Mar-1907	20-Feb-1907	John V. Ernst	Law, Catherine		
Erskine	Emily	Margaret	10-Mar-1885	20-Dec-1884	William H. Erskine	Brogan, Catherine	Patrick Brogan	Margaret Brogan
Esender	Mary	Cecelia	12-Aug-1883	06-Aug-1883	Theodora Esender	McGarrity, Catherine		Margaret McGarrity
Essender	James	Bernard	27-May-1888	24-May-1888	Charles Essender	Owens, Helen	James B. Owens	Ann Stocksdale
Essender	John	Charles	01-Jan-1900	Jan 1900	Charles Essender	Owens, Eleanor	James McCaffrey	Catherine Gray
Essender	Aureleain	Cecelia	14-Jul-1889	21-May-1889	Theodore Essender	McGarrity, Catherine		Margaret Ryan
Essender	Charles		27-Jan-1902	19-Jan-1902	Theodore Essender	McGarrity, Catherine	Charles Essender	Helen Essender
Essender	George	Aloysius	16-May-1898	02-May-1898	Theodore Essender	McGarry, Catherine		Mary McGarry
Essender	Leo	Francis	29-Mar-1902	28-May-1878	Thomas Essender	McGarity, Catherine		Mary McGarity
Eubert	William	Henry	12-Aug-1883	30-Jul-1883	John A. Eubert	Arthur, Elizabeth A.	Charles Redmond	Elizabeth Redmond
Eubert	William	Edward	8-Jul-1906	19-Jun-1906	William Henry Eubert	Schaefer, Florence	Edward A. Norton	Ann Hedge
Evans	Loretta		16-Aug-1903	02-Aug-1903	Edward M. Evans	Muldoon, M. M.	J.W. Evans	Catherine R. Evans
Evans	Franklin	Joseph	7-Sep-1913	7-Aug-1913	James Evans	Long, Ann R.	Joseph Foley	Helen Jacobs
Evans	Ann	Virginia	03-Aug-1893	About 1893	John Evans	Ferguson, Eva	Francis Evans	Mary Dempsey
Evans	John	Theodore	06-Sep-1885	23-Aug-1885	John Evans	Ferguson, Eva	Francis Evans	Eva Ferguson
Evans	Joseph	Leo	20-Dec-1891	15-Oct-1891	John Evans	Ferguson, Eva		Mary Hayden
Evans	Howard	Francis	25-Mar-1889	30-Dec-1889	John J. Evans	Ferguson, Everlina		Virginia Tarring
Evans	Mary	Evelyn	28-Sep-1883	16-Oct-1883	John J. Evans	Fergusan, Eve C.		Frances Evelyn Evans
Evans	Walter	Francis	26-Jan-1888	29-Nov-1887	John J. Evans	Ferguson, Eva		Mary Dempsey
Evans	John	Mason	29-Mar-1902	28-May-1878	Mortimer Evans	McDonald, Joan	John Miles	Catherine Miles
Evans	Mary	Eva	23-Jan-1894	24-Feb-1860	Theodore Gentry Ferguson	Cunningham, Ann Eliza	Stephen Bonetto	
Evans	Thomas		12-Jul-1903	02-Jun-1903	Thomas Evans	Burns, Margaret	George B. Evans	Ella Burns
Evans	Beatrice	Emma	6-Aug-1911	11-Jul-1911	Wesley J. Evans	Carroll, Mary E.	Thomas Jos. Birmingham	Beatrice Birmingham
Evans	Catherine	Araminta	6-Aug-1911	11-Jul-1911	Wesley J. Evans	Carroll, Mary E.	Thomas Jos. Birmingham	Beatrice Birmingham
Everett/Hazeleip	Catherine	Elizabeth	15-May-1897	05-Mar-1856	Joseph Hazeleip	Hedean, Ann Cora		Helen Hanrahan
Everist	Charles	Joseph	10-Dec-1897	30-Aug-1897	Joseph Everist	Cupe, Sarah		Mary Kerr
Everist	Viola	Carol	29-Apr-1888	20-Dec-1887	Joseph Everist	Cape, Sarah		Ann King
Ewald	Francis	Winfield	23-Aug-1912	3-Aug-1912	Francis Ewald	Farron, Mary	Joseph Farron	
Ewers	Francis	Gordon	03-Sep-1893	21-Aug-1893	Frederick August Ewers	O'Brien, Margaret Ann	Francis Ewers	Joan O'Brien
Ewers	Joseph	Carroll	13-Sep-1891	06-Sep-1891	Frederick August Ewers	O'Brien, Margaret Ann	John Ewers	Joan O'Brien
Ewers	William	Julian	23-May-1897	13-May-1897	Frederick Ewers	O'Brien, Margaret	William O'Brien	Mary J. O'Brien

37

LAST NAME	FIRST NAME	MIDDLE	BAPTISM	BIRTH	Father	Mother	SPONSORS
Ezline	Charles	Henry	11-Jun-1893	28-May-1893	Thomas Charles Eline	Keagen, Ann	Rose Ignatius Bradley
Faherty	Charles	Leo	01-Nov-1891	26-Oct-1891	John Faherty	Kremer, Mary	Ann McCormick
Faherty	Mary		17-Jan-1886	07-Jan-1886	John J. Faherty	Kremer, Mary A.	Thomas M. Broderick
Fahey	Julia	Ann	03-Mar-1884	17-Feb-1884	John Fahey	Burns, Julia	Mary Burns
Fahey	Edward		03-Feb-1901	24-Jan-1901	Michael Fahey	Keaveney, Ann	Delia Keveney
Fahey	Michael		21-May-1898	07-May-1898	Michael Fahey	Keaveney, Ann	Mary Keveney
Fahey	Walter		23-Nov-1902	10-Nov-1902	Michael Fahey	Connery, Ann	John Kelly
Fahey	Margaret	Delores	3-Aug-1913	25-Jul-1913	Thomas Fahey	Wheeler, M.	John Sturgeon
Fahey	Maud	Ann	12-Jul-1914	27-Jun-1914	Thomas Fahey	Wheeler, Maud	Charles Murphy
Fairfax	Leonard		01-Jul-1899	28-May-1899	Milton Stewart Fairfax	Hodges, Agnes Keefe	Katherine Kavanaugh
Faithful	Ann	Mary	23-Jun-1899	16-Feb-1894	Charles Faithful	Jacobs, Ann	Mary Gruner
Fallan	Mary	Teresa	22-Jul-1888	14-Jul-1888	Michael Fallan	Collins, Eleanor	Ann Collins
Fallon	Ann		13-Oct-1901	15-Sep-1901	Francis Fallon	Grogan, Catherine	Patrick Collins
Fallon	Elizabeth		25-Dec-1898	19-Nov-1898	Francis Fallon	Grogan, Catherine	Thomas Fallon
Fallon	Francis		21-Jun-1885	10-Jun-1885	Francis Fallon	Grogan, Catherine	Thomas Grogan
Fallon	Joseph		28-May-1893	10-May-1893	Francis Fallon	Grogan, Catherine	John Mulligan
Fallon	Mary	Ann	19-Nov-1882	09-Nov-1882	Francis Fallon	Grogan, Catherine	Joseph Fallon
Fallon	William		10-Aug-1890	21-Jul-1890	Francis Fallon	Grogan, Catherine	Henry Joseph Eason
Fallon	Catherine		22-Sep-1895	05-Sep-1895	Frank Fallon	[Blank], Katie	Mary Eason
Fallon	James	Leroy	15-Oct-1905	17-Sep-1905	Henry Fallon	Thompson, Gertrude	Ann Monaghan
Fallon	Catherine	Virginia	02-Dec-1900	31-Oct-1900	Joseph Fallon	Thomason, Gertrude	Elizabeth Thompson
Fallon	Magdaline		21-Jun-1903	06-May-1903	Joseph H. Fallon	Thompson, Gertrude	Catherine Hubbell
Fallon	Naomi	Beatrice	11-Apr-1915	20-Mar-1915	Joseph H. Fallon	Thompson, Gertrude	Magdaline A. Fallon
Fallon	William	Edward	23-Apr-1911	26-Mar-1911	Joseph H. Fallon	Thompson, Gertrude	Elizabeth Wellen
Fallon	Elizabeth	Naomi	13-Sep-1908	21-Aug-1908	Joseph Henry Fallon	Thompson, Gertrude	Catherine Fallon
Fallon	John	Preston	21-Nov-1886	08-Nov-1886	Joseph P. Fallon	Keenan, Helen E.	Elizabeth Mary Smith
Fallon	Joseph	Robert	02-Mar-1884	05-Feb-1884	Joseph P. Fallon	Keenan, Ellen	Alice D. Brady
Fallon	Edward	Leo	13-Sep-1891	29-Aug-1891	Joseph Patrick Fallon	Keenan, Helen Elizabeth	Ann Fallon
Fallon	Helen	Regina	21-Jul-1889	03-Jul-1889	Joseph Patrick Fallon	Keenan, Helen Elizabeth	Helen Elizabeth Keenan
Fallon	Mary		23-Mar-1890	10-Mar-1890	Michael Fallon	Duffy, Rose	Mary Agnes Fallon
Fallon	Charles	Edward	08-Jul-1884	05-Jul-1884	Peter Fallon	Conroy, Elizabeth	Mary Kelly
Fallon	E.		06-Dec-1896	26-Nov-1896	Peter Fallon	Conroy, Elizabeth	Mary Fallon
Fallon	Elizabeth		23-Nov-1890	14-Nov-1890	Peter Fallon	Conroy, Elizabeth	Hanna Neary
Fallon	Helen	Gertrude	17-Sep-1893	06-Sep-1893	Peter Fallon	Conroy, Elizabeth	Catherine Murray
Fallon	Margaret		25-Jul-1886	11-Jul-1886	Peter Fallon	Conroy, Elizabeth	Thomas Maskell
Fallon	Peter	Francis	30-Sep-1888	07-Sep-1888	Peter Fallon	Conroy, Elizabeth	Daniel J. Fallon
Faner	Henry	Bernard	29-Aug-1886	20-Aug-1886	Henry Faner	McNulty, Ann	Patrick McGovern
Fannon	Mary	Catherine	11-Mar-1888	24-Feb-1888	Frances Fannon	Grogan, Catherine	George Kolb
Fannon	Ann		11-Aug-1912	29-Jul-1912	John Fannon	McShane, Ann	Peter Kenny
Fannon	Edward	McDevitt	1-Jan-1910	23-Dec-1909	John Fannon	McShane, Ann Elizabeth	Francis McShane
Fannon	John	Patrick	14-Aug-1904	1-Aug-1904	John Fannon	McShane, Ann	Joseph McShane
Fannon	Mary	Elizabeth	4-Feb-1906	26-Jan-1906	John Fannon	McShane, Ann	John McShane
Fannon	James	Edward	21-Sep-1902	08-Sep-1902	John M. Fannon	McShane, Ann	Henry McShane
Fannon	Vincent		30-Aug-1908	23-Aug-1908	John Michael Fannon	McShane, Ann Elizabeth	Joseph Fannon
Fannon	Agnes	Carmelite	16-Jan-1898	06-Jan-1898	William Fannon	Dolan, Frances Mary	Francis McShane
Fannon	Francis		04-Feb-1894	26-Jan-1894	William Fannon	Dolan, Frances	William Klinefelter
Fannon	James	Stephen	29-Dec-1895	24-Dec-1895	William Fannon	Dolan, Frances	Edward Dolan
Fannon	Laura		06-Apr-1890	25-Mar-1890	William Fannon	Dolan, Frances	Henry Kline
Fannon	William	Edward	01-Jan-1893	20-Dec-1892	William Fannon	Dolan, Frances	Mary Deise
Fannon	William	Patrick	09-Apr-1899	02-Apr-1899	William P. Fannon	Dolan, Frances	Matilda Clark
Fannon	Mary	Elizabeth	09-Dec-1888	01-Dec-1888	William Patrick Fannon	Dolan, Frances Mary	Ellen Delaney
Farley	Francis	Michael	26-Aug-1912	11-Aug-1912	Francis Farley	Connelly, Mary	Mary Elizabeth Anderson
Farley	Joseph	Henry	31-May-1896	19-May-1896	Michael Farley	McCabe, Margaret	Mary Bannon
Farley	Julia		15-Dec-1889	04-Dec-1889	Michael Farley	McCabe, Margaret	Mary Cain
Farley	Mary		19-Sep-1897	14-Sep-1897	Michael Farley	McCabe, Margaret	Margaret Smith
Farley	Francis	Michael	08-Apr-1883	25-Mar-1883	Michael Francis Farley	Moore, Sara Ann	Rose Monaghan
Farley	Thomas	Joseph	5-Mar-1911	13-Feb-1911	Michael Francis Farley	Connelly, Rose	Margaret Farley
Farley	William		06-Jul-1902	27-Jun-1902	Michael J. Farley	McCabe, Margaret	Thomas Connelly
Farley	Catherine	Elizabeth	23-Aug-1891	08-Aug-1891	William Edward Farley	McGovern, Catherine	James Breen
Farley	Agnes		30-Dec-1908	16-Dec-1908	William F. Farley	Williams, Alice	Catherine Hoeck
Farley	Elizabeth		30-Dec-1908	16-Dec-1908	William F. Farley	Williams, Alice	Thomas Barrett
Farley	Mary	Edith	13-Feb-1887	23-Jan-1887	William Farley	McGovern, Catherine	Margaret Barrett
Farmer	John	Charles	06-Jan-1889	27-Dec-1888	James Farmer	Maxwell, Eupha	Ann McGovern
							Mary J. Rice

LAST NAME	FIRST NAME	MIDDLE	BAPTISM	BIRTH	Father	Mother	SPONSORS	
Farmer	Euphemia	Ann	19-Mar-1882	07-Mar-1882	James Francis Farmer	Maxwell, Euphemia Teresa	John Farmer	Margaret Farmer
Farran	William		04-Aug-1895	22-Jul-1895	John Farran	Hanlon, Joan		Winefred Farran
Farran	John		09-Nov-1884	13-Oct-1884	Michael Farran	Duffy, Rose Ann	Hugh Canfield	Sara Canfield
Farran	Mary	Teresa	30-Dec-1888	06-Dec-1888	Michael Farran	Hagan, Mary	James Hagan	Henrietta Bukoffsky
Farrell	John	Joseph	7-Jan-1912	28-Dec-1911	James Farrell	Donahue, Julia	Michael Hessian	Mary Donahue
Farrell	Joseph	Leon	14-Nov-1915	4-Nov-1915	James Farrell	Donahue, Julia	John Kimmett	Katherine Kimmett
Farrell	Julia	Margaret	6-Sep-1914	25-Aug-1914	James Farrell	Donahue, Judith	Patrick McGinn	Margaret Lardner
Farrell	Mary		03-Jan-1886	16-Dec-1885	James Farrell	Hanlon, Margaret	John J. Kearney	Margaret Dempsey
Farrell	Mary	Ann	02-Sep-1888	27-Aug-1888	James Farrell	Jones, Mary A.	Patrick O'Connor	Margaret Jones
Farrell	Mary	Katherine	25-Sep-1910	14-Sep-1910	James Farrell	Donahue, Julia	Laurence Maguire	Katherine Mannion
Farrell	James	Patrick	15-Aug-1909	5-Aug-1909	James Patrick Farrell	Donahue, Julia	John Farrell	Delia Donohue
Farrell	James	E.	9-Dec-1906	3-Dec-1906	John Farrell	Kimmett, Ann	Patrick Farrell	Catherine Kimmett
Farrell	Joseph	Francis	8-Jan-1905	27-Dec-1904	John Farrell	Kimmett, Ann	James McAuliffe	Ann Donoghue
Farrell	Margaret		04-Aug-1901	23-Jul-1901	John Farrell	Kimmett, Ann	Darby Dunn	Mary Farrell
Farrell	Thomas	Patrick	25-Mar-1900	10-Mar-1900	John Farrell	Kimmett, Ann	John Costello	Mary Kimmett
Farrell	Francis	Percy	14-Apr-1907	16-Feb-1907	Maurice L. Farrell	Coleman, Mary	Francis L. Coleman	Ella Gebo
Farrell	James		10-Dec-1893	28-Nov-1893	Michael Farrell	Duffy, Rose Ann	James Kiernan	Mary Murray
Farrell	William	Patrick	04-Sep-1887	24-Aug-1887	Michael Farrell	Duffy, Rose Ann	Thomas Moran	Margaret Murray
Farrell	John	Leon	18-Oct-1903	04-Oct-1903	John Farrelll	Kimmett, Ann	James Farrell	Margaret Kimmett
Farrelly	Catherine		08-Feb-1891	28-Jan-1891	Michael Farrelly	McCabe, Margaret	Patrick McCabe	Julia Farrelly
Farrelly	James	Michael	23-Sep-1894	16-Sep-1894	Michael Farrelly	McCabe, Margaret	Francis McCabe	Catherine Roche
Farrelly	Margaret		04-Dec-1892	26-Nov-1892	Michael Farrelly	McCabe, Margaret	Thomas Kernan	Mary McCabe
Farrin	John		24-Sep-1882	15-Sep-1882	Michael Farrin	Hagan, Mary	John Farran	Catherine Hagan
Farron	John		09-Mar-1890	11-Feb-1890	James Farron	Shaughnessy, Helen	Peter Farron	Genevieve Farron
Farron	Catherine	Lorraine	3-Feb-1907	12-Jan-1907	John Farron	Snyder, Ada	James Farron	Ann M. Farron
Farron	John	James	21-Nov-1886	09-Nov-1886	John Farron	Mahon, Joan	Thomas McCaffrey	Mary McCaffrey
Farron	James		28-Nov-1886	06-Nov-1886	Michael Farron	Higgins, Mary Ann	Patrick Farron	Sarah Reid
Farron	Mary	Catherine	05-Oct-1884	20-Sep-1884	Michael Farron	Higgins, Mary	Michael Hoban	Julia M. Carr
Farron	Eleanor		25-Dec-1892	21-Dec-1892	Patrick Farron	Loughter, Winifred	James King	Helen Farron
Farron	Bernard		14-Oct-1894	08-Oct-1894	Patrick James Farron	Loughter, Winifred Josephine	John Farron	Bridget Foughter
Farrow	Barbara		25-Apr-1885	15-Apr-1885	John Farrow	Hanly, Jane	James Farrow	Mary Connelly
Fauble	Cecelia		16-Jan-1898	28-Dec-1897	Elmer Fauble	Smith, Joan		Winifred Ferrer
Fay	Catherine		04-Nov-1883	23-Oct-1883	George Fay	Cullen, Hester		Elizabeth Fay
Fay	George		10-Nov-1901	15-Oct-1901	Joseph Fay	Young, Pauline	Joseph Cullen	Emma Roesinger
Fay	John	Francis	7-Mar-1915	17-Feb-1915	Joseph L. Fay	Young, Pauline	Joseph F. Messman	Etty H. Fay
Fay	Joseph	Edgar	9-Oct-1910	27-Sep-1910	Joseph L. Fay	Young, Pauline	John Cullen	Catherine Cullen
Feehan	John		02-Nov-1884	18-Oct-1884	Henry Feehan	Wells, Catherine	John Aloysius Fallon	Mary Feehan
Feehan	Joseph	Raymond	18-May-1890	01-May-1890	John T. Feehan	Wilcox, Caroline	John Fallon	Mary L. Feehan
Feehan	Helen	Mary	11-Oct-1891	28-Sep-1891	John Thomas Feehan	WillCox, Caroline	Henry Feehan	Catherine Feehan
Feehan	John	Paul	01-Apr-1894	23-Mar-1894	John Thomas Feehan	Wilcox, Caroline	Leroy Small	Susanna Hopkins
Feeney	Clarence	Patrick	27-Mar-1904	17-Mar-1904	Patrick Aloysius Feeney	Murphy, Blanch	Victor Murphy	Estelle Murphy
Feger	Franklin	Howard	29-Sep-1912	7-Sep-1912	Franklin H. Feger	Whitty, Mary C.	John B. Mallon	Margaret Wilson
Feldpush	Catherine	Estelle	20-Apr-1883	20-Sep-1883	George Feldpush	Margage, Terence		Christine Mardage
Ferciot	Thomas	Nathaniel	15-Oct-1905	6-Oct-1905	Thomas Nathaniel Ferciot	McCluskey, Mary	Thomas J. McCluskey	Mary Ferrandini
Ferran	James	Henry	11-Oct-1891	01-Oct-1891	John Janes Ferran	Hanlon, Joan	Thomas Dumphy	Mary Dumphy
Ferron	Joseph	Patrick	23-Mar-1890	20-Mar-1890	Patrick Ferron	Campbell, Winifred	Terrance Dennon	
Fertelieve	Roman	E.	23-Feb-1908	24-Jan-1908	August Fertelieve	Deer, Catherine	Louis Chassague	Eulalia Kleckholfer
Fertitta	Rose	Vincent	15-Mar-1914	5-Feb-1914	Vincent Fertitta	Caleagno, Francis	Anthony Banna	Mary Dunn
Fey	George		28-Aug-1906	08-Aug-1888	Phillip Fey	France, Ann		
Fey	Henry		13-May-1906	15-Feb-1893	Phillip Fey	France, Ann C.		Jennie Blodgett
Fible	Mary	Catherine	13-Dec-1891	03-Dec-1891	Edward Fible	Smith, John		Mary Smith
Fickinsher	Sophia	Lenore	21-Feb-1886	30-Nov-1885	Carl Fickinsher	Hayes, Mary	Carl Landers	Margaret Landers
Fiddes	J. Charles		27-Sep-1908	5-Oct-1908	J. Fiddes	Burleson, Agnes		
Fiddes	Margaret		3-Jul-1904	4-Jun-1904	John Fiddes	Burlinson, Agnes		Lily B. Clemson
Fiddes	John	Charles	5-Oct-1907	4-Oct-1907	John Joseph Fiddes	Burlinson, Agnes	Bernard Sweeney	Mary Moylan
Fiddes	Ambrose		18-Feb-1912	22-Jan-1912	Joseph Fiddes	Burlington, Agnes	William McCubbins	Mary Clemson
Fiddler	Catherine	Mary	3-Jan-1915	7-Dec-1914	John Fiddler	Burlington, Agnes	Charles Clancy	Catherine O'Neill
Fiege	John	Edward	15-Feb-1891	09-Feb-1891	Henry P. Fiege	Coonan, Ruth A.	John C.E.Fiege	Dora Coonan
Fiege	Charles	Henry	13-Jan-1889	03-Jan-1889	Henry Peter Fiege	Coonan, Ruth Agatha	Charles August Muldoon	Mary Elizabeth Muldoon
Fiege	Clara		15-Sep-1887	14-Sep-1887	Henry Peter Fiege	Coonan, Ruth A.		Clara Gross
Fields	Catherine		25-Oct-1903	26-Oct-1903	Charles B. Fields	Parrish, Margaret		Catherine Brannan
Fields	Helen	Agnes	11-May-1902	26-Apr-1902	Charles Fields	Parrish, Margaret	Edward Doud	Winifred Lanahan
Fields	Margaret	Edna	12-Aug-1900	24-Jul-1900	Charles Fields	Parrish, Margaret	Henry Parish	Mary Fields

LAST NAME	FIRST NAME	MIDDLE	BAPTISM	BIRTH	Father	Mother	SPONSORS	
Fields	Mary	Gertrude	05-Mar-1899	17-Feb-1899	Charles Fields	Parrish, Margaret	Joseph Fields	Gertrude Parrish
Fields	Grace	Victoria	11-Dec-1898	17-Nov-1898	Louis Fields	Gerhardt, Laura	George Young	Margaret Ackres
Fields	John	Joseph Patrick	30-Mar-1902	17-Mar-1902	Louis Fields	[Blank], Laura	Thomas Kelly	Margaret Ackres
Fiether	Isabelle	Blanche	20-Jun-1884	03-Jun-1883	John Nelson Fiether	McGehan, Jane	Bernard McKernan	Isabelle McKernan
Finan	Cecelia	Carmelita	06-Dec-1903	22-Nov-1903	Joseph B. Finan	Gilhart, Ann M.	Ernest J. Gilhart	Irene Gilhart
Finerty	Mary		29-Aug-1882	15-Aug-1882	Thomas Finerty	Reilly, Mary	John Reilly	Mary Welsh
Fink	Bernard	Joseph	16-Oct-1904	3-Sep-1904	Henry Fink	Fitzpatrick, Mary A.	Bernard J. Burke	Catherine Burke
Fink	Helen	Margaret	09-Aug-1897	14-Jul-1897	Henry Fink	Fitzpatrick, Mary Alice Frances		Mary McEntee
Fink	Mary	Florence	19-May-1895	03-May-1895	Henry Fink	Fitzpatrick, Mary	James Fitzpatrick	Kate Fitzpatrick
Fink	Mary	Gertrude	18-May-1902	05-May-1902	Henry Fink	Fitzpatrick, Mary		Mary Flaherty
Fink	Ann	Elizabeth	12-Sep-1887	21-Aug-1887	James Fink	Toner, Frances		Ann Bracken
Fink	Catherine	Ann	5-May-1907	22-Apr-1907	James Fink	Loewenshein, Catherine	James T. Riordan	Ann Doyle
Fink	James	Roland	18-Feb-1906	9-Feb-1906	James Fink	Lowenstein, Catherine	John F. Bracken	Ann C. Bracken
Fink	Martin		09-May-1886	29-Apr-1886	James Fink	Toner, Frances M.	James W. Hammond	Joan Hammond
Fink	Thomas	Joseph	24-Jun-1906	15-Jun-1906	John C. Fink	Hennick, Edna	John T. McCarthy	Lillian Baerschmidt
Fink	William	Bernard	11-Jun-1911	20-May-1911	John C. Fink	Hannick, Edna		Mary Elizabeth McNulty
Fink	Peter	Albert	2-Apr-1909	2-Apr-1909	John Fink	Henrick, Edna		
Fink	John	C.	30-Apr-1905	22-Apr-1905	Jophn C. Fink	Hennicks, Edna	John C. Fink	Catherine Sponsal
Fink	John	Henry	29-Sep-1884	29-Dec-1884	Phillip Fink	Farmer, Helen		Dora A. Fink
Finn	Ann		24-Dec-1882	19-Dec-1882	Michael Finn	Smith, Ann	Thomas O'Leary	Elizabeth Creen
Finn	Thomas		14-Feb-1892	07-Feb-1892	Thomas F. Finn	Brazier, Mary	Thomas Brazier	Mary Brazier
Finn	Catherine		11-Dec-1887	29-Nov-1887	Thomas Finn	Brazier, Mary	John C. Carroll	Catherine Herron
Finn	James		18-Aug-1895	06-Aug-1895	Thomas Finn	Brazier, Mary	James Davey	Mary Davey
Finn	Margaret		27-Jun-1897	18-Jun-1897	Thomas Finn	Bragier, Mary		Margaret Davey
Finn	Mary	Elizabeth	15-Dec-1889	09-Dec-1889	Thomas Finn	Bragier, Mary	Maurice Finn	Helen Brager
Finn	Mary		04-Feb-1894	22-Jan-1894	Thomas Finn	Brazier, Mary	Thomas Brazier	Elizabeth Mooney
Finn	William	John	17-Sep-1899	27-Aug-1899	Thomas Finn	Brazier, Mary	William Kelly	Mary Brazier
Finnan	Mary	E.	17-Aug-1890	28-Jul-1890	Joseph B. Finnan	Geelhaar, Ann	Samuel J. France	Julia E. Finnan
Finnan	Anita	Genevieve	31-Jul-1892	23-Jul-1892	Joseph Finnan	Geerhaar, Ann	James Logue	Marcella Finnan
Finnan	Gabrielle	Adalaide	28-Mar-1909	18-Mar-1909	Joseph Finnan	Geelhaar, Ann	Joseph A. Sutten	Ella Geelhaar
Finnan	Josephine		25-Oct-1896	17-Oct-1896	Joseph Finnan	Geerhaar, Ann Mary	Charles [Blank]	Mary Sutton
Finnegan	Edward		12-Aug-1900	30-Jul-1900	Bernard Finnegan	Connolly, Adele	Carroll Barry	Catherine Connolly
Finnegan	Francis	R.	21-May-1898	15-May-1898	Bernard Finnegan	Connolly, Adele	Michael Hessian	Sara Hession
Finnegan	Mary		18-Oct-1896	10-Oct-1896	Bernard Finnegan	Connolly, Adele	John Hessian	
Finnegan	Thomas	Edward	16-Dec-1894	06-Dec-1894	Bernard Finnegan	Connolly, Adele	J.D.Pate	Mary Finnegan
Finnegan	Ann	Mary	19-Mar-1893	08-Mar-1893	Bernard J. Finnegan	Connolly, Adele	J. Thomas Arthur	Mary Connolly
Finnegan	Mary	Elizabeth	22-Oct-1911	7-Oct-1911	Charles C. Finnegan	Fraunholz, Mary		Ann German
Finnegan	Mildred	Eugene	23-Mar-1913	11-Mar-1913	Charles Clifford Finnegan	Fraunholz, Mary E.	Charles Finnegan	Mary Euphemia McManus
Finnegan	John	Thomas	4-Sep-1910	15-Aug-1910	Charles Finnegan	Fraunholz, Mary	John Finnegan	Elsie Finnegan
Finnegan	Margaret		13-Jun-1909	2-Jun-1909	Charles Finnegan	Fraunholz, Mary	William J. Fraunholz	Carolina Fraunholz
Finnegan	Margaret	W.	08-Oct-1899	24-Sep-1899	George Finnegan	Rever, Ann	William Ruddy	Marcella Baker
Finnegan	Mary		16-Jan-1910	27-Dec-1909	James A. Finnegan	Healy, Clara	Eugene Finnegan	Mary Finnegan
Finnegan	Francis	Edmund	15-Sep-1912	27-Aug-1912	James Finnegan	Healey, Clara	Thomas Manning	Mary Manning
Finnegan	John	Bernard	30-May-1915	20-May-1913	John B. Finnegan	McGrane, Susanna	Carroll Finnegan	Mary Toner
Finnegan	John	Dempsey	04-Nov-1888	20-Oct-1888	John Finnegan	Leonard, Alice M.	Joseph Zetelle	Mary McSweeney
Finnegan	Julian	Charles	20-Nov-1892	10-Nov-1892	Laurence D. Finnegan	Ward, Susan	Thomas L. Ruckle	Marey Cole
Finnegan	Laurence	Joseph	25-Nov-1901	20-Nov-1901	Charles Finnegan	Ward, Susanna	John Carr	Elizabeth Finnegan
Finnegan	Elizabeth		03-Aug-1884	28-Jul-1884	Laurence V. Finnegan	Ward, Susanna	Patrick E. Finnegan	Ann Ward
Finnegan	Joseph	W.	28-Oct-1906	23-Oct-1906	Laurence V. Finnegan	Ward, Susanna	Charles Finnegan	Helen Finnegan
Finnegan	Margaret		28-Mar-1886	18-Mar-1886	Laurence V. Finnegan	Ward, Susan	Bernard Finnegan	Mary Finnegan
Finnegan	Helen		03-Jun-1888	22-May-1888	Laurence Valentino Finnegan	Ward, Susan	Henry Cole	Mary Ruckle
Finnegan	James	Allen	19-Oct-1890	13-Oct-1890	Lawrence Finnegan	Ward, S.	Bernard Finnegan	Basil Ruckle
Finnegan	Mary	Catherine	29-Dec-1889	26-Dec-1889	Patrick Finnegan	McGuire, Margaret	James Kennedy	Bridget Finnegan
Finnegan	Patrick	Matthew	14-Mar-1897	10-Mar-1897	Patrick Finnegan	McGuire, Margaret	William Adam	Clara Adam
Finnegan	Peter		23-Dec-1894	13-Dec-1894	Patrick Finnegan	McGuire, Margaret	Peter Duffy	Catherine Finnegan
Finneran	Ann		21-Jul-1890	08-Jul-1890	William Finnegan	Smith, Mary	George Morwood	Ida Burke
Finneran	Mary		01-Sep-1895	19-Aug-1895	William Finnegan	Smith, Mary	George Finnegan	Elizabeth Smith
Finneran	Edward	James	29-May-1910	12-May-1910	James L. Finneran	Emory, Ann	Michael W. Branaghan	Mary M. Foy
Finneran	Honora		13-Aug-1911	24-Jul-1911	James L. Finneran	Evans, Ann	John Mills	Mary A. Lundy
Finnerty	Bernard		20-Dec-1885	10-Dec-1885	Bernard Finnerty	Langan, Ann	Martin Sherrick	Catherine Sherrick
Finnerty	Brian	Joseph	12-Jan-1890	09-Jan-1890	Bernard Finnerty	Langan, Ann	Francis Cavanaugh	Sarah Lester
Finnerty	Delia	Teresa	28-Jan-1883	21-Jan-1883	Bernard Finnerty	Langan, Ann	James Gunning	Delia Langan
Finnerty	James	Bernard	13-May-1888	04-May-1888	Bernard Finnerty	Langan, Ann	Patrick Langan	Cecelia Langan

ST JOHN'S BAPTISMS 1882-1912

LAST NAME	FIRST NAME	MIDDLE	BAPTISM	BIRTH	Father	Mother	SPONSORS	
Finnerty	John	Joseph	20-Mar-1884	20-Mar-1884	Bernard Finnerty	Langan, Ann	Michael Langan	Ann Gilchrist
Finnerty	Mary	Joseph	13-May-1888	04-May-1888	Bernard Finnerty	Langan, Ann	James Gunning	Ann Finnerty
Finnerty	Julia		28-Sep-1884	16-Sep-1884	Thomas Finnerty	Kelly, Mary	James Nolan	Margaret Thornton
Finnessy	Francis		10-Aug-1913	13-Jul-1913	James Finnessy	Johnson, Grace	John Finnessy	Margaret Leland
Finney	Francis		8-Nov-1904	16-Oct-1904	Howard Finney	Friedman, Mary		Rose Agnes Ster
Finnigan	William		13-Mar-1887	07-Mar-1887	William H. Finnigan	Kauffmann, Catherine	John Kauffmann	Catherine Finnegan
Fiorentino	Francis		31-Dec-1900	23-Feb-1897	Enrico Fiorentino	Lenzi, Mary Cristina		Catherine [Blank]
Fiorentino	Mary	Louise	31-Dec-1900	28-Dec-1895	Enrico Fiorentino	Lenzi, Mary Cristina		Celeste Fiorentino
Fiorentino	Mary		31-Dec-1900	16-Sep-1898	Enrico Fiorentino	Lenzi, Mary Cristina		Catherine [Blank]
Fischer	Mary		03-Apr-1901	1-Nov-1900	Edward Fischer	Diggins, Mary		Margaret McKenna
Fischer	Edna	Elizabeth	16-Dec-1914	16-Dec-1914	Henry Fischer	Gilroy, Teresa		Loretta Gilroy
Fischer	Mary	Frances	16-Dec-1914	16-Dec-1914	Henry Fischer	Gilroy, Teresa		C.etta Gilroy
Fischer	Ethel	Mary	7-Jan-1906	26-Dec-1905	John H. Fischer	Stewart, Frances	John Gisrel	Ann Daly
Fischer	Effel	Frances	29-Oct-1893	06-Oct-1893	John Henry Fischer	Stuart, Frances Minerva	Joseph Wells Pugh	Helen Fischer
Fisher	Alma	Mary	22-Jan-1899	30-Aug-1894	Charles Fisher	Bonds, Florence		Elizabeth McKee
Fisher	William	James	28-Oct-1897	03-Nov-1885	Charles Fisher	Bonds, Florence		Thomas Leonard
Fisher	Honora		31-Jul-1904	15-Jun-1904	Edward Fisher	Diggins, Mary		Honora Diggins
Fisher	Rose		26-Oct-1902	15-Oct-1902	Edward Fisher	Diggins, Mary J.		Rose Diggins
Fisher	Ann	Mary	21-Mar-1897	18-Dec-1913	Henry Fischer	McManus, Violet		Elizabeth Mullen
Fisher	Francis		21-Mar-1897	02-Mar-1897	John Fisher	Stewart, Frances	David [Blank]	Ann O'Neill
Fisher	Helen	Irene	21-Jul-1895	04-Jul-1895	John H. Fisher	Stewart, Frances	Joseph W. Pugh	Catherine Kerr
Fisher	Elizabeth		28-Nov-1900	22-Dec-1878	Martin Fisher	Brobaker, Ann		Mrs. Peter J. Campbell
Fisher	Ann	Mary	15-Jun-1890	11-Jun-1890	Michael Fisher	Brown, Mary		
Fisher	James	Laurence	05-Jun-1887	27-May-1887	Michael Fisher	Brown, Mary	James Brown	Mary Brown
Fitzgerald	John	Catherine	10-Jul-1892	20-Jun-1892	Declano Fitzgerald	Doody, Joan	Daniel Scanlon	Alice Collins
Fitzgerald	Catherine		02-Mar-1884	27-Feb-1884	Edward Fitzgerald	Flaherty, Julia	James Daly	Margaret Flaherty
Fitzgerald	Helen		18-Feb-1912	3-Feb-1912	John Fitzgerald	Newell, Mary	Thomas Newell	Margaret McCabe
Fitzgerald	John	James	10-Jan-1915	27-Dec-1914	John J. Fitzgerald	Newell, Mary	James Newell	Katherine Newell
Fitzgerald	Cecelia		22-Apr-1888	13-Apr-1888	Stephen Fitzgerald	Rock, Eliza M.P.		
Fitzgerald	Edna		14-Jun-1885	02-Jun-1885	Stephen Fitzgerald	Rock, Elizabeth		Sara Rock
Fitzgerald	Teresa	Irene	16-Jun-1889	27-May-1889	Stephen Fitzgerald	Rock, Elizabeth	Andrew Wienkem	Mary Murphy
Fitzpatrick	James	Edward	24-May-1885	16-May-1885	James E. Fitzpatrick	Mooney, Mary	James B. Fitzpatrick	Sara Logue
Fitzpatrick	Joseph		17-Jun-1883	10-Jun-1883	James Edward Fitzpatrick	Mooney, Mary	Luke Connolly	Isabelle Swain
Fitzpatrick	Mary	Elizabeth	17-Jan-1892	31-Dec-1891	James Fitzpatrick	Quigley, Mary	Michael Reilly	Margaret O'Connor
Fitzpatrick	Mary	Gladys	02-Dec-1900	6-Nov-1900	James Fitzpatrick	Eccleston, Elle	Michael Fahey	Mary Fitzpatrick
Fitzpatrick	Mary	M.	17-Aug-1902	23-Jul-1902	James Fitzpatrick	Eccleston, Elizabeth	Peter Fitzpatrick	Winifred Geidt
Fitzpatrick	Patrick		15-May-1887	21-Apr-1887	James Fitzpatrick	Mary, Mooney,	Luke Kearney	Alice Mooney
Fitzpatrick	James	Elmer	20-Aug-1905	17-Jul-1905	James H. Fitzpatrick	Eccleston, Ella M.		Mary Cunningham
Fitzpatrick	John	Bernard	30-Jul-1899	22-Jul-1899	John L. Fitzpatrick	Riley, Mary F.	Bernard Riley	Catherine Fitzpatrick
Fitzpatrick	Joseph	Bernard	23-Aug-1908	12-Aug-1908	Joseph B. Fitzpatrick	Porter, Nellie	Charles Wells	Helen Wells
Fitzpatrick	Helen	Mary	23-Sep-1906	30-Aug-1906	Joseph Fitzpatrick	Porter, Helen	Jane Molloy	Helen Mooney
Fitzpatrick	Mary	Catherine	23-Apr-1883	13-Apr-1883	Joseph Fitzpatrick	McMechen, Emma		Mary Lyons
Fitzpatrick	Mary	Teresa	25-Apr-1885	28-Mar-1885	Joseph Fitzpatrick	Helman, Teresa	Thomas Hogan	Margaret Hogan
Fitzpatrick	Dennis		06-Oct-1884	05-Oct-1884	Michael Fitzpatrick	Dwyer, Catherine		Bridget Fitzpatrick
Fitzpatrick	John	Joseph	11-Mar-1894	05-Mar-1894	Michael Fitzpatrick	Gaynor, Mary	John Gaynor	Elizabeth Fitzpatrick
Fitzpatrick	James	Bowen	30-Nov-1905	14-Aug-1905	Michael John Fitzpatrick	Ryan, Margaret Agnes	James Josepheh Burke	Teresa Mary Burke
Fitzpatrick	Cincent	de Paulo	02-Aug-1885	19-Jul-1885	Patrick Fitzpatrick	Donlan, Bridget	Josephine Kiwy	Mary Kiwy
Fitzpatrick	Mary	Eleanor	02-Dec-1888	22-Nov-1888	Patrick Fitzpatrick	Donlan, Bridget	Michael J. Donlan	Mary E. Kirby
Fitzpatrick	Michael		30-Jul-1882	16-Jul-1882	Patrick Fitzpatrick	Donlan, Bridget	James E. Fitzpatrick	Mary Fitzpatrick
Fitzpatrick	Margaret	Mary	05-Jan-1902	21-Dec-1901	Peter Fitzpatrick	Welsh, Lena	H.J. McLenahan	Mary Fitzpatrick
Fitzpatrick	Robert	William	03-Nov-1895	19-Oct-1895	William Fitzpatrick	Colwell, Mary	Robert Thompson	Bridget Fitzpatrick
Flagherty	Edward		19-Apr-1903	31-Mar-1903	Thomas Flagherty	Donnelly, Mary	Thomas Keady	Mary Donnelly
Flaherty	Leon	Mary	22-Aug-1886	15-Aug-1886	Charles Flaherty	Hays, Anastasia	Phillip Loane	Agatha Loane
Flaherty	Julian		04-Oct-1896	11-Sep-1896	James Flaherty	Gavin, Mary		Ann Hughes
Flaherty	Margaret		07-Aug-1887	30-Jul-1887	James Flaherty	Gavin, Mary	Patrick Dunn	Mary Cody
Flaherty	Margaret		26-May-1901	15-May-1901	James Flaherty	Gavin, Mary	Ida Fitzgerald	Michael Flaherty
Flaherty	Mary	Ann	28-Dec-1890	25-Nov-1890	James Flaherty	Gavin, Mary	John Patrick MaGuire	Ann Gavin
Flaherty	Sara		08-Jan-1893	18-Dec-1893	James Flaherty	Gavin, Mary		Catherine Kelly
Flaherty	Winifred		12-Mar-1899	30-Mar-1899	James Flaherty	Gavin, Mary		Josephine Kennedy
Flaherty	John	Joseph	21-Oct-1888	06-Oct-1888	John Flaherty	Kraner, Mary	James Lee	Mary Lee
Flaherty	Mary	Veronica	1-Oct-1911	20-Sep-1911	John Flaherty	McDonnell, Ann	G. John Donnelly	Delia McDonnell
Flaherty	Mary	Catherine	09-Feb-1890	03-Feb-1890	John M. Flaherty	Eckstein, Ann	Thomas Sheridan	Mary Tivele
Flaherty	Raymond	Francis	23-Aug-1914	19-Aug-1914	Raymond Flaherty	Covahey, Katherine L.	Francis Covahey	Alice Sandman

41

LAST NAME	FIRST NAME	MIDDLE	BAPTISM	BIRTH	Father	Mother	SPONSORS	
Flaherty	James	Henry	10-Nov-1907	1-Oct-1907	Thomas Flaherty	Donnelly, Margaret	James Whelan	Mary Conway
Flaherty	John	Joseph	12-Jan-1902	24-Dec-1901	Thomas Flaherty	Donnelly, Margaret	Martin Quinn	Catherine Murray
Flaherty	Margaret	Ann	14-Aug-1904	22-Jul-1904	Thomas Flaherty	Donnelly, Margaret	Peter J. Murray	Ann Sader
Flaherty	Mary		22-Jul-1900	10-Jul-1900	Thomas Flaherty	Donnelly, Margaret	James Dudley	Elizabeth Dudley
Flaherty	Robert	Thomas	4-Feb-1906	11-Jan-1906	Thomas Flaherty	Donnelly, Margaret	Robert J. Campbell	Mary Campbell
Flaherty	Catherine	Winifred	14-Oct-1888	02-Oct-1888	William T. Flaherty	Wherrett, Catherine H.	John R. Salley	Anastasia Hayes
Flaherty	Robert	Thomas	08-Aug-1886	27-Jul-1886	William T. Flaherty	Wherrett, Catherine	A.T.McGreevey	Elizabeth Campbell
Flanagan	Elizabeth	Laura	05-Feb-1888	24-Jan-1888	John Flanagan	Edell, Mary		
Flanagan	Mary	Margaret	16-Feb-1913	2-Feb-1913	Laurence Flanagan	Burns, Ann	Miles Flanagan	Sarah Burns
Flanigan	John	Francis	18-Oct-1891	12-Oct-1891	John Flanigan	Edel, Mary	Francis Flanigan	Margaret Flanigan
Flanigan	Thomas	Aloysius	03-Jul-1898	10-Jun-1898	Thomas Flanigan	Kelly, Mary	Patrick Flanigan	Katherine Kelly
Fleming	Teresa	Mary	19-Sep-1886	08-Sep-1886	Michael Fleming	Devlin, Sara	Henry Wood	Mary Hamilton
Fleury	Elsie	Philomena	12-Dec-1897	10-Dec-1897	William Fleury	Snyder, Josephine	Joseph Snyder	Elizabeth Snyder
Flynn	Catherine	Mary	22-Jun-1913	14-Jun-1913	James Flynn	Kavanaugh, Margaret	Thomas Murtaugh	Catherine McHale
Flynn	Margaret	Mary	19-Oct-1890	22-Sep-1890	James Flynn	Hawkins, Mary	James Keller	Ellen Keller
Flynn	Michael		24-Feb-1884	18-Feb-1884	John Flynn	Ryan, Mary	Thomas Walsh	Margaret Ryan
Flynn	Ann		25-Oct-1896	11-Oct-1896	Matthew Flynn	Smith, Mary	Thomas Gaitley	Mary Kearney
Flynn	Catherine		17-Nov-1889	04-Nov-1889	Matthew Flynn	Smith, Mary	Wm Mulligan	Annie Smith
Flynn	Charles	Matthew Joseph	11-Mar-1894	23-Feb-1894	Matthew Flynn	Smith, Mary		Sara Touhy
Flynn	James	Callan	20-Sep-1891	20-Sep-1891	Michael Thomas Flynn	Callan, Catherine	Martin Callan	Sara Callan
Flynn	Julia	Catherine	15-Nov-1896	09-Sep-1896	William F. Flynn	Shannon, Mary	William Meagher	Margaret Meagher
Foard	William		06-Mar-1887	06-Sep-1846	James Foard	Foard, Henrietta	Daniel Bullock	Catherine Bullock
Foard	William		19-Oct-1912	7-Oct-1912	William Foard	Cromwell, Helen		Mary Cromwell
Foard	Leon	William	25-Aug-1914	25-Aug-1914	William R. Foard	Cromwell, Helen	Charles [Blank]	Mary Hammel
Foard	Leon		22-Aug-1914	22-Aug-1914	William R. Foard	Cromwell, Helen	Charles Gothardt	Mary Hammel
Foble	George	Joseph	1-May-1904	17-Apr-1904	Elmer Foble	Smyth, Joan	Joseph Smeykal	Mary Smeykal
Foble	Mary	Josephine	20-Jan-1895	06-Jan-1895	Elmer Foble	Smith, Joan		Alice King
Fogarty	James	Joseph	11-Aug-1901	01-Aug-1901	James Fogarty	McKewen, Ann	William McKeever	Helen Crowley
Fogarty	John	Leonard	8-Jan-1911	23-Dec-1910	James Fogarty	McKewen, Ann		
Fogarty	George	Leon	11-Mar-1906	24-Jan-1906	John Fogarty	Benton, Sarah	George Leo McCart	Mary Brentine
Fogarty	William	Burke	05-Aug-1894	22-Jun-1894	John Fogarty	Benton, Sara	Michael Vallee	Catherine Kernan
Fogerty	Sarah	Vincent	25-Jun-1905	11-Jun-1905	James J. Fogarty	Rock, Frances A.	John McFaddin	Loretta German
Foley	Joseph	Agnes	11-Apr-1894	29-Mar-1894	John Foley	Lutz, Ann	John Cassidy	Catherine Flynn
Foley	Genevieve	David	23-Mar-1897	14-Mar-1897	John Foley	Lutz, Ann	Catherine Fol	Catherine Foley
Foley	Francis	Lutz	15-Dec-1887	01-Dec-1887	John T. Foley	Lutz, Ann M.	Joan Lutz	Margaret Foley
Foley	Ann	Angela	30-Jul-1891	12-Jul-1891	John Thomas Foley	Lutz, Ann Mary	Joseph A. Lutz	Margaret B. Foley
Foley	Mary		16-Oct-1889	02-Oct-1889	John Thomas Foley	Lutz, Ann Mary	James Patrick Foley	Mary Ann Foley
Foley	Elizabeth	Margaret	01-May-1884	14-Jan-1884	Patrick Foley	Foucht, Ann	Michael Grogan	Mary Grogan
Fonshell	Mary		18-Dec-1892	25-Nov-1892	William Fonshell	Gannon, Cecelia	Francis Gray	Ella Dignan
Foos	Laura		16-Mar-1884	31-Jan-1884	Thomas Foos	Smith, Jennie		Mary Mooney
Foos/Sinclar	Francis		21-Dec-1891	11-Apr-1811	John Sinclar	Sanders, Charity		Martha Lancaster
Fopless	James	Campbell	19-Aug-1883	01-Aug-1883	George Fopless	Campbell, Isabelle	Felix Campbell	Ann Brown
Ford	James		25-Feb-1883	11-Feb-1883	John Ford	Miles, Rose	Bernard Miles	Margaret Miles
Forde	Margaret	Mary	8-Nov-1903	2-Nov-1903	Daniel A. Forde	McDonnell, Margaret	John Forde	Catherine McIntyre
Forest	Ida	Elizabeth	23-Aug-1903	26-Jul-1903	Edward Forest	Wright, Bedelia		Lillian Clemson
Forest	Thomas	William	22-Jun-1898	31-Jan-1896	Edward Forrest	Wright, Delia		Mary Wright
Forestell	John	Samuel	18-Dec-1898	20-Nov-1898	William Forestell	Six, Helen		Caroline Noll
Forrest	Edward	Ray	01-Sep-1901	23-Jan-1901	Edward Forrest	Wright, Delia	Edward Clemsen	Mary Clemsen
Forrest	Mary	Agnes	24-Jun-1898	01-Dec-1896	Edward Forrest	Wright, Delia		Mary Clemsen
Forrest	Aloysius		30-Mar-1902	26-Jan-1902	Edwin Forrest	Wright, B.		Mary Moylan
Forrest	Martin		28-May-1899	10-May-1899	Edwin Forrest	Wright, Bridget	Pascal Lincoln	Lina Serio
Forrest	John	Wesley	25-Aug-1895	03-Aug-1895	Edwin Nelson Forrest	Wright, Adelia	Wesley Forrest	Sallie McCourt
Forrest	Elizabeth		22-Sep-1910	12-Oct-1834	James Forrest	Hansen, Elizabeth		Rose Monaghan
Forrest	George		28-Apr-1897	23-Apr-1897	Martin J. Forrest	Laragy, Mary Catherine		
Forrest	Charles	Carroll	17-Oct-1901	05-Sep-1901	William Forrest	Laragy, Catherine		Bessie Smith
Forrest	Edward		26-Oct-1887	24-Oct-1887	William Forrest	Laragy, Catherine		
Forrest	Helen		07-Jun-1898	03-Jun-1898	William Forrest	Laragy, Catherine	Francis Smith	Margaret Kelly
Forrest	Julian	Ignatius	09-Aug-1899	31-Jul-1899	William Forrest	Laragy, Catherine	Eugene Kelly	Julia Smith
Forrest	Loretta		07-Jun-1898	03-Jun-1898	William Forrest	Laragy, Catherine	Julia Smith	Joseph Laragy
Forrest	William		05-Sep-1886	27-Aug-1886	William J. Forrest	Laragy, Catherine	Michael Hughes	Margaret Laragy
Forrest	Raymond	Edward	25-Feb-1894	11-Feb-1894	William John Forrest	Laragy, Mary Catherine	Jesse Charles Smith	Cecelia Laragy
Forrester	Edward	R.	30-Oct-1904	7-Oct-1904	Edward Forrester	Wright, Delia		Catherine Fitzgerald
Forstell	Leon	William	06-Aug-1901	10-Jun-1901	Walter Forstell	Six, Lena		Mrs. John Kelly

42

LAST NAME	FIRST NAME	MIDDLE	BAPTISM	BIRTH	Father	Mother	SPONSORS
Forte	John	Edward	15-Dec-1889	04-Dec-1889	Albert Forte	Smith, Joan	Alice Teresa Rock
Foster	Carl	Vinton	14-Mar-1886	25-Feb-1886	Nicholas T. Foster	Genoy, Mary	Michael Murray
Foster	Mary	Catherine	20-May-1888	10-May-1888	Nicolas Foster	Genoy, Margaret	Thomas Genoy
Fouchell	William	Jacob	17-Jun-1900	19-May-1900	William Fouchell	Gannon, Cecelia	D. Gannon
Foushell	Rose	Mary	12-Jun-1898	07-May-1898	William Foushell	Gannon, Cecelia	John Connolly
Fowler	Gertrude		29-Apr-1888	11-Mar-1888	Francis Fowler	McGriffin, Margaret A.	Joseph Walther
Fowler	Ann	Florence	05-Aug-1888	19-Jul-1888	George Fowler	McCusker, Mary J.	Mary Walther
Fowler	Bernard	Joseph	29-Mar-1896	02-Mar-1896	George Fowler	McCusker, Mary	Catherine McCusker
Fowler	Catherine	Mary	15-Jul-1894	22-Jun-1894	George Fowler	McCusker, Mary	Licia McCusker
Fowler	Helen	M.	11-Sep-1898	21-Aug-1898	George Fowler	McKusker, Mary	Ann McCusker
Fowler	Mary	Ellen	12-Jan-1890	01-Jan-1890	George Fowler	McCusker, Mary	Catherine McKusker
Fowler	William	Wesley	07-Aug-1892	23-Jul-1892	William George Fowler	McCluskey, Mary Joan	Mary Chaney
Foy	John	Richard	16-Mar-1913	24-Feb-1913	Richard Foy	Finnegan, Mary	Agnes Doory
Foy	Mary	Catherine	22-May-1910	6-May-1910	Richard Foy	Finnegan, Mary	Mary Dugan
Francis	Frederick		30-Sep-1900	18-Sep-1900	Peter Francis	Weber, Mary Lena	Honora Finneran
Frank	Mary	Ann	09-Apr-1899	06-Apr-1899	Thomas Frank	Wright, Elizabeth C.	Margaret Hogarty
Franz	William	Claude	15-Feb-1891	02-Feb-1891	Henry C. Franz	McNulty, Ann	Joseph Wright
Fraser	Robert		15-Jul-1883	05-Jul-1883	Robert Fraser	McAllister, Catherine	Thomas Franz
Frasier	Neomans	Holton	15-Jul-1894	29-Jun-1894	George Frasier	Holton, Mary	Francis Haughey
Frazer	Ida	Burch	03-Nov-1884	21-Sep-1884	Richard Frazer	Burke, Catherine	Bedela Hensil
Frazier	Mary	Genevieve	09-Apr-1882	26-Mar-1882	Henry A. Frazier	Golden, Ann	Mary Garrett
Frazier	William	Henry	17-Sep-1893	25-Aug-1893	Henry A. Frazier	Frazier, Hattie A.	Ann Hulahan
Frazier	Mary	Grace	23-Aug-1896	22-Jul-1896	Henry E. Frazier	Fink, Henrietta	Elizabeth McShane
Frazier	Richard	Burch	15-Feb-1883	21-Dec-1882	Richard Burch Frazier	Burke, Sara Catherine	Regina Koenig
Frazier	Charles		04-Jan-1889	06-Nov-1888	Richard Frazier	Burke, Catherine	Mary Berterman
Frazier	Laura		19-Jan-1882	21-Jul-1881	Richard Frazier	Burke, Catherine	Elizabeth Schrufer
Frechlin	Henry	Howard	01-Jun-1890	22-May-1890	Andrew Frechlin	Doyle, Margaret	Mary F. Burke
Frederick	Arthur	J.	17-Feb-1887	Mar 1883	Charles J. Frederick	Brown, Ella	Mary Francesca Burke
Frederick	Edward	Raymond	08-Sep-1895	21-Aug-1895	Joseph Frederick	Manning, Delia	Ann Louise McIntyre
Frederick	Joseph	Patrick	10-Apr-1898	13-Mar-1898	Joseph Frederick	Manion, Bridget	Eleanora Simmons
Frederick	Sara	Rebecca	28-Feb-1897	06-Feb-1897	Joseph Frederick	Barry, Catherine	Mary Curley
Frederick	Mary	Arthur	09-Sep-1894	23-Nov-1894	Leo Frederick	Arthur, Elizabeth	Ann McNamee
Frederick	Isabelle	Leon	04-Feb-1883	09-Dec-1882	Louis Frederick	Zoeller, Catherine	Bridget McNamara
Freedy	Edward		20-Mar-1887	08-Mar-1887	Dedrick Freedy	Kavanaugh, Catherine	Mary Berry
Freeman	Mary		21-Jul-1883	21-Jul-1883	Thomas Freeman	Kavanaugh, Catherine E.	Mary Arthur
Freeman	James	Aloysius	19-Jul-1891	14-Jul-1891	Thomas M. Freeman	Kavanaugh, Catherine E.	Mary Ann Streckfus
Freeman	Joseph	Alphonse	04-Aug-1886	04-Aug-1886	Thomas M. Freeman	Cavanaugh, Catherine E.	Mary A. Freeman
Freeman	Mary	Gertrude	03-Jun-1894	27-May-1894	Thomas Martin Freeman	Kavanaugh, Catherine	Ann Ahern
Freeman	Thomas	Joseph	22-Apr-1888	11-Apr-1888	Thomas Martin Freeman	Lavery, Ann	Catherine A. Cavanaugh
French	Ann		24-Jan-1892	11-Jan-1892	Edward French	Lavery, Ann	Mary Ann Martin
French	Bernard	Samurl	31-Jan-1909	23-Jan-1909	Edward French	Lavery, Ann	Mary Ann Lavery
French	Catherine		30-Apr-1911	20-Apr-1911	Edward French	Lavery, Ann	Bernard Lavery
French	Cecelia	Madeline	17-Jul-1904	6-Jul-1904	Edward French	Lavery, Ann	Frances Lavery
French	James		24-Feb-1907	16-Feb-1907	Edward French	Lavery, Ann	Mary Louise Grogan
French	Margaret		06-Jul-1902	28-Jun-1902	Edward French	Lavery, Ann	Mary Lidner
French	Mary	Cecelia	03-Aug-1890	22-Jul-1890	Edward French	Lavery, Ann	Helen Doolin
French	Samuel	Albert	18-Jan-1914	4-Jan-1914	Edward French	Lavery, Ann	Elizabeth Lavery
French	Thomas	Joseph	21-Aug-1915	19-Aug-1915	Raphael French	Donahue, Catherine	Elizabeth Reilly
French	Robert	Anthony	08-Jun-1902	[Blank]	Samuel French	Gilbert, Ann	Teresa Lembach
French	Rose	Francis	16-Aug-1896	07-Aug-1896	Samuel French	Gilbert, Mary	Margaret Farrell
French	Ann	Mary	11-Oct-1885	17-Aug-1885	Thomas French	McGuire, Ann E.	Katherine Mead
Freschlein	Ann	Catherine	5-Nov-1902	4-Nov-1902	Andrew Freschlein	Baird, Matilda	Ella French
Freschlein	Bridget	Ann	13-Apr-1884	07-Apr-1884	Andrew Freschlein	Doyle, Margaret	Katherine Conlehan
Freschlein	George	Thomas	14-Oct-1894	04-Oct-1894	Andrew Freschlein	Doyle, Margaret	Mary Carroll
Freshline	Mary		06-May-1888	27-Apr-1888	Andrew Freishline	Doyle, Margaret	John Coffey
Freshline	Andrew		21-Feb-1886	13-Feb-1886	Andrew Freshline	Doyle, Margaret	Thomas Colford
Freshline	Helen		11-Sep-1892	04-Sep-1892	Andrew Freshline	Doyle, Margaret	James Owens
Freshline	Mary	Elizabeth	25-Nov-1906	9-Nov-1906	Andrew Freshline	Baird, Matilda	Henry Levell
Frier	John	B.	11-May-1890	About 1812	Aaron Frier	Miller, Mary	Bernard J. McCourt
Frisby	Francis	Oliver	12-Feb-1893	01-Feb-1893	George Frisby	Dixon, Mary	Michael Freshline
Frisby	Rose	Ann	12-Feb-1893	01-Feb-1893	George Frisby	Dixon, Mary	Mary E. Kelly
Frist	Mary	Elizabeth	16-Sep-1883	03-Jul-1883	John Edgar Frist	Arthur, Margaret Ann	Mary Geigan
Fronshell	Ann	Elizabeth	29-Oct-1895	24-Sep-1895	William Fronshell	Gannon, Cecelia	Mary Tracey
							Elizabeth Hebrauk
							Martin Hayes
							Browden Beasham
							Henry Whitney
							John Dugan
							Benjamin A. Hart
							Edward Healey
							Cornelius Roach
							Bernard McCusker
							Rose Connolly
							Mary Connelly
							Mary Genoy
							Mary McKenna
							William Cain
							James S. Cunningham
							Stephen Fitzgerald
							Michael James McGovern
							James Kelly
							Michael McNamee
							Charles Reid
							William Kelly
							J. Thomas Arthur
							Leonard Streckfus
							Simon V. Cullen
							John Francis Ahern
							Martin Andrew Freeman
							Michael Grogan
							Edward French
							Daniel Leo Lavery
							Samuel J. French
							Hugh Lavery
							James Lavery
							Samuel French
							William French
							Patrick Doran
							John Casey
							James Baird
							Margaret Mitchell
							Anastasia Owens
							Martha Kendall
							Bridget McCourt
							Dennis B. Sweeney
							Dennis B. Sweeney
							John Thomas Arthur
							Elizabeth Frederick
							Ann Connolly
							John Zang

ST JOHN'S BAPTISMS 1882-1912

LAST NAME	FIRST NAME	MIDDLE	BAPTISM	BIRTH	Father	Mother	SPONSORS
Fulco	Francis		4-Jul-1915	22-Jun-1915	Joseph Fulco	Danili, Lucia	Tina Salerno
Fuller	Mary	Loretta	04-Dec-1896	24-Jun-1880	Joseph Fuller	Burgan, Josephine	Gertrude Logan
Fuller	George	Francis	06-Oct-1896	10-Mar-1825	Josephiah Fuller	Pible, Mary	George Hoen
Fuller	John	Joseph	23-Dec-1891	06-Jul-1847	Moses Fulton	Nelson, Agnes	
Fulton	Irene	Isabelle	02-Jul-1882	20-Jun-1882	William Fulton	Burke, Frances	William McClusky
Fulton	Mary	Frances	14-Dec-1884	13-Dec-1884	William N. Fulton	Burke, Frances	Clarabel Richardson
Fulton	Mary	Frances	15-Dec-1885	13-Dec-1885	William N. Fulton	Burke, Frances	Sarah Ryan
Fulton	Thomas	Hamilton	14-Dec-1884	13-Dec-1884	William N. Fulton	Burke, Frances	Sarah Ryan
Fulton	Thomas	Hamilton	15-Dec-1885	13-Dec-1885	William N. Fulton	Burke, Frances	Mary Fulton
Funk	Helen	Loretta	17-May-1914	7-May-1914	John Funk	Gallagher, Helen	Mary Fulton
Furlong	John	Cyril	11-Aug-1901	06-Aug-1901	Michael Furlong	Burns, Mary	Mary Gallagher
Furlong	Mary	Rose	16-Jul-1893	05-Jul-1893	Michael Furlong	Burns, Mary G.	Edward Burns
Furlong	Michael	Gerald	12-Dec-1897	28-Nov-1897	Michael Furlong	Burns, Mary	William Hyland
Furlong	Monica		15-Jan-1899	06-Jan-1899	Michael Furlong	Burns, Mary	Richard Byrne
Furlong	Walter	Burns	08-Sep-1895	30-Aug-1895	Michael Furlong	Burns, Mary	James Burns
Furlong	William	Edward	30-Nov-1902	21-Nov-1902	Michael Furlong	Burns, Mary	Nicholas Furlong
Furlong	Joseph	Paul	28-Feb-1904	11-Feb-1904	Michael J. Furlong	Burns, Mary G.	Michael Burns
Furlong	William		20-Jan-1884	13-Jan-1884	Patrick Furlong	Murphy, Margaret	Joseph Byrne
Furlong	Margaret	Jeannete	05-Nov-1893	27-Oct-1893	Phillip Furlong	Coffey, Ann	Richard Williams
Furlong	Catherine	Margaret	7-Dec-1913	24-Nov-1913	William V. Furlong	Sturgeon, Catherine B.	Nicholas Furlong
Furlong/Moore	Mary		04-Jul-1903	09-Oct-1832	John Furlong	[Blank]	Peter Furlong
Gady	Richard		11-Apr-1897	05-Apr-1897	John Gady	Byrne, Ann	Margaret Dyer
Gaffey	Alice		01-Apr-1885	18-Feb-1885	James Gaffey	Carroll, Bridget Ann	Mary Murphy
Gaffey	Bertha	Clara	24-Aug-1901	12-Aug-1901	James Gaffey	Feely, Mary	Joseph Carroll
Gaffey	Lucy	Virginia	03-Jan-1892	10-Dec-1891	James Gaffey	Feeley, Mary	Mary Gaffey
Gaffey	Mary	Loretta	30-Dec-1894	21-Dec-1894	James Gaffey	Feeley, Mary	Michael Gaffey
Gaffey	Rose		20-Aug-1893	05-Aug-1893	James Gaffey	Feeley, Mary	Joseph Hoden
Gaffey	Ann		21-Nov-1889	09-Nov-1889	John Gaffey	Carroll, Ann	Mary Gaffey
Gaffey	Genevieve		05-Sep-1897	22-Aug-1897	John Gaffey	Carroll, Ann	Michael Shanahan
Gaffey	John	Thomas	03-Aug-1901	28-Jul-1901	John Gaffey	Carroll, Ann	Martin Redington
Gaffey	Mary		22-Dec-1895	08-Dec-1895	John Gaffey	Carroll, Ann	William Gaffey
Gaffey	William		23-Oct-1887	21-Oct-1887	John T. Gaffey	Carroll, Ann	William Gaffey
Gaffey	Ann	Margaret	02-Dec-1894	18-Nov-1894	Michael Gaffey	Gaffney, Joan	Matthew Carroll
Gaffney	Henry	Charles	31-Jul-1887	24-Jul-1887	Michael J. Gaffney	Pinning, Joan C.	Michael Gaffey
Gaffney	Thomas	Joseph	22-Jan-1893	08-Jan-1893	Michael Joseph Gaffney	Pinning, Joan E.	John Hagerty
Gaffney	William	Thomas	21-Oct-1888	17-Oct-1888	Michael Joseph Gaffney	Pinning, Ann Elizabeth	John T. Gaffney
Gaffney	Margaret	Eleanor	21-Feb-1915	6-Feb-1915	Thomas Joseph Gaffney	Cavalier, Mary Eleanor	Michael Fitzgerald
Gagliandi	Mary	Margaret	30-Apr-1893	22-Jan-1893	John Gagliandi	Powers, Teresa	John Henry Pining
Gahan	Catherine	Pembroke	16-Jan-1887	28-Dec-1886	John Gahan	Casserly, Margaret	Henry Gaffney
Gahan	James		15-Sep-1889	27-Aug-1889	John Gahan	Casserly, Margaret	James Gagliandi
Gahan	John	Francis	08-Jan-1882	29-Dec-1881	John Gahan	Casserly, Margaret	Michael Roddy
Gahan	Margaret		01-Oct-1893	16-Sep-1893	John Gahan	Casserly, Margaret	
Gaitely	Ellenore	Elizabeth	29-Jun-1884	14-Jun-1884	John Gaitely	Healey, Margaret	John Kelly
Gaitley	Katherine	Joan	05-Jun-1887	21-May-1887	Michael Gaitley	Malone, Ann	Thomas Casserly
Gaitley	Margaret		10-May-1896	23-Apr-1896	Michael Gaitley	Malone, Ann	Michael McDermott
Gaitley	Mary	Ann	25-Sep-1887	14-Sep-1887	Michael Gaitley	Malone, Ann	William Delaney
Gaitley	Mary		09-Aug-1885	30-Jul-1885	Michael Gaitley	Malone, Ann	Henry O'Brien
Gaitley	Thomas		23-Jun-1889	04-Jun-1889	Michael Gaitley	Malone, Ann	John Furlow
Gaitly	Michael		16-Mar-1884	07-Mar-1884	John Gaitly	Malone, Ann	William Rowe
Gallagher	Charles	James	13-Sep-1891	01-Sep-1891	John Gallagher	Murphy, Mary	William Flynn
Gallagher	Francis	Patrick	13-Sep-1891	01-Sep-1891	John Gallagher	Murphy, Mary	Joan Malone
Gallagher	Nina	Elizabeth	09-Oct-1898	25-Sep-1898	Joseph Gallagher	Kelly, Mary	Martin Gaitly
Gallagher	William		04-Sep-1899	04-Sep-1899	Joseph Gallagher	Kelly, Mary	Joseph Rigney
Gallagher	Catherine		06-Mar-1892	23-Feb-1892	Patrick Gallagher	Garrity, Delia	Matthew Kelly
Gallagher	Helen		01-Apr-1886	29-Mar-1886	Patrick Gallagher	Gereghty, Delia	George Bruckheiser
Gallagher	Helen		22-Jun-1890	11-Jun-1890	Patrick Gallagher	Garrity, Bridget	David Garrity
Gallagher	Joseph	Leo	25-Jun-1893	15-Jun-1893	Patrick Gallagher	Garrity, Julia	Thomas Gereghty
Gallagher	Sara		10-Aug-1887	01-Aug-1887	Patrick Gallagher	Garrity, Delia	Malachi Kelly
Gallant	Margaret	Mary	17-May-1908	1-May-1908	Seymore A. Gallant	Bradley, Mary	George Connor
Gallant	Catherine	Albert	19-Jul-1914	3-Jul-1914	Seymour Gallant	Bradley, Mary	Alexander Bradley
Gallant	Francis	Bradley	21-Apr-1912	9-Apr-1912	Seymour Gallant	Bradley, Mary B.	George J. Eckenrode
Galligher	Mary		30-Aug-1896	19-Aug-1896	John Galligher	Mulhroy, Elizabeth	Daniel Driscoll

							Tina Salerno
							Gertrude Logan
							Clarabel Richardson
							Sarah Ryan
							Sarah Ryan
							Mary Fulton
							Mary Fulton
							Mary Fulton
							Mary Gallagher
							Mary Dunn
							Philomena Kamphaus
							Mary Byrne
							Mary Code
							Annine Burns
							Ann McManus
							Nellie M. Kelly
							Elizabeth Murphy
							Margaret Fitzpatrick
							Rose A. Sturgeon
							Mary Murphy
							Mary C. Smith
							Mary Gaffey
							Anastasia Molloy
							Teresa McNamara
							Mary Gaffey
							Mary Ann Dunn
							Mary Gaffey
							Bridget Caraugh
							Bridget Conway
							Welch, Mary
							Ann Pinning
							Ann Pinning
							Margaret Ann Collett
							Catherine Mary Collett
							Ann Gaffney
							Delores Gagliandi
							Bridget Kelly
							Mary Casserly
							Anna McDermott
							Elizabeth Larkins
							Margaret Casserly
							Mary McKenna
							Mary Flynn
							Catherine Malone
							Mary Murphy
							Ann Flynn
							Margaret Malone
							Catherine Gaitly
							Ann Murphy
							Sara McKenna
							Katherine Bruckheiser
							Margaret Garrity
							Helen Gereghty
							Rose Kelly
							Catherine Connor
							Sara Garrity
							Nettie Parr
							Caroline Siegle
							Ann Clancy
							Kavanaugh, Mary

44

LAST NAME	FIRST NAME	MIDDLE	BAPTISM	BIRTH	Father	Mother	SPONSORS
Gallop	Thomas	Martin	28-Oct-1898	06-Jan-1825	John Gallop	Coleman, Rachel	George Stemple
Galloway	Thomas	Peter	22-Jun-1890	06-Jun-1890	Thomas Galloway	Baldwin, Martha	Joseph Burton Pleasants	Emma Pleasants
Galvin	Helen	Patrick	12-Jan-1890	03-Jan-1890	John T. Galvin	Keough, Ella	Thomas Leland	Mary Keogh
Galvin	William	Leland	09-Jan-1887	27-Dec-1886	John T. Galvin	Keogh, Ella	Thomas Keough	Mary Galvin
Galvin	Mary	Helen	11-Jan-1891	30-Dec-1890	John Thomas Galvin	Keogh, Helen	Andrew Keogh	Ann Keogh
Galvin	Thomas	Keogh	10-Jan-1892	24-Dec-1891	John Thomas Galvin	Keogh, Helen	Thomas Leland	Helen Murphy
Gammie	Mary	Elizabeth	05-Aug-1900	26-Jul-1900	Charles Gammie	Ward, Sara	George Gammie	Mary Ward
Gammie	Edward		11-Apr-1882	10-Apr-1882	James Gammie	Steadman, Catherine		Mary Elizabeth Fannon
Gammie	James	Fenwick	24-Jun-1884	22-Jun-1884	James Gammie	Steadman, Catherine	Charles Gammie	Mary Gammie
Gammie	William	Dorsett	06-Sep-1896	August 1896	William E. Gammie	Cunningham, Mary Alice	Charles Gammie	Ann Hogan
Gammie	Paul	Edward Bernard	19-Aug-1894	09-Aug-1894	William Edward Jos. Gammie	Cunningham, Mary Alice	George Bernard Gammie	Emma Eve Meade
Gammitt	Ellen		13-Sep-1903	31-Aug-1903	Charles F. Gammie	Ward, Sarah E.	Leo Gammie	Mary E. Ward
Ganly	Charles		10-Jun-1906	26-May-1906	August Ganly	Kaupman, Mary	Charles Ganly	Carolina Tippett
Gannon	John	Jacob	24-Jul-1892	15-Jul-1892	John Gannon	Mahoney, Delia	William Gannon	Mary Gannon
Gannon	Ann		17-Dec-1882	10-Dec-1882	Michael Gannon	Dunn, Mary Ann	William Bavis	Alice Bavis
Gannon	Michael	Aloysius	01-Aug-1886	26-Jul-1886	Michael Gannon	Down, Mary Ann	Michael Dean	Catherine Flynn
Gannon	James	Joseph	07-Oct-1894	03-Oct-1894	Michael J. Gannon	Downs, Mary H.	George Devine	Alice Bavis
Gannon	Thomas	Joseph	17-Sep-1911	25-Aug-1911	Robert F. Gannon	Johnson, Blanche		
Ganster	Karl		13-Nov-1898	29-Oct-1898	Henry Ganster	McGraw, Sophia	John McGraw	Ann Dowd
Ganster	Mary	Dorothy	01-Jun-1902	19-May-1902	Henry Ganster	McGraw, Sarah		Mary McGraw
Ganster	Sarah	Genevieve	06-Oct-1895	23-Sep-1895	Henry W. Ganster	McGrath, Sarah	Nicholas Ganster	Ella Ganster
Ganster	Henry	Walter	24-Aug-1890	14-Aug-1890	Henry Walter Ganster	McGraw, Sara Genevieve	John McGraw	Laura Mary Ganster
Ganster	John		14-May-1893	24-Apr-1893	Henry Walter Ganster	McGraw, Sara Genevieve	Samuel Joseph Miles	Ann Elizabeth Miles
Garan	Margaret		17-Dec-1882	15-Dec-1882	Matthew Garen	Lyons, Margaret		
Gardiner	Emma	Francis	19-Jun-1887	24-May-1887	Columbo Gardiner	Carroll, Emma		Ada Carroll
Gardiner	Edward	Cleveland	03-Aug-1884	29-Jun-1884	John C. Gardiner	Harker, Rebecca	John E. Hagerty	Christina Dickerman
Gardiner	Mary	Melbey	21-Aug-1887	03-Aug-1887	John C. Gardiner	Harker, Rebecca B.		Margaret Sullivan
Gardner	Jennete	Sarah May	24-Apr-1901	02-May-1883	Richard Gardner	Freeman, Mary		Ellenor Fallon
Garrett	Joseph		11-Oct-1885	29-Sep-1885	Joseph Garrett	Connelly, Ambrosia		Mary Connelly
Garrett	John		24-Apr-1887	13-Apr-1887	Joseph T. Garrett	Connelly, Ambrosia		Julia Connolly
Garrett	Agnes		27-Nov-1904	19-Nov-1904	William C. Garrett	Rosenburger, Barbara E.	James McCarthy	Mary McCarthy
Garrett	Richard	Goff	13-Jul-1902	04-Jul-1902	William Garrett	Rosenberger, Barbara	William B. Gillen	Bridget Regina Daley
Garrett	William	F. McKay	27-Sep-1896	14-Sep-1896	William Garrett	McAleer, Nora		Elizabeth Monaghan
Garrett	Ann		23-May-1886	18-Apr-1886	William T. Garett	McCall, Mary	Edward Warfield	Sara Derry
Garrett	Mary		16-Mar-1884	23-Feb-1884	William T. Garrett	McCall, Mary	John Leilly	Jennie Doory
Garrick	James	Joseph	01-May-1902	14-Apr-1902	Peter Garrick	Croghan, Mary		
Garrigan	Catherine	Elizabeth	13-Oct-1889	02-Oct-1889	Edward Garrigan	Follan, Catherine	Owen Garrigan	Mary Agnes Kelly
Garrigan	Genevieve	Alice	21-Jul-1895	14-Jul-1895	Edward Garrigan	Follan, Catherine	Patrick Lee	Margaret Reynolds
Garrigan	Margaret		09-Jan-1898	06-Jan-1898	Edward Garrigan	Follan, Catherine	Henry Kyne	Ella Garrigan
Garrigan	Mary	Ann	24-Sep-1893	20-Sep-1893	Edward Garrigan	Follan, Catherine	Joseph Garrigan	Ann Needham
Garrigan	Ann	Margaret	26-Jul-1913	8-Jul-1913	Owen Garrigan	Golden, Ann		Mary Baker
Garrigan	Catherine		26-Jul-1913	8-Jul-1913	Owen Garrigan	Golden, Ann		Ellen Baker
Garrigan	Laurence	Jerome	30-May-1909	14-May-1909	Owen Garrigan	Golden, Ann		Nellie Garrigan
Garrigan	Helen	Jerome	4-Aug-1912	18-Jul-1912	Owen Thomas Garrigan	Richmuller, Josephine	John Eichelman	Helen Garrigan
Garritee	Edward		02-Jan-1896	13-Nov-1895	Charles Garritee	Moylan, Mary	Andrew Clayton	Rose Clayton
Garrity	Mary	Patrick	15-Mar-1896	05-Mar-1896	Andrew Garrity	Moylan, Mary E.	John Garrity	Margaret Kelleher
Garrity	John	Earl	12-Jan-1902	27-Dec-1901	Andrew J. Garrity	Pruett, Blanche	John Garrity	V. Rowland
Garrity	Bernard	Augustine	17-Jul-1910	30-Jun-1910	Bernard Garrity	Kellenstein, Elizabeth	Edward Dalton	Mary Garrity
Garrity	Edward	Elizabeth	2-Nov-1902	11-Oct-1902	Bernard Garrity	Kilchenstein, Elizabeth	William Roberts	Ann Bonlen
Garrity	Mary	Louis	22-Dec-1912	28-Nov-1912	Bernard Garrity	Kelshauskiss, Elizabeth	Joseph Watson	Mary Watson
Garrity	Robert		19-Feb-1911	30-Jan-1911	Michael Garrity	Golden, Ann		Bernardine Clarity
Garrity	Bernard		04-Feb-1902	28-Jan-1902	Michael Garrity	Love, Lilly	Patrick Garrity	Katherine Garrity
Garrity	Margaret		16-Nov-1913	28-Sep-1913	Patrick Garrity	Love, Lillian	John F. Novotny	Margaret Dalton
Garrity	Catherine	Margaret	9-Nov-1902	30-Oct-1902	Timothy Garrity	Cain, Catherine	Bernard Garrity	Ella Cain
Garrity	Agnes		22-Jan-1893	11-Jan-1893	Timothy Garrity	O'Hare, Margaret	John Ward	Mary Ann Ward
Garrity	Eleanor		11-Aug-1889	02-Aug-1889	Timothy Garrity	O'Hara, Margaret	Thomas Garrity	Mary O'Hara
Garrity	George		29-Dec-1895	15-Dec-1895	Timothy Garrity	O'Hara, Margaret	George O'Hare	Sarah Garrity
Garrity	James		01-Feb-1891	18-Jan-1891	Timothy Garrtiy	O'Hara, Margaret	Edward O'Hara	Helen Garrity
Garrity	Joseph	Sydney	28-May-1905	11-May-1905	William F. Garrity	Kilchenstein, Elizabeth	Joseph S. Watson	Elizabeth M. Watson
Garrity	Joseph		30-Jan-1911	30-Jan-1911	William Garrity	Kilchenstein, Elizabeth		
Garrity	Mary	Catherine	22-Oct-1900	12-Oct-1900	William Garrity	Kilchenstein, Elizabeth	William Braden	Catherine Garrity
Garrity	William	Joan	23-Mar-1897	01-May-1897	William Garrity	Kilchenstein, Elizabeth	George W. Bradan	Mary Kilchenstein
Garvey	Mary	C.	21-Oct-1902	21-Oct-1902	James Garvey	Koenig, Mary		Catherine Keonig

LAST NAME	FIRST NAME	MIDDLE	BAPTISM	BIRTH	Father	Mother	SPONSORS	
Garvey	Bernard		18-Aug-1889	18-Jul-1889	Thomas Garvey	Hickman, Mary	John Garvey	Margaret Garvey
Garvey	Mary	Helen	11-Jul-1886	24-May-1886	Thomas Garvey	Mangan, Mary		Susan Bishop
Garvey	Margaret	Catherine	04-May-1884	20-Apr-1884	Thomas J. Garvey	Manion, Mary Catherine	Terence McMahon	Ann McMahon
Gary	James	Edward	20-Apr-1890	08-Mar-1890	Charles Leo Gary	Kealty, Kaye		
Gassar	Adalaide		11-Jul-1912	24-Aug-1889	Joseph Gassar	[Blank] Julia		
Gassner	Francis		01-Feb-1898	25-Jan-1898	Peter Gassner	McGaffrey, Mary	Albert Schneider	Ellen Cassidy
Gateley	Ann	Nora	14-Jan-1908	15-May-1908	John Gately	Riordan, Catherine	Michael Gateley	Norah Kennedy
Gately	Vincent		15-May-1892	26-Apr-1892	Francis Bernard Gateley	Manley, Agnes Teresa	Charles Vincent Gateley	Lillian A. Manley
Gately	Francis	Raymond	08-Jul-1894	26-Jun-1894	Francis Bernard Gately	Manley, Agnes	William Gately	Gertrude Manley
Gately	William		18-Mar-1900	05-Mar-1900	Francis Gately	Manley, Agnes	William Driscoll	Barbara Driscoll
Gately	Helen	Elizabeth	12-Sep-1915	21-Aug-1915	John Gately	Riordan, Catherine		Mary Burch
Gately	Margaret		17-Sep-1891	08-Sep-1891	John Gately	Conners, Margaret	George Cooke	Rose Gately
Gately	Margaret	Mary	8-Sep-1912	7-Aug-1912	John Gately	Reardon, Catherine		Catherine Gately
Gately	John	Joseph	16-Oct-1910	23-Sep-1910	John Joseph Gately	Reardon, Catherine	Henry Fisker	Mary Gately
Gately	Mary		10-Jan-1886	07-Jan-1886	John T. Gately	Connor, Margaret A.	Francis B. Gately	Bernadette Conner
Gately	Michael		17-May-1891	27-Apr-1891	Michael Gately	Malone, Ann	James Wall	Catherine Murphy
Gates	James	E.	16-Apr-1905	5-Apr-1905	Francis P.H.Oates	Hanlon, Margaret	James Cummings	Catherine Cummings
Gaul	Michael	Joseph	10-Nov-1889	24-Oct-1889	Thomas J. Gaul	McCann, Margaret	Michael Gaul	Ann Flynn
Gaule	Margaret		20-Oct-1901	30-Sep-1901	Michael Gaule	O'Connor, Margaret	George Anderson	Alice Gaule
Gavin	James	John	23-Oct-1898	11-Oct-1898	James A. Gavin	Dunn, Alice P.	William McDevitt	Teresa Dunn
Gearen	Martha		13-Jul-1884	07-Jul-1884	Matthew Gearen	Lyons, Margaret	James F. Leach	Lily Leach
Gebhart	Josephine		21-Mar-1910	18-Nov-1910	Howard Gebhart	Dougherty, Helen Theresa		Elizabeth Dougherty
Gebhart	Howard	Joseph	09-Jan-1883	29-Dec-1882	William Gebhart	Hopkins, Ann		Sara Brown
Gebhart	Margaret		28-Apr-1895	05-Feb-1895	William Henry Gebhart	Hopkins, Ann	Samuel Gothers	Mary Carr
Geelhaar	Irene	Alvinia	19-Jan-1899	12-Jun-1886	Edward Geelhaar	Wackes, Emma		Julia Finnan
Geelhaar	Agnes	Louise	31-Jan-1904	21-Jan-1904	Ernest J. Geelhaar	Sutton, Mary	Joseph A. Sutton	Emma Finnan
Geelhaar/Finnan	Ann		27-Feb-1892	19-Aug-1871	Edward C. Geelhaar	Waskes, Emma		Julia Finnan
Gegan	Mary	Catherine	23-Mar-1903	15-Jan-1903	George Gegan	Porter, Mary	John Dyer	
Geisendaffer	Ann	Mary	19-Oct-1885	15-Sep-1885	Charles P. Geisendaffer	Dudley, Mary Helen		Ann I. Dudley
Geneste	Adele	Louise	2-Apr-1911	20-Mar-1911	Francis Geneste	Finnerty, Catherine	Joseph Finnerty	Adele R. Geneste
Geneste	Catherine	Bernardine France	28-Feb-1915	14-Feb-1915	Francis Geneste	Finnerty, Catherine	Patrick Langan	Frances Langan
Geneste	Ann	Gertrude	1-Dec-1912	16-Nov-1912	Francis J. Geneste	Finnerty, Catherine	Francis Geneste	Ann Finnerty
Gentry	Catherine	L.	16-May-1897	30-Apr-1897	Alfred Gentry	Lovele, Rose	Thomas Kennedy	Mary E. Gentry
Gentry	Mary		29-Jul-1894	15-Jul-1894	Hayden Gentry	Lavelle, Mary	Henry Lavelle	Ann M. Wright
Gentry	Pauline	Theresa	19-Jul-1891	11-Jul-1891	Hayden Gentry	Lavelle, Mary Ellen	Thomas P. Kennedy	Rose Levelle
Gentry	William	Daniel	30-Aug-1896	14-Aug-1896	Hayden Gentry	Lavelle, Mary E.	George Staab	Ann Kennedy
Geoghegan	Margaret	Elsi	15-Mar-1896	17-Feb-1896	Edward McGlone	McGlone, Margaret	Joseph McGlone	Joan York
George	Helen		8-Jul-1906	5-Feb-1906	Stephen George	Wess, Mary		Mary Shipley
George	Wilbertt	Joseph	21-May-1909	2-Nov-1909	Stephen H. George	Wess, Mary Loretta		Elizabeth Bange
Gephardt	Catherine	Adam	28-Jan-1894	25-Dec-1893	William Gephardt	Hoffman, Ann	Thomas Mulligan	Catherine Carr
Gephardt	John	Joseph	23-Nov-1884	12-Oct-1884	William Gephardt	Hopkins, Ann	Thomas Cusick	Ellen French
Gephardt	Wilber		31-Jul-1898	05-Jul-1898	William Gephardt	Hopkins, Ann	William Kelly	Rose Walters
Gephart	Catherine		25-May-1890	28-Feb-1890	Wm Gephart	Hopkins, Ann	James Goddart	Mary Hopkins
Geregthy	Andrew		11-Sep-1904	2-Sep-1904	Andrew Geregthy	Moylan, Mary	Eugene Grady	Winifred Craig
Geregthy	Catherine		08-Jul-1900	29-Jun-1900	Andrew Geregthy	Moylan, Mary	James Gereghty	Delia Rowlands
Geregthy	James		02-Apr-1899	28-Mar-1899	Andrew Geregthy	Moylan, Mary	Michael Gereghty	Mary Rowland
Geregthy	James		30-Apr-1899	28-Apr-1899	Andrew Geregthy	Moylan, Mary	Michael Gereghty	Mary Rowland
Geregthy	Margaret	Mary	31-May-1903	20-May-1903	Andrew Geregthy	Moylan, Mary	Bernard J. Rigney	Margaret Kelleher
Geregthy	Charles		10-Dec-1905	19-Nov-1905	Andrew J. Gereghty	Moylan, Mary	Michael Gereghty	Margaret Gereghty
Gereghty	James		24-Jan-1892	19-Jan-1892	James Gereghty	Russell, Catherine	Thomas Donahue	Margaret Keleher
Gereghty	Michael		02-Jun-1889	25-May-1889	James Gereghty	Russell, Catherine	Andrew Gereghty	Margaret O'Halloran
Gereghty	William		02-Nov-1890	28-Oct-1890	James Gereghty	Russell, Catherine	Michael Gereghty	Catherine Gereghty
Gereghty	Elizabeth	Cahill	01-Nov-1891	17-Oct-1891	Michael Gereghty	Reilly, Mary	James Gereghty	Ann Reilly
Gereghty	James	Michael	18-Aug-1889	09-Aug-1889	Michael Gereghty	Reilly, Mary	James Fennessy	Catherine Remmel
Gereghty	John	Joseph	28-Aug-1887	20-Aug-1887	Michael Gereghty	Reilly, Mary	John Gereghty	Elizabeth Reilly
Gerhaar	Joseph		01-Apr-1900	20-Mar-1900	Ernest Gerhaar	Sutton, Mary	Charles Sutton	Mary Kocrach
Gerhart	John	P.	11-Jul-1897	30-Jun-1897	Charles Gerhart	Ward, Mary	Felix McNulty	Catherine McNamara
Gerlach	Robert		13-Jan-1884	01-Jan-1884	John T. Gerlach	Shaw, Agnes T.		Joan (Jennie) Oursler
German	Henry	Patrick	12-May-1895	26-Apr-1895	Thomas George German	Rock, Mary Catherine	Patrick Vincent Cooney	Mary Florence Fitzgerald
German	Laura	Ethel	29-Sep-1889	20-Sep-1889	Thomas German	Rock, Mary	Stephen J. Krone	Adeline Rock
German	William	Wright	25-Dec-1892	13-Dec-1892	Thomas German	Rock, Mary	Thomas Reiley	Sara Rock
Germerhauser	Mary		28-May-1899	02-Apr-1899	William Germerhauser	Fordyce, Lula		Mary Germerhauser
Gerthey	Francis	Joseph	17-Oct-1897	08-Oct-1897	James Gerthey	Russell, Catherine	John Moylan	Mary Roland

46

LAST NAME	FIRST NAME	MIDDLE	BAPTISM	BIRTH	Father	Mother	SPONSORS	
Gessener	Mary	Helen	04-Oct-1896	25-Sep-1896	Peter Gessener	McCaffrey, Mary	James McCaffrey	Ann Quirk
Gessner	Charles	Albert	26-Feb-1893	17-Feb-1893	Henry John Gessner	Spots, Ann	Charles Albert Sumwalt	Teresa Francis Sumwalt
Gessner	Frances	Teresa	7-Jul-1907	19-Jun-1907	John G. Gessner	Skelton, Martha	Joseph Gessner	Frances Gessner
Gessner	Theodore		04-Sep-1898	28-Aug-1898	John Gessner	Bruder, Lydia	Joseph Bruder	Theodore Bruder
Gessner	Patrick	Henry	17-Mar-1910	17-Mar-1910	John Henry Gessner	Skelton, Martha	Charles Albert Sumwalt	Wilhelmina Seitz
Gessner	John		28-Jul-1907	22-Jul-1907	John J. Gessner	Bruder, Lydia	Henry Gessner	Mary Bouder
Gessner	Francis	Edward M.	12-Jul-1908	2-Jul-1908	Joseph Gessner	Jenkins, Ann May	Henry Gessner	Mary Frances Gessner
Gessner	Catherine		04-Feb-1900	26-Jan-1900	Peter Gessner	McCaffrey, Mary	John Gessler	Carolyn McCaffrey
Geyer	Agnes	Mary	10-Apr-1906	20-Jul-1904	David Geyer	Schultz, Cecelia		Philomena Carr
Giamnini	Michael		21-Mar-1915	8-May-1914	John Giamnini	Bisacci, Angelina	Salvatore Salamone	Ann L. Wilkenning
Gibbons	Francis	Leslie	14-Apr-1895	04-Apr-1895	Francis Marion Gibbons	Phillips, Sara Mary	Henry Vincent Phillips	Rose Gentry
Giblin	Catherine		29-Jul-1906	16-Jul-1906	James Giblin	Gallagher, Helen	John Gilmore	Elizabeth Loughran
Giblin	Cecelia		23-Oct-1898	14-Oct-1898	Patrick Giblin	Flanagan, Cecelia	Thomas Herron	Mary Herron
Giblin	John	Patrick	19-Apr-1891	10-Apr-1891	Patrick Giblin	Flannagen, Cecelia	Cecil Flannagen	
Giblin	Francis	Patrick	15-Dec-1895	03-Dec-1895	Patrick James Giblin	Flanigan, Cecelia	James Flanigan	Cecelia Flannigan
Gibney	Margaret		13-Sep-1890	04-Sep-1890	[Blank]	[Blank]		Margaret Gibney
Gibson	Ruth	Rebecca	03-Jan-1888	27-May-1888	[Blank]	Gibson, Emma		Catherine Schweinger
Gibson	George		16-Feb-1890	10-May-1879	Albert Gibson	Lightner, Lizzie		Emma Killan
Gibson	Robert		16-Feb-1890	11-Mar-1877	Albert Gibson	Lightner, Lizzie		Kate Leonard
Gibson	Ann		10-May-1898	26-Apr-1898	George Gibson	Connolly, Ann	Joseph Connolly	Agnes Connolly
Gibson	Edward	Gordon	15-Oct-1905	7-Oct-1905	George Gibson	Connolly, Ann	John Jennings	Winifred Jennings
Gibson	George	Robert	01-Oct-1899	25-Sep-1899	George Gibson	Connolly, Ann	Robert O'Neill	Catherine O'Neill
Gibson	Josephine	Dorothy	27-Sep-1908	10-Sep-1908	J. Gibson	Stuart, Mary	W. Gibson	Katie Cox
Gibson	Catherine	Cecelia	04-Jan-1891	23-Dec-1890	John G. Gibson	Ward, Catherine	Francis Laurie	Ellen Healey
Gibson	Robert		15-Feb-1903	31-Jan-1903	John George Gibson	Ward, Catherine	Eugene McKenna	Frances Cassidy
Gibson	Andrew		19-Oct-1902	10-Oct-1902	John Gibson	Gibson, Ann	Cornelius Thomas	Belle Gibson
Gibson	Ann		05-Dec-1897	21-Nov-1897	John Gibson	Gibson, Ann	Andrew Gibson	Mary Gibson
Gibson	Estelle		21-Nov-1897	11-Oct-1897	John Gibson	Ward, Catherine	Henry Zellers	Mary Rollman
Gibson	Gerald		23-Jun-1912	10-Jun-1912	John Gibson	Hagerty, Mary	John Gibson	Elizabeth Hagerty
Gibson	Mary		29-Jul-1888	16-Jul-1888	John Gibson	Gibson, Ann G.	Michael J. Griffin	Agnes Gibson
Gibson	Mary	Catherine	5-Apr-1908	26-Mar-1908	John Gibson	Hagerty, Mary Agnes	Andrew Giblin	Catherine Hagerty
Gibson	Joseph		23-Oct-1891	10-Oct-1891	John Joseph Gibson	Giblin, Ann Gertrude	Patrick Gibson	Mary Gibson
Gibson	Mary		23-Oct-1891	10-Oct-1891	John Joseph Gibson	Giblin, Ann Gertrude	Patrick Gibson	Mary Gibson
Gibson	Carmelita		22-May-1910	12-May-1910	John P. Gibson	Hagerty, Mary	William Bishop	Isabelle Gibson
Gibson	John	Michael	14-Oct-1906	29-Sep-1906	John P. Gibson	Hagerty, Mary A.	John Feeney	Mary Agnes Gibson
Gibson	Joseph		4-Apr-1915	22-Mar-1915	John P. Gibson	Hagerty, Margaret A.	Joseph Gibson	Ann L. Wilkenning
Gibson	Hugo	A.	7-Jan-1905	26-Dec-1904	John Patrick Gibson	Hagarty, Mary Agnes	Andrew Gibson	Margaret Frances Gibson
Gibson	Mary		2-Jul-1907	2-Jul-1907	Joseph F. Gibson	Stuart, Mary		Catherine Cannon
Gibson	Norman	Josephine	5-Jun-1910	19-May-1910	Joseph Gibson	Stewart, Mary	Charles Stewart	Helen Stewart
Gibson	James	Edward	19-Nov-1911	2-Nov-1911	Joseph W. Gibson	Stewart, Mary Ann	Edward Gibson	Ella Knell
Gibson	Andrew	Michael	17-Apr-1887	05-Apr-1887	Patrick Gibson	Flanagan, Cecelia	Andrew Gibson	Ann Gibson
Gifford	Hugo		26-May-1898	About 1817	Alexander Gifford	Johnson, Mary		
Gilbert	Margaret	Francis	05-Feb-1888	22-Jan-1888	John Coleman Gilbert	French, Margaret Eleanor	James French	Ann G. Carey
Gilbert	Wendel	Scott	18-Jan-1889	09-Jan-1889	William H. Gilbert	Scott, Mary	Charles Swinderman	Virginia Gilbert
Gilbert	William	Carroll	19-Feb-1888	02-Feb-1888	William Henry Gilbert	Scott, Mary	John Gilbert	Agnes Gilbert
Gilchrist	Leonard	Patrick	08-Apr-1883	24-Mar-1883	Patrick Gilchrist	Laughlin, Patrick [sic]	Margaret Finerty	
Gilchrist	Thomas		29-Apr-1883	25-Mar-1883	Richard Gilchrist	Randall, Sara Jane		Mary Helen Polley
Gildenfenny	Anastasia		22-Feb-1903	12-Feb-1903	Thomas F. Gildenfenny	Curtis, Mary	C.J. Gildenfenny	Ann Doyle
Gildenfenny	Helen		03-Mar-1901	15-Feb-1901	Thomas Gildenfenny	Curtis, Mary	William Gildenfenny	Bridget Curtis
Gildenfenny	Mary		07-May-1899	24-Apr-1899	Thomas Gildenfenny	Curtis, Mary	John Curtis	Mary Gildenfenny
Gilderfenny	Thomas	Ward	20-Mar-1910	28-Dec-1900	Thomas F. Gilderfenny	Smith, Ellen		
Gilhooly	Francis		20-Dec-1913	21-Dec-1913	James Gilhooly	McEvoy, Ann		Lula Henry
Gilhooly	John	Joseph	15-May-1904	3-May-1904	James Gilhooly	McEvoy, Ann	James Law	Catherine Neary
Gilhooly	Mary	Ann	23-Jul-1911	12-Jul-1911	James Gilhooly	McEvoy, Ann	Patrick Conniff	Teresa McEvoy
Gilhooly	Thomas		11-Nov-1906	30-Nov-1906	James Gilhooly	McEvoy, Ann	John Gilooley	Mary Stafford
Gilhooly	Ann	Elizabeth	8-Dec-1912	24-Nov-1912	Michael Gilhooly	Rowland, Margaret	James Gilhooly	Mary McAvoy
Gilhooly	Regina	Mary	24-Jan-1915	10-Jan-1915	Michael Gilhooly	Rowland, Margaret M.	Thomas Grady	Mary Star
Gilleade	James	Patrick	03-Jul-1887	19-Jun-1887	Patrick Gilleade	Lyons, Ida	Thomas Gilleade	Mary Hesson
Gillece	Ann	Virginia	23-Aug-1885	10-Aug-1885	Patrick Gillece	Lyle, Ida	Bernard McKenna	Rose Niemeyer
Gillece	Francis	Earle	7-Apr-1912	27-Mar-1912	Thomas L. Gillece	Welsh, Catherine	Francis Fallers	Effie Lyle
Gillece	James		27-Aug-1905	12-Aug-1905	Thomas L. Gillece	Welsh, Catherine	Edward B. Gillece	Justina Welsh
Gillece	Mary	Katherine	1-May-1910	21-Apr-1910	Thomas L. Gillece	Welsh, Catherine	Matthew J. Dunn	Ida Agnes Gillece
								Mary Marley

ST JOHN'S BAPTISMS 1882-1912

LAST NAME	FIRST NAME	MIDDLE	BAPTISM	BIRTH	Father	Mother	SPONSORS
Gillen	Andrew		04-Nov-1883	28-Oct-1883	Andrew Gillen	O'Dea, Elizabeth	John Joyce	Julia Sullivan
Gillen	Andrew		30-Jul-1891	16-Jul-1891	Andrew Gillen	O'Day, Elizabeth		Catherine Long
Gillen	Irene		09-Apr-1893	31-Mar-1893	Andrew Gillen	Long, Elizabeth		Mary Lynch
Gillen	James	Joseph	16-Mar-1884	24-Feb-1884	Joseph Gillen	Zang, Linda	Bodrick Gillen	Ann Gillen
Gillet	Sara	Ida	28-Jan-1884	12-Apr-1860	Joseph Gillet	Baumgartner, Sara		Mary Slaysman
Gilmore	Ann	Mary	29-Mar-1903	11-Mar-1903	James Gilmore	Gallagher, Helen	Michael Murray	Bridget Dolly
Gilmore	Edward	Joseph	5-May-1912	20-Apr-1912	James Gilmore	Gallagher, Ellen	Thomas B. O'Hara	Ellen O'Neill
Gilmore	Henry	James	10-Aug-1913	31-Jul-1913	James Gilmore	Gallagher, Ellen	Henry Albers	Mary Kline
Gilmore	James		03-Jan-1897	18-Dec-1896	James Gilmore	Dolly, Mary	John McDonnell	Delia Dolly
Gilmore	Michael		24-Dec-1899	Dec 1899	James Gilmore	Daily, Mary	Michael Daily	Margaret [Blank]
Gilmore	Patrick	Leon	28-Mar-1909	11-Mar-1909	James Gilmore	Gallagher, Ellen	Leo Jerome Murray	Mary Albers
Gilmore	Thomas		17-Apr-1898	06-Apr-1898	James Gilmore	Dolly, Mary	Thomas Long	Delia Long
Gilmore	William	Henry	21-Jul-1901	04-Jul-1901	James Gilmore	Galligan, Ellen	H.N.Albers	Mary Gilmore
Gilroy	Mary	Cecelia	31-Dec-1909	25-Dec-1909	[Blank]	Gilroy, Catherine		Catherine Gilroy
Gilroy	Francis		22-Nov-1899	30-Sep-1899	James Gilroy	Cain, Catherine		Emma Howe
Gilroy	Stephen	Leonard	22-Sep-1901	02-Sep-1901	James Gilroy	Cain, Catherine		Julia Gilroy
Gisrial	Frederick	George	14-Oct-1883	01-Oct-1883	John Gisrian	Coyle, Martha	George Nicholas Brian	Margaret Magraw
Gisriel	John		12-Feb-1888	25-Dec-1886	John G. Gisriel	Coyle, Martha		Mary Pool
Gisriel	John	Stewart	1-May-1910	14-Apr-1910	John Gisriel	Dailey, Ann	William Gisriel	Jennie Gisriel
Gisriel	Margaret	Beatrice	14-Jan-1912	29-Dec-1911	John Gisriel	Dailey, Ann	Ambrose Kennedy	Margaret Dailey
Gisriel	Sophia	Helen	14-Oct-1894	29-Sep-1894	John Gisriel	Coyle, Martha Agnes	Edward Burke	Mary Miller
Gisriel	William	Donelan	14-Dec-1885	20-Nov-1885	John Gisriel	Coyle, Martha	Rev.J.D. Mead	Sarah Murphy
Gisriel	Mary	Elizabeth	16-Feb-1890	20-Jan-1890	John Gisril	Coyle, Martha	Daniel Cremmins	Elizabeth Cremmins
Gisriel	Charles	Leo	14-Feb-1892	25-Jan-1892	John V. Gisriel	Coyle, Martha	Henry Miller	Margaret Coyle
Gladstone	Charles		31-Aug-1908	28-Jun-1908	Charles Talbott Gladstone	Connolly, Catherine Gertrude		Margaret Connolly
Glady	Clara	Mary	12-Dec-1886	30-Jan-1878	John H. Glady	Edell, Laura A.		Alice Brady
Glady	Laura	Lyle	12-Dec-1886	01-Oct-1879	John H. Glady	Edell, Laura A.		Catherine Burns
Glady/Edell	Laura	Genevieve	02-Nov-1884	26-Sep-1884	John Henry Glady	Edel, Laura Maryland		Elizabeth Alice Grahan
Glaser	Henry	A.	28-Nov-1886	18-Dec-1860	John Edell	Richardson, Mary J.		Catherine Lewis
Glayous	Mary		29-Jan-1882	15-Dec-1881	Henry Glaser	Wallis, Harriet	William J.A.Wallis	Mary Helen Carr
Glazer	Mary	Ann	15-Jun-1890	11-Jun-1890	William E. Glayous	Burns, Bridget	Thos. Barrett	Margaret Barrett
Gleason	William	Lavinia	28-Dec-1884	03-Dec-1884	Henry Glazer	Wallace, Harriet		Mary Catherine Wallace
Gleason	David	Thomas	09-Jan-1887	01-Jan-1887	Joseph Alexander Gleason	Slater, Ann	Thomas McGuin	Margaret McGuin
Gleason	James	Grover	06-Jun-1890	06-Jun-1890	Joseph Gleason	Slater, Ann		Elizabeth Ward
Gleason	Leon		07-Aug-1892	23-Jul-1892	Joseph Gleason	Slater, Ann	James Carter	Mary Carter
Gleason	Mary	Catherine	04-Nov-1888	30-Oct-1888	Joseph Gleason	Slater, Ann	William Slater	Catherine Gleason
Glenn	Charles	Edward	27-May-1894	19-May-1894	Joseph P. Gleason	Slater, Ann	John B. White	Caroline Bowers
Glenn	John	Patrick	9-Dec-1906	24-Nov-1906	John Glenn	O'Dea, Margaret	John Casey	Elizabeth Redington
Glenn	Joseph		11-Aug-1901	02-Aug-1901	John Glenn	O'Dea, Margaret	John Cosey	Mary Hamilton
Glenn	James	Gibbons	25-May-1882	22-May-1882	John Glenn	Jordan, Mary	John Nester	B. Nester
Glenn	Mary	G.	17-Sep-1911	7-Sep-1911	John P. Glenn	O'Dea, Margaret	John Redington	Catherine Casey
Glenn	Margaret	Regina	8-May-1904	24-Apr-1904	John P. Glenn	O'Dea, Margaret	Charles McShane	Ann O'Dea
Glorious	Mary	Edith	20-Dec-1908	9-Dec-1908	John Patrick Glenn	O'Dea, Margaret	Bridget Kavanaugh	Catherine Redington
Glorius	William		28-Aug-1892	12-Aug-1892	William Edward Glorious	Byrnes, Bridget	John Patrick Gereghty	Mary Julia Hauser
Glorius	Margaret	George	02-Sep-1888	12-Jun-1867	Martin Glorius	Berlett, Mary		Thomas Barrett
Gloyd	Charles		03-May-1891	23-Apr-1891	William Edward Glorius	Byrnes, Delia		Sara Nihill
Gloyd	Theodore		24-Mar-1895	01-Mar-1895	Charles Thomas Gloyd	Seiford, Ann	George Silversand	Kate Oliphant
Godard	Joseph		22-May-1910	10-May-1910	Thomas Gloyd	Brundette, Caroline	Patrick Smith	Frances Cook
Goetzke	Margaret	Lillian	03-Dec-1891	About 1845	Robert Godard	Pickering, Elizabeth		
Golarick	Mary	Elizabeth	3-Sep-1911	19-Aug-1911	Christian Goetzke	Spearman, Mary E.	Eugene McWhirke	Lillian Clayton
Gold	Harriett	Elizabeth	05-Mar-1899	18-Feb-1899	Joseph Golarick	McIntyre, Mary	Francis McGuire	Mary McGuire
Gold	Joseph		24-Apr-1887	22-Dec-1886	George Gold	Jackson. Amelia		Mary Hubbard
Golden	Charles	Joseph	08-Nov-1882	15-Oct-1882	George Laurence Gold	Jackson, Cornelia Rebecca		Mary Eliza Gold
Golden	Ann	Elizabeth	07-Nov-1886	31-Oct-1886	George B. Golden	Parker, Virginia D.		Margaret Guskert
Golden	James		23-Sep-1883	13-Sep-1883	John F. Golden	Slaysman, Emma J.	Henry Frasier	Ann Frazier
Goldrick	James	R.	08-Feb-1885	26-Jan-1885	John Golden	Slaysman, Emma I.	George Kilduff	Lizzie Hays
Goldrick	Joseph		05-Aug-1900	04-Jul-1900	Joseph Goldrick	McArthur, Mary	James Craig	Mary Hines
Goliardi	Rose	Theresa	24-May-1896	04-May-1896	Joseph Goldrick	McIntyre, Mary	Michael McIntyre	Margaret McIntyre
Gollardi	James	Joseph	14-Apr-1889	01-Mar-1889	John Goliardi	Goliardi, Dalade	James Caramelli	Rose Morini
Gonce	Mary	Elizabeth	07-Aug-1892	28-Jul-1892	John Louis Golliardi	Golliardi, Deliada	James Golliardi	Columba Benda
Gonce	Laura	Augusta	23-Jun-1895	28-May-1895	Thomas J. Gonce	Heise, Olivia Agnes	George Kline	Catherine Linzey
Gonder	Ann	Cecelia	06-Jan-1884	18-Dec-1883	William H. Gonce	Clautice, Alice Elizabeth	William Gonce	Mary Elizabeth Gonce
			15-Dec-1895	26-Nov-1895	Charles Gonder	McCaffrey, Agnes		Ella McCaffrey

48

LAST NAME	FIRST NAME	MIDDLE	BAPTISM	BIRTH	Father	Mother	SPONSORS
Goodman	Richars	Leon	08-Jan-1888	14-Dec-1887	Marmaduke R. Goodman	Gordon, Catherine Virginia	Emma Pryor
Goodman	Catherine		14-Oct-1883	06-Sep-1883	Marmaduke Richard Goodman	Gordon, Catherine Virginia	Mayhilda Graham
Goodman	Adalaide	Genevieve	12-Sep-1915	3-Sep-1915	William Goodman	Leonard, Genevieve	Margaret Ganghan
Goodwin	Charles	Edward	25-Oct-1905	9-Oct-1905	Brent Joseph Goodwin	Huth, Catherine E.	Emma G. Wagner
Goodwin	Joan		19-May-1897	24-Nov-1884	Thomas Goodwin	Maroney, Alice	Catherine Mooney
Gootee	Ann	Mary	9-Sep-1912	8-Aug-1912	[Blank]	Gootee, Madeline	Ann Mart Letournan
Gootee	George	Washington	05-May-1892	22-Jul-1809	John Gootee	Todd, Margaret	
Gordon	Charles	Henry	31-Jul-1892	28-Jun-1892	Charles Gordon	Rogers, Mary	Helen Gordon
Gordon	Gertrude	Leon	22-Jan-1910	21-Dec-1910	Charles Gordon	Sutton, Mary	Gertrude Gordon
Gordon	James	Edward	23-Jun-1889	09-Jun-1889	Charles Gordon	Rogers, Mary	Rose Harrison
Gordon	Matilda	Dolores	22-Jan-1911	21-Dec-1910	Charles Gordon	Sutton, Mary	Matilda Holmeyer
Gordon	Helen	Elizabeth	04-Dec-1883	27-Nov-1883	George Bernard Gordon	Parker, Virginia	Mary Macklin
Gordon	Teresa	Elizabeth	19-Apr-1891	06-Feb-1891	George Bernard Gordon	Parker, Virginia	Eva Hinkle
Gordon	Eleanor	Catherine	18-Mar-1888	29-Jan-1888	George Gordon	Parker, Virginia	Margaret Ruckert
Gordon	Mary	Virginia Cleveland	14-Dec-1884	18-Nov-1884	George Gordon	Parker, Genevieve	Louise Quinn
Gordon	Eugene	William	2-Jul-1911	20-Jun-1911	James Gordan	Behrman, Agnes	Catherine McQuillan
Gordon	Bernard	J.	31-Dec-1905	2-Dec-1905	Joseph W. Gordon	Quinn, Mary C.	Elizabeth Costello
Gordon	Charles	Leon	25-Dec-1887	07-Dec-1887	Lloyd C. Gordon	Mantly, Kaura V.	Margaret Duffy
Gordon	George	Cleveland	17-Jun-1894	05-Jun-1894	Lloyd Gordon	Mantler, Laura	Angela McDonald
Gordon	Jerome	Howard	13-Sep-1903	01-Sep-1903	Lloyd Gordon	Mantler, Laura	Laura Wethestal
Gordon	John	Lloyd	03-Mar-1901	12-Feb-1901	Lloyd Gordon	Mantler, Laura	Clara Griffin
Gordon	Joseph	L.	25-Jun-1899	03-Jun-1899	Lloyd Gordon	Mantler, Laura	Ella Brentine
Gordon	Mary	Gertrude	03-Aug-1890	18-Jul-1890	Lloyd Gordon	Mantler, Laura	Ellena Murray
Gordon	William	James	17-Jun-1894	05-Jun-1894	Lloyd Gordon	Mantler, Laura	Anastasia Parrell
Gordon	Michael	Edward	24-Aug-1884	22-Aug-1884	William J. Gordon	O'Brien, Catherine Ann	Catherine O'Brien
Gordon	Catherine	Ann	18-Nov-1888	09-Nov-1888	William Joseph Gordon	O'Brien, Catherine Ann	Mary M. Thompson
Gordon	Edward	Clarence	20-Jul-1890	13-Jul-1890	William Joseph Gordon	O'Brien, Catherine Ann	Helen Quinn
Gordon	William	Joseph	20-Aug-1882	09-Aug-1882	William Joseph Gordon	O'Brien, Catherine	Lucy Quinn
Gordon	Ed	Clarence	27-Jul-1890	13-Jul-1890	Wm Gordon	O'Brien, Cath	Lena Gutberlet
Gorman	Mary	Catherine	15-Oct-1882	30-Oct-1882	Charles Bayard Gorman	Lenft, Ann Marie	Catherine Broderick
Gorman	James		01-Jun-1902	26-May-1902	John Gorman	Summer, Bertha	Mary Patterson
Gorman	Edward	Michael	06-Sep-1891	21-Aug-1891	Michael J. Gorman	Deven, Mary Catherine	Mary A. Deven
Gormely	Henry	Richard	26-Apr-1903	11-Apr-1903	John Gormely	Conn, Ellen	Katherine Gormely
Gormley	Mary	Elizabeth	07-Jun-1891	15-May-1891	James Gormley	Moore, Roseanna	Joan Maher
Gormley	Catherine		04-Jan-1901	03-Jan-1901	John Gormley	Conn, Ann	Felix Gormley
Gorrera	Immaculata		04-Apr-1886	12-Mar-1886	Anthony Gorrera	Hortzmann, Clara	Mary Gepp
Gosman	Evan	Elizabeth	07-Feb-1897	30-Jan-1897	Ferdinand Gosman	Steer, Caroline	Helen Rowland
Gosnell	Mary	Malinda	01-May-1883	11-Apr-1883	Walter Gosnell	Trainor, Mary Malinda	Rachel Trainor
Gotts	Mary	Elizabeth	13-Feb-1898	19-Jan-1898	Robert Gotts	Connelly, Mary	Elizabeth Masson
Gotzke	B arbara	Evan	19-Oct-1913	1-Oct-1913	Christian Gotzke	Spearman, Mary Elizabeth	Barbara Mary Gotzke
Grabel	George	Henry	09-Jan-1887	01-Sep-1886	Edward Grabel	Ziegler, Joan	Barbara Grabel
Grace	Phillip		22-Feb-1914	16-Feb-1914	William Grace	Murrell, Catherine Hoch	Margaret Hagerty
Grace	William		05-Jan-1902	10-Dec-1901	William Grace	Finn , Julia	Helen Grace
Grace	William	Leon	11-Jul-1909	30-Jun-1909	William Grace	Roland, Nora	George Starr
Grace	Leon	Charles	31-Oct-1915	20-Oct-1915	Albert Graham	Kennedy, Elizabeth	Thomas Kennedy
Grace	Catherine		25-Dec-1892	12-Dec-1892	Benjamin Francis Graham	Hebrank, Mary	Henry Hebrank
Grady	Thomas		21-May-1898	10-May-1898	John Grady	Burns, Annie	Ann Griffin
Grady	Helen	Angela	3-Aug-1913	23-Jul-1913	John Grady	Byrne, Ann	Mary Mulligan
Grady	Eugene	Thomas	26-May-1912	19-May-1912	Owen Grady	Barlow, Helen M.	Agnes Barlow
Grady	Mary	Agnes	06-Apr-1890	30-Mar-1890	Owen J. Grady	Barlow, Ella M.	George J. Barlow
Grady	Nora	Mary	11-Jul-1909	10-Dec-1901	Thomas Grady	Moran, Bridget	Thomas Concannon
Graham	Edward	Thomas	31-Oct-1915	30-Jun-1909	Thomas Grady	Roland, Nora	Mary Bane
Graham	Ann	Margaret	25-Dec-1892	20-Oct-1915	Albert Graham	Kennedy, Elizabeth	Mary Starr
Graham	Elizabeth	Helen	23-Aug-1891	12-Dec-1892	Benjamin Francis Graham	Hebrank, Mary	Mary Ann Hebrank
Graham	Christopher	Edward	28-May-1887	04-Aug-1891	Benjamin Franklin Graham	Hebrand, Mary Cecelia	Lilie Genevieve Moran
Graham	Francis		11-Nov-1888	30-Apr-1887	Christopher Graham	Davis, Mary	Mary Dennert
Graham	Joseph		27-Sep-1902	22-Oct-1888	Christopher Graham	Davis, Mary Ida	Mary Quick
Graham	Charles	Cecil	18-Nov-1906	26-Sep-1902	E. L. Graham	Baker, Emma	Elizabeth McAlier
Graham	Regina	Agatha	27-Aug-1890	4-Nov-1906	Ellis C. Graham	Baker, Emma	Mary A. Thompson
Graham	William		26-Nov-1911	10-Aug-1890	Ellis C. Graham	Baker, Emma M.	Ida Baker
Graham	Edgar	Baker	24-Jun-1894	11-Nov-1911	Ellis C. Graham	Baker, Emma M.	C. Lane
Graham	Gerald	Donald	13-Sep-1903	13-Jun-1894	Ellis Constantine Graham	Baker, Emma Mary	Cecelia Baker
Graham	Kenneth	Leo	09-Sep-1900	07-Sep-1903	Ellis Graham	Baker, Emma M.	Emma Pryor
Graham				30-Aug-1900	Ellis Graham	Baker, Emma	Emma Pryor

LAST NAME	FIRST NAME	MIDDLE	BAPTISM	BIRTH	Father	Mother	SPONSORS
Graham	Ellis	Ignatius	27-Dec-1891	16-Dec-1891	Ellis Ignatius Graham	Baker, Emma Cecelia	Henry Graham
Graham	Henry	Blake	22-Jan-1893	07-Jan-1893	George Nicholson Graham	Blake, Helen	Henry Gordon Graham
Graham	William	James	04-Jul-1882	25-Jun-1882	Henry G. Graham	Kirkland, Amelia G.	
Graham	Laura	Mary	26-Dec-1886	11-Dec-1886	Henry Gordon Graham	Kirkland, Amelia	Marcus Pryor
Graham	Samuel	Crosby	25-May-1884	09-May-1884	Henry Gordon Graham	Kirkland, Amelia Grover	William Edward Graham
Graham	Albert	Casey	04-Mar-1888	01-Feb-1888	Henry Graham	Kirkland, Amelia	Joseph Kraft
Graham	John	August	19-Jun-1887	13-Jun-1887	John A. Graham	Sutherland, Sara J.	George Benson
Graham	Mary		27-Sep-1891	17-Sep-1891	John August Graham	Sutherland, Sara Josephine	Francis Fay
Graham	Samuel	Sutherland	21-Oct-1888	13-Oct-1888	John August Graham	Sutherland, Sara Josephine	Francis Aloysius Graham
Graham	Susan	Ann	08-Jul-1890	26-Jun-1890	John Graham	Sutherland, Sara	
Graham	Catherine	Agnes	14-Dec-1890	02-Dec-1890	William Graham	Pugh, Mary	William Andrew Pugh
Graham/Sutherland	Sarah	Sutherland	01-Jan-1893	26-Dec-1892	John A. Graham	Graham, Sara Josephine	James P. Lyness
Grahe	Audrey	Mary	12-Aug-1906	2-Jul-1906	Henry Grahe	Curtin, Nira	
Grannan	Margaret	E.	26-May-1889	20-May-1889	Thomas Grannan	Davis, Melvina	James M. Yarnell
Grape	Edward		19-Apr-1888	07-Aug-1854	James Grape	Cassard, Elizabeth	
Gray	James	Thomas	01-Mar-1896	08-Feb-1896	Charles Gray	Kehoe, Bridget	William Brennan
Gray	Catherine		04-Mar-1888	23-Feb-1888	Francis Gray	Owens, Catherine	John Owens
Gray	Mary	Helen	20-Aug-1882	15-Aug-1882	Francis Gray	Owens, Catherine	Charles Essender
Green	Elmer	Francis	20-Nov-1892	25-Oct-1892	Elmer Green	Dock, Catherine	Francis Neville
Green	George	Frederick	26-Jan-1913	3-Jan-1913	George Frederick Green	Miles, Mary Elizabeth	William Bernard Miles
Green	Mary	Virginia	4-Jun-1911	26-May-1911	George Frederick Green	Miles, Mary Elizabeth	Joseph Warren Kershaw
Green	Catherine	Howser	01-Oct-1882	[Blank]	Henry Green	Green, Catherine	
Green	Henry	Francis	05-Aug-1883	09-Aug-1883	John Green	Moore, Elizabeth Henrietta	
Green	Maurice	Clinton	04-Jul-1886	26-Jun-1886	John Green	Moore, Elizabeth	William T. Murphy
Green	George	Clayton	28-Apr-1901	30-Mar-1901	Maurice Green	Stephenson, E.	
Green	Margaret		05-Nov-1899	15-Oct-1899	Patrick Green	Sweeney, Mary	Joseph Green
Green	Mary	Roselie	12-Nov-1905	29-Oct-1905	Patrick J. Green	McSweeney, Mary	Andrew O'Brien
Green	Thomas	Patrick	30-Mar-1902	17-Mar-1902	Patrick Joseph Green	Sweeney, Mary	William Green
Green	Francis	G.	31-Dec-1905	16-Dec-1905	William Green	McLaughlin, Elizabeth	Charles J. Mayhan
Green	William	Joseph	14-Feb-1892	20-Aug-1883	William Green	Mileseed, Emma	
Greene	Horace	Leon	26-Jul-1903	12-Jul-1903	William Greene	McLaughlin, Elizabeth	Henry Edder
Greener	Norman		5-Aug-1906	20-Jul-1906	John F. Greener	Casserly, Agnes	
Greer	Agnes	Gerald	14-Oct-1894	12-Sep-1894	John Greer	Corcoran, Emma	
Greer	John		14-Jun-1896	07-Jun-1896	John Greer	Corcoran, Emma	
Grey	Florence	Elizabeth	10-Feb-1884	02-Feb-1884	Francis Grey	Owens, Catherine	Joseph McCaffrey
Greydam	Edward	Joseph	11-May-1907	22-Feb-1907	Joseph Greydam	Vincent, Elizabeth	
Griffen	Mary	Elizabeth	21-Jul-1901	05-Jul-1901	Thomas M. Griffen	Saffron, Mary	
Griffin	Emma		03-Aug-1903	15-Jul-1903	Eugene Griffin	McCovans, Emma	
Griffin	Catherine		05-Apr-1896	22-Mar-1896	John Griffin	Sinclair, Clara	Patrick O'Brine
Griffin	Eleanor		30-Oct-1887	28-Oct-1887	John Griffin	Keeley, Mary	James McKenna
Griffin	Thomas		01-Mar-1885	21-Feb-1885	Michael Gridfin	Conway, Mary	Michael Tierney
Griffin	Michael	Joseph	07-Aug-1887	27-Jul-1887	Michael Griffin	Comboy, Mary	Paul T. McGuire
Griffin	John		01-Jan-1882	20-Dec-1881	Thomas Griffin	Smith, Maria	Joseph Shea
Griffin	Joseph		13-Mar-1886	03-Mar-1886	Thomas Griffin	Smith, Ann	
Griffin	Joseph	R.	02-May-1886	03-Mar-1886	Thomas Griffin	Smith, Ann	
Griffin	Margaret		18-Sep-1887	23-Aug-1887	Thomas Griffin	Smith, Ann	John McAnally
Griffin	William	Helen	09-Dec-1883	23-Nov-1883	Thomas Griffin	Smith, Mary	Thomas Dowd
Griffith	Margaret	Mary	21-Jan-1911	18-Jan-1910	[Blank]	Griffith, Ann	
Griffith	Agnes	Robert	10-Jan-1897	20-Dec-1896	Robert Griffith	Gill, Alice	P. Lanahan
Grisendaffer	John		29-Nov-1914	15-Nov-1914	John Horatio Grisendaffer	Evan, Mary	Robert Grisendaffer
Grogan	John		14-Jan-1900	20-Dec-1899	Francis Grogan	Reynolds, Mary	John Greiner
Grogan	James	Thomas	07-Aug-1892	31-Jul-1892	Francis P. Grogan	Reynolds, Minnie	John Dare
Grogan	Agnes		30-Jan-1898	16-Jan-1898	Joseph Grogan	Rattray, Rachel	Charles Grogan
Grogan	Ann		04-Mar-1900	10-Feb-1900	Joseph Grogan	Rattray, Rachel	Thomas Grogan
Grogan	Mary		27-Oct-1901	18-Oct-1901	Joseph Grogan	Rattray, Rose	James Grogan
Grogan	Josephine		6-Apr-1905	29-Mar-1905	Joseph P. Grogan	Rattray, Rachel	E.J. Healy
Grogan	Agnes	R.	15-Apr-1906	7-Apr-1906	Michael Grogan	French, Helen	Edward French
Grogan	Isabelle		16-Apr-1899	26-Mar-1899	Michael Grogan	French, Ella	Andrew DeLauder
Grogan	Margaret	Helen	11-Mar-1894	01-Mar-1894	Michael Grogan	French, Helen	Thomas Grogan
Grogan	Joseph	Edward	12-Jul-1908	2-Jul-1908	Michael J. Grogan	French, Ella	Samuel French
Grogan	Mary	L.	19-Jun-1892	04-Apr-1892	Michael John Grogan	French, Mary Helen	Charles Grogan
Grogan	Catherine		10-Jan-1904	23-Dec-1903	Thomas E. Grogan	Brannan, Sara	Charles Grogan
Grogan	Edward		30-Mar-1905	21-Mar-1905	Thomas E. Grogan	Brannan, Sara	Edward J. Healy

SPONSORS (continued)
Helen Graham
Amelia Graham
Emma Pryer
Laura Graham
Cecelia Ryan
Mary Hubbel
Mary M. Keagle
Helen Keagle
Margaret Willax
Catherine Pugh
Emma C. Pryor
Josephine Curtin
Cora Yarnell
Margaret Murphy
Elizabeth Owens
Helen Essender
Mary Hendel
Catherine Klarman
Mary Sweeting
Catherine Sullivan
Elizabeth McKenna
Eugenia Frances Ruff
Joan Downey
Mary O'Brien
Catherine Connors
Agnes Crawford
Manda Murray
Catherine Edder
Catherine Casserly
Mary Agnes Dorsey
Elizabeth Sheran
Hlen McCaffrey
Mary J. Hayes
Emma Rutiger
Carolina McGreevey
Honora O'Brien
Ann Cunningham
Mary McGuire
Maria Griffin
Sarah Kehoe
Sarah Kehoe
Hannah Messenehl
Catherine Ward
Margaret Murphy
Mary Paterson
Mary Ellen Grisendaffer
Mary Kelly
Ella Grogan
Adele Farrell
Sarah Grogan
Ella Birch
Ella J. Healy
Margaret Hogan
Mary DeLauder
Margaret Grogan
Mary Kaife
Mary Grogan
Stella Grogan
Mary A. Thorton

ST JOHN'S BAPTISMS 1882-1912

LAST NAME	FIRST NAME	MIDDLE	BAPTISM	BIRTH	Father	Mother	SPONSORS
Grogan	Margaret		17-Mar-1907	25-Feb-1907	Thomas E. Grogan	Brannan, Sarah	John E. Grogan	Margaret M. Grogan
Grogan	Sara	Catherine	07-Dec-1890	27-Nov-1890	Thomas E. Grogan	Brannan, Sarah	Edward Healy	Ella French
Grogan	Joseph		07-Sep-1884	28-Aug-1884	Thomas Edward Grogan	Brannan, Sara Catherine	Joseph Grogan	Ann Kenny
Grogan	James	Gibbons	12-May-1901	01-May-1901	Thomas Grogan	Brannan, Sarah	John Brannan	Mary Ellen Dowling
Grogan	Loretta		02-Jan-1898	21-Dec-1897	Thomas Grogan	Brannan, Sara	John Brannan	Ella Burke
Grogan	Mary	Stella	03-Oct-1886	27-Sep-1886	Thomas Grogan	Brannan, Sara	Michael J. Grogan	Ellennor Brennan
Grogan	Mary	Agnes	25-Aug-1895	11-Aug-1895	Thomas Grogan	Holden, Anastasia	Joseph Grogan	Mary Agnes Holden
Grogan	Thomas	Leo	15-Apr-1894	03-Apr-1894	Thomas Grogan	Brannan, Sara	Charles Grogan	Catherine Hickey
Grogan	Thomas	Edward	15-Mar-1896	06-Mar-1896	Thomas Grogan	Brannan, Sara	Joseph Hiskey	Mary Grogan
Grogan	Carroll	Raymond	05-Apr-1891	11-Mar-1891	William Grogan	Ward, Margaret	Joseph Patrick Frogan	Catherine Agnes Golden
Grogan	Margaret	Bernadine	23-Oct-1892	08-Oct-1892	William Grogan	Ward, Margaret	Richard Higgins	Mary Roddy
Grogan	William	Leon	23-Oct-1887	09-Oct-1887	William Grogan	Ward, Margaret	Thomas Grogan	Ann Ryan
Groghan	John	Edward	09-Oct-1892	01-Oct-1892	Thomas Groghan	Brannan, Sara Catherine	Edward J. Brannan	Mary A. Brannan
Groghan	Rose		29-Jul-1888	22-Jul-1888	Thomas Groghan	Brannan, Sara	James Kelly	Rose Delaney
Gronan	Conrad	Joseph	21-Jan-1891	27-Nov-1824	Conrad Gronan	Clusman, Dorothy	John Hollfelder	
Groome	Alice		18-Feb-1894	20-Jan-1894	George Groome	Gough, Margaret		Catherine Beierlein
Groome	Christina	Ann	16-Feb-1896	01-Feb-1896	George Groome	Gough, Margaret Ann	Henry Dinan	Margaret Talbott
Groome	Margaret	Helen	16-Oct-1892	12-Oct-1892	George Groome	Gough, Margaret		Catherine Beierlein
Groome	William	George	15-Mar-1891	27-Feb-1891	George Groome	Gough, Margaret		Margaret Beirleiein
Gross	Francis		24-Jul-1883	20-Jul-1883	Bosley Gross	McBride, Mary Ann	James McBride	Margaret Bannahars
Gross	Eloise	Naomi	25-Nov-1898	04-Nov-1896	Francis Henry Gross	Wyatt, Laura		Naomi Gross
Gruner	George	John	12-Jun-1892	01-Jun-1892	George Gruner	Boden, Francis	Joseph Guthrie	Mary Joan Guthrie
Gruner	John		13-Feb-1895	13-Feb-1853	George Gruner	Stunch, Christina		
Grupert	Mary	Agnes	15-Oct-1905	29-Sep-1905	Andrew Grupert	Davey, Elizabeth	James Davey	Mary Davey
Guckert	Mary	Mildred	17-Nov-1901	1-Nov-1901	Charles Guckert	Ward, Mary		Catherine Ward
Guckert	Ann	Mary	17-Nov-1895	10-Nov-1895	Edward Guckert	Griffin, Mary	John Swain	Ann Guckert
Guckertz	Margaret		27-Feb-1898	15-Feb-1898	Edward Guckertz	Griffin, Mary	William A. McConnell	Margaret McConnell
Guerin	Charles	Jeffreys	22-Nov-1908	7-Nov-1908	John F. Guerin	Mulligan, Mary R.	Phillip Reilly	Mary Wall
Guerin	Genevieve	Mittredam	12-Jan-1908	[Blank]	John F. Guerin	Mulligan, Mary R.	Maythias B. Mulligan	Mary Burns
Guerin	John	Francis	9-Jan-1907	23-Dec-1906	John F. Guerin	Mulligan, Mary A,	Henry L. Mulligan	Ann L. Mulligan
Guerin	Mary	B.	30-Jul-1905	22-Jul-1905	John F. Guerin	Mulligan, Mary	Matthew Guerin	Margaret Guerin
Guerin	Julia	Margaret	8-Aug-1909	26-Jul-1909	Joseph M. Guerin	Tippett, Carolina	John D. Clancey	Stella Powers
Guerin	Leonora	Seagar	19-Apr-1908	29-Mar-1908	Richard Guerin	Honora Broler	Nicholas McGraw	Rose Judge
Guerin	Mary	Margaret	19-Aug-1900	04-Aug-1900	Richard Guerin	Boland, Nora	Patrick Connors	Margaret Guerin
Guerin	Richard	Matthew	29-Oct-1905	10-Oct-1905	Richard Guerin	Boland, Nora	Ignatius Eckles	Elizabeth Daly
Guerin	Sarah		18-Sep-1898	06-Sep-1894	Richard Guerin	Boland, Nora	Michael Brey	Ann Fitzpatrick
Guerin	William	Thos	13-Sep-1896	26-Aug-1896	Richard Guerin	Brolan, Nora	Daniel O'Sullivan	Mary O'Sullivan
Guffers	John	Henry	27-Jul-1890	16-Jul-1890	John J. Guffers	Feeley, Mary	Mich Guffers	Mary Guffers
Guidice	Charles		23-Jun-1907	15-Jun-1907	James Guidice	Ringlal, Alice	Charles Meade	Sidonia Ringlal
Guinan	Francis	Leon	14-Jan-1900	19-Dec-1899	John Guinan	Gensburg, Lillian	Francis Schaffer	Rose Monaghan
Guinan	John		29-Jun-1902	20-Jun-1902	John Guinan	[Blank], Elizabeth	John Ropes	Mary Kenny
Guinin	Alexander	James	15-Sep-1895	30-Aug-1895	John Guinin	Gensburg, Lillian	Alexander Scherer	Barbara Huber
Gulhaar	Charles		24-Dec-1894	02-Jun-1879	Edward C. Gulhaar	Waskes, Emma		Julia Finnan
Gulhaar	Edward	Leon	21-Dec-1894	05-Sep-1875	Edward Gulhaar	Gulhaar, Emma	Patrick John Moylan	
Gulhaar	Frederick	Russell	15-Jun-1902	04-Jun-1902	Ernest Joseph Gulhaar	Sutton, Mary	Joseph Finnan	Ann Finnan
Gulhaar	William		27-May-1906	14-May-1906	Joseph Ernest Gulhaar	Sutton, Mary Agnes	Charles J. Gulhaar	Mary Ellen Gulhaar
Gunning	Elizabeth		28-Mar-1897	26-Mar-1897	Francis Gunning	Riley, Mary	Nicholas Riley	Margaret Riley
Gunning	Elizabeth		13-Sep-1893	10-Sep-1893	James A. Gunning	Reilly, Margaret	Thomas Gunning	Mary Gill
Gunning	Francis	Xavier	15-Mar-1895	11-Mar-1895	James A. Gunning	Reilly, Margaret	Luke Sweeney	Mary A. Reilly
Gunning	Helen	Loretta	11-Sep-1896	09-Sep-1896	James A. Gunning	Reilly, Margaret	Joseph Reilly	Loretta Reilly
Gunning	Helen		26-Apr-1903	21-Apr-1903	James A. Gunning	Reilly, Margaret	Francis Gunning	Mary Gunning
Gunning	John	Brooke	3-Nov-1901	27-Oct-1901	James A. Gunning	Riley, Margaret	Joseph Gunning	Catherine Gunning
Gunning	Margaret	Helen	03-Aug-1890	27-Jul-1890	James A. Gunning	Reilly, Margaret	John J. Gunning	Catherine Naughton
Gunning	Margaret		22-Nov-1891	18-Nov-1891	James A. Gunning	Reilly, Margaret	William P. Reilly	Ann J. Garrity
Gunning	Thomas	Patrick	21-Aug-1899	20-Aug-1899	James A. Gunning	Reilly, Margaret	James Gunning	Mary Gunning
Gunning	William	Reilly	28-Nov-1897	24-Nov-1897	James A. Gunning	Reilly, Margaret		Margaret Naughton
Gunning	Catherine		16-Jun-1889	10-Jun-1889	James Augustine Gunning	Reilly, Margaret	Martin John Reilly	Catherine Gunning
Gunning	James	Ignatius	01-Aug-1886	31-Jul-1886	James Gunning	Riley, Margaret	Francis Cumming	Agnes Riley
Gunning	Joseph	Reilly	14-Oct-1900	13-Oct-1900	James Gunning	Reilly, Margaret	James Rifney	Loretta Reilly
Gunning	Phillip	Michael	8-May-1904	5-May-1904	James Gunning	Reilly, Margaret	Thomas O'Neal	Agnes Lannon
Gunning	Alena	Cecelia	27-Jan-1901	10-Jan-1901	John Gunning	Martin, Agnes	Luke Sweeney	Vera Martin
Gunning	Cecelia		03-Dec-1899	09-Oct-1899	John Gunning	Martin, Agnes	John Byrnes	Mary Byrnes
Gunning	Joseph	Wheeler	09-Oct-1898	01-Oct-1898	John Gunning	Martin, Cecelia	William Martin	Alma Martin

51

LAST NAME	FIRST NAME	MIDDLE	BAPTISM	BIRTH	Father	Mother	SPONSORS
Gunning	Roland	Ignatius	08-Aug-1897	31-Jul-1897	John J. Gunning	Martin, Agnes	Francis Casey
Gunnip	Catherine		27-Nov-1887	23-Nov-1887	Thomas Gunnip	Murray, Mary	Edward James Brannan
Gunnip	Robert	Joseph	14-Mar-1886	10-Mar-1886	Thomas Gunnip	Murray, Mary	Michael Corcoran
Gurin	Raymond	Matthew	23-Aug-1903	16-Aug-1903	John Gurin	Mulligan, Mary	Thomas Gurin
Gusimans	Nicolas		30-Dec-1890	22-Dec-1890	Joseph Gusimans	Arena, Mary	Raymond Michele
Guthrie	James	Hamilton	04-Jul-1886	22-Jun-1886	Joseph Guthrie	Boden, Mary Joan	Sylvester Hogan
Guthrie	Joseph	Henderson	14-Aug-1887	01-Aug-1887	Joseph Guthrie	Boden, Mary Joan	Slyvester Hogan
Haase/Mehling	Julian	Eugene	06-May-1888	12-Apr-1888	Henry A. Haase	Eberle, Rose E.	George Mehling
Habnicht	Myrtle	Elizabeth	21-Jun-1891	11-Jun-1891	Charles Habnicht	Hamilton, Ann	John E. Healy
Habnicht	Irene	Elizabeth	15-Oct-1905	29-Sep-1905	Walter Habnicht	Griffin, Margaret	Thomas Conway
Hackett	Frances	V.	03-Apr-1898	24-Mar-1898	Patrick Hackett	Michaels, Frances	Thomas Hackett
Hackett	Mary	Margaret	13-Oct-1901	29-Sep-1901	Patrick Hackett	Michaels, Frances	John Boyle
Hafer/Holleran	Margaret	Mary	04-Jul-1902	12-Apr-1882	Martin Hafer	Miller, Eda	Mary O'Day
Hagan	James	Edward	21-Jun-1896	03-Jun-1896	Edward Hagan	Silk, Winifred	Charles Hagan
Hagan	Margaret	Mary	23-Oct-1892	13-Oct-1892	James Edward Hagan	Silk, Winifred	John Steadman
Hagan	Peter	James	11-Nov-1890	11-Nov-1890	Michael T. Hagen	Monaghan, Bridget	Patrick Monaghan
Hagan	Agnes		01-Jun-1890	15-May-1890	Peter Hagan	McComb, Margaret	Martin C. Hennessey
Hagan	Leo		07-May-1899	10-Apr-1899	Peter Hagan	McComb, Margaret	James Hagan
Hagan	Margaret	Elizabeth	16-Aug-1896	23-Jul-1896	Peter Hagan	McComb, Margaret	
Hagan	Peter		31-Jan-1892	31-Dec-1891	Peter Hagan	McComb, Margaret	Edward Willis
Hagan	Samuel	George	31-Dec-1893	04-Dec-1893	Peter Hagan	McComb, Margaret	Joseph Henry McNally
Hagarty	Joseph		24-Feb-1895	16-Feb-1895	James J. Hagarty	Bahn, Kate	Charles O'Hara
Hagarty	John		13-May-1912	26-Apr-1912	[Blank]	Hagerty, Elizabeth	Catherine Hagerty
Hagerty	Ann		07-Mar-1886	22-Feb-1886	Hugh Hagerty	Moffat, Catherine	Mary Ann Hagerty
Hagerty	Hugh		27-Jul-1890	19-Jul-1890	Hugh Hagerty	Moffet, Catherine	Rich Hagerty
Hagerty	Helen		14-Mar-1886	02-Nov-1886	James Hagerty	Bohan, Catherine	Dennid Hagerty
Hagerty	Mary		08-Jun-1884	26-May-1884	James Hagerty	Hahn, Catherine	William Hagerty
Hagerty	Michael		31-Jul-1887	24-Jul-1887	James Hagerty	McMahon, Ida	Michael Hagerty
Hagerty	Stephen	James	05-Feb-1888	22-Jan-1888	James Hagerty	Bahn, Catherine	Stephen Bahn
Hagerty	William	Leo	22-Jan-1893	13-Jan-1893	James Hagerty	Bahn, Catherine	Charles Joseph Hart
Hagerty	Catherine		27-Jul-1890	15-Jul-1890	Jns Hagerty	Bahn, Cath	
Hagerty	James		27-Jul-1890	15-Jul-1890	Jns. Hagerty	Bahn, Cath	
Hagerty	Anastasia		16-Mar-1890	09=Mar-1890	John Hagerty	McMahon, Ida	William Reilly
Hagerty	Elizabeth		20-Oct-1885	30-Sep-1885	John Hagerty	McMaines, Isabelle	M.F. Foley
Hagerty	John		15-Jun-1890	02-Jun-1890	John Hagerty	Walsh, Mary	John Mullen
Hagerty	John		21-Jun-1896	17-Jun-1896	John Hagerty	McMahon, Ida	Barclay Keelty
Hagerty	John		29-May-1898	21-May-1898	John Hagerty	McMahon, Ida	Patrick O'Neill
Hagerty	Mary		16-Dec-1894	09-Dec-1894	John Hagerty	McMahon, Ida	Michael Keelty
Hagerty	Sara		08-May-1892	25-Apr-1892	John Hagerty	Welch, Mary	Ann Hagerty
Hagerty	James		02-Nov-1884	23-Oct-1884	John Patrick Hagerty	Killeen, Mary	James William Hagerty
Hagerty	James	Thomas	31-May-1891	17-May-1891	Patrick Hagerty	[Blank], Mary	Thomas Killeen
Hagerty	Margaret		03-Jan-1886	18-Dec-1885	Patrick Hagerty	[Blank], Mary	Thomas Killeen
Hagerty	Mary	Theresa	09-Oct-1887	25-Sep-1887	Patrick Hagerty	Killeen, Mary	Patrick J. Coughlin
Hagerty	William	Patrick	01-Jul-1883	15-Jun-1883	Patrick Hagerty	Kileen, Mary	Thomas Conway
Hagerty	Ann	Emmett	21-Apr-1889	09-Apr-1889	William Hagerty	Moylan, Margaret	Patrick Moylan
Hall	Robert	Emmett	18-Feb-1912	8-Feb-1912	George Hall	Gibbon, Ann	Catherine McLaughlin
Haine	Mary	Catherine	4-Jun-1905	25-May-1905	Patrick Haine	Kelly, Mary	Catherine Steadman
Haines	Austin		14-Feb-1904	About 1867	Charles Haines	[Blank], Elizabeth	
Hainsworth/Stockett	Eleanor		20-Apr-1893	21-Jun-1823	John Hainsworth	Wooden, Elizabeth	Sr. Caesarina
Haire	Catherine	Loretta	2-Dec-1906	26-Nov-1906	Patrick Haire	Kelly, Mary	Julia Whitty
Haire	John	Francis	02-Dec-1900	20-Nov-1900	Patrick Haire	Kelly, Mary	John Cavanaugh
Haire	Joseph		20-Apr-1902	09-Apr-1902	Patrick Haire	Kelly, Margaret	John Monaghan
Haire	Leon		02-Aug-1903	21-Jul-1903	Patrick Haire	Kelly, Mary	John J. Kelly
Hall	Edward	E.	12-Sep-1897	11-Aug-1897	Douglas Vincent Hall	Siebold, Rosa	Edward Howe
Hall	John	Vincent	22-Sep-1895	30-Aug-1895	Douglas Vincent Hall	Siebold, Rose	John Nolan
Hall	Owen	Dorsey	05-Dec-1890	01-Jun-1852	Frederick Hall	Taylor, Sara	
Hall	Samuel	Andrew	18-Jun-1882	02-May-1882	George Hall	Casby, Mary Ann	Andrew Casby
Hall	William	Leven	15-Mar-1885	05-Mar-1885	George Hall	Casby, Mary Ann	William Gardner
Hall	Grace	Isabelle	13-Apr-1890	25-Mar-1888	Henry Hall	Rogers, Mary	John Phillip Prell
Hall	Emory	Edgar Hall	9-Jun-1913	13-Nov-1882	Jesse A. Hall	Hubbard, Ann M.	
Hall	William	Bernard	22-May-1893	02-Apr-1893	Owen B. Hall	Armstrong, Mary M.	Gertrude Hall
Hall	Florence	Agnes	05-Apr-1891	24-Jan-1891	Owen Bernard Hall	Armstrong, Mary Martina	Joan McKenzie
Hall	anaBelle	Martina	14-Aug-1887	16-Jul-1887	Owen Hall	Armstrong, Martina	Mary McKenna

LAST NAME	FIRST NAME	MIDDLE	BAPTISM	BIRTH	Father	Mother	SPONSORS	
Hall	Joseph	Laura	23-Dec-1884	22-Dec-1884	Owen Hall	Armstrong, Martina		Hessie E. Kelly
Hall	Charles	Edward	21-Apr-1885	07-Feb-1885	Redmond Hall	Reeder, Elizabeth Alice		Ann Reeder
Hall	James	Claude	19-Feb-1888	24-Jan-1888	Samuel Hall	Knapp, August		Margaret Hall
Hall	Frances	De Sales	20-Mar-1910	1-Mar-1910	William Hall	Kilpatrick, Ella		Sarah Kilpatrick
Halloran	Bartholomew		22-Apr-1906	4-Apr-1906	Bartholomew Halloran	Haffer, Mary	William Dogherty	Mary Catherine Halloran
Halloran	John	Robert	14-Sep-1913	29-Aug-1913	Bartholomew Halloran	Stafer, Minny	Robert Boyle	Della Halloran
Halloran	Louise		11-Jul-1909	1-Jul-1909	Bartholomew Halloran	Haffer, Mary	James Joseph Kube	Louise Kube
Halloran	Mildred	Elizabeth	20-Mar-1904	3-Mar-1904	Bartley Halloran	Haffer, Mary	Edward W. Fitzgerald	Nora Clancy
Halloran	James		2-Jul-1911	18-Jun-1911	Bartley Halloran	Hafan, Minnie	Peter O'Dea	Virginia Knightly
Halloran	Thomas	Edward	08-Feb-1884	08-Feb-1884	John Halloran	Killilea, Julia		Sabina Killilea
Halloran	Eugene	Joseph	11-Apr-1886	19-Mar-1886	John J. Halloran	Killilea, Julia	William Halloran	Delia Halloran
Halloren	Mary	Ann	01-Nov-1891	27-Oct-1891	Martin Halloran	Nolan, Catherine	Bartholomew Halloran	Ann Joyce
Halpin	Mary	Ann	27-Jul-1902	23-Jul-1902	Bartley Joseph Halloren	Haffner, Margaret	Michael Sheridan	Mary O'Day
Halpin	Alice		04-Jun-1882	30-May-1882	Michael Halpin	Kerr, Alice	Thomas Kerr	Sara McAfee
Hamill	Louis		04-Jul-1901	24-Jun-1901	Hugh Hamill	Tidimann, Minnie	James Roche	Margaret Madden
Hamill	Wilhelmina	Margaret	13-Jan-1895	01-Jan-1895	Hugh Hamill	Tidimann, Wilhelmina	Michael Madden	Margaret Madden
Hamill	Hugo		14-Nov-1897	05-Nov-1897	Hugo Francis Hamell	Tidimann, Willhelmina Marg.	William Callender	
Hamill	Mary	Genevieve	15-Sep-1901	10-Sep-1901	John Hamill	Owens, Mary	John Owens	Mary McGinnis
Hamill	William		06-May-1884	29-Jul-1883	William Hamill	Cable, Ann		Sara Beard
Hamilton	John		27-Jun-1912	24-Dec-1888	Albert Hamilton	Scott, Ida	John Reilly	Julia Miller
Hamilton	Mary	Clair	29-Dec-1889	09-Dec-1889	C. Hamilton	McDonough, Mary	John Caveney	Ellen McDonough
Hamilton	Catherine	Teresa	20-Mar-1887	04-Mar-1887	Charles Hamilton	McDonough, Mary	Bernard Roddy	Catherine T. McDonough
Hamilton	James	Franklin	15-Feb-1903	05-Feb-1903	Francis Hamilton	McCormack, Mary	John Wall	Helen Wall
Hamilton	George	Bennet	20-Nov-1904	2-Nov-1904	George Hamilton	Hamilton, Elizabeth	Thomas Bennet	Katherine Henderson
Hamilton	James	Steward	12-Nov-1905	6-Nov-1905	George Hamilton	Henderson, Elizabeth		Agnes Cunningham
Hamilton	Mary	Elizabeth	6-Mar-1910	21-Feb-1910	George Hamilton	Henderson, Elizabeth		Elizabeth Stewart
Hamilton	Charles	Edward	21-Jan-1891	28-Feb-1863	James Hamilton	Rafter, Mary A.	Hugh Bannon	
Hamilton	Henry	Bunting	09-May-1886	12-Mar-1886	John A. Hamilton	Reilly, Mary E.		Catherine V. Reilly
Hamilton	Ann		07-Oct-1883	27-Sep-1883	Taylor Hamilton	Smith, Elizabeth Ann	James McDevitt	Ann Burke
Hamilton	William	Taylor	14-Dec-1890	23-Feb-1890	Taylor Hamilton	Smith, Elizabeth Ann		Ann Kimmett
Hammel	Charles	Edward	11-Apr-1886	13-Mar-1886	Charles Hammel	Welsh, Ellen	Martin Welsh	Delia Holmes
Hammel	Joseph	Meredith	29-Jan-1888	14-Jan-1888	Charles Hammel	Welsh, Helen	Francis Patrick McNally	Honora Holmes
Hammel	William	James	20-Apr-1890	30-Mar-1890	Charles W. Hammel	Walsh, M.		
Hammel	Edward	Michael	12-Apr-1914	21-Mar-1914	William E. Hammel	Donohue, Mary		Cecelia McAdams
Hammel	Margaret		18-Dec-1904	6-Dec-1904	William E. Hammel	Donahue, Mary A.		Mary Kirkendell
Hammell	Mary	Elizabeth	28-Jun-1891	18-May-1891	Charle Hammell	Welch, Helen	Martin John Mchale	Margaret Ryan
Hammill	Margaret		15-May-1892	21-Dec-1891	Stephen C. Hammill	McGlone, Sara		Ann McGraw
Hammit	Margaret	Ann	24-Aug-1913	4-Aug-1913	Arthur Hammit	Peters, Ann		Margaret Cooke
Hammond	Mary	Ann	21-Mar-1890	15-Mar-1811	Jacob Hammond	Hammond, Sophia		Helen Jenkins
Hampson	John	Josephine	30-May-1886	15-May-1886	John Hampson	Judge, Margaret	Francis McGuigan	Mary McGuigan
Hand	Helen	Antonia	25-Jan-1885	17-Jan-1885	Edward Hand	Lennon, Catherine B.	William Hand	Hattie Hand
Hand	Irene	Agnes	28-Jan-1883	21-Jan-1883	Edward Hand	Lennon, Catherine	John Hand	Catherine Friel
Hand	Edward	Alexander	06-Mar-1887	26-Feb-1887	Edward L. Hand	Lennon, Catherine B.	Francis Hess	Bridget Hand
Hand	Ann	Mary	21-Feb-1892	31-Jan-1892	John Hand	Cahill, Mary A.	George Norwood	Catherine Canaban
Hand	Florence	Ignatius	16-May-1886	23-Jan-1886	John Hand	Cahill, Mary	Carl Santmyer	Margaret Santmyer
Hand	George		11-Jun-1899	26-May-1899	John Hand	Scales, Mary	George Hamberger	Mary Santemyer
Hand	John	Joseph	05-Jan-1889	17-Dec-1889	John Hand	Cahill, Mary	John Leonard	Mary Scales
Hand	Joseph	Robert	7-Aug-1904	25-Jul-1904	John Hand	Scales, Mary	James R. Mitchell	Agnes Sterchcomb
Hand	Michael	Leo	22-Jul-1894	28-Jun-1894	John Hand	Scales, Mary		Mary Santmyer
Hand	Mary	Laura	04-Dec-1887	16-Nov-1887	John S. Hand	Cahill, Mary A.	Joseph B. Fitzpatrick	Catherine A. Fitzpatrick
Hand	Annabelle	Teresa	12-Mar-1893	27-Feb-1893	John Thomas Hand	Cole, Ida B.	William Giles Hand	Mary Hand
Hand	Beatrice		07-Mar-1886	26-Feb-1886	Michael Hand	Warnig, Henrietta	Edward Hand	Catherine Hand
Hand	James		03-Feb-1884	26-Jan-1884	Michael Hand	Warnick, Henrietta	John A. Fallow	Hannah Winters
Hand	Edna	Margaret	2-Apr-1904	27-Jan-1904	William L. Hand	Perrine, Sophia V.		Ella Pate
Handlan	Genevieve		28-Oct-1906	3-Oct-1906	John Handlan	Fitzpatrick, Rose		Loretta Hoyle
Handley	John	Joseph	21-Apr-1907	5-Apr-1907	John Handley	Larkins, Ella	John Slater	Agnes Handley
Handley	Thomas	Edward	23-May-1909	9-May-1909	John J. Handley	Larkins, Ellen	James Curran	Elizabeth Hughes
Handlon	Mary	Ann	11-Dec-1889	12-Nov-1889	Dennis Handlon	Waldron, Elizabeth	John Waldron	Mary Waldon
Handly	Mary	Margaret	2-Jul-1905	12-Jun-1905	John Handly	Larkins, Ella	Patrick Handly	Teresa Curran
Handrahan	Helen		23-Apr-1882	13-Apr-1882	Edward Handrahan	Hanlon, Mary	James White	Mary Roche
Handy	Margaret		25-Jan-1897	11-Jan-1860	Charles Eisman Handy	Michael, Elizabeth		Helen Ester
Handy	Caroline		21-Dec-1896	17-Apr-1893	Charles Handy	Dinan, Margaret		Ann M. Weherman
Handy	Margaret		21-Dec-1896	29-Aug-1890	Charles Handy	Dinan, Margaret		Ann M. Weherman

ST JOHN'S BAPTISMS 1882-1912

LAST NAME	FIRST NAME	MIDDLE	BAPTISM	BIRTH	Father	Mother	SPONSORS
Handy	Mary	Daisy	21-Dec-1896	15-Oct-1895	Charles Handy	Dinan, Margaret	Ann M. Werherman
Handy	Thomas		8-Nov-1905	About 1883	Thomas Handy	Franks, Isabelle	Elizabeth Clinton
Hanley	Mary	Helen	31-Dec-1882	07-Dec-1882	John Hanley	Gately, Margaret	Thomas Joiner / Julia Grimes
Hanley	Felice	Joseph	23-Jun-1912	14-Jun-1912	Joseph Hanley	McCall, Rose	William McCubbin / Elizabeth McCall
Hanlon	Dennis	Francis	02-Jun-1887	13-Dec-1886	Dennis F. Hanlon	Waldron, Elizabeth	B.D. Richardson / Ann Waldron
Hanlon	Robert	Benjamin	13-Dec-1891	19-Nov-1891	Dennis Francis Hanlon	Waldron, Elizabeth	Robert Benjamin Golden / Mary Golden
Hanlon	Carmelita		06-Dec-1903	11-Nov-1903	John Hanlon	Fitzpatrick, Rose	Charles Hiel / Ella Hiel
Hanlon	Ella		01-Dec-1901	6-Nov-1901	John Hanlon	Fitzgerald, Rose	Charles Heil / Elle Heil
Hanlon	William	Edward	24-Jan-1909	22-Dec-1908	John Hanlon	Fitzpatrick, Rose	Ella Heil
Hanlon	Michael		06-Dec-1886	03-Dec-1886	Michael Hanlon	Drew, Catherine	William Hanlon / Ann Hickey
Hanrahan	John		24-Aug-1884	17-Aug-1884	Edward Hanrahan	Hanlon, Mary	Joseph F. Haupt / Hannah Brennan
Hanshaw	Genevieve	Mary	21-Apr-1901	15-Mar-1901	Lloyd Edgar Hanshaw	McCart, Mary Alice	Genevieve McCart
Harbaugh	Charles		7-May-1911	26-Apr-1911	Charles Harbaugh	Johnson, Mary Catherine	John T. Johnson / Elizabeth Johnson
Harbler	Ann	Mary	19-Jun-1910	11-Jun-1910	Anthony Joseph Harbler	[Blank], Mary Elizabeth	Louis Harbler / Ann Mary Harbler
Hardesty	Charles	Cornelius	19-Mar-1893	About 1860	Cornelius Hardesty	[Blank], Mary	Bridget Gereghty
Hardesty	John	Clarence	19-Mar-1893	About 1880	Cornelius Hardesty	[Blank], Mary	Helen Sullivan
Harding	Mary		06-Apr-1890	17-Mar-1890	James E. Harding	McCarthy, Mary	Stephen Campbell / Mary McCarthy
Harding	Gertrude	Lillian	23-Aug-1891	24-Jul-1891	James Edward Harding	McCarthy, Mary Ignatia	Mary Ann Mariman
Harding	Agnes		16-Feb-1896	17-Jan-1896	James Harding	McCarthy, Mary	William Gammie / Mary Elizabeth Harding
Harding	Francis		11-Jul-1892	About 1820	John Harding	Harding, Frances	
Hardman	Francis	Joseph	17-Aug-1913	27-Jul-1913	Francis Hardman	Conway, Mary	Joseph [Blank] / Julia Conway
Hardman	Helen	Mary	31-Oct-1915	11-Oct-1915	Francis Hardman	Conway, Mary	Timothy O'Keife / Helen Byrne
Hardy	Margaret		28-Aug-1898	21-Aug-1898	Edward Hardy	Williams, Mary	William Cullen / Agnes Williams
Hare	Clarence	Edward	29-May-1904	21-Feb-1882	Charles Hare	Lovett, Frances	Thomas Kelly / Barbara E. Neilson
Hare	Margaret	Mary	03-Oct-1897	24-Sep-1897	Patrick Hare	Kelly, Mary	Peter Kavanaugh / Catherine Hare
Harley	William	Charles	5-Sep-1915	16-Aug-1915	Patrick Harley	Barry, Catherine E.	George Barry / Mary Murphy
Harman	Elinor		28-Oct-1906	16-Oct-1906	Andrew Harman	Gothard, Mary	Samuel Gothard / Emma Wilkins
Harmes	Elizabeth	Helen	6-Dec-1908	18-Nov-1908	William Harmes	Burrier, Margaret	John F. Novotny / Elizabeth Burrier
Harmes	Margaret	Agnes	13-Feb-1910	30-Jan-1910	William Harmes	Burrier, Margaret	William Flynn / Agnes Fitzpatrick
Harmon	Helen	Regina	11-Aug-1907	23-Jul-1907	Henry Harmon	Roddy, Ann	William McKewen / Ann Roddy
Harmon	James	Bernard	12-Jun-1904	30-May-1904	Henry Harmon	Roddy, Ann	James B. Roddy / Ann McSherry
Harner	Elizabeth	Dorothy	9-Nov-1914	21-Mar-1911	Howard L. Harner	Landburg, Jeanette	Margaret Walsh
Harner	John	Ralph	9-Nov-1914	27-Aug-1909	Howard L. Harner	Landburg, Jeanette	Ann Conroy
Harper	Charles	Hamilton	16-Dec-1888	30-Oct-1888	Andrew Jackson Harper	Heymes, Mary	Mary Louise Hagan
Harper	Florence	Virginia	21-Feb-1892	09-Feb-1892	Louis Harper	Carter, Florence	James Golden / Caroline Kendall
Harr	James		27-Jan-1889	22-Jan-1889	James Harr	Lacey, Joan	William Connolly / Catherine Connolly
Harrigan	Mary	Placida	24-Jan-1897	13-Jan-1897	M. Harrigan	Wallace, Cecilia	Stephen Miskell / Mary Ryan
Harrigan	William	Aloysius	25-Jan-1903	14-Jan-1903	Marco Harrigan	Wallace, Cecilia	Edward Meehan / Nannie McDonald
Harrigan	Ann		29-Jun-1902	20-Jun-1902	Timothy Harrigan	Doory, Ella	Robert Doyle / Holden, Mary
Harrigan	Eugene		02-Nov-1890	23-Oct-1890	Timothy Harrigan	Doory, Helen	John Harrigan / John Josephine Doory
Harrington	Thomas		05-Jan-1901	05-Jan-1901	Edward Harrington	Doory, Helen	Sarah Logan
Harrington	Catherine		21-Jul-1889	06-Jul-1889	Edward Harrington	Cooney, Catherine	John Joseph Harrington
Harris	Alice	Mary	27-Feb-1887	14-Feb-1887	Benjamin Francis Harris	Rayner, Rionora	Benjamin Griggs Harris / Eleanora Ann Harris
Harris	Edward	Joseph	16-Aug-1896	13-Jul-1896	Charles Harris	Busick, Mary	
Harris	George	Robert	18-Sep-1887	04-Aug-1887	Charles W. Harris	Busick, Mary E.	George W. Busick / Harriett Wellmore
Harris	E. Mary	Cecelia	18-Oct-1914	4-Oct-1914	Daniel Harris	Riordan, Irene V.	James Busick / Julia O'Sullivan
Harris	Mary	Norene	18-Mar-1906	1-Mar-1906	Ernest Harris	Doyle, Ann M.	Michael Doyle / Margaret Doyle
Harris	Charles	Howell	07-Dec-1884	20-Oct-1884	James Wesley Harris	Busick, Mary	James Miller
Harris	Mary	Elizabeth	3-Mar-1907	2-Feb-1907	John B. Harris	McCluskey, Teresa	Francis Auton / Emma Cecelia Pryor
Harris	Regina		25-Sep-1887	17-Sep-1887	John Francis Harris	Harris, Mary Regina	Clarence A. Noppenberger / Alice B. Connolly
Harris	John	Leroy	21-Jul-1912	7-Jul-1912	John Harris	McCluskey, Theresa	Clarence Edmund Harris / Helen Mary Harris
Harris	Laurence	Joseph	5-Sep-1909	27-Aug-1909	John Harris	McCluskey, Theresa	James McCluskey / Mary Clark
Harrison	John		25-Feb-1883	15-Jan-1883	John Wesley Harris	Busick, Mary Elizabeth	Laurence Joseph Hart / Margaret McCluskey
Harrison	Andrew		19-Jan-1892	25-Aug-1895	Andrew Harrison	Egan, Rose	John Sullivan / Eleanor Sullivan
Harrison	Frances	Cecelia	24-Jul-1910	17-Jul-1910	George Green Harrison	Kelly, Frances	Francis Dugles / Mary Agnes Meyers
Harrison	Margaret	Ann	19-Feb-1882	15-Feb-1882	John Harrison	Keller, Martha E.	Thomas Kelly / Julia McGraine
Harrison	William	Abraham	23-Sep-1884	20-Dec-1798	John Harrison	Lee, Catherine	Queenis Whitney
Harrison	William		07-Oct-1883	25-Sep-1883	Robert Harrison	McNeir, Elizabeth	James Miller / Ann Marie Kelly
Hart	Helen	Beatrice	26-Sep-1915	31-Aug-1915	John Hart	Dowd, Bridget	Catherine Byrne
Hart	John	Patrick	27-Jun-1915	16-Jun-1915	Thomas Hart	Clinton, Elizabeth	Hugo Byrne / Agnes Roach
Hart	Margaret		15-Nov-1891	11-Nov-1891	Thomas Hart	Clancy, Helen	John McTighe / Bridget Devlan
Hart	Mary	Ellen	27-Jul-1890	18-Jul-1890	Thomas Hart	Clancy, Ellen	J. Clemens / Mary Kelly
Hart	Francis	Joseph	16-Jul-1882	08-Jul-1882	William Hart	Kelly, Elizabeth	Thomas Hudson

LAST NAME	FIRST NAME	MIDDLE	BAPTISM	BIRTH	Father	Mother	SPONSORS	
Hart	Francis		18-Feb-1883	25-Jan-1883	William Hart	Kelly, Mary	John McNeil	Margaret McNeil
Hartlein	Hnry	M.	23-Oct-1887	19-Oct-1887	Henry Hartlein	Gardner, Ann	John Bracken	Ann Bracken
Hartlein	John	Michael Absalom	20-Jan-1884	18-Jan-1884	Michael Henry Hartlein	Gardner, Ann	John Mooney	Rachel Mooney
Hartman	Florence		24-May-1884	24-May-1884	Charles Hartman	Smith, Mary Catherine		
Hartman	Helen	Mary	5-Feb-1905	19-Jan-1905	Charles Hartman	Costello, Ann E.	Henry Costrllo	Mary Costello
Hartman	Adeline	Ann	20-Aug-1915	06-Jun-1915	George Hartman	[Blank], Laura	John Taylor	Ann Birbl
Hartman	Alice	Bernardine	26-Jul-1903	13-Jul-1903	Herman Hartman	Hubbell, Mary	Bernard Hubbell	Mary Hartman
Hartman	Bertha	Catherine	07-Oct-1894	29-Sep-1894	Herman J. Hartman	Hubbell, Mary	William Hubbell	Bertha Hubbell
Hartman	Mary	Elizabeth	10-Aug-1890	24-Jul-1890	Herman Joseph Hartman	Hubbell, Mary Margaret	William Joseph Hartman	Mary Catherine Hubbel
Hartman	Thomas	Francis	18-Oct-1891	14-Sep-1891	Herman Joseph Hartman	Hubbel, Mary Magdalene	Benjamin Graham	Mary Graham
Hartsock	Margaret	Mary	12-Jun-1887	30-May-1887	Marco Jesse Hartsock	Fallon, Margaret Cecilia	John Joseph Connor	Mary Agnes Fallon
Hassell	Mary	Ethel	11-Jul-1886	16-Jun-1886	William Hassell	Neser, Margaret A.		Mary Neser
Hastry	Edwin	Lewis	4-Sep-1904	14-Aug-1904	Joseph F. Hastry	Olsen, Sophia A.		Gertrude Kelly
Hastry	Mary	Louise	30-Jun-1907	11-Jun-1907	Joseph F. Hastry	Olsen, Ann Sophia		Florence Kelly
Hatch	John		05-Feb-1893	03-Feb-1893	Jame Francis Hatch	Whelan, Catherine	John Hagerty	Elizabeth Whelan
Hatch	Charles		17-Mar-1889	01-Mar-1889	James Hatch	Whelan, Catherine	Thomas Dohoney	Margaret Whelan
Hatch	James	Matthew	30-Nov-1890	15-Nov-1890	James Hatch	Whelan, Catherine	Peter Duffy	Bridget Margaret Collins
Hatfield	Terence	Edward	31-Jul-1904	6-Jul-1904	James D. Hatfield	Forward, Mary		Ella Forward
Hatfield	Jerome	Chester	14-Jun-1896	27-May-1896	James Hatfield	Norwood, Mary	James Gilroy	Ella Gilroy
Hatfield	Mary	Margaret	23-Apr-1899	14-Apr-1899	James Hatfield	Forward, Margaret	James Forward	Margaret Hanberry
Haughey	Mary	Margaret	10-Jul-1899	31-May-1899	Francis Haughey	McAllister, Mary		Joan McAllister
Hauthen	Ann	Virginia	21-Feb-1886	17-Dec-1885	John Hauthen	O'Conner, Mary	Jerome A. Keppel	Emma Collier
Havepuick	Irene	Elizabeth	29-Mar-1885	05-Mar-1885	Charles Havepuick	Egan, Mary	James McAdams	Elizabeth Jenkins
Hayden	Lucy	Bernice	10-May-1896	31-Mar-1896	Phillip Hayden	Jones, Ida E.		Mary Lathorum
Hayden	Mary	Rose	09-Oct-1887	12-Oct-1887	Phillip M. Hayden	Jones, Ida E.	Claudius Floyd	Mary R. Floyd
Haydn	William	Arthur	21-Mar-1886	02-Mar-1886	Charles Haydn	Hamilton, Alice	William Heuisler	Martha Hadyn
Hayden	Lillian	Louise	01-May-1887	20-Apr-1887	Charles Hayes	Fornes, Mary		Elizabeth Cassidy
Hayes	Mary		11-Dec-1892	29-Nov-1892	Charles Hayes	Farran, Mary	John Thomas Egan	Josephine Doory
Hayes	Charles	Joseph	31-Mar-1895	12-Mar-1895	Charles Joseph Hayes	Forns, Mary	Charles Joseph Kelly	Agnes Doory
Hayes	Martin		20-Dec-1908	5-Dec-1908	Edward Hayes	McGuiness, Margaret	Dennis [Blank]	Mary Kimmett
Hayes	Edward	Patrick	4-Jun-1905	19-May-1905	Edward Joseph Hayes	McGuiness, Margaret	John Joseph Sann	Ann [Blank]
Hayes	John	Joseph	3-Mar-1907	17-Feb-1907	Edward Joseph Hayes	McGuiness, Margaret	Edward Murphy	Mary Murphy
Hayes	Elizabeth		16-Nov-1913	3-Nov-1913	William Hayes	Clinton, Ellen	Edward Hayes	Elizabeth Clinton
Hayes	Joseph	Clinton	24-Dec-1911	7-Dec-1911	John Hayes	Clinton, Ellen	Joseph A. Muldoon	Delia Muldoon
Hayes	Laurence	Thomas	26-Dec-1898	16-Feb-1895	John Hayes	Apps, Alice	Edward Byrne	
Hayes	Mary	Ellen	13-Mar-1910	7-Mar-1910	John Hayes	Clinton, Ellen	Joseph Muldoon	Delia Muldoon
Hayes	John	Thomas	7-Feb-1909	28-Jan-1909	John Thomas Hayes	Clinton, Eleanor	Martin Hayes	Rose Gray
Hayes	Martin		27-Oct-1907	13-Oct-1907	John Thomas Hayes	Clinton, Helen	Hugo J. Byrne	Catherine Byrne
Hayes	Joseph	Edward	15-Jan-1911	12-Nov-1910	William Edward Hayes	Allen, Nellie G.		Nora Moylan
Hayes	Ellen		1-Dec-1912	29-Oct-1912	William Hayes	Allen, Ellen		Catherine Trimmings
Hayes	Florence		25-Apr-1885	05-Apr-1885	William Hayes	Harkins, Margaret	John Harkins	Helen Fahey
Hayes	Margaret	Elizabeth	20-Sep-1914	15-May-1914	William Hayes	Allen, Ellen		Elizabeth Koenig
Haynie	Francis	Joseph	13-Jan-1901	01-Jan-1901	Roswell Haynie	Rohleder, Ada	Joseph Herr	Catherine Herr
Healey	Robert	Bruce	29-Oct-1899	06-Oct-1899	Dennis Healey	Byrnes, Catherine	J.S. Pettigue	Rose McMaines
Healey	John	Joseph	28-Jul-1895	15-Jul-1895	James Healey	Byrnes, Catherine	James Connolly	Rose McKenna
Healey	Mary		09-Jan-1898	29-Dec-1897	James Healey	Halfpenny, Ann	Patrick Delaney	Catherine Clynes
Healey	Elizabeth		26-Oct-1890	09-Oct-1890	John Healey	Halpin, Ann	Frank Arthur	Joan Halpin
Healey	Earl	Charles	29-May-1910	15-May-1910	John E. Healy	Walters, Eleanor	Charles R. Elwood	Ann Noppenburger
Healy	Thomas		28-Aug-1887	26-Aug-1887	Peter Healey	Puller, Maud	James Finegan	Mary Byrnes
Healy	Dennis		15-Oct-1882	12-Oct-1882	Dennis E. Healy	Byrnes, Catherine	Martin Byrnes	Clara Healy
Healy	James	Randolph	10-Aug-1884	03-Aug-1884	Dennis Healy	Byrnes, Catherine	Patrick Byrnes	Catherine Veronica Byrnes
Healy	Mary		21-Feb-1892	10-Feb-1892	James Healy	Halfpenny, Ann	James Arthur	Mary Halfpenny
Healy	Michael	Bernard	29-Oct-1893	19-Oct-1893	James Healy	Halfpenny, Ann	Bernard Halfpenny	Bridget Halfpenny
Healy	John	Dennis	31-May-1914	15-May-1914	John E. Healy	Walters, Eleanor	Hugh F. Ward	Mary Murray
Healy	August	Joseph	18-Aug-1889	05-Aug-1889	John Edward Healy	Bertrand, Laura Virginia	Edward Healy	Sara Egan
Healy	Elmer		19-Feb-1882	09-Feb-1882	John Edward Healy	Bertrand, Laura	James B. Healy	Mary J. Healy
Healy	Helen	Gertrude	12-Jul-1885	29-Jun-1885	John Healey	Bertrand, Laura		Catherine Farron
Healy	Delia	Margaret	18-Nov-1883	30-Oct-1883	John Healy	Bertrand, Laura	James Bernard Owens	Clara Burg
Healy	Eliza	Mary	05-Dec-1886	15-Nov-1886	John Healy	Kuch, Philomena	John Stanislaus	Catherine Bertrand
Healy	George	Evangeline	06-Jul-1901	18-Dec-1898	Patrick Healy	Lindsay, Ann V.		Ann McCluskey
Heany	Maybel	Agnes	05-Jul-1898	26-May-1898	Henry A. Heany	Stehle, Agnes M.	Martin Reilly	Julia Reilly
Hebrank	Mary	Augusta	17-Aug-1890	03-Aug-1890	Joseph George Hebrank	Stehle, Agnes M.	Benjamin F. Graham	Mary H. Graham
Hebrank	Ruth		11-Dec-1892	01-Dec-1892	Joseph George Hebrank	Stehle, Mary Agnes	Frederick Stehle	Mary Agnes Stehle

LAST NAME	FIRST NAME	MIDDLE	BAPTISM	BIRTH	Father	Mother	SPONSORS	
Hechter	Charles	William	15-May-1904	6-May-1904	Charles Hechter	Smith, Virginia M.	Francis McGuire	Agnes Smith
Hechter	Virginia	Rose	29-Oct-1905	18-Oct-1905	Charles Hechter	Smith, Regina	William Smith	Mary Michael
Heiligenstadt	William	Nolan	21-Jul-1907	8-Jul-1907	John Heiligenstadt	Wood, Ann Louise		Mary Kane
Hellman	William	Wallace Slater	30-Nov-1884	12-Nov-1884	Frederick T. Hellman	Wallace, Ann E.	Owen Daily	Ann Helman
Hellman	Edgar	Arthur	21-Nov-1886	21-Jul-1886	Henry Hellman	Blaney, Caroline	Arthur Lyness	Ann Rhodes
Hellman	Irene	Matilda	18-Nov-1888	31-Aug-1888	Henry Hellman	Blaney, Caroline		Sara Joan Stedman
Helmcamp	William	Edward	06-Jan-1882	06-Dec-1881	Joseph Edward Helmcamp	Hughes, Elizabeth		Theresa Helmcamp
Henderson	Charles		07-Jun-1887	19-May-1887	Charles Henderson	Guy, Alice		Mary Gorman
Hennessy	Margaret	Ellen	24-Jan-1886	15-Jan-1886	John Hennessy	Lyons, Alice	John Cloony	Ann M. Casey
Hennessy	Sara	Elizabeth	24-Jun-1883	15-Jun-1883	John Hennessy	Lyons, Alice	James Clancy	Helen Guilfoyle
Henning	John	Curtis	2-Sep-1906	14-Jul-1906	George Henning	Taylor, Rachel		Mary Brannan
Hepburn	George	Richmond F.	29-Mar-1914	1-Mar-1914	George Hepburn	Richmond, Martha	S. Benham	Mary Sayles
Herbert	Ann	Dorothy	17-Feb-1907	5-Feb-1907	Nicholas Herbert	Christner, Margaret V.	Joseph S. Hooper	Ann Herbert
Herbert	Mary		09-Sep-1900	03-Aug-1900	Nicholas Herbert	Christner, Margaret	George Herbert	Mary Armstrong
Herbert	Raymond	Paul	04-Jul-1897	30-Jun-1897	Nicholas Herbert	Christner, Margaret	Charles Gammie	Barbara Herbert
Herbert	Nicholas	Joseph	3-Jul-1904	25-Jun-1904	Nicholas J. Herbert	Christner, Margaret	Samuel Christner	Katherine Hooper
Herbert	Priscilla		15-Mar-1891	About 1852	Thomas Herbert	[Blank]		
Herbert	Joseph	Elmer	19-May-1895	01-May-1895	William Herbert	Koerner, Ethel		
Herbes	Henry	Lee	28-Sep-1890	14-Sep-1890	Henry Herbes	Steed, Lillian	Henry Herbes	Catherine Franz
Herbes	Joseph	Adrian	04-Sep-1892	17-Aug-1892	William Henry Herbes	Steed, Lillian	Ambrose William Herbes	Agnes Byrne
Herl	Helen	Margaret	19-Sep-1915	26-Aug-1915	Anthony Herl	Brossoe, Evelyn	Rudolph [Blank]	Alice Hoben
Herlihy	Elizabeth		14-Sep-1884	01-Sep-1884	Michael Herlihy	Houlihan, Mary	John Merring	Elizabeth Fleming
Herman	Mary	Catherine	1-Oct-1905	17-Sep-1905	Andrew Herman	Gottard, Mary	Joseph Gottard	Catherine [Blank]
Hermann	Ann	Catherine	18-Dec-1899	20-May-1834	Francis Hermann	Hermann, Catherine		Mary Sorback
Herold	Dora	Cecelia	23-Dec-1907	24-Nov-1907	August Herold	Herold, Mary	George Herold	Cecelia Herold
Herring	Francis	Joseph	4-Apr-1909	19-Mar-1909	John Joseph Herring	Leimbach, Louise Catherine	Francis W. Koester	Wilhelmina A. Engelmeyer
Herron	Agnes		08-Jan-1882	01-Jan-1882	Frederick Herron	McCarthy, Bridget	James Mullen	Caroline Herron
Herron	Bridget	Ann	12-Jul-1891	27-Jun-1891	John Leo Herron	Phelps, Sophia Isabelle	Thomas John Brazier	Mary O'Sullivan
Herron	Mary	Belle	08-Sep-1895	19-Aug-1895	Leo Herron	Phillips, Belle	Bernard Mullen	Mamie Hagan
Herron	Joseph		11-Dec-1892	07-Dec-1892	Peter Herron	Miller, Mary	James Henry Mullen	Catherine Luthardt
Herron	Frederick		14-Dec-1890	10-Dec-1890	Peter Joseph Herron	Miller, Mary	John Leo Herron	Victoria Miller
Heskson	Catherine		01-Dec-1901	25-Nov-1901	John Heskson	Glynn, Mary	Thomas King	Catherine Cline
Hess	Mary		13-May-1902	10-Apr-1902	Charles Hess	Saulsbury, Rose		Rebecca Roundtree
Hess	Thomas	Irvin	04-Mar-1894	01-Feb-1894	Charles Hess	Green, Mary	Horatio Green	Florence Hess
Hess	Charles	Horatio	14-Aug-1892	29-Jul-1892	Charles Thomas Hess	Green, Mary Elizabeth	Francis Whitney Curran	Adalaide Louise Hutchins
Hess	Elizabeth	Mary	26-Dec-1885	19-Dec-1885	Isaac Hess	Miller, Mary Ann		Lucy Gordon
Hess	William	Arthur	02-Dec-1883	25-Dec-1882	Isaac Hess	Miller, Mary Ann		Elizabeth Knighton
Hessian	Gertrude	Alice	10-Apr-1887	11-Mar-1887	Phillip William Hess	Rooney, Mary	James Fitzpatrick	Alice Giblin
Hessian	Agnes	Teresa	11-Apr-1886	15-Mar-1886	John Hessian	Connors, Bridget	John Nester	Mary J. Conner
Hessian	John		02-Jun-1889	21-May-1889	John Hessian	Connors, Bridget	Michael Hessian	Mary Kelly
Hessian	Martin	Thomas	27-Nov-1887	14-Nov-1887	John Hessian	Connors, Bridget	Michael Hessian	Ann Prigon
Hessian	Mary	Catherine	22-Mar-1885	15-Mar-1885	John Hessian	Connors, Bridget		Bridget Hessian
Hession	William	Joseph	10-Jan-1894	31-May-1894	Patrick Hessian	Garrity, Mary	James Burke	Sara Hessian
Hession	Martin		13-Sep-1896	04-Sep-1896	John Hession	Glenn, Mary	John Courtney	Ella Courtney
Hession	Sarah		14-Feb-1904	28-Jan-1904	John Hession	Glenn, Mary	John Hughes	Sara Ryan
Hession	Thomas	Francis	12-Dec-1897	27-Nov-1897	John Hession	Glenn, Mary	Edward McKevitt	Winifred Glenn
Hession	Winifred		19-Nov-1899	11-Nov-1899	John Hession	Glenn, Mary	Patrick Hughes	Mary Rattigan
Hession	Catherine	Mary	29-Jan-1893	20-Jan-1893	Patrick Hession	Garrity, Mary	Andrew Gerrity	Catherine Gereghty
Hession	Margaret	Winifred	12-Jul-1891	27-Jun-1891	Patrick Hession	Garrity, Mary	Michael Hession	Mary Garrity
Hestry	Stephen		23-Jun-1901	28-May-1901	Joseph Hestry	Olsen, Ann		Mary [Blank]
Heuser/Kilduff	Mary	A.	19-Dec-1906	01-Jan-1834	Samuel Heuser	Green, Catherine		Mary A. Kilduff
Hewes	Thomas		03-May-1886	30-Apr-1886	[Blank]	Hewes, Bridget		Jennie Molloy
Heyl	George	Earnest	12-Aug-1894	31-Jul-1894	George E. Heyl	Gillen, Ann	Patrick Gillen	Margaret Winter
Heyl	Mary	Emily	17-Aug-1892	07-Aug-1892	George Ernest Heyl	Gillen, Ann		Mary A. Landers
Heyl	Charles	Vernon	10-Oct-1909	30-Sep-1909	George Heyl	Gillen, Ann		Margaret Matthews
Heyl	Hugh	Francis	17-Jul-1904	23-Jun-1904	George Heyl	Gillen, Ann	Hugh McElroy	Ann McElroy
Heyl	James	Robert	14-Dec-1902	27-Nov-1902	George Heyl	Gillen, Ann	David Kenny	Margaret Richards
Heyl	Joseph	Albert	10-Mar-1907	26-Feb-1907	George Heyl	Gillen, Ann	Thomas Watkins	Mary Kennis
Heyl	Margaret		11-Oct-1896	19-Sep-1896	George Heyl	Gillen, Ann	James Gillen	Rose O'Hara
Hickey	Henry	Raymond	02-May-1886	20-Apr-1886	Patrick Hickey	Clarke, Mary E.	Terence McMahon	Ann McMahon
Hickman	Margaret	Agnes	6-Jul-1913	18-Jun-1913	Henry Hickman	Walter, Katherine	James Connelly	Sarah Heath
Higgins	Mary		17-Feb-1884	10-Feb-1884	James Corcoran Higgins	Kearns, Mary	James Kenny	Catherine Kearns
Higgins	Edward		27-Sep-1885	14-Sep-1885	James Higgins	Kearns, Mary	James Lynch	Sarah Henry

ST JOHN'S BAPTISMS 1882-1912

LAST NAME	FIRST NAME	MIDDLE	BAPTISM	BIRTH	Father	Mother	SPONSORS	
Higgins	Margaret	Helen	06-Aug-1893	25-Jul-1893	John Higgins	Welch, Mary Helen	Michael Higgins	Mary Madden
Higgins	Mary		29-Apr-1888	11-Apr-1888	John Higgins	Welch, Mary	John J. McGuire	Mary Higgins
Higgins	William	Francis	05-Oct-1890	14-Sep-1890	John T. Higgins	Welch, Mary Helen	Michael Higgins	Margaret Higgins
Higgins	Agnes		02-Nov-1884	25-Oct-1884	Martin Higgins	Hester, Bridget	Patrick Noonan	Mary Hester
Higgins	Agnes		19-Jun-1892	03-Jun-1892	Martin Higgins	Hester, Bridget	John Colbert	Mary Grady
Higgins	Catherine		24-Nov-1889	10-Nov-1889	Martin Higgins	Hester, Bridget	Thomas Patrick O'Hara	Ann McGarvey
Higgins	Mary	Theresa	26-Feb-1888	12-Feb-1888	Martin Higgins	Hester, Bridget	Patrick Nester	Bridget McGarry
Higgins	Helen		03-Dec-1882	25-Nov-1882	Richard Edward Higgins	Nagle, Mary	Richard Higgins	Margaret Higgins
Higgins	Henry		05-May-1889	19-Apr-1889	Richard Higgins	Nagle, Mary	Michael Higgins	Joan Henry
Higgins	Richard	Edward	29-Aug-1886	18-Aug-1886	Richard Higgins	Nagle, Mary	Robert Smith	Joan Smith
Hildo	William	Edward	27-Oct-1889	Oct 1889	L.C. Hildo	Stribble, Mary		Ann Wilcox
Hill	Genevieve		12-Nov-1905	2-Nov-1905	Edward Hill	Whitney, Katherine	Francis Whitney	Elizabeth Whitney
Hill	William		25-Dec-1898	06-Dec-1898	William Hill	Donohoe, Regina	Charles Deninger	Mary Codd
Hill	Esther	Mabel	28-Jun-1896	03-Jun-1896	William J. Hill	Donohue, Esther R.	Joseph C. Dunn	Mary Rice
Hillman	Mary	Elizabeth	7-Mar-1915	18-Feb-1915	Edward F. Hillman	Shoultz, Elizabeth	James Whelan	Epulura Dougarra
Hillman	August	Stanislau	25-Oct-1885	02-Aug-1814	Zacharia Hillman	Taylor, Louise		Jon Barlow
Hiltz	Mary		10-Jan-1882	11-Dec-1881	Charles Edward Hiltz	Kenny, Mary		Mary Crescenta Miller
Hindle	Edward	Elmer	12-Oct-1902	19-Sep-1902	Edward Hindle	Whitney, Katherine	John Wood	Stella Whitney
Hines	Catherine		28-Apr-1889	17-Apr-1889	Patrick Hines	Touhy, Honora	William H. Gough	Ann Touhy
Hines	Helen		30-Nov-1890	18-Nov-1890	Patrick Hines	Touhy, Honora	John McGraw	Margaret Ann Donovan
Hines	Margaret		02-Aug-1885	21-Jul-1885	Patrick Hines	Touhy, Honora	John King	Margaret Holden
Hinkel	Joseph	Henry	26-Nov-1902	25-Oct-1902	Henry Hinkel	Potts, Eva		Mary Finn
Hinkey	Cecelia	Enez	8-Sep-1907	10-Aug-1907	William M. Hinkey	[Blank], Rose B.C.		Cecelia E. Hardesty
Hinkle	William	Francis	16-Jan-1898	10-Dec-1897	Henry Hinckle	Poat, Eva	William Callender	
Hinkle	Ann	Gertrude	10-Nov-1895	14-Oct-1895	Henry Hinkle	Poat, Mary	Daniel Crimmins	Ann Enis
Hinkle	Florence		05-May-1889	17-Apr-1889	Henry Hinkle	Poat, Eva	Leonard Honick	Rachel Honick
Hinkle	Gatium		06-Dec-1896	07-Nov-1896	Henry Hinkle	Poat, Mary		Grace Menkin
Hinkle	Henry		11-Jan-1888	01-Jan-1888	Henry Hinkle	Poat, Eva		Emma J. Meakin
Hinkle	John	Elmer	26-Nov-1900	11-Oct-1900	Henry Hinkle	Poat, Eva		Catherine McCluskey
Hinkle	Margaret	Eva	31-Jan-1892	17-Jan-1892	Henry Hinkle	Poat, Eva	Joseph J. Reilly	Margaret Hinkle
Hinkle	Rose	Teresa	13-May-1894	25-Apr-1894	Henry Hinkle	Poat, Mary Eva	William Edw. Callender	Mary Groppe
Hitchcock	William	Henry	20-May-1898	13-Jun-1828	[Blank]	[Blank]		
Hoban	Agnes	Genevieve	29-Jan-1899	18-Jan-1899	Francis Hoban	Hennessy, Barbara	Edward Hennessy	Sarah Houck
Hoban	Alice	Mary	02-Dec-1894	21-Nov-1894	Francis M. Hoban	HennessY, Barbara	Michael Curley	Mary Hennessy
Hoch	Robert	Francis	4-Feb-1906	21-Jan-1906	Christian F. Hoch	Neuhauser, Veronica	Joseph M. Lamb	Ann Lamb
Hoch	Anthony	Edgar	22-Oct-1911	7-Oct-1911	Christian Hoch	Newhouser, Veronica	Edgar [Blank]	Mary [Blank]
Hoch	John	Joseph	3-Apr-1907	13-Mar-1907	Christian Hoch	Neuhauser, Veronica	John A. Heummer	Mary Lynch
Hoch	Joseph	Christian	23-May-1909	6-May-1909	Christian Hoch	Neuhauser, Veronica	Josephine F. Busch	Helen Cline
Hoch	Veronica	Dorothy	14-Mar-1915	24-Feb-1915	Christian Hoch	Neuhauser, Veronica	Charles Hearne	Katherine Hopper
Hoch	Ann	Veronica	27-Apr-1902	17-Apr-1902	Christopher Hoch	Neuhauser, Veronica	Francis Hoffer	Mary Kernan
Hoch	Helen	M.	8-May-1904	24-Apr-1904	Christopher Hoch	Neuhauser, Veronica	Joseph Breuning	Margaret Hopper
Hoddinoff	Elizabeth		15-Jan-1882	06-Jab-1882	Elisha C. Hoddinoff	Collins, Helena	George M. Hoddinoff	Dorcas Ann Sindall
Hodges	Mary	Ann	06-Oct-1896	25-Oct-1826	Bradley H. Simpson	Brace, Hanah A.		
Hoeckel	William	Leonard	26-Feb-1911	13-Feb-1911	Francis Hoeckel	Russell, Elizabeth Mary	William Russell	Ellen Russell
Hoeckel	Ann	Celestine	19-Dec-1909	30-Nov-1909	Henry Hoeckel	Kimmett, Margaret	Thomas Kimmett	Mary Dolan
Hoeckel	Francis	Elizabeth	7-Jan-1912	26-Dec-1911	Henry Hoeckel	Kimmitt, Margaret H.	Williiam Bowes	Mary A. Bowes
Hoeckel	Mildred	Cecelia	26-Mar-1905	10-Mar-1905	John H. Hoeckel	Rowland, Mary	Howard Denn	Margaret Denn
Hoeckel	Catherine	Frances	8-Jul-1906	13-Jun-1906	John Hoeckel	Rowland, Margaret	Henry Hoeckel	Margaret Emmett
Hoen	George	Warner	26-Sep-1886	11-Sep-1886	George H. Hoen	Carey, Genevieve M.	Albert Hoen	Mary A. Landers
Hoen	Norbert	Carey	22-Jun-1884	06-Jun-1884	George H. Hoen	Carey, Jennie M.		Catherine C. McMahon
Hoen	Agnes	Teresa	16-Dec-1888	30-Nov-1888	George Henry Hoen	Carey, Joan Mary	David Francis Scott	Ida Mary Burke
Hoen	Alice	Ann	26-Jul-1891	17-Jul-1891	George Hoen	Carey, Joan	John Callaghan	Catherine Gorsuch
Hoen	Frances	Catherine S.	26-Oct-1893	12-Oct-1893	George Hoen	Carey, Joan Mary	Stephen Bonetto	Ann Chapman
Hoen	JeAnn		05-Feb-1882	07-Jan-1882	George Hoen	Carey, Joan	Thomas Carey	Margaret Healy
Hoffer	August		03-Apr-1898	28-Mar-1898	Thomas Hoffer	O'Brien, Mary A.	Eugene Hoffer	Veronica Hoffer
Hoffman	Ruth	Octavia	9-Feb-1915	11-Nov-1907	Adam Hoffman	Agnew, Eva	Richard Ormond	Julia Wolf
Hoffman	John	Leo	28-Mar-1897	19-Mar-1897	Chrs. Hoffman	Ryan, Mary	John Ryan	Jennie May
Hoffman	John	Frederick	4-Mar-1906	13-Feb-1906	Frederick C. Hoffman	May, Ann H.	John May	Catherine Kennedy
Hoffman	Henry	A.	10-Aug-1902	03-Aug-1902	John C. Hoffman	Burns, Catherine	Henry Hoffman	Elizabeth C. Hoffman
Hoffman	Theodore	Adam	28-Apr-1907	17-Apr-1907	John C. Hoffman	Burns, Catherine	Theodore A. Hoffman	Mary A. McNeal
Hoffman	Elizabeth	Mary	1-Jan-1905	18-Dec-1904	John C. Hoffman Jr.	Byrnes, Catherine	Anthony L. MAnnr	Catherine Colbert
Hoffman	Catherine		7-Mar-1909	24-Feb-1909	John Conrad Hoffman	Byrnes, Catherine	John Thomas Byrnes	Ann Hoffman
Hoffman	Ann		01-Nov-1896	22-Oct-1896	John Hoffman	Byrnes, Catherine	Adam Schevley	

ST JOHN'S BAPTISMS 1882-1912

LAST NAME	FIRST NAME	MIDDLE	BIRTH	BAPTISM	Father	Mother	SPONSORS
Hoffman	Elizabeth		05-Jun-1900	24-Jun-1900	John Hoffman	Burns, Catherine	Elizabeth Hoffman
Hoffman	George		14-Jun-1895	23-Jun-1895	John Hoffman	Byrnes, Catherine	Mary Dempsey
Hoffman	James	Paul	25-Oct-1912	3-Nov-1912	John Hoffman	Burns, Catherine	Catherine Brockmeyer
Hoffman	John	Leroy	8-Dec-1910	18-Dec-1910	John Hoffman	Byrnes, Catherine	Ella Kenny
Hoffman	Margaret	Elizabeth	7-Feb-1904	11-Nov-1904	John Hoffman	Krouse, Emma	Margaret Crismer
Hoffman	Mary		12-Aug-1898	21-Aug-1898	John Hoffman	Burns, Catherine	Mary Hoffman
Hoffman	Thomas	Joseph	3-Oct-1915	14-Feb-1915	John Hoffman	Burns, Catherine	Mary McNeill
Hoffman	Joseph		06-Aug-1895	25-Aug-1895	Louis Hoffman	Regan, Mary	Ann Conroy
Hoffmeyer	Agnes	Margaret	12-Jan-1907	3-Feb-1907	John Hoffmeyer	Ressinger, Edith Margaret	Ann McBride
Hoffmeyer	Leona	Cecelia	20-Jun-1904	10-Jul-1904	John Hoffmeyer	Keiringer, Edith	William G. Murphy
Hoffmeyer	John	Joseph	20-Apr-1902	04-May-1902	John Joseph Hoffmeyer	Reisinger, Margaret	Joseph Hoffmeyer
Hoffmeyer	Margaret	Gertrude	26-Jan-1909	21-Feb-1909	Joseph Hoffmeyer	Loman, Pauline	Mary Murphy
Hogan	Catherine	Genevieve	01-Apr-1887	03-Apr-1887	Arthur Hogan	McNamara, Margaret	Gertrude McNamara
Hogan	George		09-Nov-1888	18-Nov-1888	Arthur Hogan	McNamara, Margaret	Mary McNamara
Hogan	John	Matthew	26-May-1885	27-May-1885	Arthur Hogan	McNamara, Margaret	Catherine Ward
Hogan	James	Daniel	1-Mar-1912	17-Mar-1912	James Daniel Hogan	Sheehan, Margaret A.	Mary O'Keefe
Hogan	Mary	Margaret	30-Aug-1908	6-Sep-1908	James Daniel Hogan	McGinn, Nellie Theresa	William McDowell
Hogan	John		28-Apr-1882	30-Apr-1882	John Hogan	O'Keefe, Catherine	Mary Agnes McGinn
Hogan	Leon	Aloysius	28-Oct-1887	30-Oct-1887	John Hogan	O'Keefe, Catherine	Mary Hogan
Hogan	Margaret	Helen	7-Sep-1915	19-Sep-1915	Leon Hogan	Grogan, Margaret Elena	Mary Grogan
Hogan	Bernard		31-Jan-1897	28-Feb-1897	Michael Hogan	Hagans, Catherine	Catherine Healey
Hogan	Joseph		06-Mar-1894	03-Jun-1894	Michael Hogan	Higgins, Catherine	Mary Higgins
Hogan	Edward		28-Mar-1899	23-Apr-1899	Michael J. Hogan	Hogan, Catherine	Mary Kelley
Hogan	Michael	James	03-Aug-1895	01-Sep-1895	Michael J. Hogan	Hagans, Kate	Francis Healey
Hogan	Ann	Isabelle	03-Dec-1897	16-Jan-1898	Peter Hogan	McComas, Margaret	James Healey
Hogan	Joseph		25-Oct-1901	10-Nov-1901	Peter Hogan	McComas, Margaret	John Lee
Hogan	John	Elizabeth	15-Dec-1882	24-Dec-1882	Silvester Hogan	Caldwell, Margaret	Margaret Curley
Hogan	Ann	Beatrice	05-Mar-1885	22-Mar-1885	Sylvester Hogan	Cowell, Margaret	Mary Carroll
Hoggins	Leah		25-Jan-1884	11-Nov-1904	Robert H. Hoggins	Howard, Leah	Mary Moan
Hoggson	Hamilton	Harrison	[Blank]	15-Mar-1889	[Blank]	[Blank]	Margaret Roby
Holbrook	John	Thomas	09-May-1889	09-Jun-1889	Felice Alphonse Holbrook	Whitney, Alice	Margaret E. Montgomery
Holden	James	Vincent	20-Jun-1898	03-Jul-1898	James Holden	Kelly, Ann	Ann Kelly
Holden	Joseph	Agnes	9-Mar-1910	20-Mar-1910	James Holden	Kelly, Ann	Mary O'Connor
Holden	Mary	Margaret	18-Jun-1901	30-Jun-1901	James Holden	Kelly, Agnes	Ann Holden
Holden	Mary	Regina	16-Jan-1907	3-Feb-1907	James Holden	Kelly, Ann Agnes	Mary Kelly
Holden	Francis	Joseph	19-Jun-1895	30-Jun-1895	James Holden	Kelly, Annie	Margaret Kelly
Holden	Mary	Genevieve	5-Feb-1904	21-Feb-1904	James S. Holden	Kelly, Ann A.	Catherine Maher
Holden	Mary		30-Oct-1892	13-Nov-1892	James Stephen Holden	Kelly, Ann Agnes	William Joseph Holden
Holden	Mary		22-Dec-1888	30-Dec-1888	Peter B. Holden	Hogan, Mary	Daniel Hogan
Holden	Mary		11-May-1895	19-May-1895	Peter B. Holden	Doory, Mary	William Holden
Holden	James		11-May-1897	16-May-1897	Peter Holden	Doory, Mary C.	Rev. James Holden
Holden	Florence	Elizabeth	6-Nov-1903	8-Nov-1903	Thomas Holden	Meskill, Elizabeth	James Moore
Holden	Margaret		31-Jan-1898	12-Feb-1899	William Joseph Holden	Shanahan, Winifred	Winifred Shanahan
Holland	James	Rogers	25-Jul-1886	08-Aug-1886	James Holland	Eney, Sara France	Susan Phillips
Holland	Mary	Ann	05-Nov-1893	26-Nov-1893	Melvin Holland	O'Grady, Delia	Robert Cathell
Hollbrook	Francis	Mordecai	20-Jan-1888	19-Feb-1888	Felice Alphonsus Holbrook	Whitney, Alice	George H. Whitney
Holman	Katherine	Agnes	25-Mar-1898	02-Apr-1898	Martin Holman	Nolan, Katherine	Mary Hamilton
Holmes	Frances		April 1879	11-Oct-1903	[Blank]	Birmingham, Mary	Margaret Holmes
Holmes	Michael		August 1896	06-Sep-1896	Michael Holmes	McGarry, Bridget	Nellie Brown
Holmes	Olive	Wardell	28-Sep-1901	27-Oct-1901	Michael Holmes	McGarry, Bridget	Ann Case
Holmes	Agnes	Mary	17-Feb-1899	05-Mar-1899	Michael P. Holmes	McGarry, Bridget	Mary [Blank]
Holmes	Ann		12-Jul-1894	29-Jul-1894	Michael P. Holmes	Warner, Mary	Nellty Dunn
Holmes	Joseph	Patrick	05-May-1889	12-May-1889	Michael Patrick Holmes	McGarry, Bridget	Eleanor Nolan
Holmes	Mary	Elizabeth	1-May-1912	2-Jun-1912	William Holmes	Brewer, Cecelia	Helen Gildenfenny
Holter	John	Albert	05-Jul-1887	17-Jul-1887	Louis Holter		Agnes Birmingham
Holy	Lillian	Agnes	15-Sep-1886	12-Jun-1886	Michael Holy	Connor, Margaret	Rev.P.J. Donahue
Homick	Mary	Elizabeth	Sept 1899	15-Oct-1899	Henry Homick	Beckwith, Ida	Michael Maloney
Honeman	Catherine	Lillian	27-Nov-1888	23-Dec-1888	Herman Honeman	Ludwig, Mary	Josephine Stapleton
Hook/Dorman	Ann	Mary	About 1836	17-Dec-1907	James Hook	Warner, Mary	Catherine Honeman
Hooke	Margaret		12-Nov-1889	24-Nov-1889	Michael Hooke	McClanahan, Elizabeth Joan	Rachel Grogan
Hooke	Mary		12-Nov-1889	24-Nov-1889	Michael Hooke	McClanahan, Elizabeth Joan	Catherine McClanahan
Hooper	George	T.	7-Aug-1904	21-Aug-1904	George Colton Hooper	Coughran, Maud	Mary Helen Gately
Hooper	Joan	Virginia	30-Jan-1887	10-Apr-1887	Kemp J. Hooper	Reese, Frances	Emma Travers
							Eva Hooper

58

LAST NAME	FIRST NAME	MIDDLE	BAPTISM	BIRTH	Father	Mother	SPONSORS
Hooper	Frances	Reese	16-Feb-1890	08-Dec-1889	Kemp J.Hooper	Reese, Frances	Ann Keener
Hooper	Mary	Agnes	08-Jan-1883	07-Jan-1883	Samuel John Hooper	Rhinehart, Mary Catherine	Catherine Poidal
Hooper	William	Edward	04-May-1902	24-Apr-1902	William Edward Hooper	Nagle, Hannah C.	Catherine Barrett
Hooper	Mary	Louis	03-Aug-1884	21-Jun-1884	William J. Hooper	Waltzen, Sophia	Eva Hooper
Hopkins	Ambrose	Francis	3-Jan-1909	21-Dec-1908	Michael Hopkins	Maloney, Mary	Rose Veronica Walter
Hopkins	Catherine	Ann	10-Nov-1895	19-Oct-1895	Michael Hopkins	Maloney, Mary	Rose Ellen Dolan
Hopkins	James	A,	20-Aug-1905	8-Aug-1905	Michael Hopkins	Maloney, Mary	Mary Shipley
Hopkins	John		18-Mar-1900	20-Feb-1900	Michael Hopkins	Maloney, Mary	Catherine Dunn
Hopkins	Mary	Agnes	03-Oct-1897	16-Sep-1897	Michael Hopkins	McLaughlin, Mary	Ann Hopkins
Hopkins	Michael	Thomas	02-Apr-1894	02-Apr-1894	Michael Hopkins	Maloney, Mary	Margaret Moloney
Hopkins	Regina	Sarah	23-Jun-1907	5-Jun-1907	Michael Hopkins	Maloney, Mary	Ann Hopkins
Hopkins	Charles	Anthony	20-Dec-1914	4-Dec-1914	Michael J. Hopkins	Maloney, Mary	Margaret Leone
Hopkins	William		8-Jan-1911	29-Dec-1910	Michael J. Hopkins	Maloney, Mary	Mary Shipley
Hopkins	Joseph	B.	20-Apr-1902	23-Mar-1902	Michael James Hopkins	Maloney, Margaret	Margaret Maloney
Hopkins	Michael		16-Apr-1894	11-Mar-1894	Michael James Hopkins	Moloney, Mary Ann	Margaret Moloney
Hopkins	Bernard		22-Sep-1912	3-Sep-1912	Michael Joseph Hopkins	Maloney, Mary	Catherine O'Neill
Hopper	Catherine	Ruth	12-Feb-1893	24-Jan-1893	August Hopper	Neuhauser, Veronica	Mary Guerin
Hopper	Theresa	Gertrude	05-Jul-1891	20-Jun-1891	August Hopper	Neuhauser, Veronica	Eva Hinkle
Hopper	Ann	Louise	25-Jun-1893	27-May-1893	Louis Hopper	Carter, Florence	Catherine McIntyre
Hopper	Mary	Ellen	03-Aug-1890	25-Jul-1890	Louis Hopper	Carter, Florence	Emma Kernan
Hopper	Catherine	Froney	29-Sep-1889	27-Sep-1889	Michael August Hopper	Neuhauser, Fronay	Mary Hopper
Hopper	Thomas	Francis	20-Nov-1892	09-Nov-1892	Thomas F. Hopper	O'Brien, Mary A.	Ann O'Brien
Hopper	Catherine		14-Jul-1889	06-Jul-1889	Thomas Francis Hopper	O'Brien, Mary Ann	Rose McIntyre
Hopper	Mary		14-Nov-1886	05-Nov-1886	Thomas Francis Hopper	O'Brien, Mary Elizabeth	Augustus Hopper
Hopper	Agnes		02-Dec-1900	20-Nov-1900	Thomas Hopper	O'Brien, Mary	Joseph O'Brien
Hopper	Ann		01-Nov-1896	25-Oct-1896	Thomas Hopper	O'Brien, Mary	James [Blank]
Hopper	Francis		12-Apr-1885	28-Mar-1885	Thomas Hopper	O'Brien, Mary	Michael O'Brien
Horan	Caroline	Rebecca	10-Feb-1895	03-Feb-1895	John Horan	Boyle, Mary	Frances Cook
Horan	Frances	Ellen	10-May-1891	22-Mar-1891	John Horan	Boyle, Mary	Mary McKee
Horan	John	Joseph	15-Jun-1884	24-May-1884	John Horan	Boyle, Mary	John A. Nelson
Horan	Mary	Margaret	26-Feb-1882	14-Feb-1882	John Horan	Boyle, Mary	Mary Fitzgerald
Horan	Catherine	Grace	30-Oct-1887	15-Oct-1887	John J. Horan	Horigan, Lucy, Mary	Mary A. Keenan
Horan	Cecelia	Margaret	20-Mar-1910	10-Mar-1910	Joseph Horan	Bailey, Ada	Grace Burns
Horan	Mary		7-Oct-1906	28-Sep-1906	Joseph Horan	Bailey, Ada	Ernest Weir
Horckel	Mary	Alice	4-Aug-1912	25-Jul-1912	Francis Joseph Horckel	Russell, Mary Elizabeth	Joan Reynolds Mullen
Horigan	Martin	Joseph	18-Nov-1894	11-Nov-1894	Timothy Horigan	Doory, Ella	Francis Doyle
Horneman	Margaret	Elvie	16-Feb-1896	04-Feb-1896	Bernard Horneman	Mullen, Sophia	John Leonard
Horrigan	Mary	Wallace	18-Aug-1895	12-Aug-1895	James Horigan	Gillespie, Catherine	George Maxwell
Horrigan	Alb ert	Timothy	11-Jun-1899	20-May-1899	Timothy Horrigan	Doory, Ellen	Eugene Logan
Horrigan	Francis	Thomas	27-Aug-1893	23-Aug-1893	Timothy Horrigan	Doory, Helen Elizabeth	Peter Bernard Holden
Horrigan	John		18-Nov-1888	09-Nov-1888	Timothy Horrigan	Doory, Helen	John Joseph Clancy
Horrigan	Mary		11-Oct-1896	30-Sep-1896	Timothy Horrigan	Doory, Helen	John Horrigan
Horrigan	William	Joseph	22-Nov-1891	10-Nov-1891	Timothy Horrigan	Doory, Ellen	Daniel Horrigan
Hoshall	C. Bernard		7-Nov-1915	25-Oct-1915	Bernard Hoshall	Cotter, Sara	Julia Lee
Houchens	John	Henry	21-Aug-1882	26-Jun-1882	John F. Houchens	O'Connor, Mary E.	Catherine Bitter
Houchens	Mary	Lillian	01-May-1887	26-Mar-1887	John T. Houchens	O'Connor, Mary E.	Emma Mary Ennis
Houston	Sara	Elizabeth	02-Jul-1893	18-Jun-1893	Samuel E. Houston	Mooney, Sara	Elizabeth Radivitch
Houston	Anastasia		23-Jul-1882	22-Jun-1882	Samuel Houston	Mooney, Sara	Richard Mooney
Houston	James	Wallace	22-Aug-1886	25-Jul-1886	Samuel Houston	Mooney, Sara	Richard Charles Murphy
Houston	John	Ellsworth	08-Sep-1895	25-Aug-1895	Samuel Houston	Mooney, Sarah	John F. Finnessey
Houszman	Margaret	Florence	07-Sep-1890	18-Aug-1890	John Houszman	Mooney, Sara	John Ratroitch
Houtcher	Elizabeth	Viola	20-Apr-1902	05-Apr-1902	Henry Thomas Houtcher	Cross, Ann	Francis Mooney
Howard	Emma	Beatrice	20-Jan-1884	15-Dec-1883	Frederick Howard	Connor, Mary Helen	Martha Keyser
Howard	Margaret		09-Apr-1896	29-Mar-1896	Henry Howard	Gilchrist, Catherine	Emma Collier
Howe	Ann	Elizabeth	05-Jul-1897	03-May-1864	Edward Howe	Brown, Ann	Margaret Gilchrist
Howe	Edward	Henry	21-Dec-1913	13-Dec-1913	John Howe	Hawkins, Gertrude	Sarah Gunster
Howe	Charles	Leon	9-Feb-1908	14-Jan-1908	John Howe	McBride, Emma	Ann Bridge
Howe	Thomas		11-Dec-1898	27-Mar-1898	Thomas Howe	McBride, Emma	Ann McBride
Howe	Thomas	Joseph	17-Nov-1895	04-Nov-1895	Thomas Howe	Dohoney, Sarah	Mary Kelly
Hozer	Leon	Carter	30-Apr-1903	08-Feb-1903	Thomas Hozer	Carter, Florence	Catherine Troy
Hubbard	Marilyn		23-Feb-1883	23-Dec-1882	Charles Hubbard	McWilliams, Mary Ann	Catherine Clark
Hubbard	Charles	William	12-Jan-1882	09-Nov-1880	Charles William Hubbard	McWilliams, Mary Ann	Ann Scandlebury
Hubbard	Albert	Carr	19-Aug-1888	12-Aug-1888	George Hubbard	Mullen, Mary Joseph	Catherine McWilliams
							Mary Rigney

LAST NAME	FIRST NAME	MIDDLE	BAPTISM	BIRTH	Father	Mother	SPONSORS	
Hubbard	Ann	Matilda	21-Feb-1886	11-Feb-1886	George Hubbard	Mullen, Mary	David Shay	Joan Riley
Hubbard	James	Leo	30-Dec-1894	22-Dec-1894	George Hubbard	Mullen, Mary	Charles O'Neill	Ella Monoghan
Hubbard	Bernard	Joseph	16-Mar-1884	03-Mar-1884	George W. Hubbard	Mullen, Mary Joseph	Bernard Mullen	Mary M. Mullen
Hubbard	William		03-May-1891	24-Apr-1891	George W. Hubbard	Mullen, Mary Joseph	William Joseph Gordon	Mary Magdalene Wiedefeld
Hubbard	Agnes	Adel	17-Mar-1901	08-Mar-1901	James Hubbard	McMahon, Margaret		Blanche Hubbard
Hubbard	Catherine	Michael	02-Jun-1889	07-May-1889	James Hubbard	McMahon, Margaret	Joseph Butler	Catherine McMahon
Hubbard	Catherine	Evelyn	08-Dec-1895	24-Nov-1895	James Hubbard	McMahon, Margaret	Joseph Flynn	Catherine Flynn
Hubbard	James	Howard	24-Aug-1884	05-Aug-1884	James Hubbard	McMahon, Margaret		Catherine McMahon
Hubbard	Joseph	Edward	22-Oct-1893	13-Oct-1893	James Hubbard	McMahon, Margaret		Mary Helen Flynn
Hubbard	Mary	Gertrude	18-Dec-1898	20-Aug-1898	Jerome Hibbard	Blake, Mary Elizabeth		Catherine Foley
Hubbard	Charles		19-Sep-1909	2-Feb-1909	Jerome Hubbard	Blank, Elizabeth		Emma Gephardt
Hubbard	Mary		14-Oct-1909	5-Sep-1905	Jerome Hubbard	Hubbard, Mary Elizabeth		Ann Purcell
Hubbard	Regina		07-Jun-1896	21-Feb-1896	Jerome Hubbard	Blank, Mary Elizabeth	Thomas Leonard	Mary Magner
Hubbard	Ann		28-Oct-1883	08-Oct-1883	Samuel Hubbard	Pindell, Ann Mary	Daniel Kane	Ann Quirk
Hubbard	Isabelle	Rose	26-Feb-1893	10-Feb-1893	Samuel Hubbard	Pindle, Mary	Thomas Whalen	Mary Ann Whalen
Hubbard	Samuel	Jerome	19-Jul-1885	08-Jul-1885	Samuel Hubbard	Pindall, Mary	William Quinn	Delia Collison
Hubbard	Grace	Elizabeth	04-Feb-1883	10-Dec-1882	Thelma J. Hubbard	Pindall, Mary	Jerome Hubbard	Ann Pindall
Hubbel	Mary	Catherine	07-Aug-1887	29-Jul-1887	Bernard J. Hubbel	Philips, Sara		Selina Phillips
Hubbel	Caroline	Gertrude	16-Jun-1912	22-May-1912	Joseph Hubbel	Thomason, Mary C.	Joseph T. Groffe	Margaret Sahlender
Hubbel	Walter		26-Oct-1884	10-Oct-1884	Joseph Hubbel	Houston, Mary		Sarah Houston
Hubbell	Ann	Margaret	08-Jan-1899	18-Dec-1898	August Hubbell	Burns, Sarah	Adolph Kerchnell	Mary Hebrank
Hubbell	Mary		13-Jun-1897	10-Jun-1897	August Hubbell	Whitney, Mary		Mary Hubbell
Hubert	Evelin	Catherine	31-Jul-1904	22-Jun-1904	John Hubbert	Whitney, Mary	Francis Roberts	Emma Whitney
Huber	Mary	Catherine	14-Apr-1907	18-Mar-1907	Albert Huber	Huber, Margaret	Joseph Bowers	Catherine Roberts
Huber	Charles	Wilmer	31-May-1908	14-May-1908	Alphonse Huber	McCrier, Catherine	Alexander Chalmers	Mary Herron
Huber	Henry	Adam	16-Nov-1890	02-Nov-1890	John Huber	McLeer, Catherine	Michael Adam Huber	Helen McLeer
Huber	Elizabeth		1-Oct-1911	13-Sep-1911	Nicolas Joseph Huber	Huber, Margaret	Henry Huber	Catherine Herzing
Huber	Ellen	B.	1-May-1910	14-Apr-1910	Nicolas Joseph Huber	Mettee, Ida	Alexander Shearer	Virginia Mettee
Huber	William	Thorton	1-Oct-1911	13-Sep-1911	Nicolas Joseph Huber	Mettee, Ida	William Huber	Barbara Shearer
Hubert	Charles	Joseph	09-Jun-1889	19-May-1889	John Hubert	Mettee, Ida	Charles Hubert	Sara Mettee
Hubert	John	Michael	28-Oct-1887	14-Oct-1887	John Hubert	Huber, Margaret	Michael Huber	Catherine Herzind
Huck	John	Bernard	17-Feb-1901	06-Feb-1901	Christian Huck	Huber, Margaret	John Curran	Catherine Herzint
Huck	Thomas	Frederick	17-Feb-1901	06-Feb-1901	Christian Huck	Newhauser, Veronica	Owen Hopper	Mary Curran
Hudson	James	William	20-Nov-1887	07-Nov-1887	Charles Hudson	Newhauser, Veronica	Samuel A. Martin	Ann Traynor
Hudson	Margaret	Ann	04-Aug-1895	26-Jul-1895	George Hudson	Dowling, Francis	George McGinnity	Louise Gibson
Huesman	John	Eugene	1-May-1910	15-Apr-1910	Claude Huesman	McGinnity, Gertrude	Eugene Kelly	Bridget Lynch
Huesman	Mildred	Ann	10-Aug-1913	26-Jul-1913	Claude Huesman	Kelly, Mary	Frederick Huesman	Ann Kelly
Huesman	James	Raymond	11-Jun-1911	6-Jun-1911	Claude J. Huesman	Kelly, Mary A.		Sarah J. Henry
Huesman	Mary	Margaret	4-Apr-1915	25-Mar-1915	Claude J. Huesman	Kelly, Mary	Peter Huesman	Blanche M. Barry
Hugg	John	Leroy	14-Oct-1888	28-Jul-1888	John R. Hugg	Lipp, Laura V.	Joseph F. Lipp	Elizabeth Hawkins
Hughes	Helen	G.	26-Dec-1905	13-Dec-1905	Christopher Hughes	Spencer, Margaret	George Spencer	A. Maude McLaughlin
Hughes	Joseph		2-Aug-1914	12-Jul-1914	George F. Hughes	Murphy, Joan F.	Earl Cooke	Helen Colbert
Hughes	Mary	Elizabeth	30-Mar-1913	6-Mar-1913	George Hughes	Murphy, Joan	William Curran	Amelia Murphy
Hughes	John	Eugene	04-May-1890	22-Apr-1890	Gilbert Hughes	Fitzpatrick, Bridget	Matthew Guerin	Mary Colleran
Hughes	Mary	Agnes	01-Apr-1888	29-Mar-1888	Gilbert Hughes	Fitzpatrick, Bridget	William Kelly	Agnes Fitzpatrick
Hughes	Edward	Earle	28-Jul-1912	19-Jul-1912	James Edward Hughes	Daniels, Mary Cecelia	James Daniels	Margaret Kelly
Hughes	James	Leroy	24-Jul-1892	14-Jul-1892	James Hughes	Gately, Ella	James Maguire	Mary Elizabeth Daniels
Hughes	Mary	Josephine	21-Jun-1885	03-Jun-1885	James Hughes	Gaitly, Ella	William Gaitly	Sarah Campbell
Hughes	Rose		04-Sep-1887	22-Aug-1887	James Hughes	Gaitley, Helen	Joseph Gaitley	Lola Gaitly
Hughes	Elenore	W.	24-Aug-1890	10-Aug-1890	John Hughes	Gaitley, Ellen		Rose Gaitley
Hughes	Arthur	Joseph	11-Apr-1897	07-Apr-1897	John Michael Hughes	Ochs, Mary	Arthur Mullen	Agnes Gaitley
Hughes	Mary		08-May-1903	11-Apr-1903	Martin Hughes	Raidy, Mary		Mary Deiting
Hughes	Martin		27-Aug-1890	02-Aug-1890	Mich J. Hughes	Ochs, Frances		Elizabeth Dawson
Hughes	Anthony		22-Jun-1902	19-Jun-1902	Michael Hughes	Oches, Frances		Kate Hughes
Hughes	Catherine		11-Feb-1894	10-Feb-1894	Michael Hughes	Ochs, Frances	Charles McCabe	Catherine Hughes
Hughes	Catherine	Bogy	18-May-1902	18-Apr-1902	Michael Hughes	Bogy, Catherine	Charles Bogy	Catherine Hughes
Hughes	Francis		24-Sep-1899	21-Aug-1899	Michael Hughes	Bogy, Catherine	Charles Bogy	Francis Biddeson
Hughes	Helen		29-Dec-1896	04-Dec-1896	Michael Hughes	Bogy, Catherine	Thomas O'Reilly	Agnes Reilly
Hughes	Mary	Agnes	06-Jan-1895	17-Dec-1894	Michael Hughes	Bogy, Catherine	James Patrick McDonald	Elizabeth Bogy
Hughes	Mary		08-Jan-1899	04-Jan-1899	Michael Hughes	Ochs, Mary Frances	Peter McCourt	Angela McDonald
Hughes	Thomas	Felix	02-Apr-1893	20-Mar-1893	Michael Hughes	Bogy, Catherine	George Bogy	Margaret Mullen
Hughes	Cecelia	Elizabeth	1-Mar-1908	25-Feb-1908	Michael John Hughes	Ochs, Mary Frances	Henry N. Albers	Elizabeth Helmkamp
								Elizabeth Deoting

ST JOHN'S BAPTISMS 1882-1912

LAST NAME	FIRST NAME	MIDDLE	BAPTISM	BIRTH	Father	Mother	SPONSORS
Hughes	George	Michael	08-Dec-1895	04-Oct-1895	Michael John Hughes	Ochs, Frances	Catherine Hughes
Hughes	William	Francis	28-Jun-1903	25-Jun-1903	Micheal John Hughes	Ochs, Mary Frances	Ann M. Ochs
Hughes/Terkes	Matilda	Elizabeth	28-Nov-1886	25-Dec-1857	Frederick Terkes	Naurnrtoler, Camelia	Elizabeth Dietz
Hughston	Catherine	Blanche	26-Nov-1888	20-Jul-1888	Samuel Hughston	Mooney, Sara	Catherine Mooney
Hunt	Helen		06-Nov-1898	23-Oct-1898	Edward Hunt	Adams, Helen	Margaret Adam
Hunter	William	Alexander	3-Oct-1909	19-Aug-1909	William Alexander Hunter	Chenowith, Mary Elizabeth	Rosalie Hunter
Hurdt	Edith	Mary	07-Apr-1889	10-Mar-1889	Charles Christopher Hurdt	Piercy, Ann Teresa	Catherine Piercy
Hurley	John	William	28-Jun-1903	20-Jun-1903	John Hurley	Bowers, Margaret	Mary Agnes Myers
Hurley	Mary	Elizabeth	27-Sep-1914	21-Jul-1914	William F. Hurley	Barry, Catherine	Anastasia Hammon
Hurst	Evelyn		1-Jun-1907	26-May-1907	[Blank]	[Blank]	Mary Slaysman
Hurt	Ann	Ruth	20-Mar-1893	27-Feb-1893	Charles Hurt	Piercy, Ann	Mary McKew
Hussy	John	Joseph	22-Nov-1896	16-Nov-1896	Michael Hussy	Gereghty, Mary	
Huster	William	Wells	10-Jun-1883	28-Apr-1883	William Richard Huster	Clement, Mary Estelle	Mary Elizabeth Huster
Hutchins	Mabel	Mary	02-Aug-1903	30-Jul-1903	Willis Hutchins	Ward, Eva	Ann Ward
Hutchinson	Mary		29-Oct-1905	21-Oct-1905	Clarence Hutchinson	Ward, Veronica	Hilta Collier
Hutton	Mary		18-Oct-1896	20-Oct-1896	Elwood L. Hutton	Rohe, Mary	Mary Conners
Hyland	John	Eager	28-Nov-1897	21-Nov-1897	Daniel Hyland	Ward, Catherine	Ann Burns
Hyland	Elizabeth	Louise	03-Mar-1901	03-Jan-1901	Joseph Hyland	McClain, Josephine	Elizabeth Mullen
Hyland	Bernard		21-Apr-1901	08-Apr-1901	William Hyland	McNamara, Catherine	Mary Hyland
Hyland	Catherine		19-Apr-1903	13-Apr-1903	William Hyland	McNamara, Catherine	Richard Hyland
Hyland	Mary		24-Sep-1899	09-Sep-1899	William Hyland	McNamara, Catherine	Genevieve Hogan
Hyman	William	Joseph	13-May-1906	23-Apr-1906	William H. Hyman	Murphy, Rose C.	Ann McNamara
Hynes	Ann		03-Aug-1883	28-Jul-1883	Patrick Hynes	Touhy, Honora	Margaret McCabe
Hynes	James		10-Apr-1887	01-Apr-1887	Patrick Hynes	Touhy, Honora	Bridget Coffey
Hynes	Martin		26-Nov-1893	08-Nov-1893	Patrick Hynes	Touhy, Honora	Bridget Agnes Caffay
Hynes	William	Elizabeth	11-Sep-1892	25-Aug-1892	Patrick Hynes	Touhy, Honora	Mary Colbert
Hynes	Helen		15-Mar-1908	27-Feb-1908	Thomas L. Hynes	Zell, Ada	Catherine Touhy
Intlekfor	Agatha	Frances	14-Apr-1912	1-Apr-1912	Ludwig Intlekfor	Haugh, Elsa	Emma Seybold
Irvin	Warren		16-Aug-1896	About 1896	J. Irvin	Marble, Ann	Agatha Moore
Irvin	Mary	Helen	25-Dec-1892	13-Dec-1892	James Henry Irvin	Marble, Ann	
Irvin	John	Edward	15-May-1891	01-May-1891	James Irvin	Marble, Ann	Mary Irvin
Irving	Mary	Agnes	11-Aug-1892	06-Aug-1892	Louis Irving	Kelly, Mary Agnes	Mary Irvin
Irwin	Francis	Howard	14-Dec-1913	21-Nov-1913	James Irwin	Taylor, Rita	Mary C. Affayroux
Irwin	Irene	Leonora	14-Jul-1912	27-Jun-1912	James Irwin	Taylor, Margaret	Gladys Ward
Isensee	William		12-Aug-1894	25-Jul-1894	Charles Isensee	Rentz, Margaret	Rose Irwin
Jackson	Ann	Mary	28-Dec-1884	11-Dec-1884	Lewis Jackson	Connor, Ann	Louise Kellough
Jacobs	Helen	Veronica	11-Mar-1906	10-Feb-1906	John H. Jacobs	Rooney, Helen	Theresa Cullen
Jacobs	Ann		5-Jan-1908	1-Dec-1907	John Jacobs	Rooney, Ellen	Mary Hopper
Jacobs	Edward	Lee	20-Apr-1902	07-Apr-1902	John Jacobs	Rooney, Ella	Virginia Houch
Jacobs	Genevieve		16-Aug-1903	02-Aug-1903	John Jacobs	Rooney, Ella	Jane McKee
Jacobs	William	Francis	22-May-1892	12-May-1892	John Jacobs	Smith, Elizabeth	Ollie Hutton
Jacobs	George	Zacharia	15-Sep-1889	21-Aug-1889	Lewin H. Jacobs	Dressel, Margaret	Margaret Ryan
Jacobs	Francis	Milton	02-Apr-1893	15-Mar-1893	Lewin Henry Jacobs	Dressel, Margaret	John G. Dressel
Jacobs	Mary	Laura	13-May-1888	07-Mar-1888	Lewis Henry Jacobs	Dressel, Margaret	Francis Dressel
Jacobs	John	Lewis	29-Oct-1895	15-Oct-1895	Lewis Jacobs	Dressel, Margaret	Mary Dressel
Jacobs	William	John	17-Sep-1899	21-Aug-1899	Louis Jacobs	Dressel, Margaret	Joan Dresser
James	Gibbons		31-Oct-1897	28-Oct-1897	John Finhagen	Doyle, Ann	Mary Hamper
James	Mary	Gertrude	09-Jul-1891	28-Jun-1891	Thomas James	Ballard, Gertrude	Margaret Finhagen
James	Edward	Walter	20-Jan-1895	05-Jan-1895	Thomas Walter James	Ballard, Gertrude	Bridget O'Brien
James	Helen		01-Oct-1893	19-Sep-1893	Thomas Walter James	Ballard, Gertrude	Alexina James
James	Margaret	Elizabeth	07-May-1893	05-Apr-1893	William E. James	Tiralla, Mary A.	Rose Holmes
James	Florence	Rose	23-Aug-1891	12-Aug-1891	William Edward James	Toralla, Alexina	Ella M. Spicer
Jamison	Ann	Gertrude	02-Jan-1887	18-Dec-1886	Andrew Jamison	Griffin, Mary C.	Rose Holmes
Jamison	James	Aloysius	17-Jun-1888	08-May-1888	Andrew Jamison	Hannan, Mary Ann	Jennie V. Phillips
Jamison	John	Francis	22-May-1887	07-Apr-1887	Andrew Jamison	King, Rose Ann	Elizabeth Conners
Jamison	John	Andrew	23-Dec-1888	18-Dec-1888	Andrew Jamison	Griffin, Mary E.	Sara Stout
Jamison	Mary	Agnes	31-Aug-1884	24-Aug-1884	Andrew Jamison	Griffin, Mary Ellen	Joan Thurn
Jamison	Rose		22-Mar-1891	13-Mar-1891	Andrew Jamison	Griffin, Mary Helen	Catherine A. Griffin
Jamison	Robert	Patrick	05-Aug-1883	23-Jul-1883	Daniel Jamison	Owens, Sara	James Sullivan
Jeffers	Charles	H.	22-Oct-1905	10-Oct-1905	Henry J. Jeffers	O'Connor, Catherine	Petrouille Byrne
Jeffers	Emma	Catherine	5-Jun-1904	23-May-1904	Henry Joseph Jeffers	O'Connor, Catherine F.	Hubert D. Murray
Jefferson	Mary	Catherine	27-Sep-1891	18-Sep-1891	Andrww Jefferson	Donahue, Mary	Charles F. O'Connor
Jefferson	Howard	Francis	7-Sep-1913	29-Aug-1913	Howard Jefferson	[Blank], Edith	Patrick Joseph Roddy
							George T. Griffin
							Joan Sullivan
							Gertrude Baker
							Margaret Jeffers
							Catherine Roddy
							Rose McIntyre

61

LAST NAME	FIRST NAME	MIDDLE	BAPTISM	BIRTH	Father	Mother	SPONSORS
Jenkins	Charles		18-Jun-1899	10-Jun-1890	Charles Jenkins	Ryan, Katterina	Julia Kelly
Jenkins	Elizabeth	Josephine	18-Jun-1899	13-Mar-1885	Charles Jenkins	Ryan, Katterina	Julia Kelly
Jenkins	Albert	Fenwick	14-Jun-1893	03-Jun-1893	Charles Leo Jenkins	Ford, Helen	John Louis Burgan
Jenkins	Edward	Hamilton	28-Aug-1898	19-Aug-1898	Fenwick Jenkins	Hamilton, Agnes	James Jenkins
Jenkins	Anthony		23-May-1886	06-May-1886	Francis Jenkins	Bush, Susan	Mary Hamilton
Jenkins	Mary		07-Feb-1886	20-Jan-1886	Francis Jenkins	Duff, Mary Loretta	Mary E. Jenkins
Jenkins	Francis	Constantine	27-Feb-1887	13-Feb-1887	Francis Thomas Jenkins	Duff, Mary Laura	Joseph L. Clarkson
Jenkins	Helen	Edith	30-Sep-1888	14-Sep-1888	Francis Thomas Jenkins	Duff, Mary Laura	George Marcus Hodeinott
Jenkins	Rose		28-Jun-1891	15-Jun-1891	Francis Thomas Jenkins	Duff, Mary	Rose Ignatius Conway
Jenkins	Mary	Rita	11-Nov-1887	16-Oct-1888	Francis X. Jenkins	Bush, Susan	Cora Linn
Jenkins	Agnes		26-Apr-1887	24-Apr-1887	Henry Jenkins	Roberts, Cecelia	Mary Duff
Jenkins	George	Joseph	01-Jun-1884	22-Mar-1884	Henry Jenkins	Roberts, Cecelia	Ann Jenkins
Jenkins	Charles	Edward	06-Jan-1895	30-Dec-1894	Louis William Jenkins	Pitroff, Sophia Wilhelmina	Margaret C. Roberts
Jennings	Agnes	Winifred	20-Jun-1897	14-Jun-1897	Michael Jennings	Dorsey, Catherine	Mary C. Roberts
Jennings	Ann	T.	1-Jan-1905	27-Dec-1904	Michael Jennings	Dorsey, Catherine	Catherine Jendrech
Jennings	Catherine	Ellen	02-Jun-1895	25-May-1895	Michael Jennings	Dorsey, Kate	Agnes Dorsey
Jennings	Mary	Helen	26-Feb-1893	12-Feb-1893	Michael Jennings	Dorsey, Catherine	Mary Brannan
Jennings	Sara	Mary Angela	16-Aug-1901	10-Aug-1901	Michael Jennings	Dorsey, Katherine	Ellen Dorsey
Jennings	Thomas		25-May-1890	14-May-1890	Michael Jennings	Dorsey, Kate	Catherine Golden
Jennings	Thomas	Patrick	20-Aug-1899	12-Aug-1899	Michael Jennings	Dorsey, Catherine	Katherine Touhy
Jennings	William	Patrick	01-Apr-1894	18-Mar-1894	Michael Jennings	Dorsey, Catherine	Helen Dorsey
Jennings	Joan	Laura	01-Sep-1889	19-Aug-1889	Patrick Jennings	Holland, Mary	Mary Dorsey
Jennings	Julia	Theresa	06-Feb-1887	28-Jan-1887	Patrick Jennings	Holland, Mary	Ann Collins
Jennings	Margaret	Ann	01-Oct-1882	22-Sep-1882	Patrick Jennings	Holland, Mary	Julia Quinn
Jennings	Michael	Patrick	05-Oct-1884	28-Sep-1884	Patrick Jennings	Holland, Mary	Michael Holmes
Jennings	Catherine	T.	9-Jul-1905	30-Jun-1905	Thomas Jennings	Logue, Mary	Michael Burke
Jennings	John	Patrick	29-Jul-1906	9-Jul-1906	Thomas Jennings	Logue, Mary	John Carmody
Jimenez	Eva	Mayilkda	19-Apr-1891	14-Mar-1891	Lino Joseph de Jimenez	Casters, Felicitas	John Jennings
Joens	Sophia		4-Aug-1912	24-Jul-1912	William Robert Joens	Schneider, Clara Mary	Edward Jennings
Johanson	H.		26-Oct-1896	15-Oct-1896	William Johnson	Keogh, Mary	Catherine Jennings
Johns	Thomas		05-Nov-1888	27-Jul-1888	Robert Johns	Ahern, Margaret	Phillip Herrera deComanho
Johnson	Charles		24-May-1885	15-Apr-1885	Angelo Johnson	O'Brien, Margaret	Sophia Cath. Schneider
Johnson	Hilda		06-Oct-1896	About 1880	Charles Robinson (sic)	Powel, Leah	William Schneider
Johnson	Eugene		17-Feb-1889	20-Dec-1888	Charles W. Johnson	Kernan, Mary J.	Sarah Higgins
Johnson	Elmer	Yarborough	17-Feb-1895	06-Feb-1895	Edward Aloysius Johnson	Evert, Ann Genevieve	Charlotte McConer
Johnson	Patrick		16-Dec-1907	14-Dec-1907	Francis Johnson	McEvoy, Mary	Mary Dougherty
Johnson	Joseph	Edward	22-Dec-1889	18-Dec-1889	Frederick A. Johnson	Rosensteel, Clara A.	Ann R. Kearney
Johnson	Regina	Mary	27-Nov-1887	20-Nov-1887	Frederick A. Johnson	Rosensteel, Clara A.	Gertrude Bentz
Johnson	Francis		19-Feb-1893	12-Feb-1893	Frederick Johnson	Rosensteel, Clara A.	James McDevitt
Johnson	Pauline		19-Feb-1893	12-Feb-1893	Frederick Johnson	Rosensteel, Clara A.	
Johnson	Mary	Bridget	26-Jan-1913	9-Jan-1913	George Johnson	Ash, Sarah E.	Margaret R. Seim
Johnson	George	John	11-Aug-1889	17-Jul-1889	Henry Johnson	Hughson, Mary	Francis Rosensteel
Johnson	Henry		20-Mar-1887	03-Mar-1887	Henry Johnson	Granell, Helen	J. Leo Rosensteel
Johnson	Sarah	Ellen	21-Apr-1901	09-Apr-1901	Jerome Johnson	O'Neill, Sarah	Charles S. Rosensteel
Johnson	Leon	Henry	24-Sep-1911	10-Sep-1911	John F. Stark	Keegan, Elizabeth	Constance Rosensteel
Johnson	Leonard	Leroy	26-Jun-1892	30-May-1892	Leandro Laurence Johnson	Rogerson, Ann Frances	Margaret Cook
Johnson	Gregory		07-May-1893	28-Apr-1893	William A. Johnson	Keogh, Mary J.	Augusta Gunter
Johnson	William	Aloysius	13-Sep-1891	05-Sep-1891	William Aloysius Johnson	Keogh, Mary	Mary Holden
Johnson	Mary	Celeste	03-Nov-1895	23-Oct-1895	William Johnson	Keogh, Mary	Catherine McGinnity
Johnson	Walter	Joseph	12-Aug-1894	03-Aug-1894	William Johnson	Keogh, Mary	Mary Ray
Johnson	Blanche	Cecelia	21-Jun-1891	07-Jun-1891	William Joseph Johnson	Lawson, Laura Viola	Rose Ursula Stephens
Johnson/Bassett	Mary	Lucretia	24-Nov-1897	14-Jan-1844	Thomas Johnson	Dickson, Elizabeth	Cecelia Johnson
Johnston	Charles	Joseph	29-Aug-1897	19-Aug-1897	Jerome H. Johnston	O'Neill, Sarah	Catherine Josephine Keogh
Johnston	Mary		13-Nov-1898	29-Oct-1898	Jerome Johnston	O'Neill, Sara	Mary Carle
Jones	Rachael		11-Apr-1901	25-Aug-1866	Albert Jones	McCadden, Rose	Mary Reirdon
Jones	Elizabeth		18-Jan-1903	27-Dec-1902	Charles Jones	Phelps, Elizabeth	Genevieve Weldon
Jones	Robert	Emmet	07-Mar-1883	09-Nov-1842	George Harrison Jones	Hoffman, Caroline Louise	Mary Golloway
Jones	George	Thomas	29-Nov-1891	18-Nov-1891	Henry James Jones	Bacon, Joan Agatha	Bridget Kelly
Jones	Lillian		26-Feb-1899	04-Feb-1899	Henry Jones	Bason, Genevieve	Mary Kelly
Jones	Joseph	F. Paul	25-Jan-1888	02-Oct-1888	John Jones	Cole, Sara	Margaret Leland
Jones	Teresa	Margaret	21-Apr-1901	26-Aug-1866	Joseph Jones	Jones, Sarah	Elizabeth Phelps
Jones	Thomas	Edward	14-Sep-1902	03-Aug-1902	Joseph Jones	[Blank], Sara	Ann Josephine Bryson
Jones	Elizabeth	Ann	13-Aug-1882	23-Jul-1882	Levin K. Jones	Robinson, Elizabeth	Julia Toomey

Additional sponsor column entries (right side):

SPONSORS (continued)
Margaret C. Roberts
Catherine Jendrech
Michael Dorsey
Winifred Jennings
Catherine Jennings
John Delaney
Thomas Long
Margaret Collins
Edward Jennings
Thomas Jennings
Thomas Jennings
Michael O'Neill
Thomas Murphy
Michael J. McCourt
Francis Cary
Joseph Branty
Charles Thomas O'Connell
Michael O'Neill
William Clarence Murphy
Leo H. Dunn
Susanna F. Rosensteel
Clara Rosensteel
J. Leo Rosensteel
Thomas Leonard
James Cullan
Michael O'Neill
Thomas Bacon
Richard Gutberlet
Roise Gutberlet
Josephine Cubb
Joan Miner
Thomas Miner
Benjamin Jones
Mary Jones

LAST NAME	FIRST NAME	MIDDLE	BAPTISM	BIRTH	Father	Mother	SPONSORS	
Jones	Sarah	Mary	11-Oct-1885	22-Aug-1885	Levin K. Jones	Robinson, Elizabeth A.	Francis Graham	Alice A. Graham
Jones	William	Benjamin	15-Jun-1884	08-May-1884	Levin Katon Jones	Robinson, Elizabeth Ann	William Graham	Elizabeth Jones
Jones	Edward		27-Apr-1890	08-Apr-1890	Thomas C. Jones	Dignan, Mary E.	Eugene McIntyre	Elizabeth Good
Jones	Francis	Leo	16-Aug-1891	31-Jul-1891	Thomas C. Jones	Dignan, Mary Ellen	John Cohen	Ann McIntyre
Jones	John	Thomas	24-Apr-1884	06-Apr-1884	Thomas C. Jones	Dignan, Mary E.		Margaret Ellen Connelly
Jones	Mary	Elizabeth	05-Jul-1895	22-Jun-1895	Thomas C. Jones	Dignan, Mary E.		Mary Elizabeth Good
Jones	Charles	Dennis	13-Dec-1896	24-Nov-1896	Thomas Jones	Dignan, Mary Helen	Daniel Whelan	Mary Whelan
Jones	David		03-Sep-1886	09-Aug-1886	Thomas Jones	Degnan, Clara		Elizabeth Goode
Jones	James	William	03-Jun-1888	13-May-1888	Thomas Jones	Dignan, Mary	William Mulligan	Mary McGiveney
Jones	Joseph		15-Jan-1893	19-Dec-1892	Thomas Jones	Dignan, Mary Helen	Edward Connolly	Mary Potts
Jones	Sara	Reisman	11-Feb-1883	15-Jan-1883	Thomas Jones	Dignan, Mary Helen	James Cohen	Mary Cohen
Jones	John		01-Dec-1887	Circa 1865	Uria Jones	Mincher, Ann	William Reisman Jones	
Jones	Adalaide		18-Feb-1906	11-Feb-1906	William I. Jones	Rock, Adalaide	George Wall	Loretta German
Jones	Ann	Beatrice	17-Nov-1895	30-Oct-1895	William Jones	Rock, Adelina	James Fogarty	Ann Rock
Jones	Laurence	Quenton	20-Nov-1904	31-Oct-1904	William Jones	Rock, Adelina	Charles Rock	Mary German
Jones	Oliver	Edward	31-May-1903	17-May-1903	William Jones	Rock, Adalaide	Edward Affayroux	Maud German
Jones	William	R.	7-Nov-1915	23-Oct-1915	William Jones	Cousins, Mary		Catherine Neilson
Jones	Virginia	Mary	16-Jul-1914	11-Jul-1914	William Russell Jones	Cousin, Margaret Alice		Ann Teresa Gannon
Jones/Ruff	Sara	Matilda	21-Mar-1890	About 1820	William Jones	Grace, Mary	James Hays	
Jordan	Elizabeth	Ethel	9-May-1915	21-Apr-1915	Charles Jordan	Nippard, C.	Robert Colbert	Mary Colbert
Jordan	Walter		21-May-1882	13-May-1882	James H. Jordan	Dowd, M. Ann	James Glenn	Ann Dowd
Jordan	John		26-Mar-1882	12-Mar-1882	William Jordan	Engel, Margaret	R. Houck	
Joseph	William	Edgar	20-Aug-1899	26-Jul-1899	Howard Joseph	Lavelmann, Christina M.	William Lavelmann	Elizabeth McGraw
Joseph	Ann	Emelia	4-Feb-1906	28-Jan-1906	James B. Joseph	O'Connell, Elizabeth	Martin O'Connell	Harriet O'Neill
Joseph	Cecelia		13-Mar-1904	8-Mar-1904	James B. Joseph	O'Connor, Elizabeth C.	Edward Maskill	Cecelia O'Connor
Joseph	Edward		10-Oct-1915	30-Sep-1915	James Joseph	Connor, Elizabeth	John O'Connor	Catherine Meskill
Joseph	Elizabeth		03-Jan-1897	25-Dec-1896	James Joseph	O'Connor, Elizabeth		Martin O'Connor
Joseph	Ellen		24-Jan-1909	20-Dec-1909	James Joseph	Conners, Elizabeth Joseph	John Connors	Catherine Connors
Joseph	Esther	Joseph	17-Mar-1901	04-Mar-1901	James Joseph	Connor, Elizabeth	Michael Connor	Margaret Murray
Joseph	James		12-Feb-1911	30-Jan-1911	James Joseph	Connor, Elizabeth	Martin Comer	Margaret Morris
Joseph	Margaret		27-Jul-1902	05-Jul-1902	James Joseph	O'Connor, Elizabeth	Martin O'Connor	Margaret O'Connor
Joseph	Mary	Ann	05-Feb-1899	28-Jan-1899	James Joseph	O'Connor, Elizabeth	Martin O'Connor	Bridget O'Connor
Joseph	Elizabeth	Hoffman	14-Mar-1897	09-Mar-1897	Matthew Joseph	Owens, Elizabeth	John Dunn	Joan Owens
Joseph/Kilduff	Dorothy		23-Jan-1888	23-Jan-1860	James Joseph	Umphreys, Mary Ann		Mary Kilduff
Judge	Sara		13-Aug-1887	05-Aug-1887	[Blank]	Judge, Mary Ann		Helen Reilly
Judge	John		11-Jan-1883	24-Dec-1882	John Judge	Judge, Mary		Mary E. Vick
Judge	Elizabeth	Ann	14-Jan-1906	1-Jan-1906	Michael A. Judge	McSherry, Catherine	John J.D. McGraw	Sadie P. McGraw
Judge	Ann		14-Jan-1900	31-Dec-1899	Michael Judge	McSherry, Catherine	Michael McKenna	Mary Byrnes
Judge	Catherine		15-Dec-1901	02-Dec-1901	Michael Judge	McSherry, Catherine	Neil Judge	Catherine Judge
Judge	William	James	3-Mar-1907	14-Feb-1907	William Judge	Sherry, Rose	James Anderson	Jenie McGuire
Julius	Mary	Elizabeth	7-Apr-1914	9-May-1913	Robert Julius	[Blank]		Emma Smith
Jungers	Gertrude	Elizabeth	25-Mar-1883	21-Jan-1883	John Jungers	Russell, Georgia Honora		Joan Kerr
Kachel	Mary	Elizabeth	23-Jun-1895	06-Jun-1895	Gustave Kachel	Faetch, Ann		Ann Faetch
Kagee	George		30-May-1900	20-Feb-1900	Charles Kagee	Justina, Mary		
Kahl	Henry	Aloysius	18-Jul-1905	16-May-1905	Tillman Kahl	Mitchell, Sadie		Mary Pattyerson
Kahlbaugh	Mary		02-Nov-1884	01-Nov-1884	George Kahlbaugh	Kiley, Helen	James Brazier	Mary Walsh
Kaidy	Michael	Joan	09-Oct-1887	27-Sep-1887	Patrick Kaidy	McKenna, Ann	James Clancy	Sarah Johnston
Kain	Charles	Lloyd	27-Dec-1903	06-Dec-1903	James J. Kain	Page, Sara	Charles Eastine	Francis C. Kelly
Kaiser	George		19-Apr-1887	22-Feb-1822	George Kaiser	[Blank]		
Kampe	William	Henry	3-Apr-1915	20-Oct-1893	James F. Kampe	Mitchell, Helen	John W. Tracey	
Kane	Ann	Elizabeth	13-Feb-1887	31-Jan-1887	Daniel Kane	Quirk, Ann Elizabeth		Ann Elizabeth Strott
Kane	John	Daniel	04-Jan-1885	27-Dec-1884	Daniel Kane	Quirk, Ann A.	John Henry Stalls	
Kane	Catherine	Mary	26-Feb-1905	9-Feb-1905	John Kane	Akers, Margaret K.		Mary Ziegler
Kane	William	M.	18-Jul-1886	John Kane	John Kane	Morewood, Agnes	Patrick Delaney	Elizabeth Morewood
Kapp	Charles	Howard	29-Jul-1894	04-Jul-1894	William Kapp	Poole, Mary	Charles Poole	Catherine Able
Karrigan	Joseph		21-Jul-1901	13-Jul-1901	John Karrigan	Kelleher, Ellen	Patrick Lehane	Catherine Leahey
Kassakatis	Leonard	Vernon	29-May-1892	20-Nov-1891	Albert Kassakatis	Schuster, Elizabeth		Mary Elizabeth Richter
Kassakatis	Leonard	George	13-Jul-1884	13-Apr-1884	Albert Kassakatis	Schuster, Elizabeth	Leonard G. Schuster	Mary Ebel
Kassakatis	Mary	Bertha	29-Oct-1882	27-Aug-1882	Albert Kassakatis	Schuster, Elizabeth		Mary Ann Schuster
Kassakatis	William	Albert	12-Jun-1887	05-Apr-1887	Albert Kassakatis	Schuster, Elizabeth		Mary Pohler
Katz	Louis	Leroy	25-Sep-1892	06-Sep-1892	David Katz	Moylan, Esther		Francis Moylan
Katzberger	Leo	Milton	14-Apr-1895	10-Apr-1895	John Louis Katzberger	McCoy, Mary Joan	George Louis Strongbow	Anastasia Walsh
Katzenberger	Henry	Raymond	19-Sep-1897	16-Sep-1897	John Katzenberger	McCoy, Mary	Claudus Murphy	Catherine Fitzpatrick

63

LAST NAME	FIRST NAME	MIDDLE	BAPTISM	BIRTH	Father	Mother	SPONSORS
Katzenberger	Alice		02-Feb-1890	23-Jan-1890	John L. Katzenberger	McCoy, Mary J.	John Golden	Alice Katzenberger
Katzenburger	Margaret	Regina	02-Oct-1887	28-Sep-1887	John L. Katzenburger	McCoy, Mary J.	John F. Connor	Mary Glenn
Katzenburger	Thomas	W.	29-Nov-1885	20-Nov-1885	John L. Katzenburger	McCoy, Mary Joan	James Golden	Emma McAleer
Katzenburger	John	Joseph	13-May-1883	12-May-1883	John Louis Katzenburger	McCoy, Mary J.	Daniel Giles Blessing	Catherine Agnes Golden
Kavanaugh	Edward		8-Nov-1914	24-Oct-1914	[Blank]	Kavanaugh, Lillian	Edward Mckee	Sarah Sinnott
Kavanaugh	Ann	Elizabeth	26-Feb-1893	17-Feb-1893	Benedict Kavanaugh	McCormick, Elizabeth	Laurence Kavanaugh	Ann McCormick
Kavanaugh	Helen	Genevieve	19-Jan-1896	08-Jan-1896	Benedict Kavanaugh	McCormick, Elizabeth	Samuel McCormick	Catherine McCormick
Kavanaugh	John	H.	03-Aug-1902	22-Jul-1902	Benedict Kavanaugh	McCormick, Elizabeth	F.P. Kavanaugh	Ann Connolly
Kavanaugh	Mary	Agnes	03-Jun-1894	24-May-1894	Benedict Kavanaugh	McCormick, Elizabeth	Thomas McCormick	Florence Kavanaugh
Kavanaugh	Rose		20-Jan-1901	09-Jan-1901	Benedict Kavanaugh	McCormick, Elizabeth	John McCale	Lene Gossman
Kavanaugh	Thomas	LeRoy	02-Oct-1898	21-Sep-1898	Benedict Kavanaugh	McCormick, Elizabeth	Thomas McCormick	Mary McCormick
Kavanaugh	Francis	Dennis	29-Jul-1894	19-Jul-1894	Francis Kavanaugh	Cassidy, Mary B.	Dennis Kavanaugh	Catherine Cassidy
Kavanaugh	Francis	Paul	04-Feb-1900	25-Jan-1900	Francis Kavanaugh	Cassidy, Mary	Samuel McCormick	Catherine Cassidy
Kavanaugh	Catherine	Jenette	21-Feb-1904	8-Feb-1904	Francis Patrick Kavanaugh	Cassidy, Mary		Philomena Vanzant
Kavanaugh	Mary	Helen	16-Jul-1890	10-Jul-1890	Francis Patrick Kavanaugh	Cassidy, Mary	James McDevitt	Catherine McCormick
Kavanaugh	Florence	Mary	11-Jun-1914	13-Dec-1899	James Kavanaugh	Eisenach, Elizabeth		Katherine Loughran
Kavanaugh	Irene	Stella	11-Jun-1914	16-Aug-1901	James Kavanaugh	Eisenach, Elizabeth		Bernadette Casey
Kavanaugh	Ann		21-Nov-1886	19-Nov-1886	Matthew Kavanaugh	Murtagh, Mary	James Michaels	Mary Ward
Kavanaugh	Mary		21-Nov-1886	19-Nov-1886	Matthew Kavanaugh	Murtagh, Mary	Michael H. Welch	Ann Murtagh
Kavey	Caroline	Agnes	18-Apr-1915	26-Mar-1915	Charles K. Kavey	Clemson, Elizabeth	William [Blank]	Ann Moylan
Keagle	Elizabeth	Irene	03-Mar-1889	14-Feb-1889	Charles Keagle	Volk, Mary	Daniel J. Volk	Elizabeth Nellert
Keagle	John	Charles	04-Jan-1891	12-Dec-1890	Charles Keagle	Volk, Mary	John Bankerd	Josephine Bankerd
Keagle	William		27-Aug-1894	18-Aug-1894	Charles Keagle	Volk, Mary		G. W. Devine
Keagle	Mary		06-May-1896	23-Mar-1896	Charlews Keagle	Volk, Mary		Mary Broughton
Keagle	William		13-Jun-1895	19-Dec-1848	George Keagle	Smith, Elizabeth	John Moylan	
Keagle	Aloysius		05-Oct-1890	21-Sep-1890	William A. Keagle	Meek, Mabel Frances	Aloysius C. Smith	Mary E. Smith
Keagle	Mary Agnes		29-Jan-1882	13-Jan-1882	William Andrew Keagle	Meek, Mabel Frances		Jeanie Johnson
Keagle	Catherine	Laura	31-Jul-1887	19-Jul-1887	William Keagle	Meek, Mabel		Catherine Kearney
Keagle	Clara	Mary	04-Jan-1885	22-Dec-1884	William Keagle	Meek, Mabel		Joan Guntman
Kealy	Mary		11-Aug-1901	27-Jul-1901	Lawrence Kealy	Malone, Mary	John Kealy	Margaret Kealy
Kearney	Andrew	Redding	15-Apr-1900	06-Apr-1900	Andrew Kearney	Redding, Mary	Michael Kearney	Mary Austin
Kearney	Mary	Genevieve	12-Jun-1904	26-May-1904	Charles Kearney	Carter, Sarah	John J. Carter	Ann Smith
Kearney	Andrew		28-Apr-1890	28-Apr-1890	Dennis J. Kearney	Kearney, Mary E.		
Kearney	Mary		03-Jan-1892	26-Dec-1891	Dennis Kearney	Kearney, Mary	James Kearney	Mary Kearney
Kearney	Albert		13-Feb-1898	07-Feb-1898	John G. Kearney	Costello, Mary	A.S. Papka	Ann O'Neill
Kearney	Leo	Leahy	17-Apr-1892	11-Apr-1892	John G. Kearney	Costello, Mary A.	Martin J. Leahy	Mary E. Leahy
Kearney	John	Melton	20-Jul-1890	07-Jul-1890	John J. Kearney	Costello, Mary	Patrick Etridge	Ann Etridge
Kearney	Mary	Angela	7-Nov-1909	20-Oct-1909	John J. Kearney	Nagel, Catherine Gertrude	John D. Ruck	Elizabeth Ruck
Kearney	Charles	Joseph	02-Sep-1888	22-Aug-1888	John Kearney	Dalton, Mary E.	Francis Kearney	Margaret Kearney
Kearney	Francis		15-Dec-1889	04-Dec-1889	John Kearney	Dalton, Mary Helen	John Michael Mears	Catherine Kearney
Kearney	Leona	Jane	24-Jan-1909	5-Jan-1909	John Kearney	Kearney, Catherine	Charles Guckert	Mary Guckert
Kearney	Teresa		22-Nov-1914	5-Nov-1914	John Kearney	Shelley, Catherine	Edward McGrogan	Teresa McGrogan
Kearney	James	P.	27-Apr-1905	19-Oct-1903	John T. Kearney	Shelley, Catherine		Catherine Kearney
Kearney	Ann	Catherine	1-Aug-1907	11-Mar-1905	John Thomas Kearney	Shelley, Catherine		Catherine Kearney
Kearney	Elizabeth	Mary	9-Jun-1912	21-May-1912	John Thomas Kearney	Shelley, Catherine	Hugh Ward	Sarah Johnson
Kearney	John	Thomas	26-Mar-1911	21-Feb-1911	John Thomas Kearney	Shelley, Catherine Ann	John V. Ward	Margaret Ward
Kearney	Margaret		1-Aug-1907	6-Oct-1906	John Thomas Kearney	Shelley, Catherine		Catherine Hogan
Kearney	Mary	Ellen	12-May-1901	02-May-1901	John Thomas Kearney	Shelley, Catherine	Thomas K. Barrett	Catherine Burke
Kearney	Elizabeth		16-Sep-1894	09-Sep-1894	Luke Kearney	Callan, Margaret	John V. [Blank]	Catherine Naughton
Kearney	Ellen		11-Feb-1900	03-Feb-1900	Luke Kearney	Callan, Margaret	Mortimer Quinn	Ellen Smith
Kearney	Loretta		02-Aug-1903	30-Jul-1903	Luke Kearney	Kearney, Margaret	John Quinn	Agnes Kearney
Kearney	Luke	Joseph	03-Apr-1892	24-Mar-1892	Luke Kearney	Callan, Margaret	William Kearney	Mary Hogan
Kearney	Margaret		25-Jul-1897	22-Jul-1897	Luke Kearney	Callan, Margaret	Francis Hogan	Mary Kearney
Kearney	Mary	Agnes	27-Jan-1889	22-Jan-1889	Luke Kearney	Callan, Margaret	Thomas Kirby	Mary Kearney
Kearney	Mary		14-Apr-1907	10-Apr-1907	Luke Kearney	Callan, Margaret	Michael Kearney	Mary Kearney
Kearney	Michael	Joseph	30-Aug-1896	19-Aug-1896	Michael Kearney	Keiley, Hannah	Luke J. Kearney	Agnes Dougherty
Kearney	William	Paul	07-Jul-1889	29-Jun-1889	Michael Kearney	Reilly, Hannah	Luke Kearney	Catherine Mullen
Kearney	Helen		23-Mar-1913	17-Jan-1913	Robert H. Kearney	Aukward, Ida	William Grund	Helen Grund
Keating	John		08-Jan-1885	18-Nov-1884	Thomas Keating	Burkins, Clara		Sarah McGuigan
Keating	John	Henry	16-Mar-1902	05-Mar-1902	William Keating	McGraw, Joan	John Brown	Mary Flynn
Kebler	Herman	Joseph	12-Aug-1906	27-Jul-1906	Howard Joseph Kebler	Havelman, Charistina	Herman Havelman	Elizabeth O'Rourke
Keelan	Catherine		03-Dec-1899	25-Nov-1899	James Keelan	Sinnott, Anastasia	Richard Williams	Ella Keenan
Keelan	Elizabeth	Agnes	31-Oct-1897	20-Oct-1897	James Keelan	Sinnott, Ann	Thomas Keelan	Mary Williams

LAST NAME	FIRST NAME	MIDDLE	BAPTISM	BIRTH	Father	Mother	SPONSORS
Keelan	James		04-Jan-1891	24-Dec-1890	James Keelan	Sinnott, Ann	Laura Sinnott
Keelan	Joan		24-Jan-1892	19-Jan-1892	James Keelan	Sinnott, Ann	Lauren Sinnott
Keelan	Margaret	M.	14-Dec-1902	30-Nov-1902	James Keelan	Sinnott, Anastasia	Thomas Monaghan
Keelan	Michael		25-Aug-1895	12-Aug-1895	James Keelan	Sinnott, Ann	Michael Keelan
Keelan	Thomas	Aquinas	27-Mar-1892	15-Mar-1892	Thomas A. Keelan	Leonard, Catherine M.	James F. Leach
Keelan	Vincent	Leonard	21-Nov-1890	01-Nov-1890	Thomas A. Keelan	Leonard, Catherine M.	B. Vincent Keelan
Keelan	Catherine	Frances	18-May-1883	[Blank]	George O. Colt	Snow, Fannie A.	Rev. M.F. Foley
Keenan	Helen		11-Jan-1898	08-Jan-1898	Joseph P. Keenan	[Blank], Katherine	Mary Mulgrew
Keenan	Alice	Genevieve	04-Mar-1888	02-Mar-1888	Paul Keenan	[Blank], Ann	Mary Hanan
Keenan	Felix		13-Aug-1882	09-Aug-1882	Paul Keenan	McGovern, Ann	Timothy Donohoe
Keenan	James		25-Jan-1891	21-Jan-1891	Paul Keenan	McGovern, Ann	John Moan
Keenan	Mary	Ann	11-Jul-1886	10-Jul-1886	Paul Keenan	McGovern, Ann	Felix McNally
Keenan	Paul		31-May-1885	28-May-1885	Paul Keenan	McGovern, Ann	Hugh McLaughlin
Keenan	Sara	Jane	04-Nov-1883	31-Oct-1883	Paul Keenan	McGovern, Ann	Joan McNally
Keenan	Susan	Catherine	08-Jan-1893	04-Jan-1893	Paul Keenan	McGovern, Ann	William McManus
Keenan	Francis	Edward	10-Jun-1900	10-May-1900	Preston Keenan	Hudson, Sarah	Thomas Nevin
Keenan	Mary		27-Jan-1901	21-Jan-1901	Stephen Keenan	McNally, Mary	Joseph McHern
Keenan	Edward	Nicolas	11-Jun-1893	26-May-1893	Vincent Keenan	Dollard, Margaret	James Edward Dollard
Keene	Mary	Cecelia	13-May-1906	1-May-1906	James Keene	Reardon, Ann E.	Sarah M. Munchel
Keene	Phillip	Marion	13-Oct-1901	20-Sep-1901	James Keene	Riordan, Ella	Lottie Riordan
Keever	William	Henry	16-Dec-1894	20-Dec-1856	James Keever	Rose, Margaret	Phillip Riordan
Kehm	Elizabeth		07-Jun-1891	26-May-1891	[Blank]	Kehm, Stella	James McDevitt
Kehoe	Ann	Mary	12-Feb-1882	[Blank]	Andrew Shannon	[Blank]	Elizabeth Owens
Kehoe	Edmund	Leonard	22-Nov-1903	6-Nov-1903	James J. Kehoe	Giblin, Margaret	Catherine Agnes Kehoe
Kehoe	Joseph	Patrick	12-Mar-1893	03-Mar-1893	James Joseph Kehoe	Giblin, Margaret Louise	Julia Miller
Kehoe	Ann	Mary	10-Jan-1897	23-Dec-1896	James Kehoe	Giblin, Margaret	Catherine Tibbett
Kehoe	George		19-Mar-1899	03-Mar-1899	James Kehoe	Giblin, Margaret	Mary McCormick
Kehoe	James		03-Mar-1895	22-Feb-1895	James Kehoe	Giblin, Margaret	Mary Conroy
Kehoe	Mary	Regina	19-Jan-1902	06-Jan-1902	James Kehoe	Giblin, Margaret	Sara Giblin
Kehoe	Anastasia		05-May-1895	21-Apr-1895	John Kehoe	Vondersmith, Ann	John McCormick
Kehoe	Blanche		23-Oct-1898	09-Oct-1898	John Kehoe	Vondersmith, Ann	John Edelman
Kehoe	Daniel		28-Apr-1900	19-Apr-1900	John Kehoe	Vondersmith, Ann	Frank Laughlin
Kehoe	Edward		06-Jun-1897	22-May-1897	John Kehoe	Vondersmith, Ann	Francis Kelly
Kehoe	John		26-Jun-1903	26-Jun-1903	John Kehoe	Vondersmith, Ann	James Jehoe
Kehoe	Margaret	Mary	23-Oct-1892	09-Oct-1892	John Kehoe	Vondersmith, Ann	Ann Simpson
Kehoe	Agnes		10-Jan-1886	01-Jan-1886	Patrick Kehoe	Noonan, Catherine	Margaret Kehoe
Kehoe	August		08-Oct-1893	29-Sep-1893	Patrick Kehoe	Shanahan, Catherine	Emma Burke
Kehoe	Cornelius		25-Sep-1892	16-Sep-1892	Patrick Kehoe	Shanahan, Catherine	Elizabeth Elwood
Kehoe	James	Joseph	02-Jun-1895	22-May-1895	Patrick Kehoe	Mooney, Helen	Rose Way
Kehoe	John	Francis	27-Dec-1891	16-Dec-1891	Patrick Kehoe	Dorgan, Helen	Ann Finnegan
Kehoe	Edward	Leon	23-Sep-1889	10-Sep-1889	Peter Kehoe	Noonan, Catherine	Richard Usher
Keigle	Mary	L.	13-Sep-1896	13-Aug-1896	Joseph Keigle	Noonan, Catherine	Patrick McCarthy
Keikel	Genevieve		27-Sep-1914	23-Sep-1914	Frederick Keikel	Duff, Mary	Albert Burke
Keil	Elizabeth		8-Jan-1911	1-Jan-1911	William Keil	Stein, Catherine	William Dean
Keiley	Mary	Elizabeth	01-Mar-1898	09-Nov-1894	James Keiley	Dorsey, Ellen	Frederick Stein
Keith	Margaret	Esther	12-Aug-1894	30-Jul-1894	James Keith	Brown, Elizabeth	William Dorsey
Keleher	Catherine		02-Mar-1890	12-Feb-1890	Michael Keleher	Cousin, Ella V.	Charles Les Brown
Keleher	Helen	Viola	18-Jan-1885	11-Jan-1885	Michael Keleher	[Blank], Ellen	Matthew Valentine
Keleher	Joseph	Patrick	27-Mar-1887	17-Mar-1887	Michael Keleher	Dorgan, Helen	Catherine Keleher
Keleher	Mary	Elizabeth	11-Mar-1883	03-Mar-1883	Michael Keleher	Dorgan, Eleanor	Mary Smith
Kell	Nora		1-Mar-1908	15-Jan-1887	Philip Kell	Vamos, Mary	Michael Minton
Keller	Herbert	Elmer	26-Jun-1913	8-Apr-1913	Charles H. Keller	Vondersmith, Ann	Malachi Lyons
Keller	Joseph	Andrew	06-May-1883	12-Apr-1883	George Alphonse Keller	McManus, Leila E.	Catherine Deck
Keller	Vyrill	Alexander	30-Mar-1890	29-Mar-1890	George Alphonse Keller	Nugent, Elizabeth Agnes	Catherine Stack
Keller	John	Henry	20-Oct-1907	30-Sep-1907	Henry Wilmer Keller	Nugent, Elizabeth Agnes	Elizabeth Douglas
Keller	Joan	Honora	09-Mar-1890	11-Jan-1890	John Keller	Brown, Emma Florence	Helen Simmons
Keller	Lillian		11-Aug-1895	11-Jul-1895	John M. Keller	Umlauff, Eleanor	Julia Keller
Keller	Ellennor	Margaret	08-Jul-1894	06-Jun-1894	John Magill Keller	Umlauff, Elenor	Elizabeth Douglas
Keller	Julia	Margaret	13-Sep-1891	14-Aug-1891	John Magill Keller	Umlauf, Helen	Margaret Keller
Keller	Leo	Eva	25-Jun-1893	28-May-1893	John Magill Keller	Umlauff, Helen	Mary Isabelle Keller
Keller	Mary	Eva	06-Nov-1887	23-Oct-1887	John McGill Keller	Umlauf, Helen	Mary Joseph Eliz. Keller
Kelley	Francis	Aloysius	12-Jul-1896	27-Jun-1896	Edward Kelly	Coyne, Bridget M.	James Crowley
Kelley	Edward	Martin	11-Oct-1896	01-Oct-1896	George J. Kelley	Schilough, Mary	John E. Kelley

LAST NAME	FIRST NAME	MIDDLE	BAPTISM	BIRTH	Father	Mother	SPONSORS	
Kelley	Elizabeth		06-Dec-1885	28-Nov-1885	John Kelley	Henry, Mary A.	Thomas Hawkins	Catherine Hawkins
Kelley	Elizabeth	Winnie	06-Sep-1885	27-Aug-1885	Michael Kelly	Willis, Mary Ann	John Mee	Alice Kendall
Kellough	Edward	Alexander	04-Sep-1892	12-Aug-1892	Alexander Kellough	Roesinzer, Louise		Ann Roesinzer
Kelly	Agnes	Dorothy	13-Jun-1910	10-Feb-1910	[Blank]	Kelly, Ann		Elsie Elizabeth Kratz
Kelly	Catherine	Estelle	08-Dec-1889	26-Nov-1889	[Blank] Kelly	Challion, Mary	Albert Evans	Kate Kelly
Kelly	Charles	Bernard	20-Sep-1914	10-Sep-1914	Charles B. Kelly	Ross, Mary	James J. Kelly	Margarer Ragan
Kelly	Charles	Vincent	24-Jun-1900	10-Jun-1900	Charles V. Kelly	Lyons, Mary G.	J. Thomas Lyons	Mary Kelly
Kelly	Mary	Margaret	07-Nov-1897	05-Nov-1897	Edward Kelly	Coyne, Bridget	Daniel Carbery	Helen Coyne
Kelly	Norman		06-Aug-1899	16-Jul-1899	Edward Kelly	Davis, Ann	Michael Kelly	Catherine Kane
Kelly	John	Patrick	12-May-1912	1-Apr-1912	Eugene Kelly	Hagerty, Theresa	William Hagerty	Mary Kelly
Kelly	Ann	C.	13-Dec-1903	28-Nov-1903	Francis Kelly	Fisher, Mary	James W. Kelly	Sarah Rooney
Kelly	Thomas	Leon	08-Sep-1901	24-Aug-1901	Francis Kelly	Fisher, Mary	John T. Mullen	Mary Cullen
Kelly	Mary	Loretta	5-Apr-1908	19-Mar-1908	Francis P. Kelly	Fisher, Mary	Percy Campbell	Mignon Campbeell
Kelly	Francis	Patrick	26-Nov-1905	15-Nov-1905	Francis Patrick Kelly	Fisher, Mary	John Kelly	Susannah Kelly
Kelly	Mary	Elizabeth	12-Feb-1888	04-Feb-1888	George J. Kelly	[BlankJ, Mary	Eugene Kelly	
Kelly	Margaret		23-Jul-1893	09-Jul-1893	George Joseph Kelly	Challion, Mary	Francis Patrick Kelly	Mary Kelly
Kelly	Lillian	Mary	11-Oct-1891	25-Sep-1891	George Kelly	Challion, Mary	George Chaillon	Mary Chaillon
Kelly	Catherine	Mary	23-Sep-1883	19-Sep-1883	James J. Kelly	McCabe, Margaret	John Kelly	Catherine Roche
Kelly	Alice	Mary	08-Jun-1884	29-May-1884	James Kelly	Corrigan, Catherine	Joseph Wicker	Alice Kelly
Kelly	Charles	Bernard	24-Jun-1888	18-Jun-1888	James Kelly	McCabe, Margaret	Charles McCabe	Mary McCabe
Kelly	James	Patrick	14-Mar-1886	10-Mar-1886	James Kelly	McCabe, Margaret	Joan McCabe	Mary McCabe
Kelly	James		18-Jan-1891	13-Jan-1891	James Kelly	Brannan, Ellen	Henry Schmidt	Hannah Brannan
Kelly	Leo		08-Jan-1893	29-Dec-1892	James Kelly	Brannan, Helen	John Patrick Brannan	August Gunter
Kelly	Margaret		15-Feb-1885	10-Feb-1885	James Kelly	McCabe, Margaret	Simon McCabe	Margaret Smith
Kelly	Mary		11-Aug-1889	05-Aug-1889	James Kelly	Brennan, Eleanor	John Kelly	Eleanor Kelly
Kelly	Mildred		10-Nov-1912	29-Oct-1912	James L. Kelly	Siebold, Ellen	Henry Siebold	Catherine [Blank]
Kelly	Robert	Thomas	10-Nov-1912	29-Oct-1912	James L. Kelly	Siebold, Ellen	Edward Gordon	Margaret McQuillen
Kelly	John	Edward	25-Jan-1891	15-Jan-1891	John E. Kelly	Hagerty, Margaret M.	Francis P. Kelly	Mary E. Boyle
Kelly	William	Henry	10-Jul-1892	29-Jun-1892	John E. Kelly	Hagerty, Margaret M.	Terence Kelly	Catherine Kelly
Kelly	Owen	Patrick	27-Nov-1887	20-Nov-1887	John Edward Kelly	Hagerty, Margaret Martin	William Hagerty	Mary Agnes Kelly
Kelly	Charles	Woodruff	14-Jan-1894	23-Jan-1894	John F. Kelly	Smith, Mary V.	James Brennan	Mary Davis
Kelly	Charles	Simon	14-Jan-1894	07-Jan-1894	John J. Kelly	Kelly, Ellen M.	Charles W. Kelly	Mary Kelly
Kelly	Ellen	Elizabeth	23-Jun-1895	11-Jun-1895	John J. Kelly	Kelly, Ellen	James Kelly	Mary Bowes
Kelly	James	Joseph	16-Mar-1890	09-Mar-1890	John J. Kelly	Kelly, Ella	Michael Furlong	Helen Scott
Kelly	Jerome	Howard	2-Dec-1906	27-Nov-1906	John J. Kelly	Kelly, Helen	Gibbons Scott	Catherine Elizabeth Kelly
Kelly	Mary	Melicent	10-Jan-1892	02-Dec-1891	John Joseph Kelly	Kelly, Helen	Simon Michael Kelly	Mary Dunn
Kelly	Alice	Regina	23-Dec-1900	17-Dec-1900	John Kelly	Kelly, Ella	Norbert Dunn	Mary Valentine
Kelly	Eugene		27-May-1888	14-May-1888	John Kelly	Henry, Mary A.	Charles A. Hawkins	Joan Henry
Kelly	Jerome		20-Jul-1890	05-Jul-1890	John Kelly	Henry, Mary A.	John McGinn	Mary Gilroy
Kelly	John	Joseph	22-Sep-1895	15-Sep-1895	John Kelly	McMahon, Mary Ann	John Gormley	Mary King
Kelly	Joseph		05-Jun-1898	22-May-1898	John Kelly	Kelly, Ella	John Dunn	Mary Kelly
Kelly	Joseph	Leon	20-Jan-1884	30-Dec-1883	John Kelly	Henry, Mary	John Kelly	Ann Fahey
Kelly	Joseph	Edward	16-May-1915	3-May-1915	John Kelly	Keaveny, Mary	Thomas Donnellan	Mary McNally
Kelly	Mary	Ann	06-Aug-1893	25-Jul-1893	John Kelly	Henry, Mary Ann	George Satterfield	Mary Colton
Kelly	Rose	Milley	26-Nov-1911	20-Oct-1911	John Kelly	Subode, Ann	Robert Subode	Elizabeth McGinn
Kelly	William	Edward	05-Feb-1882	26-Jan-1882	John Kelly	Henry, Mary Ann	Thomas McGinn	Catherine Bamberger
Kelly	Charles	Edward	25-Nov-1905	24-Nov-1905	John P. Kelly	Miller, Mary E.	Charles E. Miller	Elizabeth Kelly
Kelly	Elizabeth	Sylvia	26-Sep-1909	15-Sep-1909	John W. Kelly	Gephardt, Sylvia	William J. Kelly	Mary Kennedy
Kelly	Mary	Ann	10-Jan-1897	17-Dec-1897	Joseph E. Kelly	Hagerty, Margaret	George Kelly	Ann O'Brien
Kelly	Alice	Catherine	02-Sep-1883	17-Aug-1883	Joseph Kelly	Eisenock, Susan	Robert Campbell	Helen Walsh
Kelly	Ann	Mary	31-Aug-1902	08-Aug-1902	Joseph Kelly	Quigley, Catherine	James Quigley	Mary Campbell
Kelly	Catherine		17-Mar-1907	3-Mar-1907	Joseph Kelly	Leonard, Ann	Edward McCormack	Alice Vereker
Kelly	Mary		04-Nov-1888	28-Sep-1888	Joseph Kelly	Eisenock, Susanna	Robert Campbell	Catherine Oates
Kelly	Margaret	Mary	15-Sep-1907	25-Aug-1905	Joseph L. Kelly	Jenkins, Elizabeth	James Vereker	Ella McGee
Kelly	Catherine	Bernardine	17-Aug-1913	6-Aug-1913	Joseph Leon Kelly	Jenkins, Elizabeth	William Oates	J. Mooney
Kelly	Catherine		25-Oct-1908	11-Oct-1908	Martin Joseph Kelly	Bannon, Catherine	J. Dumphy	Mary Owens
Kelly	Agnes		2-Feb-1913	5-Jan-1913	Martin Kelly	Donahue, Catherine		Margaret Kelly
Kelly	Martin	Joseph	07-Sep-1884	30-Aug-1884	Martin Kelly	Bodkin, Mary	Thomas Patrick Kelly	Mary Clensen
Kelly	Martin	Joseph	03-May-1896	22-Apr-1896	Martin Kelly	McNulty, Bridget	John Lillis	Agnes Banahan
Kelly	Thomas	Martin	16-Jul-1905	10-Jul-1905	Martin Kelly	Banahan, Catherine	Edward Brady	Mary Murray
Kelly	Bridget		08-Jan-1882	07-Jan-1882	Matthew Kelly	Clancy, Catherine	Patrick Kelly	Catherine Murray
Kelly	Julia		17-May-1885	15-May-1885	Matthew Kelly	Clancey, Catherine	Patrick Kelly	

LAST NAME	FIRST NAME	MIDDLE	BAPTISM	BIRTH	Father	Mother	SPONSORS	
Kelly	John	Francis	18-Oct-1914	29-Sep-1914	Michael F. Kelly	Donnelly, Marcella R.	John Kelly	Mary L. Donnelly
Kelly	Marcella	M.	19-Feb-1911	24-Jan-1911	Michael F. Kelly	Donnelly, Marcella R.	John J. Kelly	Delia Martin
Kelly	Michael	Joseph	21-Jul-1912	30-Jun-1912	Michael Francis Kelly	Donnelly, Marcella Regina	Michael Ward	Ann Richards
Kelly	Ignatius		20-Aug-1882	28-Jul-1882	Michael Kelly	Hughes, Catherine	Charles Joseph Brooks	Helen Hughes
Kelly	John		14-Nov-1886	09-Nov-1886	Michael Kelly	Scott, Catherine	John McMahon	Elizabeth McMahon
Kelly	John	Joseph	13-Apr-1890	04-Apr-1890	Michael Kelly	Ward, Bridget	Michael Ward	Catherine Ward
Kelly	Mary	Ann	08-Apr-1883	30-Mar-1883	Michael Kelly	Willis, Mary Ann	William Willis	Elizabeth Willis
Kelly	Michael		10-Nov-1883	09-Nov-1883	Michael Kelly	Ward, Delia		Mary Ward
Kelly	Michael	Francis	13-Sep-1885	05-Sep-1885	Michael Kelly	Ward, Bridget	Michael Ward	Catherine Ward
Kelly	Michael	Leon	8-Feb-1914	22-Dec-1913	Michael Kelly	Halligan, Ann		Ursula Sinnott
Kelly	Joseph		07-Jul-1889	25-Jun-1889	Patrick Kelly	Colford, Mary E.	Adrian Fitzpatrick	Mary Eagan
Kelly	Joseph		05-Jan-1896	16-Dec-1895	Patrick Kelly	Calford, Mary	Joseph Vaughan	Mary Egan
Kelly	Leo		19-Apr-1891	05-Apr-1891	Patrick Kelly	Colford, Mary Helen	John Nicholson Kelly	Margaret Quirk
Kelly	Margaret	Helen	16-Nov-1884	08-Nov-1884	Patrick Kelly	Colford, Mary Helen	Thomas Kavanaugh	Joan Moore
Kelly	Mary	Ann	19-Sep-1886	10-Sep-1886	Patrick Kelly	Colford, Mary E.	Andrew Rock	Mary Rettay
Kelly	Mary	Genevieve	22-Jan-1893	12-Jan-1893	Patrick Kelly	Colford, Mary Helen	Michael Fitzgerald	Mary Quirk
Kelly	Thomas	Patrick	14-May-1882	05-May-1882	Patrick Kelly	Colford, Mary Helen	Thomas Colford	Catherine Colford
Kelly	Edward	Joseph	16-Aug-1903	01-Aug-1903	Peter J. Kelly	Cassidy, Nellie E.	Edward G. Keely	Nellie A. Kelly
Kelly	Charles	Joseph	03-Mar-1901	13-Feb-1901	Peter Joseph Kelly	Cassidy, Ellen	Michael Logue	Mamie Cassidy
Kelly	C.	Mary	20-Mar-1898	13-Mar-1898	S. Michael Kelly	Ridgley, Mary	Joseph Kelly	Catherine Morris
Kelly	Eugene		27-Sep-1896	18-Sep-1896	Terence Kelly	Sullivan, Helen	Joseph Murphy	Mary Murphy
Kelly	William		16-Oct-1898	10-Oct-1898	Terence Kelly	Sullivan, Ellen	Joseph Murphy	Julia Sullivan
Kelly	Terence	S.	5-Mar-1905	17-Jun-1905	Terence S. Kelly	Elizabeth Noonan	James J. Quillan	Mary Arminger
Kelly	Charles	Aloysius	23-Oct-1887	13-Oct-1887	Thomas H. Kelly	Donnelly, Alice B.	Charles Biddle	Ann A.T. Starrs
Kelly	Thomas		18-Mar-1883	14-Mar-1883	Thomas H. Kelly	Donnelly, Alice	Catherine Grop	Philomena Sarbacher
Kelly	Alice	Teresa	09-Mar-1890	23-Feb-1890	Thomas Kelly	Donnelly, Alice Bernardine	James Donnelly	Teresa Salesia McKenna
Kelly	John	Ward	22-Nov-1885	20-Nov-1885	Thomas Kelly	Donley, Alice	James Cullen	Catherine Amrein
Kelly	John		17-Aug-1887	27-Jul-1887	Thomas Kelly	Morisey, Ellenor	William Dwyer	Delia Ward
Kelly	Thomas	Joseph	27-Aug-1899	12-Aug-1899	Thomas Kelly	Murray, Catherine	John Kelly	Bridget Kelly
Kelly	Edward	Joseph	07-Oct-1883	02-Oct-1883	William Alphonse Kelly	Kelly, Joan Elizabeth	Peter Kelly	Mary Burns
Kelly	Rosalin	Cecelia	23-Aug-1891	13-Aug-1891	William Alphonse Kelly	Kelly, Joan Elizabeth	Ignatius Loritz	Cecelia Loritz
Kelly	Helen		11-Feb-1894	23-Jan-1894	William Henry Kelly	Kelly, Joan	Thomas Colford	Sara Agnes Stewart
Kelly	Ann	Daisy	19-Aug-1883	02-Nov-1878	William Kelly	Dorsey, Mary		Ann Hulavan
Kelly	Catherine		26-Apr-1885	25-Apr-1885	William Kelly	Hughes, Margaret	John Kelly	Elizabeth Hughes
Kelly	Ellen	Catherine	4-Nov-1900	21-Oct-1900	William Kelly	Fay, Susanna	H.J. Fay	Ann [Blank]
Kelly	Mary		29-Aug-1886	19-Aug-1886	William Kelly	Kelly, Joan	Frederick Hinder	Mary Hinder
Kelly	Mary		11-Jul-1897	22-Jun-1897	William Kelly	Fahey, Susanna	John Kelly	Sara Rooney
Kelly	Theresa		02-Dec-1896	20-Nov-1896	William Kelly	Kelly, Joan		Mary Burns
Kelly	William		06-Aug-1882	24-Jun-1882	William Kelly	Kelly, Joan	Patrick Kavanaugh	Catherine Conway
Kelly	William	Francis	03-Mar-1895	20-Feb-1895	William Kelly	Fay, Susan	Francis Patrick Kelly	Sara Rooney
Kemno	Claudia	V.	02-Dec-1888	30-Oct-1888	Henry L. Kemno	Reed, Lula Estelle B.	Walter F. Mitchell	
Kendall	Edward	Joseph	11-Oct-1888	24-Sep-1896	T. L. Kendall	Kolb, Dora	Henry Barton	Emelia Kendall
Kendall	Ann	Mary	03-Aug-1898	20-Jul-1898	Terence Kendall	Kolb, Dora		Mary Kendall
Kendell	Frederick	Clarence	13-Oct-1898	08-Oct-1898	Frederick Kendell	Cousins, Ella		Mary Watson
Kenealy	Eugene		22-Nov-1903	9-Nov-1903	Donald Kenealy	Golden, Catherine	Joseph Katzenderfer	Elizabeth Bailey
Kenly	Albert	L.	4-Feb-1906	29-Dec-1905	Albert Kenly	Fink, M. Catherine		Emma Ennis
Kennedy	Ambrose		22-Jan-1893	07-Jan-1893	Ambrose Kennedy	McDonald, Ann	James Egan	Mary Ann Collins
Kennedy	Ann		06-Jan-1889	30-Dec-1888	Ambrose Kennedy	McDonald, Ann	Ambrose McDonald	Joan McDonald
Kennedy	Daniel		11-Oct-1896	29-Sep-1896	Ambrose Kennedy	McDonald, Ann	Marcus Sinnott	Amanda Harvey
Kennedy	Gertrude		16-Mar-1894	16-Mar-1894	Ambrose Kennedy	McDonnell, Ann		Bridget Eagan
Kennedy	John		17-Jul-1890	04-Jul-1890	Ambrose Kennedy	McDonald, Ann	Nicolas Caton	Mary McDonald
Kennedy	Margaret		24-Mar-1895	12-Mar-1895	Ambrose Kennedy	McDonald, Ann	Michael Hagerty	Ann Hagerty
Kennedy	Margaret	Agnes	30-Nov-1913	23-Nov-1913	Ambrose Kennedy	Dailey, Mary	Daniel Kennedy	Ann Kennedy
Kennedy	Mary		03-Apr-1887	23-Mar-1887	Ambrose Kennedy	McDonald, Ann	John O'Sullivan	Helen Doyle
Kennedy	Mary	Bernardine	11-Dec-1910	29-Nov-1910	Ambrose Kennedy	Dailey, Mary	John Kennedy	Margaret Kennedy
Kennedy	Michael		02-Jan-1898	25-Dec-1897	Ambrose Kennedy	McDonnell, Ann	John Logan	Bridget Logan
Kennedy	Helen	Rose	18-Jul-1897	06-Jul-1897	Daniel Kennedy	O'Connor, Mary	Hollins Brooks	Mary Brooks
Kennedy	Bernard		20-Oct-1907	5-Oct-1907	Dennis Kennedy	Connors, Mary	Herman Miller	Elizabeth Daley
Kennedy	Dennis	Edward	25-Jan-1903	15-Jan-1903	Dennis Kennedy	Connors, Mary	James Connors	Nellie Colbert
Kennedy	Edward		04-Dec-1901	27-Nov-1901	Dennis Kennedy	Connors, Mary		Mary Calhern
Kennedy	John		05-Feb-1899	24-Jan-1899	Dennis Kennedy	O'Connor, Mary	John Smith	Adelina Smith
Kennedy	Leon	Francis	7-Feb-1915	3-Feb-1915	Dennis Kennedy	O'Connor, Mary		Ann Daily
Kennedy	Mary	Christian	05-Jan-1896	25-Dec-1895	Dennis Kennedy	O'Connor, Mary		

LAST NAME	FIRST NAME	MIDDLE	BAPTISM	BIRTH	Father	Mother	SPONSORS	
Kennedy	Rose	Genevieve	13-Aug-1905	2-Aug-1905	Dennis P. Kennedy	Connors, Mary	Henry G. Bersterman	Rose Bersterman
Kennedy	Joseph		10-Jun-1894	29-May-1894	Dennis Patrick Kennedy	Connors, Mary	Charles August Boyle	Delia Conner
Kennedy	Genevieve		24-Dec-1899	13-Dec-1899	James Quinlan	Kennedy, Mary	Matthias Gahan	Margaret Rooney
Kennedy	Austin		26-Nov-1899	08-Nov-1899	John Kennedy	O'Donnell, Mary		Mary Yoe
Kennedy	Elizabeth		26-Feb-1899	14-Feb-1899	John Kennedy	Couch, Catherine	Joseph Kennedy	Mary Kennedy
Kennedy	Mary		18-Dec-1887	28-Nov-1887	John Thomas Kennedy	O'Donnell, Winifred	Daniel Lucey	Ann Margaret Biebel
Kennedy	Catherine		19-Oct-1884	08-Oct-1884	Joseph Kennedy	Hart, Catherine	George Grogan	Catherine Kelty
Kennedy	Josephine		19-Mar-1882	10-Mar-1882	Joseph Kennedy	Hart, Catherine	Edward Rogers	Ann Grogan
Kennedy	Ann		14-Sep-1890	03-Sep-1890	Martin Kennedy	Cashen, Bridget	Patrick Cashen	Mary Cashen
Kennedy	Ann	Elizabeth	20-Oct-1895	05-Oct-1895	Martin Kennedy	Cashen, Bridget	William Tunny	Delia Tunney
Kennedy	Cecelia	Elizabeth	31-Dec-1893	19-Dec-1893	Martin Kennedy	Cashen, Bridget	Patrick Carroll	Catherine Maher
Kennedy	Martin	Joseph	15-May-1892	06-May-1892	Martin Kennedy	Cashen, Bridget	Edward Cashen	Mary Ann Tunney
Kennedy	Thomas	Michael	29-Oct-1899	19-Oct-1899	Martin Kennedy	Cashen, Bridget	Patrick Cashen	Bridget Cashen
Kennedy	Edward		07-Feb-1886	31-Jan-1886	Patrick Kennedy	McKeone, Mary	George L. Bogy	Ann Barry
Kennedy	John		03-Feb-1884	27-Jan-1884	Patrick Kennedy	McKewen, Mary	Peter Creamer	Mary McKewen
Kennedy	William		16-Jul-1893	16-Jul-1893	Peter A. Kennedy	Ferguson, Rose G.		Mary Phoebus
Kennedy	William	Ferguson	23-Jul-1893	16-Jul-1893	Peter Ambrose Kennedy	Ferguson, Rose Gertrude	Richard Cronan	Mary Phoebus
Kennedy	Edwin	Thomas	17-Apr-1892	29-Mar-1892	Thomas Kennedy	O'Donnell, Winifred	Joseph O'Donnell	Bertha Driscoll
Kennedy	Winifred		10-Nov-1889	31-Oct-1889	Thomas Kennedy	O'Donnell, Winifred	Patrick Dougherty	Agnes O'Donnell
Kennelly	Daniel	Joseph	23-Nov-1902	5-Nov-1902	Daniel J. Kennelly	Golden, Catherine	James Golden	Catherine Golden
Kennelly	Joan	Mary	27-Aug-1893	20-Aug-1893	Daniel Joseph Kennelly	Golden, Catherine Agnes	John Thomas Golden	Georgia L. Katzenberger
Kennelly	Catherine	McCoy	16-Jun-1895	11-Jun-1895	Daniel Kennelly	Golden, Catherine	Charles McDonald	Mary Cain
Kennelly	Margaret		13-Feb-1898	09-Feb-1898	Daniel Kennelly	Golden, Catherine	George Katzenberger	Mary Katzenberger
Kennelly	Thomas	Francis	04-Oct-1896	02-Oct-1896	Daniel Kennelly	Golden, Catherine	John Katzenberger	Agnes Macken
Kennelly	Ella	Regina	01-Sep-1901	25-Aug-1901	Donald Kennelly	Golden, Catherine	Charles Guckert	Ellen Watson
Kennelly	William	James	11-Feb-1900	07-Feb-1900	Donald Kennelly	Golden, Catherine		Catherine Golden
Kenney	John	M.	09-Jan-1898	17-Dec-1897	John Kenney	Brown, Margaret	Martin Kenney	L.P. Brown
Kenney	Paul	Dailes	8-Jul-1906	27-Jun-1906	David D. Kenny	Gillen, Mary	Joseph Samsel	Myrtle Hyle
Kenney	Anthony	Neal	16-Jul-1905	23-Jun-1905	Davis Kenny	Gillen, Mary	Patrick Gillen	Elizabeth Gereghty
Kenny	James	Louis	7-Apr-1912	22-Mar-1912	James Joseph Kenny	Burrier, Mary	Louis Burrier	Ezliabeth Burrier
Kenny	Joseph	Daniel	26-Mar-1882	19-Mar-1882	James Kenny	Corrigan, Catherine	Thomas Grogan	Helen Brannan
Kenny	John		24-Feb-1884	12-Feb-1884	John Kenny	Ratigan, Mary	Patrick O'Brien	Francis Ratigan
Kenny	William	Joseph	7-Mar-1909	15-Feb-1909	Joseph Kenny	Burrier, Mary	John Burrier	Catherine Kenny
Kenny	Catherine		30-Jul-1893	21-Jul-1893	Michael Kenny	Birmingham, Catherine	John Barry	Mary Birmingham
Kenny	Rose	Francis	19-Jul-1891	24-Jun-1891	Michael Kenny	Birmingham, Catherine	Joseph Donahue	Ann Kenny
Kenny	William	A.	13-Oct-1907	27-Sep-1907	William Kenny	McDonald, Esther	Edward Murphy	Margaret Murphy
Kenrick	Elizabeth		21-Jan-1906	12-Jan-1906	Dennis J. Kenrick	Mahoney, Margaret	Charles Mooney	Mary Mooney
Kenrick	Margaret		17-Dec-1899	09-Dec-1899	Dennis Kenrick	Mahoney, Margaret	Thomas Mahoney	Elizabeth Mahoney
Kenrick	William	Thomas	13-Apr-1902	07-Apr-1902	Dennis Kenrick	Mahoney, Margaret	Dennis Don	Ann Lehane
Kent	Philip	R.	26-Jun-1898	30-Apr-1895	Philip Kent	Smith, Stella		Ann Webb
Keogh	Margaret	Genevieve	14-Nov-1908	14-Nov-1908	James Joseph Keogh	Giblin, Margaret Louise	Patrick B. Kelly	Ann Raphael Daley
Keogh	Margaret	Genevieve	20-Dec-1908	14-Nov-1908	James Joseph Keogh	Giblin, Margaret Louise		
Keogh	Gerald		6-May-1906	19-Feb-1906	James Keogh	Giblin, Margaret		Mary Daily
Kerchner	James	Albert	05-Jan-1902	30-Dec-1901	J. Frederick Kerchner	Mullehey, Mary	James Mullehey	Mary Burke
Kerchner	William	Ferdinand	08-Jan-1899	29-Dec-1898	John Kerchner	Malloy, Mary	William Kerchner	Agnes Malloy
Kern	Gertrude		09-Oct-1898	01-Oct-1898	John Kern	Gorman, Mary	Eugene Finnigan	Susanna McGraw
Kern	Helen	Mary	17-Feb-1895	10-Feb-1895	John Kern	Gorman, Mary	William McGraw	Ann Trainor
Kern	Mary	Gertrude	24-May-1896	19-May-1896	John Kern	Gorman, Mary	Felix Reilly	Nora Kern
Kern	Catherine	Rosalie	05-Aug-1894	15-Apr-1894	Edward Kernan	Kimmerlein, Rose Catherine		Ruth Fiege
Kernan	Mary	Helen	12-Jun-1910	4-May-1910	Eugene Kernan	Clautice, Ella May	Eugene Kernan	Mary V. O'Brien
Kernan	Bernard		14-Jun-1885	30-May-1885	John Joseph Kernan	Hall, Catherine	Thomas Hopper	Margaret Quirk
Kernan	Joan	Lily	09-Sep-1883	28-Aug-1883	John Joseph Kernan	Hall, Catherine	Bernard James Kernan	Helen Callender
Kernan	Elizabeth	Edward	22-Dec-1889	09-Dec-1889	John Kernan	Hall, Catherine	Bernard James Kernan	Mary Kernan
Kernan	John	James	24-Aug-1902	14-Aug-1902	John Kernan	Gorman, Mary	Felix Owens	Gertrude Owens
Kernan	Joseph	Hall	26-Mar-1893	21-Mar-1893	John Kernan	Hall, Catherine	William Edward Anderson	Ann Quirk
Kernan	William	Burke	27-Nov-1887	15-Nov-1887	John Kernan	Hall, Catherine	James Mulligan	Mary Mitchell
Kernan	Francis	Regis Aloysius	28-Jun-1891	16-Jun-1891	Philip Edward Kernan	Fitzgerald, Catherine	Michael Thomas Carney	Mary Ann Duffy
Kernan	Philip	Edward	07-Feb-1897	24-Jan-1897	Philip Edward Kernan	Fitzgerald, Catherine	John Hildebrand	Mary Helen Kerly

LAST NAME	FIRST NAME	MIDDLE	BAPTISM	BIRTH	Father	Mother	SPONSORS
Kernan	Joseph	Leo	11-Feb-1900	04-Feb-1900	Philip Kernan	Fitzpatrick, Catherine	Charles O'Neill, Ann Carney
Kernan	Catherine	Laura	24-Mar-1889	10-Mar-1889	Phillip Edward Kernan	Fitzgerald, Catherine	Charles O'Neill, John O'Neill
Kernan	James	Patrick F.	25-Nov-1886	15-Nov-1886	Phillip Edward Kernan	Fitzgerald, Catherine	James Patrick Fitzgerald, Elizabeth Kernan
Kernan	Mary	Joan	06-Jul-1884	01-Jun-1884	Phillip Edward Kernan	Fitzgerald, Catherine	Michael Joseph Duffin, Susan Thomas Phillips
Kernan	Mary	Margaret	12-Nov-1893	02-Nov-1893	Phillip Edward Kernan	Fitzgerald, Catherine	Joseph O'Neill, Helen Carney
Kernan	Henry		19-Sep-1897	10-Sep-1897	Preston P. Kernan	Hudson, Sara E.	Henry Burse, Sara O'Donnell
Kerney	Francis		5-Nov-1911	25-Nov-1911	John Joseph Kerney	Nagle, Catherine	Francis Nagle, Lauretta Nagle
Kerney	William	James	06-Sep-1885	30-Aug-1885	John Kerney	Dalton, Mary Ann	James Kerney, Sarah Kerney
Kerns	Bernard	Joseph	10-Sep-1899	18-Aug-1899	Bernard Kerns	Peterson, Ida	William Burke, Mary Burke
Kerns	Emma	Elizabeth	24-Jul-1892	18-Jun-1892	Bernard Kerns	Peterson, Ida	Charles Bavis, Anastasia Parrell
Kerns	James	Bernard	05-Oct-1890	09-Sep-1890	Bernard Kerns	Peterson, Ida Louise	James J. Kerns, Catherine Kerns
Kerns	Laura	Isabelle	02-Dec-1894	17-Nov-1894	Bernard Kerns	Peterson, Ida L.	John Kerns, Margaret Kerns
Kerns	William	Thomas	15-Dec-1901	30-Nov-1901	Bernard Kerns	Monley, Frances	Patrick Burns, Margaret Burns
Kerns	Frances	Isabelle	12-Nov-1893	01-Nov-1893	Francis Kerns	Monley, Frances	James Kerns, Margaret McCusker
Kerns	Edward	Joseph	20-Mar-1892	11-Mar-1892	William Kerns	Curran, Sara Cecelia	James Clancy, Ann Owens
Kerr	James	Edward	26-Jul-1896	11-Jul-1896	Edward C. Kerr	Murray, Mary Helen	John Clay, Mary Coolahan
Kerr	Catherine		03-Feb-1895	20-Jan-1895	Edward Kerr	Murray, Mary	Charles Bavis, Susan Hasson
Kerrigan	Elizabeth	Helen	10-May-1896	05-May-1896	John Kerrigan	Kerrigan, Helen	Humphrey Golden, Elizabeth Lehan
Kerrigan	Margaret		18-Nov-1898	28-Oct-1898	John Kerrigan	Keleher, Ella	William Bennett, Ann Hughes
Kerrigan	Mary	Ellen	20-Apr-1890	14-Mar-1890	John Kerrigan	Kelleher, Ellen	Bridget Kerrigan
Kesseling	Dora	Agnes	04-May-1882	24-Apr-1882	Joseph Kesseling	Westcamp, Helen	Elizabeth Kegner
Ketler	Elizabeth	Lillian	16-Feb-1908	28-Jan-1907	Howard J. Ketler	Haverman, Cristina	Michael O'Rourke, Elisabeth O'Rourke
Ketler	Ann	Loretta	13-Sep-1903	28-Aug-1903	Howard Ketler	Havener, Christina	Herman Havener, Josephetta Havener
Kevenay	Thomas	Bernard	27-Jan-1889	14-Jan-1889	James Kivenay	McDonough, Catherine	Bernard Roddy, Mary Hamilton
Keyes	Mary	Catherine	29-Sep-1912	22-Sep-1912	James J. Keyes	Byrne, Mary E.	Laurence Malloy, Catherine Roche
Keyes	Francis	Xavier	24-May-1914	10-May-1914	James Keyes	Byrne, Mary E.	Laurence Byrne, Elizabeth O'Connor
Keyhan	Walter		27-Dec-1885	Jan 1878	Joseph Keyhan	Bunting, Cornelia	William H. McBride
Kidd	Wilfred		24-Oct-1886	04-Oct-1886	James Kidd	Hammell, Rose	Michael Kidd, Sara Kidd
Kidd	Esther		30-Dec-1888	27-Dec-1888	Michael Francis Kidd	Quigley, Sara	Michael Laughlin, Joan Hagerty
Kiely	Mary	Frances	25-Mar-1883	23-Mar-1883	Dennis Kiely	Flaherty, Margaret	Patrick McAuliffe, Catherine Flaherty
Kildorf	William	Carey	18-Oct-1891	29-Sep-1891	Thomas J. Kildorf	Carey, Catherine Agnes	Hermann Hartman, Catherine McClenahan
Kilduff	John	Arthur	18-Sep-1910	31-Aug-1910	Arthur Joseph Kilduff	Colley, Sarah	Stephen J. Kilduff, Irene M. Gannon
Kilduff	Bernard	Francis	25-Feb-1894	31-Jan-1894	Bernard Joseph Kilduff	Fortman, Rosalie Angel	Francis Patrick Arthur, Regina Magdalene Fortman
Kilduff	Henry	M.	13-Dec-1896	16-Nov-1896	Bernard Kilduff	Fortman, Mary Rose	Nicholas Merryman, Mary R. Butler
Kilduff	Mary	Caroline	07-Apr-1891	20-Jul-1887	Francis Hoen	[Blank], Sophia	Stephen Kilduff, Ellen Kilduff
Kilduff	James	Charles	17-Jul-1887	05-Jul-1887	John Kilduff	Edwards, Bella	Patrick H. Gibbons, Mary Butler
Kilduff	Walter	L.	25-Jun-1899	24-May-1899	John Kilduff	Edwards, Anabelle	Michael Droney, Elizabeth Giblin
Kilduff	Albert		21-Aug-1894	19-Aug-1894	John Thomas	Hoffman, Dorothy	Mary Kilduff
Kilduff	Albert	Raymond Elmer	16-Sep-1894	19-Aug-1894	John Thomas Kilduff	Joseph, Dorothy	John Kilduff, Mary Kilduff
Kilduff	Agnes		29-Apr-1883	22-Mar-1883	Joseph Kilduff	McCarthy, Catherine	Daniel Joseph McCarthy, Ann Creaghan
Kilduff	Agnes	Loretta	22-Jun-1884	14-Jun-1884	Joseph Kilduff	Hoen, Carrie	George Kaufmann, Magdalena Kaufmann
Kilduff	Catherine	Agnes	31-Jan-1889	21-Jan-1889	Joseph Kilduff	McCarthy, Catherine	Eugene McCarthy, Ann Creagan
Kilduff	Francis	Rebecca	25-Feb-1887	16-Feb-1887	Joseph Kilduff	McCarthy, Catherine	Elizabeth Tully
Kilduff	Stephen	George	14-Nov-1886	26-Oct-1886	Stephen Joseph Kilduff	Hoen, Caroline	George Stephen Kilduff, Catherine Rock
Kilduff	Arthur		19-May-1889	04-May-1889	Stephen Kilduff	Hoen, Caroline	Arthur Kilduff, Joan Kilduff
Kilduff	Helen	Regina	09-Oct-1892	26-Sep-1892	Stephen Kilduff	Hahn, Mary Caroline	Nicholas Buxmeyer, Ella A. White
Kilduff	Mary	Elizabeth	19-Feb-1882	06-Feb-1882	Thomas J. Kilduff	Hoen, Caroline	Thomas Bell, Mary Elizabeth Kammerell
Kilduff	Martin	Carey	18-Mar-1888	18-Feb-1888	Thomas J. Kilduff	Carey, Catherine A.	Martin Carey, Ann Thompson
Kilduff	Mary		24-Mar-1894	23-Mar-1894	Thomas Kilduff	Carey, Catherine A.	
Kilduff	Gertrude	Lee	08-Jan-1890	25-Dec-1889	Thomas Kilduff	Carey, Catherine	Cecelia Maguire
Kilduff	Gertrude		02-Mar-1890	25-Mar-1889	Thomas Kilduff	Carey, Catherine	Thomas Kelly
Kilduff	Mildred	Emily	22-Mar-1903	04-Mar-1903	Thomas Kilduff	Donovan, Mary	U.F. Hamill, Mary Finn
Kilfoyle	Elizabeth		23-Apr-1882	09-Apr-1882	Thomas Kilfoyle	O'Keefe, Catherine	
Kilfoyle	Emma	Cecelia	28-Oct-1883	19-Oct-1883	Thomas Kilfoyle	O'Keefe, Catherine	Martin Hennesy, Catherine Waldman
Kilkenny	Donald	Francis	18-Sep-1910	31-Aug-1910	John W. Kilkenny	McGoughran, Mary	Francis J. Kilkenny, Catherine Murphy
Killeen	Mary	Helen	29-Jan-1882	17-Jan-1882	John Killeen	Cusick, Julia	John Flynn, Mary Killeen
Kilroy	Francis		12-May-1899	09-Apr-1899	[Blank]	Kilroy, Margaret	Catherine Kilroy
Kimball	John	Michael	28-Jun-1891	15-Jun-1891	Joseph Kimball	Clancy, Julia	John Michael Kimball, Mary Rooney
Kimball	Joseph	Willis	30-Apr-1893	14-Apr-1893	Joseph Willis Kimball	Clancy, Julia	Francis Zellers, Mary Clancy
Kimball	Ann	Mary	17-May-1896	03-May-1896	Joseph Kimball	Clancey, Julia	John Durkan, Catherine Clansey
Kimberly	Catherine	Emma	17-Jul-1884	30-Jun-1884	Henry Kimberly	Wade, Elizabeth Joan	Emma Joan Irving
Kimlein	Matilda	Teresa	08-Aug-1886	18-Jul-1886	John Kinlein	Huber, Mary	John Freide, Matilda Kimlinstein
Kimmet	Charles	Andrew	21-Dec-1884	26-Sep-1884	August Kimmet	Stoffer, Ann Margaret	Francis G. Rosensteel, Elizabeth Steck

LAST NAME	FIRST NAME	MIDDLE	BAPTISM	BIRTH	Father	Mother	SPONSORS
Kimmet	James	Laurence	10-Dec-1882	22-Nov-1882	Gustave Kimmet	Stoffer, Margaret Ann	James McDevitt	Ann Marue King
Kimmet	Alma	Regina	30-May-1886	28-Apr-1886	Gustavus Kimmet	Stoffer, Margaret	Joseph Belshon	Clara E. Mitchell
Kimmett	Eugene	Leon	28-May-1887	29-Aug-1874	Gustave Kimmett	Stoffer, Margaret	James McDevitt	Emily Cecelia Gamble
Kimmett	William		23-Oct-1887	01-Jan-1876	Gustave Kimmett	Stoffer, Margaret Ann		Clara A. Mitchell
Kimmett	James	Bernard	18-Feb-1912	6-Feb-1912	John Kimmett	Farrell, Catherine	James Farrell	Mary Kimmett
Kimmett	John	Patrick	10-Aug-1902	27-Jul-1902	John Kimmett	Farrell, Catherine	John Costello	Margaret McGuinnis
Kimmett	Margaret		28-Jul-1889	18-Jul-1889	John Kimmett	Donahue, Ann	Michael Kimmett	Mary Nicholson
Kimmett	Mary	Catherine	2-Sep-1906	19-Aug-1906	John Kimmett	Farrell, Catherine	Thomas Kimmett	Helen Farnen
Kimmett	Thomas	Paul	19-Jun-1892	05-Jun-1892	John Kimmett	Donohue, Ann	Patrick Donohoe	Helen Donohoe
Kimmett	Genevieve		30-Dec-1906	9-Dec-1906	Roger F. Kimmett	Kelly, Mary	Thomas Moylan	Margaret Byrnes
Kimmett	Edna	Mary	30-Aug-1914	10-Aug-1914	Roger Kimmett	Kelly, Mary	Edward A. Fitzgerald	Mary Brennan
Kimmett	Roger	Thomas	14-Aug-1910	13-Jul-1910	Roger Kimmett	Kelly, Mary A.		Lillian Murphy
Kines	Eleanor		13-Oct-1895	29-Sep-1895	William Kines	Rogers, Nelly	Thomas Slater	Catherine Doyle
King	Edward		01-Feb-1891	13-Jan-1891	Emerson John King	Shaughnessy, Catherine	Sigmund Stephen	Mary Teresa Hynes
King	George	Henry	12-Jan-1913	15-Dec-1912	George King	Barrett, Mary		Mary Ann Cook
King	Albert	William	6-Dec-1914	21-Sep-1888	James Albert King	Hindle, Margaret	James J. Murphy	Margaret L. Crone
King	Elizabeth		7-Apr-1907	26-Mar-1907	James E. King	Reilly, Margaret	John K. Wess	Elizabeth O'Malley
King	James		23-Dec-1894	13-Dec-1894	James Edward King	Reilly, Margaret Blanche	John Francis King	Catherine Mary O'Malley
King	Alice	Genevieve	13-Mar-1904	22-Feb-1904	James King	Keenan, Alice Agnes	James Joseph Farnen	Helen Farnen
King	Ann	Mary	26-Nov-1893	12-Nov-1893	James King	Keenan, Alice	James Farron	Winifred Farrom
King	Catherine	Christine	08-Dec-1895	29-Nov-1895	James King	Keenan, Alice	Patrick Farron	Mary Gallagher
King	James		17-Dec-1899	01-Dec-1899	James King	Keenan, Alice	James McCrony	Margaret Reilly
King	James	Morris	09-Dec-1900	05-Dec-1900	James King	Morris, Mary	John Connolly	Nora Connolly
King	John	Edward	30-May-1896	16-May-1896	James King	Reilly, Margaret B.		Hannah Creagan
King	John		31-Oct-1897	18-Oct-1897	James King	Kernan, Alice	Peter Kernan	Ella Brown
King	Joseph		31-Mar-1901	15-Mar-1901	James King	Reilly, Margaret	John Colbert	Ann King
King	Louis	Wilmer	10-Jan-1909	25-Dec-1908	James King	Keenan, Alice		Ann King
King	William		18-Jul-1897	03-Jul-1897	James King	Reilly, Margaret	Edward Healey	
King	Samuel	Raymond	12-Jun-1904	30-May-1904	John F. King	McCourt, Mary	Eugene McCourt	Isabelle McCourt
King	Alice	Isabelle	8-Nov-1908	31-Oct-1908	John Francis King	[Blank], Mary Josephine	James [Blank]	Mary Isabelle Shea
King	Ann	Augusta	21-May-1905	11-May-1905	John King	McComb, Mary J.	Samuel McComb	Ann McComb
King	John	Emerson	20-Nov-1887	04-Nov-1887	John King	Shaughnessy, Catherine	James McGovern	Clara McGovern
King	John	Thorndyke	22-Jun-1890	29-Apr-1890	John King	Moffett, Virginia	John McCormick	Ann Beard
King	Margaret	Francis	01-Jan-1899	13-Apr-1903	John King	McComb, Mary	Francis McComb	Adlina McComb
King	Margaret		01-Jan-1899	18-Dec-1898	John King	Riley, Margaret	John Riley	Mary Hubbard
King	Mary	Catherine	25-Aug-1901	02-Aug-1901	John King	McComb, Mary	James McComb	Ann McComb
King	Honora		03-Dec-1899	20-Nov-1899	Martin King	Redington, Nora	Valentine King	Margaret McHale
King	Margaret	Joseph	19-Jun-1898	07-Jul-1898	Martin King	Redington, Honora	Anthony Nolan	Bridget Nolan
King	Stephen		29-Dec-1901	22-Dec-1901	Martin King	Redington, Nora	Anthony Nolan	Bridget Nolan
King	Ann	Mary	30-Oct-1892	23-Oct-1892	Patrick King	Gahan, Margaret	Thomas King	Margaret Connor
King	John	Patrick	01-Mar-1896	16-Feb-1896	Patrick King	Gahan, Margaret	William Curley	Margaret Curley
King	Margaret	Helen	16-Jan-1898	29-Dec-1897	Patrick King	Gahan, Margaret	Clement Fuller	Margaret Fuller
King	Michael	James	13-Oct-1889	29-Sep-1889	Patrick King	Gahan, Margaret	Thomas Curley	Bridget Curly
King	Mary	Matilda	22-Jan-1882	22-Aug-1881	Peter King	Hutchison, Virginia	David O'Neal	Carlotta King
King	Bernard		09-Mar-1890	06-Msr-1890	Stephen King	McNally, Mary Ann	John Coogan	Rose Coogan
King	James		24-May-1903	23-May-1903	Stephen King	McNally, Mary	James Hagerty	Elizabeth Finn
King	Mary		15-Jul-1894	10-Jul-1894	Stephen King	McNally, Mary		Helene McNally
Kinsella	Ann	Elizabeth	6-Jul-1913	25-Jun-1913	Patrick Kinsella	Bynes, Mary		Margaret Byrnes
Kinsella	Patrick		8-Aug-1915	23-Jul-1915	Patrick Kinsella	Kelly, Theresa	Robert Dunworth	Elizabeth Dunworth
Kirby	Florence	Mary	16-Aug-1903	28-Jul-1903	John F. Kirby	Finegan, Ann	John A. McKenna	Mary Kelly
Kirby	Catherine	Rose	03-Oct-1886	26-Sep-1886	John Kirby	Stark, Lillian	Richard Hughes	Margaret Kelly
Kirby	Frances	Estelle	14-Sep-1913	16-Aug-1913	Raymond Kirby	Stark, Lillian	Joseph Stark	Ida Harrison
Kirby	John	Raymond	20-Nov-1909	12-May-1909	Raymond Kirby	Stark, Lillian	William Fraunholz	Ann McCourt
Kirby	Lillian	Margaret	24-Sep-1911	3-Sep-1911	Raymond Kirby	Stark, Lillian	John F. Stark	Ann McComb
Kirby	Mary	Naomi	14-May-1914	1-Nov-1907	Raymond Kirby			Margaret Ward
Kirby	Luke	Aloysius	07-Jun-1891	29-May-1891	Thomas P. Kirby	Kearney, Mary	William J. Kirby	Catherine Naughton
Kirby	Helen	M.	31-Jul-1904	14-Jul-1904	William Joseph Kirby	Footman, Regina E.	Michael J. Kirby	Ellen L. Kirby
Kirby	William	Joseph	22-Dec-1901	06-Dec-1901	William Joseph Kirby	Fortman, Regina Elizabeth	Thomas P. Kirby	Mollie Kirby
Kirby	Regina	Beatrice	19-Feb-1899	24-Jan-1899	William Kirby	Fortner, Regina	John Kirby	Rose Fortner
Kirch	Evelyn	Agnes	14-Nov-1914	03-Jul-1897	Frederick Kirch	Castella, Agnes		Rose Curran
Kirch	Gladys	Mary	14-Nov-1914	31-Dec-1899	Frederick Kirch	Castella, Agnes		Rose Curran
Kirchner	Ellen	Teresa	8-Feb-1914	30-Jan-1914	Leon Kirchner	Hoffman, Emma	Henry Allsruhe	Ellen Kirchner
Kirk	John	Edward	02-Oct-1887	23-Sep-1887	Michael Kirk	Sadtler, Emma	Charles B. Plummer	Margaret Quirk

LAST NAME	FIRST NAME	MIDDLE	BAPTISM	BIRTH	Father	Mother	SPONSORS
Kirns	George	William	17-Oct-1897	18-Sep-1897	Bernard Kirns	Peterson, Idela Louise	William B. Turner
Kirsch	Florence		29-Oct-1882	12-Oct-1882	Frederick Kirsch	Schuler, Mary	Margaret Bingel
Kirsch	Margaret	Helen	15-Mar-1903	05-Feb-1903	Frederick Kirsch	Costello, Agnes	Mrs. Albert Philbin
Kirsch/Radford	Dora	Radford	08-Feb-1894	20-Sep-1869	Charles Kirsch	Vorverk, Wilhelmina	Ann Radford
Kirwan	Agnes		06-May-1897	30-Apr-1897	John Kirwan	Finegan, Ann	A.S. Papka
Kirwan	Ann	Elizabeth	27-Jan-1885	05-Jan-1885	John Kirwan	Finegan, Ann	Isabelle Ficke
Kirwan	Joseph		20-Sep-1891	13-Aug-1891	John Kirwan	Finnegan, Ann	Mary Guerin
Kirwan	Mary	Frances	24-Aug-1889	24-Aug-1889	John Kirwan	Finnegan, Ann	Margaret Garvey
Kirwan	Mary	Frances	08-Sep-1889	24-Aug-1889	John Kirwan	Finnegan, Ann	Margaret Garvey
Kirwan	Thomas		30-Oct-1882	17-Oct-1882	John Kirwan	Finnegan, Ann	Helen Dowd
Kirwan	Bernard	James	29-Jul-1906	17-Jul-1906	Patrick Kirwan	Byrnes, Mary	Evelyn A. Leonard
Kirwan	Patrick	B.	4-Sep-1904	25-Aug-1904	Patrick Kirwan	Byrnes, Mary C.	Mary E. Byrnes
Kirwan	John	Gilbert	1-Oct-1905	16-Sep-1905	Thomas Kirwan	Gamnie, Elizabeth	John B. Ward
Kirwin	John	Theodore	2-Aug-1908	10-Jul-1908	William Kirwin	Craddock, Mary	Mary R. Sturgeon
Kirwin	William	Joseph	15-Mar-1903	01-Mar-1903	William P. Kirwin	Craddock, Mary E.	Mary Carr
Kitzinger	Martin		29-Mar-1899	08-Oct-1848	Frederick Kitzinger	Hubner, Margaret	Bridget Dunlevy
Kleintank	Gertrude	Irene	15-Nov-1903	16-Oct-1903	Henry Kleintank	McCosker, Gertrude	Mary McCosker
Klinefelter	Estelle		17-Feb-1889	09-Feb-1889	Jerome Klinefelter	Anderson, Joan	Mary E. Anderson
Klinefelter	Helen	Angel	25-Oct-1891	14-Oct-1891	Jerome Klinefelter	Henderson, Joan	Mary Ward
Klinefelter	Jerome		16-Dec-1883	07-Dec-1883	Jerome Klinefelter	Anderson, Joan (Jane)	Margaret Kerley
Klinefelter	Mary	Elizabeth	23-May-1886	05-May-1886	Jerome Klinefelter	Anderson, Joan (Jane)	Mary Kelleher
Klinefelter	Mary	M.	20-Aug-1905	10-Aug-1905	William J. Klinefelter	Bossom, Genevieve F.	Margaret Klinefelter
Klinefelter	William	Joseph	30-Jul-1911	18-Jul-1911	William J. Klinefelter	Bosson, Jennie F.	Genevieve Cath. Klinefelter
Klinefelter	Helen	Gertrude	6-Jun-1909	29-May-1909	William Kliinefelter	Bosson, Joan	Ella Dailey
Klitch	Hugo	Douglas	15-Feb-1891	06-Dec-1891	Richard Klitch	Bradley, Eleanor	Ann Canby
Knabler	Joseph	John	12-Apr-1888	05-Mar-1888	George Knabler	Buscher, Matilda	
Knapp	John	Joseph	19-Dec-1909	6-Dec-1909	James Knapp	Murray, Mary	Ann Miller
Knapp	William		12-Apr-1891	25-Mar-1891	William J. Knapp	Poole, Mary C.	Alice Little
Knapp	John	Henry	15-Dec-1889	03-Dec-1889	William James Knapp	Poole, Mary Christina	Amelia Eliz. Digelmann
Knapp	James	Frederick	15-Dec-1889	03-Dec-1889	William Joseph Knapp	Poole, Mary Christina	Mary Ann Grevelding
Knauer	Catherine		03-Mar-1889	17-Feb-1889	Charles Knauer	Bearsley, Ann	Catherine Knauer
Knauer	Herbert		12-Aug-1883	02-Aug-1883	John Knauer	Stengel, Ann	Margaret Popp
Knight	Ann	Olivia	14-Nov-1886	23-Oct-1886	Theodore Knight	Heim, Elizabeth Cecelia	Ann Bowen
Knight	Elizabeth	Heim	20-May-1883	04-May-1883	Theodore Knight	Heim, Elizabeth	Agnes Gonce
Knight	James	McCabe	23-Oct-1892	08-Oct-1892	Theodore Knight	Heim, Elizabeth	Gertrude McCabe
Knighton	Mary	Mildred	10-May-1908	29-Feb-1908	James Pence Knighton	St. John, Viola	Mary Smerkel
Knighton	Catherine		02-May-1897	28-Oct-1897	John Knighton	St. John, Violet	Elizabeth Knighton
Knighton	Mary	Elizabeth	23-Jun-1901	18-May-1901	John Knighton	St. John, Viola	Mary St John
Knighton	Herbert	John	24-May-1886	23-Jul-1884	John T. Knighton	Pentz, Margaret	Elizabeth Knighton
Knighton	Howard	Josephine	24-May-1886	23-Jul-1884	John T. Knighton	Pentz, Margaret	Mary Knighton
Knighton	Laura	Catherine	02-Dec-1883	16-Mar-1881	John T. Knighton	Pentz, Margaret A.	Elizabeth Knighton
Knighton	Daniel	Van Trump	04-May-1883	05-Mar-1877	John Thomas Knighton	Pentz, Margaret	Elizabeth Knighton
Knighton	James	Fenhagen	09-May-1883	18-Dec-1874	John Thomas Knighton	Pentz, Margaret	Elizabeth Knighton
Knighton	Margaret		04-Mar-1883	01-Sep-1872	John Thomas Knighton	Pentz, Margaret	
Knopf	Joseph	Rupert	22-Feb-1891	28-Jan-1891	John Knopf	Baker, Margaret	Catherine Elizabeth Grogan
Knott	Francis	Xavier	21-Apr-1912	3-Apr-1912	Henry A. Knott	Doyle, Martha	Joan Donahue
Knott	Henry	Joseph	11-Nov-1906	2-Nov-1906	Henry A. Knott	Doyle, Martha	Elizabeth McGrath
Knott	Charles	Arthur	19-Jun-1910	31-May-1910	Henry Knott	Doyle, Martha	Bridie Ribby
Knott	Martin	Francis	15-Dec-1907	3-Dec-1907	Henry Knott	Doyle, Martha	Mary Weldon
Knox	Albert	Aloysius	01-Mar-1891	11-Feb-1891	Albert Knox	Griffin, Mary	Bridget Griffin
Knox	Alan	John	18-Jun-1899	0-Jun-1899	Alfred Knox	Griffin, Mary	Margaret Conlon
Koban	Barbara		08-Nov-1896	26-Oct-1896	Francis M. Koban	Hennessey, Barbara	
Kober	Joseph	John	17-Feb-1895	04-Feb-1895	John Henry Kober	Bahlman, Josephine	Catherine Kober
Koch	John	Joseph	2-May-1915	19-Apr-1915	John Koch	McKenna, Ann	Grace Harner
Kocher	Mary	Edna	14-May-1914	7-Mar-1914	George Kocher	Murphy, Lillian Francis	Mary Mueller
Koenig	Elizabeth		03-Nov-1895	25-Oct-1895	[Blank] Koenig	Willis, Elizabeth	Ellen Richards
Koenig	Ann		27-Feb-1898	15-Feb-1898	George Koenig	Willis, Elizabeth	Winifred Kelly
Koenig	Henry	Robert	17-Jul-1887	07-Jul-1887	George Koenig	Willis, Elizabeth	Margaret Griffin
Koenig	M. Mary		24-Feb-1901	09-Feb-1901	George Koenig	Willis, Eliza	Mary Muller
Koenig	Mary	A.	26-Jun-1904	17-Jun-1904	George L. Koenig	Willis, Elizabeth	James Willis
Koenig	Leo	George	23-Aug-1891	14-Aug-1891	George Leo Koenig	Willis, Elizabeth Cecelia	Jerome Cronin
Koenig	George		15-Apr-1889	03-Apr-1864	Henry Koenig	Snyder, Catherine	Qilliam Curley
Koester	John	Whitcomb	21-Nov-1909	4-Nov-1909	Charles A. Koester	Mullen, Agnes M.	John W. Shock Mary A. Shock

71

LAST NAME	FIRST NAME	MIDDLE	BAPTISM	BIRTH	Father	Mother	SPONSORS
Kohler	Daniel	Webster	17-Dec-1882	03-Dec-1882	Daniel Webster Kohler	McKenna, Mary Helen Agnes	James McKenna	Elizabeth McKenna
Kohler	James	Walter	22-Feb-1885	01-Feb-1885	Daniel Webster Kohler	McKenna, Mary Ellen	Michael J. O'Connor	Delia McKenna
Kohler	Margaret	Ann	01-May-1892	19-Apr-1892	George E. Kohler	Farrell, Helen	James Joseph McKenna	Catherine McKenna
Kohler	Ann	Helen	13-Sep-1914	28-Aug-1914	George Kohler	Daily, Mary	James Kehoe	Katherine Daily
Kohler	Joan	Mary	02-Jun-1889	15-May-1889	George Kohler	Farrell, Helen	John Barrett	Joan Reid
Kohler	John	George	15-Sep-1912	4-Sep-1912	George Kohler	Daily, Mary	William Kohler	Margaret Daily
Kohler	William	Vincent	07-Oct-1894	16-Sep-1894	George Kohler	Farrell, Mary	Patrick V. Freeman	Mary Bittner
Kohler	George	Timothy	30-Oct-1910	23-Oct-1910	George Thomas Kohler	Dailey, Farr, Maryell	Timothy Dailey	Florence Kohler
Kohler	Rose	Ann	17-May-1896	28-Apr-1896	James Kohler	Hoader, Mary Elizabeth Helen		Rose Ann Angela Hoader
Kohrs	William	F.	20-Aug-1905	15-Aug-1905	Frederick J. Kohrs	Blum , Ann R.	William Blum	Cecelia Blum
Koontz	Edward	Lilly	15-May-1887	24-Apr-1887	Edward Koontz	Krener, Robert[sic] B.	George F. Colbert	Mary Koontz
Kramer	John	E.	08-Feb-1888	15-Jan-1888	George Kramer	[Blank]		
Krause	Mary	Matthew	20-Mar-1910	22-Feb-1910	John Michael Krause	Novodnorsky, Mary	John Novodnorsky	Mary Quinlan
Krein	Mary	Catherine	27-Aug-1905	16-Aug-1905	Stephen K. Krein	Kennedy, Elizabeth	Joseph A. Krein	Mary Kennedy
Krein	Charles	Edward	28-Jul-1907	20-Jul-1907	Stephen Krein	Kennedy, Elizabeth G.	Edward E. Kennedy	Mrs. Jerome Collins
Krener	Rose		05-Jul-1885	22-Jun-1885	George A. Krener	Kelly, Mary E.	James F. Considine	Ann H. Kelly
Krichton	Alfred		06-Dec-1885	04-Nov-1885	George A. Krichton	Huboner, Henrietta	James Cassidy	Mary Miner
Krichton	Charles	Bernard	10-Feb-1884	30-Nov-1883	Joseph Aloysius Krichton	Barringer, Anastasia	George Ambrose	Carlotta Krichton
Krimmelbein	Sophia	Mary	22-Oct-1893	07-Oct-1893	Ferdinand Krimmelbein	Lawrence, F.		Catherine Egan
Kucher	John	Joseph	8-Oct-1911	22-Sep-1911	Joseph Kucher	Lang, Frances	John Mack	Ann Kucher
Kuchling	William	Henry	25-Jul-1901	25-Jul-1901	Francis Kuchling	Waldeck, Mary	Henry Shoemaker	
Kuhne	George	Charles	15-Feb-1885	04-Feb-1885	George Kuhne	Lipp, Catherine	Joseph Lipp	Gertrude Lipp
Kunkel	Elizabeth	Mary	15-Aug-1909	6-Aug-1909	Frederick J. Kunkel	Napfel, Mary	Benjamin D. Richardson	Elizabeth Napfel
Kunkel	Mary	Louise	2-Jun-1907	23-May-1907	Frederick Kunkel	Napfel, Mary r.	James J. Kube	Mary L. Kube
Kunkel	Mary	Agnes	5-Mar-1911	17-Feb-1911	Frederick Kunkel	Napfel, Mary	Benjamin Richardson	Mary Kinkel
Kunkel	Frederick	Joseph	26-Apr-1908	16-Apr-1908	Joseph Kunkel	Napfel, Mary	Edward J. McKee	Elizabeth Napfel
Kunkle	Lillian	Mary	14-Dec-1898	16-Mar-1889	Charles Kunkel	[Blank], Clara		Margaret Dyer
Kunst	Edward		4-Jul-1915	22-Jun-1915	William Kunst	Willis, Mary	Edward Willis	Mary Willis
Kuper	Rose	Cecelia	12-Jul-1914	12-Jun-1914	Francis J. Kuper	Simms, Mary Elizabeth	Albert Uzmeed	Rose Mary Hanlon
Kurtz	Elizabeth	M.	28-Nov-1887	01-Feb-1870	John F. Kurtz	Bates, Ann		Elizabeth Kelly
La Guiza	George		9-Feb-1914	5-Feb-1914	Joseph La Guiza	Scrabanay, Mary		Mary Fizella
La Manna	Andrew		1-Dec-1912	28-Aug-1912	Charles La Manna	Kraus, Margaret	Andrew Kraus	Mary Kraus
Lacey	Augusta	Cecelia	20-Feb-1896	20-Jan-1896	John Lacey	Quinn, Mary	Francis Lacey	Amelia Arnick
Lacey	John	Francis	07-Sep-1885	05-Sep-1885	John Lacey	Colgan, Mary		Margaret Colgan
Lacey	Thomas		01-Sep-1901	22-Aug-1901	Joseph Lacey	Bryan, Mary	J.J. Codd	Agnes Codd
Lacher	Edwin	Francis	5-Sep-1909	25-Aug-1909	Edwin Lacher	Donohue, Margaret	John Gadden	Margaret A. Dyer
Lackey	James	Patrick	13-Jul-1913	27-Jun-1913	James Lackey	Welby, Mary	James Welby	Joan Bruce
Lackey	Mary	Cecelia	16-Apr-1911	4-Apr-1911	James Lackey	Logue, Mary	John Lorby	Teresa Dolan
Lacy	Ann	Margaret	09-Oct-1898	01-Oct-1898	Joseph Lacey	Golden, Margaret	William Carmody	Ann Barron
Lacy	Mary	Angela	14-Mar-1897	05-Mar-1897	Thomas Lacy	Dreyer, Clara	Hugh Lennartz	Ann Lenhartz
Lader	Gertrude		03-Nov-1884	10-Oct-1884	William Lader	Hays, Mary Elizabeth		Elizabeth A. Arthur
Laglan	Samuel	Joseph	26-Mar-1890	About 1819	Darby Laglan	Cutts, Susannah		
Lahey	Cecelia	Margaret	26-Jul-1891	18-Jul-1891	Thomas Lahey	Cavanaugh, Cecelia		Margaret Lahey
Lamana	Camille		21-Dec-1902	16-Dec-1902	Charles Lamana	Clifford, Cecelia	John Clifford	Joan Sticker
Lamana	Cecelia	Mary	16-Sep-1900	03-Sep-1900	Charles Lamana	Clifford, Cecelia	Joseph Cadaro	Ann Miles
Lamana	Francis	John	18-Jul-1915	28-May-1915	Charles Lamana	Kraus, Molly	Francis Kraus	Marcella Kraus
Lamana	James	Leo	28-Aug-1898	07-Aug-1898	Charles Lamana	Clifford, Cecelia	Andrew Loretta	Ellen McAleer
Lamana	Margaret		21-Dec-1902	16-Dec-1902	Charles Lamana	Clifford, Cecelia		Margaret Clifford
Lamax	Madaline	B.	06-Jul-1897	25-May-1897	James Lamax	[Blank]		
Lamb	Ann		23-Jun-1904	09-Aug-1866	John Lamb	Lewis, Ann E.	Henry Dunkirk	Ann Davern
Lamb	Edward	Joseph	11-Nov-1906	22-Oct-1906	Joseph Lamb	Trainor, Ann	James Lamb	Veronica Hoch
Lamb	Helen	Gertrude	5-Apr-1908	20-Mar-1908	Joseph Lamb	Trainor, Ann	William P. McGraw	Bertha Owens
Lamp	Frances	Viola	03-May-1885	15-Mar-1885	Aloysius Lamp	Wilson, Mary	Nicholas Lamp	Francis Moylan
Lamp	Thomas	Stapleton	13-May-1894	08-May-1894	Louis Lamp	Murphy, Margaret	Timothy Murphy	Catherine Murphy
Lamp/McCrory	Bertha	Mary	7-Dec-1910	08-Oct-1884	Conrad Lamp	Starkey, Elizabeth Joan		Elizabeth Miller
Lanagan	Matthew		25-Nov-1894	17-Nov-1894	John Lanagan	O'Keefe, Mary	Daniel Tierney	Catherine Abbott
Lanahan	August		09-Nov-1896	22-Oct-1896	Charles Lanahan	Clifford, C.	John Clifford	Catherine Lanahan
Lanahan	Ann	Elizabeth	29-Aug-1886	25-Aug-1886	John A. Lanahan	Senft, Eva	Carl Gorman	Ann Gorman
Lanahan	Daniel	Stephenie	06-Jan-1889	26-Dec-1888	John Lanahan	O'Keefe, Mary	John Fitzgerald	Mary Keleher
Lanahan	John		21-Sep-1890	09-Sep-1890	John Lanahan	O'Keefe, Mary	Patrick O'Keefe	Catherine O'Keefe
Lanahan	Leo	Patrick	16-May-1897	03-May-1897	John Lanahan	O'Keefe, Mary		Julia Ring
Lanahan	Mary		04-Sep-1892	26-Aug-1892	John Lanahan	Caveny, Helen	Daniel Crimmins	Catherine Gormely
Lanahan	William	Joseph	29-Mar-1883	27-Mar-1883	Thomas Lanahan			Catherine Egan

72

LAST NAME	FIRST NAME	MIDDLE	BAPTISM	BIRTH	Father	Mother	SPONSORS	
Lancaster	William	George	06-Oct-1901	24-Sep-1901	William Lancaster	Bealzer, Agnes	George Bealzer	Martha Lancaster
Landenslager	Genevieve	hazel	23-Aug-1909	27-Nov-1909	Edward Landenslager	Cairy, Elizabeth Genevieve		Mary Agnes Flora
Lander	Frances	Estelle	26-Jul-1896	02-Jun-1896	John Lander	Petit, Mary		Frances Simon
Landerkin	Ann		22-Mar-1909	20-Mar-1909	James Landerkin	Redmond, Mary		
Landerkin	Catherine		01-Sep-1895	20-Aug-1895	James Landerkin	Redmond, Mary	Michael Monogue	Lizzie Foal
Landerkin	Francis	Edward	15-Apr-1906	3-Apr-1906	James Landerkin	Redmond, Mary	Allen Blake	Margaret Dolan
Landerkin	Gertrude		29-Nov-1903	15-Nov-1903	James Landerkin	Redmond, Mary	Edward Brannan	Catherine Dolan
Landerkin	James		03-Oct-1897	24-Sep-1897	James Landerkin	Redmond, Mary	Andrew O'Brien	Margaret Reilly
Landerkin	Mary		01-Dec-1901	13-Nov-1901	James Landerkin	Redmond, Mary	Bernrd J. McGuire	Ella Hanrahan
Landers	Joseph	Thomas	4-Nov-1900	3-Nov-1900	Bernard Joseph Landers	Shirk, Wilhelmina	Thomas Grogan	Ann McGee
Landin	Gertrude	Ann	02-Aug-1895	23-Jun-1895	Barton Landin	Barton, Pauline	Joseph Barton	
Landrigan	John	Joseph	10-Sep-1899	27-Aug-1899	James Landrigan	Redmond, Mary	Ann Touhy	John Touhy
Lang	Catherine	Mary	10-May-1911	25-Nov-1889	Charles Lang	[Blank]		Theresa Tarr
Lang	George		15-Jun-1895	05-Apr-1890	John Lang	Kloetsch, Mary		Catherine Kloetsch
Lannan	Margaret	Mary	15-Mar-1896	07-Mar-1896	James Lannan	Reilly, Sarah	Martin Reilly	Ella Lannan
Lannan	Florence	Mary	02-Mar-1895	02-Mar-1895	Terence Lannan	Bradley, Rose		Mary Regan
Lannan	Florence		09-Sep-1900	04-Sep-1900	Terence Lannan	Bradley, Rose	James Lannan	Catherine Bradley
Lannan	Francis		18-Sep-1898	08-Sep-1898	Terence Lannan	Bradley, Rose	Edward Hayes	Mary Lannan
Lannan	Terence		01-Aug-1897	23-Jul-1897	Terence Lannan	Bradley, Rose	John Lannan	Blanche Lannan
Lannon	James	John	25-Sep-1904	19-Sep-1904	Clarence V. Lannon	Bradley, Rose I.	John Lannon	Mary A. Bradley
Lannon	Mary	Elizabeth	16-Oct-1898	08-Oct-1898	James J. Lannon	Reilly, Sarah	William P. Reilly	Laura Reilly
Lannon	Elizabeth		16-Nov-1902	8-Nov-1902	James J. Lannon	Reilly, Sarah A.	John Lannon	Elizabeth Lannon
Lannon	Francis	Xavier	22-Sep-1907	13-Sep-1907	James J. Lannon	Reilly, Agnes	Thomas O'Neill	Mary Gunning
Lannon	Catherine		25-Aug-1901	22-Aug-1901	James Lannon	Reilly, Agnes	James Gunning	Catherine Gunning
Lannon	Helen	Agnes	10-Jun-1900	05-Jun-1900	James Lannon	Reilly, Agnes	Joseph Riley	Mary Lannon
Lannon	James	Reardon	20-Jun-1897	17-Jun-1897	James Lannon	Reilly, Sarah	James A. Gunning	Margaret Gunning
Lannon	Francis	Edward	31-Aug-1890	19-Aug-1890	John Lannon	Mullen, Julia	Clarence Lannon	John Vansant
Lannon	John	Joseph	21-Aug-1887	13-Aug-1887	John Lannon	Mullen, Julia A.	Terence Lannon	Elizabeth Lannan
Lannon	Mary	Elizabeth	24-Sep-1905	19-Sep-1905	John P. Lannon	Mullen, Julia A.	Edward Mullen	Catherine Killilea
Lannon	Edward		01-Mar-1896	23-Feb-1896	Terence Lannon	Bradley, Rose	Yerence Lannon	Elizabeth Lannon
Lannon	Margaret		28-Mar-1915	13-Mar-1915	Thomas Lannon	Kimmett, Margaret	Charles Dolan	Margaret Brennan
Laragy	Regina	Mary	22-May-1884	10-May-1884	William James Laragy	Renehan, Elizabeth		Catherine Laragy
Laragy	Genevieve		04-Feb-1883	20-Jan-1883	William Laragy	Keenan, Elizabeth	Joseph Woods	Margaret Hagerty
Lardner	Catherine		29-Sep-1901	16-Sep-1901	John Lardner	Cryan, Catherine	Joseph Donnelly	Beatrice Donnelly
Lardner	Dennis		17-Nov-1895	07-Nov-1895	John Lardner	Cryan, Catherine	Patrick Cryan	Catherine O'Hara
Lardner	Ellen		21-Feb-1909	9-Feb-1909	John Lardner	Cryan, Catherine	William Minton	Mary Minton
Lardner	John	Joseph	22-Oct-1893	09-Oct-1893	John Lardner	Cryan, Catherine	Thomas Henrihan	Bridget Joseph Lardner
Lardner	Joseph		29-Oct-1899	16-Oct-1899	John Lardner	Cryan, Catherine	John Cornelius Kilcoyne	Catherine Kilcoyne
Lardner	Mary	E.	13-May-1906	2-May-1906	John Lardner	Cryan, Catherine A.	Thomas Porter	Mary Davey
Lardner	Michael		24-Apr-1904	16-Apr-1904	John Lardner	Cryan, Catherine A.	George O'Keefe	Mary A. Davey
Lardner	Thomas		29-Aug-1897	15-Aug-1897	John Lardner	Cryan, Catherine	Bartholomew Hanihan	Mary Kimmett
Larkin	Clara		22-Oct-1911	6-Oct-1911	John Larkin	[Blank], Alminia	William Jones	Mary Jones
Larkin	Genevieve		09-Aug-1896	26-Jul-1896	John Larkin	Gilchrist, Ann	James Gilchrist	Joan Boland
Larkin	John		10-Dec-1893	26-Nov-1893	John Larkin	Gilchrist, Ann	Patrick Larkin	Bridget Larkin
Larkin	Joseph		07-Apr-1895	24-Mar-1895	John Larkin	Gilchrist, Ann	James Carr	Cecelia Gilchrist
Larkin	Laura		20-Jul-1884	07-Jul-1884	John Larkin	Gilchrist, Ann	William Larkin	Margaret Gilchrist
Larkins	Mary		29-Jan-1886	09-Jan-1886	James Larkins	Rockfort, Mary	John J. Connolly	Ann Connolly
Larron	James	Joseph	02-Jul-1892	26-Jun-1892	James Larron	Shaughnessy, Ellen	Winifred Larron	
Lashrown	Sara		05-Sep-1897	09-Aug-1897	Leon Lashrown	Odie, Mary	Philip Kaden	Virginia Leach
Lauf	William	Henry	14-Aug-1908	12-Aug-1908	Charles Lauf	Brentine, Mary		Sarah Yeakle
Laughran	Rose		27-Jan-1901	09-Jan-1901	James Laughran	Smith, Elizabeth	John Smith	Ann Smith
Lavery	Bernard		11-May-1884	09-May-1884	James Lavery	O'Hanlon, Mary Ann	J. Thomas Golden	Ann Lavery
Lavery	Hugh		12-Feb-1882	09-Feb-1882	James Lavery	O'Hanlon, Mary Ann	James I. Quinn	Ann Lavery
Lavery	Margaret	Joan	22-May-1887	16-May-1887	James Lavery	O'Hanlon, Mary Ann	William McPherson	Catherine Dempsey
Lavery	Mary		05-Apr-1891	24-Mar-1891	James Lavery	O'Hanlon, Mary Ann	George Lavery	Ann French
Lavignon	Edward		16-Sep-1888	21-Aug-1888	William G. Lavignon	Lynch, Margaret	John McKewen	Mary Virginia Jeanty
Lavin	Agnes	Mary	16-May-1909	3-May-1909	Michael Lavin	Elwood, Helen	Thomas Law	Agnes Elwood
Lavin	Charles		12-Feb-1911	3-Feb-1911	Michael Lavin	Elwood, Eleanor	John Lavin	Winifred Elwood
Lavin	Mary	Agnes	26-Jan-1890	17-Jan-1890	Michael Lavin	Mullen, Mary	Michael Mullen	Ann Norton
Lawernson	John	Robert	1-Jan-1905	24-Dec-1904	James Lawernson	Kain, Catherine	Dennis Driscoll	Catherine Driscoll
Lawkin	Agnes	Cleveland	14-Dec-1884	08-Nov-1884	Thomas A. Lawkin	Cunningham, Mary Agnes		Agnes Aaron
Lawrence	Mary	Augustine	12-Jul-1884	11-Jul-1884	August Lawrence	Smith, Elizabeth		Sarah Osburne
Lawrence	Isabelle	Mary	24-Oct-1897	20-Oct-1897	Engelbert Lawrence	Heyer, Ann		Mary Heyer

73

LAST NAME	FIRST NAME	MIDDLE	BAPTISM	BIRTH	Father	Mother	SPONSORS
Lawrence	Helen	Catherine	27-Mar-1898	05-Mar-1898	James Clifford Lawrence	Bennior, Mary Agnes	Ella Bennoir
Lawry	Catherine	Mary	27-Aug-1905	19-Jul-1905	Howard Lawry	Freeburger, Mary Frances	James Dunn
Leach	John	Walter	25-Jan-1914	15-Dec-1913	Benjamin Franklin Leach	Clark, Mary Isabelle	Mary Smith
Leach	Charles	Benjamin	14-Aug-1910	14-Jul-1910	Benjamin Leach	Clark, Belle	John William Leach
Leach	George	Joseph	07-May-1884	06-May-1884	John Leach	Waddell, Mary Jane	Elizabeth Itzel
Lear	James	Joseph	3-Feb-1907	13-Dec-1906	James Lear	Snyder, Elizabeth	Emma Tarlton
Leary	Mary	Teresa	02-Mar-1884	24-Feb-1884	James Joseph Leary	Cunningham, Ann Catherine	Ann Leach
Leary	Mary Teresa		25-Mar-1884	24-Feb-1884	James Joseph Leary	Cunningham, Catherine	Jane Furlong
Leasure	Emory		06-Sep-1891	30-Aug-1891	Emory Leasure	[Blank], Ella	Florence Clark
Lebrun	Mary	Adele	31-Dec-1882	23-Dec-1882	Alphonse Peter Lebrun	Cole, Emma Olivia	Florence Clark
LeBrun/Cole	Emma	Olivia	02-Jan-1883	25-Jun-1883	William Cole	Whittiker, Susan	Florence Leasure
Leccombe	Mary	August	06-Apr-1884	19-Mar-1884	John Leccombe	Patrick, Elizabeth Cecelia	Ann Prevost
Leckey/Magness	Isabelle	Beard	25-May-1883	08-Sep-1810	John Leckey	Beard, Isabelle	Susan Abby Koop
Leckner	Louis	Leon	26-Jan-1890	03-Jan-1890	Louis Leckner	Ward, Catherine	William E. Gammie
Lederer/Seifert	Amelia		23-Oct-1887	07-Jul-1867	John M. Lederer	Schlegel, Mary L.	Isabelle Crouch
Ledonne	Anthony		18-Aug-1907	24-Jan-1907	Serverino Ledonne	Damico, Rose	Helen McCabe
Lee	Julian	Lee	25-May-1905	11-May-1845	Andrew Scott	Burnan, Catherine	Catherine Rochfort
Lee	Bernard	James	10-May-1914	28-Apr-1914	Bernard J. Lee	Bailey, Sarah	Rose DeDominici
Lee	Mary	Catherine	16-May-1909	6-May-1909	Bernard J. Lee	Bailey, Sarah	Martha Cotter
Lee	Mary	Bernadette	21-Aug-1910	12-Aug-1910	Bernard J. Lee	Bailey, Sarah	Mary Ralston
Lee	Mary	Eleanor	23-Jun-1912	17-Jun-1912	Bernard Lee	Brady, Sarah	Ann M. Bailey
Lee	Helen		21-Apr-1889	28-Jan-1889	Henry Lee	Wyatt, Catherine	Theresa V. Bailey
Lee	Julia	Louise	29-May-1887	24-Mar-1887	Henry Lee	Wyatt, Catherine	Mary Swick
Lee	Bernard	Curtis	17-Feb-1901	06-Feb-1901	Patrick Joseph Lee	Neeham, Ann	Mary Driscoll
Lee	Mary	Alice	21-Apr-1902	16-Apr-1902	Patrick Lee	Needham, Ann	Martha Lee
Lee	Ceceia	Mary	03-Feb-1889	07-Jan-1889	Robert E. Lee	Larkin, Virginia	Catherine Lee
Lee	Robert	Edward	31-Jul-1892	07-Jul-1892	Robert Edward Lee	Larkins, Virginia	Winifred Hagan
Leeland	Elizabeth		02-Mar-1884	16-Feb-1884	Michael Leeland	Timothy, Mary	Stella Lee
Lehr	George	Louis	12-Apr-1908	31-Mar-1908	Phillip Lehr	Garrett, Ann	Mary Slaysman
Leibold	Ann	Thelma	12-Apr-1908	3-Apr-1908	Louis Leibold	Silverson, Mary E.	Ann Leeland
Leibold	Teresa	Clara	05-Jan-1902	20-Dec-1901	Louis Leibold	Silverson, Mary	Mary Elizabeth Eisenhauer
Leidensahl	Charles		30-Aug-1891	18-Aug-1891	Charles Leidensahl	Quinn, Helen	Ann A. Paul
Leidensahl	Helen	Margaret	24-Jun-1894	19-Jun-1894	Charles Leidensahl	Quinn, Helen	Catherine Silverson
Leimatre	Mary	Elizabeth	10-Dec-1893	19-Nov-1893	George H. Leimatre	Maley, Ann	Mary Goldrick
Leimbach	Catherine	Elizabeth	14-Nov-1896	09-Feb-1875	Paul Leimbach	Meuller, Catherine E.	Helen Donhander
Leimbach	Frances	Margaret	07-Jun-1903	17-May-1903	William Leimbach	King, Rose	Julia Myers
Leipold	Henry	V.	10-Apr-1904	14-Mar-1904	William Leipold	O'Rourke, Sara	Laura M. Crouch
Leipold	Marc		24-Jun-1906	27-May-1906	William Leipold	O'Rourke, Sarah	Frances Hoffnagle
Leist	Mary	Ernestine	13-Jul-1898	[Blank]	Theodore Leist	Howe, Mary	Mary Sinnott
Leitner	Elizabeth	Lula	5-Apr-1914	13-Oct-1897	James Leitner	Leitner, Louise	Ellen Kerr
Leitzen	Adalaide	Elizabeth	21-Dec-1902	17-Dec-1902	Joseph Leitzen	Kassakatus, Bertha	James F. Kelly
Leitzer	Joseph	Leonard	11-Mar-1900	02-Feb-1900	Joseph Leitzer	Kassakatis, Elizabeth	Francis Mooney
Leland	Ann	Louise	20-Dec-1885	03-Dec-1885	Michael Leland	Timothy, Mary	Leonard Kassakatis
Leland	Robert	Patrick	30-Sep-1899	21-Aug-1899	Patrick Leland	Sullivan, Margaret	Joseph Egan
Leland	Michael	Cornelius	4-Dec-1910	24-Nov-1910	Robert Leland	Leland, Rose	Timothy Roddy
Leland	Florence	Elizabeth	01-Feb-1885	22-Jan-1885	Thomas Leland	Timothy, Catherine	Thomas McGovern
Leland	Thomas	Andrew	17-Dec-1882	03-Dec-1882	Thomas Leland	Timothy, Catherine	John Galvin
Lembach	Charles	William	14-Dec-1894	23-Sep-1894	Henry Lembach	Amreihn, Christina	Patrick Flatley
Lembach	Henry	Jacob	14-Sep-1890	02-Sep-1890	William F. Lembach	Jamison, Rose	Ann Leland
Lembach	Robert	Matthew	8-Apr-1906	2 yrs old	William Frederick Lembach	Jamison, Rose	Catherine Lembach
Lembach	Ann	Louise	14-Jul-1895	06-Jun-1895	William Lembach	Jamison, Rose	Mary Noonan
Lembach	Charles	Cecil	14-Jul-1895	09-Apr-1894	William Lembach	Jamison, Rose	Ann Elizabeth Cox
Lemback	Charles	A.	21-Jan-1906	27-Dec-1905	William Lembach	Jameson, Rose	Louise Napfel
Lemback	William	Jacob	30-Jun-1890	01-Apr-1889	William Lemback	Jamison, Rose	Charles Myers
LeMetre	Florence	Ann	10-Apr-1898	10-Mar-1898	George LeMetre	Malloy, Ann	Charles Myers
Lemmon	John		07-Oct-1888	04-Sep-1864	B. L. Lemmon	Davis, Jane	Albert Passagno
Lemmon	John	U.	07-Apr-1895	30-Mar-1895	John U. Lemmon	Hannafice, Agnes	Agnes Reilly
Lemmon	John	Uhler	09-Apr-1893	01-Apr-1893	John Uhler Lemmon	Hanafin, Agnes John	Ann Carr
Lemmon	Mary	Joan	09-Aug-1891	02-Aug-1891	John Uhley Lemmon	Hanafin, Agnes Joan	Ann Hannafice
Lemp	Louis	Howard	21-Apr-1889	22-Mar-1889	Louis Lemp	Wilson, Mary	Richard Higgins
Lenahan	Mary	Dorothy	24-Apr-1910	6-Apr-1910	Daniel Lenahan	Kelly, Mary	William James Hanafin
Lenahan	William	Joseph	22-Apr-1883	27-Mar-1883	Thomas Lenahan	Keveny, Helen	Thomas J. Lemmon
Lenahan	Mary		28-May-1882	14-May-1882	Timothy Lenahan	Kirby, Honora	Mary Agnes O'Brien

Additional SPONSORS entries (right column continued):
							Charles Patrick McGinn
							Rosalie Kelly
							Catherine Egan
							Catherine Kirby

LAST NAME	FIRST NAME	MIDDLE	BAPTISM	BIRTH	Father	Mother	SPONSORS	
Lender	Mary	Grace	26-Apr-1891	23-Mar-1891	William Lender	Petit, Mary	Andrew Bradley	Margaret Bradley
Lenderkin	Mary	Catherine	03-Oct-1893	October 1893	James Lenderkin	Redmond, Mary	Nicolas Redmond	Helen Reilly
Lennon	Joseph		07-Sep-1902	29-Aug-1902	Clarence Lennon	Bradley, Rose	John Lennon	Lillian Hayes
Lennon	Helen	Ann	5-Feb-1905	29-Jan-1905	James Lennon	Reiley, Sarah A.	Clarence Lennon	Loretta Reiley
Leonard	James		17-Jun-1883	08-Jun-1883	James Leonard	Smyth, Catherine	Peter Brosnan	Mary Keleher
Leonard	Francis		25-Dec-1887	14-Dec-1887	John J. Leonard	Seward, Eleanor	Michael J. Seward	Mary Byrnes
Leonard	Mary		07-Feb-1886	01-Feb-1886	John Joseph Leonard	Seward, Helen	Michael Leonard	Catherine Pepp
Leonard	Adam		30-Apr-1899	10-Apr-1899	John Leonard	McGlone, Alice	William McGlone	Ann Collins
Leonard	Alice	Lillian	10-Feb-1895	31-Jan-1895	John Leonard	McGlone, Alice	Joseph McGlone	Mary Stitehow
Leonard	Edward	Jeannete	26-Sep-1897	09-Sep-1897	John Leonard	McGlone, Alice	Francis McGlone	Margaret Geoghegen
Leonard	Ellen	Francis	07-Dec-1890	24-Nov-1890	John Leonard	Seward, Ellen	Hugh O'Neill	Elizabeth O'Neill
Leonard	John	Ignatius	10-Aug-1884	31-Jul-1884	John Leonard	Seward, Ellen	John Flannagan	Margaret Flannagan
Leonard	Joseph	Thomas	09-Jan-1887	19-Dec-1886	John Leonard	McGlone, Alice	William McGlone	Mary Leonard
Leonard	Margaret	Florence	16-Nov-1902	08-Nov-1902	John Leonard	McGlone, Alice	Thomas McGlone	Margaret Stabb
Leonard	Mary	Loretta	18-May-1890	04-May-1890	John Leonard	McGlone, Alice A.	Francis McGlone	Mary York
Leonard	John Leo		30-Oct-1892	23-Oct-1892	Joseph Leonard	McGlone, Alice Ann	Francis Leonard	Margaret McGlone
Leonard	Mary	Catherine	17-Oct-1886	30-Sep-1886	Michael Leonard	McKenna, Helen	Francis Leonard	Catherine McKenna
Leonard	Ambrose		9-Mar-1912	About 1863	Thomas Leonard	Wayne, Sarah	Edward Willis	Mary Willis
Lessner	Mary	Genevieve	20-Aug-1893	09-Aug-1893	John Lessner	Brady, Elizabeth		Mary King
Leuthardt	John	Joseph	10-Mar-1895	28-Feb-1895	George Leuthardt	Herron, Kate	John Bennett	Ella Herron
Levin	Thomas		29-Dec-1912	22-Dec-1912	Michael Levin	Elwood, Helen	Charles Elwood	Elizabeth Elwood
Lewin	John	Blake	25-Feb-1883	13-Feb-1883	Charles Lewin	Blake, Elizabeth		Elizabeth Wright
Lewin	Margaret	Rose	31-Aug-1884	27-Aug-1884	Charles Lewin	Blake, Elizabeth		Margaret Coright
Lewin	Laurence	Joseph	04-Apr-1886	29-Mar-1886	Charles W. Lewin	Blake, Elizabeth	Henry Blake	Catherine Ann Blake
Lewin	Charles	Charles	01-May-1893	30-Oct-1852	William Lewin	Cork, Ann	Jams Blake	Catherine Blake
Lewis	Mary	Virginia	04-Dec-1887	21-Nov-1887	Charles Lewis	Hart, Emma Virginia		Virginia Hauptman
Lewis	John	Edward	8-Nov-1914	28-Oct-1914	Chester Edward Lewis	Yahn, Elizabeth	John Yahn	Catherine Truelove
Lewis	Mary	Helen	23-Jan-1887	09-Aug-1886	Henry Lewis	Larkin, Mary	Patrick McDermott	Mary Crawford
Lewis	Mary		27-Oct-1889	21-Oct-1889	James Thomas Lewis	Maher, Mary Elizabeth	John Vincent Lewis	Julia Maher
Lewis	Ann	Mary	03-Mar-1901	25-Feb-1901	Joseph Francis Lewis	Napfel, Mary Louise	Patrick Rafferty	Mary Napfel
Lewis	Joseph	Francis	31-Dec-1899	18-Dec-1899	Joseph Francis Lewis	Napfel, Mary	Benjamin Richardson	Christina Napfel
Lewis	Thomas	Albert	05-Oct-1902	28-Sep-1902	Joseph Lewis	Napfel, Mary L.	Thomas Kavanaugh	Tillie Kavanaugh
Lieber	Phillip	Charles	27-Feb-1887	20-Jan-1887	Charles Lieber	Quinn, Ann	Phillip Robert Champness	Margaret Champness
Liebolt	Mary		31-Jul-1910	17-Jul-1910	Louis Liebolt	Silverson, Mary Elizabeth	Michael Charles Silverson	Mary Charles Silverson Leonard
Lillis	Catherine	Bridget	22-Mar-1903	10-Mar-1903	John W. Lillis	Flanagan, Mary A.	Lawrence J. Kavanaugh	Dora Flanagan
Lillis	John	Thomas	4-Dec-1904	24-Nov-1904	John W. Lillis	Flanagan, Mary A.	Hugo Cavanaugh	Mary A. Cummings
Limbach	Margaret	William	08-Mar-1903	23-Nov-1900	Charles J. Limbach	Amerein, Katherine	John Bloberger	Elizabeth Connors
Limbach	Margaret	Julia	07-Oct-1900	02-Jun-1900	William Linbach	Quinn, Rose	Henry Campbell	Jane Phillips
Lingelbach	Helen	Mary	16-Sep-1894	26-Aug-1894	Theodore Lingelbach	Phillips, Helen Virginia	Francis Martin Kerney	Catherine Granger
Lingner	George	Francis	10-Jun-1888	01-Jun-1888	George Frederick Lingner	Owens, Agnes Margaret	Francis Vaeth	Margaret Hall
Linhard	Helen	O'Gorman	24-Feb-1884	09-Feb-1884	Edward Vallette Linhard	McDonald, Catherine	Francis Xavier Donnelly	Helen McDonald
Link	Mary	Edna	09-Aug-1891	25-Jul-1891	Godefride Link	Fussell, Mary Lelinda	Charles Roedlein	Mary Wess
Link	Mary		07-Sep-1884	18-Aug-1884	Godefrido Adam Link	Russell, Zalindia	Peter Bernard Holden	Mary Russell
Link	John	Joseph	16-Mar-1890	08-Mar-1890	Godfrey Link	Fussell, Zelinda	John F. Nugent	Clarissa Fussell
Linzey	Gerge	Washington	27-Apr-1902	17-Nov-1901	John Henry Linzey	Vausant, Margaret Ann	Henry Buntz	
Lipscomb	Charles		07-Apr-1902	08-Oct-1870	William Lipscomb	Holland, Henrietta		Rebecca Blaine
Littig	William		12-Feb-1890	20-Nov-1854	Luthur Littig	Gittings, Louise	Andrew Franz	
Little	Edward	Joseph	4-Nov-1906	13-Oct-1906	Edward G. Little	McCreer, Ann	Joseph H. Little	Catherine McCreer
Little	Joseph	August	19-Nov-1913	17-Oct-1913	John Little	Hubbard, Florence		Mary Elizabeth Hubbard
Little	Mary		18-Jul-1915	14-May-1918	John Little	Hubbard, Florence		Mary Hubbard
Little	Joseph		25-May-1890	12-May-1890	M. Little	Lea, Alice		
Litz	George	Henry	12-Jun-1904	26-May-1904	George Litz	Ritzen, Mary	George Lily	Ella Mullen
Litzinger	Joseph	Arlington	9-Nov-1913	26-Oct-1913	Arlington Litzinger	Tagney, Margaret	Dennis Tagney	Ann Tagney
Livingston	Francis	Leon	08-Mar-1885	22-Feb-1885	William Livingston	Gardner, Mary Virginia	Robert Courtney	Emma S. Walsh
Livingston	Victoria	Dobbin	08-Mar-1885	21-Feb-1885	William Livingston	Gardner, Mary Virginia	Jefferson J. Walsh	Agnes McNules
Lloyd	Catherine	Ann	15-Nov-1891	23-Oct-1891	Elizabeth Lloyd	Lynch, Margaret	John Bankerd	Angelina Bankerd
Loane	James	Richard	01-Oct-1893	22-Sep-1893	Charles M. Loane	Bowers, Theresa	Thomas Cassidy	Agnes Fenley
Loane	Charles	Michael	13-Sep-1891	28-Aug-1891	Charles Michael Loane	Bowers, Theresa	Charles James Murphy	Mary Catherine Berger
Loane	Helen	Theresa	05-Feb-1882	10-Jan-1882	Charles Michael Loane	Bowers, Theresa		Emma Bowers
Loane	Catherine	Agnes	1-Aug-1909	25-Mar-1909	Joseph Loane	Lacher, C. Pauline		
Lober	Frederick	John	3-Oct-1915	15-Sep-1915	Francis Lober	Gallagher, Ann	John H. Horton	Agnes O'Connor
Lober	Walter	John	6-Dec-1914	22-Nov-1886	John Lober	Smith, Ann	William Reilly	Agnes O'Connor
Lockard	Josephine		3-Apr-1904	6-Apr-1904	W.J. Lockard	Berlinson, Emily		Mary Farrelly

LAST NAME	FIRST NAME	MIDDLE	BAPTISM	BIRTH	Father	Mother	SPONSORS	
Lockard	John	Thomas	17-Dec-1905	26-Nov-1905	Walter J. Lockard	Burmington, Emily	E. Mullan	
Lockwood	Hilda	Frances	27-Sep-1903	14-Sep-1903	William Lockwood	Gillen, Mary	George B. Bailey	Susanna F. Bailey
Loeffler	Edith	Ray	22-Apr-1894	20-Apr-1894	Joseph Loeffler	Hunt, Florence	Henry Lanft	Mary Loeffler
Loeffler	Joseph	Phillip	03-Jun-1888	20-May-1888	Joseph Phillip Loeffler	Hunt, Florence		Mary Loeffler
Loewstein	Michael		12-Jul-1908	6-Jul-1908	Charles Loewstein	Reinfelder, Elizabeth	John Clinton	Ann Reinfelder
Logan	Dolores		22-Jan-1905	16-Jan-1905	Eugene J. Logan	Doory, Sara Gertrude	Francis G. Doyle	Gertrude Logan
Logan	Margaret	M.	29-Nov-1903	26-Nov-1903	Eugene J. Logan	Doory, Sarah G.		Ann McLaughlin
Logan	Ann	Gertrude	28-Jul-1901	25-Jul-1901	Eugene Logan	Doory, Sarah	Charles McGraw	Catherine Doyle
Logan	Eugene		12-Aug-1894	10-Aug-1894	Eugene Logan	Doory, Sara	Walter Logan	Margaret Logan
Logan	Joan		05-Jan-1896	30-Dec-1895	Eugene Logan	Doory, Sarah	William Peach	Estelle Logan
Logan	Walter		12-Sep-1897	07-Aug-1897	Eugene Logan	Doory, Sarah	Walter Logan	Agnes Doory
Loge	William	Andrew	17-Oct-1897	19-Sep-1897	Joseph Loge	Collins, Ann	Andrew Freshlein	Ann McGee
Logne	Mary		14-Aug-1892	04-Aug-1892	Joseph Logne	Colran, Ann	John Lawler	Mary Kelly
Logue	William	Henry	19-Dec-1887	19-Dec-1887	James A. Logue	Lucas, Harriet C.		Ann Winter
Logue	Alice	Regina	09-Mar-1890	27-Feb-1890	James Ambrose Logue	Lucas, Henrietta Cecelia	James Carroll Ahern	Ann Catherine Winster
Logue	James		16-Feb-1908	3-Feb-1908	James C. Logue	McEvoy, Agnes	Joseph Stafford	Mary Rafferty
Logue	Ann		27-Aug-1893	25-Aug-1893	James Logue	Kelly, Ann	Ignatius Aloysius Russell	Bridget H. Monaghan
Logue	Catherine		29-Dec-1895	24-Dec-1895	James Logue	Kelly, Ann	John Logue	Catherine Logue
Logue	Clara	Joseph	06-Jan-1884	22-Dec-1883	James Logue	Lucas, Henrietta Harriet Cecelia	David Peter Kernan	Mary Josephine O'Donald
Logue	James	Joseph	09-Mar-1890	08-Mar-1890	James Logue	Kelly, Ann	Patrick Logue	Joan Logue
Logue	John		27-Nov-1898	21-Nov-1898	James Logue	Kelly, Ann	James Logue	Joan Logue
Logue	Mary		17-May-1891	15-May-1891	James Logue	Kelly, Ann	Michael Logue	Mary Kelly
Logue	Catherine		17-Sep-1899	22-Aug-1899	Joseph Logue	Collins, Ann	Edward Kronyager	Agnes Kronyager
Logue	Michael		01-Sep-1901	12-Aug-1901	Joseph Logue	Collins, Ann	John Carroll	Elizabeth Frishline
Logue	Ellen		25-Oct-1903	06-Oct-1903	Joseph P. Logue	Collins, Ann	Felix Logue	Agnes Brenahan
Logue	John		10-Oct-1897	03-Oct-1897	Philip Logue	Donahue, Mary	John Ratigan	Marcella Finnan
Logue	Mary	Agnes	20-Nov-1898	12-Nov-1898	Philip Logue	Donohue, Mary	John Donegan	Julia Donegan
Logue	Joseph	Leon	22-Jan-1882	05-Jan-1882	William Henry Logue	Mommonier, Pamela Joan	E. Curran	
Loney	Margaret	Joan	24-Feb-1885	10-Feb-1885	George Loney	Glenn, Elizabeth		Margaret Fallon
Loney	Adam	Adele Elizabeth	30-Dec-1883	01-Dec-1883	George W. Loney	Glenn, Elizabeth	Edward Fussell	Mary Fussell
Long	William	Edward	12-Feb-1882	03-Jan-1882	George Long	Jones, Mary		Ann Mulligan
Long	Ann	Dominic	29-Jun-1882	[Blank]	Samuel Long	Killam, Elizabeth		
Long	Catherine	Edna	11-Sep-1887	02-Sep-1887	William C. Long	Voeglin, Ann C.		Catherine E. Roach
Long	Margaret		27-Dec-1885	15-Dec-1885	William C. Long	Voeglein, Ann G.		Mary C. Voeglein
Long	Lola	Ann	18-Nov-1883	10-Nov-1883	William Long	Voeglin, Ann		Mary Voeglin
Long	Mary		21-Nov-1897	11-Nov-1897	William Long	Voeglein, Ann		
Loritz	Genevieve		03-Jan-1892	24-Dec-1891	John Loritz	Feeley, Mary		
Loughlan	Catherine		01-Mar-1885	07-Feb-1885	Patrick Loughlan	Gilchrist, Ann	Bernard O'Boy	Catherine O'Boy
Loughlan	Francis	Winfeld	24-Sep-1882	13-Sep-1882	Patrick Loughlan	Gilchrist, Ann	Thomas Reynolds	Bridget Reynolds
Loughran	Elizabeth		08-Oct-1893	20-Sep-1893	James J. Loughran	Smith, Elizabeth	Charles F. Pierce	Mary Maythau
Loughran	Hubert		20-Feb-1896	18-Jan-1896	James Loughran	Smith, Elizabeth	John Loughran	Ann Smith
Louis	Bernard	Edward	10-May-1892	17-Apr-1892	John Louis	Fitzpatrick, Mary		Rose Fitzpatrick
Love	William	Russell	10-Feb-1902	24-Jan-1902	Clifford Love	Sadler, Carolina		Carolina Sadler
Love	George		25-Dec-1893	[Blank]	George Love	Spencer, Sara	John Smith	
Love	Joseph	Lyndon	05-Jun-1889	02-May-1889	James B. Love	McCormick, Emma L.		Elizabeth A. Love
Love	Mary	H.	11-Feb-1906	14-Jan-1906	Thomas C. Love	Sadler, Carrie A.		Mary Sullivan
Love	Thomas	Kenneth Clifford	08-Jan-1893	22-Dec-1892	Thomas Clifford Love	Sadler, Caroline Amelia		Mary Agnes Sadler
Love	Leo	Clifford	15-Jul-1900	30-Jun-1900	Thomas Love	Sadler, C.		Eliza Sadler
Love	Ann		09-Jan-1898	28-Dec-1897	William Love	McKee, Mary	William Brown	Margaret [Blank]
Love	Blanch	Cecelia	16-Dec-1903	11-Dec-1903	William Love	McKee, Agnes		Nellie Buchannon
Love	Edwin	Joseph	25-Nov-1901	7-Nov-1901	William Love	McKee, Agnes		Mary Horan
Love	George	Edward	01-Jan-1899	22-Dec-1898	William Love	McKee, Agnes	Joseph Herbert	Mary McCourt
Love	John	Raymond	24-Dec-1905	3-Dec-1905	William Love	McKee, Mary Agnes	Edward McKee	Elizabeth Herbert
Love	William		27-May-1900	12-May-1900	William Love	McKee, Agnes		Margaret McKee
Love/Shelley	Margaret	Howard	09-Nov-1892	26-May-1847	William Love	Smallwood, Serena Agnes		Margaret Taylor
Lowry	Michael	Howard	04-Mar-1884	26-Feb-1884	Howard Lowry	Campbell, Bridget		Ellen Courtney
Luby	Frances	Andrew	20-Aug-1911	10-Aug-1911	John J. Luby	Satterfield, Florence A.	Francis J. Weggen	Pearl Luby
Luby	Clara	Susannah	25-Dec-1904	17-Dec-1904	John Luby	Bloom, Rose	Tofe Skolenski	Susana Rachubinske
Luby	John	Malvin	20-Jun-1915	27-Jan-1913	John Luby	Satterfield, Florence		Elizabeth McGraw
Lucas	Francis	Graham	22-Jun-1907	3-Jun-1907	Cornelius Lucas	Samuels, Edith		Agnes Koester
Lucas	Francis	Henry	12-Jul-1898	01-Jul-1898	George T. Lucas	Poncet, Mary		Mary Chesagne
Lucey	Mary	Catherine	21-Jul-1890	30-Jun-1890	Daniel Lucey	McDonald, E.	Michael Murphy	Mary Murphy
Lucey	Julia		6-Mar-1904	9-Feb-1904	Jerome Lucey	Toner, Mary E.	Daniel J. Kelleher	Ann McKenna

76

LAST NAME	FIRST NAME	MIDDLE	BAPTISM	BIRTH	Father	Mother	SPONSORS
Lucy	Bernard		23-Jun-1895	08-Jun-1895	Jerome Lucy	Toner, Mary A.	Michael Murphy
Lucy	Mary	Catherine	28-Nov-1897	18-Nov-1897	Jerome Lucy	Toner, Mary	Hugh Toner
Ludsburg	Margaret	Joan	21-Oct-1889	24-Sep-1889	Joseph August Ludsburg	Desch, Margaret Catherine	Mary Ludsburg
Ludwig	Catherine	Maud Louise	17-Jul-1904	1-Jun-1904	George C. Ludwig	Callahan, Maud	William L. Callahan
Ludwig	Charles	Howard	08-Jun-1902	13-May-1902	Lincoln Ludwig	Ward, Agnes	Raymond Collier
Ludwig	Elmer	Allan	21-Apr-1889	13-Apr-1889	Lincoln Ludwig	Ward, Agnes	Bernard Ward
Ludwig	Ethel	Mary	25-Sep-1887	13-Sep-1887	Lincoln Ludwig	Ward, Agnes	Henry McKewen
Ludwig	Helen	Genevieve	24-Jan-1892	03-Jan-1892	Lincoln Ludwig	Ward, Agnes	Peer Ward
Luke	Henry		18-Mar-1906	5-Mar-1906	Charles Luke	Parrish, Margaret	Henry C. Parrish
Lusby	Penelope	Theresa	28-Feb-1904	13-Feb-1904	William H. Lusby	Walsh, Margaret	James McTague
Lusby	William	Henry	23-May-1905	15-Apr-1905	William H. Lusby	Walsh, Mary	
Lusby	Catherine	Bernardine	20-Feb-1910	4-Feb-1910	William Lusby	Welsh, Margaret	James Curran
Lusby	Cecelia	Agnes	29-Mar-1908	5-Mar-1908	William Lusby	Welsh, Margaret	C. Anstine
Lush	Mary	Lillian	31-Mar-1912	20-Jan-1912	Benjamin Lush	Clarke, Mary	
Luthardt	Ann	Irene	16-Jul-1893	06-Jul-1893	George Luthardt	Herron, Catherine	Peter Herron
Luthardt	Helen	Mary	21-Feb-1892	17-Feb-1892	George Luthardt	Herron, Catherine	John Leo Herron
Lutts	Eliza		19-Mar-1893	04-Mar-1893	William J. Lutts	Collins, Mary E.	Henry Wilkins
Lutts	Charles		26-Jun-1899	15-Jun-1899	William Lutts	Collins, Elizabeth	Thomas Collins
Lutz	Ann	Leona	8-Aug-1909	20-Jul-1909	Henry Lutz	Dietzway, Cecelia	
Lutz	Barbara	Mildred	29-Sep-1907	12-Sep-1907	Henry Lutz	Dietzway, Cecelia	
Lutz	Margaret	C.	25-Jun-1905	7-Jun-1905	Henry Lutz	Dietzway, Cecelia M.	Nicholas Dietzway
Lutz	John	William McCrary	16-Jul-1893	04-Jul-1893	John Lutz	Booth, Mary	
Lutz	Lillian		24-Sep-1900	05-Sep-1900	Walter Lutz	Captain, Emelia	
Lyman	Charles		14-Jan-1900	08-Dec-1899	Charles Lyman	Keenan, Flora	William Keenan
Lynch	Mary		9-Aug-1908	29-Jul-1908	[Blank]	Lynch, Elizabeth	
Lynch	James	E.	08-Feb-1885	28-Jan-1885	Bernard Lynch	Moylan, Frances	Christopher Engel
Lynch	Loretta		20-Feb-1887	10-Feb-1887	Bernard Lynch	Moylan, Frances B.	William Lynch
Lynch	Mary	Loretta	30-Dec-1883	19-Dec-1883	Bernard Lynch	Moylan, Frances	Peter Smith
Lynch	Francis		26-Jan-1908	13-Jan-1908	Charles H. Lynch	Penning, Bertha Catherine	Francis Snowmann
Lynch	Gennetta	W	17-Sep-1905	29-Aug-1905	Charles H. Lynch	Penning, Bertha C.	John J. McWhirter
Lynch	Mary		1-Nov-1903	03-Oct-1903	Charles H. Lynch	Penning, Katherine B.	Albert Lynch
Lynch	Bernard		03-Aug-1884	17-Jul-1884	Daniel Lynch	O'Donnell, Mia	Bernard Lynch
Lynch	Charles	Edward	06-Jan-1895	22-Dec-1894	Francis Lynch	Rowles, Rose Helen	John Thomas Rogers
Lynch	Helen		04-Aug-1901	28-Jul-1901	Francis Lynch	Rowles, Rosella	John Gallagher
Lynch	Ignatius		06-Aug-1898	20-Aug-1898	Francis Lynch	Rowles, Rosetta	William Griffin
Lynch	Joseph	Leonard	30-Sep-1888	12-Sep-1888	Francis Lynch	Powers, Rosetta	Henry Parish
Lynch	Martin	Viola	21-Mar-1909	7-Mar-1909	George M. Lynch	Kendale, Caroline	Edward Kendale
Lynch	Mary	V.	22-Nov-1891	11-Nov-1891	John S. Lynch	Murnane, Adelaid	James Keenan
Lynch	Cecelia	Mary	05-Nov-1899	25-Oct-1899	Joseph Lynch	Byrnes, Joan	
Lynch	Edna	Rosalin	08-Jun-1890	29-May-1890	Francis T. Lynch	Rowle, Rose E. M.	James McCaffrey
Lynch	Francis	Pierce	27-Dec-1903	12-Dec-1903	Francis T. Lynch	Rowles, Rosella M.	Thomas C. Lynch
Lynch	Matthew	Andrew	06-Aug-1893	25-Jul-1893	Francis Thomas Lynch	Rolles, Rosalie	Francis Gillen
Lynch	Mary	Alice	30-Sep-1888	12-Sep-1888	Francis Thomas Lynch	Rolles, Rosalie	Peter James Heron
Lynch	Mary		2-Jun-1912	18-May-1912	George M. Lynch	Kendale, Caroline	Edward Kendale
Lynch	Robert	Ensor	11-Aug-1887	10-Jul-1887	John S. Lynch	Byrnes, Joan	James Keenan
Lynch	Mary	Rosalie	19-Feb-1911	23-Jan-1911	Joseph Lynch	Kuper, Mary E.	Francis T. Lynch
Lynch	Matilda	Teresa	15-Mar-1914	6-Feb-1914	Matthew Lynch	Kuper, Mary	John Hanlon
Lynch	Elizabeth		03-Apr-1887	10-Mar-1887	Joseph Lynch	Gilley, Mary	
Lynes	Agnes		21-May-1903	19-May-1903	James Lyng	Carberry, Helen	Edward O'Brien
Lyng	James		30-Jun-1902	28-Jun-1902	James Lyng	Carberry, Helen	Thomas Lyng
Lyng	Michael		30-Jun-1902	28-Jun-1902	James Lyng	Carberry, Helen	John Lyng
Lyng	Agnes	B.	5-Aug-1906	25-Jul-1906	John Lyng	Leary, Margaret	Thomas Lyng
Lyng	Elizabeth		11-Oct-1908	4-Oct-1908	John Lyng	Leary, Margaret	John Leary
Lyng	Margaret	Mary	17-Dec-1911	2-Dec-1911	John Lyng	Leary, Mary	James Curran
Lyons	George	Everhardt	2-Dec-1906	28-Oct-1906	Henry Lyons	Colburn, Grace	Samuel N. Colvin
Lyons	Grace	Mary	2-Oct-1904	18-Aug-1904	Henry Lyons	Coleman, Grace	Thomas Lyons
Lyons	Henry	Richard	26-Apr-1903	03-Apr-1903	Henry Lyons	Colburn, Grace	Michael Gumbert
Lyons	Ann	Bridget	2-Nov-1907	11-Oct-1907	John Lyons	McCrae, Ann	James Mooney
Lyons	Ellen	Elizabeth	27-Jul-1902	11-Jul-1902	John Lyons	McCrea, Ann	John Hattigan
Lyons	John	Leon	25-Sep-1904	10-Sep-1904	John Lyons	McCrea, Ann	John McNamara
Lyons	Peter	James	22-Jan-1893	12-Sep-1892	John Thomas Lyons	Heffernan, Mary Agnes	Michael Sullivan
Lyons	Catherine	Ann	16-Mar-1884	06-Mar-1884	Malachi Lyons	Gwynn, Margaret	Daniel W. Sullivan
Lyons	Mary	Josephine	16-Jul-1882	06-Jul-1882	Malachi Lyons	Winn, Margaret	Michael Keleher

							Mary Murphy
							Mary McKenna
							Mary Ludsburg
							Mary Callahan
							Eva Ward
							Mary Collier
							Margaret Ward
							Gertrude Ward
							Mary Fields
							Napy Walsh
							Mary Hanly
							Theresa Curran
							Mary Dowling
							Mary Long
							Mary McGuire
							Caroline Walker
							Catherine England
							Ann G. Collins
							Ann Kohnlein
							Cecelia Dietzway
							Margaret Burch
							Elizabeth Smith
							Ellen Ward
							Catherine Keenan
							Mary Slomessman
							Elizabeth Smith
							Mary McMauliffiff
							Helen Smith
							Ann E. Penning
							Ann Penning
							Mary Lynch
							Frances Lynch
							Mary McCaffrey
							Elizabeth Mulroy
							Ellen Murray
							Agnes Coltart
							Ella Lynch
							Mary Rogers
							Catherine Rutler
							Ann Lynch
							Mary Lynch
							Mary Clark
							Sarah Murnane
							Elizabeth Byrnes
							Emma M. Rogers
							Ann Hanlon
							Elizabeth Gilley
							Bridget Holden
							Mary Stedman
							Ann Maloney
							Mary Leary
							Elizabeth Leary
							Elizabeth Leary
							Cecelia Gumbert
							Rose Hamill
							Margaret Gumbert
							Delia Hellyan
							Genevieve Gisriel
							Mary H. Quirk
							Mary Eberle
							Mary A. Sullivan
							Joan Ormond

LAST NAME	FIRST NAME	MIDDLE	BAPTISM	BIRTH	Father	Mother	SPONSORS
Lyons	Thomas	Leonard	25-Oct-1885	17-Oct-1885	Malachi Lyons	Winn, Margaret	William Keefe	Ann Slattery
Lyons	Elizabeth		19-Jun-1887	10-Jun-1887	Patrick Lyons	Sullivan, Mary	William Cain	Mary Landragan
Lyons	Francis	Ignatius	04-Oct-1891	19-Sep-1891	Patrick Lyons	Sullivan, Mary	John Carmody	Mary McCabe
Lytle	Charles	Albert	10-Oct-1886	10-Sep-1886	Charles Lytle	Henderson, Margaret		Nora E. Hesterman
MacCubbin	Thomas	Patrick	6-Jun-1909	20-May-1909	William MacCubbin	Mullin, Isabelle	Thomas H. MacCubbin	Mary Lewis
MacGregor	Rose		24-Jan-1904	11-Jan-1904	William H. MacGregor	McCourt, Mary	John Rooney	Rose Finnegan
MacGregor	John	David	29-Jan-1888	19-Jan-1888	William Henry MacGregor	McCourt, Mary Catherine	Peter Joseph McCourt	Margaret McCourt
MacGregor	Mary	Ann	04-Aug-1889	27-Jul-1889	William Henry MacGregor	McCourt, Mary Catherine	Bernard Joseph McCourt	Margaret McCourt
MacGregor	William	Joseph	10-Jun-1894	01-Jun-1894	William Henry MacGregor	McCourt, Mary Catherine	James Rooney	Catherine McCourt
MacGregor	David	McCourt	22-Nov-1891	10-Nov-1891	William MacGregor	McCourt, Mary	Charles McCourt	Susdan Rooney
Mackabee	Joseph	Henry	20-Mar-1892	11-Feb-1892	Joseph T. Mackabee	Downes, Susan	Henry Franz	
Mackereth	Ann	Augusta	04-Sep-1892	08-Aug-1892	John James Mackereth	Knockey, Mary Agnes		Mary Lyons
Mackin	Francis	Michael	13-Feb-1910	30-Jan-1910	James F. Mackin	McKay, Mary Sarah		Catherine Mackin
Mackin	Joseph	Cornelius	11-Aug-1907	31-Jul-1907	James Mackin	McKay, Sarah	Cornelius Dailey	E. M. Dailey
MacKreeth	William	Joseph	08-Oct-1893	21-Sep-1893	John MacKreeth	Knockey, Augusta"		Agnes Haid
Madden	Agnes		15-Jan-1898	15-Jan-1898	John Madden	Kennedy, Elizabeth	James Moylan	Elizabeth Talbott
Madden	John	William	22-Nov-1896	06-Nov-1896	John Madden	Kennedy, Elizabeth	William J. Carrick	Agnes Kennedy
Madden	John	Thomas	13-May-1900	21-Apr-1900	John Madden	Kennedy, Elizabeth	Thomas Madden	Rose Kennedy
Madden	John	Thomas	22-Jun-1902	06-Jun-1902	John Madden	Kennedy, Elizabeth	John Kline	Catherine Fannon
Madden	Martin		08-Oct-1893	13-Sep-1893	John Madden	Kennedy, Elizabeth	Charles Long	Charlotte Miller
Madden	Mary	Agnes	17-Apr-1892	02-Apr-1892	John Madden	Kennedy, Elizabeth	Joseph Bracken	Elizabeth Miller
Madden	Mary	Elizabeth	01-Sep-1895	21-Aug-1895	John Madden	Kennedy, Elizabeth	John Kennedy	Rose Miller
Madden	Catherine		08-May-1892	02-May-1892	Patrick Madden	Welch, Catherine	Matthias Connolly	Margaret Melia
Madden	Margaret		02-Dec-1883	14-Nov-1883	Patrick Madden	Welsh, Catherine	John Clancy	Catherine Clancy
Madden	Helen		28-Mar-1909	17-Mar-1909	Thomas J. Madden	McKenna, Rose	James Baird	Helen Bishop
Madden	Rose		30-Apr-1905	22-Apr-1905	Thomas J. Madden	McKenna, Rose	Bernard McKenna	Elizabeth Murphy
Madden	Bernard		11-Dec-1898	02-Dec-1898	Thomas Joseph Madden	McKenna, Rose	Bernard McKenna	Ella Colbert
Madden	Catherine		14-Jan-1900	31-Dec-1899	Thomas Madden	McKenna, Rose	Peter Byrnes	Mary Dorsey
Madden	James		07-Mar-1897	25-Feb-1897	Thomas Madden	McKenna, Rose	John Hynes	Rose Hynes
Madden	Margaret	Elizabeth	10-Dec-1911	24-Nov-1911	Thomas Madden	McKenna, Rose	John Dailey	Mary McKenna
Madden	Mary		16-Feb-1902	10-Feb-1902	Thomas Madden	McKenna, Rose	Francis Metcalf	Mary McNulty
Madden	Thomas		11-Jan-1914	29-Dec-1913	Thomas Madden	McKenna, Rose	Bernard McKenna	Margaret Coyle
Madden	William		5-May-1907	24-Apr-1907	Thomas Madden	McKenna, Rose	Peter J. Byrnes	Mary Ward
Madigan	Ann		26-Sep-1897	07-Sep-1897	Daniel Madigan	Enright, Catherine	Patrick Murnane	Hannah Madigan
Madigan	Catherine		04-Aug-1895	22-Jul-1895	Daniel Madigan	Enright, Catherine	John Murnane	Honora Murnane
Madigan	Daniel		15-Sep-1901	25-Aug-1901	Daniel Madigan	Enright, Catherine	James Madigan	Alice Moran
Madigan	James		13-Dec-1891	28-Nov-1891	Daniel Madigan	Enright, Catherine	Michael Madigan	Delia Madigan
Madigan	James	Aloysius	09-Jul-1899	21-Jun-1899	Daniel Madigan	Enright, Catherine	Patrick Madigan	Ann Madigan
Madigan	Mary	Alice	01-Oct-1893	11-Sep-1893	Daniel Madigan	Enright, Catherine	Patrick Howard	Ann Madigan
Madigan	Catherine		17-Feb-1895	03-Feb-1895	Michael Madigan	Golden, Ann	Humphrey Golden	Catherine Golden
Madigan	Catherine		8-Mar-1908	28-Feb-1908	Michael Madigan	Golden, Ann	John Joseph Luby	Helen Madigan
Madigan	Daniel		15-Jan-1905	1-Jan-1905	Michael Madigan	Golden, Ann	Daniel Luberg	Honora Madigan
Madigan	Eleanor		04-Dec-1892	24-Nov-1892	Michael Madigan	Golden, Hanna	James Madigan	Catherine Madigan
Madigan	James		19-Apr-1896	01-Apr-1896	Michael Madigan	Golden, Ann	Danile Madigan	Catherine Abbott
Madigan	James	Joseph	13-Jan-1901	01-Jan-1901	Michael Madigan	Golden, Ann	Patrick Madigan	Catherine Golden
Madigan	Margaret	M.	14-Dec-1902	21-Nov-1902	Michael Madigan	Golden, Ann	James Monaghan	Delia Monaghan
Madigan	Mary	Agnes	17-Feb-1895	03-Feb-1895	Michael Madigan	Golden, Ann	Michael Rooney	Elizabeth Lehane
Madigan	Mary	Adam	24-Apr-1910	17-Apr-1910	Michael Madigan	Golden, Ann	James P. Monaghan	Delia Monaghan
Madigan	Michael	John	3-Feb-1907	6-Jan-1907	Michael Madigan	Golden, Ann	Dennis Kehoe	Catherine Kelliher
Madigan	Agnes		10-Mar-1895	03-Mar-1895	Patrick Madigan	Hartnett, Hannah	Edward Rooney	Mary Hartnett
Madigan	James	Joseph	30-Oct-1898	10-Oct-1898	Patrick Madigan	Hartnett, Hannah	James Madigan	Catherine Madigan
Madigan	Julia		31-Jan-1897	20-Jan-1897	Patrick Madigan	Hartnett, Hanna	Patrick O'Connell	Julia O'Connell
Madigan	Margaret		12-Nov-1893	22-Oct-1893	Patrick Madigan	Hartnett, Ann	Michael Madigan	Delia Madigan
Magarity	Charles	Edwin	30-Apr-1886	12-Sep-1853	John Magarity	Mummy, Susan		
Magee	Stephen	Lee	22-Jan-1911	9-Jan-1911	Samuel Lee Magee	McConnell, Stella F.	Percy J. McConnell	Mary F. Toher
Magner	Margaret		10-Nov-1886	30-Oot-1886	Davis Magner	Driscoll, Mary	John Casey	Catherine Driscoll
Magness	Ambrose	Marechal	16-Apr-1882	05-Apr-1882	John M. Magness	Parnell, Mary J.		
Magness	Ambrose	Marichal	11-Sep-1882	05-Apr-1882	John M. Magness	McAlese, Josephine		Margaret Holmes
Magness	William	Edgar	23-Jan-1887	12-Jan-1887	John M. Magness	McAlese, Josephine		Mary Brennan
Magness	George	Milton	14-Oct-1883	22-Aug-1883	John Magness	McAleese, Josephine		
Magness	John	William	27-Feb-1885	02-Nov-1884	John Magness	McAleese, Josephine		Ann Davis
Magness	Mary	Ann	15-Dec-1889	24-Nov-1889	John Magness	McAlese, Josephine	John Bertrand	Mary Bertrand
Magness	William	Howard	08-Sep-1901	22-Aug-1901	William Magness	McGraw, Margaret	John Guinan	Mary Irvin

78

ST JOHN'S BAPTISMS 1882-1912

LAST NAME	FIRST NAME	MIDDLE	BAPTISM	BIRTH	Father	Mother	SPONSORS
Magraw	Catherine		20-May-1883	10-May-1883	James Magraw	Connolly, Sara	William Conway / Mary Ann Magraw
Magraw	William		28-Mar-1886	12-Mar-1886	James Magraw	Connelly, Sarah E.	John F. Burke / Sarah Patterson
Magraw	Mary	Elizabeth	09-Sep-1883	05-Sep-1883	Richard James Magraw	Lane, Ann	John Joseph O'Brien / Ann King
Magrogan	Gertrude	Elizabeth	11-Jan-1914	27-Dec-1913	Edward Magrogan	Shamber, Teresa	Frederick Mehl / Gertrude Mehl
Maguire	Lillian		21-Dec-1895	17-Aug-1892	Daniel Maguire	Parish, Amelia	Robert Burns
Maguire	Albert	Leo	14-Feb-1892	07-Feb-1892	Edward Maguire	O'Neill, Susan	Hugh Ray / Ann Maguire
Maguire	Mary		18-Aug-1895	07-Aug-1895	Edward Maguire	O'Neal, Susan	Owen Hopper / Florence Hopper
Maguire	Mary	Virginia	30-Oct-1892	18-Oct-1892	John Francis Maguire	Phillips, Emelia Joan	Mary Phillips
Maguire	Agnes		17-Feb-1891	04-Feb-1891	John Maguire	Hopkins, Cecelia	Mary Davey
Maguire	Catherine		18-Nov-1887	28-Oct-1887	John Maguire	Hopkins, Cecelia	Ann Gebhart
Maguire	Elizabeth		25-Sep-1888	23-Sep-1888	John Maguire	Hopkins, Cecelia	Agnes Kearney
Maguire	Gertrude		11-Oct-1889	06-Oct-1889	John Maguire	Hopkins, Cecelia	Elizabeth Murphy
Maguire	John	Edward	01-Oct-1893	17-Sep-1893	John Maguire	Phillips, Emma Joan	Edward Talbott / Lillie Sturgeon
Maguire	Julia		01-Jul-1892	19-Jun-1892	John Maguire	Hopkins, Cecelia	Catherine Judge
Maguire	Lillian		11-Aug-1886	30-Jul-1886	John Maguire	Hopkins, Cecelia	Catherine Hobnicht
Maguire	Mary	Ann	01-Jul-1883	23-Jun-1883	John Maguire	Hopkins, Cecelia	Edward Petit / Bridget Reilly
Maguire	Michael	Patrick	27-Jul-1898	10-Jul-1898	John Maguire	Hopkins, Cecelia	Mary Fannon / P.C. Gavin
Maguire	Ann		12-Oct-1902	02-Oct-1902	Patrick Maguire	Black, Mary	Charles Buchette / Mary McMcAuliffiff
Maguire	Catherine		18-Nov-1894	10-Nov-1894	Patrick Maguire	Black, Mary	William Gough / Ann McCale
Maguire	Eugene	Gregory	5-Dec-1909	17-Nov-1909	Patrick Maguire	Black, Mary	Matthew Maguire / Margaret Brown
Maguire	Rose	Gertrude	2-Dec-1906	15-Nov-1906	Patrick Maguire	Black, Mary	John Delea / Mary O'Hanlon
Maguire	Thomas	Patrick	17-Mar-1895	07-Mar-1895	Patrick Maguire	Mulryan, Margaret	Henry Nuth / Margaret Graley
Maguire	Thomas	Patrick	21-Dec-1902	11-Dec-1902	Patrick T. Maguire	Mulryan, Margaret	Martin Jennings / Katherine Jennings
Maguire	Margaret	Helen	29-Jan-1905	16-Jan-1905	Patrick Thomas Maguire	Mulryan, Margaret	Ann Gannon / Joan Gannon
Maguire	Michael	Joseph	10-Sep-1893	26-Aug-1893	Patrick Thomas Maguire	Mulryan, Margaret	Owen Thomas Griffin / Margaret Gertrude Griffin
Maguire	Thomas	Edgar	19-May-1890	18-Nov-1886	Thomas Maguire	Ege, Laura Emma	Elizabeth Maguire
Maguire	Sarah	Elizabeth	01-Jul-1888	15-Jun-1888	William J. Maguire	Hartman, Catherine E.	Eva Bautz
Maher	John	Francis	26-Sep-1887	15-Feb-1887	John Maher	Pfister, Ann	Catherine McNamara
Maher	Edward	Francis	21-Sep-1913	14-Sep-1913	Richard Maher	Ragan, Mary Elizabeth	Phillip H. Maher / Agnes Ragan
Maher	Alice		2-Jul-1905	19-Jun-1905	William J. Maher	Way, Rose	James Way / Margaret Maher
Maher	John	Carroll	19-Sep-1909	10-Sep-1909	William J. Maher	Way, Rosanna	Patrick Bannon / Mary Agnes Rosensteel
Maher	William	Way	18-Aug-1907	8-Aug-1907	William J. Maher	Way, Rose E.	John A. Way / Ann Maher
Maher	Edward		15-Dec-1901	01-Dec-1901	William Maher	Way, Rose	Thomas Way / Alice Way
Maher	Margaret	Mildred	4-Nov-1900	23-Oct-1900	William Maher	Way, Rose	Carlisle Way / Catherine Maher
Mahon	James		10-Jul-1897	08-Jul-1897	James Mahon	Hughes, Emma	Henry Hughes / Agnes Mahon
Mahon	James		29-Aug-1897	08-Jul-1897	James Mahon	Hughes, Emma	Henry E. Hughes / Agnes Mahon
Mahon	William	Hughes	24-Oct-1909	1-Oct-1909	James Mahon	Hughes, Emma	Francis X. Dailey / Mary Hession
Mahone	Thomas	Francis	27-Sep-1891	14-Sep-1891	Thomas Mahone	Moylan, Catherine	Daniel Moylan / Catherine McDonnell
Mahoney	Ann	Mary	21-Feb-1889	22-Feb-1845	Aloysius Mahoney	Walsh, Elizabeth	Esther Fay
Mahoney	James	Whitney	09-Nov-1883	15-Apr-1878	James Mahoney	Mahoney, Elizabeth	
Mahoney	John	Michael	04-Dec-1887	23-Nov-1887	Thomas J. Mahoney	Moylan, Catherine	Thomas Moylan / Mary Moylan
Mahoney	Genevieve		29-Aug-1897	19-Aug-1897	William Mahoney	Cook, Matilda	William Reynolds / Mary Cook
Mahony	Leonard		21-Jan-1900	09-Jan-1900	William Mahoney	Cook, Matilda	William Lueck / Mary Monaghan
Mahony	James	George	20-Dec-1901	16-Dec-1901	William Mahoney	Cook, Matilda	Katherine Cook
Mahony	Thomas		15-Mar-1886	15-Mar-1886	John A. Mailer	Hamilton, Julia A.	Ann M. Kerchner
Mailer	Joseph		14-May-1889	22-Sep-1888	William James Maitland	Byrne, Evangeline Frances	James J. Murphy / Blanche Moore
Maitland	Evangeline	Florence	26-Oct-1884	16-Oct-1884	Jonathan Mallalien	Tucker, Emma V.	William H. King / Rose Jamison
Mallalien	Jennelle		21-Jan-1883	22-Dec-1882	Jonathan Mallalien	Tucker, Emma	George Cook / Jennie King
Mallon	Charles	McLane	30-May-1909	17-May-1909	John B. Mallon	Mallon, Margaret	James Donnelly / Mary Whittle
Mallon	John	Vincent	30-Jul-1911	14-Jul-1911	John B. Mallon	Kelly, Margaret	Patrick Reilly / Catherine M. Kelly
Mallon	Mary		8-Dec-1907	20-Nov-1907	John B. Mallon	Kelly, Margaret	John V. Stedman / Mary Stedman
Mallon	Gertrude	Agnes	24-Nov-1912	11-Nov-1912	John Bernard Mallon	Kelly, Margaret	John Kelly / Alice Kendall
Mallon	Thomas		05-Feb-1882	02-Feb-1882	Thomas Francis Mallon	McCluskey, Theresa	John Joseph Martin / Joan McCluskey
Mallon	Margaret		07-Sep-1884	23-Aug-1884	Thomas Mallon	McCluskey, Teresa	Charles Kearney / Catherine Kearney
Mallon	Mary	Catherine	10-Jun-1883	21-May-1883	Thomas Mallon	McCluskey, Teresa	Edward McCluskey / Ann C. Kery
Malloy	Elizabeth		10-Aug-1884	03-Aug-1884	Edward Malloy	Lee, Mary	Patricia Lee / Julia Clancy
Malloy	John	Matthew	27-Jul-1885	25-Jul-1885	John Malloy	Mullen, Mary	Bridget Mullen
Malloy	Anastasia	Regina	10-Feb-1901	03-Feb-1901	Laurence Malloy	Kirkland, Mary	Michael Drooney / Philomena Ward
Malloy	John	Joseph	01-Jun-1890	26-May-1890	Laurence Malloy	Kirkland, Mary Joan	Thomas Joseph Walsh / Joan Malloy
Malloy	Margaret	Mary	01-Jun-1890	26-May-1890	Laurence Malloy	Kirkland, Mary Joan	James Riordan / Margaret Sinnott
Malloy	Mary		24-Apr-1898	16-Apr-1898	Thomas Malloy	Donahue, Margaret	William Byrne / Mary Donahue
Malone	James	R.	25-Oct-1914	13-Oct-1914	James R. Malone	Shea, Mary	Leo J. Sullivan / Bernard Casey

79

LAST NAME	FIRST NAME	MIDDLE	BAPTISM	BIRTH	Father	Mother	SPONSORS
Malone	James	William	10-Dec-1911	27-Nov-1911	James Richard Malone	Shea, Mary Isabelle	William Malone	Kathleen Shea
Malone	Mary	Thelma	6-Aug-1905	20-May-1905	John Joseph Malone	Sweeney, Ann	James Malone	Honora Malone
Malone	Edward		24-Jul-1898	03-Jul-1898	John L. Malone	Cummins, Elizabeth	Daniel Cummins	Catherine O'Neill
Malone	Ann		15-Nov-1908	29-Oct-1908	John Laurence Malone	Cummins, Elizabeth	Danile Cremins	Mary R. Cremins
Malone	Thomas	James	02-Nov-1884	21-Oct-1884	John Malone	Gately, Catherine	James Wall	Bridget Malon
Malony	Bridget	Agnes	18-May-1884	28-Jan-1883	John Malony	O'Brien, Bridget Agnes		Mary Parrell
Malthan	Charles	Bernard	29-May-1889	13-May-1889	Charles Malthan	Loughran, Mary Ann		Mary O'Hara
Malthan	Henry		21-Jan-1888	31-Dec-1887	Charles Malthan	Loughran, Mary A.		Ann McFee
Mancusa	Mary	Grace	27-Dec-1914	23-Mar-1914	Cannelo Mancusa	Panatella, Josephine		Mary Mancusa
Mancuso	Louise	Antonio	16-Mar-1910	27-Feb-1910	C.Mancuso	Laporto, Camilla	Nicholas Rudolpho	Mary Rudolpho
Mancuso	Vincent		14-Mar-1909	15-Feb-1909	Camilla Mancuso	La Porta, Camilla	Vincent Mancuso	Mary Fridolpha
Mancuso	Francis	Elmira	29-Jul-1913	28-Jul-1911	Sigmund Mancuso	Montalto, Mary	Nicholas Rudolpho	Mary Rudolpho
Mancuso	Vincenza	Antionette	19-Apr-1908	11-Oct-1907	Sigmund R. Mancuso	Montalto, Mary	Joseph Rudolpho	Carmelle Mancuso
Mancuso	Grace	V.	16-Jun-1912	16-Feb-1912	Vincent Mancuso	Barrassi, Petrini Scia	Charles Raimondi	Teresa Raimondi
Mancuso	M.	Vincent	11-Oct-1914	12-Sep-1914	Vincent Mancuso	[Blank], Petrina		
Mandellowitz	Catherine	Dora	1-Jun-1913	24-May-1913	James Mandellowitz	Wagner, Frances		Catherine Lorder
Mandley	Emma	Mary	18-May-1911	25-Apr-1910	Frederick Norman Mandley	Parrish, Emma Estelle		Rose Monaghan
Mandley	Frederick		18-May-1911	10-Jul-1906	Frederick Norman Mandley	Parrish, Emma Estelle		Rose Monaghan
Mangano	Mary	Francis	23-May-1915	10-May-1915	Louis Mangano	Romano, Pauline	George Davis	Mary Davis
Mangano	Rose	Mary	2-Aug-1908	8-Jul-1908	Louis Mangano	Romano, Pauline	Martin Kavanaugh	Rosetta Moscati
Marion	Patrick	Henry	07-Dec-1884	27-Nov-1884	James Manion	Buckley, Mary	Michael Joseph O'Keefe	Ann O'Keefe
Marion	Ann	Mary	2-Dec-1906	19-Nov-1906	Stephen Manion	Casey, Mary	James Curran	Bridget Murray
Marion	Catherine	L.	10-Apr-1904	30-Mar-1904	Stephen Manion	Casey, Mary		Catherine Clynes
Manley	George		05-Mar-1899	10-Feb-1899	John Manley	Becker, Frieda	Francis Gately	Agnes Gately
Manner	Catherine		31-Dec-1911	8-Dec-1911	Charles Manner	O'Connor, Margaret		Catherine [Blank]
Manners	Charles	Augustus	6-Feb-1910	15-Jan-1910	Charles Manners	O'Connor, Margaret		Rose O'Connor
Manning	Edward	Eugene	30-Jul-1911	19-Jul-1911	Edmund Eugene Manning	Dennis, Margaret	John Dennis	Sue M. Dennis
Manning	Edward	Alfred	26-Nov-1882	05-Nov-1882	Edward Alfred Manning	Callopy, Ann	J. McDevitt	Ann Somerville
Manning	Francis	William	20-Jul-1913	1-Jul-1913	Edward Eugene Manning	Dennis, Catherine	William M. Burns	Catherine Cardwell
Manning	Mary	Catherine	11-Apr-1915	25-Mar-1915	Eugene Manning	Davis, Elizabeth	James Dennis	Ann Dennis
Manning	Margaret		25-Dec-1910	22-Dec-1910	James Manning, A.	Maher, Catherine	John Carroll	Catherine Manning
Manning	Mary		6-Oct-1912	2-Oct-1912	James Manning, A.	Maher, Catherine	Joseph McCafferty	Joan Veazy
Manning	Mary		07-Jun-1891	About 1869	James Flahart Manning	Jones, Mary A.		
Manning	John	Joseph	12-Nov-1882	11-Nov-1882	James Henry Manning	Buckley, Mary	Luke Danaher	Helen Hurlihay
Manning	John Laurnece		10-Dec-1882	21-Nov-1882	James Manning	Hughes, Margaret	John Meagher	Agnes Manning
Manning	Mary	Agnes	30-Apr-1893	16-Apr-1893	James Manning	Buckley, Mary	Benjamin Barry	Catherine Barry
Manning	Michael	Ignatius	22-Feb-1891	02-Feb-1891	James Manning	Buckley, Mary	John Bannon	Mary Helen Coyne
Manning	Florence	Elizabeth	02-Nov-1890	30-Oct-1890	William Manning	Fitzpatrick, Margaret	Michael Lally	Helen McManus
Manning	James	Gibbons	15-Oct-1893	21-Sep-1893	William Manning	Healy, Clara	Thomas Aspinwall	Clara Johnson
Manning	Mary	Irene	06-Jan-1889	28-Dec-1888	William Manning	Fitzpatrick, Margaret	James Manning	Mary Donohue
Manning	William	Martin	01-May-1892	06-Apr-1892	William Manning	Healy, Clara	Robert Edward Carroll	Elizabeth Carroll
Manning	William	Raymond	06-Sep-1885	22-Aug-1885	William Manning	Fitzpatrick, Margaret	Michale Fitzpatrick	Catherine McClenahan
Mannion	Elizabeth		01-Jun-1884	18-May-1884	James Mannion	Maher, Margaret	Henry McGraw	Ann Byrnes
Mannion	Joan	Catherine	25-Mar-1888	06-Mar-1888	James Mannion	Maher, Margaret	James Maguire	Ann A. Smith
Mannion	John	Paul	01-Jul-1900	19-Jun-1900	Stephen Mannion	Casey, Mary	Patrick Corrigan	Sarah Holmes
Mannion	Stephen	Joseph	11-Oct-1908	26-Sep-1908	Stephen Mannion	Casey, Mary	Patrick Kelley	Mary Quinn
Mannion	Thomas		17-Jul-1898	07-Jul-1898	Stephen Mannion	Casey, Mary	John Costello	Kate Casey
Mannion	William		23-Mar-1902	10-Mar-1902	Stephen Mannion	Casey, Mary	Patrick Reilly	Delia McHale
Mannon	James	Nicholas	26-Jul-1914	10-Jul-1914	James Mansberger	Casey, Mary	James Burke	Ann Dolan
Mansberger	Josephine		16-Aug-1910	[Blank]	James Mansberger	Thomas, Mary		
Manson	James	H.	11-Feb-1906	25-Jan-1906	Joseph Manson	Kenny, Alice Maria	Patrick Breen	Maygarey Manson
Marconi	Mary	J.	10-Nov-1902	02-May-1902	Vincent Marconi	Barsotle, Geneva		Catherine Mullahy
Marler	Jesse	Thomas	3-Nov-1912	29-Oct-1912	Jesse Marler	Blum, Mary Cecelia	John Gordon	Regina Blum
Marr	Ann	Lee	10-Jun-1908	03-Feb-1889	Henry P. Marr	Dorsey, Lee, Ann	William Schwartz	Elenora Roland
Marsh	Percy	Edward Leonard	18-Dec-1910	29-Mar-1890	Charles Oscar Marsh	Beatty, Ann	C.J. Ripple	Alma Elizabeth Phillips
Marshall	William		19-Aug-1891	13-Nov-1810	[Blank] Marshall	[Blank]	James Hayes	
Martin	Agnes	Rosalie	24-Jan-1915	13-Jan-1915	Bernard L. Martin	Kelly, Julia	Leo Kearney	Rose Curran
Martin	Joseph	Walter	06-Jan-1889	01-Dec-1888	George Martin	Connolly, Winifred	Michael Connolly	Catherine Connolly
Martin	John	Joseph	30-Apr-1882	24-Apr-1882	John Martin	Meena, Isabelle	Augustine Rudjet	Helen Rudy
Martin	John	Thomas	18-Feb-1883	14-Jan-1883	John Martin	Devalin, Mary	Joseph Inglemeyer	Mary Wering
Martin	Mary	Estelle	19-Apr-1903	04-Jan-1903	John Martin	Wooters, Laura Router	Charles Premmer	Estelle Oates
Martin	[Blank]		29-Dec-1908	18-Dec-1908	Joseph P. Martin	Ogden, Ann Wright	John F. O'Connor	Mary Martin
Martin	Joseph	Patrick	27-Oct-1907	19-Oct-1907	Joseph Patrick Martin	Wright, Ann	John Evans	Margaret Evans

LAST NAME	FIRST NAME	MIDDLE	BAPTISM	BIRTH	Father	Mother	SPONSORS
Martin	Paul	Alma	24-Sep-1882	06-Aug-1882	Michael Martin	Vick, Paulina	Michael Buckley	Mary Jennings
Martin	Ann	Mary Margaret	23-Nov-1913	23-Oct-1913	Thomas H. Martin	Bailey, Rose	Joseph Horan	Ada Horan
Martin	Thomas	Joseph	13-Mar-1910	22-Feb-1910	Thomas H. Martin	Bailey, Rose K.	James J. Hagan	Margaret Hagan
Martin	Augusta	Mildred	5-Dec-1909	14-Nov-1909	Thomas Joseph Martin	Jordan, Bridget M.	Charles Edward Jordan	Mary Martin
Martin	Francis	Thomas Martin	14-Mar-1905	29-Nov-1838	William C. Martin	Young, Elizabeth	James Conor	
Martin	Bernard	Leon	06-Mar-1887	21-Jan-1887	William H. Martin	Costello, Margaret	Charles Kelly	Mary Kelly
Martin	Rosalie		15-Apr-1883	16-Mar-1883	William Henry Martin	Costello, Margaret	Charles Graham	Catherine Rock
Martin	William	Henry	07-Jun-1885	25-Apr-1885	William Martin	Costello, Margaret	Joseph Donohue	Mary Kelly
Martin/Callender	Laura		07-Nov-1886	26-Feb-1863	Ephraim Martin	Pierce, Rachel		Ann Ahearn
Martindale	Catherine		2-Nov-1907	13-Oct-1907	Fielder Martindale	McNeigh, Margaret	Conrad Baumgartner	Mary A. Baumgartner
Martingale	Cora	Margaret	18-May-1902	08-Apr-1902	Fielder Martindale	McNeigh, Margaret		Mary Taylor
Marucci	Louis		14-Jun-1915	27-May-1914	Anthony Marucci	Jamonocho, Carmela	Vincent Siampagli	Emilia Ciochetti
Mason	Francis		03-Apr-1892	11-Mar-1892	Charles Mason	Burke, Mary Ann	Francis McKeever	Ella Burke
Mason	Herman		17-Sep-1882	05-Sep-1882	Charles Mason	Bourke, Mary Ann	William Horatio McBride	Helen McGerrigan
Mason	James		01-Jan-1900	25-Nov-1899	James Mason	Goods, Elizabeth	James Murphy	Katerina O'Neill
Mason	William	Charles	11-Oct-1885	03-Oct-1885	William Charles Mason	Burke, Mary A.	Henry A. Murphy	Margaret McGarigle
Mason	Laurence		19-Dec-1897	14-Nov-1897	William Mason	Goods, Elizabeth		Alice Kneslein
Massey	Margaret		07-Jun-1903	17-May-1903	John J. Massey	Martin, Margaret	John Sinnott	Catherine Sinnott
Massey	Helen	Genevieve	13-Mar-1887	02-Mar-1887	William Massey	Fitzpatrick, Margaret	Michael Fahey	Agnes Fitzpatrick
Masterson	Margaret		05-Oct-1890	22-Sep-1890	John Masterson	Edwards, Mary	John Bannan	Mary Flaherty
Mathison	Elizabeth		25-Mar-1894	14-Mar-1894	George Ignatius Mathison	Lacy, Catherine	John Ignatius Graham	Elizabeth Wherrett
Mathison	George		05-Nov-1882	05-Oct-1882	George Ignatius Mathison	Lacy, Catherine Elizabeth	John Francis Doyle	Catherine Lacy
Mathison	George	Henry	13-Oct-1907	20-Sep-1907	George Mathison	Taylor, Addie	James Mathison	Barbara E. Mathison
Mathison	Henry	Lacy	07-Nov-1897	22-Oct-1897	George Mathison	Lacy, Catherine	Joseph Graham	Marcella Lacy
Mathison	John	Leo	23-May-1892	10-May-1892	George Mathison	Lacy, Catherine	James McLaughlin	Leocadia Lacy
Mathison	Josephine		12-Sep-1908	22-Jun-1908	Joseph Mathison	Pfaff, Clara		Mary Mersman
Matthews	John	Joseph	09-Oct-1898	29-Sep-1898	Andrew Matthews	Owens, Elizabeth	August Dunn	Joan Owens
Matthews	Mary	Rita	26-Sep-1909	16-Sep-1909	Andrew Matthews	Dunn, Mary	James A. Slaysman	Elizabeth Daily
Matthews	John		19-Feb-1901	19-Feb-1901	Nolan Matthews	Laregy, Ann		Julia Smith
Matthews/Lorenz	Ann	Mary	13-Mar-1898	25-Dec-1850	Henry Matthews	[Blank], Margaret		Florence Lorenz
Mauwood	Margaret	Elizabeth	12-Aug-1900	30-Jul-1900	William Mauwood	Casey, Catherine	William Delaney	Ann Delaney
May	Ann	Lillian	11-Feb-1906	5-Feb-1906	George A. May	Montgomery, Lillian M.	Francis Wiseman	Ann Wiseman
May	Teresa		12-Jul-1908	23-Jun-1908	George Ambrose May	Montgomery, Lillian	Frank M. May	Teresa A. Stole
May	Michael	Stevenson	08-Apr-1890	02-Apr-1890	Peter May	Powers, Elizabeth		Michael Malone
Mayberry	Martha	Loretta	26-Aug-1883	25-Jan-1887	Thomas Mayberry	Fitzpatrick, Mary	Joseph Fitzpatrick	Margaret Fitzpatrick
Maycumber	Mary	Helen	7-Apr-1906	19-Aug-1891	Richmond Maycumber	Hart, Josephine		Julia Doyle
Mayted	Mary	Katherine	14-Mar-1915	25-Feb-1915	William F. Mayted	Dagenhardt, Mary		Mary Decker
Maytee	William	R.	30-Jan-1898	06-Jan-1898	William Maytee	Lawlor, Alice	Richard Brockmeyer	Mary Lawler
Maytern	William	James	18-Jul-1915	17-Jun-1915	William Maytern	Hulse, Mary	John Ward	Margaret Leonard
Maythias	John	August	16-Jun-1901	04-Jun-1901	August Maythias	Cullen, Ellen	William Cullen	Margaret Cullen
Maythias	Stewart	Newton	16-May-1888	17-Apr-1888	George Edward Maythias	Helmcamp, Frances		Teresa Smith
Maytison	Joseph		15-Mar-1885	26-Feb-1885	George Maytison	Lacy, Catherine	Joseph Lacy	Margaret Marriman
McAdam	Margaret	Joseph	25-Oct-1891	10-Oct-1891	James McAdam	Corcoran, Winifred	Martin Gallagher	Margaret Smith
McAdams	Rose		28-Oct-1883	11-Oct-1883	James McAdams	Tidings, Catherine	Peter McAdams	Ann Hullivan
McAdams	Eugene	George	04-Dec-1892	11-Nov-1892	Peter McAdams	Donohue, Cecelia	Charles Donohue	Catherine Bodka
McAdams	Mary	Ann	25-Jan-1885	01-Jan-1885	Peter McAdams	Donohue, Cecelia		Mollie McConnell
McAdams	Rose	Veronica	24-Oct-1886	07-Oct-1886	Peter McAdams	Donohue, Cecelia	Thomas Gray	Rose McManus
McAdams	Sara		20-Aug-1899	08-Aug-1899	Peter McAdams	Donohue, Cecelia	James R. Kenly	Hannah Bremmer
McAleer	Mary	Dolores	12-Jan-1913	27-Dec-1912	Dennis C. McAleer	Schaefer, Mary A.	Joseph A. Carey	Grace Agnes Fields
McAleer	Ellen	Rose	18-Feb-1883	[Blank]	Philip McAleer	Kelleher, Catherine	Herman Graham	Ellen McAleer
McAleer	Mary	John	06-Jun-1886	01-Jun-1886	Phillip McAleer	Keleher, Catherine	Samuel Eppler	John Moore
McAlenney	George	Henry	14-Apr-1882	01-Apr-1882	Bernard McAlenney	Cook, Ann		Margaret Tierney
McAler	John		24-Aug-1890	17-Aug-1890	C. McAler	Kuler, Mary		Mary J. Richardson
McAler	Margaret		01-Jan-1899	21-Dec-1898	Joseph McAler	Amos, Margaret	John McAler	Margaret McAler
McAllister	Ruth	Mary	16-Jun-1907	7-Jun-1907	Joseph B. McAlister	Marshall, Virgill[sic]	John Schaefer	Mary J. Decker
McAllister	Joseph	Bernard	25-Feb-1906	13-Feb-1906	Joseph B. McAllister	Marshall, Virgill[sic]	Francis X. Marshall	Mary E. Decker
McArthur	Margaret		29-Nov-1896	02-Nov-1896	William McArthur	Burke, Mary		
McAuliffe	Mary	Irene	16-Sep-1894	07-Sep-1894	Cornelius McAuliffe	Doran, Mary	Patrick Vaughan	Briget McAuliffe
McAuliffe	Michael	Joseph	31-Dec-1895	17-Dec-1895	Cornelius McAuliffe	Doran, Mary	Patrick Byrne	Bridget Doran
McAvoy	Gladys	Agnes	4-May-1913	5-Apr-1913	Henry McAvoy	Cooper, Catherine	Charles R. McAvoy	Agnes Kavanaugh
McBride	Catherine	Elizabeth	07-Sep-1884	16-Aug-1884	Francis McBride	Keefe, Mary Ann	Christopher Keefe	Helen Kelly
McBride	Mary	Elizabeth	18-Jun-1883	10-May-1883	Francis McBride	Keefe, Mary		Mary Catherine Scott
McBride	James	Ernest	9-Aug-1914	27-Jul-1914	James McBride	Werneth, Pearl	Philip Arges	Gertrude McBride

LAST NAME	FIRST NAME	MIDDLE	BAPTISM	BIRTH	Father	Mother	SPONSORS
McBride	John	Francis	12-Jun-1883	25-May-1880	John McBride	McCourt, Sara	Mary Whitney
McBride	Ann		28-Apr-1889	10-Apr-1889	Thomas McBride	Clifford, Mary	Catherine McBride
McBride	Daniel		10-Jan-1897	28-Dec-1896	Thomas McBride	Clifford, Mary	Sara O'Brien
McBride	Francis		04-Oct-1891	15-Sep-1891	Thomas McBride	Clifford, Mary	Margaret Little
McBride	Francis	Gertrude	20-Nov-1892	08-Nov-1892	Thomas McBride	Clifford, Mary	Martin F. Mooney
McBride	James		12-Jul-1885	02-Jul-1885	Thomas McBride	Clifford, Mary	John Reynolds
McBride	Ann	Mary	27-Dec-1885	15-Dec-1885	William H. McBride	Keyhan, Catherine	James McBride
McCabe	Agnes	Veronica	05-May-1889	16-Apr-1889	Charles McCabe	McIntyre, Helen	Peter Dunn
McCabe	Ann	Loretta	08-Nov-1891	24-Oct-1891	Charles McCabe	McIntyre, Ellen	Phillip McIntyre
McCabe	Catherine	Genevieve	16-Sep-1894	13-Sep-1894	Charles McCabe	McIntyre, Helen	Daniel Cremins
McCabe	Elizabeth		29-Nov-1891	15-Nov-1891	Charles McCabe	Brady, Mary	Eugene McIntyre
McCabe	Joseph	Anthony	12-Sep-1887	31-Aug-1887	Charles McCabe	McIntyre, Eleanor	Bernard Reilly
McCabe	Lucy	Margaret	01-Mar-1896	29-Feb-1896	Charles McCabe	McIntyre, Helen	Eugene McIntyre
McCabe	Mary	Teresa	15-Oct-1882	07-Oct-1882	Charles McCabe	McIntyre, Helen	Joseph Riley
McCabe	Mary	Catherine	31-Mar-1889	18-Mar-1889	Charles McCabe	Brady, Mary	Owen McIntyre
McCabe	William	Francis	04-Jan-1885	21-Dec-1884	Charles McCabe	McIntyre, Ella	Peter McCabe
McCabe	Mary		19-Jan-1890	12-Jan-1890	J. McCabe	[Blank]	Francis Regan
McCabe	Agnes		05-Feb-1882	09-Dec-1881	James McCabe	Ryan, Mary	John Connor
McCabe	Bernard		06-Aug-1899	13-Jul-1899	James McCabe	Doyle, Rose	James McCabe
McCabe	James		03-Feb-1895	25-Jan-1895	James McCabe	Doyle, Rose Genevieve	Hubert Conroy
McCabe	Margaret		07-Mar-1897	01-Feb-1897	James McCabe	Doyle, Rose	James Edward Berry
McCabe	John	Samuel	15-Dec-1901	27-Nov-1901	John Joseph McCabe	Leary, Mary	Francis McCabe
McCabe	Catherine	Mary	16-Jan-1898	05-Jan-1898	John McCabe	Finnigan, Mary	Thomas Sheridan
McCabe	James	Patrick	15-Mar-1903	04-Mar-1903	John McCabe	Finnegan, Mary	William H. Cain
McCabe	John	Joseph	02-Sep-1900	25-Aug-1900	John McCabe	Finnegan, Mary	James Morgan
McCabe	Margaret	Bridget	15-Mar-1903	04-Mar-1903	John McCabe	Finnegan, Mary	John Cain
McCabe	Margaret	Josephine	28-Jun-1903	10-Jun-1903	John McCabe	Leary, Mary	Thomas Donoghue
McCabe	Mary		07-Dec-1898	18-Nov-1898	John McCabe	O'Leary, Mary	John Flaherty
McCabe	Nicholas		11-Mar-1900	02-Mar-1900	John McCabe	Leary, Mary	Nicholas McGraw
McCabe	Catherine		20-Nov-1892	13-Nov-1892	Joseph McCabe	Doyle, Rose	Edward J. Radigan
McCabe	John		09-Feb-1896	02-Feb-1896	Simon McCabe	McCall, Margaret	Michael Monaghan
McCabe	Margaret		18-Feb-1900	12-Feb-1900	Simon McCabe	McCall, Margaret	Francis McCabe
McCabe	Mary		17-Dec-1893	08-Dec-1893	Simon McCabe	McCall, Margaret	John McCabe
McCabe	Michael		06-Apr-1890	01-Apr-1890	Simon McCabe	McCall, Margaret	Patrick McCabe
McCafferty	Elmer	Mary	07-Feb-1886	26-Jan-1886	John McCafferty	McIntyre, Elizabeth	James Mellen
McCafferty	James	Elliott	3-Apr-1904	15-Mar-1904	Thomas M. McCafferty	Elliott, Delia	Joseph P. Flaherty
McCaffrey	Catherine	Ella	05-May-1895	23-Apr-1895	James McCaffrey	Lynch, Mary	Pat. McCaffrey
McCaffrey	Cecelia	Mary	01-Apr-1894	20-Mar-1894	James McCaffrey	Lynch, Mary	John McCaffrey
McCaffrey	James		04-Apr-1900	28-Mar-1900	James McCaffrey	Lynch, Mary	Francis Lynch
McCaffrey	Mary	Gertrude	21-Mar-1897	11-Mar-1897	John McCaffrey	Lynch, Mary Gertrude	Charles Lynch
McCaffrey	Patrick	William	08-Jul-1888	23-Jun-1888	Thomas McCaffrey	Daily, Mary E.	George Eichner
McCalley	Ethel	Lassell	23-Feb-1896	17-Feb-1896	Robert L. McCailley	Jordon, Isabelle	Louis Jordan
McCambridge	Mary		11-Sep-1898	30-Aug-1898	John McCambridge	Roche, Margaret	John Roche
McCann	James	Edward	22-Jun-1902	10-Jun-1902	Edward McCann	O'Connell, Ella	James O'Donnell
McCann	Julia		08-Jul-1900	28-Jun-1900	Edward McCann	O'Connell, Ellen	Leo McCann
McCann	John		19-Jan-1891	07-Jan-1891	George McCann	Swift, Margaret	
McCann	Edward		26-Jun-1892	20-Jun-1892	John McCann	Diller, Helen	Charles Dowd
McCann	John		26-Jun-1892	20-Jun-1892	John McCann	Dillon, Helen	Dennis Manion
McCann	John	Joseph	29-Aug-1897	24-Aug-1897	John McCann	Dillon, Helen	Thomas Leonard
McCann	Mary		24-Oct-1886	17-Oct-1886	John McCann	[Blank], Laura	James Mackin
McCann	Mary		25-Sep-1887	17-Sep-1887	John McCann	Dillon, Helen	Patrick McCann
McCann	Thomas		25-Jun-1899	20-Jun-1899	John McCann	Dillon, Ella	Francis Hoffer
McCarb	James		22-Jun-1884	06-Jun-1884	William McCarb	Smith, Mary	Charles McCarb
McCardell	Catherine	Eleanor	24-Jul-1910	8-Jun-1910	Ernest J. McCardell	Brown, Ferdie	Catherine Hughes
McCardell	William	Eugene	07-Dec-1890	28-Nov-1890-	William E. McCardell	Brown, Mary A.	Mary B. Trambo
McCart	Edgar	Andrew	10-Jan-1915	15-Dec-1914	Andrew McCart	McCluskey, Mary	Edgar Joseph Thomas
McCart	John	Dorman	19-Oct-1913	6-Oct-1913	Andrew McCart	McCluskey, Mary E.	John McCluskey
McCart	Mary	Elizabeth	19-Oct-1913	6-Oct-1913	Andrew McCart	McCluskey, Mary E.	James McCluskey
McCart	James	Leon	10-Nov-1889	21-Oct-1889	Charles William McCart	Stark, Lydia	Joseph McCart
McCart	Terrance	Joseph	10-May-1883	08-May-1883	William McCart	Smith, Mary	Ann McCart
McCarthy	Jerome	Donald	17-Jul-1904	8-Jul-1904	Edward McCarthy	Fitzpatrick, Margaret	Martha Kendall
McCarthy	Francis		11-Apr-1915	3-Apr-1915	Francis D. McCarthy	Ludwig, Mary E.	Michael Fitzpatrick
McCarthy	John	Patrick	02-Jun-1895	31-May-1895	James McCarthy	O'Keefe, Mary	Elmer A. Ludwig
							James Dalton
							Hannah Reardon

LAST NAME	FIRST NAME	MIDDLE	BAPTISM	BIRTH	Father	Mother	SPONSORS	
McCarthy	John	Stephen	02-Oct-1887	17-Sep-1887	Patrick McCarthy	Conway, Cecelia	Terence E. Fitzpatrick	Mary D. Collins
McCarthy	Mary	Gertrude	10-Jul-1892	24-Jun-1892	Patrick McCarthy	Conway, Cecelia	James Kernan	Catherine Thompson
McCarthy	Rose	Agnes	18-Aug-1889	05-Aug-1889	Patrick McCarthy	Conway, Cecelia	Felix Gormley	Christina Kelly
McClain	Francis		11-Aug-1901	29-Jul-1901	Francis O'Brien	[Blank], Minnie	Henry Shafer	Mary Shafer
McClary	George	Robinson	3-Sep-1911	14-Aug-1911	George McClary	Stewart, Isabelle	John L. Stewart	Sabina Concannon
McClary	John	Joseph	17-Nov-1912	4-Nov-1912	George McClary	Stewart, Isabelle	Thomas Enright	Helen Sheridan
McClary	Robert	Alexander	29-Mar-1914	15-Mar-1914	George R. McClary	Stewart, Isabelle Mary	Laurence Quinlan	Mary Ellen Concannon
McClasky	Joseph	Leon	27-Dec-1903	09-Dec-1903	William E. McClasky	McEamley, Sara		Sara McClasky
McClellan	Joseph	Louis Adams	27-Nov-1887	24-Oct-1887	James Robert McClellan	Bonnett, Alice Henry	Francis Meyer Bonnett	Ann Catherine Bonnett
McClelland	Edward		05-Dec-1897	25-Nov-1897	David McClelland	Jackson, Mary	John O'Connor	Bridget Kelly
McClelland	Elizabeth	Napier	01-Jan-1882	10-Dec-1881	David McClelland	Jackson, Maria E.	Arthur Napier	Helen Weldon
McClintock	Sara	Josephine	19-Mar-1887	11-Oct-1858	Robert McClintock	Lee, Elizabeth		Alberta Mobley
McClure	Clarence		26-Apr-1886	26-Mar-1886	William McClure	Keenan, Elizabeth		Ann Winters
McCluskey	Cornelius	Dudley	7-Jun-1908	8-May-1908	Bernard J. McCluskey	Blake, Ann E.		Mary Fowler
McCluskey	Bernard	Joseph	13-May-1906	17-Apr-1906	Bernard McCluskey	Blake, Ann	William J. Fowler	Catherine McCluskey
McCluskey	John		26-Aug-1912	2-Aug-1912	Bernard McCluskey	Welzel, Ann		Margaret Sneider
McCluskey	John		20-Dec-1903	06-Dec-1903	John McCluskey	Kane, Ella	Charles Carey	Bessie Kane
McCluskey	Mary	Elizabeth	04-Oct-1891	24-Sep-1891	Joseph McCluskey	Evans, Margaret	James Broughton	Elizabeth McCluskey
McCluskey	Ann		10-Apr-1892	04-Apr-1892	Michael McCluskey	Healy, Ann	Daniel Haney	Agnes Coogan
McCluskey	Catherine		18-Nov-1883	08-Nov-1883	Michael McCluskey	Healy, Ann	James McCourt	Bridget McCourt
McCluskey	James	Thomas	26-Oct-1890	21-Oct-1890	Michael McCluskey	Healy, Ann	Thomas Manning	MarCecelia Finnan
McCluskey	Michael	Joseph	23-May-1897	19-May-1897	Michael McCluskey	Healy, Ann	Thomas Jos. McCluskey	Mary McCluskey
McCluskey	Teresa		24-Apr-1887	15-Apr-1887	Muchael McCluskey	Healy, Ann	Martin F. Haly	Sara G. McGang
McCluskey	Barbara		3-May-1908	22-Apr-1908	William C. McCluskey	Leimbach, Catherine	John Guilta	Barbara Guilta
McCluskey	Ann	Joan	11-Dec-1887	06-Dec-1887	William McCluskey	Keane, Catherine	Patrick McCabe	Ann McCluskey
McCluskey	Margaret	Elizabeth	15-Apr-1906	30-Mar-1906	William McCluskey	McCalley, Sara A.		Sara McCluskey
McCluskey	Mary	Sara	08-Apr-1883	31-Mar-1883	William McCluskey	Kane, Catherine	John McNally	Mary McNally
McCluskey	Mary	Catherine	28-Jul-1901	17-Jul-1901	William McCluskey	Leimbach, Elizabeth	Edward Boyle	Catherine Boyle
McCluskey	Thomas	Joseph	05-Oct-1884	24-Sep-1884	William McCluskey	Kane, Catherine	Michael McCluskey	Mary A. McCluskey
McCluskey	William	D.	27-Sep-1893	22-Nov-1846	William McCluskey	[Blank]		Margaret McCluskey
McColm	Robert	Louise	30-Apr-1899	24-Apr-1899	Robert L. McColm	Leimbach, Elizabeth	Joseph Emory	Sara Hilberg
McComas/Cole	Mary	Frances	21-Jan-1894	09-Jan-1894	Aquilla McComas	Meegan, Alice F.		Mary Hebrank
McComb	Samuel		31-Jan-1886	08-Feb-1855	James McComb	Slade, Elizabeth		
McComb	Catherine	A.	27-Nov-1912	27-Jul-1860	Samuel McComb	Cook, Mary		
McComb	Catherine	A.	05-Mar-1886	16-Feb-1886	Samuel McComb	McDermott, Ann B.	Mary Fox	Mary Fox
McComb	Isabelle	Laura	25-Apr-1886	16-Feb-1886	Samuel McComb	McDermott, Ann B.	Edward McDermott	Catherine McDermott
McComb	Joseph	Carroll	27-Nov-1887	11-Nov-1887	Samuel McComb	McDermott, Ann	Francis McComb	Mary McDermott
McComb	Samuel		28-Jan-1894	12-Jan-1894	Samuel McComb	McDermott, Ann		
McComb	Susan		12-Nov-1904	10-Dec-1842	Samuel McComb	McComb, Sara	James E. McComb	
McComb	Matthew	Elizabeth	01-Mar-1882	14-Feb-1882	Samuel McComb	McDonald, Ann		IdaBella Mary McComb
McCombs	Irene		19-Sep-1892	29-Aug-1892	Joseph McCombs	Judge, Mary		Catherine Bertrand
McCombs	Margaret		05-Mar-1889	01-Jan-1889	William McCombs	Judge, Mary Ann		Eleanor Riley
McCombs/Hagan	Margaret		20-Dec-1906	01-Dec-1860	James McCombs	Clark, Agnes		
McConkey	Mary		27-Sep-1883	27-Apr-1883	George McConkey	Mee, Catherine Frances	James Rigney	Helen Rigney
McConnell	Joseph		16-Jul-1893	30-Jun-1893	Joseph McConnell	Dare, Ada	Thomas Evans	Catherine McConnell
McCord	Thomas	Leo	28-Oct-1900	20-Oct-1900	Peter McCord	Fahey, Ellen	Thomas J. Dohoney	Ellen Davey
McCormick	John		08-Apr-1883	04-Apr-1883	John McCormick	Krener, Sarah	George Krener	Catherine Krener
McCormick	John		14-Aug-1904	1-Aug-1904	John McCormick	Gaynor, Ann G.	Francis McCormick	Margaret Gaynor
McCormick	Mary	Elizabeth	28-Dec-1890	20-Dec-1890	John McCormick	Krener, Ann Margaret	George Michael Skipper	Elizabeth McCormick
McCormick	Matthew		12-Jan-1902	21-Dec-1901	John McCormick	McCormick, Mary	Thomas Cullan	Julia Gillespie
McCormick	Mary	Elizabeth	3-Dec-1905	20-Nov-1905	Peter J. McCormick	Lynch, Cecelia M.	Eugene C. Shipley	Mary Shipley
McCormick	Elizabeth	Ann	21-Jan-1906	12-Jan-1906	Thomas Edward McCormick	Lannon, Blance	John McCormick	Mary Lannon
McCosker	Edward	Charles	13-Sep-1914	30-Aug-1914	Bernard McCosker	Blake, Ann	Edward Healey	Margaret Healey
McCourt	Henry		20-Sep-1903	13-Sep-1903	Bernard J. McCourt	Wright, Margaret	John Wright	Mary Wright
McCourt	Mary	Elizabeth	24-Oct-1897	19-Oct-1897	Bernard J. McCourt	Wright, Margaret	Henry J. Wright	Ann Wright
McCourt	Joseph	Bernard	20-Sep-1891	14-Aug-1891	Bernard Joseph McCourt	Wright, Margaret	Adam Joseph Wright	Margaret Wright
McCourt	Bernard	Joseph	07-Jul-1901	27-Jun-1901	Bernard McCourt	Wright, Margaret	William Burke	Mary Quinn
McCourt	David	Leo	25-Feb-1900	21-Feb-1900	Bernard McCourt	Wright, Margaret	Cornelius Sullivan	Ann Sullivan
McCourt	Mary	Ann	30-Sep-1883	23-Sep-1883	Charles Henry McCourt	McCall, Mary Ann Elizabeth	David McCourt	Mary McCollum
McCourt	Eugene	F.	02-May-1897	24-Apr-1897	Charles McCourt	McCall, Mary	William Adam	Catherine McIntyre
McCourt	Margaret	Regina	24-May-1891	15-May-1891	Charles McCourt	McCall, Mary M.	Michael J. McCourt	Rose McCall
McCourt	Myles	Joseph	28-Mar-1886	25-Mar-1886	Charles McCourt	McCall, Mary Ann	Peter J. McCourt	Bridget McCall
McCourt	Rose	Elizabeth	03-Jun-1888	25-May-1888	Charles McCourt	McCall, Mary Ann	Patrick McGuire	Margaret McFall

LAST NAME	FIRST NAME	MIDDLE	BAPTISM	BIRTH	Father	Mother	SPONSORS
McCourt	Theresa	Bridget	01-Oct-1893	23-Sep-1893	Charles McCourt	McCall, Mary	James Duffy
McCourt	Joseph		07-May-1882	30-Apr-1882	Edward McCourt	Hagerty, Susan	George Bishop
McCourt	William	John	07-May-1882	01-May-1882	Edward McCourt	Hagerty, Susan	Francis Hagerty
McCourt	Helen	Catherine	26-Jan-1913	9-Jan-1913	Joseph Edward McCourt	Hart, Catherine	Thomas Hart
McCourt	Margaret	Agnes	14-Feb-1915	1-Feb-1915	Joseph Edward McCourt	Hart, Catherine	Henry Coyne
McCourt	Mary	``	10-Sep-1882	03-Sep-1882	Michael J. McCourt	Appleton, Mary	Edward Hogan
McCourt	Rose	Ann	25-Jan-1885	20-Jan-1885	Michael J. McCourt	Appleton, Mary	Thomas Appleton
McCourt	Thomas	Edward	19-Dec-1886	14-Dec-1886	Michael McCourt	Appleton, Mary	Thomas Appleton
McCourt	David		22-Jun-1890	14-Jun-1890	Peter Joseph McCourt	Fahey, Helen	James Flynn
McCourt	Matthew		14-Apr-1895	04-Apr-1895	Peter Joseph McCourt	Fahey, Helen	James Mulligan
McCourt	Bernard		21-Nov-1897	30-Oct-1897	Peter McCourt	Fahey, Helen	
McCourt	Peter	Wilmer	09-Oct-1892	30-Sep-1892	Peter McCourt	Fahey, Helen	Francis J. Kimmett
McCoy	Elmer	Louis	7-Feb-1915	28-Jan-1915	Robert E. McCoy	Reller, Stela	Anthony L. Campo
McCray	Ann	Cecelia	12-Sep-1915	20-Aug-1915	James McCray	Lamp, Bertha E.	Bernard Lavery
McCready	Lillian		15-Mar-1891	02-Feb-1891	Samuel McCready	McCall, Sara J.	
McCreer	Edward		12-Feb-1882	09-Jan-1882	Thomas McCreer	Crimmins, Mary	J. Carroll
McCrory	John		08-Mar-1885	27-Feb-1885	William McCrory	Clarke, Hannah	James McCourt
McCrory	William	Joseph	27-Feb-1887	0-Feb-1887	William McCrory	Clarke, Ann	Patrick McCabe
McCrory	James	Edward	24-Jul-1883	19-Jun-1883	William Rogers McCrory	Clark, Ann	John Patrick Clark
McCrory	Mary	Ann	02-Aug-1891	24-Jul-1891	William Thomas McCrory	Clarke, Ann	Edward McCrory
McCubbin	Mary		25-Jul-1904	21-Jul-1904	Parke McCubbin	Thurn, Estelle	Dr. Pound
McCubbin	Agnes	Ellen	01-Dec-1901	15-Nov-1901	William McCubbin	Mullen, Isabelle	Francis Pohler
McCubbin	Charles	Henry	06-May-1900	April 1900	William McCubbin	Mullen, Isabelle	Henry Rudiger
McCubbin	Francis	Xavier	26-Apr-1903	14-Apr-1903	William McCubbin	Mullen, Elizabeth	August Rudiger
McCubbin	Helen	Francis	5-Feb-1905	9-Jan-1905	William McCubbin	Mullen, Isabelle	Julian Rudiger
McCubbin	Henry	Rudiger	17-Mar-1912	29-Feb-1912	William McCubbin	Mullen, Isabelle	George J. Roney
McCubbin	Joan	V.	9-Nov-1913	20-Oct-1913	William McCubbin	Mullen, Isabelle	Joseph Macgregor
McCubbin	William	Edward	01-Apr-1894	21-Mar-1894	William Thomas McCubbin	Mullen, Isabelle	Patrick Mullen
McCue	Lydia		02-Nov-1894	24-Aug-1864	Israeli S. Cambaugh	Minnigh, Elina	G. W. Devine
McCue	Ellen		27-May-1894	15-May-1894	Patrick McCue	Stumbaugh, Lydia C.	Joseph Dunn
McCullough	Joseph	Andrew	13-Dec-1903	26-Nov-1903	Henry McCullough	Donohue, Catherine	Andrew J. Gereghty
McCullough	Mary	Connelly	25-Aug-1901	02-Aug-1901	Henry McCullough	Donohue, Catherine	Thomas Brazier
McCullough	Catherine		2-Nov-1907	25-Oct-1907	William A. McCullough	Quinn, Delia	Thomas Leland
McCullough	John		15-Dec-1894	17-Jun-1890	William McCullough	Stiley, Ann	James McDevitt
McCusker	Caroline		19-Aug-1906	25-Jul-1906	John McCusker	McCusker, Caroline	Michael McCusker
McCusker	Mary	Agnes	22-Sep-1904	12-Sep-1904	Luca McCusker	Flemming, Delia	Patrick McCusker
McCusker	Luke	Fleming	9-Sep-1906	27-Aug-1906	Luke McCusker	Flemming, Delia	Michael Sweeney
McDaniel	Joseph	Milton	09-Mar-1902	01-Mar-1902	Joseph McDaniel	Katzenberger, Georgia	John Katzenberger
McDermott	S.		06-Jul-1890	17-Jun-1890	E. McDermott	Myers, Philomena	John McComb
McDermott	Edward	Donald	20-Aug-1905	10-Aug-1905	Edward F. McDermott	Myers, Philomena	James W. Shea
McDermott	Ann	B.	11-Jun-1899	24-May-1899	Edward McDermott	Myers, Philomena	Charles M Kohlerman
McDermott	Kathleen		15-Dec-1901	09-Dec-1901	Edward McDermott	Myers, Minnie	John Shea
McDermott	Mary	Gertrude	09-Sep-1894	20-Aug-1894	Edward McDermott	Myers, Philomena	Nicolas Kohlerman
McDermott	Ann	Mary	20-Nov-1904	4-Nov-1904	James McDermott	Smith, Gladys	Charles Gothard
McDermott	Edward	Gregory	03-Apr-1887	12-Mar-1887	James McDermott	Hart, Ann	James McComb
McDermott	Joseph	Jerome	13-Jan-1884	22-Dec-1883	James McDermott	Hart, Ann	James McComb
McDermott	Leon	Joseph	10-Apr-1889	10-Apr-1889	James McDermott	Sheehan, Mary	
McDermott	Mary	Joseph	03-Apr-1892	17-Mar-1892	James McDermott	Sheehan. Susan	Henry Vincent Sheehan
McDermott	Owen	Charles	27-Jan-1901	09-Jan-1901	James McDermott	Sheehan. Susan	James McDermott
McDermott	Wilbur		05-Jan-1890	27-Dec-1889	Patrick Joseph McDermott	Carroll, Edward[sic]	Ida Crawford
McDermott	Edward	Crawford	15-Jul-1888	24-Jun-1888	Patrick McDermott	Crawford, Mary Helen	William DouBell Smith
McDermott	George	Eldridge	30-Jul-1899	20-Jul-1899	Patrick McDermott	Crawford, Mary	Clarence Wamsley
McDermott	Catherine		30-Oct-1904	23-Sep-1904	William P. McDermott	Garrick, Bridget	Michael Davey
McDermott	Honora		18-Feb-1906	28-Jan-1906	William P. McDermott	Carrick, Bridget	Michael Holmes
McDermott	William		26-Jan-1908	6-Jan-1908	William P. McDermott	Carrick, Delia	Michael Moylan
McDevitt	Owen	Morris	06-Jun-1890	25-May-1890	Wm McDermott	Shane, Fanny	
McDevitt	Arthur		07-Aug-1887	18-Jul-1887	Arthur McDevitt	Courtney, Mary	John Courtney
McDonald	Catherine		06-Oct-1889	29-Sep-1889	Edward Edgar McDonald	McIntyre, Mary E.	Edward J. Fields
McDonald	Emma	Pearl	22-Oct-1893	07-Oct-1893	Edward McDonald	McIntyre, Helen	Charles Fields
McDonald	John	Thomas	15-Jul-1888	07-Jul-1888	Edward McDonald	McIntire, Mary Helen	John McIntyre
McDonald	Margaret		16-Feb-1908	18-Jan-1908	Edward McDonald	McIntire, Mary	William E. Mackessy
McDonald	Eleanor	Louise	5-Mar-1911	19-Feb-1911	James E. McDonald	McCann, Beulah	Owen Murphy
McDonald	Helen		26-Sep-1909	12-Sep-1909	James E. McDonald	McCahan, Beulah	Patrick Murphy

| Bridget Finnegan |
| Susan Hagery |
| Ann Hagerty |
| Sarah Ryan |
| Christina Ryan |
| Mary Smith |
| Catherine Appleton |
| Ann Sullivan |
| Helen Davey |
| Helen Mulligan |
| |
| Catherine King |
| Ids J. Campo |
| Ann N. French |
| Mary J. Murphy |
| Ann Murphy |
| Ann McCart |
| Sara Corrigan |
| Catherine McCourt |
| Susan Clarke |
| |
| Agnes Bretner |
| Sarah Mullen |
| Blanche Mallon |
| Emma Rudiger |
| Helen Rudiger |
| Joan Rooney |
| Emma Blondel |
| |
| Theresa E. Hoff |
| Lilia Dobbins |
| Mary Green |
| Mary O'Sullivan |
| James McDevitt |
| Mary Agnes McCusker |
| Mary Sherman |
| Mary Ryan |
| Mary Katzenberger |
| Fannie Allen |
| Mary B. Shea |
| Mary Kohlerman |
| Mary Shea |
| Mary G. Kohlerman |
| Mary Gothard |
| Mary McComb |
| Isabelle McComb |
| Mary Molloy |
| Augustina McComb |
| Mary Sheehan |
| Mary Seales |
| Mary McDermott |
| Anastasia Parell |
| Mary Barrett |
| Bridget K. Holmes |
| Ella McNally |
| Mary Kelly |
| Mary Courtney |
| Margaret O'Hara |
| Ann McIntyre |
| Catherine Callaghan |
| Sinevera McDonald |
| Rita McDonald |
| Elizabeth O'Neill |

84

LAST NAME	FIRST NAME	MIDDLE	BAPTISM	BIRTH	Father	Mother	SPONSORS	
McDonald	James	Edmund	16-Nov-1913	29-Oct-1913	James E. McDonald	McCann, Beulah	Peter E. McDonald	Loretta Kirby
McDonald	Frances		4-Aug-1912	7-Jul-1912	James Edward McDonald	McCann, Beulah	Henry Joseph Kirby	Loretta Catherine Kirby
McDonald	Helen	Mary	11-Mar-1901	11-Mar-1901	James McDonald	Herron, Ellen		Mary Hepler
McDonald	James		10-Feb-1900	10-Feb-1900	James McDonald	Harran, Nellie		Mrs. Slaughter
McDonald	James	L.	18-Jan-1903	05-Jan-1903	James McDonald	Narron, Helen J.	P.J. Narron	Catherine Narxron
McDonald	James	Francis	22-Aug-1909	6-Aug-1909	James McDonald	Dunn, Nellie V.	Thomas D. McDonald	Nellie McDonald
McDonald	James		1-Nov-1911	[Blank]	James McDonald	McDonald, Sarah		
McDonald	Charles		22-Sep-1907	12-Sep-1907	John Feeney	Feeney, Agnes	James O'Hara	Ann O'Hara
McDonald	Edward		14-Oct-1883	02-Oct-1883	John McDonald	Hyland, Lydia	James Hyland	Catherine McDonald
McDonald	James	Joseph	10-Aug-1902	27-Jul-1902	John McDonald	Feeney, Bridget	James Gilmour	Margart O'Hara
McDonald	Margaret	Agnes	30-Aug-1896	19-Aug-1896	John McDonald	Feeney, Agnes	James Gilmore	Mary Feeney
McDonald	Mary		24-Dec-1893	13-Dec-1893	John McDonald	Feeney, Bridget	Patxrick McDonald	Sara McDonald
McDonald	Mary		17-Feb-1901	12-Feb-1901	Patrick McDonald	Egan, Marjorie	Jerome O'Connor	Hanah Egan
McDonald	Patrick		8-Nov-1914	22-Oct-1914	Patrick McDonald	McCuen, Mary	John McDonal	Ann Callaghan
McDonald	Ann	Rosalie	11-May-1913	27-Apr-1913	Thomas D. McDonald	Timmins, Ellen	James Timmins	Anita Jennings
McDonald	Thomas	Edward	26-Feb-1911	12-Feb-1911	Thomas D. McDonald	Timmons, Nellie	James McDonald	Julia Whitty
McDonald	James		21-Jan-1883	14-Jan-1883	Thomas McDonald	Ward, Rose	R. Burke	Mary A. Flynn
McDonald	John	Francis	31-Oct-1915	17-Oct-1915	Thomas McDonald	Timmons, Helen	John Miller	Catherine Daly
McDonald	Mary	Gertrude	30-Jan-1887	23-Jan-1887	Thomas McDonald	Ward, Rose Ann	John Guerin	Mary Agnes Gill
McDonald	Thomas	Bernard	30-Nov-1884	15-Nov-1884	Thomas McDonald	Ward, Rose Ann	Henry Donovan	Emma Clark
McDonnell	Edward		13-Feb-1898	Jan 1898	Edward McDonnell	McIntyre, Ellen	James Gorman	Mary Gleason
McDonnell	Helen	Genevieve	23-Dec-1894	10-Dec-1894	Edward McDonnell	McIntyre, Mary Helen	John McIntyre	Margaret Mee
McDonnell	James	Gilbert	6-Nov-1904	9-Oct-1904	Edward McDonnell	McIntyre, Helen	Philip Peters	Mary Agnes Peters
McDonnell	Helen	Kinsella	13-Jan-1889	28-Dec-1888	James Edward McDonnell	Kuper, Bernardine	John Joseph McDonnell	Helen Veronica McDonnell
McDonnell	Catherine	Anthony	8-Jan-1905	24-Dec-1904	John McDonnell	Sweeney, Bridget	Richard Murphy	Mary Lundy
McDonnell	Edward	Joseph	24-Feb-1892	25-Dec-1860	John McDonnell	Jones, Emma	Timothy Riordon	
McDonnell	John		11-Jun-1899	01-Jun-1899	John McDonnell	Feeney, Agnes	Martha Garrity	Mary Garrity
McDonnell	John	Joseph	25-Nov-1906	6-Nov-1906	Patrick McDonnell	Egan, Margaret	Maurice Moore	Katherine Moore
McDonnell	John	Joseph	12-Jul-1908	28-Jun-1908	Patrick McDonnell	McKewen, Mary	John Clinton	Frances Smith
McDonnell	Mary	Agnes	5-May-1912	22-Apr-1912	Patrick McDonnell	McKewen, Mary	Michael J. McDonnell	Mary McDonnell
McDonnell	William	Anthony	11-Jan-1903	31-Dec-1902	Patrick McDonnell	Egan, Margaret	John Butler	Sara Butler
McDonough	George	Francis	17-Jan-1904	10-Jan-1904	George Francis McDonough	Kohler, Catherine	Charles Kohler	Mary Kohler
McDonough	Irene	Rosaline	15-Sep-1901	04-Sep-1901	George McDonough	Kohler, Catherine	John Young	Irene Kohler
McDonough	Genevieve		03-Jul-1898	23-Jun-1898	Joan McDonough	Regan, Julia	Martin Regan	Agnes [Blank]
McDonough	Patrick		10-Aug-1899	31-Jul-1899	Patrick McDonough	Eagan, Margaret	John McDonough	Sara McDonough
McDowell/Tydings	Joan		28-Nov-1886	Oct 1862	Robert McDowell	McMullen, Sara		Margaret Holmes
McEnroe	Mary		03-Oct-1886	26-Sep-1886	Patrick McEnroe	Owens, Delia	Peter McEnroe	Mary Owens
McEntee	Ann		18-Dec-1887	12-Dec-1887	Daniel McEntee	Grant, Mary	Henry Wigger	Ann Hamilton
McEntee	Catherine		11-Oct-1885	01-Oct-1885	Daniel McEntee	Grant, Mary	Charles Reagan	Mary Reagan
McEntee	Margaret		18-Mar-1883	04-Mar-1883	Daniel McEntee	Grant, Mary	Peter Grant	Margaret Grant
McEntee	Mary		20-Jul-1890	10-Jul-1890	Daniel McEntee	Egan, Margaret	William Pierce	Margaret Fitzpatrick
McEntee	Catherine	Margaret	26-Jul-1896	10-Jul-1896	Joseph McEntee	Amos, Margaret	Charles Fields	Margaret Parish
McEntee	Joseph	Edward	17-Jun-1900	02-Jun-1900	Joseph McEntee	Amos, Margaret	James Holden	Mary Kraus
McEntee	Mary		20-Jan-1895	05-Jan-1895	Joseph McEntee	Amos, Margaret	Daniel McEntee	Ann Hartman
McEvoy	Patrick		18-Oct-1908	11-Oct-1908	Patrick McElvoy	Brady, Catherine	Edward J. Brady	Agnes Banahan
McEvoy	Mary		6-Jan-1907	31-Dec-1906	Patrick McEvoy	Brady, Catherine	James C. Logue	Agnes Banahan
McEvoy	Joseph		10-Nov-1907	27-Oct-1907	Peter McEvoy	McEvoy, Ann	Joseph Krastel	Ann Finnegan
McEvoy	Leonard		11-Nov-1906	1-Nov-1906	Peter McEvoy	Krester, Ann	Leonard Parker	Ann Finnegan
McFadden	Joseph	John	26-Oct-1913	14-Oct-1913	John McFadden	Kelleher, Catherine	Joseph B. Kelleher	Ellen McFadden
McFarland	James	M.	16-Oct-1904	2-Oct-1904	James M. McFarland	McGee, Mary Cecelia	Edward Curran	Catherine McKenna
McFlin	John	Thomas	19-Oct-1890	27-Sep-1890	James McFlin	Ryan, Kate		Kate Bennett
McGainey	Catherine		25-Jun-1893	13-Jun-1893	James McGainey	Reilly, Ann	John Charles McManus	Catherine Reilly
McGall	Henry	Jerome	06-Mar-1898	12-Dec-1867	Henry McGall	Gamball, Sarah		
McGann	Helen	Frances	01-Aug-1886	14-Jul-1886	Michael J. McGann	Mahoney, Mary Teresa		Mary O'Neil
McGann	Margaret		05-Aug-1888	27-Jul-1888	Michael J. McGann	Mahoney, Mary T.		Eleanor Buckley
McGann	Mary		09-Aug-1885	25-Jul-1885	Michael J. McGann	Mahoney, Mary Teresa		Mary Fitzmaurice
McGann	John	Galvin	28-Sep-1890	17-Sep-1890	Michael James McGann	Mahoney, Mary Teresa	John Galvin	Elizabeth Galvin
McGann	Henry	Donovan	24-Jul-1892	10-Jul-1892	Michael McGann	Mahoney, Mary	David Walsh	Ann Doolin
McGann	William	Morris	04-Aug-1901	28-Jul-1901	William McGann	Boland, Helen	John Boland	Susan Boland
McGarey	Elizabeth		25-Nov-1883	10-Nov-1883	Matthew McGarry	Norray, Mary Ann	Timothy Burns	Mary Cox
McGarrey	Mary	Joseph	14-Dec-1884	22-Dec-1884	Matthew McGarrey	Norray, Mary Ann	Patrick Norray	Ellen Norray
McGarry	Daniel	Carroll	28-Aug-1887	19-Aug-1887	Thomas McGarry	McManus, Mary	Daniel McGarry	Eleanor McManus
McGarry	Leo		29-May-1892	18-May-1892	Thomas McGarry	McManey, Catherine	Henry Nolan	Isabelle Lacy

LAST NAME	FIRST NAME	MIDDLE	BAPTISM	BIRTH	Father	Mother	SPONSORS
McGarvey	Mary		23-Nov-1890	17-Nov-1890	John J. McGarvey	Ward, Ann	Michael McGarvey	Elizabeth Ward
McGarvey	Annabelle		28-Jan-1894	23-Jan-1894	John McGarvey	Ward, Ann	Edward Ward	Margaret Ward
McGarvey	Joseph	Timothy	6-Dec-1914	18-Nov-1914	John McGarvey	O'Hara, Agnes	Timothy Sullivan	Ellen M. Straney
McGarvey	Julian		27-Mar-1898	22-Mar-1898	John McGarvey	Ward, Ann	George Norwood	Mary Ward
McGaw	John	Joseph	05-May-1895	23-Apr-1895	John McGaw	Burke, Mary	William McGaw	Mary Spellman
McGaw	Catherine		24-Jan-1892	10-Jan-1892	Richard McGaw	Gunther, Barbara	Henry Gunther	Catherine Butke
McGaw/Valentine	Mary		13-Nov-1887	13-Jan-1850	William McGaw	Flahart, Mary	Patrick Mason	Julia Mason
McGee	James		25-Feb-1883	[Blank]	Patrick McGee	Cassidy, Elizabeth	John Cassidy	Rolanna McDonald
McGee	James	Elizabeth	20-May-1883	25-Feb-1883	Patrick McGee	Cassidy, Elizabeth	Joan Cassidy	Mary Hopper
McGee	Mary		16-Aug-1885	05-Aug-1885	Patrick McGee	Cassidy, Elizabeth	Thomas McGee	Sarah Ehm
McGee	Genevieve		06-Mar-1893	17-Mar-1879	William McGee	Nace, Elizabeth		Ellen Doyle
McGeeney	Robert	Emmett John	25-Sep-1892	09-Sep-1892	Robert E.J. McGeeney	Young, Gertrude	Johnson McCarthy	Mary McGeeney
McGeeney	Francis	Mary	07-Nov-1897	16-Oct-1897	Robert McGeeney	Young, Gertrude	Leo McGeeney	Ann Quinn
McGill	Richard	Columbus	19-Feb-1882	29-Dec-1881	John William McGill	Ogle, Catherine Theresa		Ida Frederica Ogle
McGin	Edward	Francis	13-Feb-1887	28-Jan-1887	Patrick F. McGin	Lafferty, Mary	John McKew	
McGinn	Aloysius	James	21-Jun-1892	25-Feb-1892	Patrick McGinn	Hand, Joan	Helen Nagle	
McGinn	Anthony		19-Feb-1888	16-Feb-1888	Patrick McGinn	Hand, Joan	Anthony Hand	Helen Hand
McGinn	Bernard	Joseph	12-Jun-1898	23-May-1898	Patrick McGinn	Hand, Joan		Bridget Sheehan
McGinn	John	Leo	14-Mar-1894	11-Feb-1894	Patrick McGinn	Hand, Joan		Julia Tirrala
McGinn	Michael	Joseph	14-Mar-1894	11-Feb-1894	Patrick McGinn	Hand, Joan		Mary Landers
McGinn	Patrick		23-Jun-1895	11-Jun-1895	Patrick McGinn	Hand, Joan	James McKewen	Elizabeth McKewen
McGinn	Edward	James	17-Feb-1884	14-Feb-1884	Thomas McGinn	Hagan, Julia	Francis McGinn	Mary Toland
McGinn	Julia	Virginia	10-Feb-1889	14-Jan-1889	Thomas McGinn	Hogan, Julia Ann	Joseph McGinn	Agnes Dalrymple
McGinn	Samuel	Leona	17-Oct-1886	27-Sep-1886	Thomas McGinn	Hogan, Julia		Mary McGinn
McGinnerty	Elizabeth Virginia		23-Dec-1900	29-Nov-1900	Bernard McGinnerty	O'Keefe, Mary	John O'Keefe	Catherine Jackson
McGinnis	Mary	Agnes	04-Jan-1886	27-Dec-1885	Charles McGinnis	Fox, Rose Ann		Ann Lally
McGinnis	Mary	Agnes	03-May-1896	16-Apr-1896	James McGinnis	Phillips, Mary	Joseph J. Carr	Agnes Cotter
McGinnity	Bernard		21-Aug-1898	10-Aug-1898	Bernard McGinnity	O'Keefe, Mary	Robert Brown	Catherine Jackson
McGinnity	Frances	Elizabeth	05-Jan-1896	21-Dec-1895	Bernard McGinnity	O'Keefe, Mary	James Murname	Catherine Hogan
McGinnity	Mary		04-Oct-1891	28-Sep-1891	Bernard McGinnity	O'Keefe, Mary Agnes	Eager Crosby	Mary McGinnity
McGinnity	Henry		04-Feb-1900	19-Jan-1900	George McGinnity	Lamp, Catherine	Patrick McNamara	Mary Guerin
McGinnity	Francis		05-Feb-1888	18-Jan-1888	Henry McGinnity	Schellenberger, Catherine	Hugh Caulfield	Sara O'Neill
McGinnity	James		18-Feb-1883	10-Feb-1883	Henry McGinnity	Schellenberger, Catherine	James McCluskey	Joan Gelhausen
McGinnity	Teresa		19-Oct-1884	04-Oct-1884	Henry McGinnity	Schellenberger, Catherine	Joan Schellenberger	Virginia Gallahauser
McGinny	Margaret		08-May-1883	22-Apr-1883	Michael McGinny	Smith, Mary Helen	James Washington	Joan Hammack
McGirr	Mary	Alice	29-Jan-1888	12-Jan-1888	Patrick Francis McGirr	Lafferty, Mary Sabino	John William Gallagher	Margaret Colgan
McGlennon	Elizabeth		21-Dec-1886	06-Jan-1886	Michael McGlennon	Schimp, Elizabeth	John Joseph Dunn	Margaret Dunn
McGlone	John	Francis	6-Jul-1913	25-Jun-1913	Joseph McGlone	Walsh, Margaret	George Emge	Margaret Emge
McGlone	Joseph	Martin	7-Nov-1909	29-Oct-1909	Joseph McGlone	Walsh, Margaret	John McGlone	Catherine Walsh
McGlone	Charles	Leon	10-Apr-1904	26-Feb-1904	William T. McGlone	Kearns, Ann Loretta		Catherine Heard
McGlone	Edward	Francis	22-Oct-1893	15-Oct-1893	William Thomas McGlone	Collins, Ann	Francis Charles McGlone	Mary Joan York
McGonigle	Elizabeth	Leona	25-Oct-1903	06-Oct-1903	James L. McGonigle	Culleton, Elizabeth	Laurence J. Callahan	Helen E. Culleton
McGonnigan	Mary	Elizabeth	05-Jun-1883	08-Apr-1883	James McGonnigan	Killeen, Ann		Catherine Havnicht
McGonnigle	Margaret	Matilda	28-Dec-1886	26-Dec-1886	James McGonnigle	Killeen, Ann Bridget	Michael Joseph Owens	Catherine Wetherstine
McGough	Francis	John	16-Oct-1892	05-Oct-1892	Hugh McGough	Ryan, Mary A.		Catherine Ryan
McGovern	John		21-Jun-1885	03-Jun-1885	James F. McGovern	Shaughnessy, Clara M.	Anthony Welby	Mary Ann Dunn
McGovern	Catherine		27-Apr-1913	7-Apr-1913	Thomas McGovern	Leland, Emma	John Redington	Mary Ann Dunn
McGovern	Janette	Rose	14-Oct-1900	11-Oct-1900	Thomas McGovern	Leland, Emma	Patrick Reilly	Fanny Redington
McGovern	Clara		12-Jan-1896	31-Dec-1895	James McGovern	Shaughnessy, Clara	Martin Redington	
McGovern	John	Patrick	17-May-1908	2-May-1908	Thomas McGovern	Leland, Emma	Patrick Leland	Ann McGovern
McGovern	Elizabeth		09-Oct-1887	25-Sep-1887	James P. McGovern	Shaughnessy, Clara	Joseph Shaughnessy	Elizabeth Shaughnessy
McGovern	Mary	Emily	17-Apr-1910	5-Apr-1910	Thomas McGovern	Leland, Emily Theresa	Robert Leland	Bridge Agnes McGovern
McGovern	Raymond	Key	29-Sep-1889	13-Sep-1889	James P. McGovern	Shaughnessy, Clara M.	John Schwind	Joan Schwind
McGovern	Monica		21-Apr-1912	25-Mar-1912	Thomas McGovern	Leland, Emma	Robert Lelend	Margaret Leland
McGovern	James		06-Aug-1882	28-Jul-1882	James Paul McGovern	Shaughnessy, Clara Magdalene	Michael Joseph Owens	Julia Aloysius Tirallo
McGovern	Mildred	Cecelia	10-Apr-1898	29-Mar-1898	Thomas Joseph McGrain	Lanahan, Mary	Thomas Leonard	Cecelia Dolan
McGovern	Julia			05-Oct-1892	James Paul McGovern	Shaughnessy, Clara		Helen Agnes Clara Hynes
McGrain	Thomas	Joseph	22-Mar-1896	12-Mar-1896	Thomas Joseph McGrain	Lanahan, Mary	James McGrain	Mary Ryan
McGrain	Ann	Regina	20-Aug-1893	11-Aug-1893	Thomas McGrain	Lanahan, Mary	John McGrain	Mary Dolan
McGrain	John	Leo	11-May-1890	05-May-1890	Thomas McGrain	Lanahan, Mary	John McGrain	Bridget Lanahan
McGrain	Mary	Catherine	27-Sep-1891	14-Sep-1891	Thomas McGrain	Lanahan, Mary	Daniel Dolan	Ann Dolan
McGran	Catherine		20-Mar-1887	02-Mar-1887	Francis McGran	Donohue, Julia	George Nolan	Bridget Ann Dolan
McGran	Elizabeth		17-Nov-1889	05-Nov-1889	Richard McGran	Gunther, Barbara		

LAST NAME	FIRST NAME	MIDDLE	BAPTISM	BIRTH	Father	Mother	SPONSORS
McGran	Catherine	E.	17-Nov-1889	25-Oct-1889	Wm J. McGran	Hagerty, Teresa	
McGrane	Robert	Lee	04-Dec-1892	20-Nov-1892	William F. McGrane	Holmes, Mary	Frances McGrane
McGrane	Joseph	Edward	08-Jun-1890	28-May-1890	William McGrane	Holmes, Mary	Frances Toner
McGrane	Mary	Ruth	09-Aug-1891	24-Jul-1891	William McGrane	Holmes, Mary	Susan Toner
McGrann	Louis	Andrew	30-Sep-1883	14-Sep-1883	Francis McGrann	Donohoe, Bridget	Joseph Edward Toner
McGrann	Theresa	Elizabeth	02-Feb-1890	12-Jan-1890	Francis McGrann	Donahue, Julia	James Kelly
McGrath	John	Ambrose	28-Dec-1884	07-Dec-1884	John T.V. McGrath	McGrath, Julia	James P. Thornton
McGrath	Catherine		06-Mar-1892	18-Feb-1892	Thomas Joseph McGrath	Manax, Helen	James Hannan
McGraw	Helen		20-Dec-1896	05-Dec-1896	Bernard McGraw	Tensfield, Eugenia	Mary McGrath
McGraw	Rosalind		21-Jul-1895	06-Jul-1895	Bernard McGraw	Murphy, Mary	Wilhelmina Sertz
McGraw	Michael		30-Nov-1890	01-Nov-1890	Jerome Joseph McGraw	McSherry, Alice	Ann Wright
McGraw	Cecelia		29-Mar-1903	04-Mar-1903	Jerome McGraw	Sherry, Alice	Sara McGraw
McGraw	John	Patrick	16-Sep-1888	12-Jul-1888	Jerome McGraw	McSherry, Alice	Cecelia Shaw
McGraw	Leonora	St John	18-Dec-1887	07-Nov-1887	John McGraw	Smith, Frances	Mary Davey
McGraw	Mary		27-Sep-1885	03-Sep-1885	John McGraw	Smith, Frances	Mary Reinhardt
McGraw	Sara		05-May-1889	30-Mar-1889	John McGraw	McGrath, Mary	Ann McGraw
McGraw	William		22-Nov-1883	20-Nov-1883	John McGraw	McGraw, Mary	Mary Quirk
McGraw	John		19-Oct-1902	29-Jun-1902	Nicholas McGraw	Furlong, Margaret	Mary McGraw
McGraw	John	Timothy	12-Jan-1913	28-Dec-1912	Nicholas McGraw	Murphy, Catherine	Katherine Egan
McGraw	Margaret		25-Jul-1897	11-Jul-1897	Nicholas McGraw	Furlong, Margaret	Mary E. Murphy
McGraw	Nicholas		2-Jul-1911	14-Jun-1911	Nicholas McGraw	Murphy, Katherine	Mary Ellis
McGraw	Thomas		24-Apr-1914	18-Apr-1914	Nicholas McGraw	Murphy, Catherine	Margaret McGraw
McGraw	John		29-Dec-1895	18-Dec-1895	Nicolas McGraw	Furlong, Margaret	Margaret McGraw
McGraw	Joseph		07-Oct-1894	25-Sep-1894	Nicolas McGraw	Furlong, Margaret	Catherine Furlong
McGraw	Margaret	Sara	19-Jan-1908	9-Jan-1908	Nicolas McGraw	Murphy, Catherine	Jennie Molloy
McGraw	Thomas		08-May-1892	25-Apr-1892	Nicolas McGraw	Furlong, Margaret	Mary M. Barry
McGraw	Alice		31-Oct-1887	21-Oct-1887	Richard McGraw	Gunther, Barbara	Helen McGraw
McGraw	Florence	May	10-May-1885	29-Apr-1885	Richard McGraw	Gunther, Barbara	Ann McGraw
McGraw	George	Thomas	23-Nov-1890	07-Nov-1890	Thomas McGraw	Cavanaugh, Helen L.	Elizabeth McGraw
McGraw	Catherine	Loretta	30-May-1886	27-May-1886	William McGraw	McKernan, Margaret	Alice E. Cavanaugh
McGraw	Helen	Mary	19-Aug-1900	07-Aug-1900	William McGraw	O'Connor, Mary	Susan McGraw
McGraw	James	Leon	05-Aug-1888	23-Jul-1888	William McGraw	Kernan, Margaret A.	Susie McGraw
McGraw	William		21-Oct-1883	11-Oct-1883	William McGraw	McKernan, Margaret	Ann Owens
McGreevey	Catherine		17-Mar-1889	08-Mar-1889	George L. McGreevey	Griffin, Catherine	Catherine Maguire
McGreevey	George	Louis	26-Jul-1896	14-Jul-1896	George L. McGreevey	Griffin, Catherine	Mary Murray
McGreevey	Helen		22-Nov-1890	14-Nov-1890	George L. McGreevey	Griffin, Catherine	Ann Griffin
McGreevey	James	Francis	06-Mar-1887	21-Feb-1887	George L. McGreevey	Griffin, Catherine	Mary Griffin
McGreevey	Caroline		10-Apr-1883	10-Apr-1883	George Louis McGreevey	Griffin, Catherine	Mary Cummings
McGreevey	Mary	Loretta	23-Aug-1885	15-Aug-1885	George McGreevey	Griffin, Catherine	Margaret Murphy
McGreevey	John	Arthur	20-Jul-1902	20-Jul-1902	John A. McGreevey	Phillips, Nellie	Mary Tate
McGreevey	Edward	Leon	23-Oct-1904	11-Oct-1904	John Arthur McGreevey	Phillips, Elizabeth	Helen Chrystal
McGreevey	Helen	Bernardine	22-Mar-1896	26-Feb-1896	John Arthur McGreevey	Phillips, Elizabeth Mary	Catherine McGreevey
McGreevey	Henry	John	02-Oct-1892	16-Sep-1892	John Arthur McGreevey	Phillips, Elizabeth Mary	Ann Elizabeth Phillips
McGreevey	Mary	Grace	01-Apr-1894	09-Mar-1894	John Arthur McGreevey	Phillips, Elizabeth Mary	Ann Phillips
McGreevey	George	Estelle	16-Sep-1883	27-Aug-1883	Solomon McGreevey	Salsbury, Susan Isabelle	Catherine Moss
McGreevey	Henry		16-Sep-1883	27-Aug-1883	Solomon McGreevey	Salsbury, Susan Isabelle	Catherine Moss
McGreevey	Thomas	Hugh	18-Apr-1905	13-Apr-1880	Thomas McGreevey	Daughton, Martha	Catherine McGreevey
McGreevey	William		28-Dec-1892	03-Sep-1891	Thomas McGreevey	Daughton, Marthy	Rose Cassidy
McGuigan	Catherine		12-Sep-1886	26-Aug-1886	John McGuigan	Baldwin, Caroline	Sara McGuigan
McGuigan	Sarah		12-Sep-1886	26-Aug-1886	John McGuigan	Baldwin, Caroline	Ann Eppler
McGuigan	James	Benjamin	03-Aug-1884	27-Jun-1884	Thomas McGuigan	Murray, Emma	Ann Moan
McGuiness	Ethel	Adele	14-Aug-1898	July 1898	James McGuiness	Phillips, Ann	Helen Sturgeon
McGuiness	Helen	Genevieve	22-Oct-1900	07-Oct-1900	James McGuiness	Phillips, Ann Virginia	Mary Agnes Reilly
McGuiness	Mary	Joseph	13-Dec-1891	02-Dec-1891	Michael Patrick H. McGuiness	McNamara, Mary Ann	Edward E. McNamara
McGuire	Edward		2-May-1911	12-Apr-1911	[Blank]	McGuire, Elizabeth	C. McGinn
McGuire	Genevieve		25-Jan-1905	17-Mar-1902	Daniel T. McGuire	Parish, Emelia	Ellen C. Costella
McGuire	Charles	Franklin	14-Jan-1912	28-Dec-1911	Edgar McGuire	Tompkins, Lillian	Ann Cook
McGuire	Joseph	Albert	16-Mar-1913	21-Feb-1913	Edgar McGuire	Tomkin, Bridget A.	Ann Collins
McGuire	John	William	20-Dec-1885	01-Dec-1885	Edward McGuire	O'Neill, Susan	Mary O'Neill
McGuire	Joseph	Francis	16-Apr-1893	02-Apr-1893	Edward McGuire	O'Neill, Susan	Mary Garvey
McGuire	Mary	Agnes	13-Jan-1889	29-Dec-1888	Edward McGuire	O'Neill, Susan Agnes	Agnes Rigley
McGuire	Susanna		15-Jun-1890	06-Jun-1890	Edward McGuire	O'Neill, Susannah	Francis Patrick Rigley
McGuire	Thomas	Patrick	29-Mar-1885	14-Mar-1885	Edward McGuire	Barron, Mary	Catherine Barron

LAST NAME	FIRST NAME	MIDDLE	BAPTISM	BIRTH	Father	Mother	SPONSORS	
McGuire	Thomas		30-Jul-1896	About 1896	John McGuire	Hopkins, Cecelia		Mary McGuire
McGuire	Ann	Teresa	21-Oct-1906	13-Oct-1906	Patrick McGuire	Mulryan, Margaret	George A. Hall	Mary McKenna
McGuire	Genevieve		02-May-1897	22-Apr-1897	Patrick McGuire	Black, Mary	Peter Duffy	Ann McGuire
McGuire	Helen		26-Feb-1888	12-Feb-1888	Patrick McGuire	Eagan, Mary	John Joseph Woods	Bridget Sweeney
McGuire	Honora		3-Jan-1909	22-Dec-1908	Patrick McGuire	Mulryan, Margaret	Owen McGuire	Mary Eleanor Graley
McGuire	James	Patrick	15-Oct-1899	06-Oct-1899	Patrick McGuire	Black, Mary	Patrick Monaghan	Mary [Blank]
McGuire	John		10-Jan-1897	20-Dec-1896	Patrick McGuire	Muligan, Margaret	Michael Murray	Margaret Murray
McGuire	Mary		04-Sep-1892	29-Aug-1892	Patrick McGuire	Black, Mary	James Logue	Margaret McNally
McGuire	Mary	Ann	27-Nov-1898	14-Nov-1898	Patrick McGuire	[Blank], Margaret	John McKenna	Helen McKenna
McGuire	Matthew		09-Nov-1890	21-Oct-1890	Patrick McGuire	Black, Mary	John Fitzgerald	Ella Fitzgerald
McGuire	James		28-Apr-1901	26-Apr-1901	Patrick Thomas McGuire	Muligan, Margaret		Mary McKenna
McGuire	Charles	Albert	21-Sep-1890	05-Sep-1890	Thomas McGuire	Ege, Laura	Carlisle Penna	Laura White
McHale	Ann		07-Jan-1894	25-Dec-1893	Martin McHale	Holmes, Delia	Stephen Manning	Catherine McCabe
McHale	James	Laurence	01-Aug-1897	30-Jul-1897	Martin McHale	Holmes, Delia	Michael Donahue	Nelly Hamil
McHale	Thomas	Michael	29-Sep-1901	16-Sep-1901	Martin McHale	Holmes, Delia	Robert Colbert	Catherine Casey
McHale	Martin	Thomas	08-Sep-1895	28-Aug-1895	Patrick McHale	Holmes, Delia	Stephen Manion	Sarah Holmes
McHenry	Rebecca		12-Aug-1897	[Blank]	[Blank]	Canby, Susanna	James Reardon	Mary Thompson
McHibin	Matilda	Mary	06-Jul-1897	28-Jun-1897	Ambrose McHibin	Bates, Mary		Mary Cronan
McHugh	Mary		13-Oct-1889	18-Sep-1889	John McHugh	Coffay, Catherine	Michael Kelly	Mary Kelly
McHugh	Thomas		07-Oct-1888	23-Sep-1888	John McHugh	Coffay, Catherine	William Coffay	Mary Coffay
McIntire	Coleman		18-Mar-1900	08-Mar-1900	Ambrose McIntire	[Blank], Catherine	James McIntire	Helen Banaghan
McIntire	Mary		12-Oct-1890	02-Oct-1890	Ambrose McIntire	Hopper, Catherine M.		
McIntyre	Ambrose		31-Jul-1887	19-Jul-1887	AmbMcIntyre, Rose	Hopper, Catherine M.	Thomas Hopper	Mary Kernan
McIntyre	Ambrose		11-Jan-1914	28-Dec-1913	AmbMcIntyre, Rose	Schleifer, Ann	Rose McIntyre	Catherine McIntyre
McIntyre	Ann		16-Dec-1894	08-Dec-1894	AmbMcIntyre, Rose	Hopper, Catherine	Nicolas McIntyre	Mary Hopper
McIntyre	Caherine		06-Nov-1892	25-Oct-1892	AmbMcIntyre, Rose	Hopper, Catherine M.	Owen Hopper	Mary McIntyre
McIntyre	Edward		09-Jun-1901	28-May-1901	AmbMcIntyre, Rose	Hopper, Catherine	Louis Hopper	Veronica Hough
McIntyre	Francis		27-Dec-1885	13-Dec-1885	AmbMcIntyre, Rose	Hopper, Catherine M.	James Glenn	Margaret Giblin
McIntyre	James		04-May-1884	20-Apr-1884	AmbMcIntyre, Rose	Hopper, Catherine	James McIntyre	Mary O'Brien
McIntyre	Elizabeth		18-Apr-1886	17-Nov-1885	Edward McIntyre	[Blank]		Ida E. Scully
McIntyre	James	Leon	25-Apr-1886	18-Apr-1886	Michael McIntyre	Dooris, Joan	Teresa McGann	Joan Dawson
McIntyre	Joseph	Patrick	19-Mar-1882	11-Mar-1882	Michael McIntyre	Dooris, Joan	Phillip McIntyre	Bridget Dalton
McIntyre	Rose	Mary	15-Jun-1884	23-May-1884	Michael McIntyre	Dooris, Joan	John Thomas Northousez	Mary Connolly
McIntyre	Edward	Fabian	3-Feb-1907	21-Jan-1907	Phillip McIntyre	Gallagher, Mary		Mary McGuire
McIntyre	Eugene	Vincent	20-Oct-1882	30-Sep-1882	William McIntyre	Joynes, Margaret Estelle		
McIntyre	Thomas		03-Feb-1884	20-Jan-1884	William McIntyre	Joiner, Margaret	William Joiner	Julia Hanley
McIntyre	William		18-Jul-1886	03-Jul-1886	William McIntyre	Joiner, Margaret	Carl McCabe	Helen McCabe
McKee	Edward	Joseph	05-Aug-1883	01-Aug-1883	Edward McKee	Turgable, Margaret	James Mulligan	Ann Zurgable
McKee	Margaret	Gable	04-Mar-1887	20-Feb-1887	Edward McKee	Gable, Margaret		Margaret Bird
McKenna	Joseph		19-Oct-1902	13-Oct-1902	[Blank] McKenna	Dawson, Mary	George Brown	Catherine McKenna
McKenna	Helen		7-Apr-1907	25-Mar-1907	Bernard J. McKenna	Dorsey, Mary	Wilfred Kidd	Honora Burns
McKenna	James		1-Jun-1911	23-Dec-1910	Bernard Joseph McKenna	Dorsey, Mary	James J. McNulty	Mary McNulty
McKenna	Bernard		4-Nov-1900	23-Oct-1900	Bernard McKenna	Dorsey, Mary	Patrick Mullen	Elizabeth Mullen
McKenna	Bernard		23-Feb-1913	8-Feb-1913	Bernard McKenna	Dorsey, Mary	Bernard McNulty	Elizabeth Koenig
McKenna	Catherine		30-Apr-1899	18-Apr-1899	Bernard McKenna	Dorsey, Mary	Joseph Bryan	Rose Madden
McKenna	Charles		22-Nov-1908	9-Nov-1908	Bernard McKenna	Dawson, Mary	Francis [Blank]	Elizabeth Mullin
McKenna	Elizabeth		7-Jan-1906	29-Dec-1905	Bernard McKenna	Dawson, Mary	William A. Dawson	Helen Dawson
McKenna	Mary		14-Mar-1897	03-Mar-1897	Bernard McKenna	Dorsey, Mary	Peter McKenna	Lily Byrnes
McKenna	Thomas		17-Apr-1904	4-Apr-1904	Bernard McKenna	Dorsey, Mary Agnes	Francis Medcalf	Nora Madden
McKenna	Ann	Mary	09-Nov-1884	01-Nov-1884	Charles McKenna	McCormack, Mary	Hugh Jones	Mary Toner
McKenna	Thomas	Edward	14-Dec-1913	5-Dec-1913	Dennis J. McKenna	Killila, Mary	William Killila	Rose McKenna
McKenna	Mary	Ellen	08-Nov-1891	01-Nov-1891	Felice McKenna	Smith, Anastasia	John Greer	Ellen McKenna
McKenna	Francis	Patrick	11-Apr-1897	28-Mar-1897	Felix McKenna	[Blank], Anastasia	Francis McKenna	Margaret McKenna
McKenna	Margaret		17-Feb-1889	17-Feb-1889	Felix McKenna	Smith, Rose	Thomas Mullen	Rose Kennedy
McKenna	Elizabeth		16-Feb-1913	3-Feb-1913	Francis McKenna	Shipley, Ann	John S. McKenna	Elizabeth Shipley
McKenna	Mary	Elizabeth	15-Oct-1893	02-Oct-1893	James Joseph McKenna	Hebrank, Margaret Mary	Joseph Hebrank	Mary C. Graham
McKenna	Ann		16-Nov-1890	06-Nov-1890	James McKenna	Wiegand, Ann		Teresa Wiegand
McKenna	Carroll	Leo	15-Nov-1891	04-Nov-1891	James McKenna	Murray, Mary Agnes	John Gormly	Catherine Murrary
McKenna	Edward		31-Oct-1897	21-Oct-1897	James McKenna	[Blank], Mary	George Adams	Emma Hamilton
McKenna	Elizabeth	Alice	17-Mar-1895	16-Mar-1895	James McKenna	Hebrank, Mary Margaret	Henry Kline	Elizabeth Alice Moran
McKenna	James	August	30-May-1886	23-May-1886	James McKenna	Wiegand, Ann	James McKenna	Teresa Wiegand
McKenna	John	William	24-Mar-1907	16-Mar-1907	James McKenna	Murray, Mary	Daniel Murray	Catherine Adams
McKenna	Joseph	Eugene	22-Sep-1901	14-Sep-1901	James McKenna	Murray, Mary	Eugene McKenna	Margaret McKenna

LAST NAME	FIRST NAME	MIDDLE	BAPTISM	BIRTH	Father	Mother	SPONSORS
McKenna	Katherine		01-Apr-1900	19-Mar-1900	James McKenna	Murray, Mary	Thomas Grogan, Ann Murray
McKenna	Margaret	Genevieve	8-Jan-1905	27-Dec-1904	James McKenna	Murray, Mary	Albert McKenna, Ann Bishop
McKenna	Mary	Agnes	22-Mar-1896	06-Mar-1896	James McKenna	Hebrank, Margaret	Henry Hebrank, Mary Agnes Hebrank
McKenna	Mary	Irene	23-Feb-1896	15-Feb-1896	James McKenna	Murray, Mary	Daniel Murray, Helen Murray
McKenna	Theresa		01-Jul-1888	27-Jun-1888	James McKenna	Wiegand, Ann	Charles Wiegand, Theresa Wiegand
McKenna	John	Alfred	08-Apr-1894	26-Mar-1894	John Alfred McKenna	Doyle, Agnes	Joseph Jerome Peters, Alice Davis
McKenna	Julia		01-May-1892	22-Apr-1892	John Alfred McKenna	Doyle, Agnes Teresa	William C. Cunningham, Mary Eliz. Cunningham
McKenna	Edward		28-Apr-1889	13-Apr-1889	John E. McKenna	Jeans, Laura	Ida Dellone
McKenna	Edmund	Eugene	02-Jun-1889	31-May-1889	John James McKenna	Ward, Margaret	James McKenna, Mary Ward
McKenna	James	Albert	11-Jun-1893	09-Jun-1893	John James McKenna	Ward, Margaret	John Gibson, Catherine Gibson
McKenna	John	Francis	06-Sep-1891	30-Aug-1891	John James McKenna	Ward, Margaret	Francis Ward, Mary McKenna
McKenna	Catherine	Helen	28-Mar-1897	14-Mar-1897	John McKenna	Ward, Margaret	Francis Ward, Mary McKenna
McKenna	Elizabeth		08-Jul-1894	25-Jun-1894	John McKenna	Murray, Mary Ann	Daniel Donahue, Mary Helen Graley
McKenna	Helen		15-Feb-1885	11-Feb-1885	John McKenna	Murray, Mary	John Murray, Cecelia Flannigan
McKenna	Helen		13-Oct-1896	06-Oct-1896	John McKenna	Doyle, Agnes	
McKenna	James		12-Aug-1900	31-Jul-1900	John McKenna	Heinmiller, Lotta	John Coogan, Rose Coogan
McKenna	Laura	Catherine	25-May-1884	27-Apr-1884	John McKenna	Jeans, Laura	John McShane, Sara Affayroux
McKenna	Margaret		20-Nov-1892	06-Nov-1892	John McKenna	Murray, Mary A.	Michael Murray, Margaret Murray
McKenna	Margaret		23-Feb-1902	19-Feb-1902	John McKenna	Ward, Margaret A.	C.O. Gipson, Mary Kavanaugh
McKenna	Mary		18-Nov-1888	26-Oct-1888	John McKenna	Murray, Mary Ann	Michael McKenna, Mary McKenna
McKenna	Owen		15-Mar-1896	29-Feb-1896	John McKenna	Murray, Mary	John Glenn, Catherine Glenn
McKenna	Catherine		15-Jan-1898	15-Jan-1898	Michael McKenna	[Blank]	William McKenna, Sarah Giblin
McKenna	Edward	Charles	02-Jun-1895	20-May-1895	Michael McKenna	Curry, Mary E.	Chas. W. Hoffert, Mary Price
McKenna	Eugene		07-Oct-1883	25-Sep-1883	Michael McKenna	Curry, Mary Elizabeth	Margaret Hinges
McKenna	Francis	Patrick	16-Jul-1899	03-Jul-1899	Michael McKenna	Curry, Mary	William McKenna, Mary McKenna
McKenna	Helen		07-Feb-1892	17-Jan-1892	Michael McKenna	Curry, Mary Helen	John McKenna, Mary Ann McKenna
McKenna	Ignatius		18-Aug-1889	29-Jul-1889	Michael McKenna	Curry, Mary	John McKenna, Mary McKenna
McKenna	John		03-Oct-1886	23-Sep-1886	Michael McKenna	Curry, Mary E.	John McKenna, Mary McKenna
McKenna	Bernard	J.	28-Sep-1902	08-Sep-1902	Peter F. McKenna	Dawson, Catherine	Bernard McKenna, Helen Dawson
McKenna	Josephine	Calesane	25-Jun-1910	27-Aug-1909	Peter Francis McKenna	Dorsey, Catherine	Bernard Joseph McNulty, Rose Monaghan
McKenna	Elizabeth	Chantal	26-Aug-1913	6-Jun-1913	Peter McKenna	Fitzgerald, Joan	Joan Hughes
McKenna	James		17-May-1904	13-Apr-1904	Peter McKenna	McKenna, Mary	Margaret McFadden
McKenna	Margaret	Bernadette	9-Feb-1908	16-Jan-1908	Peter McKenna	Dorsey, Catherine	Margaret McFadden
McKenna	Mary	Agnes	07-May-1899	27-Apr-1899	Peter McKenna	Dorsey, Catherine	William Dorsey, Mary McNulty
McKenna	Michael	Matthew	16-Feb-1896	05-Feb-1896	Peter McKenna	Dorsey, Catherine	Thomas Madden, Mary Dorsey
McKenna	Peter	Francis	12-Sep-1897	05-Sep-1897	Peter McKenna	Dorsey, Catherine	William Dorsey, Elizabeth Dorsey
McKenna	Rose		16-Dec-1894	07-Dec-1894	Peter McKenna	Dorsey, Catherine	Thomas Madden, Mary McKenna
McKenna	William		09-Dec-1900	24-Nov-1900	Robert McKenna	Sweeney, Eleanor	Bernard McKenna, Rose Madden
McKenna	Eleanor		24-Jan-1886	17-Jan-1886	Robert McKenna	Sweeney, Catherine	Dennis J. Sweeney, Kate A. Sullivan
McKenna	John		14-Feb-1886	02-Feb-1886	William McKenna	McKenna, Mary	Joan Ryan
McKenna	Francis	Patreck	18-Jul-1897	20-Jun-1897	William McKenna	Schuyler, Mary	Elizabeth Anderson
McKenna	Loretta	Beatrice	04-Oct-1891	19-Sep-1891	William McKenna	McEnroe, Mary Theresa	Felix McKenna, Laura V. Connors
McKenna	Mary	Ann	03-Jan-1886	29-Dec-1885	William Owen McKenna	Undress, Minnie	Charles Edward Dalton, Mary Ann Ryan
McKenner	Ann		27-Aug-1890	18-Aug-1890	John M Kenner	Murray, Mary Ann	Patrick Glynn, Ann Glynn
McKeon	Bridget		16-Dec-1888	10-Dec-1888	James McKeon	Hand, Elizabeth	Patrick McGinn, Catherine Shevlin
McKeown	Edward		24-Feb-1884	14-Feb-1884	Felice McKeown	McKeown, Mary	Edward McKeown, Sarah Tohar
McKernan	Edgar		15-Jul-1894	05-Jul-1894	John McKernan	Hawkins, Mary	Frederick Henry, Nelly M. Shields
McKernan	John		06-Dec-1891	04-Nov-1891	John McKernan	Hawkins, Mary	Edgar A. McKenna, Margaret Donnelly
McKernan	Louis		09-Feb-1896	19-Jan-1896	John McKernan	Hawkins, Mary	John Donnelly, Mary Henry
McKevitt	Ann	Mary	8-Sep-1912	7-Sep-1912	Arthur J. McKevitt	McEnroe, Mary	Ann McEnroe
McKevitt	Joseph	Edward	14-Sep-1913	6-Sep-1913	Arthur J. McKevitt	McEnroe, Mary	Thomas Conroy, Mary Conroy
McKevitt	Arthur	Joseph	28-Jun-1908	18-Jun-1908	Arthur Joseph McKevitt	McEnroe, Mary Theresa	J.J. Dillon, Ann McEvoy
McKevitt	Edward	Patrick	7-Feb-1915	30-Jan-1915	Arthur Joseph McKevitt	McEnroe, Mary	Joseph Hintenmack, Margaret Hintenmack
McKevitt	Bridget	Dolores	9-Apr-1911	7-Apr-1911	Arthur McKevitt	McEnroe, Mary	Bridget McEnsor
McKevitt	Catherine		19-May-1889	07-May-1889	Arthur McKevitt	Courtney, Mary	Patrick Hughes, Catherine Hines
McKevitt	Edward		25-May-1883	04-Mar-1883	Arthur McKevitt	Courtney, Mary	James Courtney, Catherine Courtney
McKevitt	Helen		24-Jan-1892	10-Jan-1892	Arthur McKevitt	Courtney, Mary	Joseph Haughhey, Margaret Hoban
McKevitt	Julia		04-Aug-1895	24-Jul-1895	Arthur McKevitt	Courtney, Mary	John Hassian, Ann Baker
McKevitt	Mary	Magdalene	20-Jun-1909	14-Jun-1909	Arthur McKevitt	McEnroe, Margaret	George Lipp, Pauline Hoffman
McKevitt	Catherine		08-Aug-1883	20-May-1883	Edward McKevitt	Welsh, Sara	Mary Russell
McKew	Margaret	Philomena	03-Feb-1889	15-Jan-1889	Luke McKew	Oleson, Harriett	William McKew, Margaret McKew
McKew	Mary		25-Apr-1886	01-Apr-1886	Luke McKew	Oleson, Harriet	John McKew, Mary McKew
McKew	John		13-Dec-1885	06-Dec-1885	Patrick McKew	Dugan, Joan	Charles McKew, Mary Ryan

LAST NAME	FIRST NAME	MIDDLE	BAPTISM	BIRTH	Father	Mother	SPONSORS	
McKew	Thomas	Henry	1-Oct-1905	22-Sep-1905	Thomas H. McKew	O'Neill, Elizabeth	James O'Neill	Margaret McKew
McKew	Harriet		28-Jan-1897	[Blank]	William Henry Oldson McKew	Armstrong, Elizabeth	A. Murray	Jennette McKew
McKewen	Elizabeth		28-Feb-1892	18-Feb-1892	James McKewen	Hand, Elizabeth	Michael Corbit	Mary Clarke
McKewen	James	Leo	29-Jul-1894	18-Jul-1894	James McKewen	Hand, Elizabeth	Patrick McGinn	Joan McGinn
McKewen	Mary		16-Nov-1890	07-Nov-1890	James McKewen	Hand, Elizabeth	Edward French	Ann French
McKewen	Alice	Gertrude	21-Jan-1894	09-Jan-1894	John McKewen	Kelly, Susan	Thomas P. Kennedy	Theresa Kennedy
McKewen	Thomas	Joseph	21-Aug-1892	11-Aug-1892	John McKewen	Kelly, Susan	Thomas Hayden	Mary Kelly
McKewen	Thomas	M.	26-Mar-1905	14-Mar-1905	Michael. F. McKewen	Grogan, Ella	Thomas Fogerty	Ann Fogerty
McKewen	Helen	M.	30-Sep-1906	10-Sep-1906	Michael McKewen	Croghan, Ellen	Arthur Byrnes	Ann Byrnes
McKewen	William	Francis	17-Feb-1909	16-Feb-1909	Michael McKewen	Grogan, Ella		
McKewen	Edward		17-Feb-1884	11-Feb-1884	Patrick McKewen	Dugan, Joan	William Toher	Margaret McKewen
McKewen	John		02-Jan-1887	28-Dec-1886	Patrick McKewen	Dugan, Joan	Charles McKewen	Emma Wernsing
McKlaskey	Sarah	Ann	14-Feb-1897	29-Jan-1897	William McKlaskey	Leimbach, Elizabeth	John M. Harkins	Bridget Harkins
McKoitt	Mary		24-May-1885	10-May-1885	Arthur McKoitt	Courtney, Mary	Pascal Serio	Julia Serio
McKuen	John		07-Mar-1886	28-Feb-1886	Felice McKuen	McKuen, Mary	William Tohey	Joan (Jane) McKuen
McLain	Bernard	V.	22-Oct-1905	12-Oct-1905	Francis E. McLain	Wamback, Minnie	Bernard V. Kelly	Frances Kelly
McLain	Agnes	Teresa	18-Jan-1903	07-Jan-1903	Francis McLain	Wanbach, Filomena	O.J. Kelly	Mary Manning
McLain	Arthur	Eugene	09-May-1897	23-Apr-1897	Francis McLain	Wamback, Mary	Peter Smith	Mary Kelly
McLain	Catherine		14-Jul-1889	04-Jul-1889	Francis McLain	Wanebach, Wilhelmina	Patrick McLain	Catherine McLain
McLain	Eugene	Edward	15-Apr-1900	25-Mar-1900	Francis McLain	Wamback, Minnie	Eugene Murphy	Ann Adler
McLain	George		03-Apr-1887	26-Mar-1887	Francis McLain	Wamback, Mary	George Wamback	Mary Kelly
McLain	Margaret	Catherine	02-Dec-1894	16-Nov-1894	Francis McLain	Wamback, Mary	Patrick McLain	Catherine McLain
McLain	Mary	Agnes	03-Dec-1885	29-Nov-1885	Francis McLain	Wamback, Wilhelmina		GeorgeAnn Glenn Demske
McLain	Robert	Cleveland	23-Nov-1890	15-Nov-1890	Francis McLain	Wamback, Wilhelmina	Edward A. Ruckle	Sarah Kelly
McLain	William	Patrick	11-Mar-1896	10-Mar-1896	Francis McLain	Wamback, Mary		
McLain	William	Patrick	09-Oct-1898	21-Sep-1898	Francis McLain	Wamback, Mary	Patrick McLain	Katherine McLain
McLain	Helen	Laura	15-Jan-1893	30-Dec-1892	George McLane	Wamback, Wilhelmina	John Kelly	Mary Kelly
McLain	George	Francis	2-Feb-1913	12-Feb-1913	George McLain	Shanahan, Mary		Loretta McLain
McLaughlin	Catherine		13-Jul-1890	07-Jul-1890	[Blank]	McLaughlin, Helen		Mary Elizabeth McLaughlin
McLaughlin	Adalaide	Celeste	09-Oct-1893	27-Sep-1893	Charles J. McLaughlin	Bishop, Adalaide		Isabelle McLaughlin
McLaughlin	Mary	Josephine	12-Jun-1898	01-Jun-1898	Charles J. McLaughlin	Bishop, Adalaide		Celest McLaughlin
McLaughlin	Charles	Alexander Jordan	25-Aug-1907	11-Aug-1907	Charles McLaughlin	Bishop, Adalaide		Celeste McLaughlin
McLaughlin	Irene	Isabelle	10-Dec-1895	16-Nov-1895	Charles McLaughlin	Bishop, Adalaide		Mary McLaughlin
McLaughlin	Lucy	Cecelia	25-May-1902	18-May-1902	Charles McLaughlin	Bishop, Adalaide		Celeste McLaughlin
McLaughlin	James		16-Sep-1900	07-Sep-1900	Groden McLaughlin	Morris, Delia	Thomas Colbert	Katherine Connell
McLaughlin	Mary		16-Sep-1897	03-Mar-1897	Grovan Joseph McLaughlin	Morris, Ada	Matthew J. Connolly	Nora O'Connell
McLaughlin	James	Francis	19-Mar-1893	03-Mar-1893	Hugh McLaughlin	Murphy, Mary E.	Charles Murphy	Agnes Murphy
McLaughlin	Mary	Agnes	12-May-1895	01-May-1895	Hugh McLaughlin	Murphy, Mary Helen	Joseph Murphy	Mary Hooper
McLaughlin	Genevieve		29-Apr-1900	13-Apr-1900	Hugo McLaughlin	Murphy, Mary	James Hooper	Mary Hooper
McLaughlin	Ann		20-Aug-1899	14-Aug-1899	James McLaughlin	McGannon, Catherine	John Burns	Margaret Burns
McLaughlin	James		10-May-1891	02-May-1891	James McLaughlin	Gannon, Catherine	John Logue	Mary Wess
McLaughlin	John	Patrick	12-Dec-1897	08-Dec-1897	James McLaughlin	Gannon, Catherine Winifred	John Burns	Margaret Byrnes
McLaughlin	Mary		14-Aug-1892	08-Aug-1892	James McLaughlin	Gannon, Catherine Winifred	Thomas Comella	Ann Comella
McLaughlin	Thomas	Joseph	01-Sep-1901	11-Aug-1901	James McLaughlin	Gannon, Catherine	Joseph Mills	Mary O'Day
McLaughlin	William	Edward	14-Aug-1904	11-Aug-1904	James McLaughlin	Gannon, Catherine	William Gannon	Isabelle Caton
McLaughlin	James	Frederick Floyd	24-Dec-1893	05-Dec-1893	Peter McLaughlin	Bourne, Catherine	William McLaughlin	Rose Tierney
McLaughlin	Thomas		11-Jun-1911	29-May-1911	Thomas F. McLaughlin	Watkins, Elizabeth	Thomas G. Watkins	Mary Burgison
McLaughlin	William	James	12-Jun-1910	1-Jun-1910	Thomas McLaughlin	Watkins, Elizabeth	James McLaughlin	Mary Watkins
McLean	William	West	22-Dec-1885	14-Oct-1885	William B. McLean	Cropsey, Deborah A.		George Ann McLean
McLinden	John	Joseph	29-Dec-1889	15-Dec-1889	John McLinden	O'Brien, Lizzie	John Crowley	
McMahon	Mary		24-Apr-1898	13-Apr-1898	Arthur McMahon	Eagan, Mary	Bernard McMahon	Ann McMahon
McMahon	Genevieve		27-Jul-1890	18-Jul-1890	Bernard McMahon	Gillen, Mary	G. McMahon	M. Gerrity
McMahon	Leo	Bernard	17-Feb-1895	13-Feb-1895	Bernard McMahon	Gillen, Mary	Patrick Gillen	Mary Maynes
McMahon	Thomas	James	26-Nov-1893	19-Nov-1893	Felice Patrick McMahon	Conlon, Elizabeth	Andrew Conlon	Mary Kenny
McMahon	Catherine	Mary	16-Mar-1913	16-Dec-1898	George McMahon	McCleary, V.	Michael [Blank]	Mary Catherine [Blank]
McMahon	Charles	William	16-Sep-1894	31-Aug-1894	James McMahon	Strassberger, Mary		Elizabeth Seibert
McMahon	Mary	Elizabeth	10-Feb-1901	27-Jan-1901	James McMahon	Strassberger, Mary	John Snyder	Elizabeth Snyder
McMahon	Francis	Xavier	3-Oct-1909	15-Sep-1909	James W. McMahon	Strassberger, Mary		Mary Whitney
McMahon	Joseph	Francis	3-Oct-1909	15-Sep-1909	James W. McMahon	Strassberger, Mary		Mary Whitney
McMahon	Charles	Francis	18-Jul-1909	19-Aug-1902	James William McMahon	Strassberger, Mary		Mary Whitney
McMahon	Helen	Loretta	13-Mar-1898	20-Feb-1898	James William McMahon	Strassberger, Ann Philomena		Helen Strassberger
McMahon	Mary	Ruth	11-Jul-1909	2-Mar-1905	James William McMahon	Strassberger, Mary		Mary Whitney
McMahon	Mildred	Catherine	17-Jan-1904	1-Jan-1904	John Joseph McMahon	O'Neill, Ann		Mary Manlon

LAST NAME	FIRST NAME	MIDDLE	BAPTISM	BIRTH	Father	Mother	SPONSORS
McMahon	Helen		17-Nov-1895	06-Nov-1895	John McMahon	Holden, Mary	John Russell	Mary Ann Kelly
McMahon	John	Howard	17-Jan-1892	03-Jan-1892	John McMahon	Hogan, Mary E.	Thomas Hogan	Ellen Tracey
McMahon	Leonard		13-Nov-1898	05-Nov-1898	John McMahon	Hogan, Mary		Ann Brown
McMahon	Wilmer		15-Dec-1889	08-Dec-1889	John McMahon	Hogan, Mary Helen	William Hogan	Agnes O'Neill
McMahon	Mary	Margaret	05-Jun-1887	04-May-1887	John T. McMahon	Hogan, Mary B.	William Gough	Catherine McMahon
McMahon	Austin	Joseph	23-Oct-1901	9-Nov-1900	Joseph McMahon	Hanlon, Martha		Margaret Miller
McMahon	Mary	Rose	17-Oct-1887	03-Aug-1897	Joseph McMahon	Henlon, Martha	William Oats	Alice Oats
McMahon	Catherine		4-Dec-1904	5-Nov-1904	Phillip J. McMahon	Murphy, Ann	James McMahon	Mary McNulty
McMahon	Mary	Regina	08-Jan-1899	26-Dec-1898	Thomas McMahon	Wentz, Theresa	James Manning	M.M. Snopor
McMaines	Rose	Mary	25-Apr-1915	9-Apr-1915	William McMaines	Wolsey, Ann	James Mullin	Mary Russell
McManus	Joseph		17-Oct-1915	5-Oct-1915	[Blank]	McManus, Violetta		Elizabeth Mullen
McManus	John	Francis	16-Mar-1884	10-Mar-1884	Bernard McManus	O'Connell, Hannah	John McManus	Margaret O'Connell
McManus	Alice	Theresa	29-Jun-1884	23-Jun-1884	Henry McManus	Minahan, Alice	John Minahan	Joan Reedy
McManus	Francis		22-Oct-1885	12-Oct-1885	John McManus	Linton, Elizabeth		Mary McManus
McManus	John		18-Feb-1883	[Blank]	John McManus	Linton, Elizabeth	John Hogan	Catherine Welsh
McManus	Lydia		21-Nov-1889	19-Oct-1868	John McManus	Moss, Mary		
McManus	Catherine		23-Feb-1887	08-Feb-1887	John T. McManus	Linton, Elizabeth		Catherine C. Kelly
McManus	Ann		18-Aug-1889	29-Jul-1889	John Thomas McManus	Linton, Elizabeth	Hugh McManus	Margaret Melie
McManus	James	Lindsay	20-Sep-1885	05-Sep-1885	Martin J. McManus	Lindsay, Margaret	Henry J. Campbell	Ella R. Ward
McManus	Leon	Gibbons	27-Apr-1902	07-Apr-1902	Martin J. McManus	Lindsay, Margaret	James McManus	Ann Gage
McManus	Martin		24-May-1891	13-May-1891	Martin J. McManus	Lindsay, Mary	John Kelly	Euphenia Lindsay
McManus	Vincent	Alexander	15-Oct-1893	27-Sep-1893	Martin Joseph McManus	Lindsay, Margaret G.	John N. Nelligan	Ann Gage
McManus	Charles	Eugene	07-Nov-1897	19-Oct-1897	Martin McManus	Lindsay, Margaret	Patrick McManus	Mary McManus
McManus	Mary	Euphemian	18-Mar-1888	05-Mar-1888	Martin McManus	Lindsay, Margaret	Michael Lynch	Mary McManus
McManus	Martin	Joseph	20-Mar-1887	06-Mar-1887	Patrick James McManus	O'Keefe, Mary	Martin McManus	Margaret McManus
McManus	Bernard	Emmett	21-May-1882	09-May-1882	Patrick McManus	O'Keefe, Mary	James B. Riordan	Susan T. Eagan
McManus	Robert		09-Nov-1884	26-Oct-1884	Patrick McManus	O'Keefe, Mary	John Kilfoyle	Helen Kilfoyle
McManus	William		24-Aug-1882	22-Aug-1882	William Sinnott	Bubbons, Mary Jane		
McNally	Clara		05-Dec-1899	23-Nov-1899	Alice McNally	Healy, Clara	Francis Nugent	Mary Keenan
McNally	Edgar	Phillip	11-Apr-1909	4-Apr-1909	Bernard A. McNally	Herzog, Bertha	Phillip Herzog	Bertha Herzog
McNally	Hugo	Bernard	12-Jan-1908	29-Dec-1907	Bernard A. McNally	Herzold, Bertha	Anthony Albert	Mary McNally
McNally	Joseph	John	17-Sep-1882	04-Sep-1882	Bernard McNally	Gutberlet, Teresa	Joseph Gutberlet	Florence Gutberlet
McNally	Charles	A.	21-Aug-1904	15-Aug-1904	Charles P. McNally	Connolly, Stella	John Connolly	Teresa McNally
McNally	Ellen	Loretta	19-Sep-1909	13-Sep-1909	Charles P. McNally	Connolly, Stella	Frank Connelly	Florence McNally
McNally	Cecelia		19-Apr-1903	04-Apr-1903	Felice A. McNally	Healy, Clara	Louis Sherman	Elizabeth Sherman
McNally	Edward		11-Apr-1897	03-Apr-1897	Felice A. McNally	Healy, Clara	William McLaughlin	Rose Lawler
McNally	James	Joseph	19-Apr-1903	04-Apr-1903	Felice A. McNally	Healy, Clara	James Healy	Genevieve Keenan
McNally	Alice		22-Mar-1896	06-Mar-1896	Felice McNally	Healy, Clara	Hugh Callahan	Emma Hanlon
McNally	Mary		12-Jun-1898	08-Jun-1898	Felice McNally	Healy, Clara	Edward Healy	Alice McNally
McNally	Mary	Agnes	14-May-1882	02-May-1882	Henry McNally	Flynn, Julia	Thomas Campbell	Mary McNally
McNally	Mary		20-Mar-1892	11-Mar-1892	John Francis McNally	Clines, Elizabeth Amelia	Felix McNally	Ann McNally
McNally	John		02-Feb-1890	25-Feb-1890	John McNally	Cline, Lizzie	John McNally	Alice McNally
McNally	Francis	Xavier	09-Dec-1888	08-Dec-1888	Joseph Henry McNally	Hoban, Helen A.	Francis Michael Hoban	Anastasia Laura Malloy
McNally	John		26-Nov-1893	15-Nov-1893	Joseph Henry McNally	Hoban, Helen A.	Michael Joseph Martin	Catherine Cain
McNally	Mary		14-Dec-1884	05-Dec-1884	Joseph Martin McNally	Hoban, Helen A.	John McNally	Sarah E. Hoban
McNally	Jesse	Francis	21-Feb-1886	14-May-1885	Joseph McNally	Marsh, Frances	Michael Cassidy	Winifred Connolly
McNally	Joseph		02-May-1886	24-Apr-1886	Joseph McNally	Hoban, Eldora	John Delaney	Mary Ward
McNally	Sara		01-Mar-1891	26-Feb-1891	Joseph McNally	Hoban, Ella	John J. Rock	Elizabeth Hoban
McNally	Mary	Francis	02-Jun-1895	26-May-1895	Edward McKenna	Casey, Kate	Bart. Gehardz	Agnes Casey
McNamara	Ann	Mary	04-Sep-1898	23-Aug-1898	Edward McNamara	Casey, Catherine	James Conlon	Margaret Nevin
McNamara	Edward	Aloysius	21-Jun-1891	15-Jun-1891	Edward McNamara	Cassidy, Catherine	Michael P. McGuiness	Gertrude Casey
McNamara	Joseph		08-Mar-1893	07-Mar-1893	Edward McNamara	Casey, Catherine	Dunn, Mary igan	Laurence Carton
McNamara	A. Walsh		3-Jul-1904	28-Jun-1904	Patrick J. McNamara	Walsh, Anastasia	Michael Molloy	Margaret Guerins
McNamara	Mary	Loretta	25-Feb-1900	20-Feb-1900	Patrick McNamara	Walsh, Ann	John McNamara	Catherine Walsh
McNamee	Ann		28-May-1882	21-May-1882	James McNamee	Almony, Catherine		Ann Williams
McNamee	Elizabeth	Frances	01-May-1887	18-Apr-1887	James McNamee	Almony, Catherine		Ann Helling
McNamee	Martin		27-Apr-1884	19-Apr-1884	James McNamee	Almony, Catherine	Martin Gosman	Ann Mears
McNamera	Patrick	Joseph	23-Jun-1901	21-Jun-1901	Patrick Joseph McNamera	Walsh, Anastasia	Timothy McNamera	Honora McNamera
McNeal	Julia		10-May-1885	06-May-1885	Michael McNeal	Burns, Ann	Patrick McNeal	Agnes Gill
McNeil	Walter		12-May-1894	02-Aug-1894	George E. McNeil	Bennett, Elizabeth	Walter McCardel	Margaret Anderson
McNeil	Michael	Thomas	27-Nov-1887	20-Nov-1887	Michael McNeil	Byrne, Ann	Patrick McNeil	Catherine Mears
McNeill	Ann	Ellen	09-Mar-1884	07-Mar-1884	Michael McNeill	Burns, Ann	John W. Gallagher	Mary Murray
McNeir	Lillian		26-Jun-1898	10-Jun-1898	Andrew McNeir	Jenkins, Mary M.	Joseph Dunn	Ann Dietrich

LAST NAME	FIRST NAME	MIDDLE	BAPTISM	BIRTH	Father	Mother	SPONSORS	
McNever	John	Andrew	11-Aug-1901	29-Jul-1901	Andrew McNever	Jenkins, Mary	Francis Jenkins	Margaret Jenkins
McNicholas	Richard		15-Dec-1889	07-Dec-1889	Thomas McNicholas	Hughes, Bridget	Gilbert Hughes	Elizabeth McDonough
McNulty	Joseph		01-Feb-1898	27-Jan-1898	Bernard McNulty	McKenna, Mary	John Clifford	Katherine Meehan
McNulty	Brian	Bernard	04-Aug-1895	24-Jul-1895	Brian McNulty	McKenna, Mary	Bernard McKenna	Elizebeth Hoban
McNulty	Leo	Patrick	22-Apr-1900	08-Apr-1900	Brian McNulty	McKenna, Mary Elizabeth	Thomas Flaherty	Mamie O'Sullivan
McNulty	Andrew		14-Oct-1888	30-Sep-1888	Daniel McNulty	Dennert, Catherine	Andrew Dennert	Esther Day
McNulty	Elroy	Edward	30-Mar-1890	03-Mar-1890	Daniel McNulty	Dennert, Catherine	John Hoffman	Margaret Parrish
McNulty	Gertrude	Mary	04-Sep-1892	19-Aug-1892	Daniel McNulty	Dennert, Catherine		Mary Parrish
McNulty	Margaret		05-Sep-1897	19-Aug-1897	Daniel McNulty	Dennert, Catherine	Henry Parish	Catherine Fay
McNulty	William	Henry	11-Apr-1886	31-Mar-1886	Daniel McNulty	Bond, Georgia	Henry Nolan	Sara McNulty
McNulty	Thomas	Burnett	24-Apr-1892	30-Mar-1892	Henry C. McNulty	Bond, Georgia	Thomas McNulty	Virginia McNulty
McNulty	Genevieve	Bond	04-Jan-1891	05-Dec-1890	Henry McNulty	Bond, Georgia	John T. Mooney	Margaret Trainor
McNulty	Mary	Virginia	16-Mar-1884	24-Jan-1884	Henry McNulty	Bond, Georgia		Mary Ott
McNulty	Ann	Elizabeth	15-May-1887	27-Apr-1887	Henry William McNulty	Bond, Georgia		Mary Kolb
McNulty	George	Bond	22-Apr-1894	04-Mar-1894	Henry William McNulty	Bond, Georgia		Margaret Ann Trainor
McNulty	Ann		13-Jun-1897	05-Jun-1897	James McNulty	O'Neill, Rose	Louis O'Neill	Bridget Mannion
McNulty	Elena		06-Aug-1899	29-Jul-1899	James McNulty	O'Neill, Rose	James McDonnell	Catherine Bannon
McNulty	George	Michael	15-Oct-1882	01-Oct-1882	James McNulty	Ellis, Emma	William Michael Keleher	Mary McNamara
McNulty	James		27-Jul-1902	20-Jul-1902	James McNulty	O'Neil, Rose	Patrick O'Neil	Frances O'Neil
McNulty	John	Edward	27-Dec-1885	12-Dec-1885	James McNulty	Bell, Emma	John McNamara	Genevieve McNamara
McNulty	Rose		13-Aug-1905	6-Aug-1905	James McNulty	O'Neill, Rose	Hugh Bannon	Helen O'Neil
McNulty	James	Michael	27-May-1888	10-May-1888	James P. McNulty	Ellis, Emma	Michael J. Scully	Catherine Connolly
McNulty	Patrick		21-Mar-1895	17-Mar-1895	K. McNulty	Scott, David		Kate McNulty
McNulty	Annabelle	Mary	16-Dec-1888	06-Dec-1888	Thomas Francis McNulty	McNulty, Clare, Mary	John Andrew McGarry	Catherine McGarrity
McNulty	Eliza	Genevieve	25-Mar-1883	04-Mar-1883	Thomas Francis McNulty	McGarrity, Clara	James Edward McGarrity	Elizabeth Jones
McPhee	John	Victor	24-Apr-1887	21-Apr-1887	Hugh McPhee	McKenney, Helen	James B. McGoldrick	Catherine McKenney
McPherson	Mary	Grace	15-Oct-1893	27-Sep-1893	David L. McPherson	Hooper, Everista	Julia Kemp	Mary L. Kemp
McPherson	Everista		14-Apr-1889	02-Apr-1889	David McPherson	Hooper, Everista		Mary Hooper
McPoland	Lillian	Mary	20-Sep-1914	29-Aug-1914	Charles McPoland	Simms, Ida M.	Louis Klein	Lillian Lemon
McQuade	Ann	Mary	11-Mar-1906	20-Feb-1906	Francis McQuade	Barry, Elizabeth		Mary McDonald
McQuade	James	Edward	6-Dec-1908	23-Nov-1908	James Edward McQuade	Barry, Elizabeth Mary		Eleanor Dailey
McQuaid	Charles	Michael	16-Sep-1900	14-Aug-1900	James McQuaid	Kelledy, Mary	Michael Birmingham	Mary Birmingham
McQuaid	Catherine		9-Jul-1911	25-May-1911	James McQuaid	Killety, Elizabeth		Della Halloran
McQuaid	James		20-Mar-1898	28-Feb-1898	James McQuaid	[Blank], Elizabeth	William Holden	Elizabeth Holden
McQuillan	Catherine		11-Feb-1894	05-Feb-1894	Edward McQuillan	Clarke, Mary Ann	Patrick McGlone	Margaret Connolly
McQuillan	Francis	Edmund	27-May-1894	13-May-1894	Hugh McQuillan	Cavanaugh, Mary	John F. Cain	Mary E. Cain
McQuillan	Mary	Elizabeth	16-Sep-1891	10-Aug-1891	Hugh McQuillan	Kavanaugh, Mary	Francis McGinnis	Joan McGinnis
McQuillan	Hugh		26-Dec-1886	16-Dec-1886	John McQuillan	O'Brien, Mary	Henry McGinnis	Mary McGinnis
McQuillan	Margaret	Mary	21-Oct-1883	09-Oct-1883	John McQuillan	O'Brien, Mary	Francis McGinnis	Ann King
McRory	William		2-Nov-1907	13-Oct-1907	James Joseph McRory	Lamp, Bertha	Walter Sturgeon	Irene Sturgeon
McShane	Alice		26-Aug-1900	09-Aug-1900	Charles McShane	Glenn, Catherine	John P. Glean	Martha Wallace
McShane	Arthur		29-Nov-1896	17-Nov-1896	Charles McShane	Glenn, Catherine	John Casey	Margaret Casey
McShane	Charles		05-Jan-1890	30-Dec-1889	Charles McShane	Glenn, Kate	William B. Demfay	Mamie [Blank]
McShane	John		04-Sep-1898	20-Aug-1898	Charles McShane	Glenn, Katherine	Martin Freeman	Bridget McShane
McShane	Mary		07-May-1893	26-Apr-1893	Charles McShane	Glenn, Catherine	Edward J. Wallace	Mary Ryan
McShane	Elizabeth		25-Jan-1897	About 1870	James Patterson McShane	Alexander, Joan		Catherine Mettee
McShane	Francis	Peter	16-Jul-1893	28-Jun-1893	John F. McShane	Affayroux, Mary Joan	Thomas McVay	Sarah McVay
McShane	Joseph	Terence	31-Mar-1889	19-Mar-1889	John F. McShane	Affayroux, Mary J.	Charles J. Hayes	Ann Canby
McShane	C.inne	Mary	23-Jul-1882	08-Jul-1882	John Francis McShane	Affayroux, Mary Joan	Joan Frances Affayroux	Mary Catherine McCarron
McShane	Charles	Elizabeth	20-Mar-1887	04-Mar-1887	John Francis McShane	Affayroux, Mary Joan	Patrick McCarthy	Joan Cook
McShane	Henry	Francis	21-Sep-1884	31-Aug-1884	John McShane	Affayroux, Mary Jane	Charles McShane	Sallie Affayroux
McShane	Thomas	Julian	12-Apr-1891	24-Mar-1891	John McShane	Affayroux, Mary J.	Charles Lynch	Elizabeth McShane
McShane	Albert		24-May-1882	08-Apr-1882	Peter Alex. Charles McShane	Case, Sara Lucy	James McDevitt	Catherine Lacy
McShane	Walter	Hiram	24-May-1882	08-Apr-1882	Peter Alex. Charles McShane	Case, Sara Lucy	James McDevitt	Mary Lacy
McShane	William	Aloysius	19-Sep-1897	03-Sep-1897	Timothy McShane	Paterson, Elizabeth Mary	John McComb	Catherine McComb
McShane	Ann		25-Aug-1896	04-Mar-1824	William [Blank]	Pugh, Ester		
McSweeney	Daniel		20-Dec-1885	12-Dec-1885	William McSweeney	Hurley, Ann	John McAuliffe	Nora Hurley
McSweeney	William		18-May-1884	13-May-1884	William McSweeny	Herlihy, Ann	John McKenna	Ann McKenna
McTighe	Margaret		10-Apr-1898	26-Mar-1898	John McTighe	Nolan, Margaret	Michael Nolan	Catherine Nolan
McTighe	Mary		05-Aug-1900	18-Jul-1900	John McTighe	Nolan, Margaret	James Clancy	Elizabeth McMahon
McTighe	Patrick	Leon	27-Mar-1904	11-Mar-1904	John McTighe	Nolan, Margaret	Edward Nolan	Mary Casserly
McVay	Lillian	Mary	21-Jan-1894	03-Jan-1894	Thomas McVay	Affayroux, Sara	John S. Corcoran	Catherine Corcoran
McWhirter	Albert	Eugene	14-Apr-1891	06-Apr-1891	John J. McWhirter	Lynch, Elizabeth		

LAST NAME	FIRST NAME	MIDDLE	BAPTISM	BIRTH	Father	Mother	SPONSORS
McWhirter	Mary	Helen	09-Jul-1893	16-Jun-1893	John Joseph McWhirter	Lynch, Elizabeth	Charles Lynch / Alice Crowley
McWhirter	Elizabeth	Helen	19-Jul-1896	08-Jul-1896	John McWhirter	Lynch, Elizabeth	Charles Lynch / Elizabeth Crowley
McWhirter	Matilda		04-Sep-1887	26-Aug-1887	John McWhirter	Lynch, Elizabeth	James Wallace / Catherine Shaughnessy
McWilliams	James		29-Dec-1907	29-Dec-1907	John McWilliams	Hart, Mary	
McWilliams	Joseph	Patrick	21-Apr-1912	2-Apr-1912	John McWilliams	Hart, Martha	James Hart / Ann [Blank]
McWilliams	Mary	Catherine	13-May-1906	1-May-1906	John McWilliams	Hart, Joan	John J. Craven / Catherine Dowd
McWilliams	Rose		03-Aug-1902	16-Jul-1902	John McWilliams	Hart, Joan	James Hart / Catherine Crage
McWilliams	Agnes	Teresa	10-Jan-1909	28-Dec-1908	John Thomas McWilliams	Hart, Mary Jane	John Mulroy / Catherine Hart
McWilliams	John	Thomas	26-Jun-1904	13-Jun-1904	John Thomas McWilliams	Hart, Jane	Maurice Hoppert / Mary Craben
Mea	Mary	Loretta	13-Jan-1884	21-Dec-1883	James Mea	Quigley, Mary Angela	George Blondell / Mary May
Meade	Rose Ann		1-Aug-1915	16-Jul-1915	Charles Meade	Gunder, Ann	Grace Hall
Meade	Emma	Cordelia	13-Apr-1883	18-Aug-1883	John Meade	Johnson, Susan	Susan Somerville
Meagher	Mary	Margaret	26-Aug-1883	13-Aug-1883	Patrick Joseph Meagher	Leahey, Mary	James Leahey / Mary Shanahan
Medary	George	Curtis	11-Jun-1899	09-Feb-1899	John Medary	Rock, Catherine	Matilda Rock
Medshank	Catherine		05-Jan-1896	28-Dec-1895	Timothy Medshank	Patterson, Elizabeth	Minnie Patterson
Mee	Joseph		31-May-1914	22-May-1914	Luke Joseph Mee	O'Neill, Ann Mary	Milton Gross / Katherine O'Neill
Meehan	Charles	Edward	12-Jun-1887	27-May-1887	James Meehan	Sullivan, Sarah	James P. O'Connor / Agnes Sullivan
Meehan	James	William	07-Mar-1886	19-Feb-1886	James Meehan	Sullivan, Sarah	Edward Meehan / Margaret Sullivan
Meehan	Sarah	Katherine	21-Oct-1897	06-Oct-1897	James Meehan	Sullivan, Sarah	William Sullivan / Florence Brady
Meehan	Jerome		03-Jul-1892	11-Jun-1892	James V. Meehan	Sullivan, Sara	John Brady / Mary Moylan
Meehan	Raymond		23-Dec-1888	10-Dec-1888	James V. Meehan	Sullivan, Sara	Edward Meehan / Florence C. Sullivan
Meehan	Robert		27-May-1894	15-May-1894	James V. Meehan	Sullivan, Sara J.	John J. Moylan / Ellen Moylan
Meehan	Ellen	Moylan	12-Nov-1884	25-Oct-1884	John Moylan	Meehan, Mary Ann	James Moylan / Mary McKenna
Meers	Agnes	Jane	25-Oct-1903	20-Oct-1903	John M. Meers	Lemmon, Mary E.	James McKenna / Jane Agnes O'Donnell
Meers	Mary	Virginia	16-Oct-1910	3-Oct-1910	John M. Meers	Lemmon, Mary	James M. Daily / Mary B. Lemmon
Meers	James		05-Feb-1899	23-Jan-1899	Martin Meers	Ward, Catherine	Bernard P. Wess / Ann Meers
Meers	John	Joseph	23-Sep-1888	09-Sep-1888	Mortimer F. Meers	Ward, Catherine	Michael Fitzpatrick / Mary Cuddy
Meers	Mark		01-Aug-1886	16-Jul-1886	Mortimer F. Meers	Ward, Catherine	John J. Ward / Catherine McClelland
Meers	Michael	James	10-Dec-1895	19-Nov-1895	Mortimer Francis Meers	Ward, Catherine	John P. Byrnes / Margaret Burns
Meers	Francis	C.	06-Oct-1901	25-Sep-1901	Mortimer Meers	Ward, Catherine	John M. Meers / Helen Halloran
Meers	Sara		15-Mar-1891	09-Mar-1891	Mortimer Meers	Ward, Catherine	Mortimer Carroll / Mary Anderson
Mehling	George	James	19-Dec-1886	10-Dec-1886	Henry Mehling	Eberle, Rose	Michael Meers / Mary J. Mehling
Mehling	Mary	Josephine	13-Jan-1884	02-Dec-1883	Henry Mehling	Eberle, Rose	George J. Mehling / Mary Joseph Mehling
Mehrbrei	Frederick	James	01-Dec-1895	21-Nov-1895	Ambrose Mehrbrei	Bates, Mary	Frederick Schipley / Catherine Mehrbrei
Mehrbrei	Helen	Francis	03-Jun-1894	31-May-1894	Ambrose Mehrbrei	Bates, Mary Francis	Ann Roth
Mei	Henry		24-Jan-1904	11-Jan-1904	Henry Mei	Murray, Elizabeth	Mary McKenna
Menekhein	Elizabeth	Mary	30-Jun-1895	10-May-1895	Ernest H. Menekhein	Emge, Mary	John McKenna / Elizabeth Beckermeier
Menekhein	Margaret	R.	17-Sep-1905	27-Aug-1905	Henry Menekhein	Emge, Mary	Margaret Belz
Menikheim	Andrew	Leroy	08-Feb-1903	27-Nov-1902	Henry Menikheim	Emge, Mary	Louis Menikheim / Catherine Fox
Menikheim	Ernest	Henry	08-Feb-1903	27-Nov-1902	Henry Menikheim	Emge, Mary	Louis Menikheim / Mary Culleton
Menitor	Margaret	Mary	18-Jul-1897	04-Jul-1897	Thomas Menitor	Wright, Elizabeth	Joseph Wright / Mary Wright
Menton	Charles		26-Sep-1886	11-Sep-1886	Patrick Menton	Fay, Margaret	Michael Kearney / Mary Byrnes
Mercer	William	Outen	12-Jan-1890	19-Nov-1889	George P. Mercer	Dwiley, Mary S.	William Mercer / Mary J. Mercer
Mercer	Daniel	Benedict	25-May-1890	15-May-1890	Joseph Mercer	Booth, Frances	
Mercer	Stanislaw	Norfleet	16-Jan-1887	08-Jan-1887	Joseph Plunkett Mercer	Booth, Frances Teresa C.	James McDevitt / Mary Joan Mercer
Meredith	Francis	Edward	03-Feb-1901	24-Jan-1901	Henry Meredith	Birmingham, Agnes	P.F. Hackett / Catherine Birmingham
Mergler	Ann	Catherine	15-Aug-1885	06-Oct-1861	John Burket	Dobson, Rebecca	Caroline Mergler
Merriman	Helen	Mary	21-Jan-1906	5-Jan-1906	John H. Merriman	Brazer, Catherine	James P. Monaghan / Mary Brazer
Merriman	Catherine		3-Mar-1907	18-Feb-1907	John Merriman	Bariger, Catherine	Thomas Finn / Elizabeth Finn
Mersmann	Joseph	Frederick	19-Aug-1883	28-Jul-1883	Patrick Merrsmann	Leary, Mary	Frederick Merrsmann / Josephine Edelsta
Meskill	Edmund		25-Mar-1906	14-Mar-1906	Edmund J. Meskill	O'Connor, Catherine	John Evans / Margaret Evans
Meskill	Mercedes		02-Jun-1901	09-May-1901	Edmund Meskill	O'Connor, Catherine	
Meskill	Catherine		18-Jun-1899	11-Jun-1899	Edward Meskill	O'Connor, Catherine	James O'Keefe / Mary O'Keefe
Meskill	Clara		30-Jan-1898	17-Jan-1898	John Meskill	[Blank], Augusta	Patrick Meskill / Ann Meskill
Meskill	John	William	02-Jan-1893	23-Dec-1892	Michael Joseph Meskill	Manning, Ann Mary	Thomas McCrystal / Mary A. Meskill
Meskill	William		17-Aug-1884	07-Aug-1884	Michael Meskill	Noonan, Mary	Patrick Meskill / Mary Shea
Messenzehl	Gertrude	Estelle	08-Feb-1885	20-Jan-1885	Joseph Messenzehl	Devane, Hanna	William H. Rowley / Lilly Hogan
Messick	James	Henry	30-Jun-1902	06-Mar-1832	Solomon Messick	Park, Mary	Matthew Geen / Margaret [Blank]
Mettee	John		27-Mar-1892	19-Feb-1892	James R. Mettee	Ryan, Mary Catherine	Timothy McShane / Catherine McShane
Mettee	James	Edward	03-Jun-1894	17-May-1894	James Richard Mettee	Ryan, Catherine	James Edward McShane / Mary Agnes McShane
Mettee	James		29-Jan-1897	28-Dec-1866	John Mettee	Summerson, Eliza J.	William Powers
Mettee	M.	Henry	20-Aug-1899	[Blank]	John Mettee	[Blank], Sara Ann	
Mettee	Elsie	Adabelle	13-Apr-1908	12-Mar-1890	John Paul Mettee	Hennick, Sarah	

LAST NAME	FIRST NAME	MIDDLE	BIRTH	BAPTISM	Father	Mother	SPONSORS
Mettee	John	George	10-Jul-1896	26-Jul-1896	William Mettee	Lawler, Alice	George Hoffman	Ann Machenstein
Metz	George	Albert	30-Aug-1901	08-Sep-1901	John Joseph Metz	Koher, Catherine	George West	Margaret West
Metz	Margaret	Alice	7-Aug-1907	25-Aug-1907	Thomas Metz	Murphy, Margaret	Gerald McGraw	Mary Barrett
Meyd	George	Vincent	19-Jul-1908	26-Jul-1908	John F. Meyd	Conroy, Margaret	George A. Meyd	Ann C. Moran
Meyd	Dorothy	Mary	6-Feb-1907	17-Feb-1907	John Meyd	Conroy, Margaret	John Meyd	Emma Conroy
Meyd	Margaret	Gladys	23-Jun-1910	3-Jul-1910	John Meyd	Conroy, Margaret	John A. Meyd	Frances S. Meyd
Meyer	Edith	Cecelia	02-Apr-1884	13-Apr-1884	Carl Meyer	Lipp, Carlotta Elizabeth	Caroline Lipp	Louise Lipp
Meyer	Charlotte	Estelle	26-Aug-1890	07-Sep-1890	Charles Meyer	Lipp, Charlotte Elizabeth	James Kuhn	Mary Lipp
Meyers	August		03-Jun-1893	11-Jun-1893	August Meyers	McCanley, Catherine	Charles McCanley	Mary Ann McCanley
Meyers	James	Vincent	11-Jan-1898	16-Jan-1898	August Meyers	[Blank], Catherine	Charles Meyers	Mary Meyers
Meyers	Mary	Estelle	24-Aug-1891	28-Aug-1891	August Meyers	McCanley, Catherine	Charles McCanley	Martha McCanley
Meyers	Elizabeth	Mary	27-Apr-1886	16-May-1886	Carl Myers	McLaughlin, Ann	William Cremen	Margaret McLaughlin
Meyers	John	Frederick	14-May-1892	22-May-1892	Charles Meyers	Lipp, Lottie		Agatha Groeson
Meyers	James	Joseph	19-Mar-1883	01-Apr-1883	George W. Myers	Taggard, Theresa		Mary Fay
Meyers	John		25-Jun-1892	25-Jun-1892	William Myers	Melia, Julia		
Miles	Mary		17-Jul-1900	22-Jul-1900	Charles Miles	McGraw, Margaret	Frederick [Blank]	Mary Miles
Miles	George		30-Sep-1893	24-Dec-1893	Eugene Miles	Clifford, Ann	James Clifford	Hannah Clifford
Miles	Mary	Elizabeth	30-Aug-1887	18-Sep-1887	Lemuel J. Miles	Sands, Ann	Eugene A. Hannan	Sara McGraw
Miles	Stephen	A.	23-Sep-1902	12-Oct-1902	Lemuel Miles	Sands, Ann		Katherine Ryan
Miles	John		24-Apr-1899	14-May-1899	Lemuel Towers Miles	Sands, Ann	Bernard Miles	Catherine Miles
Miles	Eugene		[Blank]	27-Jul-1897	Leo Eugene Miles	Clifford, Ann	Charles J. Lannan	Elizabeth Clifford
Miles	Agnes	Elizabeth	29-Oct-1893	12-Nov-1893	Samuel Miles	Sands, Ann	John McGraw	Ann McGraw
Miles	Ann	Estelle	01-Feb-1896	16-Feb-1896	Samuel Miles	Sands, Ann	William Ryan	Sarah Ryan
Miles	Pattie	Agnes	18-Jan-1901	10-Feb-1901	William Miles	Stevens, Ada Estelle		Ann Miles
Millar/Ayers	Thomas		20-Jan-1827	30-May-1884	Jacob Ayers	Sellman, Sedonia		Margaret B. Foley
Miller	John	James	16-Jan-1882	20-Jan-1882	Adam Miller	Towers, Elizabeth		Catherine Towers
Miller	Mary		12-Oct-1891	12-Apr-1914	Albert Francis Miller	[Blank], Rosina	Emory McCourt	
Miller	Florence		22-Oct-1888	11-Nov-1888	Aloysius Miller	Gesner, Christina		W. Gesner
Miller	George	Neal	20-Jul-1875	19-Nov-1904	George Miller	Miller, Alice		Mary Forrell
Miller	John	H.	11-Jul-1894	16-Feb-1898	George Miller	Phillips, Bernice B.		
Miller	Mary	Catherine	16-Jan-1905	22-Jan-1905	Henry J. Miller	Kearney, Margaret	Joseph Miller	Catherine Miller
Miller	Francis	William	3-Sep-1907	8-Sep-1907	Henry J. Miller	Kearney, Margaret C.	James H. Miller	Catherine A. Miller
Miller	Henry	Joseph	26-Sep-1900	30-Sep-1900	Henry Miller	Kearney, Margaret Catherine	Joseph Rank	Margaret Rank
Miller	Margaret	Elizabeth	14-Jul-1898	17-Jul-1898	Henry Miller	Kearney, Margaret	H. Miller	Mary Kearney
Miller	Mary		18-Feb-1896	23-Feb-1896	Henry Miller	Kearney, Margaret	Joseph Miller	Mary Miller
Miller	William	Raymond	13-Jun-1912	16-Jun-1912	Henry Miller	[Blank], Mary		Mary [Blank]
Miller	Ann		31-Aug-1902	07-Sep-1902	Henry Miller	Kearney, Margaret	James Miller	Elizabeth Kearney
Miller	Agnes		10-Jun-1898	26-Jun-1898	Herbert Miller	Rigger, M.	F. Rigger	Rose Rigger
Miller	Mary	Dorothy	26-Sep-1915	3-Oct-1915	J. Omar Miller	Wyatt, Agnes M.	Francis P. Wyatt	Mary K. Wyatt
Miller	Mary	Josepha	21-Jan-1909	31-Jan-1909	James Henry Miller	McCourt, Catherine	Michael J. McCourt	Mary Josepha McCourt
Miller	Emma	Elizabeth	16-Apr-1888	29-Apr-1888	John Miller	Ohm, Elizabeth	James Murphy	Mary Clemsen
Miller	William		25-Apr-1881	04-Feb-1883	John R. Miller	Schreiner, Mary	M. Pryer	Emma Pryer
Miller	James	Francis	25-Feb-1911	5-Mar-1911	Joseph Miller	Collins, Ann C.		Catherine Dugan
Mills	Joseph		10-Feb-1895	24-Feb-1895	John Mills	McLaughlin, Ann	James FitzGibbons	Maud Mercer
Mills	David		08-Jan-1883	21-Jan-1883	John Mills	McLaughlin, Anastasia		Susan McLaughlin
Mills	Sara		05-May-1827	29-Sep-1901	Joseph Mills	Caulwell, Sarah		
Mills/Carey	Cecelia		19-Jun-1889	23-Jun-1889	Lemuel Miles	Sands, Ann	George Connors	Sara Ryan
Miner	Mary		06-May-1873	25-Jul-1897	Robert Mills	Turner, Sophia	Joseph Kelly	Helen Cassidy
Miner	Monica		31-Aug-1892	11-Sep-1892	John A. Miner	Bonahan, Bridget	John Pidano	Mary Welch
Miner	Helen	F.	04-Oct-1894	14-Oct-1894	John Ambrose Miner	Bonahan, Bridget Agnes	John Laurence Burns	Mary Laura Grogan
Miner	Thomas		22-Jul-1899	10-Aug-1899	John Miner	Banahan, Bridget	Joseph Flynn	Mary Flynn
Minor	Elizabeth	Catherine	20-Mar-1890	30-Mar-1890	John Miner	Banahan, Bridget	John Moore	Catherine Miner
Minitor	Elizabeth	Catherine	15-Jul-1900	17-Jul-1900	Thomas Minitor	Wright, Elizabeth Catherine		Mary Catherine Quinn
Minitor	Loretta		15-Jul-1900	29-Jul-1900	Thomas Minitor	Wright, Elizabeth	B.J. McCourt	Mary Quinn
Minners	Helen		08-Dec-1902	09-Dec-1902	Thomas Minitor	Wright, Elizabeth E.		Ann C. Wright
Minnick	George	Robert	31-Jan-1908	16-Feb-1908	Charles Minners	O'Connor, Margaret	John Farley	Nellie O'Connor
Minnick	George	Robert	05-Jan-1883	11-Feb-1883	George Robert Minnick	Staylor, Patrick[sic]	Henry Reilly	Mary Dillaway
Minnick	John	Henry	21-Jun-1913	5-Jul-1913	George Robert Minnick	Cannon, Henrietta Mary	Francis P. McManis	Mary Oliver
Minnick	John		29-Dec-1886	09-Jan-1887	John Minnick	Blair, Sara	James T. Reardon	Mary Minnick
Minnick	Naomi	Anastasia	30-Mar-1820	24-Mar-1895	John Minnick	Eigenbrot, Frederica		
Minor	John		19-Sep-1909	10-Oct-1909	Louis N. Minnick	Imhoff, Margaret N.	Theodore Rohleder	Anastasia Imhoff
Minor	Catherine		29-Oct-1896	08-Nov-1896	John Minor	Banahan, Bridget	Mary Kelly
Minor	Catherine		13-Sep-1899	24-Sep-1899	William Minor	Clifford, Elizabeth	Thomas Cronan	Margaret [Blank]

94

LAST NAME	FIRST NAME	MIDDLE	BAPTISM	BIRTH	Father	Mother	SPONSORS	
Minor	Mary		12-Jun-1898	03-Jun-1898	William Minor	Clifford, Elizabeth		Ann Miles
Minton	Catherine		19-Feb-1882	06-Feb-1882	Patrick Minton	Fahy, Margaret	Patrick Fury	Sara Egan
Minton	Mary		26-Apr-1885	10-Apr-1885	Patrick Minton	Feeley, Margaret	Bernard Haskey	Teresa Hanson
Mitchel	Mary	Catherine	25-Nov-1883	05-Nov-1883	Lloyd Mitchel	Kernan, Mary Ann	Edward Hawkins	Catherine Kernan
Mitchell	Rose		19-Jun-1914	15-Apr-1914	[Blank]	Mitchell, Ellen Spollen	John Spollen	Ellen Spollen
Mitchell	Francis		14-Sep-1891	09-Aug-1883	James E. Mitchell	Smith, Ella		Sarah Dolan
Mitchell	William		26-Jun-1887	11-Aug-1879	James E. Mitchell	Smith, Helen		Sara H. Dolan
Mitchell	Sara	Catherine	30-May-1886	22-Apr-1886	John James Mitchell	Wallace, Henrietta		Sara Wallace
Mitchell	Joseph	Marr	10-May-1888	30-Dec-1887	John Mitchell	Wallace, Harriet		Mary Parrell
Mitchell	Mary	Lillian	28-Feb-1892	11-Feb-1892	Joseph B. Mitchell	Smick, Elizabeth S.		Mary J. Sindall
Mitchell	Joseph	Wallace	10-Dec-1908	10-Dec-1908	Joseph Mitchell	Travely, Ann		Margaret Samsel
Mitchell	Catherine	Loretta	19-Nov-1909	9-Sep-1909	Joseph Patrick Mitchell	Travely, Ann	Catherine Kirby	
Mitchell	Edward	Hawkins	16-Sep-1888	28-Aug-1888	Lloyd E. Mitchell	Kernan, Mary	Edward Hawkins	Catherine Hawkins
Mitchell	George	Washington	28-Jul-1895	10-Jul-1895	Lloyd Emerson Mitchell	Kernan, Mary C.	Patrick Breen	Eliza Hawkins
Mitchell	William	Emerson	16-Oct-1892	25-Sep-1892	Lloyd Emerson Mitchell	Kernan, Mary	Henry Loeller	Teresa Connolly
Mitchell	Francis		05-Dec-1897	16-Nov-1897	Lloyd Mitchell	Kernan, Mary		
Mitchell	Mary	Helen	11-Jul-1890	24-Oct-1866	Robert Mitchell	Williams, Mary Helen	Emma Williams	Rose Mitchell
Mitchell	William	Henry Patrick	18-Apr-1888	11-May-1840	William James Mitchell	Haines, Elizabeth		Joan Colford
Mittendorf	Henry	Frederick	13-Sep-1891	14-Jul-1891	Herman Mittendorf	Everle, Mary Ann	Henry Frederick Funk	Joan Julia Mittendorf
Mittendorf	Frederick	Cleveland	15-Aug-1884	01-Aug-1884	John H. Mittendorf	Eberle, Mary A.	Frederick Dierken	Mary E. Logan
Mittendorf	Mary	Teresa Catherine	05-May-1887	23-Nov-1886	John H. Mittendorf	Eberly, Mary A.		Bridget Harkins
Moan	Mary	Margaret	02-Aug-1903	19-Jul-1903	James J. Moan	Reilly, Margaret	Bernard E. Moan	Mary Schreufer
Moan	William		20-Feb-1905	13-Feb-1905	James J. Moan	Reilly, Margaret	Charles Moan	Catherine Crosby
Moan	Alice		06-Mar-1887	05-Feb-1887	James Moan	Hughes, Mary A.	John T. Gaffney	Ann Gaffney
Moan	Bernard	Vincent	15-Apr-1883	24-Mar-1883	James Moan	Hughes, Mary Ann	Edward French	Mary Moon
Moan	George	Thomas	04-Nov-1888	14-Oct-1888	James Moan	Hughes, Mary A.	John Logue	Margaret V. Donohue
Moan	Mary	Catherine	17-May-1885	29-Apr-1885	James Moan	Hughes, Mary A.	Ignatius Hughes	Catherine Crosby
Moan	Terence	Ardle	18-Dec-1892	02-Dec-1892	James Moan	Hughes, Mary Ann	Michael Moan	Alice Moan
Mobley	Edward	Carver	09-Feb-1890	30-Nov-1844	Edward M. Mobley	Carver, Ellen C.	Francis Kelly	
Moffett	Edward	Howard	4-Jul-1915	18-Jun-1915	George H. Moffett	Henninger, Ann		Esther Morris
Moffitt/Annen	Eleanor	Isabelle	04-Nov-1888	31-Dec-1868	George W. Moffitt	Wren, Mary J.		Ann Ross
Mohr	John	Francis	08-Mar-1891	06-Mar-1891	John Henry Mohr	McMahon, Ann	John Francis Byrnes	Margaret Wise
Mohr	Mildred	Caroline	12-Nov-1911	28-Oct-1911	Louis Mohr	Pruet, Catherine	Frederick Mohr	Carolina Mohr
Molloy	Catherine	Agnes	02-Sep-1883	25-Aug-1883	John Molloy	Mary Molloy	Thomas Barrett	Bridget Mullen
Molloy	James	Patrick	17-Feb-1884	12-Feb-1884	John Molloy	Ennis, Sara	James Joseph Codd	Margaret Sinnot
Molloy	Mary		03-Sep-1882	01-Sep-1882	John Molloy	Ennis, Sara	Peter Holden	Catherine O'Neal
Molloy	Ann	Margaret	02-Aug-1891	22-Jul-1891	Laurence Malloy	Kirkland, Mary J.	Thomas J. Walsh	John Molloy
Molloy	Charles		27-Aug-1893	20-Aug-1893	Laurence Molloy	Kirkland, Mary Joan	Patrick Molloy	Margaret Molloy
Molloy	Laurence		13-Dec-1885	30-Nov-1885	Laurence Molloy	Kirkland, Mary Joan	John McGraw	Isabelle Jones
Molloy	Mary		15-Dec-1895	09-Dec-1895	Laurence Molloy	Kirkland, Mary Joan	Marcus Sinnott	Catherine Geary
Molloy	Michael		04-May-1884	25-Apr-1884	Laurence Molloy	Kirkland, Mary Joan	M. Murphy	Margaret Sinnott
Molloy	William	Leon	15-Jan-1888	09-Jan-1888	Lawrence Molloy	Kirkland, Mary J.	Michael Wallace	Helen McGraw
Molloy	Alice		23-Oct-1898	16-Oct-1898	Lawrence Molloy	Kirkland, Mary	John Kenny	Mary Williams
Molloy	L.	Joseph	22-Nov-1891	06-Nov-1891	Thomas Molloy	Donohue, Margaret	Michael Donohue	Delia Molloy
Molloy	Thomas	Patrick	23-Apr-1893	11-Apr-1893	Thomas Molloy	Donohue, Margaret	Patrick Quinn	Mary Molloy
Molloy	Luke	Francis	9-Nov-1913	23-Oct-1913	Thomas P. Molloy	Finn, Mary Elizabeth	James Blake	Joan Gisriel
Monaghan	Ann		18-Jul-1886	11-Jul-1886	Francis Monaghan	Buckley, Ann	James Leach	Ann Dawson
Monaghan	Catherine		04-Mar-1900	18-Feb-1900	Francis Monaghan	Buckley, Ann Elizabeth	James Biddison	Catherine Biddison
Monaghan	Elizabeth		18-Jul-1886	11-Jul-1886	Francis Monaghan	Buckley, Ann	Michael Sweeney	Catherine Mahon
Monaghan	Helen		26-Feb-1893	14-Feb-1893	Francis Monaghan	Buckley, Ann	Thomas Larkin	Ann Reilly
Monaghan	John		20-Jan-1889	07-Jan-1889	Francis Monaghan	Buckley, Ann	Michael J. McGann	Matilda Mahoney
Monaghan	Joseph		27-Aug-1904	15-Aug-1904	Francis Monaghan	Buckley, Ann	William Keneally	Mary Mahoney
Monaghan	Margaret		22-Feb-1891	08-Feb-1891	Francis Monaghan	Buckley, Ann	Joseph Thomas Norton	Helen Tracy
Monaghan	Mary		13-Jan-1884	02-Jan-1884	Francis Monaghan	Buckley, Ann C.	William Maloney	Helen Buckley
Monaghan	Rose		06-Jun-1897	24-May-1897	Francis Monaghan	Buckley, Ann	William Grogan	Mary Larkin
Monaghan	Elizabeth	Laura	01-Dec-1889	22-Nov-1889	James Monaghan	Kinross, Margaret E.	Thomas Collins	Margaret Colgan
Monaghan	Peter		12-Nov-1887	06-Nov-1887	James Monaghan	Kinross, Margaret		Mary E. Cain
Monaghan	Margaret	Lousdale	15-Apr-1906	30-Mar-1906	John J. Monaghan	Terrel, Julia	Edward J. Burke	Mary Monagahan
Monaghan	Martin	David	24-Jan-1893	20-Jan-1893	John Monaghan	Lansdale, Sara Joan	Martin Monaghan	Bridget Kerigan
Monaghan	Rose		14-Nov-1886	08-Nov-1886	John Monaghan	Rites, Laura	James Patrick Monaghan	Margaret Corcoran
Monaghan	John	Thomas	01-Jun-1890	20-May-1890	John Thomas Monaghan	Rites, Laura Joan	John Thomas Arthur	Mary Agnes Kelly
Monaghan	Mary	Helen	31-Jul-1892	20-Jul-1892	John Thomas Monaghan	Rites, Laura Joan	Thomas Silvester Moore	Helen Rose Moore
Montgomery	Frances		19-Jan-1908	2-Jan-1908	Henry Montgomery	Heise, Louise		Mary Blessing

ST JOHN'S BAPTISMS 1882-1912

LAST NAME	FIRST NAME	MIDDLE	BAPTISM	BIRTH	Father	Mother	SPONSORS
Montgomery	Mary	William	28-May-1899	09-May-1899	Henry Montgomery	Heise, Lillian	Mary Montgomery
Montrose	Frederick	George	08-Mar-1896	21-Feb-1896	Joseph Montrose	Kelly, Catherine	Mary Mulledy
Mooney	Ann	Gertrude	03-Jun-1900	15-May-1900	Charles Mooney	Kenrick, Mary	George Mooney
Mooney	George		05-Dec-1897	01-Dec-1897	Charles Mooney	Kenrick, Mary	Henry Hartlein
Mooney	Mary		22-Jan-1899	08-Jan-1899	Charles Mooney	Kenrick, Mary	Dennis Kenrick
Mooney	Charles	Alexander	8-Dec-1907	26-Nov-1907	Charles W. Mooney	Kenrick, Mary Helen	Mary Madigan
Mooney	John	Melchon	14-Feb-1904	11-Feb-1904	Eurolo W. Mooney	Kenrick, Mary E,	Martha Kenrick
Mooney	Mary	Irene	21-Jun-1891	12-Jun-1891	Francis G. Mooney	Murphy, Margaret	William Crawford
Mooney	Estelle		8-Apr-1906	10-Mar-1906	Francis Joseph Mooney	Murphy, Margaret	Adell Grogan
Mooney	George	Patrick	13-Mar-1904	27-Feb-1904	Francis Mooney	Murphy, Margaret	Mary E. Murphy
Mooney	John		30-Apr-1902	24-Mar-1902	Francis Mooney	Murphy, Margaret	Catherine Mooney
Mooney	Margaret		18-Dec-1892	03-Dec-1892	Francis Mooney	Murphy, Margaret	Mary Lacey
Mooney	Ann	Gertrude	12-Jan-1896	30-Dec-1895	James Mooney	Leary, Ann	Mary Hagerty
Mooney	Edward	Joseph	10-Sep-1882	30-Aug-1882	James Mooney	Lyman, Ann	Smith, Mary
Mooney	James	Patrick	29-Jun-1884	22-Jun-1884	James Mooney	Lyman, Ann	Martin Holmes
Mooney	John	Francis	21-Mar-1886	14-Mar-1886	James Mooney	Lyman, Ann	Catherine Philbin
Mooney	William	Henry	01-Jan-1888	15-Dec-1887	James Mooney	Lynan, Ann	Mary Brown
Mooney	Margaret	Elizabeth	1-Aug-1915	24-Jul-1915	John M. Moony	Smeykal, Mary	Margaret Smeykal
Mooney	Dolores		2-Nov-1902	22-Oct-1902	John Mooney	Arringdale, Catherine	Elizabeth Cossett
Mooney	Lenore		27-Mar-1898	24-Feb-1898	John Mooney	Dunnigan, Agnes	Nora O'Connell
Mooney	Wilfred	Joseph	21-Oct-1906	12-Oct-1906	John Mooney	Arringdale, Catherine	Margaret M. Corbett
Mooney	Alice	Loretta	26-Aug-1883	28-Jul-1883	Joseph Mooney	Wrenn, Sara	Ann Ross
Mooney	Martin	John	01-Nov-1891	21-Oct-1891	Martin Mooney	Grady, Ann	Julia Brady
Mooney	Edward		15-Apr-1905	11-Apr-1905	Martin T. Mooney	Brady, Ann	Mary O'Sullivan
Mooney	Honora		13-Apr-1905	11-Apr-1905	Martin T. Mooney	Brady, Ann	Mary O'Sullivan
Mooney	Mary	Agnes	17-Apr-1892	04-Apr-1892	Richard Joseph Mooney	Banahan, Mary Agnes	Joan Banahan
Mooney	Richard	Joseph	9-Jul-1905	25-Jun-1905	Richard Joseph Mooney	O'Grady, Mary Elizabeth	Julia Gobright
Mooney	Ann		04-Dec-1898	02-Nov-1898	Richard Mooney	Banahan, Mary	Ann Banahan
Mooney	Mary	Joseph	28-Mar-1886	19-Mar-1886	Richard Mooney	O'Grady, Catherine	Mary C. O'Grady
Mooney	Raymond	Ignatius	07-Aug-1892	30-Jul-1892	Richard Mooney	Grady, Catherine	Margaret Rusk
Mooney	Richard	Joseph	10-Apr-1900	19-Mar-1900	Richard Mooney	Banaghan, Mary	Catherine Banaghan
Mooney	Thomas		28-Jun-1896	14-Jun-1896	Richard Mooney	Banehan, Mary	Ann Mooney
Mooney	Thomas		06-May-1896	06-May-1896	Thomas J. Mooney	Finn, Elizabeth	Mary Davey
Mooney	William	Patrick	10-Feb-1889	01-Feb-1889	Thomas Joseph Mooney	Finn, Elizabeth	Edward Joseph Roche
Mooney	John	Maurice	17-Aug-1890	10-Aug-1890	Thomas Mooney	Finn, Elizabeth	Thomas Finn
Mooney	Mary		31-Jan-1892	19-Jan-1892	Thomas Mooney	Finn, Elizabeth	Dennis Creem
Moore	Ann	Margaret	12-Aug-1906	27-Jul-1906	August Moore	O'Connor, Margaret	Laurence O'Connor
Moore	Mary	Elizabeth	29-Aug-1886	18-Aug-1886	Frederick Moore	Menon, Margaret Eliz.	Patrick Deeris
Moore	Mary	Catherine	04-Aug-1889	21-Jul-1889	Henry Moore	Dietzwieg, Ann	Francis Segrist
Moore	Marcella		01-Apr-1900	15-Mar-1900	James Moore	Courtney, Marcella	Thomas Way
Moore	Mary		26-Feb-1899	11-Feb-1899	James Moore	Courtney, Marcella	Thomas Moore
Moore	Ann	Elizabeth	07-Jul-1889	05-Jul-1889	John H. Moore	McMahon, Ann	Henry Moore
Moore	John	Laurence	22-Apr-1888	15-Apr-1888	John Henry Moore	McMahon, Ann	John McMahon
Moore	John		29-Apr-1900	22-Apr-1900	John Moore	Carmody, Mary	Henry Carmody
Moore	Mary	Agatha	15-Nov-1885	27-Oct-1885	John O. Moore	Carmody, Mary	William A. Delahunt
Moore	Gerald	Vincent	03-Aug-1890	19-Jul-1890	John Orlando Moore	Carmody, Mary Joan	
Moore	John	Charles	16-Oct-1887	03-Oct-1887	John Orlando Moore	Carmody, Mary Joan	Joan A. Moore
Moore	Mary	Laura	18-Sep-1884	04-Sep-1884	John Orlando Moore	Carmody, Mary J.	Henry Carmody
Moore	Robert	A.	11-Jul-1893	10-Jul-1893	John Orlando Moore	Carmody, Mary Joan	Helen Moore
Moore	Wilfred		19-Jan-1884	[Blank]	L. Moore	Milburn, E.	
Moore	Phillip	Joseph	5-Dec-1910	26-Nov-1910	Max Moore	Leonard, Mary	Carmel Donatelli
Moore	Ann	Gertrude	17-May-1914	28-Feb-1914	Phillip Moore	Winn, Catherine	Rose Miller
Moore	Catherine	Elizabeth	15-Dec-1912	3-Aug-1912	Samuel Moore	Cotter, Catherine Mary	James Mullen
Moore	Eleanor		26-Apr-1914	13-Jan-1914	Samuel Moore	Cotter, Catherine E.	William Williams
Moore	Elizabeth	Sedonia	14-May-1889	11-Apr-1889	William Moore	Byrne, Blache	Evangeline F. Byrne
Moore	John	Soloman	18-Oct-1891	24-Sep-1891	William Moore	McKenna, Rose	Sedonia Brown
Moore	John	Robert	29-Jan-1888	06-Jan-1888	William Moore	McKenna, Rose	Felix McKenna
Moore	William	Howard	10-Nov-1889	06-Nov-1889	William Moore	McKenna, Rose	John Ceovo
Moore	Edward		5-Oct-1913	20-Jun-1913	William Moore	Lynn, Alberta	Joseph Kelly
Moorwood	Edward		20-Sep-1903	16-Sep-1903	George Moorwood	Ward, Mary	John Moorwood
Moran	Catherine		14-Feb-1897	28-Jan-1897	Bernard Moran	Hawkins, Matilda	John Farmer
Moran	Edward	Joseph	24-Mar-1895	07-Mar-1895	Bernard Moran	Hawkins, Matilda C.	Henry Brehm
Moran	Matilda	Caroline	08-May-1892	15-Apr-1892	Bernard Moran	Hawkins, Matilda	John N. Biddingmayer

LAST NAME	FIRST NAME	MIDDLE	BAPTISM	BIRTH	Father	Mother	SPONSORS
Moran	Mary	Elizabeth	30-Nov-1902	18-Nov-1902	Charles H. Moran	Rigney, Katherine	James Rigney / Mary Dohoney
Moran	Charles		2-Jun-1907	21-May-1907	Charles Harrison Moran	Rigney, Catherine	John Moran / Mary Moran
Moran	Margaret	Riquey	28-May-1905	21-May-1905	Charles Harrison Moran	Rigney, Catherine Regina	Thomas J. Doheny / Teresa Matilda Moran
Moran	John	Francis	12-Dec-1886	20-Nov-1886	John F. Moran	Graham, Alice E.	William E. Graham / Ada Graham
Moran	Alice	M.	24-Jun-1888	12-Jun-1888	John Francis Moran	Graham, Alice Elizabeth	Benjamin Francis Graham / Mary Antonia Zink
Moran	Alice		12-Mar-1882	08-Mar-1882	John Moran	Enright, Honora	Patrick Moran / Mary Donovan
Moran	Charles	Steward	12-Oct-1890	26-Oct-1890	John Moran	Hughes, Mary	F. Kelly / Mary Trainor
Moran	Mary	Dolores	12-Oct-1902	28-Sep-1902	John Moran	Conroy, Ann	William Curran / Mary Curren
Moran	Joseph		10-Aug-1882	06-Aug-1882	Michael Moran	Hogan, Mary	
Moran	Mary	Elizabeth	08-Jul-1883	30-Jun-1883	Michael Moran	Moran, Mary	Michael Kearney / Mary Kearney
Moran	James		21-Dec-1884	17-Dec-1884	Patrick Moran	Enright, Alice	John Moran / Mary Enright
Moran	William	Patrick	16-Mar-1884	09-Mar-1884	Patrick Moran	Dolan, Mary	John Moran / Ann Byrnes
Moran	Edward	August	23-Jan-1887	11-Jan-1887	William T. Moran	Rafferty, Rosetta	John T. Gray / Catherine Rafferty
Moran	Mary	Elizabeth	26-Aug-1888	05-Aug-1888	William Thomas Moran	Rafferty, Rose	Ambrose August Ryan / Olivia Hughes
More	Margaret	Mary	13-Feb-1894	13-Jan-1894	William More	McKenna, Rose	Margaret Murphy
Morgan	Charles	Francis	3-Oct-1915	20-Sep-1915	Charles Francis Morgan	Adams, S.	Elizabeth Morgan
Morgan	Henry	Leon	6-Nov-1910	23-Sep-1910	Charles H. Morgan	Smith, Ann	Terrance L. Kendall / Mary Clark
Morgan	Alice		24-Nov-1912	24-Oct-1912	Charles Henry Morgan	Smith, Ann Cecelia	Floyd Smith / Catherine Clifford
Morgan	Ethel	Hartly Mary	05-Jun-1887	29-Apr-1887	Charles Morgan	Callaghan, Ann V.	James E, McGinley / Margaret Gallagher
Morgan	Francis	Harrison	11-Oct-1888	05-Sep-1888	Charles Morgan	Callahan, Ann V.	Margaret O. Little
Morgan	U. Ann		23-Jul-1914	19-May-1914	Henry D. Morgan	Smith, Ann	Alice A. Kendall
Morgan	Dorothy	Lillian	9-Feb-1908	29-Jan-1908	Henry J. Morgan	Smith, Ann	Robert Young / Caroline Kendall
Morgan	Helen	Catherine	05-Jul-1897	[Blank]	Henry Morgan	McManus, [Blank]	
Morgan	Ann		24-Jun-1883	14-Jun-1883	James Francis Morgan	Caffrey, Helen	Patrick Nugent / Alice Murphy
Morgan	Laura		18-Dec-1892	07-Dec-1892	James Francis Morgan	McCaffrey, Helen	Daniel A. O'Connor / Mary A. Murray
Morgan	Theresa		18-Oct-1896	07-Oct-1896	James Magan	Caffrey, Ella	Ann Dudley
Morgan	James		10-May-1885	30-Apr-1885	James Morgan	Caffrey, Helen	John Morgan / Margaret Shields
Morgan	Joseph		07-Jul-1895	24-Jun-1895	James Morgan	McCaffrey, Ellen	William Armen / Bridget Dudley
Morgan	Elizabeth	Agnes	18-Oct-1885	03-Oct-1885	John Morgan	Burns, Mary	John F. Shields / Bridget Shields
Morgan	Loretta	Susannah	14-Mar-1915	7-Feb-1915	W. Morgan	Cummings, Loretta	Leonard J. City / Olivia City
Morgan	Catherine		03-Jun-1885	23-Jan-1885	Wakeman F. Morgan	Davis, Ludia A.	Mary Farrell
Morgan	Margaret	Elizabeth	13-Oct-1907	1-Oct-1907	Winifred B. Morgan	Cummings, Mary Loretta	James O. Lyness / Lattie Cummings
Morgan	Edna	Frances	15-Aug-1909	1-Aug-1909	Winnie Morgan	Cummings, Loretta	Mary Collins
Moriarty	Eugene		31-May-1885	28-May-1885	John C. Moriarty	Killilea, Catherine	Joseph B. Moriarty / Sabina Burke
Morris	Joseph	Alonzo	10-Apr-1909	28-Feb-1886	Alonzo D. Morris	Shipley, Alice Mary	James E. Murphy / Catherine Murphy
Morris	Mary	Mildred	5-Jun-1910	18-May-1910	Alonzo Joseph Morris	Mooney, Mary Joseph	Raymond Morris / Catherine Mooney
Morris	Bernard		12-Feb-1911	12-Jan-1911	Edward Morris	Conroy, Margaret	Bernard Croghan / Mary Rooney
Morris	Katherine		28-Oct-1906	12-Oct-1906	Edward Morris	Conroy, Margaret	Ann Walters
Morris	Margaret	Cecelia	27-Nov-1904	7-Nov-1904	Edward Morris	Conroy, Margaret	Fanny Reilly
Morris	Catherine	Mary	16-Dec-1894	30-Nov-1894	Frederick Morris	Maley, Julia	James Maley / Catherine Maley
Morris	Mary	Agnes	13-Apr-1884	04-Apr-1884	Henry Morris	McLaughlin, Ann	Patrick Joseph McLaughlin / Martha McLaughlin
Morris	Mary	Jane	18-Jul-1909	28-Jun-1909	Martin Morris	Brady, Christina	Frank Snyder / Kate Salter
Morris	Margaret	Etta	17-Aug-1913	22-May-1913	William Morris	Weatherstine, Ann	Julia Farrelly
Morris	Mary	Helen	16-Sep-1906	17-Aug-1906	William Morris	Wetherstine, Ann	Robert Shanks / Genevieve Wetherstine
Morris	William		15-Dec-1894	18-May-1847	James Morrow	Cameron, Sara	James McDevitt
Morrow	George	Alfred	11-Mar-1894	13-Feb-1894	William Joseph Morrow	Marshall, Ceratia	John Consiff / Catherine Fitzpatrick
Morrow	Andrew		15-Jan-1888	09-Jan-1888	William Joseph Morrow	Lavery, Mary A.	Thomas Guerin / Catherine Morrow
Morrow	Florence		11-Aug-1895	11-Jun-1895	William Morrow	Hayes, Margaret	
Morrow	Joseph	Bernardine	05-Jul-1886	05-Jul-1886	William Morrow	Lavery, Mary	Margaret Geringer
Morton	Michael	Anthony	27-Jan-1884	14-Jan-1884	John Morton	Tighe, Mary	James Morrow / Ann Tighe
Morwood	Margaret	A.	26-Mar-1905	21-Mar-1905	George Morwood	Ward, Mary	William Harrington / Elizabeth Ward
Morwood	Agnes	M.	16-Apr-1899	08-Apr-1899	William Morwood	Casey, Catherine	Cornelius Morwood / Ann Casey
Morwood	Ann	Agnes	14-Feb-1886	09-Feb-1886	William Morwood	Casey, Catherine T.	George Morwood / Agnes Casey
Morwood	Katherine	Frances	09-May-1897	27-Apr-1897	William Morwood	Casey, Katherine	Cornelius Morwood / Agnes Casey
Morwood	Mary	Helen	10-Aug-1887	03-Aug-1887	William Morwood	Casey, Catherine	Jerome Kuhan / Mary McAdams
Mosbella	Mary		3-May-1914	9-Apr-1914	[Blank]	Mosbella, Clara	Mary Romano
Moscate	Mary	Viola	18-Sep-1910	4-Apr-1910	Paschale Moscate	Romano, Rosair	Joseph Moscate / Blanche Johnson
Mosco	Mary	Henderson	27-Feb-1910	14-Feb-1910	Joseph Mosco	Johnson, Laura	Robert Gannon / Mary E. Schmeckelier
Moser	George	Franklin	20-Sep-1896	04-Sep-1896	Louis Moser	Henderson, Margaret	George McNeill / Ann Brady
Mosher	William	Albert	19-May-1883	03-May-1883	William Mosher	Brady, Ellen	Edward Brady / Catherine Miles
Most	Charles	Joseph	13-Apr-1888	01-Feb-1888	Joseph Alexander Most	Moran, Margaret	Harriet Creaney
Mounie	Henry	Helen	11-Jan-1903	26-Nov-1902	John Mounie	Creaney, Elizabeth	Charles Creaney / Mary O'Sullivan
Moxley	Mary		18-Aug-1889	08-Aug-1889	Jonathan Eldridge Moxley	O'Sullivan, Mary	Daniel Geran

ST JOHN'S BAPTISMS 1882-1912

LAST NAME	FIRST NAME	MIDDLE	BAPTISM	BIRTH	Father	Mother	SPONSORS	
Moylan	Josephine		06-Jul-1890	26-Jun-1890	J. Moylan	[Blank], Mary		Mary O'Keefe
Moylan	Catherine	Agnes	23-Nov-1880	07-Nov-1890	James Moylan	Harvey, Margaret	Thomas J. McCarty	Fanny Moylan
Moylan	Edward	Milton	21-Dec-1902	02-Dec-1902	James Moylan	Harvey, Katherine	Francis Sellers	Hester Kates
Moylan	Henry		08-Feb-1898	02-Feb-1898	James Moylan	Harvey, Catherine		Harriet Moylan
Moylan	James	Joseph	02-Dec-1888	08-Nov-1888	James Moylan	Harvey, Catherine		Rose Gavin
Moylan	Joan		08-Oct-1882	28-Sep-1882	James Moylan	Kelly, Ann	John P. Moran	Frances Moylan
Moylan	John	Joseph	06-Mar-1887	17-Feb-1887	James Moylan	Harvey, Catherine	John J. Rock	Margaret Zeller
Moylan	Margaret	Smith	10-Nov-1895	21-Oct-1895	James Moylan	Harvey, Katie	Frank Zeller	Josephine Gardill
Moylan	Mary	Virginia	03-May-1885	05-Apr-1885	James Moylan	Harvey, Catherine	Peter Harvey	Ann Herford
Moylan	William	H.	7-Aug-1904	17-Jul-1904	James Moylan	Harvey, Catherine	John Moylan	Agnes Filter
Moylan	Mary	Cecelia	14-May-1905	14-May-1905	John G. Moylan	Moran, Sann	Bernard Sweeney	Mary Moylan
Moylan	Edward	Joseph	28-Oct-1888	13-Oct-1888	John Joseph Moylan	Meehan, Mary Ann	James Moylan	Catherine Fitzgerald
Moylan	John	Joseph	27-Sep-1891	18-Sep-1891	John Joseph Moylan	Dignan, Mary	Thomas Moylan	Catherine Brooks
Moylan	Agnes		02-Apr-1894	01-Apr-1894	John Moylan	Meehan, Mary A.	Edward J. Meehan	Catherine Glenn
Moylan	Ann	Mary	08-Apr-1888	29-Mar-1888	John Moylan	Dignan, Mary	Joseph Moylan	Hannah Moylan
Moylan	Ann	Mary	18-Mar-1900	27-Feb-1900	John Moylan	Wright, Mary	Daniel Moylan	Catherine McKenna
Moylan	Catherine		09-Aug-1891	[Blank]	John Moylan	Meehan, Mary	James A. Brady	Mary McDonnell
Moylan	Francis		20-Oct-1898	22-Oct-1898	John Moylan	Dignan, Mary		Ann Dignan
Moylan	Genevieve		13-Aug-1893	25-Jul-1893	John Moylan	Dignan, Mary		Mary Moylan
Moylan	Gertrude		20-Nov-1892	06-Nov-1892	John Moylan	Meehan, Mary	Joseph Smith	Catherine McDonnell
Moylan	Helen		19-Sep-1897	27-Aug-1897	John Moylan	Dignan, Mary	Edward McDonnell	Blanche Sindal
Moylan	James	Courtney	27-Nov-1904	11-Nov-1904	John Moylan	Moylan, Nora	Howard Sindal	Mary Moylan
Moylan	John		18-Feb-1883	06-Feb-1883	John Moylan	Meehan, Mary	Timothy Moylan	Julia McLaughlin
Moylan	Julia		24-May-1896	20-May-1896	John Moylan	Dignan, Mary		Catherine Freeman
Moylan	Laura		14-Apr-1889	08-Apr-1889	John Moylan	Dignan, Mary	Thomas Freeman	Ella Smith
Moylan	Leon		16-Feb-1890	02-Feb-1890	John Moylan	Meehan, Mary	Peter Smith	Catherine Farrell
Moylan	Margaret	Catherine	14-Jul-1901	20-Jun-1901	John Moylan	Wright, Mary	William Miller	Julia Dignan
Moylan	Mary	Laura	07-Nov-1886	31-Oct-1886	John Moylan	Dignan, Mary A.	John McDonnell	Catherine Dignan
Moylan	Mary		17-Mar-1895	20-Feb-1895	John Moylan	Dignan, Mary		Margaret Healy
Moylan	Theresa		12-Sep-1886	29-Aug-1886	John Moylan	Moylan, Mary	Martin Healy	Lillian V. Clemson
Moylan	Martin	Wright	2-Dec-1906	12-Nov-1906	John T. Moylan	Wright, Mary T.	James Moylan	RoseAnn Farrell
Moylan	Veronica	E.	19-Jul-1903	25-Jun-1903	John T. Moylan	Wright, Mary T.	William Farrell	Margaret McDonnell
Moylan	Ann		13-Oct-1911	29-Sep-1911	M. Moylan	Handy, Mary M.	John Finnegan	Margaret McDonald
Moylan	Catherine		2-Feb-1913	17-Jan-1913	Maurice Moylan	Hanley, Mary M.	John McDonald	Margaret B. McDonnell
Moylan	Mary	Bridget	28-Mar-1909	14-Mar-1909	Maurice Moylan	Hanley, Margaret	Joseph E. Murphy	Frances Fischer
Moylan	Mildred	Francis	30-Aug-1914	5-Aug-1914	Maurice Moylan	Hanley, Mary	John McDonnell	Mary Nagle
Moylan	Catherine		02-Mar-1902	13-Feb-1902	Thomas Moylan	Barrett, Hanna	Edward Barrett	Margaret Barrett
Moylan	Helen	Francis	16-Apr-1893	02-Apr-1893	Thomas Moylan	Barrett, Honora	Edward Barrett	Margaret Moylan
Moylan	Honora	Matilda	03-May-1896	10-Apr-1896	Thomas Moylan	Barrett, Honora	William Barrett	Bridget Worthington
Moylan	Margaret		10-Apr-1898	25-Mar-1898	Thomas Moylan	Barrett, Honora	Patrick Barrett	Joan Mulligan Nagle
Moylan	Mary		10-Apr-1898	25-Mar-1898	Thomas Moylan	Barrett, Honora	John Barrett	William Barrett
Moylan	Thomas		24-Dec-1899	Dec 1899	Thomas Moylan	Barrett, Nora	Barrett, Margaret	Margaret Moylen
Moylen	Cornelius		13-Mar-1904	24-Feb-1904	Thomas Moylen	Barnett, Honora	John Moylen	Margaret Dorsey
Mueler	Theodore	Henry	8-Nov-1914	28-Oct-1914	Henry D. Mueler	Dorsey, Mary E.	Theodore Mueler	Ann Ward
Mulcahey	Edward	Herman	17-Dec-1893	08-Dec-1893	Patrick Mulcahey	Colleran, Mary	Peter Coughlin	Mary Elizabeth Muldoon
Muldoon	Helen	Culbert	15-Dec-1889	19-Nov-1889	Jerome Muldoon	Muldoon, Ada Rebecca	Charles Muldoon	Catherine Roche
Mulgrew	George		24-Jul-1910	4-Jul-1910	Edward F. Mulgrew	Murphy, Mary	Dennis Roche	Harriet O'Neill
Mulgrew	John	Joseph	03-May-1903	23-Apr-1903	Edward F. Mulgrew	Murphy, Mary J.	John Wright	Winifred Kelly
Mulgrew	Mary	R.	9-Sep-1906	1-Sep-1906	Edward F. Mulgrew	Murphy, Mary J.	William E. Brown	Loretta [Blank]
Mulgrew	Paul		27-Nov-1904	20-Nov-1904	Edward F. Mulgrew	Murphy, Mary J.	Joseph Whelan	Catherine Kerm
Mulgrew	David	Warfield	17-Apr-1898	07-Apr-1898	Edward Mulgrew	Murphy, Mary Joan	Leo McGinnity	Catherine Roche
Mulgrew	Edward		05-Dec-1899	19-Nov-1899	Edward Mulgrew	Murphy, Ann	Dennis Roche	Margaret Murphy
Mulgrew	Margaret		11-Oct-1896	24-Sep-1896	Edward Mulgrew	Murphy, Mary Joan	William Ward	Mary Maynes
Mulgrew	Michael	Leon	23-Jun-1901	15-Jun-1901	Edward Mulgrew	Murphy, Mary	Francis Maynes	Sadie Mills
Mulgrew	Thomas	Leonard	28-Jun-1908	20-Jun-1908	Edward Mulgrew	Murphy, Mary Jane	Henry J. Burns	Margaret Colleran
Mulhahy	William	August	13-Jan-1884	06-Jan-1884	Patrick Mulhahy	Callahan, Mary	Martin Colleran	Katerina Montrose
Mullady	Hugo		01-Jan-1899	14-Dec-1898	Thomas Mullady	Kelly, Mary	George Montrose	Bridget Shea
Mullahy	Catherine	Lauren	15-Apr-1888	08-Apr-1888	Patrick Mullahey	Colleren, Mary	James F. Connaughton	Catherine Readdy
Mullahy	Thomas	Benson	14-Mar-1886	02-Mar-1886	Patrick Mullahy	Colleran, Mary	Thomas Colleran	Nellie Mullan
Mullan	John	William	4-Oct-1914	24-Sep-1914	Frederick Mullan	McManus, Elizabeth	William Gisriel	Ann Maher
Mulledy	Mary	Ann	28-Jul-1895	14-Jul-1895	Thomas Mulledy	Kelly, Mary	James Shanahan	Helen Fahey
Mulledy	Michael	Josephine	21-Mar-1897	05-Mar-1897	Thomas Mulledy	Kelly, Mary	John Mulledy	E. Jennings
Mullehy	Martin	Leo	15-Jun-1890	01-Jun-1890	Patrick Mullehy	Coleman, Mary	Andrew Rock	

98

LAST NAME	FIRST NAME	MIDDLE	BAPTISM	BIRTH	Father	Mother	SPONSORS	
Mullen	Victor	Ignatius	07-Jun-1896	25-May-1896	[Blank] Joseph Mullen	Grady, Mary Agnes	James William Carroll	Catherine Mooney
Mullen	Joseph	Elder	01-Oct-1893	11-Sep-1893	Ambrose B. Mullen	Evans, Carrie A.	Read McCaffrey	P. McCaffrey
Mullen	Joseph	Leon	24-Nov-1889	10-Nov-1889	Ambrose Beauregard Mullen	Evan, Caroline	Henry Francis Evans	Louis Evans
Mullen	Arthur		05-Sep-1886	23-Aug-1886	Arthur Mullen	McWilliams, Cecilia	John Mullen	Catherine Mullen
Mullen	Bernard		28-Feb-1897	16-Feb-1897	Arthur Mullen	McWilliams, Ann	George McElroy	Catherine McElroy
Mullen	Charles	Carroll	15-Jul-1900	04-Jul-1900	Arthur Mullen	McWilliams, Ann	Charles Burger	Margaret Burger
Mullen	John		11-Jan-1885	27-Nov-1884	Arthur Mullen	McWilliams, Ann	John McGuire	Rose McGuire
Mullen	Joseph		15-Oct-1882	19-Sep-1882	Arthur Mullen	McWilliams, Ann	George McWilliams	Bridget Harkins
Mullen	Mary	Rose	09-Sep-1888	30-Aug-1888	Arthur Mullen	McWilliams, Ann	Bernard J. Mullen	Catherine Halpin
Mullen	Ann	Mary Isabelle	04-Jun-1893	16-Mar-1893	Arthur T. Mullen	McWilliams, Ann C.	John McElroy	Mary McElroy
Mullen	George	Albert	08-Mar-1891	23-Feb-1891	Arthur Thomas Mullen	McWilliams, Ann Cecelia	George McWilliams	Margaret Mullen
Mullen	Joan		25-Nov-1894	17-Nov-1894	Arthur Thomas Mullen	McWilliams, Ann Cecelia	Francis Patrick Kelly	Mary Joan Kelly
Mullen	Joan	Reynolds	15-Oct-1893	03-Oct-1893	Bernard Ignatius Mullen	Reynolds, Mary E.	Felix Reilly	Alice Reynolds
Mullen	Catherine	Grace	23-Jan-1898	13-Jan-1898	Bernard J. Mullen	Reynolds, Mary E.	James Mullen	Mary A. Byren
Mullen	Bernard	Arthur	22-Nov-1891	09-Nov-1891	Bernard Mullen	Reynolds, Mary E.	Arthur Mullen	Mary Reynolds
Mullen	John		10-Jul-1887	01-Jul-1887	Bernard Mullen	Reynolds, Mary B.	George W. Hubbard	Ann O'Neill
Mullen	Margaret	Dolores	28-Apr-1912	6-Mar-1912	Bernard Mullen	McAuliffe, Elizabeth	William McGrain	Mary Lanahan
Mullen	Mary	Alice	14-Apr-1889	05-Apr-1889	Bernard Mullen	Reynolds, Mary E.	Peter B. Mullen	Bridget Jennings
Mullen	Margaret		20-Sep-1908	1-Aug-1908	Charles Mullen	Powers, Margaret		Julia Helen Mullen
Mullen	Thomas	Tynan	04-Mar-1885	01-Mar-1885	Edward F. Mullen	Bulger, Emma A.	Louis Blondell	Sarah Teresa Mullen
Mullen	Eugene	Thomas	19-Oct-1902	06-Oct-1902	Emory J. Mullen	Grady, Mary	Joseph Mullen	Gertrude Hogan
Mullen	Bernard	Walter	01-Nov-1891	25-Oct-1891	Emory Joseph Mullen	Grady, Mary Agnes	James McLaughlin	Stella Logan
Mullen	Joseph	Arunah	19-Mar-1884	21-Feb-1884	Emory Joseph Mullen	Grady, Mary A.	Eugene Logan	Agnes O'Neil
Mullen	James	E.	06-Nov-1885	06-Oct-1885	Emory Mullen	Grady, Mary A.	Edward M. McKenna	Julia McHenry
Mullen	Mary	Catherine	20-Jan-1901	24-Dec-1900	Gregory Mullen	Perkins, Rose	John Perkins	Rose Perkins
Mullen	James	Leon	06-Mar-1887	19-Feb-1887	James H. Mullen	McCartney, Ann	John L. Herron	Isabelle Caldwell
Mullen	Frederick	Cleveland	08-Mar-1885	05-Mar-1885	James Mullen	McCarthy, Ann	Andrew Jennings	Margaret Mygan
Mullen	Nellie	Mary	04-Mar-1900	17-Feb-1900	John B. Mullen	Noonan, Ann	Frederick Mullen	Julia Mullen
Mullen	Ann		18-Sep-1886	13-Sep-1886	John Mullen	McCann, Mary		Catherine Miner
Mullen	Arthur		14-Jan-1883	05-Jan-1883	John Mullen	Shea, Catherine	Arthur Napier	Helen Napier
Mullen	Bernard	Joseph	9-Nov-1913	25-Oct-1913	John Mullen	Beck, Ann	Bernard Mullen	Mary Mullen
Mullen	Mary	Catherine	19-Jan-1904	6-Jun-1904	John Mullen	Cullen, Mary	Thomas Connors	Mary Mullen
Mullen	Catherine	Mary	12-Apr-1903	03-Apr-1903	John T. Mullen	Flanagan, Catherine M.	James J. Mullen	Alice Flanagan
Mullen	Mary		17-Jul-1887	05-Jul-1887	John T. Mullen	Shea, Catherine	James E. Shea	Mary Shea
Mullen	Helen	Evelyn	4-Aug-1912	18-Jul-1912	Joseph A. Mullen	Hafer, Francis Mary	Thomas Patrick Finn	Mary Dolan
Mullen	Charles	Edward	26-Jan-1902	18-Jan-1902	Patrick J. Mullen	Dorsey, Elizabeth	Bernard McKenna	Mayr McKenna
Mullen	Bridget		08-Jun-1885	03-Jun-1885	Patrick Mullen	McElhannay, Bridget		Mary Fannon
Mullen	Bridget		24-Aug-1885	03-Jun-1885	Patrick Mullen	McElhannay, Bridget		Mary Fannon
Mullen	Catherine	Mary	13-Jan-1889	08-Jan-1888	Patrick Mullen	McKenna, Ann	James Joseph Kerns	Catherine Kerns
Mullen	Ellen	Elizabeth	23-Feb-1890	19-Feb-1890	Patrick Mullen	McKenna, Ann		Mary McKinn
Mullen	Joseph	Patrick	05-Jul-1891	23-Jun-1891	Patrick Mullen	McKenny, Ann J.	John Maynes	Mary Mullen
Mullen	William		08-Feb-1891	30-Jan-1891	Peter Bernard Mullen	Russell, Margaret	William H. Ryan	Morris Elizabeth Memmert
Mullen	Joseph	Leo	21-Jun-1896	07-Jun-1896	Peter C. Mullen	Russell, Margaret	Joseph August Mullen	Ann Mullen
Mullen	Edward		22-Aug-1897	18-Aug-1897	Peter Mullen	Russell, Margaret	Edward Healy	Margaret Doud
Mullen	Mary		14-Jan-1894	02-Jan-1894	Peter Mullen	Russell, Margaret	Edward Dowd	Mary A. Hopper
Mullen	Mary	Celeste	2-Jan-1910	25-Dec-1909	Wilbur V. Mullen	Hynes, Ann	Elmer Mullen	Mary Hynes
Mullen	Helen		15-Jan-1882	14-Dec-1881	William Mullen	Chester, Helen	William Kelly	Susan Fay
Mullen	James	Wilbur	28-Jun-1908	18-Jun-1908	William Wilbur Mullen	Hynes, Ann H.	James Hynes	Bessie McGill
Mulligan	Margaret	Ann	01-Jan-1893	20-Dec-1892	James Edward Mulligan	Kerr, Ann H.	William P. Mulligan	Mary McGivney
Mulligan	Mary	Laura	27-Dec-1891	08-Dec-1891	James Edward Mulligan	Kerr, Mary Cecel	Matthew Michael Fox	Genevieve Bosson
Mulligan	Ann		05-Apr-1891	24-Mar-1891	James Mulligan	Burns, Ann	John Thomas Nolan	Margaret McDevitt
Mulligan	Edward		04-Aug-1889	26-Jul-1889	James Mulligan	Byrne, Anns	Edward Burke	Margaret Gormly
Mulligan	James		03-Jan-1888	15-May-1888	James Mulligan	Burns, Ann	John Kernan	Ann Clifford
Mulligan	Janes	Joseph	22-Apr-1900	10-Apr-1900	James Mulligan	O'Connell, Catherine	Edward Mulligan	Mary Sinnott
Mulligan	Margaret		10-Jan-1886	03-Jan-1886	James Mulligan	Carter, Margaret A.	William McGierney	Mary Tierney
Mulligan	Matthew	Joseph	14-Oct-1883	07-Oct-1883	James Mulligan	Carter, Margaret	Joseph Tragesser	Ann Tragesser
Mulligan	Patrick	Josephine	12-Apr-1885	29-Mar-1885	James Mulligan	Burns, Ann	August Hopper	Ann Binger
Mulligan	John	Thomas	22-May-1887	16-May-1887	James Thomas Mulligan	Byrne, Anns	James Clifford	Lucia Byrnes
Mulligan	Ann		22-Nov-1885	26-Oct-1885	John Mulligan	Grogan, Mary	Francis Fallow	Catherine Fallow
Mulligan	James	Joseph	15-Apr-1888	25-Mar-1888	John Mulligan	Grogan, Mary	William Grogan	Catherine Eason
Mulligan	Thomas	Joseph	23-Mar-1890	17-Mar-1890	John Mulligan	[Blank], Mary	R. Kenny	P. Kenny
Mulligan	Mary	Estelle	26-Dec-1905	2-Dec-1905	Joseph M. Mulligan	Thornhill, Mary J.	Edward L. Henry	Mary Agnes Henry
Mulligan	Ann		08-Apr-1883	27-Mar-1883	Matthew Mulligan	Burns, Ann	Thomas Burns	Mary Glenn

ST JOHN'S BAPTISMS 1882-1912

LAST NAME	FIRST NAME	MIDDLE	BAPTISM	BIRTH	Father	Mother	SPONSORS
Mulligan	Henry	Cleveland	06-Sep-1885	31-Aug-1885	Matthew Mulligan	Burns, Ann	Burns, Ann
Mulligan	Margaret		06-Apr-1890	30-Mar-1890	Matthew Mulligan	Byrne, Anns	Charles Duffey
Mulligan	Ann	'	26-Oct-1902	24-Oct-1902	Patrick Mulligan	Byrnes, Mary	John Byrnes
Mulligan	Catherine		13-Feb-1887	05-Jan-1887	Patrick Mulligan	Byrne, Mary	John Daily
Mulligan	Ella		27-Jan-1895	15-Jan-1895	Patrick Mulligan	Byrnes, Mary	John Mulligan
Mulligan	Henry		15-Dec-1889	02-Dec-1889	Patrick Mulligan	Byrnes, Mary	Henry Byrnes
Mulligan	James		08-Nov-1885	01-Nov-1885	Patrick Mulligan	Burns, Mary	Daniel Quigley
Mulligan	John		08-Nov-1885	07-Nov-1885	Patrick Mulligan	Burns, Mary	Edward Mulligan
Mulligan	John		06-Aug-1899	24-Jul-1899	Patrick Mulligan	Burns, Mary	John Burns
Mulligan	Mary		24-Aug-1884	18-Aug-1884	Patrick Mulligan	Burns, Mary	William McGiveny
Mulligan	Margaret	Elizabeth	10-Jul-1898	30-Jun-1898	William Mulligan	Reynolds, Laura	John Reynolds
Mullin	Joan	Irene	14-Jul-1907	28-Jun-1907	Bernard Mullin	McAuliffe, Elizabeth	James Cremin
Mullin	Charles	Anthony	16-Sep-1906	3-Sep-1906	Patrick Mullin	Dorsey, Elizabeth	Charles Koester
Mullin	Mary	Elizabeth	23-Nov-1913	23-Oct-1913	Thomas Mullin	Powers, Margaret	James Walsh
Mullonee	Evelyn	Virginia	29-Sep-1907	3-Sep-1907	Lawrence Mellonee	Burns, Catherine	
Mumma	Ann	Mary	02-Jan-1889	12-Dec-1888	David Marion Mumma	Weaver, Bertha	
Mumma	David	Reilly	16-Aug-1886	24-Jul-1886	David Mumma	Weaver, Bertha	
Mumma	Joseph	Jerome	01-Dec-1892	14-Nov-1892	David Mumma	Weaver, Bernardine	
Mumma/Walter	Edith	Mary	24-Dec-1913	03-Jan-1893	John D. Mumma	Brown, Emma	
Munchel	Joan		10-Jul-1898	29-Jun-1898	Joseph Munchel	Frey, Sarah	Johan M. Schellenberger
Munchel	Vincent	George	19-Jan-1908	8-Jan-1908	Joseph Munchel	Frey, Sara M.	William Munchel
Munchel	Leon	Lindlay	19-Mar-1905	4-Mar-1905	Joseph Munchell	Frey, Sara M.	James Lindlay Keene
Munchell	Sarah	Mary	26-Jun-1904	About 1868	Samuel Frey	Sherlinger, Sarah	Ann Keane
Murnane	Joseph		24-Jan-1897	03-Jan-1897	John Murnane	Enright, Honora	Margaret Tierney
Murnane	Alice	Caroline	11-Aug-1907	18-Jul-1907	Daniel Murnane	Slaysman, Carolina	William Neary
Murnane	Daniel		23-Nov-1889	23-Nov-1889	John Murnane	Enright, Honora	James Landerkin
Murnane	Honora		16-Jul-1893	27-Jun-1893	John Murnane	Enright, Honora	John Hagerty
Murnane	James	Delaney	25-Nov-1883	01-Nov-1883	John Murnane	Enright, Honora	Michael Kelly
Murnane	John		27-Nov-1887	28-Oct-1887	John Murnane	Enright, Honora	Simon Dowling
Murnane	Mary		07-Feb-1892	11-Jan-1892	John Murnane	Enright, Honora	Edward Murnane
Murnane	Patrick		09-Apr-1899	17-Mar-1899	John Murnane	Enright, Nora	
Murnane	Danile		15-Dec-1889	23-Nov-1889	Joseph Murnane	Enright, Honora	John Murnane
Murnane	Alice		12-Jan-1890	01-Jan-1890	Patrick Murnane	Enright, Alice	John McGanon
Murnane	Catherine		[Blank]	28-Feb-1888	Patrick Murnane	Enright, Alice	Patrick O'Donnell
Murnane	Daniel	Franklin	21-Feb-1886	11-Feb-1886	Patrick Murnane	Enright, Alice	Joseph Evans
Murnane	Patrick		15-Jan-1893	01-Jan-1893	Patrick Murnane	Enright, Alice	Patrick Walsh
Murohy	Patrick		07-Mar-1886	04-Mar-1886	Patrick Murphy	Murphy, Mary	John Crone
Murphy	Catherine		17-Apr-1904	9-Mar-1904	Charles E. Murphy	Jacob, Elizabeth	
Murphy	Mary	Anastasia	20-Feb-1889	29-Jan-1889	Charles J. Murphy	Steinbacher, Margaret	John Murphy
Murphy	Thomas	Frederick	25-Jul-1886	28-Jun-1886	Charles J. Murphy	Steinbacher, Margaret A.	Joseph Slater
Murphy	John		23-Oct-1887	02-Oct-1887	Charles Murphy	Steinbacher, Margaret	Joseph Hysan
Murphy	Claudia		22-Jan-1882	16-Jan-1882	Charles William Lamar	Armstrong, Helen Francis	Louis Murphy
Murphy	Louis	Oliver	11-Jun-1911	24-May-1911	Claude C. Murphy	Furda, Margaret	Daniel Broderick
Murphy	Joseph	Ignatius	24-Mar-1913	7-Mar-1913	Claude Murphy	Fulda, Margaret Louise	John Gunning
Murphy	Catherine	Frances	20-Nov-1887	06-Nov-1887	David J. Murphy	Hackett, Mary	Thomas Murphy
Murphy	Elizabeth		16-May-1886	23-Apr-1886	David James Murphy	Hackett, Mary E.	
Murphy	James		04-Nov-1887	22-Nov-1880	David James Murphy	Hackett, Mary Helen	
Murphy	Edward	George	24-Jul-1892	04-Jul-1892	Edward Murphy	Furlong, Rose	George Eline
Murphy	Edward	Allan	7-Feb-1915	26-Jan-1915	Edward Murphy	Saunders, Clara	Allan Landers
Murphy	Mary	Katherine	10-Jan-1915	29-Dec-1914	Eugene E. Murphy	Lembach, Margaret	Charles J. Lembach
Murphy	Owen	John	30-Jun-1912	18-Jun-1912	Eugene E. Murphy	Lembach, Margaret Catherine	Owen John Murphy
Murphy	John	Brooke	28-Jun-1903	21-Jun-1903	Eugene J. Murphy	White, Helen	William White
Murphy	Eugene		22-Jan-1888	19-Jan-1888	Eugene Murphy	Brennan, Margaret Ann	Joseph Wesler
Murphy	John	Golden	06-Mar-1887	06-Jan-1887	Eugene Murphy	Golden, Mary	John Synnott
Murphy	Mary		18-Apr-1915	25-Mar-1915	Henry Murphy	Schellengberger, Eva	
Murphy	Clara	Ann	16-Mar-1884	11-Mar-1884	James Murphy	Whelan, Sarah	Joseph H. Whelan
Murphy	Clement		20-Jan-1889	15-Jan-1889	James Murphy	Whelan, Sara E.	Joseph Hardiman
Murphy	Edward		29-Oct-1882	15-Oct-1882	James Murphy	Hackett, Mary Helen	James McDevitt
Murphy	Helen	Mary	28-Mar-1897	10-Mar-1897	James Murphy	Delaney, Martha	James Duggan
Murphy	John	Thomas	17-Nov-1887	06-Nov-1887	James Murphy	Hackett, Mary	
Murphy	Leon	Joseph	24-Oct-1886	20-Oct-1886	James Murphy	Whelan, Sara	Thomas Hayden
Murphy	Margaret	Helen	12-Oct-1884	06-Jun-1884	James Murphy	Delaney, Martha	James Brady
Murphy	Mary	Jeannete	05-Nov-1893	03-Nov-1893	James Murphy	Whelan, Sara E.	John Murphy

| Patricia Mulligan |
| Mary Conroy |
| Mary Mulligan |
| Mary Tierney |
| Ella Byrnes |
| Margaret Elwood |
| Bridget Kedy |
| Mary Mulligan |
| Nora Barrett |
| Mary Tierney |
| Helen Reynolds |
| Catherine Cremin |
| Agnes Koester |
| Mary Katherine Orr |
| Catherine Mellonee |
| Mary Joan Weaver |
| Mary Parrell |
| Mary Purnell |
| Rose McIntyre |
| Mary Donohue |
| Ann Doyle |
| Ann M. Keene |
| Ann Keane |
| Margaret Tierney |
| Sadie Murnane |
| Catherine |
| Mary Hagerty |
| Mary Maddigan |
| Elizabeth Evesson |
| Catherine Murphy |
| Catherine Abbott |
| Catherine Donavan |
| Catherine Enright |
| Ann Lavery |
| Catherine Madigan |
| Mary Walsh |
| Ann Crone |
| Anastasia Clonkling |
| Mary Murphy |
| Elizabeth Kenny |
| Georgia Hysan |
| Victoria Murphy |
| Francis E. Oliver |
| Mary Gunning |
| Mary Murphy |
| Mary Sheehan |
| Catherine Furlong |
| Margaret Murphy |
| Mary Colleran |
| Ella A. Murphy |
| Helen M. Hanrahan |
| Ann Delaney |
| Elzabeth Fitzpatrick |
| Margaret Murphy |
| Mary A. Gahgan |
| Mary Donahue |
| Catherine Murphy |
| |
| Mary Wright |
| Ann King |
| Ann Donohue |
| Mary Wess |

100

LAST NAME	FIRST NAME	MIDDLE	BAPTISM	BIRTH	Father	Mother	SPONSORS
Murphy	Mary Edna		08-May-1898	30-Apr-1898	James Murphy	Whelan, Sarah	Albert Murphy / Margaret Meers
Murphy	Robert	Lee	08-Jan-1890	[Blank]	James Murphy	Furlong, Rose	Cecelia Maguire
Murphy	Thomas	Leonard	08-May-1898	30-Apr-1898	James Murphy	Whelan, Sara	Patrick Mason / Catherine Foley
Murphy	Vincent	Wallace	19-Jul-1891	10-Jul-1891	James Murphy	Whelan, Sara	John Moylan / Ann M. May
Murphy	Walter	David	25-Aug-1889	14-Aug-1889	James Murphy	Hackett, Mary	Thomas Hackett / Mary Hackett
Murphy	Ann		16-Apr-1893	04-Apr-1893	Jerome Murphy	Fenton, Ann	David O'Connor / Mary Fenton
Murphy	Daniel		12-Aug-1888	07-Aug-1888	Jerome Murphy	Fenton, Hannah	Dennis Driscoll / Mary Keys
Murphy	Helen		30-Aug-1894	17-Sep-1894	Jerome Murphy	Fenton, Hanna	Dennis O'Connell / Elizabeth Carroll
Murphy	James		12-Jan-1896	08-Dec-1895	Jerome Murphy	Fenton, Hannah	Thomas Nolan / Hanna Quinlan
Murphy	Jerome		16-Oct-1892	20-Sep-1892	Jerome Murphy	McClellan, Mary	Mary Dunn
Murphy	Jerome		28-Nov-1897	15-Nov-1897	Jerome Murphy	Fenton, Ann	Margaret Murphy
Murphy	John		25-Jan-1891	11-Jan-1891	Jerome Murphy	Fenton, Hannah	John McAuliffe / Catherine Driscoll
Murphy	Margaret		31-May-1891	17-May-1891	Jerome Murphy	McClennan, Mary	Winfield Scott Bell / Catherine Bell
Murphy	Joseph	Edward	30-Jun-1912	18-Jun-1912	John Joseph Murphy	Anderson, Elizabeth	John Thomas Hogan / Catherine Corrigan
Murphy	Katherine		1-Nov-1914	23-Oct-1914	John Joseph Murphy	Anderson, Elizabeth	William Kennedy
Murphy	Mary		1-Nov-1914	23-Oct-1914	John Joseph Murphy	Anderson, Elizabeth	Matthew Murphy / Mary Anderson
Murphy	Marcellum		06-Aug-1882	01-Aug-1882	John Murphy	Oliver, Lucy	Cassandra Murphy
Murphy	Thomas	William	20-Nov-1887	15-Nov-1887	John Murphy	Murphy, Ann	Catherine Wilson
Murphy	John	Victoria	24-Feb-1884	19-Feb-1884	Joseph B. Murphy	Oliver, Philomena	Peter Woods / Margaret Ward
Murphy	Mary	Estelle	02-May-1886	29-Apr-1886	Joseph B. Murphy	Oliver, Philomena	James H. Sheridan / Mary Leonard
Murphy	Cecelia		17-Jun-1906	24-May-1906	Joseph E. Murphy	Mooney, Alice	Henry A. Murphy / Irene Mooney
Murphy	Lillian	Frances	11-Aug-1895	20-Jul-1895	Joseph G. Murphy	Kelly, Agnes	Joseph P. Murphy / Catherine Murphy
Murphy	Mary		20-Aug-1893	05-Aug-1893	Joseph George Murphy	Kelly, Mary Agnes	Bartholomew Shea / Catherine Kelly
Murphy	Alice	Margaret	20-May-1900	03-May-1900	Joseph Murphy	Mooney, Alice	George J. Kelly / Margaret Ruck
Murphy	Allison	Joseph	22-Apr-1904	22-Apr-1904	Joseph Murphy	Mooney, Alicia	A. Boedeke / Mary Mooney
Murphy	Catherine	Edna	5-Jun-1904	15-May-1904	Joseph Murphy	Kenny, Mary Agnes	Patrick Murphy / Catherine McComb
Murphy	Eugene		18-Mar-1900	27-Feb-1900	Joseph Murphy	Kelly, Mary	Timothy P. Cronin / Mary Kelly
Murphy	Margaret		17-Aug-1902	29-Jul-1902	Joseph Murphy	Kelly, Mary A.	Eugene Kelly / Mary Burns
Murphy	Mary		21-Mar-1902	09-Feb-1902	Joseph Murphy	Mooney, Alice	James B. Meehan / Catherine Mooney
Murphy	Mary		25-Oct-1896	05-Oct-1896	Martin Murphy	Hughes, Catherine	Bernard Hughes / Elizabeth Doyle
Murphy	Matthew		04-Oct-1903	17-Sep-1903	Matthew J. Murphy	Blair, Mary L.	Charles Wills / Mary Wills
Murphy	William		17-Apr-1902	16-Apr-1902	Mayhew James Murphy	Blair, Lee, Mary	
Murphy	Amelia	Ella	19-Apr-1903	13-Mar-1903	Michael E. Murphy	Hayemeyer, Mabel P.	Francis Kernan / Ann Ritter
Murphy	Charles	Henry	03-Jul-1898	31-May-1898	Michael Murohy	Hegemyer, Mabel	Joseph Murphy / Alice Murphy
Murphy	Alice	Julia	16-Oct-1892	20-Sep-1892	Michael Murphy	Lucey, Mary	Jerome Lucey / Mary Ann Toner
Murphy	Bernard		18-May-1890	19-Apr-1890	Michael Murphy	Lacey, Mary	Daniel E. Lacey / Alice Murphy
Murphy	John	Joseph	11-Sep-1888	10-Sep-1888	Michael Murphy	Lucy, Mary	
Murphy	Joseph		01-Apr-1900	19-Mar-1900	Michael Murphy	McCourt, Sarah	Richard Murphy / Margaret Hagerty
Murphy	Mary	E.	26-Jan-1908	26-Dec-1907	Michael Murphy	Hagemeyer, Mabel	Joseph McInerney / Irene Mooney
Murphy	Pauline	Gertrude	11-Nov-1900	13-Oct-1900	Michael Murphy	Hagemyer, Mabel	William Welsh / Catherine Bahn
Murphy	Richard	Joseph	03-Aug-1902	21-Jul-1902	Michael Murphy	McCourt, Sarah	Joseph McCourt / Catherine Hagerty
Murphy	William		18-Sep-1906	15-Nov-1914	Michael Murphy	Hagemeyer, Paulina	Adalaide Murphy
Murphy	Margaret	Mary	30-Sep-1906	26-Sep-1906	Owen J. Murphy	White, Ellen A.	John Regan / Dorothy Regan
Murphy	Ann		25-Dec-1885	23-Oct-1885	Owen Murphy	Golden, Mary A.	Edward J. Barrow / Margaret Golden
Murphy	Helen		29-Apr-1883	23-Apr-1883	Owen Murphy	Brennan, Mary Ann	John Logue / Helen Brannan
Murphy	James		14-Dec-1884	08-Dec-1884	Owen Murphy	Brennan, Mary Ann	John Sinnott / Catherine Broderick
Murphy	Margaret	Elizabeth	16-Jun-1901	10-Jun-1901	Owen Murphy	White, Ellen	John White / Mary Agnes Shea
Murphy	Emma	Helen	28-Mar-1889	13-Mar-1889	Patrick F. Murphy	Quinn, Mary J.	Emma E. Lyness
Murphy	James	Joseph	18-Sep-1892	08-Sep-1892	Patrick Francis Murphy	Lacy, Catherine Teresa	John Patrick Lacy / Margaret Elizabeth Lacy
Murphy	James	Thomas	15-Aug-1886	30-Jul-1886	Patrick J. Murphy	Doyle, Mary	James J. Byrnes / Mary E. Egan
Murphy	Margaret	Catherine	22-Dec-1889	07-Dec-1889	Patrick J. Murphy	Doyle, Mary A.	John J. Doyle / Margaret T. Doyle
Murphy	Mary	Laura	04-Dec-1887	21-Nov-1887	Patrick J. Murphy	Doyle, Mary A.	Patrick Doyle / Sara E. Ratican
Murphy	Matthew	Edwin	30-Oct-1892	13-Oct-1892	Patrick John Murphy	Doyle, Agnes	James Patrick Doyle / Catherine Doyle
Murphy	Agnes	Genevieve	22-Mar-1885	08-Mar-1885	Patrick Murphy	Quinn, Mary Joan	John J. Dugan / Mary Ann Murphy
Murphy	Ann		15-Oct-1896	07-Oct-1896	Patrick Murphy	Lacy, Mary	Theresa Mary Flaherty
Murphy	Daniel	Patrick	29-Jan-1888	13-Jan-1888	Patrick Murphy	Quinn, Mary Joan	James Rogers Kearney / Mary Elizabeth Kearney
Murphy	John	Leon	23-Aug-1886	16-Aug-1886	Patrick Murphy	Quinn, Mary Joan	Catherine Murphy
Murphy	Vincent	Joseph	04-Jun-1882	20-May-1882	Patrick Murphy	Quinn, Mary Joan	James Patrick Feeney / Rose Quinn
Murphy	Elizabeth		06-Jan-1883	06-Jan-1883	Richard Murphy	Quirk, Margaret	Elizabeth Ryan
Murphy	John	Francis	11-Nov-1883	04-Nov-1883	Richard Murphy	McNeil, Bridget	Francis McNeil / Rose McNeil
Murphy	Mary		16-Jan-1882	06-Jan-1882	Richard Murphy	Quirk, Margaret	M.F. Foley
Murphy	Catherine		06-Mar-1898	16-Feb-1898	Thomas Murphy	Kennedy, Margaret	Henry Kent / Catherine Gary
Murphy	Helen		29-Oct-1895	13-Oct-1895	Thomas Murphy	Kennedy, Margaret	Peter Kane / Ann McGee

LAST NAME	FIRST NAME	MIDDLE	BAPTISM	BIRTH	Father	Mother	SPONSORS	
Murphy	John	Thomas	09-Dec-1888	25-Nov-1888	Thomas Murphy	Kennedy, Margaret	Edward French	Mary Dunt
Murphy	Martin		01-Oct-1893	18-Sep-1893	Thomas Murphy	Kennedy, Margaret	Ambrose McDonald	Helen Slattery
Murphy	Mary	Ellen	25-Jan-1891	12-Jan-1891	Thomas Murphy	Kennedy, Margaret	William Murphy	Julia Doyle
Murphy	Margaret	Sarah	12-Oct-1890	27-Sep-1890	Tim Murphy	Kenneally, Margaret	James Murphy	Mary Kenneally
Murphy	Catherine		07-May-1882	24-Apr-1882	Timothy Murphy	Kennedy, Margaret	Phillip O'Keefe	Catherine O'Keefe
Murphy	Catherine		26-Feb-1888	03-Dec-1887	Timothy Murphy	Kenneally, Margaret	Daniel Moylan	Honora Clorthy
Murphy	Catherine		16-Oct-1891	10-Oct-1891	Timothy Murphy	Drumgoole, Joan		Helen Murrphy
Murphy	John	Joseph	23-Aug-1885	09-Aug-1885	Timothy Murphy	Doyle, Catherine	Moses Murphy	Ann Gaitley
Murphy	Joseph		14-May-1899	05-May-1899	Timothy Murphy	Halloran, Margaret	William Morrow	Mary McNamara
Murphy	Mary		14-Mar-1886	09-Mar-1886	Timothy Murphy	Keneally, Margaret	John Daily	Margaret Daily
Murphy	Theresa	Cecelia	21-Jun-1885	07-Jun-1885	Timothy Murphy	Drumgoole, Jennie	Martin Drumgoole	Ann Drumgoole
Murphy	Timothy		04-Nov-1883	19-Oct-1883	Timothy Murphy	Drumgoole, Ann	Thomas Murphy	Bridget Murphy
Murphy	William		29-Nov-1903	18-Nov-1903	Timothy S. Murphy	[Blank]	David S. Ward	Margaret Murphy
Murphy	Ira	Raymond	22-Jul-1890	30-Apr-1890	William C. Murphy	Dean, Ann B.		Mary L. Murphy
Murphy	Margaret	J.	24-Sep-1905	5-Sep-1905	William G. Murphy	Hoffmeyer, Mary	William Russell	Ann Hynes
Murphy	Alice	Agnes	8-Mar-1912	28-Dec-1899	William Henry Murphy	Helbing, Catherine	James Anderson	Nora Dinan
Murphy	Louis	James	8-Mar-1912	05-Apr-1889	William Henry Murphy	Helbing, Catherine	James E. Anderson	Nora Dinan
Murphy	William	Thomas	8-Mar-1912	12-Apr-1887	William Henry Murphy	Helbing, Catherine	James C. Anderson	Nora Dinan
Murphy	William	Louis	2-Mar-1913	1-Feb-1913	William Henry Murphy	Hartman, Mary Rose	Louis James Murphy	Catherine Hartman
Murphy	James	P.	28-Oct-1909	23-Oct-1909	William John Murphy	Farrell, Anastasia Theresa	Murphy, Mary	Thomas J. Murphy
Murphy	Daniel	Elmer	29-Aug-1909	6-Aug-1909	William Murphy	Hoffmeyer, Mary	Joseph Murphy	Mary Sweykal
Murphy	George	Hillman	7-Mar-1915	13-Feb-1915	William Murphy	Hoffmeyer, Mary C.	George Dillman	Mary Hoffmayer
Murphy	Helen	Cecelia	21-Jun-1903	11-Jun-1903	William Murphy	Hoffmeyer, Mary	John Hoffmeyer	Edith Hoffmeyer
Murphy	Mary	Ann	2-Nov-1907	18-Oct-1907	William Murphy	Hoffmeyer, Mary	Thomas McBride	Mary McBride
Murphy	Robert		25-Apr-1913	6-Apr-1913	William Murphy	[Blank], Catherine		
Murphy	Stephen	LeRoy	6-Oct-1912	16-Sep-1912	William Murphy	Hoffmeyer, Mary	William Morrell	Margaret Smykel
Murphy	Thomas	Joseph	7-Aug-1912	24-Jul-1912	William Murphy	Parcell, Anastasia	Rev Thomas J. Murphy	Mary L. Kilkenny
Murphy	Dora	Ann	20-Sep-1896	14-Jun-1896	George Murray	Diehlmann, Hannah	Edward C. Kerr	Rose Martin
Murray	Mary	Ann	18-Mar-1888	07-Mar-1888	James Murray	Nolan, Ann	John Pendergast	Ann Shay
Murray	Teresa	Joan	29-Oct-1882	16-Oct-1882	James Murray	Concannon, Joan	Michael Concannon	Susan Dawson
Murray	William	Henry	16-Mar-1887	31-Aug-1833	James Murray	Spriggs, Elizabeth	John Collins	
Murray	John	Patrick	26-Apr-1903	15-Apr-1903	John M. Murray	Gavin, Mary	John Maguire	Nora Waters
Murray	Elizabeth		02-Apr-1882	29-Mar-1882	John Murray	Maguire, Cecilia	Thomas Clark	Ann Clarl
Murray	Florence		23-Dec-1883	15-Dec-1883	Martin Murray	Murray, Ann	Robert Jerome Rochfort	Catherine Murrary
Murray	Margaret		15-Oct-1882	06-Oct-1882	Martin Murray	Murray, Ann	James Murray	Mary McDonough
Murray	Michael		29-Nov-1891	27-Nov-1891	Michael Murray	Maguire, Sara	John Maguire	Sara Maguire
Murray	Ann	Alice	01-Aug-1886	10-Jul-1886	Patrick Murray	Cawfield, Mary		Margaret Preston
Murray	Eugene	Hannan	19-Dec-1887	17-Dec-1887	Patrick Murray	Gordon, Ann Ceceilia		Catherine Kelly
Murray	Florence	James	29-Jan-1886	08-Jan-1886	Patrick Murray	Gordon, Ann	Samuel France	Ann Byrnes
Murray	Francis	Patrick	06-Jan-1883	28-Dec-1883	Patrick Murray	Gordon, Ann	Edward R. Sudsbury	Ann Frantz
Murray	Joseph	Wilbur	9-Jun-1912	20-May-1912	Patrick Murray	Barrett, Mary	Laurence Metz	Honora Barrett
Murray	Mary		7-Sep-1913	11-Aug-1913	Patrick Murray	Barrett, Mary	Michael Barrett	Ann Starr
Murray	John		30-Jun-1893	15-Jun-1893	Peter Murray	Dugan, Mary		Amanda Harvey
Murray	John	Thomas	12-Jul-1885	16-Jun-1885	Robert A. Murray	Washburn, Elizabeth		Elizabeth C. Kelly
Murray	Ann	Elizabeth	10-Apr-1887	01-Dec-1886	Robert August Murray	Washburn, Elizabeth		Elizabeth Cecelia Kelly
Murray	James	Roger	25-Nov-1883	20-Oct-1883	Robert Augustine Murray	Washburn, Elizabeth		Elizabeth Cecelia Kelly
Murray	Mary	Alice	04-Nov-1888	19-Oct-1888	Robert Murray	Washbourne, Elizabeth		Elizabeth C. Kelly
Murray	Michael	James	05-Apr-1891	04-Feb-1891	Thomas Murray	Walsh, Anastasia		Mary Murray
Murray	Thomas	Joseph	28-Oct-1894	07-Oct-1894	Thomas Murray	Walsh, Anastasia	Joseph Daniel Maguire	Margaret M. Rechielt
Musey	Mary	Magdalene	13-Jun-1900	10-Mar-1900	William Musey	Schleigh, Elizabeth		Mary Schleigh
Musey	William	Lorain	29-Dec-1901	9-Nov-1901	William Musey	Schleigh, Elizabeth		Delia Cosby
Muth	Mary	Grace	23-Aug-1914	10-Aug-1914	Henry B. Muth	Fallon, Katherine Elizabeth	John A. Muth	Margaret O'Brien
Muth	Henry	Eugene	19-May-1912	14-May-1912	Henry Bernard Muth	Muth, Catherine Elizabeth	John Muth	Loretta Fallon
Muth	Elizabeth	Adalaide	21-Jun-1908	16-Jun-1908	Henry Muth	Fallon, Catherine	Peter Fallon	Philomena Muth
Myers	Joseph	Lee	21-Apr-1895	08-Apr-1895	August Myers	McCamley, Catherine	Danile Myers	Mary Myers
Myers	Charles	Henry Albert	21-Mar-1886	13-Mar-1886	Charles A.A. Myers	Lipp, Lottie E.	Joseph F. Lipp	Laura Lipp
Myers	Francis	Maurice	26-Feb-1888	11-Feb-1888	Charles Myers	Lipp, Lotta	Francis Austindorff	Laura Lipp
Myers	Mary	Louise	21-Aug-1887	08-Aug-1887	Daniel E. Myers	Quinn, Mary	James Rock	Mary L. Rock
Myers	William		08-Oct-1893	22-Sep-1893	Frederick Myers	Mealey, Julia	John Mealey	Catherine Dempsey
Myers	John	Taylor	15-May-1886	27-Apr-1866	John Myers	Taylor, Mary R.	John F. Hunter	
Myers	John	Taylor	08-Apr-1900	04-Feb-1900	John Myers	Zang, Ann	John Myers	Frances Taylor
Myers	Charles	Henry	17-Dec-1907	24-Jan-1859	William Myers	Myers, Mary	James Clancy	
Myers	Margaret		25-Oct-1896	07-Oct-1896	William Myers	Maley, Julia	Thomas Lackey	M. Lackey

LAST NAME	FIRST NAME	MIDDLE	BAPTISM	BIRTH	Father	Mother	SPONSORS
Nagel	Joan	Margaret	3-Jan-1915	22-Dec-1914	John Nagel	Clinton, Helen	Joseph Muldoone
Nagle	Julia	Margaret	23-Jun-1895	13-Jun-1895	Charles Nagle	Flemmings, Bridget	Mary Clemson
Nagle	Charles	William	8-May-1914	13-Feb-1871	Charles William Nagle	Wilcox, Ann K.	Mary Jeanette Sindall
Naguire	Mary	Margaret	25-Sep-1888	23-Sep-1888	John Maguire	Hopkins, Cecelia	Mary Rohe
Napfel	Adolph	Joseph	17-Feb-1907	8-Feb-1907	Thomas J. Napfel	Guckert, Margaret	Margaret McComas
Napfel	Charles	Joseph	26-Apr-1902	22-Mar-1902	Thomas Napfel	Guckert, Margaret	A.J. Napfel
Napfel	Christopher		13-Nov-1904	30-Oct-1904	Thomas Napfel	Guckert, Margaret	Charles Koester
Napfel	Edward		02-Jan-1898	24-Dec-1897	Thomas Napfel	Guckert, Margaret	Christopher Guckert
Napfel	Thomas	Joseph	25-Mar-1900	16-Mar-1900	Thomas Napfel	Guckert, Margaret	Edward Guckert
Napier	Ann		03-Sep-1893	22-Aug-1893	Arthur Napier	Weldon, Ann	Thomas Huths
Napier	Arthur	Joseph	26-Jun-1887	20-Jun-1887	Arthur Napier	Weldon, Helen	Martin Rudolph
Napier	Edward		25-Nov-1883	14-Nov-1883	Arthur Napier	Weldon, Helen	Joseph Klein
Napier	Edward	Francis	05-Dec-1883	01-May-1862	Arthur Napier	Balmet, Joan (Jane)	Francis Schaefer
Napier	Rose	Mary	14-Jun-1885	05-Jun-1885	Arthur Napier	Weldon, Helen	Francis Schaefer
Napier	Francis	Teresa	25-Oct-1891	15-Oct-1891	Terence O'Neill	Whitly, Catherine	Michael Weldon
Napoleone	Elizabeth		18-Feb-1906	10-Feb-1906	George Napoleone	Rossi, Emma	Felix Gormly
Nary	Albert	Gibbons	11-Jul-1886	25-Jun-1886	Michael Nary	Kane, Sara	Anthony Didominis
Naylor	James	Albert	1-Nov-1903	22-Oct-1903	William Naylor	Welsh, Florence	Henry Flynn
Neary	Catherine		17-Jan-1892	06-Jan-1892	Michael Neary	Kane, Sara	James Kaestler
Neary	Edward	Aloysius	09-Jun-1889	31-May-1889	Michael Neary	Kane, Sara	John Neary
Neary	Francis	Patrick	20-Apr-1884	12-Apr-1884	Michael Neary	Kane, Sara	Michael Ward
Neary	Helen		20-Nov-1887	09-Nov-1887	Michael Neary	Kane, Sara	Michael Cain
Neary	Thomas		28-Jan-1883	17-Jan-1883	Michael Neary	Kane, Sara	John Duffy
Neary	Ann		1-May-1910	21-Apr-1910	Thomas Neary	McAvoy, Katherine	James Thomas Lewis
Neary	Helen		24-Aug-1913	13-Aug-1913	Thomas Neary	McEvoy, Catherine	James Logue
Neibeck	Charles		21-Apr-1913	26-Jan-1880	Charles Niebeck	Kerns, Catherine	James Gilhooly
NeidHammell	Mary	Catherine	14-Dec-1890	03-Dec-1890	Henry Bernard NeidHammell	Kelly, Alice Gertrude	William Edward Kelly
Neil	William	H.	17-Jul-1910	11-Jun-1910	Joseph M. Neil	Fallong, Adelina Haugh	
Nelligan	Thomas	Joseph	02-May-1895	20-Apr-1895	Thomas Nelligan	Turner, Mary E.	John Rock
Neothen	Elizabeth	Louise	15-Jan-1901	23-Nov-1900	John Neothen	Kline, Alice	
Nestor	William	Francis	18-Feb-1883	09-Feb-1883	Frederick Nestor	Hays, Bridget	James Glenn
Nestor	Mary	Elena	10-Aug-1899	02-Jul-1899	John Nestor	Eagers, Mary	James Nestor
Nevill	Catherine		31-Jul-1902	19-Jul-1902	Edward Nevill	Furlong, Catherine	
Nevill	Helen		02-Aug-1902	19-Jul-1902	Edward Nevill	Furlong, Catherine	
Neville	Ann		14-Sep-1906	11-Aug-1906	Edward Neville	Furlong, Catherine	
Neville	Catherine	Helen	27-Aug-1905	2-Aug-1905	Edward Neville	Furlong, Catherine	James P. Barry
Neville	Edward		21-Aug-1898	10-Aug-1898	Edward Neville	Furlong, Catherine	Nicholas McGraw
Neville	Mary		17-Dec-1899	29-Nov-1899	Edward Neville	Furlong, Catherine	
Neville	Thomas		10-Apr-1897	05-Apr-1897	Edward Neville	Furlong, Catherine	Peter McCabe
Neville	Elizabeth		19-Sep-1886	09-Sep-1886	William H. Neville	Ryan, Mary	Bernard McKenna
Neville	Helen	Grace	10-Aug-1890	28-Jul-1890	William Neville	Ryan, Mary	Matthew McDermott
Nevins	John	Michael	10-Feb-1901	13-Jan-1901	Edward Nevins	[Blank], Catherine	John Dumphy
Newell	Bridget	Catherine	09-Aug-1903	02-Aug-1903	James J. Newell	Kavanaugh, Ann	Catherine Roddy
Newell	James	J.	17-Dec-1905	9-Dec-1905	James J. Newell	Kavanaugh, Ann	Patrick Reilly
Newman	John	Carroll	04-Aug-1901	29-Jul-1901	John Newman	Rock, Sarah	Edward Affraux
Nice	Edward	Vincent	06-Feb-1887	20-Jan-1887	Howard M. Nice	Connolly, Mary	Edward Connolly
Nice	Ann	Agnes	03-Aug-1883	21-Jul-1883	Howard Milton Nice	Connolly, Mary	Patrick Connolly
Nichols	Charles	Thomas	04-Feb-1887	26-Jan-1887	Charles Nichols	Murphy, Mary Helen	Thomas Murphy
Nichols	Helen		09-Dec-1888	25-Nov-1888	Charles Nichols	Murphy, Mary Helen	Michael Murphy
Nichols/Thompson	Louise		16-Feb-1892	[Blank]	James Nichols	Perkins, Patty	
Niemeyer	Francis	Martin	11-Jan-1885	29-Nov-1884	Frederick G. Niemeyer	Glesse, Rose	Martin Solek
Niemeyer	Charles	Edward	01-Jul-1888	11-Jun-1888	Frederick Niemeyer	Gillese, Rose	John Carroll
Niemeyer	Eugene	Charles	09-Feb-1890	08-Jan-1890	Frederick Niemeyer	Gillece, Rose Mary	John J. Tighe
Niemeyer	Ann	Magdalene	08-Nov-1891	18-Oct-1891	Frederick William Niemeyer	Geleese, Rose Mary	John Tighe
Niemeyer	Frederick	William	19-Mar-1882	04-Mar-1882	Frederick William Niemeyer	Galespe, Rose Mary	Patrick Donohoe
Niemeyer	George	Louis	04-Oct-1883	25-Sep-1883	Frederick William Niemeyer	Gillece, Rose	George Itzel
Niemeyer	Rose		17-Oct-1886	09-Jul-1886	William F. Niemeyer	[Blank], Rose	Michael Gillease
Nigart	Emma	Catherine	15-Jul-1886	25-Jun-1886	Henry M. Nigart	Raborg, Emma Catherine	
Nighl	John	Ryan	13-Mar-1887	07-Mar-1887	Frederick A. Nighl	Smith, Margaret	John R. Sheehan
Nighl	Catherine	Cecelia	12-Jul-1885	01-Jul-1885	Frederick Nighl	Sincoe, Margaret	Jsoeph Dignan
Nighl	Elizabeth	Margaret	28-Oct-1888	12-Oct-1888	Frederick Nighl	Sincoe, Margaret	Richard Joseph Driscoll
Nippard	Mary	Irene	22-Dec-1912	26-May-1894	George Oliver Nippard	Meise, Eloise	
Nixon	Elizabeth	Margaret	24-Oct-1888	06-Oct-1888	Hugh Nixon	Gernhardt, Elizabeth	Agnes Edell

SPONSORS (col 9)
Mary Cassidy
Mary Clemson
Mary Jeanette Sindall
Mary Rohe
Margaret McComas
Elizabeth Napfel
Mary Haire
Josephine Guckert
Mary Deise
Rose Weldon
Agnes Oens
Agnes Carey
Ann Doolan
Elizabeth Keenan
Roser Didominis
Elizabeth Byrne
Ann Kaestler
Ann Neary
Catherine Ryan
Ann Flynn
Catherine O'Hara
Judy Kennedy
Ann McAvoy
Mary McAvoy
Mary Bailey
Joan J. Neil
Mary Rock
Sarah Yeakle
Mary Glenn
Mary Burns
Mary Kavanaugh
Margaret Bray
Mary E. Graley
Josephine Barry
Margaret Bray
Margaret Dumphy
Ella Neville
Alice Mason
Helen McDermott
Ellen Leary
Thomas P. Kavanaugh
Mary Newell
Adalaide Jones
Margaret McNally
Mary Connolly
Mary Enge
Rachel Battray
Ann Glesse
Rose Carroll
Ann Gillece
Ann Geleese
Mary Catherine White
Ann Gilleace
Alicia Raborg
Joan Lawrence
Catherine Sincoe
Elizabeth Sincoe
Bridget Martin

LAST NAME	FIRST NAME	MIDDLE	BAPTISM	BIRTH	Father	Mother	SPONSORS
Noakes	Cecelia	Joan	06-Oct-1888	08-Mar-1869	James G. Noakes	Britton, Ella Virginia	Catherine C. Pfister
Noctor	Ann	Elizabeth	11-Nov-1911	11-Nov-1911	Matthew Noctor	Curran, Bertha	Mary Noctor
Noctor	Catherine	Mary	24-Apr-1910	15-Apr-1910	Matthew Noctor	Curran, Delia	Mary Quinn
Noctor	Eileen		10-May-1914	25-Apr-1914	Matthew Noctor	Curran, Bridget	Katherine McCormick
Noctor	James		29-Dec-1908	15-Dec-1908	Matthew Noctor	Curran, Delia	Thomas Lannon
Nolan	Eleanor	Margaret	14-May-1893	05-May-1893	John Thomas Nolan	Seobold, Louise	Frederick Siebold
Nolan	James	Albert	20-Jan-1895	02-Jan-1895	John Thomas Nolan	Siebold, Louise	George Joseph Nolan
Nolan	John		07-Mar-1897	01-Mar-1897	Martin Nolan	Banahan, Mary	Michael Nolan
Noon	Catherine		16-Jul-1882	07-Jul-1882	John Noon	McWilliams, Emma	Michael Noon, Jr.
Noonan	Mary	Elizabeth	16-Mar-1890	06-Mar-1890	Daniel Noonan	Clarke, Margaret A.	Samuel A. Moore
Noonan	Catherine	Honora	30-Mar-1913	20-Mar-1913	Edmund Noonan	Whitty, Julia	Thomas Eagan
Noonan	Mary	Regina	21-Jun-1914	11-Jun-1914	Edward Noonan	Whitty, Julia	Patrick Noonan
Noonan	Joseph	Donald	12-Aug-1888	02-Aug-1888	Jerome Joseph Noonan	McWilliams, Emma	Howard Smith
Noonan	Carl		19-Dec-1886	15-Dec-1886	Jerome Noonan	Hennesey, Mary	William Noonan
Noonan	John	Joseph	30-Mar-1884	22-Mar-1884	John Joseph Noonan	McWilliams, Emily	Jonathan Mallalien
Noonan	Loretta	Eula	07-Mar-1886	25-Feb-1886	John Noonan	McWilliams, Emma	Thomas J. Noonan
Noonan	Francis	Allan	2-Aug-1908	8-Jul-1908	Pat Noonan	Barrett, Mary	Frank P. [Blank]
Noonan	Eugene		19-May-1912	20-Apr-1912	Patrick J. Noonan	Barrett, Morris[sic]	Francis P. McGramm
Noonan	Jerome	Anthony	27-Jul-1902	10-Jul-1902	Patrick Noonan	Barrett, Mary	William Curran
Noonan	Mary		2-Oct-1904	9-Sep-1904	Patrick Noonan	Barrett, Mary	Julia Barrett
Noonan	Helen		15-Jan-1882	13-Jan-1882	William Noonan	Quirk, Honora	Thomas Brazier
Noonan	Patrick		20-Mar-1887	12-Mar-1887	William Noonan	Quirk, Honora	Patrick Meskill
Noonan	William		25-Jun-1909	25-Jun-1909	William Noonan	Hawkins, Mary	Joan Shea
Norman	Henry	John	22-Jan-1905	5-Jan-1905	William Norman	Hotem, Mary	Catherine Hotem
Norris	Ann	Mary	24-Jun-1885	04-Jun-1885	Charles Norris	McCabe, Rose	Emma Crosby
Norris	Sophia	Teresa	06-Jan-1890	12-Dec-1889	Charles Norris	McCabe, Rose	Margaret Holmes
Norton	Vincent	Paul	21-Nov-1915	12-Nov-1915	James Norton	Doxen, Ruth	Mary Kenealy
Norton	Catherine		06-May-1888	28-Apr-1888	John Norton	Whelan, Eliza	Margaret McMunuls
Norton	John		27-Aug-1893	15-Aug-1893	Martin Norton	Griffin, Bridget	Mary Norton
Norton	Angela	Rose	24-Jul-1910	12-Jul-1910	Micharl Norton	Conlon, Bridget	Frances Norton
Norton	John	Patrick	16-Sep-1894	28-Aug-1894	Patrick Norton	Keedy, Catherine	Catherine Kelly
Norton/Green	Mary	Estelle	08-Dec-1900	02-Sep-1879	John Norton	[Blank], Margaret	Mary [Blank]
Norwood	Mary	Ann	28-Mar-1915	11-Mar-1915	William F. Norwood	Ely, Susanna	Elizabeth Norwood
Norwood	Emilie	Joan	05-Aug-1894	19-Jul-1894	William F. Norwood	Casey, Catherine Teresa	John Norwood
Norwood	William	Francis	13-Oct-1889	03-Oct-1889	William Norwood	Casey, Catherine	Henry Burgun
Norwood	William	Francis	16-Mar-1913	28-Feb-1913	William Norwood	Ely, Susanna	Helen Norwood
Nossel	Francis	Joseph	3-Oct-1915	25-Sep-1915	Francis John Nossel	Quinn, Eleanor Agnes	John Bernard Nossel
Nottingham	Gladys	Mary	03-May-1884	12-Mar-1871	William Nottingham	Beale, Mary	Mary E. Quinn
Oaks	Catherine	Mary	23-Jul-1911	18-Jul-1911	William F. Oaks	Freeman, Catherine M.	Mary E. Drane
Oates	Patrick		24-Jun-1891	24-Jun-1891	Francis Oates	Hanlon, Margaret	Mary Freeman
Oates	Margaret		27-May-1883	15-May-1883	Mary Oates	McGivey, Bridget	Mary Hester
Oates	William	Francis	11-Apr-1886	30-Mar-1886	Patrick F. Oates	Hanlon, Margaret	Alice Hanlon
Oates	Ella		25-Oct-1896	15-Oct-1896	Patrick Oates	Hanlon, Margaret	Ella Nagle
Oates	Mary	Dorothy	21-Jun-1908	6-Jun-1908	William F. Oates	Freeman, Catherine	Alice Oates
Oates	William	Francis	31-May-1914	22-May-1914	William Oates	Foreman, Katherine Josephine	Mary Elizabeth Rodgers
Oats	Mary		14-Jun-1900	13-Jun-1900	Francis Oats	Hanlon, Margaret	Ellen Fanon
O'Brien	Mary	Catherine	24-Jul-1910	24-Jun-1910	Daniel O'Brien	Bremmer, Nora	Cecelia Hisky
O'Brien	Helen		30-Nov-1884	02-Nov-1884	Francis O'Brien	Rebel, Bridget	Mollie McKewen
O'Brien	Margaret		03-Sep-1882	16-Aug-1882	James O'Brien	McShane, Margaret	Ann O'Brien
O'Brien	Joseph	Patrick	09-Sep-1883	26-Aug-1883	John Joseph O'Brien	Harper, Mary Helen	William Grogan
O'Brien	Thomas	August	10-Nov-1895	24-Oct-1895	John Joseph O'Brien	Hopper, Mary Ellen	Patricck Donohoe
O'Brien	Mary	Louise	10-Nov-1907	4-Oct-1907	John M. O'Brien	Alexander, Rebecca	August Alexander
O'Brien	Agnes		28-Sep-1890	22-Sep-1890	John O'Brien	Steadman, Mary	John Steadman
O'Brien	Agnes		8-Jan-1905	22-Dec-1904	John O'Brien	McCourt, Margaret	Joseph Cavanaugh
O'Brien	Ann		27-Mar-1898	13-Mar-1898	John O'Brien	Clarke, Ann	John Cullan
O'Brien	Bernard		29-Jan-1909	9-Jan-1909	John O'Brien	McCourt, Margaret	Peter McCourt
O'Brien	Bernardine	Elizabeth	20-Nov-1898	31-Oct-1898	John O'Brien	Hopper, Mary	Francis Hess
O'Brien	Bernardine		25-Nov-1900	7-Nov-1900	John O'Brien	McCourt, Margaret	Joseph McCabe
O'Brien	Catherine	Philomena	21-Jul-1895	05-Jul-1895	John O'Brien	McCourt, Margaret	Donald Kennedy
O'Brien	Eleanor		18-Mar-1888	26-Feb-1888	John O'Brien	Clarke, Ann	Michael O'Brien
O'Brien	John	Ellen	12-Jan-1890	23-Dec-1890	John O'Brien	Clarke, Ann	William O'Brien
O'Brien	Joseph		08-Jul-1888	01-Jul-1888	John O'Brien	Steadman, Mary J.	Edward Steadman
O'Brien	Joseph	Leo	13-Mar-1898	03-Mar-1898	John O'Brien	McCourt, Margaret	Charles McCourt

LAST NAME	FIRST NAME	MIDDLE	BAPTISM	BIRTH	Father	Mother	SPONSORS
O'Brien	Mary	Josephine	11-Sep-1892	31-Aug-1892	John O'Brien	Clarke, Ann	Michael O'Brien / Elizabeth Ruppert
O'Brien	Mary		01-Jan-1893	20-Dec-1892	John O'Brien	McCourt, Margaret	Patrick Curran / Mary Curran
O'Brien	Rebecca	Agnes	12-Aug-1903	09-Jul-1903	John O'Brien	Alexander, Rebecca M.	Augusta Alexander
O'Brien	Thomas		31-Oct-1886	22-Oct-1886	John O'Brien	Clarke, Ann	Patrick Clarke / Margaret Clarke
O'Brien	James	W.	14-Jun-1903	04-Jun-1903	John P. Brien	McCourt, Margaret	William MacGregor / Mary MacGregor
O'Brien	John	Patrick	01-Feb-1891	17-Jan-1891	John Patrick O'Brien	McCourt, Margaret	William P. O'Brien / Catherine O'Brien
O'Brien	Helen		19-Feb-1893	24-Jan-1893	Joseph O'Brien	Hopper, Mary E.	Thomas Grogan / Catherine McQuillan
O'Brien	John	Francis	16-Jun-1889	05-Jun-1889	Joseph O'Brien	Hopper, Mary	John Francis Guerin / Catherine McCluskey
O'Brien	Mary	Ann	11-Jan-1891	29-Dec-1890	Joseph O'Brien	Hopper, Mary Helen	Franklin Hopper / Margaret Gaven
O'Brien	Michael	Francis	31-Oct-1886	11-Oct-1886	Joseph O'Brien	Hopper, Mary E.	Owen Hopper / Maggie McCusker
O'Brien	Wilmer	Joseph	18-Feb-1894	12-Feb-1894	Michael J. O'Brien	McCormick, Ann	John McCormick / Catherine Owens
O'Brien	Brandan		12-Jun-1892	02-Jun-1892	Michael Joseph O'Brien	McCormick, Ann	Thomas Francis Hopper / Mary Ann Hopper
O'Brien	John	E.	12-Dec-1896	09-Dec-1896	Michael Joseph O'Brien	McCormick, Ann	Francis Hoffer / Catherine Cammick
O'Brien	Allan		28-Oct-1900	16-Oct-1900	Michael O'Brien	McCormick, Ann	James Hyland / Mary Hamilton
O'Brien	Mary		16-Sep-1895	16-Sep-1895	Michael O'Brien	McCormick, Ann	Thomas Burke / Mary Ellen Hess
O'Brien	William	Jennings	15-Oct-1899	15-Oct-1899	Michael O'Brien	McCormick, Ann	James Gately / Ellen McCormick
O'Brien	Jerome		31-Oct-1886	24-Oct-1886	Patrick O'Brien	Flaherty, Catherine	Dennis Kelly / Margaret Kelly
O'Brien	Edward		14-Sep-1884	04-Sep-1884	Peter O'Brien	Hannigan, Henrietta Virginia	George Laurence Gold / Mary Helen Crawford
O'Brien	Margaret		26-Feb-1882	05-Feb-1882	Peter O'Brien	Harrigan, Virginia	Alexander Lange / Margaret Lange
O'Brien	Joseph	Anthony	9-Jun-1907	27-May-1907	Thomas J. O'Brien	Snyder, Margaret	Joseph Zimmerman
O'Brien	Margaret	Bridget	7-Jan-1906	23-Dec-1905	Thomas J. O'Brien	Snyder, Margaret	Charles J. O'Brien / Bridget Snyder
O'Brien	Mary	Agnes	8-Nov-1908	27-Oct-1908	Thomas J. O'Brien	Snyder, Margaret	Francis Thorne / Mary Zimmerman
O'Brien	Dennis		16-Aug-1891	08-Aug-1891	Thomas O'Brien	Shea, Julia	Francis Morrell / Margaret Neville
O'Brien	Francis		04-Jun-1899	12-May-1899	Thomas O'Brien	Shea, Julia	Peter Lally / Ann Lally
O'Brien	Honora		01-Mar-1896	20-Feb-1896	Thomas O'Brien	Shea, Julia	Michael Ruckley / Helen Noonan
O'Brien	John	Richard	15-Dec-1889	04-Dec-1889	Thomas O'Brien	Harrington, Mary	John Gruner / Mary Becker
O'Brien	Mary		17-Dec-1893	03-Dec-1893	Thomas O'Brien	O'Shea, Julia	John Michael Finn / Catherine Finn
O'Brien	Thomas		29-Jan-1886	27-Jan-1886	Thomas O'Brien	Shea, Julia	Dennis Shea / Mary O'Brien
O'Brien	Catherine		03-Aug-1902	21-Jul-1902	William J. O'Brien	Kelly, Mary	Thomas P. Kelly / Catherine McKay
O'Brien	Catherine		01-Jan-1899	21-Dec-1898	William O'Brien	Kelly, Mary	James O'Brien / Catherine Kelly
O'Brien	Daniel	Francis	07-Jun-1885	29-May-1885	William O'Brien	Donohue, Mary	Michael Conway / Mary Ryan
O'Brien	Mary	Genevieve	07-Oct-1900	25-Sep-1900	William O'Brien	Kelly, Mary	Francis Tracey / Margaret O'Brien
O'Brien	Michael		07-Jun-1885	29-May-1885	William O'Brien	Donohue, Mary	John O'Connor / Catherine Donegan
O'Connell	Ann	B.	19-Nov-1899	03-Nov-1899	Charles O'Connell	Frazier, Ann	Francis Quinn / Ella Noor
O'Connell	Francis	Xavier	24-Jul-1887	08-Jul-1887	John Joseph O'Connell	Daily, Helen Laura	James Cotter / Frances Cecelia Roche
O'Connell	Joseph		28-Oct-1883	15-Oct-1883	John Joseph O'Connell	Daly, Helen	Henry Fay / Mary Maguire
O'Connell	Isabelle		25-Nov-1888	16-Nov-1888	John O'Connell	Murray, Elizabeth	James O'Connell / Isabelle O'Connell
O'Connell	Maurice		25-Apr-1885	03-Apr-1885	John O'Connell	Daly, Helen	John Smith / Catherine Smith
O'Connor	Mary	Catherine	03-Jun-1894	21-May-1894	William Joseph O'Connell	Thornton, Margaret	Patrick Francis Reilly / Mary Foley
O'Connor	Agnes		17-Oct-1897	01-Oct-1897	William O'Connell	Thornton, Margaret	James Thornton / Mary Donoghoe
O'Connor	Bridget	Mary Gertrude	25-Sep-1892	07-Sep-1892	William O'Connell	Thornton, Margaret	James P. Thornton / Catherine Thornton
O'Connor	Margaret		05-Jun-1895	15-May-1895	William O'Connell	Thornton, Margaret	James Thorton / Bridget Thorton
O'Conner	Mary	Loretta	14-Nov-1883	14-Nov-1883	Joseph O'Connell	Reilly, Mary Elizabeth	James O'Conner / Margaret Reilly
O'Connor	Joseph	Howard	5-Dec-1909	21-Nov-1909	Charles Matthew O'Connor	Silver, Netter	Howard T. Curran / Mary Mulligan
O'Connor	Charles	Vincent	27-Sep-1896	10-Sep-1896	Charles O'Connor	[Blank], Margaret	James O'Connor / Catherine McFarland
O'Connor	Alice	Louise	05-Mar-1899	22-Feb-1899	Charles V. O'Connor	Hardy, Margaret	James O'Connor / Mary Agnes O'Connor
O'Connor	Francis		08-Mar-1885	11-Feb-1885	Francis O'Connor	Clarke, Katherine	William Smith / Ann Smith
O'Connor	Ann		12-Jan-1896	01-Jan-1896	George O'Connor	McDermott, Mary	John Browning / Ann Browning
O'Connor	Catherine	Loretta	17-Apr-1904	5-Apr-1904	George O'Connor	McDermott, Mary Agnes	Thomas F. Ronan / Catherine Ronan
O'Connor	George	Patrick	29-Aug-1897	19-Aug-1897	George O'Connor	McDermott, Mary	James Kestler / Mary McDermott
O'Connor	Mary	Helen	27-Aug-1899	19-Aug-1899	George O'Connor	McDermott, Mary	John McMahon / Catherine Halpin
O'Connor	John	Brook	12-Oct-1902	29-Sep-1902	George P. O'Connor	McDermott, Mary A.	Thomas Gollery / Ellen Daly
O'Connor	Mary		23-Dec-1895	23-Dec-1895	James Connor	Galvin, Mary		
O'Connor	Mary	Eleanor	01-Jun-1899	21-May-1899	James O'Connor	Galvin, Mary A.	William O'Connor / Julia O'Connor
O'Connor	Thomas	Herbert	22-Nov-1896	17-Nov-1896	James O'Connor	Galvin, Mary A.	James O'Connor / Sara Egan
O'Connor	William	Joseph	11-Mar-1894	28-Feb-1894	James O'Connor	Galvin, Mary	Michael James O'Connor / Sara Helen O'Connor
O'Connor	John	Joseph	21-Aug-1904	18-Aug-1904	James P. O'Connor	Galvin, Mary	Timothy Roddy / Catherine O'Connor
O'Connor	Robert		05-Jan-1902	31-Dec-1901	James P. O'Connor	Galvin, Mary Ann	William Galvin / Margaret Leland
O'Connor	Helen	Romula	16-Apr-1906	13-Apr-1906	James P.A. O'Connor	Galvin, Mary Ann	Thomas K. Galvin / Mary A. O'Connor
O'Connor	James	Galvin	22-Nov-1891	09-Nov-1891	James P.A. O'Connor	Galvin, Mary A.	Thomas J. O'Connor / Ann Roddy
O'Connor	Mary	Ann	13-Jul-1890	05-Jul-1890	James Patrick August O'Connor	Galvin, Mary Ann	John Thomas Galvin / Mary Aloysius O'Connor
O'Connor	John	Joseph	23-Mar-1913	11-Mar-1913	John Joseph O'Connor	Connolly, Ann	Michael Ward / Isabelle Connolly
O'Connor	Catherine		28-May-1905	13-May-1905	John O'Connor	Mears, Catherine	Richard Upman / Rose Connelly

LAST NAME	FIRST NAME	MIDDLE	BAPTISM	BIRTH	Father	Mother	SPONSORS	
O'Connor	Elizabeth		2-Oct-1904	21-Sep-1904	John O'Connor	Lanahan, Bertha	Ann Lanahan	Martin O'Connor
O'Connor	John		25-Nov-1906	9-Nov-1906	John O'Connor	Lanahan, Bertha	Margaret O'Connor	Edmund Meskill
O'Connor	Mary		08-Oct-1893	01-Oct-1893	John O'Connor	Mears, Catherine	Mary Mears	Alphonsus Birkenbacher
O'Connor	Teresa		28-May-1905	13-May-1905	John O'Connor	Mears, Catherine	Elizabeth Ryan	Walter Upman
O'Connor	Elizabeth	M.	27-Aug-1905	13-Aug-1905	Joseph B. O'Connor	Smith, Margaret	Sarah Weakle	Stephn H. Campbell
O'Connor	Ada		11-Jul-1900	01-Jul-1900	Joseph O'Connor	Smith, Margaret	Adalina Smith	John Smith
O'Connor	Ann		23-Aug-1896	09-Aug-1896	Joseph O'Connor	Smith, Margaret	Elizabeth McAuliffe	Stephen King
O'Connor	Francis		15-Feb-1895	11-Feb-1895	Joseph O'Connor	Smith, Margaret	Elizabeth Loughran	John Patrick Smith
O'Connor	John		26-Apr-1885	17-Apr-1885	Joseph O'Connor	Smith, Margaret	Cecelia Lacey	James Owens
O'Connor	Joseph		22-Dec-1889	08-Dec-1889	Joseph O'Connor	Smith, Margaret	Ann Smith	Daniel Sheeley
O'Connor	Margaret		06-Jul-1902	27-Jun-1902	Joseph O'Connor	Smith, Margaret	Mary Dunn	Charles Gulhaar
O'Connor	Mary		03-Jul-1892	23-Jun-1892	Joseph O'Connor	Smith, Margaret	Elizabeth Smith	James Lochran
O'Connor	Mary		30-Jan-1898	06-Jan-1898	Joseph O'Connor	Smith, Margaret	Ann Smith	Francis Lynch
O'Connor	Esther		22-Aug-1897	20-Jul-1897	Laurence O'Connor	Ward, Mary E.	Rose Doyle	
O'Connor	J.	Agnes	14-Mar-1909	13-Feb-1909	Laurence O'Connor	Ward, Mary	Agnes Caffery	
O'Connor	Laurence	Leonard V.	25-Mar-1900	26-Feb-1900	Laurence O'Connor	Ward, Mary	Emma Ward	
O'Connor	Margaret		9-Jul-1905	10-Jun-1905	Laurence O'Connor	Ward, Mary E.	Mary Whelan	James Whelan
O'Connor	Gerald	Stewart	19-Jul-1908	21-May-1908	Martin O'Connor	Beard, Sarah L.	Mary Kaife	Gerald O'Connor
O'Connor	Mary	Louise	17-Mar-1912	11-Mar-1912	Martin P. O'Connor	Ehrhart, Clara	Mary Evans	John Evans
O'Connor	Dennis		09-Mar-1902	23-Feb-1902	Michael J. O'Connor	Mears, Catherine	Sara Collins	Henry Bowen
O'Connor	Margaret		28-Apr-1895	18-Apr-1895	Michael John O'Connor	Mears, Catherine	Margaret Gordon	William Augustus Malia
O'Connor	Hugo		2-Nov-1902	24-Oct-1902	Michael O'Connor	Doyle, Mary	Mary Ritter	
O'Connor	James	Arthur	24-Mar-1901	13-Mar-1901	Michael O'Connor	Doyle, Mary	Ann Quigley	
O'Connor	Thomas		20-Nov-1898	31-Oct-1898	Michael O'Connor	Mears, Catherine	Mary O'Brien	Andrew O'Brien
O'Connor	James	Joseph	11-Jun-1893	31-May-1893	Miles O'Connor	O'Connell, Mary	Margaret O'Connor	Charles McKernen
O'Connor	Mary		18-Aug-1895	14-Aug-1895	Patrick O'Connor	McGovern, Mary	Rose McGovern	Michael McGovern
O'Connor	Peter		06-May-1883	04-May-1883	Patrick O'Connor	McGovern, Mary	Margaret McGovern	Robert Burns
O'Connor	T.	Mary	09-Oct-1898	24-Sep-1898	Patrick O'Connor	McGovern, Mary	Elizabeth Dunleavy	John Hennessey
O'Connor	Mary	Theresa	25-Sep-1892	08-Sep-1892	William O'Connor	O'Brien, Mary	Theresa O'Connor	Edward O'Conner
O'Day	Bridget		03-Dec-1882	22-Nov-1882	John O'Day	Halloran, Mary	Mary Gill	Thomas O'Day
O'Day	Catherine	Ann	21-Nov-1886	13-Nov-1886	John O'Day	Holleran, Mary	Elenora McGovern	Patrick Halloran
O'Day	Mary		31-Aug-1884	25-Aug-1884	John O'Day	Halloran, Mary	Bridget Halloran	Patrick Halloran
O'Day	Michael		06-Dec-1885	31-Nov-1885	Michael O'Day	Welby, Margaret	Catherine Madden	Nicholas Barry
O'Day	Bridget		14-Nov-1886	04-Nov-1886	Thomas O'Day	Gill, Mary	Ann Toole	Martin Halloran
O'Day	Peter		06-Nov-1887	03-Nov-1887	Michael O'Day	Gill, Mary	Mary Clancy	John O'Day
O'Dea	John		17-Feb-1884	16-Jan-1884	Michael O'Dea	Welby, Margaret	Catherine Madden	Nicholas Barret
O'Dea	Thomas	Joseph	09-Nov-1890	27-Oct-1890	Michael O'Dea	Welby, Margaret	Ella Welby	Thomas Hurney
O'Dea	Catherine		29-Sep-1895	15-Sep-1895	Thomas P. O'Dea	Gill, Mary	Margaret Welby	
Odendahl	John	Laurence	15-Dec-1901	01-Oct-1901	John Odendahl	Ruhl, Elizabeth		
O'Donohue	James		05-Aug-1888	24-Jul-1888	Samuel O'Donahue	Frank, Bertha	Susan Diggs	John O'Donohue
O'Donnell	Catherine	Rosalie	27-Jun-1915	15-Jun-1915	Charles O'Donnell	Haydock, Agnes	Catherine Chambers	Robert Chambers
O'Donnell	Winifred	Frances	29-Oct-1911	17-Oct-1911	Edward J. O'Donnell	Roche, Abigail	Catherine K. McGeady	Edward F. McGeady
O'Donnell	Abigail		16-Dec-1906	6-Nov-1906	Edward O'Donnell	McCambridge, Abigail (Roche)	Margaret Roche	Samuel Kane
O'Donnell	James	Henry	14-Oct-1906	2-Oct-1906	James P. O'Donnell	Klasmeyer, Agnes	Mary Emge	Henry Klasmyer
O'Donnell	Teresa	Dolores	5-Sep-1915	16-Aug-1915	John E. O'Donnell	Ehm, Amelia	Ann Ehm	William L. O'Donnell
O'Donnell	Margaret		17-Aug-1902	03-Jul-1902	John J. O'Donnell	Hughes, Mary E.	Mary Hughes	
O'Donnell	Paul	Leon	27-Nov-1887	12-Oct-1887	John O'Donnell	Devlin, Ann	Mary Ann O'Brien	George Yakel
O'Farrell	Margaret	Agnes	30-Mar-1890	21-Mar-1890	James O'Farrell	Janes, Mary	Margaret Jones	
O'Hanlon	Walter		21-Jul-1889	13-Jul-1889	Michael O'Hanlon	Drew, Catherine	Margaret Sheehan	Jerome Cronin
O'Hara	Charles	Edward	21-Jul-1911	27-May-1911	Francis Edward O'Hara	Weckresser, Augusta	Mary Smeykal	
O'Hara	Mary	O'Hara	28-Feb-1915	15-Apr-1913	Francis O'Hara	[Blank], Bertha	Catherine Essinger	
O'Hara	Bernard		22-Nov-1914	7-Nov-1914	John F. O'Hara	Bosson, Helen	Ann O'Hara	James O'Hara
O'Hara	Ann	Helen	1-Apr-1906	21-Mar-1906	John O'Hara	Bosson, Ann	Martha Murphy	James O'Hara
O'Hara	Catherine	Elizabeth	26-Oct-1913	17-Oct-1913	John O'Hara	Bosson, Honora	Mary Mueller	Charles H. Mueller
O'Hara	Charles	James	24-Nov-1907	8-Nov-1907	John O'Hara	Bosson, Ann	Mary A. Baumgartner	George M. Hogan
O'Hara	Margaret		1-May-1910	11-Apr-1910	John O'Hara	Bosson, Ann	Mary Hagerty	James O'Hara
O'Hara	Marion		16-Apr-1911	29-Mar-1911	John O'Hara	Bosson, Ann	Ann O'Hara	James O'Hara
O'Hara	Mary		12-Nov-1904	10-Nov-1904	John O'Hara	Bosson, Ann		
O'Hara	Mildred	Eleanor	17-Nov-1912	9-Nov-1912	John O'Hara	Bosson, Ann	Elizabeth [Blank]	William Boylan
O'Hara	James	Bosson	18-Apr-1909	31-Mar-1909	John Thomas O'Hara	Bosson, Helen Ann	Edith Bosson	James Garrity
O'Hara	Mary	Mildred	29-Oct-1893	21-Oct-1893	Patrick Arthur O'Hara	Sheeler, Ann	Ann Simms	Edward O'Hara
O'Hara	Agnes	Isabelle	29-Nov-1891	12-Nov-1891	Patrick O'Hara	Sheeler, Ann	Genevieve O'Hara	Bernard O'Hara
O'Hara	Ann	Elizabeth	24-Jan-1886	06-Jan-1886	Patrick O'Hara	Sheeler, Ann	Margaret O'Hara	Thomas Sheeler

LAST NAME	FIRST NAME	MIDDLE	BAPTISM	BIRTH	Father	Mother	SPONSORS
O'Hara	Edward	Louis	18-May-1890	05-May-1890	Patrick O'Hara	Sheeler, Ann	Thomas Sheeler	Mary O'Hara
O'Hara	James	Gibbons	13-May-1888	03-May-1888	Patrick O'Hara	Sheeler, Ann	John Sheeler	Mary O'Hara
O'Hara	Mary	Agnes	05-Jun-1887	15-May-1887	Patrick O'Hara	Sheeler, Ann	William Garrity	Eleanor Sheeler
O'Hara	Margaret		08-Mar-1891	10-Feb-1891	William Charles O'Hara	Carron, Rose	Deidrich Linnenbom	Mary Irvin
O'Keefe	John	Michael	29-Jun-1884	19-Jun-1884	David O'Keefe	Welby, Mary	Michael F. Conway	Ellen Welby
O'Keefe	John		27-Sep-1885	24-Sep-1885	David O'Keefe	Welby, Mary	John Welby	Catherine Welby
O'Keefe	Margaret	Collins	11-Jun-1893	08-Jun-1893	David O'Keefe	Welby, Mary	John Callahan	Margaret Collins
O'Keefe	Ann	Elizabeth	08-Jan-1899	06-Jan-1899	James O'Keefe	Carroll, Margaret	Vincent O'Keefe	Matilda Carroll
O'Keefe	Mary	Regina	23-Aug-1896	18-Aug-1896	James O'Keefe	Carroll, Margaret	Henry Douthat	Regina Douthat
O'Keefe	Edward	Vincent	18-Mar-1894	01-Mar-1894	James W. O'Keefe	Carroll, Margaret		Elizabeth Byrnes
O'Keefe	Catherine	Loretta	16-Jun-1889	02-Jun-1889	William O'Keefe	Slattery, Ann	Robert Knight	Sophia McQuade
O'Keefe	Eleanora		06-Mar-1887	23-Feb-1887	William O'Keefe	Daily, Catherine	Bridget Slattery	Joan O'Keefe
O'Keefe	James	John	02-Oct-1898	23-Sep-1898	William O'Keefe	Slattery, Ann M.	John Lauer	Mary Lyons
O'Keefe	Maurice		25-Feb-1894	17-Feb-1894	William O'Keefe	Slattery, Ann	David O'Keefe	Mary Boyle
O'Keefe	William		19-Jul-1891	09-Jul-1891	William T. O'Keefe	Slattery, Ann M.	William J. Hanley	Ann Nagerty
O'Keefe	Thomas		02-May-1897	23-Apr-1897	William Thomas O'Keefe	Slattery, Ann Mary	Henry McQuaid	Catherine Ryan
O'Leary	Ann		06-Aug-1899	27-Jul-1899	Patrick O'Leary	Dumphy, Elena	Timothy Ward	
O'Leary	John	Michael	17-Jul-1904	6-Jul-1904	Patrick O'Leary	Dumphy, Ellen	John Dumphy	Mary Cullen
O'Leary	Mary	Josephine	16-Mar-1902	14-Mar-1902	Patrick O'Leary	Duffy, Ellen	Margaret Duffy	Joan Duffy
Oliver	Helen		28-Nov-1893	October 1891	Charles Oliver	Mulcahey, Ann		Catherine McDougall
Oliver	Henry	Stephen	26-Nov-1893	11-Oct-1893	Charles Oliver	Mulcahey, Ann		Emma Chambland
Oliver	Laura	Faustina	30-Aug-1885	10-Aug-1885	Charles Oliver	Mulcahey, Ann	Daniekl McDougal	Catherine McDougal
Oliver	Joseph	Edward	22-Jun-1902	09-Jun-1902	Edward Olmer	Albert, Mary	Joseph Snyder	Delia Snyder
Olmer	Gertrude		22-May-1904	4-May-1904	C. O'Mailey	Austen, Mary E.	John A. O'Mailey	Gertrude O'Mailey
O'Mailey	John	Albert	13-Jan-1884	05-Jan-1884	John Albert O'Malley	Hamilton, Julia	James O'Mailey	Mary Margaret Hamilton
O'Malley	Patrick	James	03-Jan-1886	29-Dec-1885	Edward O'Malley	Lee, Mary	John O'Toole	Mary Clancy
O'Neal	Theresa		27-Apr-1884	21-Apr-1884	James O'Neal	Hagerty, Margaret	John Hagerty	Bridget Caddau
O'Neal	Francis	Edward	04-Oct-1903	26-Sep-1903	Patrick F. O'Neal	Teevan, Margaret	Patrick O'Neal	Mary Robinson
O'Neal	Joseph		3-Oct-1909	23-Sep-1909	Patrick O'Neal	O'Brien, Ellen	Jeremaih Daley	Ellen Finn
O'Neil	Mary		17-Jun-1883	14-Jun-1883	Dennis O'Neil	Auliffe, Ann	Caroline O'Neil	Honora Herlihy
O'Neil	Celeste		24-Sep-1892	21-Sep-1892	James O'Neil	Hagerty, Margaret		Nelly O'Neil
O'Neil	Elizabeth		05-Sep-1887	10-May-1887	John O'Neil	Bannan, Ann	Daniel Cremen	Ann O'Neil
O'Neil	John		25-Mar-1883	03-Mar-1883	John Vincent O'Neil	Bannon, Ann	Hugh Francis Bannop	Elizabeth O'Neil
O'Neil	Mary	Joseph	07-Dec-1902	26-Nov-1902	Patrick O'Neil	Moore, Ellen	Henry Barnes	Nora Flanigan
O'Neil	Terence	Joseph	12-Jan-1902	05-Jan-1902	Patrick O'Neil	O'Brien, Ellen	Philip Bannon	Catherine Bannon
O'Neill	Catherine	Agnes	02-Mar-1884	13-Feb-1884	Terence O'Neil	Whitty, Catherine	John Wall	Mary O'Neil
O'Neill	John	Leon	22-Apr-1888	11-Apr-1888	Terence O'Neil	Whitty, Catherine	John O'Neil	Catherine O'Neil
O'Neill	Thomas	Francis	27-Nov-1887	09-Nov-1887	Thomas Francis O'Neil	Hitzelberger, Annette Virginia	Martin Patrick O'Neil	Margaret Teresa Burke
O'Neill	Mary		29-Dec-1889	17-Dec-1889	Catherine O'Neill[sic]	Luran, Mary	John O'Neill	Mary [Blank]
O'Neill	Charles	Francis	11-Feb-1912	4-Feb-1912	Charles O'Neill	Carney, Mary	James P. O'Neill	Ann Carney
O'Neill	Elizabeth	Ann	01-Jun-1884	27-May-1884	Dennis O'Neill	McAuliffe, Joan	James McAuliffe	Helen McAuliffe
O'Neill	William		01-Sep-1889	10-Aug-1889	Hugh F. O'Neill	Higgins, Elizabeth	John Higgins	Mary A. Gereghty
O'Neill	Harriet	Frances De Sales	17-Jul-1887	27-Jun-1887	Hugh O'Neill	Higgins, Elizabeth	Phillip Logue	Ellennor Leonard
O'Neill	Mary	Elizabeth	10-Sep-1893	18-Aug-1893	Hugh O'Neill	Higgins, Elizabeth	John Roddy	Margaret Roddy
O'Neill	Richard	Daniel	11-Aug-1895	28-Jul-1895	Hugo O'Neill	Higgins, Elizabeth	George McLaughlin	Delia McLaughlin
O'Neill	Gerald	Francis	14-Jul-1912	2-Jul-1912	Hugo O'Neill	Dunphy, Margaret	Martin Dunphy	Helen Kelly
O'Neill	John	Joseph	29-Nov-1914	22-Nov-1914	John Joseph O'Neill	Dunphy, Margaret	Richard O'Neill	Elizabeth McCabe
O'Neill	Mildred	Mary	02-Oct-1892	11-Sep-1892	James Joseph O'Neill	O'Neill, Joan Frances		Teresa Elizabeth O'Neill
O'Neill	James	Edward	31-Jul-1887	22-Jul-1887	James O'Neill	Hagerty, Margaret	David O'Neill	Mary A. Dignan
O'Neill	Joseph	Martin	21-Sep-1913	6-Sep-1913	James P. O'Neill	McGreevey, Mary A.	Peter McGreevey	Joan O'Neill
O'Neill	James	Patrick	29-Aug-1915	15-Aug-1915	James Patrick O'Neill	McGrevey, Mary A.	Charles Wilson	Catherine Barrett
O'Neill	James	Daniel	11-Oct-1903	22-Sep-1903	James Thomas O'Neill	Lee, Essie		Elizabeth Crow
O'Neill	William		14-Aug-1910	17-Jul-1910	John E. O'Neill	Lynch, Cecelia	Albert Rogers	Cecelia McCaffery
O'Neill	Charles	Joseph	30-Nov-1890	06-Oct-1890	John Joseph O'Neill	McGraw, Ann	William John McGraw	Helen O'Neill
O'Neill	Catherine		08-Mar-1885	20-Feb-1885	John O'Neill	Bannon, Ann Mary	John Bannon	Mary Edwards
O'Neill	Catherine	M.	18-Sep-1904	11-Sep-1904	John O'Neill	Quillen, Elizabeth	Thomas O'Neill	Mary Quillen
O'Neill	Charles	Boneparte	29-Dec-1889	16-Dec-1889	John O'Neill	Bannor, Ann	John Kennedy	Mary Cremens
O'Neill	Ellen	Katherine	2-Jul-1911	12-Jun-1911	John O'Neill	Clark, Emma	Thomas [Blank]	Mary Lewis
O'Neill	Joan		08-May-1898	18-Apr-1898	John O'Neill	Lynch, Cecelia	Francis Lynch	Mary McCaffrey
O'Neill	Lorreta		12-Nov-1899	26-Oct-1899	John O'Neill	Lynch, Cecelia	Charles Lynch	Ann Rutter
O'Neill	Margaret	Rosetta	13-Dec-1891	26-Nov-1891	John O'Neill	Bannon, Ann Mary	John Murtz	Emma Murtz
O'Neill	Margaret	Edith	11-Aug-1912	23-Jul-1912	John O'Neill	Clarke, Emma L.	Henry Parrish	Ida Parrish
O'Neill	Joseph		20-Apr-1884	07-Apr-1884	Martin O'Neill	Cunningham, Mary J.	Andrew J. Alluisi	Mary Alluisi

LAST NAME	FIRST NAME	MIDDLE	BIRTH	BAPTISM	Father	Mother	SPONSORS
O'Neill	Henry	Thomas	16-Aug-1896	30-Aug-1896	Michael J. O'Neil	Stinchcum, Grace A.	Francis Fitzpatrick / Mary Pugni
O'Neill	John	Patrick	31-Aug-1883	09-Sep-1883	Michael O'Neil	Redington, Catherine	Michael Connell / Mary Redington
O'Neill	Elizabeth	Elenora	08-Nov-1886	21-Nov-1886	Michael O'Neil	Redington, Catherine	Martin Redington / Margaret O'Neill
O'Neill	Frances	Catherine	15-Dec-1891	03-Jan-1892	Michael O'Neil	Riddington, Catherine	Patrick Redington / Mary O'Neill
O'Neill	Mary	Virginia	27-May-1890	15-Jun-1890	Michael O'Neil	Redington, Catherine	Thomas O'Neill / Fanny Redington
O'Neill	Catherine	Euginia	14-Jan-1894	21-Jan-1894	Patrick Francis O'Neill	Teevan, Margaret	Andrew M. Norton / Elizabeth Teevan
O'Neill	Elizabeth	Ann	06-Jun-1896	21-Jun-1896	Patrick Francis O'Neill	[Blank], Margaret	Andrew Norton / Catherine McDonald
O'Neill	Margaret	Teresa	17-Sep-1891	27-Sep-1891	Patrick Francis O'Neill	Teevan, Margaret	Terence Cusick / Catherine Teevan
O'Neill	Mary	Gertrude	31-Jul-1888	19-Aug-1888	Patrick Francis O'Neill	Teevin, Margaret	Terence O'Neill / Margaret Shea
O'Neill	Alice	Loretta	05-Mar-1901	17-Mar-1901	Patrick O'Neill	Teevan, Margaret	Bernard King / Elizabeth Teevan
O'Neill	James	Patrick	14-Jan-1897	17-Jan-1897	Patrick O'Neill	O'Brien, Helen	Hughes Bannon / Ann O'Neill
O'Neill	John	Patrick	27-Sep-1898	09-Oct-1898	Patrick O'Neill	Gevan, Margaret	Johna McDonald / Katherine Gevan
O'Neill	John		23-Aug-1899	27-Aug-1899	Patrick O'Neill	O'Brien, Helen	James McNulty / Catherine Kennedy
O'Neill	Margaret	Christmam	7-Apr-1907	14-Apr-1907	Patrick O'Neill	Brey, Ann	Edward Cusick / Mary Bannon
O'Neill	Mary	Ellen	18-Dec-1891	20-Dec-1891	Patrick O'Neill	O'Brien, Ann	Richard O'Neill / Margaret Binstead
O'Neill	Mary		1-Jul-1904	10-Jul-1904	Patrick O'Neill	Moore, Helen	Edward Cusick / Rose McNulty
O'Neill	Patrick	Francis	17-Mar-1904	20-Mar-1904	Patrick O'Neill	Brey, Ann	John Mulligan / Helen Costello
O'Neill	Thomas	Michael	31-Aug-1893	03-Sep-1893	Patrick O'Neill	O'Brien, Ella	William Brey / Mary Brey
O'Neill	Thomas		19-Jun-1898	26-Jun-1898	Patrick O'Neill	Moore, Ellen	James McDonnell / Margaret McDonnell
O'Neill	Thomas	Edward	22-Aug-1901	01-Sep-1901	Patrick O'Neill	Whitty, Catherine	Edward Carroll / Mary O'Donnell
O'Neill	Ann	Mary	28-Jul-1899	20-Aug-1899	Terence O'Neill	Whitty, Catherine	William Whitty / Lillian Whitty
O'Neill	Mary		04-Dec-1885	27-Dec-1885	Terence O'Neill	Reilly, Loretta Mary	Patrick O'Neill / Eleanor Rossiter
O'Neill	Mary	Isabelle	11-Dec-1906	13-Jan-1907	Thomas F. O'Neill	Hilzelburger, Annette V.	James A. Gunning / Margaret A. Gunning
O'Neill	John	Owen	14-Dec-1885	25-Dec-1885	Thomas O'Neill	Maloney, Ann	John Simmet / Catherine Kielty
O'Neill	Mary	Helen	12-Nov-1901	24-Nov-1901	Thomas O'Neill	Reilly, Loretta	Patrick Maloney / Emme Neville
O'Neill	Mary	Frances	7-Dec-1907	13-Dec-1907	Thomas O'Neill		John H. O'Neill / Agnes Lannon
O'Rourke	James	Koseph	04-Apr-1890	27-Apr-1890	Joseph O'Rourke	Hall, Mary	James O'Rourke / Margaret O'Rourke
O'Rourke	John	William	08-May-1882	21-May-1882	Patrick O'Rourke	Shanahan, Mary	James Snee / Bridget Snee
O'Rourke	Margaret		20-Aug-1886	05-Sep-1886	Patrick O'Rourke	Shanahan, Mary A.	Charles Giffuss / Bridget Quirk
O'Rourke	Mary	Catherine	28-May-1885	14-Jun-1885	Patrick O'Rourke	Shanahan, Mary	John Quirk / Bridget Quirk
O'Rourke	Paul	Patrick	19-Jun-1915	4-Jul-1915	Patrick Paul O'Rourke	Schmidt, Lottie	Michael O'Rourke / Elizabeth O'Rourke
O'Rourke	Loretta	Elizabeth	08-Apr-1886	16-May-1886	William O'Rourke	McGuire, Mary G.	/ Catherine McCann
Orr	Helen	Viola	17-May-1915	30-May-1915	Nelson Orr	Mullen, Mary C.	Thomas Mullen / Helen Donhauser
Orr	Mary	Helen	14-May-1911	21-Jan-1912	Nelson Orr	Mullin, Mary Catherine	Thomas Mullin / Helen Mullin
O'Shaughnessy	Mary	Margaret	23-Feb-1894	04-Mar-1894	James O'Shaughnessy	Roberts, Clare	Michael Brady / Mary Bolander
Ostendorf	Catherine	Mary	07-Aug-1895	08-Sep-1895	Henry C. Oatendorf	Seklaugh, Mary	/ Catherine Seklaugh
Osterman	Joseph	Edward	30-Jul-1905	13-Aug-1905	Francis J. Osterman	Tyler, Emme	William Bowes / Sophia Slater
Osterman	John	Gallow	7-Oct-1906	14-Oct-1906	Francis Osterman	Tyler, Emma	John Barrett / Norah Barrett
Ostermann	Henry	Bernard	12-Feb-1904	13-Mar-1904	Francis I. Ostermann	Taylor, Emma	James J. Farnen /
O'Sullivan	Bernard	Joseph	13-Nov-1884	23-Nov-1884	Daniel O'Sullivan	McAlister, Eliza	Joseph Drane / Mary Drane
O'Sullivan	Catherine		15-Jan-1908	26-Jan-1908	Daniel O'Sullivan	Riordon, Julia	John J. Cullen / Catherine Cullen
O'Sullivan	D.	Edward	31-Jul-1911	13-Aug-1911	Daniel O'Sullivan	Reardon, Julia A.	John F. Walker / Rose Leach
O'Sullivan	Elizabeth		17-Apr-1882	23-Apr-1882	Daniel O'Sullivan	McAlister, Elizabeth	John King / Mary Ann King
O'Sullivan	Leon		26-Jul-1886	08-Aug-1886	Daniel O'Sullivan	McAllister, Eliza	John J. McDonnell / Mary King
O'Sullivan	Margaret	Adele	9-Feb-1909	21-Feb-1909	Daniel V. O'Sullivan	Reardon, Julia	James B. Riordan / Margaret Riordan
O'Sullivan	Elizabeth		22-Feb-1906	4-Mar-1906	Daniel V. O'Sullivan	Reardon, Julia	James T. Dunn / Joan Dunn
O'Sullivan	Cornelius	William	04-Dec-1882	31-Dec-1882	Michael J. O'Sullivan	Hochner, Mary	Phillip Joseph McCormack / Caroline Virginia Frank
Oswald	James	William	24-Dec-1882	14-Jan-1883	William Oswald	Lynch, Elizabeth	Alfred Edwards / Sara Edwards
Otis	Francis	James	1-Oct-1910	9-Oct-1910	John Daniel Otis	Riley, Freda	James P. Rooney / Nellie Finnerty
O'Toole	Elizabeth	Mary	13-May-1894	20-May-1894	John O'Toole	Lee, Margaret	Patrick O'Malley / Elizabeth O'Malley
O'Toole	William	Joseph	21-Oct-1896	01-Nov-1896	John O'Toole	Lee, Margaret	Michael Kelly / Mary O'Malley
O'Toole	James		20-Oct-1884	09-Nov-1884	Michael Francis O'Toole	Hall, Mary	James Hall / Helen Hall
O'Toole	Mary	Frances	07-Sep-1886	26-Sep-1886	Michael O'Toole	Hall, Mary	Michael Kearney / Mary Barnes
O'Toole	Michael	Francis	15-Oct-1888	28-Oct-1888	Michael O'Toole	Hall, Mary Helen	Thomas Cummings / Ann Kelly
O'Toole	William		20-Sep-1882	08-Oct-1882	Michael O'Toole	Hall, Mary Elizabeth	John McDonald / Catherine McDonald
Ott	John		15-Nov-1873	16-Mar-1884	Joseph Ott	Nippard, Mary	/ Emma Pryor
Oursler	Ethel	Margaret	20-Jan-1881	30-Sep-1899	Tobia Oursler	Manning, Loretta	/
Oursler	Mary	Curley	03-Apr-1898	03-Apr-1898	Tobia Oursler	Manning, A.	/ Mary Lemmon
Owens	Joseph	Raymond	29-Nov-1890	07-Dec-1890	Bailey Ham Owens	Braker, Theresa (Yakel)	Andrew M. Yakel / Philomena Yakel
Owens	Francis	Carroll	19-Dec-1892	08-Jan-1893	Daniel Joseph Owens	Lyle, Effie Genevieve	Bernard Owens / Elizabeth O'Keefe
Owens	Joseph	De Paul	20-Mar-1907	31-Mar-1907	Daniel Joseph Owens	McElroy, Mary Helen	Bernard J. McEvoy / Ann Cecil Mullen
Owens	Bernard	Franklin	12-Oct-1902	19-Oct-1902	Daniel Owens	Owens, Mary	John Gray / Katherine McElroy
Owens	Elizabeth	Anthony	03-Jun-1900	17-Jun-1900	Daniel Owens	McElroy, Mary	Bernard NcElroy / Elizabeth Burk

LAST NAME	FIRST NAME	MIDDLE	BAPTISM	BIRTH	Father	Mother	SPONSORS
Owens	Genevieve	Agnes	2-Oct-1904	21-Sep-1904	Daniel Owens	McElroy, Mary	Estelle McElroy
Owens	Margaret	Lillian	2-Jan-1910	13-Dec-1909	Daniel Owens	Walsh, Mary	Mary Casserly
Owens	James	Bernard	26-Nov-1882	14-Nov-1882	James Bernard Owens	Colford, Anastasia	Joan Moore
Owens	Charles	Patrick	29-Nov-1891	11-Nov-1891	James Owens	Colford, Anastasia	Joan Colford
Owens	Daniel	Edward	20-Aug-1882	17-Aug-1882	James Owens	Neville, Mary	Catherine Neville
Owens	James	Ham	23-Dec-1891	24-Dec-1891	James Wesley Owens	Ham, Lucretia	Edward Vincent O'Keefe	Henrietta Yakel
Owens	Mary		02-Jan-1898	12-Dec-1898	John D. Owens	McElroy, Mary A.	John McCluskey	Margaret Gray
Owens	Elizabeth	Rose	4-May-1913	20-Apr-1913	Patrick J. Owens	Dunn, Mary F.		Mary Staney
Owens	James	A.	18-Nov-1906	8-Nov-1906	Patrick J. Owens	Dunn, Mary F.	John Hamill	Mary Hamill
Owens	Joseph	Ray	18-Apr-1909	9-Mar-1909	Patrick J. Owens	Dunn, Mary F.	Francis Miller	Crescentia Miller
Owens	George	Edward	3-Apr-1910	24-Mar-1910	Patrick Joseph Owens	Dunn, Mary	Robert Henry Dunn	Eleanor Conners
Owens	John	Augustine	22-Dec-1901	16-Dec-1901	Patrick Joseph Owens	Dunn, Mary F.	James Dunn	Mary Dunn
Owens	Catherine	Mary	31-Dec-1899	24-Dec-1899	Patrick Owens	Dunn, Mary	Matthew Dunn	Catherine Krous
Owens	Rita		25-Feb-1912	12-Feb-1912	Patrick Owens	Dunn, Mary	Adam Brown	Catherine Fleckenstein
Owens	Vincent	Gregory	12-Jan-1908	4-Jan-1908	Patrick Owens	Dunn, Mary	John Owens	Mary Connor
Owings	Thomas		29-Mar-1896	28-Feb-1896	Thomas Owings	Gilchrist, Delia	Patrick Gilchrist	Margaret Gilchrist
Painter	Sophia	Florence	18-May-1884	17-Apr-1884	Edward August Painter	Felzman, Mary		Mary Sophia McQuade
Painter	Edward	August	10-Aug-1888	15-Jul-1888	Edward Painter	[Blank], Mary		Susan English
Painter	Edward	August	29-Jul-1900	15-Jul-1988	Edward Painter	Felzman, Mary	Edward Stresenski	Antoinette Stresenski
Palen	William	Robert	25-Jun-1908	16-May-1908	William Robert Palen	Butler, Helen		Mary E. Nolte
Palmer	Joseph	Regina	23-Sep-1915	8-Jul-1915	Claude Palmer	Barrett, Margaret		Frances Barrett
Palmer	Thelma	Helen	18-May-1913	25-Nov-1910	Daniel Palmer	Meyer, Caroline		Margaret Tragesser
Palmer	Margaret	Elizabeth	17-Dec-1907	08-Oct-1891	Henry R. Palmer	Patterson, Florence		Grace Patterson
Palmer/Ward	Margaret		12-Jan-1892	08-Jan-1892	William Palmer	Marvel, Mary		Agnes Saunders
Parker	Emma	Cecelia	27-Jul-1890	21-Jul-1890	Geo Parker	Maher, Ann	Wm Maher	Emma Maher
Parks	Beatrice		11-Apr-1897	01-Apr-1897	William Parks	Nestor, Mary	John Parks	Sarah Nestor
Parks	Milton	Alexander	12-May-1911	25-Nov-1900	William Parks	Parks, Cora	James McCarthy	Rose Monaghan
Parks	George	Dawson	10-Apr-1911	4-Apr-1911	Albert H. Parlett	Dawson, Mary	George A. Dawson	Ann Dawson
Parlett	William	Henry	17-Aug-1884	13-Jul-1884	Daniel Henry Parlett	Clark, Mary Virginia	William Thomas Clark	Mary Matilda Clark
Parlett	Edward		22-Dec-1895	07-Oct-1852	Thomas Parlett	Price, Elizabeth	Dennis Dore	
Parlett/Parlette	Mary	Virginia	18-May-1885	08-Jan-1863	George Clarke	Parlette, Laura		Ann McCart
Parlette	David	Clarke	04-May-1887	01-Oct-1886	Daniel Parlette	Clarke, Genevieve M.		Mary M. Clarke
Parr	William	Albert	03-Apr-1892	21-Mar-1892	Albert Parr	Gittings, Margaret		Ann Isabelle Dudley
Parr	Martin	Edwin	16-Feb-1908	21-Jan-1908	Andrew J. Parr	Manning, Bridget J.	Martin Parr	Mary E. Herbert
Parr	Worman	Clara Estelle	19-Oct1885	22-Sep-1885	George Parr	Webb, Estelle		Louise Cunningham
Parr	Frederick	Edward	27-Jun-1915	10-Jun-1915	George R. Parr	McBride, Ann	Frederick Hanamiller	Mary Bell
Parr	George	John	5-Jan-1913	27-Dec-1912	George Robert Parr	McBride, Ann	John Joseph Moylan	Mary Irving
Parr	Henry		02-Aug-1891	03-Jul-1891	John Parr	Kelly, Catherine	Matthew McManus	Mary Connolly
Parr	William		16-Jul-1893	17-Jun-1893	John Parr	Kelly, Catherine	Bernard Connolly	Margaret Connolly
Parr	Joseph		10-Oct-1886	10-Oct-1886	Joseph Parr	Driscoll, Mary	Nicholas Parr	Mary Kohler
Parr	Mary	Catherine	20-Jul-1884	05-Jul-1884	Joseph Parr	Driscoll, Mary	Alexander Carr	Mary O'Halloran
Parrell	Anastasia		01-Oct-1882	22-Sep-1882	James Parrell	Conway, Margaret	Laurence Malloy	Catherine Coulahan
Parrell	Mary		10-May-1885	28-Apr-1885	James Parrell	Conway, Margaret	William Smith	Mary McGovern
Parrish	James	Gedeon	11-Mar-1883	03-Mar-1883	Henry Clay Parrish	Matthews, Mary	James Kearney	Rebecca Dignan
Parrish	James	Louis	30-Jan-1910	20-Jan-1910	James Gideon Parrish	Schlang, Susan	Louis Baker	Gertrude Baker
Parsons	John	Emory	02-Mar-1899	01-Feb-1899	Guy W. Parsons	Gallagher, Estelle		Rose Gallagher
Parsons	William	Joseph	16-Aug-1903	18-Jul-1903	William W. Parsons	Gallagher, Mary Stella	William Joseph Tierney	Clara V. Sappington
Pate	Catherine	Mildred	12-Sep-1897	29-Aug-1897	Jefferson Davis Pate	Rigney, Helen	John Rigney	Mary Pate
Pate	John	Thomas	14-May-1905	30-Apr-1905	John Jefferson Pate	Rigney, Helen	Edward J. Burns	Mary Moran
Patrick	leo	Eugene	14-Jul-1895	04-Jul-1895	Joseph Patrick	Magness, Isabelle	Williaim Waldman	Mary Falvey
Patrick	Francis	Xavier	03-Jun-1900	04-May-1900	Thomas Joseph Patrick	Magness, Isabelle	Harry E. Douthat	Regina Douthat
Patten	Margaret	Ellen	25-Oct-1890	About 1859	William Patten	Gordon, Margaret		
Patterson	Mabel		30-Aug-1885	15-May-1885	Albert J. Patterson	McDermott, Elizabeth G.		Joan Carr
Patterson	Mary	Rose	27-Feb-1887	02-Feb-1887	Albert Patterson	McDermott, Elizabeth		Susan Murphy
Patterson	Wesley	Albert	01-Jul-1883	14-Jun-1883	Albert Patterson	McDermott, Elizabeth	Patrick McDermott	Mary McDermott
Patterson	George	Harvey Carlyl	10-May-1914	2-Apr-1914	Harvey Patterson	Wilson, Lillian	George Huber	Murial Wilson
Patterson	Susan	Mary	17-Mar-1892	02-Mar-1874	Robert Patterson	Deveney, Mary	Henry C. Franz	Mary Litz
Pattison	Charles	Carroll	24-Jun-1883	14-Jun-1883	Richard Edward Pattison	Masterman, Mary Elizabeth	Charles A. Masterman	Mary Florence Patttison
Paul	Edward		02-Dec-1900	22-Oct-1900	Edward Paul	Brady, Nellie	John Brady	Ann Brady
Paul	Mary		02-Mar-1890	12-Jan-1890	L. Paul	Wilson, Mary	Richard Paul	Josephine Wilson
Paul	Frances	Jennings	04-Sep-1887	06-Jul-1887	Luke Thompson Paul	Wilson, Mary Ann	Robert Graham Paul	Mary Virginia Wilson
Peach	Elizabeth		11-Jan-1894	18-Nov-1883	William Joseph Peach	Doory, Margaret	John J. Doory	Mary Peach
Peach	Josephine	Mary	03-Apr-1892	25-Mar-1892	William Parr	Doory, Margaret	Frederick Peach	Catherine Latchford

LAST NAME	FIRST NAME	MIDDLE	BAPTISM	BIRTH	Father	Mother	SPONSORS
Peacock	Elizabeth		14-Jul-1884	08-Jul-1884	Samuel Peacock	Melstone, Elizabeth	Helen Magmier
Pearce	Charles	Franklin	26-Jan-1902	18-Jan-1902	Charles F. Pearce	Smith, Ann	Ella Staples
Pearce	Helen	Pearce	13-Dec-1896	28-Nov-1896	William Pearce	McEntee, Helen	William P. Staples	Mary Brannan
Pearce	Joan	William	11-Feb-1894	26-Jan-1894	William Pearce	McIntre, Helen	James C. Kilauff	Mary McAleer
Peat	William	Anthony	18-Nov-1900	18-Nov-1900	John Peat	Fallon, Mary	John Browning	Margaret Fallon
Pecora	Camelia		31-Aug-1912	23-Jul-1912	M. Pecora	Kiler, Virginia	Michael Fallon	Ida Begona
Peed	Ida		25-Mar-1888	31-Jan-1866	Richard Peed	Ramey, Sara		
Pellens	Francis	Frederick	03-Dec-1893	20-Nov-1893	Francis Frederick Pellens	Carey, Mary Helen	Andrew James Carey	Caroline Francis Dunn
Pellens	Albert		03-Jan-1886	24-Dec-1885	Frederick Pellens	Carey, Mary Helen	Edward Carey	Teresa Dunn
Pence	Florence	Loretta	18-Sep-1898	27-Aug-1898	William Pence	McEntee, Ella Ann	Patrick McEntee	Margaret English
Penn	Mary	Edna	07-Feb-1888	15-Jan-1888	Charles Penn	Jones, Mary		Ann Jones
Penning	Martin	E.	04-Jan-1903	15-Dec-1902	John Penning	Evans, Ann	Edward Evans	Teresa M. Callaghan
Pentz/Brindella	Rebecca		21-Aug-1886	08-Feb-1861	Henry B. Pentz	Humphries, Elizabeth		Ella Pentz
Pepino	John	Edward	19-Feb-1882	04-Feb-1882	Charles Edward Pepino	Stout, Joan	Thelma B. Campbell	Sara Stout
Percy	Margaret		30-Oct-1904	1-Oct-1904	Robert F. Percy	Fogarty, Emma C.	Joseph L. Dunn	Ann Dunn
Percy	James	Leo	08-Oct-1899	29-Sep-1899	Robert Percy	Fogarty, Emma	James Fogarty	Catherine Clark
Percy	John	Raymond	09-Mar-1902	09-Mar-1902	Robert Percy	Fogarty, Emma	John Clark	Ellen Clark
Percy	Mary	Vincent	17-Apr-1892	05-Apr-1892	Robert Percy	Fogarty, Emma	Nicolaus Fogarty	Margaret Quirk
Percy	Catherine	Gerald	03-Jun-1894	25-May-1894	Robert Thomas Percy	Fogarty, Emma Catherine	Phillip Fogarty	Mary Fogarty
Perrine	Mary	Piquett	23-Oct-1884	12-Oct-1884	William H. Perrine	Burns, Margaret J.		Mary Kigney
Perrine	Bertha	Virginia	21-Sep-1893	03-Aug-1893	William Henry Perrine	Sann, Louise Virginia		Eva Margaret Meridith
Perry	Robert	Henry	09-Jan-1887	01-Sep-1886	Carl Perry	Phillips, Ann	John T. Coady	Margaret Burke
Perry	Catherine	Ruby	25-May-1884	19-Apr-1884	Charles Perry	Phillips, . Elizabeth Ann		Ida Phillips
Perry	Thomas	Patrick	21-Jul-1901	06-Jul-1901	William H. Perry	Lynch, Ellen	Thomas P. Walsh	Catherine Lynch
Peter	Elizabeth	Catherine	11-Nov-1882	[Blank]	Frederick August Nichols	Wills, Caroline		Catherine Moylan
Peters	Agnes		04-Oct-1891	22-Sep-1891	George Peters	Owens, Agnes	William Kelly	Helen Croghan
Peters	Catherine	Stella	13-Mar-1887	24-Feb-1887	George Peters	Owens, Agnes	John Owens	Catherine O'Neill
Peters	Joseph	Leonard	09-Mar-1902	19-Feb-1902	George Peters	Owens, Agnes	Thomas Donnelly	Cecelia Croghan
Peters	William	Patrick	21-Mar-1909	25-Feb-1909	John G. Peters	Keenan, Catherine	John Keenan	Winifred Geldt
Peters	Charles		01-Mar-1896	09-Feb-1896	John George Peters	Owens, Agnes		Margaret Gosnell
Peters	Hoan	Genevieve	24-Jan-1897	27-Jan-1859	John George Peters	Sorgelier, Augusta	Francis Kelly	
Peters	Joan	George	11-Feb-1894	22-Jan-1894	John George Peters	Owens, Agnes	Adam Itzel	Mary Agnes Lacy
Peters	Mary	Ellen	08-May-1898	18-Apr-1898	John George Peters	Owens, Agnes	Peter Elwood	Elizabeth Coffey
Peters	Mary		20-May-1900	24-Apr-1900	John Peters	Owens, Agnes	Peter Joseph McGovern	Margaret Owens
Pethie	Bridget	Delia	27-Jul-1884	14-Jul-1884	Edward Pethie	Reilly, Bridget	Nicolas Herbert	Joan Ebeline
Petted	Mary	Ann	26-Apr-1883	24-Apr-1883	Edward Petted	Riley, Bridget		Mary Ann Murray
Pfeffer	Mary	Elizabeth	07-Oct-1885	20-Sep-1885	Charles H. Pfeffer	Riley, Mary Rose		Mary Parrell
Pfeil	James	Allen	15-Sep-1889	02-Sep-1889	August Pfeil	McDermott, Catherine	James McComb	Philomena Myers
Pfenning	Ann	Mary	13-Oct-1913	12-Dec-1908	Daniel Pfenning	Thompson, Clara		Elizabeth Bonce
Pfenning	Daniel		13-Oct-1913	5-Jul-1911	Daniel Pfenning	Thompson, Clara		Amelia Barton
Pfenning	Edward	John	13-Oct-1913	30-Aug-1912	Daniel Pfenning	Thompson, Clara		Ann Bonce
Pfenning	Elizabeth	Dorothy	13-Oct-1913	6-Mar-1910	Daniel Pfenning	Thompson, Clara	George Brockmeyer	Alice Bonce
Phebus	Catherine	Eva	11-Jan-1885	24-Dec-1884	John Phebus	Hannan, Isabelle		Rose Hannan
Phennecia/Byrne	Grace	Cathedra Frances	3-Mar-1911	25-Dec-1891	Francis Phennecia	Hoose, Ann		Martha Byrne
Phiel	Mary		12-Oct-1890	26-Sep-1890	August Phiel	McDermott, Kate	E. McDermott	Mary Byrnes
Philips	Joseph	Anderson	12-Oct-1902	25-Sep-1902	Charles Philips	Gemison, Genevieve	Joseph Novotny	Louise Gordis
Philips	Agnes	Regina	5-Nov-1911	25-Oct-1911	George F. Philips	Rhyknapp, Mary M.	Lep Simms	Ann Clark
Philips	John	Edmund	06-May-1888	27-Apr-1888	Thomas Philips	Jamison, Josephine G.	John Kelly	Mary Jamison
Philip	Alma	Elizabeth	08-May-1887	27-Apr-1887	James Philllips	Cairns, Ann	Owen Donegan	Hannah Creaghan
Phillips	Charles	LeRoy	15-Apr-1900	01-Apr-1900	Charles Phillips	Jamison, James[sic]	George Brockmeyer	Lena Franz
Phillips	George	Thomas	22-Jun-1884	05-Jun-1884	Charles Phillips	Jamison, Jane		Catherine Flannigan
Phillips	Genevieve	Margaret	13-Jul-1890	28-Jun-1890	Charles Thomas Phillips	Jamison, Josephine	Frederick C. Schanberger	Ann McGinnis
Phillips	Mary	Elizabeth	30-Sep-1888	17-Sep-1888	Charles Wesley Phillips	Schwelkert, Mary Helen	Edward Paul Duffy	Elizabeth Agnes Smith
Phillips	Charles	Leon	6-Jul-1913	16-Jun-1913	George Phillips	Rhnknapp, Mary	George McCast	Katherine Watson
Phillips	George	Joseph	20-Dec-1908	4-Dec-1908	George Phillips	Rhnknapp, Mary	Joseph James McCart	Ann McCart
Phillips	John	Aloysius	20-Oct-1912	29-Sep-1912	George Phillips	Manley, Frances	John Mayers	Margaret Phillips
Phillips	Mary	Elizabeth	9-Sep-1907	7-Sep-1907	George Phillips	Rymknapp, Margaret M.	William Vickers	Teresa Ann Pula
Phillips	Mary	Alice	19-Dec-1909	9-Dec-1909	George Phillips	Rhnknapp, Margaret	George Leo McCarthy	Mary McRoy
Phillips	Genevieve	Margaret	27-Feb-1910	9-Feb-1910	George Thomas Phillips	Manley, Fannie	William J. Anderson	Genevieve M. Phillips
Phillips	Clinton	Jerome	30-Dec-1883	12-Dec-1883	Isaac Phillips	Corcoran, Alicia A.	William Watson	Catherine Davis
Phillips	Julia	Gertrude	21-Mar-1886	04-Mar-1886	Isaac Phillips	Corcoran, Alicia A.	William A. Gobright	Julia A. Gibright
Phillips	Regina		15-Apr-1894	03-Apr-1894	James P. Phillips	Cairns, Ann	Joseph P. Fallon	Ellen Friel
Phillips	Ann	Estelle	18-Aug-1889	09-Aug-1889	James Patrick Phillips	Cairns, Ann Genevieve	Edward Joseph Phillips	Sara Kenny

LAST NAME	FIRST NAME	MIDDLE	BAPTISM	BIRTH	Father	Mother	SPONSORS	
Phillips	Francis	Xavier	20-Nov-1904	8-Nov-1904	James Phillips	Kerns, Ann	Joseph Creaghan	Alma Phillips
Phillips	James	Edward	08-Jan-1899	22-Dec-1898	James Phillips	Cairns, Ann	Henry McClelland	Helen Daily
Phillips	Mary	Ellen	13-Mar-1892	03-Mar-1892	James Phillips	Cairns, Ann G.	John McGreevey	Mary McGreevey
Phillips	Mary	Elizabeth	09-Nov-1896	27-Aug-1896	Thomas Phillips	DeLacy, Grace		
Phillips	Helen		24-Jun-1883	23-Jun-1883	William J. Phillips	McKenna, Rose M.	William Collins	Mary Kavanaugh
Phoebus	Camilla	Estelle	26-Jul-1896	17-Jul-1896	John F. Phoebus	Hannan, Isabelle		Mary Rosenburger
Phoebus	Eugene	Leroy	24-Feb-1895	12-Feb-1895	John F. Phoebus	Hannan, Isabelle H.	Daniel Volk	Mimmie Foige
Phoebus	Herbert	Irving	29-Jan-1893	15-Jan-1893	John Francis Phoebus	Hannan, Isabelle Agnes	John Kennedy	Mary Kennedy
Phoebus	Helen	Gertrude	13-Feb-1887	01-Feb-1887	John Phoebus	Hannan, Isabelle	Peter Kennedy	Rose Ferguson
Phoebus	Isabelle		28-Sep-1890	17-Sep-1890	John Phoebus	Hannan, Isabelle	John Kennedy	Mary Kennedy
Phoebus	James	Harrison	18-Mar-1888	01-Mar-1888	John Phoebus	Hannan, Isabelle	Richard Cronin	Mary Volk
Phoebus	John	Henry	03-Sep-1882	13-Aug-1882	John Phoebus	Hannan, Isabelle	John Harrison	Mary Hannan
Picciotti	Camilla		19-May-1907	24-Mar-1907	John Picciotti	Russo, Mary	Samuel Picciotti	Camilla Picciotti
Picciotto	Salvatore		24-Dec-1911	11-Nov-1911	John Picciotto	Russo, Mary	Francis Russo	Catherine Russo
Pidaino	M.		11-Jun-1911	25-Oct-1910	E. Pidaino	Messina, Josephine	Salvatore PIdaino	Cynthia Cappitano
Pierce	Ann	Smith	6-Jun-1909	26-May-1909	Charles F. Pierce	Smith, Ann	John Smith	Addi Smith
Pierce	John	Charles	18-Aug-1907	4-Aug-1907	Charles F. Pierce	Smith, Ann	Joseph O'Connor	Blanche M. Pierce
Pierce	Helen		23-Oct-1904	18-Oct-1904	Charles Franklin Pierce	Smith, Ann	Francis M. Quinn	Amanda M. Pierce
Pierce	Elizabeth	Agnes	28-Jul-1899	12-Jul-1899	Charles Pierce	Smyth, Ann	James Lochran	Agnes Killian
Pierce	John	Patrick	5-Jun-1910	19-May-1910	Charles Pierce	Smith, Ann	Herbert Loughran	Elizabeth Loughran
Pierce	John	Charles	28-Oct-1898	24-Apr-1839	David Pierce	Dooley, Elizabeth	George Stemple	
Pierce	Mary		30-Jan-1910	19-Dec-1909	George J. Pierce	Brownall, Sadie E.	Frederick Mullen	Salina O'Brien
Pierce	William	Gorman	4-Dec-1908	3-Nov-1908	George Pierce	Brown, Sadie		Catherine Moylan
Pierce	William	Wallace	15-Dec-1889	07-Sep-1866	John T. Pierce	Smith, Ann E.	Henry Wigger	
Pierce	Ann	Mary	09-Oct-1892	17-Sep-1892	William Pierce	McEntee, Helen	Daniel McEntee	Ann E. Pierce
Pierce	Joseph	Edgar	24-May-1891	11-May-1891	William Pierce	McEntee, Ellen	Joseph McEntee	Margaret Amos
Pierce	Margaret	Ann	12-May-1901	25-Apr-1901	William Pierce	McEntee, Helen	George E. Price	Margaret McEntee
Pierce	William		11-Aug-1895	30-Jul-1895	William Pierce	McEntee, Ella	James McEntee	Ann Douglas
Piercy	Mary	Catherine	04-Jun-1887	22-Sep-1885	Lemuel P. Piercy	Spies, Alice V.		Catherine J.Piercy
Piercy	Arthur	Matthew	13-Jan-1896	16-Oct-1895	Samuel Piercy	Spies, Alice		Mulligan, Mary
Piercy	Samuel	Debou	05-Mar-1890	25-Jan-1890	Samuel Piercy	Spies, Ann		Catherine Piercy
Piercy	William	Paul	13-Jan-1896	16-Oct-1895	Samuel Piercy	Spies, Alice		Helen Haron
Pike	Helen	Mary	23-Jun-1901	30-May-1901	Walter Pike	Connolly, Mary	Joseph Connolly	Ann Connolly
Pinning	John	Joseph	24-Mar-1907	23-Feb-1907	John H. Pinning	Evans, Ann B.		Ann E. Pinning
Pinning	Michael	Irvin	26-Jun-1904	31-May-1904	John H. Pinning	Evans, Susanna B.		Mary Pinning
Pinning	Ann	Helen	08-Aug-1897	31-Jul-1897	John Pinning	Evans, Ann Blanche		Ann Pinning
Piorier	Catherine	Rose Ella	7-Feb-1909	29-Jan-1909	Noel Poirier	Leary, Catherine	John Doyle	Martha Knott
Pipino	Henry	Francis	04-Jan-1885	16-Dec-1884	Charles Edward Pipino	Stout, Theresa J.		Catherine Connor
Pipino	Helen		12-Jul-1883	17-Jul-1883	Edward Pipino	Stout, Joan	Nicholas Stickler	Sara Stout
Pipino	Theresa		07-Aug-1887	21-Jul-1887	Edward Pipino	Stout, Theresa		Sara Stout
Piraino	Amanda		14-Jun-1914	25-Oct-1913	Tiglio Piraino	Messina, Guiseppna	Charles Bagiotan	Antoinette Faraino
Piranno	Teresa	S.	24-Jan-1909	15-Sep-1908	Emmannuel Piranno	Piranno, Josephine	Samuel Russo	Santo Piranno
Pletch	Mary	Agnes	23-Feb-1908	21-Jan-1908	Louis Pletch	Winter, Emma L.		Mary A. Sullivan
Pletsch	Aloysius	Leroy	24-Jul-1888	24-Jul-1888	Aloysius Pletsch	Waldman, Catherine	James F. King	Mary Waldman
Plitch	John	Theodore	22-May-1910	1-May-1908	[Blank] Plitch	Wagner, Jeanette		Mary Wagner
Plum	Joseph	Clifford	24-Nov-1889	12-Nov-1889	Oscar Plum	Trapp, Mary Elizabeth	Joseph Wenger	Philomena Leiben
Plummer/Rodeleder	Elsi	Mary	26-May-1901	23-Dec-1881	Edward Plummer	Prettyman, Lida	Francis Herr	Catherine Herr
Plunkett	Edward	Thomas	10-Feb-1907	21-Jan-1907	Edward Julian Plunkett	O'Brien, Elizabeth	Thomas Jefferson Brien	Alice Elizabeth Brien
Plunkett	Francis		22-Oct-1905	9-Oct-1905	Francis J. Plunkett	Fitzsimmons, Ann	James P. Fitzsimmons	Elizabeth A. Fogerty
Plunkett	Mary	E.	10-Feb-1907	23-Jan-1907	Francis Joseph Plunkett	Fitzsimmons, Ann Cecelia	James Pat. Fitzsimmons	Ann Fitzsimmons
Plunkett	William	Joseph	27-Mar-1904	7-Mar-1904	Francis Joseph Plunkett	Fitzsimmons, Ann Cecelia	William T. Meagher	Mary Murphy
Plunnett	Ann	Cecelia	4-Jul-1909	18-Jun-1909	Francis Joseph Plunnett	Fitzsimmons, Ann Cecelia	William Dumphy	Catherine Dumphy
Poehler	Florence	Margaret	10-Apr-1887	05-Feb-1887	Francis H. Poehler	Shuster, Mary A.		Margaret R. Clark
Pohl	John	Francis	02-Aug-1903	16-Jul-1903	Francis Pohl	Charton, Blanche	J.J. Brannan	Mary Pohl
Pohler	Edward	Philip	16-Sep-1900	03-Sep-1900	Edward Pohler	Clarke, Mary	Adam Pohler	Honora Flemming
Pohlman	Ann	Pauline	19-Jul-1885	05-Aug-1867	Nicolas Pohlman	Caspar, Ann		Catherine L. Pate
Poisal	Ignatius	Wilbur	28-Mar-1883	31-Jul-1882	Wilbur F. PoIsal	Hooper, Etta Catherine		Ann B. Hooper
Poisal	Samuel	John Hooper	29-Jul-1883	08-Jul-1883	Wilbur F. Poisal	Hooper, Catherine		Florence Offner
Polor	Francis	Henry	12-Jan-1893	30-Dec-1892	Henry Polor	Clarke, Mary		Mary Clarke
Pool	Mary		08-Oct-1889	17-Apr-1889	Benjamin Pool	Reynolds, Mary		Margaret Rourke
Pool	Thomas	Ben James	08-Oct-1889	02-Mar-1886	Benjamin Pool	Reynolds, Mary		Margaret Rourke
Poole	Charles	Raymond	12-May-1895	05-Apr-1895	Charles Peter Poole	Smith, Carlotta Irene	Thomas Magnes	Mary Florence Fitzgerald
Poole	Elizabeth	Amelia	03-Dec-1893	18-Nov-1893	Charles Peter Poole	Smith, Carlotta R.		Mary Christian Knapp

LAST NAME	FIRST NAME	MIDDLE	BAPTISM	BIRTH	Father	Mother	SPONSORS	
Popp	Florence	Genevieve	29-Jan-1888	17-Jan-1888	George Popp	Leonard, Catherine	Eugene Joseph O'Neill	Mary Joan Bradley
Popp	Mary	Loretta	19-Nov-1884	29-Oct-1884	George Popp	Seward, Catherine		Cecelia Flanagan
Port	William	Richard	13-Jun-1897	05-Jun-1897	Joseph Port	Gunning, Mary	Richard Doody	Zela Doody
Portas	Louis	Francis	18-Aug-1912	13-Jul-1912	Louis Portas	Orban, Margaret	Francis Boga	Teresa Boga
Porter	Adam (Ada)	Genevieve	29-Jun-1882	14-May-1863	William Porter	Dodd, Ada	Rev. M.F. Foley	Mary Bryan
Potter	Grafton	Joseph	13-Mar-1892	06-Mar-1820	Thomas Potter	Wilson, Charlotte	George Hoen	
Potts	Emma	Eugenia	14-Oct-1886	23-Sep-1886	Henry A. Potts	Green, Sara L.		Mary J. Connolly
Potts	Henry	August	18-Mar-1888	19-Jan-1888	Henry A. Potts	Green, Sara L.		Margaret Sapp
Potts	John	Russelll	9-Aug-1914	26-Jul-1914	Henry Potts	Kerns, Ellen		Elsie Deganhardt
Potts	Edward		04-Jun-1893	20-May-1893	Robert Potts	Connolly, Mary E.	Edward Connolly	Bridget Connelly
Potts	Loretta		07-Jul-1901	13-Jun-1901	Robert Potts	Connolly, Mary	John Jones	Sarah Jones
Potts	Margaret		28-Oct-1894	07-Oct-1894	Robert Potts	Connolly, Mary Elizabeth	Edward Connolly	Delia Holmes
Potts	Ann	Elizabeth	28-May-1893	18-May-1893	William Potts	Kilchenstein, Catherine	John Benjamin Schuman	Mary Bittner
Potts	Edward	Frank	15-Sep-1895	06-Sep-1895	William Potts	Kilchenstein, Catherine	Conrad Bittner	Nora Shipley
Power	Rose	Edith	28-Jan-1894	08-Jan-1894	Thomas Power	Langhran, Sara	James Thomas Lewis	Mary Edith Lewis
Power	William	Henry	07-Sep-1891	04-Apr-1890	William Henry Power	Smackum, Rose		Ida Mason
Powers	Agnes		02-Oct-1898	17-Sep-1898	Joseph Powers	Burke, Bridget	William Powers	Mary Clemsen
Powers	Ann	Mary	25-Nov-1900	2-Nov-1900	Joseph Powers	Burke, Bridget	William Powers	Mary Powers
Powers	Catherine	Sabina	21-Mar-1897	18-Feb-1897	Joseph Powers	Burke, Bridget	Michael Burke	Mary Powers
Powers	Helen	Nora	21-Jul-1895	02-Jul-1895	Joseph Powers	Burke, Bridget	William Powers	Mary Powers
Powers	Catherine	Anthony	29-Jan-1899	20-Jan-1899	Peter Powers	Martin, Catherine	Thomas O'Neill	Catherine Mettee
Powers	William	Cecelia	19-May-1901	07-May-1901	Peter Powers	Martin, Katherine	Martin Jennings	Katherine Jennings
Powers	Sarah	Mary	14-Sep-1890	30-Aug-1890	Thomas F. Powers	McLaughlin, Sara	John P. Gaynor	Mary A. Hitchcock
Powers	Ann		28-Jun-1896	09-Jun-1896	Thomas Powers	Laughran, Sara Cecelia	Edward Briggs	Julia Landers
Powers	Edward	Loughran	06-Aug-1882	19-Jul-1882	Thomas Powers	Laughlin, Sara Cecelia	Richard Williams	Ann Wahl
Powers	Joseph	Loretta	27-Jun-1886	18-Jun-1886	Thomas Powers	Loughran, Sara Cecelia	John J. Cassidy	Catherine Latchfoot
Powers	Margaret	Francis	13-Jul-1884	25-Jun-1884	Thomas Powers	Loughran, Sara	John Lewis	Margaret Lynch
Powers	Thomas		24-Jun-1888	31-Mar-1888	Thomas Powers	Laughran, Sara Cecelia	Francis Patrick Curtis	Elizabeth O'Neill
Powers	Catherine		03-Dec-1899	30-Oct-1899	William Powers	Ryan, Anastasia	James Mettee	Mary McShane
Powers	Edward	Gertrude	20-Sep-1907	1-Sep-1907	William Powers	Ryan, Anastasia		Catherine Mettee
Powers	Helen	Carroll	17-Sep-1882	20-Aug-1882	William Powers	Fagan, Catherine	Fagan, Catherine	Helen Powers
Powers	James		07-Oct-1888	11-Sep-1888	William Powers	Fagan, Catherine		Mary Dunn
Powers	Jane	Mary	05-Apr-1901	25-Mar-1901	William Powers	Ryan, Anastasia	Joseph Powers	Margaret Powers
Powers	Michael	Edward	29-May-1898	15-May-1898	William Powers	Ryan, Anastasia	Peter Powers	Mary Powers
Powers	William		11-Oct-1903	07-Sep-1903	William Powers	Ryan, Anastasia	Michael Ryan	Mary Powers
Preuger	Catherine	Eileen	6-Feb-1910	23-Jan-1910	Henry Preuger	Coyne, Mary	Edmund Coyne	Ann Preuger
Preuger	John	Theodore	19-Jul-1908	8-Jul-1908	Henry R. Preuger	Coyne, Mary J.	Ambrose Coyne	Lillian Preuger
Price	Ann	Eva	29-Jun-1886	31-Jan-1886	Carl W. Price	Hattrick, Cornelia		Mary Parrell
Price	Cornelia	Louise	13-Sep-1888	18-Jun-1888	Charles W. Price	Hattrick, Cornelia		Ann M. Wood
Price	Stephen	Wesley	19-Aug-1883	28-May-1883	Charles W. Price	Hattrich, Cornelia L.	Edward J. Whiting	Cornelia A. Whiting
Price	James	Edwin	02-Apr-1893	03-Mar-1893	James Price	Mighan, Ann M.		Theres Quirk
Price	Mary		02-Apr-1882	25-Dec-1881	James Price	Migan, Ann		Anastasia Holden
Price	Helen	Mary	28-May-1888	June 1861	Joseph Price	Pritchard, Elizabeth		Catherine Agnes Foley
Price	Allen	Mobley (Paul)	25-Jan-1888	28-Jul-1807	Richard Price	Mobley, Elizabeth		
Pritchard	Ann	Mary	10-Dec-1899	29-Jun-1899	Maurice Pritchard	Waldeck, Catherine		Mary Fanon
Pritchard	Mary	Theresa	10-Dec-1899	21-Sep-1897	Maurice Pritchard	Waldeck, Catherine		Mary Fanon
Proctor	Agnes		07-Mar-1886	17-Feb-1886	Joan Proctor	Donald, Ann		Florence Heimiller
Pruett	Catherine		19-Jun-1892	12-Jun-1892	George Washington Pruett	Giblin, Alice Gertrude	James Michael Fitzpatrick	Bridget Cath. Fitzpatrick
Pruill	Bernard		14-Jan-1900	03-Jan-1900	George Pruill	Giblin, Alice	John St. Ledger	Alice Giblin
Pruitt	George	Bernard	03-Mar-1895	20-Feb-1895	George Washington Pruitt	Giblin, Alice Gertrude	John Saint Leger	Catherine Gert. Fitzpatrick
Pryor	Arthur	Bernard	16-Oct-1908	07-May-1882	[Blank] Pryor	[Blank], Margaret		Mary Kennedy
Pryor	Genevieve		25-Jul-1886	18-Jul-1886	George H. Pryor	Busick, Emma T.		Emma C. Pryor
Pryor	George	Edward	18-Sep-1887	19-Aug-1887	George H. Pryor	Busick, Emma T.		Elizabeth A. Busick
Pryor	Henry	Elroy	23-Jul-1893	13-Jul-1893	Henry Pryor	Forrest, Ann	Henry Deppish	Emma Pryor
Pryor	Clara		27-Jul-1885	21-May-1885	Singleton Pryor	Tetherstone, Margaret		Mary Kennedy
Pscherer	Agnes	R.	15-Nov-1903	29-Oct-1903	Francis B. Pscherer	McGainy, Rose Lee	John J. Cassidy	Agnes Cassidy
Pugh	Mary	E.	11-Oct-1896	12-Sep-1896	Joseph Pugh	Lane, Eva		Mary Matthews
Pugh	Edward	William	17-Apr-1904	2-Apr-1904	William A. Pugh	McMillan, Catherine		Catherine Graham
Pugh	Walter	John	02-Oct-1898	12-Sep-1898	William A. Pugh	McMillan, Catherine		Catherine Pugh
Pugh	Catherine	Anastasia	7-Jan-1906	10-Dec-1905	William Pugh	McMillan, Katherine	William Graham	Mary Graham
Pugh	Edna	Catherine	27-Apr-1902	28-Feb-1902	William Pugh	McMillen, Katherine	William McMillen	Ann Connelly
Pugh	William		16-Aug-1896	29-Jul-1896	William Pugh	McMullen, Catherine		
Puhl	Ann		21-Nov-1886	31-Oct-1886	Frederick Puhl	Murray, Alice	James Smith	Ann H. Hooper

LAST NAME	FIRST NAME	MIDDLE	BAPTISM	BIRTH	Father	Mother	SPONSORS	
Puhl	Charles	Brennan	18-Jan-1883	01-Jan-1883	Frederick Puhl	Murray, Alice	Michael Emmet Brennan	Alice Mary Carroll
Puhl	Frederick		07-Jul-1893	21-May-1893	Frederick Puhl	Murray, Alice		Mary Affeld
Purnis	William		6-Nov-1904	28-Nov-1901	John Purnis	[Blank], Elizabeth	William R. Salmon	Rachael Salmon
Purser	Loretta	Mary	09-Oct-1892	25-Sep-1892	George P. Purser	Williams, Martha Ann	George Purser	Mary Purser
Queen	James	Donohue	28-Oct-1886	15-Oct-1886	[Blank]	Queen, Isabelle		Ann Magnes
Quigley	Ann	Mary	04-May-1902	23-Apr-1902	Daniel Quigley	Lynch, Ann M.	John Sherry	Catherine McManus
Quigley	James	Joseph	12-Jan-1896	02-Jan-1896	Daniel Quigley	Lynch, Ann	James Lynch	Mary Lynch
Quigley	Agnes		03-Dec-1893	20-Nov-1893	Edward Quigley	O'Rourke, Bridget	Patrick O'Rourke	Catherine O'Rourke
Quigley	Ann	Mary	06-Feb-1894	25-Jan-1894	Edward Quigley	Cullen, Ellen	James Quigley	Bridget Quigley
Quigley	Ellen	Margaret	06-Mar-1891	06-Mar-1891	Edward Quigley	Cullen, Ella		Bridget Quigley
Quigley	Helen	Regina	24-Oct-1906	8-Oct-1906	Edward Quigley	Quigley, Helen	Frank C. Woods	Edward P. McAdams
Quigley	James	Aloysius	19-May-1900	03-May-1900	Edward Quigley	Cullen, Ella		
Quigley	Margaret	Mary	31-Mar-1897	23-Mar-1897	James Quigley	Cullen, Ella	Edward Cullen	Mary Cullen
Quigley	James	Laurence	25-May-1900	16-May-1900	James Quigley	Roche, Mary		Margaret Smith
Quigley	Martin		26-Jun-1898	11-Jun-1898	James Quigley	Burke, Mary	John Redmond	Isabelle O'Brien
Quigley	Mary	Helen	29-Jun-1902	17-Jun-1902	James Quigley	Roche, Mary	Charles Hagan	Ann Quigley
Quigley	Bernard	James	22-Jun-1884	12-Jun-1884	John Quigley	Shields, Mary	Francis Deppish	Emma Boyle
Quigley	Emma	Mary	22-Jun-1884	12-Jun-1884	John Quigley	Shields, Mary	John Boyle	Emma Boyle
Quigley	Laura	Josephine	10-Mar-1889	02-Mar-1889	John Quigley	Shields, Mary Elizabeth	James Shields	Mary Ann Shields
Quillan	James	Edward	01-Dec-1889	26-Nov-1889	Edward Quillan	Clarke, Mary, Ann	George Kelly	Margaret Clarke
Quillan	Sarah	Mary	23-Aug-1896	14-Aug-1896	Edward Quillan	Clark, Ann	Peter Connelly	Sarah Connelly
Quillan	Anita		26-Feb-1899	19-Feb-1899	James Quillan	Clark, Mary	Laurence Quinn	Mary Russell
Quinlan	Catherine		13-Nov-1898	23-Oct-1898	James Quinlan	Kennedy, Mary	Thomas Kennedy	Mary Kennedy
Quinlan	Elizabeth		09-Dec-1900	27-Nov-1900	James Quinlan	Kennedy, Mary		Mary Armstrong
Quinlan	Helen		19-Sep-1897	09-Aug-1897	James Quinlan	Kennedy, Mary	Martin Kennedy	Ella Rooney
Quinlan	James	Conway	15-Jun-1902	01-Jun-1902	James Quinlan	Kennedy, Mary	Patrick Roche	Mary Roche
Quinlan	Margaret	Regina	23-Sep-1896	13-Aug-1896	James Quinlan	Kennedy, Mary	John Reardon	Ella Kennedy
Quinlan	Mary	Alma	04-Aug-1895	26-Jul-1895	James Quinlan	Kennedy, Mary	James Whelan	Margaret Quinlan
Quinn	Ann	Adalaide	10-Nov-1885	04-Nov-1885	[Blank]	Quinn, Louise		Ella Essender
Quinn	Sara	Mary	7-Aug-1910	29-Jul-1910	Francis M. Quinn	Smith, Elizabeth	Harry K. Schoen	Lillian Edelman
Quinn	Alana	Ellen	26-Apr-1908	15-Apr-1908	Francis McAbee Quinn	Smith, Elizabeth	William J. Quinn	Ann Smith
Quinn	Catherine	M.	4-Nov-1900	22-Oct-1900	Francis Quinn	Porter, Emma	Charles Gordon	Louise Quinn
Quinn	Francis	McAlee	8-Aug-1915	25-Jul-1915	Francis Quinn	Smith, Elizabeth	Martin Quinn	Ann Smith
Quinn	John	Patrick	18-Mar-1906	5-Mar-1906	Francis Quinn	Smith, Elizabeth	Joseph McNally	Margaret O'Conner
Quinn	Elizabeth		13-Mar-1904	4-Mar-1904	Francis Quinn	Smith, Elizabeth		Mary Mulligan
Quinn	William	Joseph	14-Mar-1913	29-Oct-1904	George Quinn	Griffin, Annette	James O'Hara	Jeanette [Blank]
Quinn	Catherine		9-Jun-1907	25-May-1907	James E. Quinn	Doolin, Ann	James Casserly	Ann Quinn
Quinn	Helen		04-Jan-1903	19-Dec-1902	James J. Quinn	Dowling, Ann	Thomas L. Kenny	Mary Quinn
Quinn	Ann	Isabelle	13-Mar-1904	24-Feb-1904	James P. Quinn	Devine, Norah	William P. Colbert	Margaret Magner
Quinn	Catherine		14-Aug-1904	4-Aug-1904	James Quinn	Doolin, Ann	Thomas Croghan	Helen Dooling
Quinn	Elizabeth	M.	03-Sep-1882	20-Aug-1882	James Quinn	Hubbard, Isabelle	George Wash. Blondell	Catherine Wooden
Quinn	James		27-Nov-1902	25-Nov-1902	James Quinn	Dunn, Honora		Mary McGuire
Quinn	Jennie		2-Jan-1910	9-Dec-1909	James Quinn	Doolin, Ann	Francis Dooling	Margaret Airey
Quinn	Mary		19-Aug-1900	03-Aug-1900	James Quinn	Quinn, Nora	James Mooney	Margaret Donohue
Quinn	Mary	Isabelle	17-Nov-1887	06-Nov-1887	James Quinn	Hubbard, Isabelle	Richard Mooney	Agnes Martin
Quinn	V.A. Quinn	Agnes	07-Aug-1898	19-Jul-1898	James Quinn	Dunn, Honora	Patrick Donahue	Mary Quinn
Quinn	Mary		28-Jan-1906	12-Jan-1906	James Quinn	Doolin, Ann	Robert Joseph Samsel	Mary Samsel
Quinn	John		29-Nov-1896	09-Nov-1896	James Quinn	Dunn, Nora	Charles Dowd	Mary Colbert
Quinn	Elizabeth		25-Sep-1910	14-Sep-1910	John King	Quinn, Katherine	William Enright	Katherine Enright
Quinn	James	Joseph	04-Mar-1888	01-Mar-1888	John P. Quinn	McCluskey, Mary	George McElroy	Elizabeth McCluskey
Quinn	John		24-Jan-1886	19-Jan-1886	John Quinn	Gunnip, Mary	Charles McCabe	Catherine Hanlon
Quinn	John		26-Nov-1882	17-Nov-1882	John Quinn	McCluskey, Mary	Bernard McCluskey	Mary Quinn
Quinn	Mary		01-Apr-1888	23-Mar-1888	John Quinn	Gunnip, Mary	James Gereghty	Ann O'Connor
Quinn	Sara		20-Jun-1886	18-Jun-1886	John Quinn	McCluskey, Mary	Joseph McCluskey	Ella F. Quinn
Quinn	Elizabeth	Paricia	05-Oct-1884	30-Sep-1884	John Quinn	McCluskey, Mary A.	John McCluskey	Helen (Ellen) McCluskey
Quinn	Mary	Elizabeth	29-Mar-1914	17-Mar-1914	Martin Dunn	Brogan, Elizabeth	John Delaney	Sarah Brogan
Quinn	Catherine	Laura	26-Feb-1888	14-Feb-1888	Martin F. Quinn	Young, Joan	Like Kearney	Delia Brandt
Quinn	Helen		15-May-1892	02-May-1892	Martin Quinn	Young, Joan	John Thomas McGuire	Mary Agnes Hackett
Quinn	James	Joseph	22-Jun-1890	08-Jun-1890	Martin Quinn	Young, Joan	William Devine	Mary Joan McGuire
Quinn	John	Patrick	12-Jul-1908	20-Jun-1908	Martin Quinn	Brogan, Elizabeth	James Quinn	Mary Quinn
Quinn	Martin	Anthony	18-Mar-1883	08-Mar-1883	Martin Quinn	Young, Joan	John T. Hogan	Mary Moran
Quinn	Martin	Francis	02-Aug-1896	12-Jul-1896	Martin Quinn	Young, Joan	William Young	Ida M. Kelly
Quinn			15-Jul-1906	26-Jun-1906	Martin Quinn	Henne, Mary	Patrick Hogan	Margaret Roddy

LAST NAME	FIRST NAME	MIDDLE	BAPTISM	BIRTH	Father	Mother	SPONSORS
Quinn	Martin	John	27-Nov-1910	18-Nov-1910	Martin Quinn	Brogan, Elizabeth	Patrick Brogan / Carmella Bursella
Quinn	Mary		17-Dec-1899	03-Dec-1899	Martin Quinn	Brogan, Elizabeth	John Delaney / Mary Quinn
Quinn	Michael	Patrick	18-Oct-1903	03-Oct-1903	Martin Quinn	Brogan, Bessie	James Quinn / Ann E. Quinn
Quinn	Mary	Catherine	25-Nov-1883	19-Nov-1883	Timothy Quinn	McSweeny, Honora	Patrick Aloysius Sullivan / Catherine Sullivan
Quinn	William	Dennis	13-Nov-1887	06-Nov-1887	Timothy Quinn	Sweeney, Hannah	John Miller / Elizabeth Miller
Quinn	Elizabeth	Mary	25-Jul-1913	30-Jun-1913	William J. Quinn	McAleer, Mary	/ Elizabeth M. Smith
Quinn	Mary	Catherine	28-Apr-1907	14-Apr-1907	William J. Quinn	McAleer, Mary J.	John A. Quinn / Lucy Quinn
Quinn	Teresa		10-Jan-1915	20-Dec-1914	William J. Quinn	Quinn, Mary J.	Charles M. Mueller / Teresa Mueller
Quinn	William	Joseph	1-Jan-1905	18-Dec-1904	William J. Quinn	McAleer, Mary	William Burns / Ella Rudolph
Quinn	William		20-Apr-1906	20-Apr-1906	William J. Quinn	McAleer, Mary	William Kelleher / Ella Rudolph
Quinn	Agnes	Estelle	3-Oct-1909	23-Sep-1909	William Quinn	Meehan, Nellie	Alfonsus M. Burger / Rose Catherine Batchelor
Rabe	John	Joseph	18-Apr-1909	5-Apr-1909	George William Rabe	O'Leary, Josephine	John Joseph Rabe / Rosaline McGrew
Raber	Mary	Thelma	14-Mar-1897	02-Jan-1897	Daniel Raber	Graham, Etta	/ Mary Graham
Rachell	Francis	Andrew	09-Dec-1883	30-Nov-1883	Francis Rachell	Dolan, Margaret	Edward John Dunn / Mary Teresa Wright
Rachensberger	Francis	Edward	29-Jun-1913	21-Jun-1913	John Rachensberger	Fridel, Clara	Francis Rachensberger / Catherine Willis
Rachensberger	Joseph		2-Jul-1912	2-Jul-1912	John Rachensberger	Fridel, Clara	
Radcliffe	Estelle	Rose	17-May-1891	14-May-1891	William J. Radcliffe	Wyvel, Sarah	/ Ann Parker
Radcliffe	Henry		01-May-1892	21-Apr-1892	William James Radcliffe	Wyvel, Sara	/ Susan Slater
Radford	Joseph		05-Aug-1900	28-Jul-1900	William Radford	O'Connor, Ann	James Radford / Elle Ellis
Radford	Joseph		6-May-1906	29-Apr-1906	William Radford	Conor, Ann O.	G.W. Devine / Mary Radford
Radford	Mary		21-Nov-1897	07-Nov-1897	William Radford	O'Connor, Ann	William Calender / Ann O'Connor
Radford	William		05-Aug-1900	28-Jul-1900	William Radford	O'Connor, Ann	
Radivitch	John	Bell	5-Jul-1908	5-Jul-1908	[Blank]	[Blank]	
Radivitch	Mary	Bell	14-Oct-1900	03-Oct-1900	Harry A. Radivitch	Connolly, Rose	Edward Burke / Mary Monaghan
Radivitch	George	LeRoy	26-Oct-1902	25-Oct-1902	Henry Radivitch	Connolly, Rose	George C. Radivitch / Elizabeth Radivitch
Radivitch	Mildred	Catherine	24-Sep-1905	21-Sep-1905	Henry Radivitch	Connolly, Ruth	John Radivitch / Ann Connolly
Radoff	William	James	13-May-1882	06-Dec-1869	William Radoff	Burns, Esther	/ Julia Tiralla
Rae	William	Joseph	17-Jan-1904	17-Jan-1904	William Rae	Simms, Mary	Michael Joseph Simms / Mary Ann Simms
Rafferty	William	James	25-Mar-1906	7-Mar-1906	James B. Rafferty	Harcourt, Josephine	Henry Rafferty / Loretta Quigley
Rafferty	James	Boyle	27-Sep-1885	18-Sep-1885	James R. Rafferty	Boyle, Emma	Samuel Boyle / Elizabeth Boyle
Rafferty	Michael	Joseph Patrick	06-Jun-1898	28-May-1898	Michael Rafferty	McDonald, Ann	Patrick McDonnell / Margaret Eagan
Rafferty	Sara	Ann	30-Mar-1902	17-Mar-1902	Michael Rafferty	McDonald, Ann	Charles Murray / Delia McDonald
Rafferty	William		10-May-1900	27-Apr-1900	Michael Rafferty	McDonald, Ann	William Dennison / Mary McDonald
Rafferty	Mary	S. Josephine	19-Nov-1882	28-Oct-1882	Peter Rafferty	Rafferty, Catherine	John Hagerty / Catherine Kennedy
Rafferty	Francis	Edward	22-Mar-1885	12-Mar-1875	William J. Rafferty	Boyle, Mary Ann	John E. Shields / Mary Shields
Ragan	James		2-Apr-1911	21-Mar-1911	Francis P. Ragan	Kelly, Margaret M.	James J. Kelly / Agne Ragan
Ragan	Margaret	Mary	11-Nov-1888	28-Oct-1888	Francis P. Ragan	Kelly, Mary	Martin E. Kelly / Margaret Kelly
Ragan	Mary	Elizabeth	6-Feb-1910	24-Jan-1910	Francis P. Ragan	Kelly, Margaret M.	Charles Kelly / Elizabeth Ragan
Ragan	Paul	James	18-Jan-1891	05-Jan-1891	Francis P. Ragan	Kelly, Mary	James P. Guinan / Mary A. Gahan
Ragan	Agnes	Cecelia	10-May-1896	03-May-1896	Francis P. Ragan	Kelly, Mary	Terence Lannan / Ann McGee
Ragan	Francis	Edward	31-Jan-1892	17-Jan-1892	Francis Ragan	Kelly, Mary	Thomas Doheny / Clara Elliott
Ragan	James	Joseph	18-Oct-1885	12-Oct-1885	Francis Ragan	Kelly, Margaret	Edward Kelly / Catherine Hughes
Ragan	Martin	Henry	9-Nov-1913	25-Oct-1913	Francis Ragan	Kelly, Margaret	Joseph A. Caldwell / Margaret A. Kelly
Ragan	Catherine		19-Dec-1886	16-Dec-1886	Francis Ragan	Kelly, Mary	James Kelly / Mary Gahan
Rahla	Joseph		24-Sep-1886	20-Sep-1886	Jermiah Ragan	Sullivan, Mary	/ Roseann Farrell
Raimondi	Phillip		26-Jul-1885	18-May-1885	Adam Rahla	Rose, Catherine	/ Honora Mooney
Rainey	Edward		25-Nov-1907	16-Nov-1907	Louis Raimondi	Sylvester, Rose	Francis Cusimano /
Rainey	Charles		13-Dec-1903	26-Oct-1903	Francis Rainey	Stirley, Louise	/ Amelia Gummet
Rainey	Edward	Seigfrist	2-Dec-1906	25-Aug-1906	John Rainey	Stirley, Louise	/ Mamie Trainor
Rainey	John		24-Mar-1897	04-Mar-1897	John Rainey	Stirley, Louise	Bernard Trainor / Margaret Trainor
Rainone	Joan		17-Mar-1895	05-Mar-1895	John Rainey	Stirley, Louise	John Gabriel Bannon / Mary Eugenia Bannon
Rainone	Ralph		3-Oct-1915	20-Jul-1915	Louis Rainone	Sequillant, Ann	Louis Laponzina / Giacoma Fassalaque
Ramar	Charles	Henry	5-Jul-1914	28-Jan-1914	Louis Rainone	Squillauba, Ann	William Ehrlein / Rachel Ehrlein
Ramhild	Rose		07-Jul-1893	05-Dec-1892	Charles H. Ramar	Tankwert, Catherine	/ Margaret Parrell
Ramsay	Edna	Mary	14-Apr-1889	27-Oct-1888	Henry Ramhild	Cuccia, Clara	/ Rose Magan
Ramsay	Sara	Margaret	03-Feb-1901	03-Jan-1901	Edward Mortimer Ramsay	Phelps, Mary Louise	James Phelps / Gertrude Judge
Ramsey	Thomas	L.	17-Aug-1885	Aug 1885	Robert Ramsey	Dolan, Emma	/ Mary Browning
Ramsey	Matthew		07-Dec-1902	17-Nov-1902	Thomas L. Ramsey	Woods, Ave Maris	/ Regina Mary Phelps
Rankin	Gertrude	Mary	04-Sep-1895	24-Feb-1813	Thomas Ramsay	Walsh, Elizabeth	
Rankin	John	Leon	2-Oct-1904	23-Sep-1904	Hugh Rankin	Cadden, Frances	John Cadden / Mary Bachelor
Rankin	George	Thomas	26-Jul-1903	11-Jul-1903	Hugh Rankin	Cadden, Frances	John Rankin / Margaret O'Neill
Rankin	Francis	Gerlad	24-Oct-1909	14-Oct-1909	Hugo F. Rankin	Cadden, Frances H.	Patrick J. Rankin / Mary O'Donnell
Rankin			19-Jul-1914	6-Jul-1914	Hugo Rankin	Cadden, Frances	Joseph M. Dignan / Mary E. Dignan

114

LAST NAME	FIRST NAME	MIDDLE	BAPTISM	BIRTH	Father	Mother	SPONSORS	
Ratchfort	Ann		04-Sep-1895	01-Sep-1893	John Ratchfort	[Blank]	Ellen Byrnes	
Ratican	Thomas		01-Jun-1890	24-May-1890	John Joseph Ratican	Doyle, Ann Loretta	James Francis McCabe	Loretta Timmons
Ratican	James	Hubert	03-Jul-1892	29-Jun-1892	John Ratican	Doyle, Ann Loretta	Hubert Couroyet	Ann Doyle
Ratigan	Ann	Loretta	09-Jan-1887	02-Jan-1887	John Ratigan	Doyle, Ann	James Doyle	Rose Doyle
Ratigan	Francis	Leon	11-Jan-1885	04-Jan-1885	John Ratigan	Doyle, Ann	John Conroy	Bridget Conroy
Ratigan	Joseph	Patrick	25-Mar-1883	23-Mar-1883	John Ratigan	Doyle, Ann	James Conroy	Bridget Donohue
Ratigan	Mary	Josephine	22-Jul-1894	13-Jul-1894	Michael Ratigan	Flemming, Honora	John Murray	Mary Kenny
Ratray	Ann		29-Aug-1898	About 1871	[Blank]	[Blank]		
Rauh	Joseph	Michael	17-Nov-1907	10-Nov-1907	Joseph A. Rauh	Guerin, Margaret	Charles Debes	Mary Codd
Ray	James		12-Oct-1884	29-Sep-1884	Adam Ray	Clarke, Isabelle	John William Kane	Mary Clark
Ray	Clara		15-Apr-1906	12-Apr-1906	Hugo Ray	Morris, Atta		Anastatia Parrell
Ray	John		16-Apr-1911	30-Mar-1911	James Ray	Conston, Mary	John T. Clark	Florence Clark
Ray	Ann	Elizabeth	22-Mar-1914	13-Mar-1914	William Ray	Simms, Mary	Leo A. Simms	Mary Burns
Ray	Gordon		4-Oct-1908	20-Sep-1908	William Ray	Sims, M. Mary	Michael Sims	J. Coulter
Ray	Robert		26-Sep-1909	20-Sep-1909	William Ray	Simms, Mary	Michael J. Simms	Sara Coulter
Ray	Thomas	Edward	18-Jun-1905	4-Jun-1905	William Ray	Simms, Mary G.	William P. Hagerty	Catherine Simms
Ray	William		4-Aug-1912	28-Jul-1912	William Ray	Simms, Mary Gertrude	Michael Joseph Simms	Genevieve Simms
Ready	Richard		06-Jan-1901	26-Dec-1900	John Reddy	Murphy, Mary	Thomas Murphy	Margaret Murphy
Real	Agnes	Ann	12-May-1907	28-Apr-1907	William J. Real	Blummer, Catherine	Louis W. Gates	Ann Laura Bates
Reardon	Cecelia		26-Jun-1892	08-Jun-1892	James Bernard Reardon	Donohue, Carlotta	William Henry Donohue	Julia Agnes Reordan
Reardon	Ida	Regina	18-Oct-1893	12-Sep-1893	James Bernard Reardon	Donohue, Charlotte	Cornelius Dinan	Margaret Reardon
Reardon	James	Phillip	29-Jan-1905	19-Jan-1905	James Bernard Reardon	Donaghoe, Charlotte	James Edward Donaghoe	Annie Keene
Reardon	Helen	Elizabeth	18-Oct-1896	18-Sep-1896	James Reardon	Donahue, Mary L.	Daniel O'Connor	Fannie Malloy
Reardon	Mabel	Mary	24-May-1891	14-May-1891	James Reardon	Donahue, Mary L.	Dennis E. Reardon	Margaret R. McNeal
Reardon	Alice		16-Apr-1885	07-Apr-1885	Thomas R. Reardan	Curand, Alice C.		Mary E. Cook
Reardon	Grace	Agnes	12-Nov-1882	09-Nov-1882	Timothy Reardon	Schweitzer, Emma		Agnes O'Malley
Recheilll	Carl		24-Oct-1886	14-Oct-1886	Francis Reichell	Dolan, Margaret		Catherine Broderick
Recheilll	Mary	C.	05-Apr-1896	01-Apr-1896	William Recheilll	Blum, Catherine		Mary Blum
Reddy	Agnes	Catherine	03-Jan-1897	19-Dec-1897	John Reddy	Murphy, Mary	Thomas Murphy	Catherine Murphy
Reddy	Mary	Elizabeth	13-Jan-1895	03-Jan-1895	John Reddy	Murphy, Mary	William Cullen	Ann Cullen
Reddy	Richard	Joseph	21-Mar-1909	8-Mar-1909	Richard Joseph Reddy	Eberle, Mary Teresa	John Coffey	Agnes K. Croghan
Reddy	Catherine	Elizabeth	26-Jun-1904	25-May-1907	Richard Reddy	Eberle, Mary	Peter Furlong	Agnes Eberle
Reddy	Margaret	Theresa	10-Nov-1901	11-Jun-1904	Thomas Reddy	Keene, Mary	Patrick J. Moran	Mary Reddy
Redford	Elizabeth		05-Jan-1896	2-Nov-1901	Thomas Reddy	Keelan, Mary	Richard Reddy	Margaret Keelan
Redgrave	Margaret	Joan	18-May-1902	26-Dec-1895	William Redford	O'Connel, Ann	John Redford	Mary Redford
Redington	Catherine		15-Dec-1901	12-Apr-1902	Walter Redgrave	Goodwin, Joan	James Patterson	Mary Patterson
Redington	Edward		10-Oct-1897	02-Dec-1901	John Redington	O'Dea, Catherine	William White	Sara White
Redington	Elizabeth		19-Apr-1891	20-Sep-1897	John Redington	O'Dea, Catherine	John Keeley	Mary McCormick
Redington	John		13-May-1894	04-Apr-1891	John Redington	O'Dea, Catherine	Martin Redington	Catherine O'Neill
Redington	Martin		16-Oct-1892	26-Apr-1894	John Redington	O'Dea, Catherine	Bartholomew Jos. Fahey	Honora Flood
Redington	Mary		05-Aug-1900	04-Oct-1892	John Redington	O'Dea, Catherine	Patrick Keelty	Delia O'Day
Redmond	Charles	Patrick	24-Feb-1884	19-Jul-1900	Charles Redmond	O'Dea, Catherine	John O'Neill	Mary Ann Dunn
Redmond	Edward		13-Aug-1882	14-Feb-1884	Charles Redmond	Callaghan, Bridget	Edward Callahan	Mary Callahan
Redmond	James	Albert	05-Jul-1885	06-Aug-1882	Charles Redmond	Callaghan, Elizabeth	William Connelly	Elizabeth O'Neill
Redmond	James		21-May-1899	25-Jun-1885	John Redmond	Callaghan, Elizabeth	James McDonald	Mary Parrish
Redmond	Mary		16-Dec-1900	06-May-1899	John Redmond	Elliott, Mary	James Landrigan	Margaret Elliott
Reed	Mary		04-May-1891	05-Dec-1900	Michael J. Reed	Elliott, Mary	Francis Ward	Delia Elliott
Reed	Margaret	H.	11-Feb-1906	02-Apr-1891	Richard C. Reed	Thrope, Mary		Sara Reed
Reed	Charles	Harvey	29-Jun-1913	29-Jan-1906	Richard Reed	Vogt, Dora	James Harvey	Margaret Harvey
Reed/Stowe	Ida	H.	10-Sep-1903	13-Apr-1913	James H. Reed	Donaldson, Elizabeth	Joseph Fabe	Margaret Bell
Reese	Gertrude	Landerice	15-Oct-1905	08-Sep-1865	John A. Reese	Palley, Sarah		Edward Hulse
Reese	John		09-Jan-1898	5-Oct-1905	John A. Reese	[Blank]	Arthur P. Turner	Sarah Turner
Reese	Henry	Aloysius	11-Feb-1900	25-Dec-1897	John Reese	Turner, Eva	John Turner	Agnes Kelly
Reese	Leonard	Augustine	05-Jan-1902	01-Feb-1900	John Reese	Turner, Eva	John Turner	Clara Boughton
Reese	Mary	E.	11-Feb-1900	21-Dec-1901	John Reese	Turner, Eva	William Turner	Ella Turner
Reese	Walter	Ambrose	26-Aug-1894	01-Feb-1900	John Reese	Turner, Eva	John Turner	Sara Turner
Reese	William	Perry	02-Aug-1896	24-Aug-1894	John Reese	Turner, Eva	John Turner	Sara Turner
Reese	Mary		22-Feb-1914	26-Jul-1896	Richard Reese	Turner, Eva	John Turner	Sarah Turner
Reever	James	Edgar	17-Jul-1892	17-Sep-1873	William Henry Reever	[Blank], Catherine		Grace Weigman
Reeves	Catherine	Irenne	01-Nov-1896	05-Jul-1892	Richard Reeves	Eline, Julia Marie	James Eline	Ann Eline
Regan	Catherine		17-Oct-1886	22-Oct-1896	Jerome Regan	O'Brien, Ann Sarah	John Sullivan	Mary Chaillon
Regan	T.	Richard	27-Nov-1898	26-Sep-1886	Jerome Regan	Sullivan, Mary	Henry Evans	Roseann Farrell
Regan				06-Nov-1898		McKenna, Susanna		Sarah Giblin

115

LAST NAME	FIRST NAME	MIDDLE	BAPTISM	BIRTH	Father	Mother	SPONSORS
Reichielll	Viola	Cecelia	08-May-1898	04-May-1898	William Reichell	Blum, Catherine	Adam Blum
							Ann Blum
Reichielll	Helen	Gertrude	03-Mar-1901	22-Feb-1901	William Reichell	Blum, Catherine	Frances Sofski
							Catherine Sofski
Reid	Richard	Connor Paul	23-Jul-1911	29-Jun-1911	Richard C. Reid	Delaney, Elizabeth	E.L. Devine
							Sarah H. McAfee
Reid	Agnes	Elizabeth	14-Mar-1915	25-Feb-1915	Whiteford Reid	McKenna, Julia	John Dempsey
							Mary Flynn
Reilly	Joseph	William	01-Nov-1886	04-Oct-1886	David Reilly	Glenn, Rose	
							Ellenora Glenn
Reilly	Francis	Howard	09-Aug-1883	28-May-1883	Francis Howard Reilly	Staylor, Honora	Emma Staylor
Reilly	Andrew	George	03-Jun-1894	11-Apr-1894	Henry Reilly	Staylor, Honora	Andrew George Prell
							Elizabeth Connors
Reilly	Francis	William	08-Mar-1891	02-Feb-1891	Henry Reilly	Staylor, Honora	Francis Campbell
Reilly	Henry	Edward	06-Feb-1887	03-Jan-1887	Henry Reilly	Staylor, Honora	George E. Staylor
							Frances Campbell
Reilly	Joseph	Warner	02-Jun-1889	20-Apr-1889	Henry Reilly	Staylor, Honora	Michael Hopkins
							Frances Campbell
Reilly	James	Patrick	12-Feb-1888	08-Feb-1888	James Reilly	Kelly, Mary Joan	Martin J. Reilly
							Helen Smith
Reilly	Joseph	Vincent	07-Apr-1889	04-Apr-1889	James Reilly	Kennedy, Mary Joan	Hugh McConville
							Agnes Reilly
Reilly	Mary	Ellennor	07-Nov-1886	02-Nov-1886	James Reilly	Kennedy, Mary J.	Vincent Reilly
							Rose Reilly
Reilly	William	Albert	26-Apr-1891	22-Apr-1891	James Reilly	Kennedy, Mary Jane	Patrick Reilly
Reilly	Francis	Merriman	05-Jul-1891	22-Jun-1891	John Joseph Reilly	Duff, Ellen B.	James Murphy
							Ann Murphy
Reilly	William	Joseph	15-Apr-1888	05-Mar-1888	John Martin Reilly	Durkin, Catherine	William Wallace
							Helen Durkin
Reilly	Edward		05-Jun-1887	22-May-1887	John R. Reilly	Mea, Mary	John Mea
							Hannah Mea
Reilly	Francis	Charles	15-Jun-1884	04-Jun-1884	John Reilly	Carroll, Mary	Catherine Carroll
Reilly	John	M.	01-Jun-1902	06-May-1902	Joseph Reilly	McMahon, Mary	William Francis Reilly
							James McMahon
Reilly	Mary	Margaret	17-Jul-1904	2-Jul-1904	Joseph Reilly	McMahon, Mary	Philip McMahon
							Catherine Keenan
Reilly	Agnes	Matilda	22-Jun-1890	13-Jun-1890	Michael Reilly	McGrue, Helen	James Donahue
							Julia Griffin
Reilly	Michael	Edward	01-Jan-1888	25-Dec-1887	Michael Reilly	McGraw, Helen	John White
							Catherine Eliz. McKernan
Reilly	Sarah	E.	19-Jul-1886	12-Jul-1886	Michael Reilly	McGraw, Helen	William Judge
							Mary Reilly
Reilly	Catherine	Eleanor	05-Apr-1888	20-Mar-1888	Patrick Reilly	Spriggs, Mary A.	Catherine Arata
							Bridget McGraw
Reilly	Francis	Joseph	03-Jan-1892	17-Dec-1891	Patrick Reilly	Fahey, Catherine	Francis Fahey
							Margaret Ryan
Reilly	Helen	Mary	04-Aug-1889	01-Jul-1889	Patrick Reilly	Fahey, Catherine	Thomas Fahey
							Margaret Donahue
Reilly	James	Patrick	20-May-1894	03-May-1894	Patrick Reilly	Fahey, Catherine	James A. Fahey
							Aberilla Horner
Reilly	Sarah	Catherine	14-Nov-1897	04-Nov-1897	Patrick Reilly	Fahey, Catherine	James Gunning
							Mary Ann Ryan
Reilly	Ann		14-Jun-1903	30-May-1903	William P. Reilly	Grady, Mary	Patrick Hester
							Margaret Gray
Reilly	Mary	Catherine	21-Jul-1901	07-Jul-1901	William P. Reilly	Grady, Mary	William Melin
							Mary Owens
Reilly	Gladys	Mary	23-Dec-1900	09-Dec-1900	William Reilly	Krouse, Mary	Henry Burlege
							Elizabeth Reilly
Reilly	Margaret		2-Oct-1904	20-Sep-1904	William Reilly	Grady, Mary	Andrew Garity
							Margaret Kelleher
Reilly	William	Luke	27-Aug-1899	17-Aug-1899	William Reilly	Grady, Mary	Patrick Grady
							Mary Gereghty
Reilly	William		08-Oct-1899	17-Sep-1899	William Reilly	Krouse, Mary	John Coffey
							Blanche Love
Reinhard	Catherine		25-Apr-1908	01-Dec-1886	John Reinhard	Dittus, Mary	Agnes Dellone
Reinhardt	Elizabeth		16-May-1886	10-Mar-1886	Frederick Reinhardt	Magraw, Elizabeth	Elizabeth Shae
Reinhardt	Charles	W.	29-Jul-1896	About 1859	George Reinhardt	[Blank]	
Reinhardt	Charles	Campbell	24-May-1891	15-May-1891	William M. Reinhardt	Campbell, Philomena A.	August C. Reinhardt
							Mary Reinhardt
Reinhardt	Edward	Coulter	23-Sep-1906	6-Sep-1906	William M. Reinhardt	Campbell, Philomena A.	Thomas D. Campbell
							Catherine M. Tighe
Reinhardt	Louise	Bennett	7-Feb-1904	22-Jan-1904	William M. Reinhardt	Campbell, Philomena A.	Francis Dunn
							Ella W. Reinhardt
Reinhardt	Philomena		01-Jul-1894	14-Jun-1894	William M. Reinhardt	Campbell, Philomena A.	August Reinhardt
							Virginia Campbell
Reinhardt	Margaret	Virginia	23-Oct-1892	12-Oct-1892	William Michael Reinhardt	Campbell, Philomena Agnes	Stephen Campbell
							Catherine Campbell
Reinhardt	Catherine	V.	25-Jun-1899	09-Jun-1899	William Reinhardt	Campbell, Philomena	
							Catherine Cavanaugh
Reinhardt	William	August	19-Apr-1896	About 1896	William Reinhardt	Campbell, Philomena	William Dunn
							Mary Reinhardt
Reirdon	Charlotte	Agnes	29-Sep-1895	14-Sep-1895	James Riordan	Donahue, Charlotte	John Riordan
							Mary Riordan
Reitmuller	Cecelia	Laura	09-Sep-1888	28-Aug-1888	Henry Reitmuller	Oliver, Cecelia M.	James Henry
							Genevieve Henry
Releh	William		20-Nov-1887	05-Nov-1887	William Releh	Rose, Catherine	William McGiveney
							Honora Mooney
Remmel	John	Joseph	16-Oct-1892	04-Oct-1892	John Remmel	Kelly, Teresa Small	James McDevitt
							Alice Brady
Renmey	Mary	Ann	02-Feb-1895	17-Oct-1829	Samuel Renmey	Lawrence, Mary	John Gaynor
Renner	Lillian	Mary	12-Mar-1893	18-Feb-1893	George Washington Renner	Schlang, Margaret	
							Elizabeth Schlang
Renner	Howard	Leo	07-May-1893	28-Apr-1893	Joseph Renner	Boyle, Mary A.	John Boyle
							Mary A. Boyle
Renner	John		25-Apr-1886	14-Apr-1886	Joseph Renner	Boyle, Mary	John O'Brien
							Laura Kennedy
Renner	Catherine		25-Feb-1883	17-Feb-1883	Josepheh Renner	Boyle, Mary	William Boyle
							Ann Coulehan
Renner	Catherine	Agnes	02-Nov-1890	19-Oct-1890	Thomas Renner	Gleason, Mary	Patrick McGee
							Mary Helen Gleason
Renner	Thomas		29-Aug-1886	13-Aug-1886	Thomas Renner	Gleason, Mary	Mary Renner
Renschling	George		2-Nov-1914	14-Feb-1903	William Renschling	Vincent, Josephine	Roger Wooden
Renschling	William		2-Nov-1914	19-Mar-1900	William Renschling	Vincent, Josephine	Leo Armstrong
Reskensburger	Mary		18-Jul-1909	9-Jul-1909	John Reskensburger	Friedel, Clara	Edward Willis
							Mary Willis
Reus	Henry	Joseph	10-Jan-1909	1-Jan-1909	George Oscar Reus	Adler, Dorothy	Henry Joseph Adler
							Sophia Adler
Reuschling	Mabel	Elizabeth	8-Aug-1915	19-Jul-1915	William Reuschling	Dwyer, Joan	Charles Keagle
							Mabel Keagle
Reuter	Catherine	Agnes	29-Sep-1901	15-Sep-1901	August Reuter	Burket, Catherine	James Monaghan
							Delia Monaghan
Reuter	Christina	Dolores	2-Oct-1904	10-Sep-1904	August Reuter	Burket, Catherine	Michael Hart
							Stella Sanders
Reuter	Genevieve	Margaret	08-Sep-1895	03-Sep-1895	August Reuter	Burket, Katie	Genevieve Reuter

LAST NAME	FIRST NAME	MIDDLE	BAPTISM	BIRTH	Father	Mother	SPONSORS	
Reuter	Mary	Cecelia	24-Oct-1897	09-Oct-1897	August Reuter	Burket, Katherine		Mary Burket
Reynolds	William	Leon	31-Jan-1902	10-Nov-1901	Charles Reynolds	Welch, Mary		Katherine Earle
Reynolds	John	Thomas	22-Jun-1902	11-Jun-1902	Edward Reynolds	Gannon, Mary	Thomas Migan	Katherine Gormley
Reynolds	Catherine		7-May-1905	23-Apr-1905	Edward T. Reynolds	Gannon, Mary	David Russell	Margaret Russell
Reynolds	Eugene	Raymond	10-Nov-1900	29-Oct-1900	Francis Reynolds	Brattan, Jane		Margaret Duffy
Reynolds	James		21-Oct-1889	03-Aug-1889	James Reynolds	Dempsey, Ann		
Reynolds	Nora	Lucy	04-Oct-1894	19-Dec-1890	James Reynolds	Andrews, Ann		Margaret Dailey
Reynolds	Rose	Ellen	04-Oct-1894	30-Mar-1894	James Reynolds	Andrews, Ann		Margaret Dailey
Reynolds	Genevieve		08-Aug-1897	29-Jul-1897	John Reynolds	Murphy, Catherine		Mary Murphy
Reynolds	George		13-Feb-1896	About 1878	John Reynolds	Reynolds, Ann		
Reynolds	John	Michael	13-Jan-1895	16-Dec-1894	John Reynolds	Murphy, Kate		Agnes Kennedy
Reynolds	George		22-Jan-1893	07-Jan-1893	Michael Joseph Reynolds	Mason, Mary	Michael Reynolds	Mary Leech
Reynolds	Catherine		11-Sep-1892	01-Sep-1892	Patrick Reynolds	Conroy, Mary	William Law	Margaret Conny
Reynolds	Margaret		10-Feb-1901	28-Jan-1901	Patrick Reynolds	Conroy, Mary	John Wood	Mary Wood
Reynolds	Patrick	Thomas	26-Jan-1902	10-Jan-1902	Patrick Reynolds	Conroy, Mary	Anthony Welby	Mary Casserly
Reynolds	Sarah	Irene	26-Oct-1914	2-Jul-1914	Thomas M. Reynolds	Coates, Irene	Gerald Burroughs	A. Burroughs
Rhatigan	Mary	A.	23-Jul-1902	13-May-1901	John Rhatigan	Rifkan, Ann		Ann Hededinger
Rhodes	Benjamin	Adams	2-Mar-1912	16-Oct-1842	William Rhodes	[Blank]	John F. Sealy	
Rhynknap	John	Clark	05-Sep-1884	25-Oct-1882	Laurence Rhynknap	Clark, Elizabeth		Ann A. McCarb
Rice	Flora	Mary	12-Sep-1886	12-Nov-1884	William O. Rice	Tessender, Philura		Margaret Coyle
Richard	Robert	Willis	11-Nov-1888	29-Oct-1888	Edward Richard	Conroy, Catherine	Edward J. Willis	Jennie Tracey
Richards	Francis	Wilson	20-Feb-1887	08-Feb-1887	Edward B. Richards	Conroy, Catherine	James H. Conroy	Margaret Connelly
Richards	Winifred	Ester	18-Jan-1903	05-Jan-1903	Edward Richard	Ward, Ann	Edward Reardon	Ellen Richards
Richards	James	Conroy	09-Mar-1884	02-Mar-1884	Edward Richards	Conroy, Catherine	Frederick Seebold	Catherine Green
Richards	Mary	Catherine	19-Feb-1905	5-Feb-1905	Edward Richards	Ward, Ann	Timothy Ward	Frances Wilson
Richardson	John	Joseph	11-Apr-1909	8-Mar-1909	Calvin Jacob Richardson	Mettee, Joan Catherine	Frederick Mullen	Elizabeth Ann Healy
Richardson	Matilda	Gertrude	31-Oct-1894	26-Oct-1894	Charles H. Richardson	Post, Marion		Elizabeth White
Richardson	Grace	Honora	13-Apr-1890	28-Jan-1890	Charles Richardson	Pout, Mary	William Joseph Pout	Emma Grace Meakin
Richardson	Dorothy	Regina	3-Dec-1911	12-Nov-1911	Joseph Richardson	Williams, Minnie		Ella Garrity
Richardson	Joseph	William	15-Sep-1912	2-Aug-1912	Joseph Richardson	William, Wilhelmina	Charles Murphy	Amelia Fiddel
Richardson	Morton	H. Clair	31-Dec-1882	13-Nov-1882	William Richardson	Frazier, Martha W.		Mary Joseph Hubbard
Richmond/Connolly	Catherine	Mary	7-Dec-1884	19-Oct-1884	Daniel Richmond	Kerns, Jennie		Ann Leland
Rick	George	Charles	7-Nov-1915	24-Oct-1915	George Rick	McMann, Mary E.	George Mehenickle	Catherine Tucker
Ridenour	Joseph	Edward	27-Aug-1905	20-Aug-1905	Charles Ridenour	Murray, Ann		Mary Lanahan
Rider	Ann	Virginia	15-Nov-1908	20-Oct-1908	August C. Rider	Simms, Mary Ann	Osborne Rider	Laura Callender
Rider	Mary	Theresa	06-Oct-1895	03-Sep-1895	August C. Rider	Simms, Ann	Samuel Simms	Catherine Simms
Ridgeway	Thomas		11-Jun-1882	29-Apr-1882	William Henry Ridgeway	McCabe, Catherine		Alice Coughlan
Ridgeway	John	Albert	02-Jul-1884	26-Feb-1884	William Ridgeway	McCall, Catherine	Joseph A. Foley	
Ridnour	Francis	Melvin	29-Sep-1907	23-Sep-1907	Charles Ridnour	Murray, Ann	Thomas Lundy	Helen Dolan
Riehl	Frances	Mildred	02-Aug-1903	28-Jul-1903	William Riehl	Blum, Catherine	Thomas Blum	Maud Blum
Riethmuller	Catherine		01-Mar-1891	16-Feb-1891	Henry Riethmuller	Oliver, Cecelia		Mary Smith
Riethmuller	Veronica	Gertrude	13-Nov-1892	04-Nov-1892	Henry Riethmuller	Oliver, Cecelia		Mary Smith
Rightmuller	Ann	Mary	19-Mar-1893	12-Mar-1893	John L. Rightmiller	[Blank], Catherine		Ann Barlage
Riley	Florence		08-Jan-1888	23-Nov-1887	David McKenzie Riley	Glenn, Rose		Mary Glenn
Riley	Helen	Mary	07-Jun-1885	01-May-1885	Henry Riley	Staylor, Honora	Georgia Staylor	Mary Staylor
Riley	George		19-Sep-1886	22-Jul-1886	John M. Riley	Carroll, Mary		Ella Carroll
Riley	Helen		20-Jul-1884	16-Jul-1884	John Riley	Quinn, Margaret E.	Patrick Quinn	Margaret Quinn
Riley	James		10-Dec-1899	27-Nov-1899	Joseph Riley	McMahon, Mary	Philip McMahon	Nora Kern
Riley	Thomas		28-Aug-1887	14-Aug-1887	Patrick Riley	Fahey, Catherine	Peter Fahey	Catherine Murrary
Rinehart	Henry		11-Jun-1883	22-Apr-1883	Frederick Rinehart	McGraw, Mary		Margaret Connelly
Ringleben/Otto	Emily		12-Dec-1901	07-Oct-1860	John Ringleben	Hohenstein, Rose	Ambrose Tauer	Marcella Kearney
Ringler	Alice	Mary	20-Aug-1884	14-Sep-1889	William Henry Ringler	Cleer, Sedonia		Mary Cleer
Ringsdorfer	Josephine	Lambert	13-Nov-1910	4-Nov-1910	James L. Ringsdorfer	Willis, Mary A.	William Moffett	Florence Cecelia Callahan
Rink	Phillip	Edward	6-Apr-1913	29-Mar-1913	Albert Rink	Martin, Helen	Winfred Camy	T. Rink
Riordan	Edward	Francis	25-Aug-1901	19-Aug-1901	Dennis Reardon	Cullen, Ann	Daniel Riordan	Mary Cullen
Riordan	Elizabeth	Matthew	06-Dec-1903	19-Nov-1903	John Riordan	Lowenstein, Dora	Thomas Riordan	Katherine McNally
Riordan	John		8-Dec-1907	26-Nov-1907	John Riordan	Lowenstein, Dora	Timothy Riordan	Helen Whittie
Riordan	Mary	D.	17-Sep-1905	1-Sep-1905	John T. Riordan	Lowenstein, Dora	Edward Reardon	Margaret McAnnally
Riordan	Catherine	Laura	02-Oct-1889	14-Sep-1889	Thomas Riordan	Carr, Alice		Kate O'Malley
Riordan	Dennis		15-Aug-1886	11-Aug-1886	Timothy Riordan	Whelan, Elizabeth	Charles Holmes	Margaret Whelan
Riordan	Thomas		15-Aug-1886	11-Aug-1886	Timothy Riordan	Whelan, Elizabeth	John Riordan	Catherine Kearney
Riordan	Timothy		27-Jan-1884	15-Jan-1884	Timothy Riordan	Whelan, Elizabeth	James Moan	Mary Whelan
Riordan	Vincent		20-Jan-1889	16-Jan-1889	Timothy Riordan	Whelan, Elizabeth	James Quinlan	Margaret Holmes

LAST NAME	FIRST NAME	MIDDLE	BAPTISM	BIRTH	Father	Mother	SPONSORS
Ripken	Ann	Margaret	26-Oct-1902	12-Oct-1902	Henry Ripken	Silverson, Aneneta	John Silverson	Mary M. Leibold
Ripken	John	Michael	20-Feb-1898	01-Feb-1898	Henry Ripken	Silverson, Ann	John Silverson	Helen City
Ripken	Teresa		04-Feb-1900	22-Jan-1900	William Ripken	Silverson, Ann	John Silverson	Carolyn Silverson
Ripley	Paul		07-Mar-1893	03-Mar-1893	Caspar Shipley	Cook, Emma	Parul Shipley	Dorothy Rappold
Rippard	George		23-Dec-1891	04-Nov-1868	William Rippard	Gwynn, Mary	James Laughlin	
Ripple	Mary	Katherine	10-May-1914	6-May-1914	John Michael Ripple	McCarthy, Agnes	Leo McCarthy	Mary Katherine Carr
Ritter	Charles	Gilbert	1-Aug-1909	18-Jul-1909	Edward Ritter	Brosnan, Mary	Daniel Brosnan	Agnes Brosnan
Ritter	Mary		1-Jun-1914	29-May-1914	Edward Ritter	Brosnan, Mary	Martin Smith	Agnes Brosnan
Roach	Mary	Agnes	18-Apr-1909	4-Apr-1909	August Eugene Roach	Hammell, Mary Nied	John J. Kelly	Mary Hoffman
Roach	Cornelius		30-Oct-1904	15-Oct-1901	Cornelius F. Roach	McCusker, Lucy	Bernard McCusker	Ann Fowler
Roach	Thomas	L.	16-Oct-1904	1-Oct-1904	James L. Roach	Horrigan, Mary E.	Thomas E. Roach	Ann Roach
Roach	Dennis		12-Jul-1891	25-Jun-1891	John Roach	Hart, Agnes	James Roach	Mary Hart
Roach	Francis	Xavier	18-Jan-1886	18-Jan-1886	John Roach	Grender, Mary E.		Ann Brown
Roache	August	Edward	26-Feb-1911	6-Feb-1911	August Eugene Roache	[Blank], Mary Catherine	Edward J. Batterdan	Mary E. Batterdan
Roache	John		03-Feb-1901	10-Jan-1901	Cornelius Roach	McCusker, Roach	John McCambridge	Abigail McCambridge
Roache	Catherine	Margaret	26-Jul-1896	12-Jul-1896	James L. Roache	Horgan, Mary E.	Richard Horgan	Margaret Roache
Roache	John	Dennis	28-Aug-1898	19-Aug-1898	James Roache	Horrigan, Mary	Dennis Roache	Catherine Roache
Robbins	Andrew	Russell	16-Aug-1885	10-May-1885	Henry Russell Robbins	McNeal, Ida Harriet		Mary Monica Robbins
Roberts	Margaret		10-May-1885	19-Apr-1885	Henry Roberts	Smith, Catherine		Mary Roddy
Roberts	Sara		30-Jul-1882	30-Jun-1882	Henry Roberts	Smith, Catherine	William McCart	Catherine Smith
Roberts	Rosalie	Thelma	28-Aug-1900	30-Jul-1900	Isaac Roberts	O'Neill, Matilda		Ann O'Neill
Roberts	John	Edward	15-Aug-1915	5-Aug-1915	John Edward Roberts	O'Connell, Bridget	Edward Hughes	Mary McLaughlin
Roberts	Andrew	William	27-Apr-1903	28-Feb-1903	Joseph Roberts	Hyde, Sara		Mary Catherine Quinn
Roberts	William	Isaac	6-Oct-1912	2-Sep-1912	Rutherford Roberts	O'Connell, Julia		Teresa Farrell
Roberts/Clifford	Harriett	Ann	22-Nov-1900	15-Jun-1869	James Roberts	Miskelly, Josephine		Rose McDonald
Robertson	Arthur	Vincent	10-Apr-1910	27-May-1906	Henry Ellsworth Robertson	Myers, Louise Mary		Rose Monaghan
Robertson	Ethel	Mary	10-Apr-1910	30-Mar-1910	Henry Ellsworth Robertson	Myers, Louise Mary		Margaret Regina McCourt
Robertson	Mary	Eleanor	26-Jul-1888	22-Jul-1888	William G. Robertson	Diggs, Eleanor	Francis T. Diggs	Emily R. Diggs
Robertson	Mary	Victoria	26-Jul-1888	15-May-1885	William G. Robertson	Diggs, Eleanor		Mary J. Robertson
Robinson	Robert	Hays	29-Nov-1896	[Blank]	James Robinson	Hays, Mary		Francis Lauer
Rocca	Angela		16-Feb-1915	16-Oct-1914	Francis Rocca	Lautring, Carmelo	Andrew Kawzymistei	Teresa Sciaterrasi
Roche	Catherine	Genevieve	19-May-1912	27-Apr-1912	August Roche	[Blank], Mary Catherine	Anthony Lauting	Ella O'Brien
Roche	Bernard		19-Nov-1899	08-Nov-1899	C. Roche	McKusker, Lucy	August [Blank]	Mary Fowler
Roche	Rose		09-Oct-1898	25-Sep-1898	Charles Roche	Wells, Catherine	Bernard McKenna	
Roche	Mary	Thelma	17-Sep-1906	9-Sep-1906	Cornelius F. Roach	McCusker, Lucy	Edward Healey	Margaret Healey
Roche	Cornelius		1-Oct-1910	22-Sep-1910	Cornelius Francis Roche	McCosker, Lucia Placidia	Edward J. Healy	Margaret Ann Healy
Roche	Daniel	Wilmer	27-Feb-1898	18-Feb-1898	Cornelius Roche	McCusker, Lucy	Thomas Roche	Catherine McCusker
Roche	Edward	Joseph	10-Jun-1906	24-May-1906	James L. Roche	Harrigan, Mary	Edward O'Donnell	Abigail O'Donnell
Roche	James		25-Aug-1901	13-Aug-1901	James Roche	Horrigan, Mary	Cornelius Roche	Mary Gentry
Roche	Julia	Elizabeth	22-Aug-1897	10-Aug-1897	John Laurence Roche	Horrigan, Mary	Edward Horrigan	Ann Roche
Roche	James	Rose	05-Feb-1899	28-Jan-1899	Thomas Roche	Valee, Ann	Michael Vallee	Margaret Roche
Rochfort	John	Edgar	16-Feb-1882	07-Jan-1882	John E. Rochfort	Gallagher, Catherine	Michael Welsh	Alice Hardy
Rock	John	Joseph	02-Oct-1892	21-Sep-1892	Andrew Francis Rock	Smith, Barbara	John Joseph Rock	Mary Dunn
Roche	Leonard		25-Dec-1896	24-Dec-1896	Andrew Rock	Smith, Barbara		
Rock	John	William	18-Feb-1894	05-Feb-1894	George Rock	O'Connell, Catherine	O'Connell, Mary	Margaret Healey
Rock	Ann	Mary	10-Aug-1890	03-Aug-1890	James Rock	Delaney, Rose Agnes	Joseph Bernard Rock	Alice Kernan
Rock	James		16-Oct-1892	11-Oct-1892	James Rock	Delaney, Rose Agnes	Richard Cronan	Ann Delaney
Rock	Rose		30-Sep-1894	22-Sep-1894	James Rock	Delaney, Rose Agnes	Jerome Kuhan	Ann Delaney
Rock	Clara	Virginia	25-Nov-1894	17-Oct-1894	John Rock	Dwyer, Margaret		Alice Rock
Rock	Ann	Rose	01-Mar-1903	22-Feb-1903	Joseph B. Rock	Kernan, Alice E.	Thomas J. Kernan	Margaret Cook
Rock	Joseph	Frederick	29-Jan-1905	19-Jan-1905	Joseph B. Rock	Kernan, Alice	Hannah Kernan	Patrick [Blank]
Rock	Ellen	Bernardine	29-Sep-1901	23-Sep-1901	Joseph Rock	Kernan, Alice	Edward Cook	Emma Kernan
Rock	Emma	Mary	21-Apr-1907	16-Apr-1907	Joseph Rock	Kernan, Alice	J.H. Kernan	Margaret Carroll
Rockford	John	Howard	4-Apr-1907	19-Jul-1907	Edward L. Rockford	Sella, Mary A.	James Stickline	Adeline Sella
Rockford	Louise		09-Aug-1896	12-Jul-1896	George Rockford	Barry, Margaret	Helen Patterson	Mary Patterson
Rockford	Mary		19-Jul-1891	08-Jul-1891	George Rockford	Barry, Margaret		Martha Hunter
Rocks	John	Adam	22-May-1893	27-Apr-1893	John A. Rocks	Dwyer, Margaret		Louise Hunter
Rocks	William	Dwyer	07-Aug-1898	29-Apr-1898	John A. Rocks	Dwyer, Margaret	James Hunter	Jenenie Goodwin
Rocks	Alice		28-Dec-1895	24-Oct-1895	John Rocks	Dwyer, Margaret		
Rocks	Frank		21-Feb-1897	22-Jan-1897	John Rocks	Dwyer, Margaret Helen	James Hunter	Louise Hunter
Roddy	James	Hunter	15-Feb-1885	05-Feb-1885	Bernard Roddy	Lally, Susan	Patrick Roddy	Mary McDonough
Roddy	Susan	Joseph	21-Jan-1883	12-Jan-1883	Bernard Roddy	Lally, Susan	Timothy Roddy	Ann O'Conner
Roddy	Thomas							

LAST NAME	FIRST NAME	MIDDLE	BAPTISM	BIRTH	Father	Mother	SPONSORS	
Roddy	John	Joseph	20-Nov-1904	11-Oct-1904	James B. Roddy	Knauer, Ann B.	Thomas J. Roddy	Katherine Frank
Roddy	Mary	Mildred	22-Feb-1903	20-Feb-1903	James G. Roddy	Knauer, Mary	William McKenna	Nannie Harmon
Roddy	Thomas		13-May-1883	04-May-1883	John Roddy	Norton, Mary	Thomas Roddy	Mary Norton
Roddy	John	Joseph	8-Apr-1906	28-Mar-1906	Luke J. Roddy	Tighe, Margaret M.	John Roddy	Catherine Tighe
Roddy	Michael	Henry	29-Mar-1908	15-Mar-1908	Luke J. Roddy	Tighe, Margaret	Michael J. Roddy	Catherine Feeney
Roddy	Margaret		02-May-1886	27-Apr-1886	Michael Roddy	Moran, Sarah	Michael Roddy	Margaret Roddy
Roddy	Michael	Henry	24-Jun-1888	10-Jun-1888	Michael Roddy	Moran, Sara	Thomas Joseph Roddy	Bridget Noon
Roddy	Bridget		13-Oct-1889	19-Sep-1889	Richard Roddy	Moran, Sara	Luke Roddy	Margaret Roddy
Rode	Charles		15-Jul-1894	24-Jun-1894	Alfred A. Rode	Dunn, Amelia	Charles Dunn	Catherine Dunn
Rode	Henry		15-Jul-1894	24-Jun-1894	Alfred A. Rode	Dunn, Amelia	Henry Dunn	Catherine Dunn
Roder	Ann	Elizabeth	02-Jan-1888	29-Nov-1887	William Roder	Mannion, Mary		Parr, Maryell
Roder	Mary	Viola	19-May-1889	08-May-1889	William Roder	Mannion, Mary Agnes	Charles V. Bamburger	Ann Bamburger
Roe	Charles	Benjamin	14-Dec-1884	17-Nov-1884	Benjamin Roe	Hart, Rose	Michael J. Lauer	Philomena Cavanaugh
Roe	Alice	Cecelia	29-Oct-1905	4-Oct-1905	William Roe	Coyne, Ann	Joseph B. Sandman	Mary Alice Sandman
Roe	Catherine	Teresa	29-Sep-1907	7-Sep-1907	William Roe	Coyne, Ann	Martin Hickey	Margaret Clinton
Roe	Martin		19-Jan-1913	27-Dec-1912	William Roe	Coyne, Ann	Henry Coyne	Ann Laud
Roe	Mary	Olive	30-Oct-1904	10-Oct-1904	William Roe	Coyne, Ann	David Coyne	Mary Coyne
Roe	Mary	Catherine	7-Apr-1907	31-Mar-1907	William Roe	Simms, Mary Catherine	William Simms	Teresa Hagerty
Roe	William	Hayward	21-May-1911	2-May-1911	William Roe	Coyne, Ann	John J. Owens	Beatrice Nutcalf
Rogers	Mary	Stella	06-Apr-1884	29-Dec-1883	[Blank]	Rogers, Margaret		Mary Franz
Rogers	Albert		01-Sep-1889	22-Aug-1889	John T. Rogers	Lynch, Mary	Thomas Lynch	Sarah McNally
Rogers	Charles	William	26-Jun-1892	17-Jun-1892	John Thomas Rogers	Lynch, Mary Helen	William Bernard Holden	Helen Lynch
Rogers	Emma	Mary	08-Apr-1894	30-Mar-1894	John Thomas Rogers	Lynch, Mary Helen	James Gillen	Emma McCormick
Rogers	William	Bernard	15-Jul-1900	30-Jun-1900	William Kines	Rogers, Mary	John Rogers	Mary Tighe
Rogers/Watts	Emma	Charlotte	13-Apr-1908	19-Oct-1889	James Rogers	Burrier, Elizabeth	Joseph L. Carroll	Alice E. Gaffey
Rogge	Lillian	Cecelia	12-Jan-1902	22-Dec-1901	Bernard A. Rogge	O'Keefe, Elizabeth	John Stewart	Ellen Stewart
Rohrbaugh	Leonard	Luther	22-Aug-1908	May 1887	Charles L. Rohrbaugh	Ford, Sarah	Leonard Ripple	Margaret E. Killeen
Roland	John	Joseph	05-Feb-1900	20-Jan-1900	[Blank]	Roland, Mary		Elizabeth White
Roland	Emma	Elizabeth	31-Aug-1898	28-Aug-1898	Michael Roland	Durham, Ella		Mary Shea
Romar	Mary	Beatrice	03-Dec-1893	24-Jan-1892	Joseph Thomas Romar	Eller, Louise		Mary Helen Donohue
Rook	Leo		06-Mar-1898	20-Feb-1898	Joseph Rook	McAleer, Emma	Joseph Riley	Margaret Ryan
Rooney	Mary		23-Aug-1891	18-Aug-1891	Edward Rooney	Madigan, Mary	James Madigan	Ann Madigan
Rooney	James	Evan	27-Sep-1914	7-Sep-1914	Evan Rooney	Driscoll, Helen	James Eaton	Mary O'Connor
Rooney	Shella	Alma	5-Jul-1908	24-Jun-1908	James P. Rooney	Oakes, Shella Alma	John D.Oakes	Ann M. Parlett
Rooney	Agnes	Mary	20-Jan-1884	07-Jan-1884	John Thomas Rooney	McGregor, Susan	John O'Brien	Catherine McCourt
Rose	Dorothy	R.	12-Dec-1897	18-Jun-1897	W. Louis Rose	Larmour, Virginia		Edith Pentz
Rosendale	Mary	Evelyn	3-Dec-1911	16-Nov-1911	George Rosendale	Ross, Evelyn	Joseph Rosendale	Mary O'Hara
Rosensteel	Alice		22-Apr-1888	21-Apr-1888	Charles Rosensteel	Murphy, Catherine H.	J. Lee Rosensteel	Frances Rosensteel
Rosensteel	Clara	Margaret	29-May-1892	24-May-1892	Charles Rosensteel	Murphy, Catherine	Edwin Rosensteel	Constance Rosensteel
Rosensteel	Frank		15-Sep-1895	12-Sep-1895	Charles Rosensteel	Murphy, Kate		Amelia Adenhaur
Rosensteel	Helen		09-Mar-1890	03-Mar-1890	Charles Rosensteel	Murphy, Catherine	Samuel Leo Baterman	Samuel R. Seim
Rosensteel	Hilda		24-Jan-1897	16-Jan-1897	Charles Rosensteel	Murphy, Catherine	Joseph Leo Rosensteel	Margaret Rosensteel
Rosensteel	Charles	Alvin	18-May-1884	16-May-1884	Charles S. Rosensteel	Murphy, Catherine Helen	Francis S. Rosensteel	Clara Amelia Rosensteel
Rosensteel	Joseph	Leo	14-Jan-1894	05-Jan-1894	Charles S. Rosensteel	Murphy, Catherine	Terence McMahon	Margaret Meers
Rosensteel	Thomas	Julian	09-May-1886	01-May-1886	Charles S. Rosensteel	Murphy, Catherine H.	Thomas J. Murphy	Mary H. Geary
Rosensteel	Joseph	Leon	1-Mar-1908	21-Feb-1908	Edwin H. Rosensteel	Duffy, Gertrude R.	Thomas F. O'Neill	Catherine F. Guerin
Rosensteel	Margaret		13-Jun-1915	13-Jun-1915	Joseph L. Rosensteel	Maher, Mary A.	Edward Rosensteel	Margaret Maher
Rosensteel	Robert		6-Nov-1904	2-Nov-1904	Joseph Leon Rosensteel	Maher, Mary Agnes	William Maher	Florence Rosensteel
Rosensteel	Julian	Ellsworth	22-Mar-1914	10-Mar-1914	Thomas Rosensteel	Smith, Jeanette V.	Charles A. Rosensteel	
Ross	Nicolas		08-Jun-1891	About 1865	Peter Ross	Euler, Mary Magdalene		Joan Callaghan
Rossi	George		17-Jul-1904	26-Mar-1904	P. Rossi	Rossi, Lena	Philip Longa	Mary Cunningham
Rosso	Joan		7-Mar-1909	28-Feb-1909	Joseph Rosso	Stephens, Mary	James Rosso	Mary Domico
Rosso	Sarah		6-Mar-1909	28-Feb-1909	Joseph Rosso	Stephens, Mary	Vincent Stephens	Theresa Rosso
Roth	Margaret		21-Mar-1910	8-Dec-1909	Henry Roth	Pfister, Mary		Margaret Buckley
Rouh	Mary	Josephine	29-Nov-1906	17-Nov-1906	Joseph A. Rouh	Guerin, Margaret	James Smith	Julia Guerin
Rourke	Margaret	Ignatius	26-Apr-1891	22-Apr-1891	Joseph Rourke	Hall, Mary	James O'Rourke	Teresa O'Rourke
Rowe	Laurence		05-Dec-1897	26-Nov-1897	Thomas Rowe	Dohoney, Sarah	Edward Martin	Mary Martin
Rowe	Ida		1-Dec-1913	25-Jun-1884	William Rowe	Paul, Mary E.		Margaret Rowe
Rowland	Catherine		10-Jul-1910	18-Jun-1910	William Eugene Rowland	Marr, Ann Lee	John Hoeckel	Margaret Hoeckel
Rowland	Mary		05-Jun-1900	05-Jun-1900	William Rowland	Hogan, Mary		Ann Kennedy
Rowland	William	Eugene	5-Nov-1911	5-Nov-1911	William Rowland	Lee, Ann		
Rowling	Mary	Dorothy	28-Sep-1913	15-Sep-1913	William E. Rowling	Marr, Ann Lee	Henry Rowling	Mary Rowling
Royster	James	Clifford	20-Oct-1908	11-Dec-1907	James Goodrich Royster	Clifford, Eleanor		Beatrice Clifford

LAST NAME	FIRST NAME	MIDDLE	BAPTISM	BIRTH	Father	Mother	SPONSORS
Royston	Leo	Wilson	11-Oct-1896	18-Sep-1896	Charles Royston	[Blank], Ida	Mary Gorman
Ruah	Mary		6-Apr-1905	10-Apr-1905	Joseph A. Ruah	Meers, Margaret	
Ruchman	Edmund	Murray	28-Nov-1897	16-Nov-1897	William Ruchman	Murray, Mary Theresa	Thomas Kernan
Ruckle	Ann		17-Aug-1884	26-Jul-1884	James S. Ruckle	Kehoe, Mary Elizabeth	Ann Kehoe
Ruckle	Joseph	Henry	03-Dec-1882	12-Nov-1882	James Sinclair Ruckle	Kehoe, Mary Elizabeth	Helen Kehoe
Ruckle	Elsie	Mary	09-Aug-1903	21-Jul-1903	Thomas L. Ruckle	McGreevey, Margaret	Charles W. Price	Agnes McCabe
Ruckle	Margaret		15-Oct-1905	3-Oct-1905	Thomas L. Ruckle	McGreevey, Margaret	Edward Ruckle	Mary Smith
Ruckle	Adam		21-Nov-1886	09-Nov-1886	Thomas Ruckle	Ward, Mary A.	John McGarvey	Elizabeth Ward
Ruckle	Mary	Florence	08-Jul-1883	20-Jun-1883	Thomas Ruckle	Ward, Mary	Laurence Finnegan	Mary Fallon
Rudiger	Mary	J. Ellen	24-Jan-1904	4-Jan-1904	John E. Rudiger	Blondell, Emma		Sara T. Mullen
Rudiger	Charles	Edward	6-Mar-1910	17-Feb-1910	Julian Rudiger	Blondell, Emma	Charles H. Poat	Blanche Mallon
Rudolph	Mary	Helen	23-Apr-1905	10-Apr-1905	John Rudolph	McLeer, Helen	Philip H. McLeer	Helen Rudolph
Ruffino	Ellen	Mary	05-Jan-1889	15-Dec-1889	Edward Ruffino	Stout, Teresa		Sara Stout
Rummel	John	Joseph	2-Feb-1913	16-Jan-1913	John P. Rummel	Howe, Mary	John Breymeyer	Mary Byrne
Rummell	George	Edward	30-Aug-1914	12-Aug-1914	John Rummell	Howe, Mary G.	John Howe	Margaret Smallwood
Rupert	Mary		19-Jan-1882	24-Sep-1881	John Rupert	Hilbus, Susan		Mary Parrell
Ruppert	James	Timothy	13-Aug-1893	08-Jul-1893	John William Ruppert	Clark, Elizabeth		Ann O'Brien
Ruppert	Elizabeth		10-Dec-1886	29-Nov-1886	William Ruppert	Clark, Elizabeth		Ann O'Brien
Ruppert	Francis	Hittle	12-Jan-1890	25-Nov-1889	William Ruppert	Clark, Elizabeth	John O'Brien	Ella Cullen
Ruppert	John	William	02-Jan-1888	15-Dec-1887	William Ruppert	Clark, Elizabeth	Andrew Wilson	Margaret Clark
Ruppert	Louis	Albert	13-Sep-1891	08-Aug-1891	William Ruppert	Clark, Elizabeth		Ann O'Brien
Rusk	Arthur		13-Nov-1898	06-Oct-1898	Edward Rusk	Bugester, Genevieve	Edward Rusk	Mary O'Dea
Rusk	Edward	Francis	5-Apr-1914	1-Apr-1914	Howard F. Rusk	Hyatt, Florence	Francis Wyatt	Margaret Bosson
Rusk	Mary	Theresa	18-Oct-1903	14-Oct-1903	John D. Rusk	Kearney, Elizabeth	Joseph Rusk	Margaret Echert
Rusk	Joseph		23-Sep-1883	07-Sep-1883	Joseph H. Rusk	Mooney, Margaret A.	Francis Mooney	Ann McMahon
Rusk	Edward	Washington	20-Sep-1885	03-Sep-1885	Joseph Rusk	Mooney, Margaret	Joseph Carroll	Sarah Houston
Rusk	Leon	Howard	21-Jul-1889	08-Jul-1889	Joseph Rusk	Mooney, Margaret	Francis Mooney	Barbara Rusk
Russell	Edward	Heffner	30-Sep-1883	29-Aug-1883	Alexander Russell	Baker, Sara Elizabeth	James Bernard Shields	Mary Ann Shields
Russell	Elizabeth		06-May-1888	01-Apr-1888	Alexander Russell	Baker, Elizabeth		Jennie Walsh
Russell	Francis	Joseph	29-Jan-1886	24-Dec-1885	Alexander Russell	Baker, Sara Elizabeth	Francis T. Butler	Mary Donovan
Russell	David	Terence	26-Jul-1908	10-Jul-1908	David Russell	Reynolds, Margaret J.	Bernaes J. Mullen	Mary E. Mullen
Russell	Francis	Xavier	20-Mar-1910	8-Mar-1910	David Russell	Reynolds, Margaret J.	Charles O'Neill	Mary A. Mullen
Russell	Mary	Octavia	28-Apr-1907	15-Apr-1907	David Russell	Reynolds, Margaret E.	John F. Muller	Helen Rose
Russell	Mary	Ann	11-Feb-1894	07-Feb-1894	James Russell	Murray, Mary Joan	James Mead	Margaret Byrne
Russell	John		21-May-1911	1-Jun-1910	Richard B. Russell	Dillon, Joan	Francis Russell	Lucia Russell
Russell	Herman	Jerome	19-Jun-1887	03-Jun-1887	William R. Russell	Burke, Ella	M.J. McArdle	Ella Burke
Russell	Charles	Kirk	14-Apr-1889	02-Apr-1889	William Russell	Burke, Ella	Charles Hayes	Mary Hayes
Russell	Charles		04-Aug-1895	21-Jul-1895	William Russell	Burke, Helen	Frederick Russell	Ann Leonard
Russell	Francis	Morrison	02-Apr-1900	30-Mar-1900	William Russell	Burke, Ellen	Thomas Russell	Ann Delaney
Russell	Helen	Patterson	24-Apr-1898	04-Apr-1898	William Russell	Burke, Helen	James Russell	Helen Patterson
Russell	James	Anderson	18-Jan-1885	04-Jan-1885	William T. Russell	Burke, Helen	John Gunning	Mary Liveney
Russell	Mary	Barry	15-Feb-1891	03-Feb-1891	William T. Russell	Burke, Ellen	John Stanton	Ann Stanton
Russell	John		25-Jun-1893	14-Jun-1893	William Thomas Russell	Burke, Helen	Francis Thomas Hogan	Mary Hogan
Ruther	Catherine	Ellen	14-Jan-1911	20-Dec-1910	William Ruther	Bray, Ellen		Margaret Bray
Ruthmuller	August	Henry	03-Apr-1887	27-Mar-1887	Henry Ruthmiller	Oliver, Cecella	William Moore	Catherine Campbell
Ryan	Mary	V.	17-Jun-1883	20-May-1883	Ambrose Augustus Ryan	Moran, Catherine	John Moan	Mary Ryan
Ryan	Cyril	Jeffries	04-Aug-1901	15-Jul-1901	Ambrose Ryan	Moran, Catherine	Edward Scheil	Mary Reilly
Ryan	Catherine		18-Nov-1886	18-Nov-1886	Cornelius Ryan	Slattery, Catherine		Mary Ann Magan
Ryan	Cornelius		02-Mar-1888	02-Feb-1888	Cornelius Ryan	Slattery, Catherine	Jermiah Joseph Maguire	Bridget Slattery
Ryan	Mary	Elizabeth	13-Mar-1892	29-Feb-1892	Francis Ryan	Edell, Mary E.	Vincent Lyons	Margaret Ryan
Ryan	Sarah	Regina	14-Sep-1913	26-Aug-1913	Joseph J. Ryan	Kearney, Mary	Charles Ryan	Mary Ryan
Ryan	Mary	Joseph	24-Feb-1901	13-Feb-1901	Joseph Ryan	Donnelly, Bridget	J. Harry Byrne	Mary Ryan
Ryan	John		22-Oct-1900	09-Oct-1900	Michael Ryan	Murray, Mary	John Murray	Mary Ryan
Ryan	Genevieve	May	13-Nov-1898	29-Oct-1898	Michael Ryan	[Blank], Mary	John Ryan	Elizabeth Shane
Ryan	Thomas		07-Jun-1891	09-May-1891	Robert L. Ryan	White, Rose	Michael J. Groghan	John Ryan
Ryan	James	Michael	29-Jan-1905	17-Jan-1905	Robert L. Ryan	[Blank], Rose	Joseph Moroney	Mary E. Moroney
Ryan	Rose		04-Jan-1895	21-Dec-1894	Robert Ryan	White, Rose		James McDevitt
Ryan/Reilly	Marcella	Frances	06-Jul-1902	26-Jun-1902	William E. Ryan	Mouse, Mary		Ann Wicks
Sadler	Arthur	Herman	10-Dec-1893	28-Nov-1893	Charles Henry Sadler	Jones, Alice Elizabeth		Bridget Eagan
Sadler	Robert	Leroy	03-Apr-1898	22-Mar-1898	Charles Sadler	Jones, Alice		Catherine Shea
Sadler	Hugh	Henry	16-Jun-1895	06-Jun-1895	John E. Sadler	Eagan, Ann	Michael Ward	Bridget Eagan
Sadler	Francis	Elmer	15-Sep-1900	03-Sep-1900	John Sadler	Eagan, Ann	John Ward	Ann Ward

LAST NAME	FIRST NAME	MIDDLE	BAPTISM	BIRTH	Father	Mother	SPONSORS	
Sadler	Laurence	Wilson	21-Jan-1892	16-Jan-1892	John Wilson Sadler	Eager, Francis	Hugh Eager	Francis Eager
Sadler	Alfred	John	20-Jun-1889	29-Apr-1889	Thomas Sadler	Ryan, Anastasia		Mary E. McKenna
Sadlier	Joseph	Ambrose	02-Jan-1887	04-Mar-1886	Thomas Sadlier	Ryan, Anastasia		Ann Kirby
Sahlender	Martin	Eugene	02-Aug-1896	13-Jul-1896	Martin Sahlender	Smith, Ann	Patrick O'Neill	Mary Teevan
Salsbury	Edward		15-Apr-1889	02-Nov-1888	Charles Salsbury	Harrigan, Rose		Elizabeth Harrigan
Salsbury	Rose	Helen	17-Nov-1884	12-Jan-1884	Charles Salsbury	Harrigan, Rose McClennan		Elizabeth Harrigan
Samsel	John	Milton	29-Mar-1902	21-Aug-1875	George Samsel	Riley, Elizabeth	John Byrnes	Julia McGrane
Samsel	Lydia		25-Oct-1907	About 1881	George Samsel	Riley, Elizabeth		Ann Hyle
Samsel	Robert		12-Nov-1904	07-Feb-1882	George Samsel	Riley, Elizabeth	Robert	Margaret Samsel
Samsel	Catherine	Mary	05-Feb-1901	11-Jan-1901	John Samsel	Tierney, Catherine		Joan Fogle
Samsel	Margaret		5-Nov-1905	25-Oct-1905	Robert J. Samsel	Croghan, Mary	John J. Samsel	Mary Raftury
Samsel	Mary		11-Aug-1907	27-Jul-1907	Robert Samsel	Croghan, Mary	Patrick Burns	Margaret Croghan
Samuel	Margaret		21-Dec-1902	06-Dec-1902	John M. Samuel	Tierney, Margaret	Robert Samuel	Margaret Connors
Samuels	John	Lillian	20-Nov-1898	09-Nov-1898	John Samuels	McGee, Ann	Martin Doyle	Sarah Holmes
Sanders	Mary	Francis	08-Feb-1885	28-Jan-1885	John W. Sanders	Adams, Frances D.	Thomas W. Slater	Elizabeth Sanders
Sanders/Smeper	Ann		28-Jul-1915	Aug 1829	Joseph Sanders	[Blank], Matilda Eliz		
Sandman	Joseph	Bernard	20-Sep-1891	09-Sep-1891	Henry Joseph Sandman	Morris, Bridget	Bernard Sandman	Margaret Keane
Sandman	Mary	Alice	06-Aug-1893	23-Jul-1893	Henry Joseph Sandman	Morris, Bridget	Charles Schaub	Mary Connor
Sanner	Martin		09-Oct-1887	02-Sep-1887	James B. Sanner	Adde, Louise	James S. Sanner	Mary Bohlman
Sanner	Laura	Celeste	18-Apr-1886	25-Feb-1886	James B. Sannerer	Adde, Louise		Caroline Sanner
Sanner	Felicitas	Antoinnette	23-Dec-1884	20-Dec-1884	James Sanner	Adde, Louise	Sidney Sann	Lillian Sann
Sanner	Loretta		24-Feb-1886	23-Feb-1886	James Sannerer	Adde, Louise		Caroline Sanner
Sapp	Edward	Charles	24-Jun-1888	14-Feb-1869	Edward Charles Sapp	Dowd, Catherine	Arthur Seipp	Catherine Carroll
Sappington	Mary	Catherine	2-Nov-1913	23-Oct-1913	Edward C. Sappington	Snyder, Mary	Edward [Blank]	Catherine Snyder
Sappington	Edward	Calvert	7-Jul-1907	1-Jul-1907	Edward Calvert Sappington	Snyder, Mary G.	Joseph Snyder	
Sarin	Ann		07-Dec-1890	28-Nov-1890	Edward Sarin	Dyer, Mary	John Dyer	Ann Dyer
Sasscer	Genevieve		22-Feb-1891	23-Jan-1891	William Sasscer	Donegan, Catherine		Mary Slaysman
Satterfield	Francis		21-Nov-1886	10-Nov-1886	Edward L. Satterfield	White, Catherine	Thomas Hawkins	Joan Henry
Satterfield	Albert		26-Aug-1906	18-Aug-1906	Edward Lyman Satterfield	Callan, Catherine	Edward Satterfield	Mary Elizabeth Silberson
Satterfield	Catherine	Callan	30-Sep-1900	10-Sep-1900	Edward Lyman Satterfield	Callan, Catherine White	Francis Satterfield	Mary Quinn
Satterfield	Charles	Eugene	23-Aug-1891	15-Aug-1891	Edward Lyman Satterfield	White, Catherine	William Joseph Quinn	Ann McCluskey
Satterfield	Clara		24-May-1896	17-May-1896	Edward Lyman Satterfield	White, Catherine	Michael McCluskey	Clar White
Satterfield	Edward	Lyman	08-Jun-1884	22-May-1884	Edward Lyman Satterfield	White, Catherine A.	Francis A. Broderick	Mary Devon
Satterfield	George	A.	14-May-1882	02-May-1882	Edward Lyman Satterfield	White, Catherine	John Morwood	Mary White
Satterfield	Mary	Catherine	09-Dec-1894	05-Dec-1894	Edward Lyman Satterfield	White, Catherine Agnes	Charles Satterfield	Mary Satterfield
Satterfield	John	Wilmer	10-Apr-1898	24-Mar-1898	Lyman Satterfield	White, Catherine	William Kelly	Rose Ryan
Satterfield	William	Joseph	23-Dec-1888	15-Dec-1888	Lyman Satterfield	White, Catherine	Thomas McGinn	Margaret McGinn
Sauer	Bernard	James	28-Jul-1912	13-Jul-1912	Joseph L. Sauer	Gallagher, Mary C.	Bernard Gallagher	Mary Gallagher
Saunders	George		27-Jan-1884	15-Dec-1883	Arthur Saunders	McCarron, Rose	John F. Affayroux	Mary Affayroux
Saunders	Peter		19-Mar-1882	07-Mar-1882	Arthur Saunders	McCarron, Rose	John Goulder	Mary Gallagher
Saunders/Schmidt	Ann	Isabelle	7-Dec-1910	23-Aug-1882	William Saunders	Saunders, Sarah	Michael Schmidt	Mary Flavet
Saure	Mary	Jeanette	12-Jul-1914	4-Jun-1914	Joseph H. Saure	Gallagher, Mary	Milton Gallagher	Emma Gallagher
Saurin	Mary	Louise	30-Jun-1895	01-Jun-1895	E. Saurin	Dyer, Mary	John McGuire	Emma McGuire
Saurin	Irvin	James	17-Dec-1905	3-Dec-1905	Edmund H. Saurin	Dyer, Mary		Elizabeth Butze
Sauter	Margaret	Helen	01-Jun-1884	18-May-1884	Henry R. Sauter	Ruckle, Catherine L.	James H. Sheridan	Mary E. Mahony
Savage	Ann		13-Aug-1882	01-Aug-1882	John Savage	Duffy, Elizabeth	Thomas Gunnip	Mary Clark
Savage	George	Thomas	19-Oct-1884	11-Oct-1884	John Savage	Duffy, Elizabeth	John Gorman	Ann Magee
Savignol	Mary		23-Dec-1883	28-Oct-1883	William Savignol	Lynch, Margaret	Michael Corcoran	Margaret Corcoran
Sayles	Helen	Mary	19-Jan-1908	7-Jan-1908	John Sayles	Hepburn, Mary	George L. Hepburn	Rose H. Darr
Scales	Ann	Elizabeth	19-Jan-1896	02-Jan-1896	Joseph Scales	Smith, Mary		Margaret Coyne
Scales	Stella		24-Apr-1898	13-Apr-1898	Joseph Scales	Smith, Mary		Mary Scales
Scales	William	Joseph	16-Aug-1885	23-Jul-1885	Joseph Scales	Smith, Mary		Margaret Coyne
Scales	Genevieve		29-Jan-1893	11-Jan-1893	Stephen Scales	Connolly, Margaret	Joseph Patrick Fields	Mary Joan Tracey
Scales	James		10-Dec-1895	09-Nov-1895	Stephen Scales	Connolly, Margaret	John Connolly	Elizabeth Daubert
Scales	Joan	Joseph	03-Nov-1889	29-Oct-1889	Stephen Scales	Connolly, Margaret Mary	Frederick William Miller	Mary Miller
Scales	Joseph	Bernard	22-Mar-1891	14-Mar-1891	Stephen Scales	Connolly, Margaret	Bernard O'Boy	Margaret O'Connor
Scally	John	Laurence	19-Mar-1905	13-Mar-1905	John F. Scally	Coogan, Agnes B.	Laurence Scully	Florence Truelove
Scarborough	Elizabeth		18-Nov-1904	14-Feb-1884	William Scarborough	Kinsey, Emma C.		Mary F. Hushon
Schadewald	Albert	Henry	29-Jul-1888	08-Jul-1888	August Schadewald	Fales, Sara E.	William Lauer	Louise Lauer
Schadewald	John	August Charles	14-Nov-1886	02-Nov-1886	August Schadewald	Fales, Sara Elizabeth	John Joseph Lauer	Mary Elizabrth Lauer
Schadewald	Mary	Emily	13-Apr-1884	25-Mar-1884	August Schadewald	Fales, Sara	Michael John Lauer	Mary Caroline Lauer
Schadewald	William	Stanley	18-May-1890	21-Mar-1890	August Schadewald	Fales, Sara	William Lauer	Agnes Lauer
Schaefer	George	Aloysius	18-Sep-1887	02-Sep-1887	Francis J. Schaefer	Carey, Elizabeth	John J. Mohler	Eva Carey

LAST NAME	FIRST NAME	MIDDLE	BAPTISM	BIRTH	Father	Mother	SPONSORS
Schaefer	Lillian	Rita	11-Nov-1888	27-Oct-1888	Henry F. Schaefer	Clare, Mary	Laurence Cotter / Elizabeth Clare
Schaeffer	George	Franklin	31-Dec-1882	25-Nov-1882	William B. Schaeffer	Dressel, Virginia	Francis George Dressel
Schaeffer	Helen	Virginia	30-Mar-1884	11-Mar-1884	William John Schaeffer	Chridall, Sara Elizabeth	James McDevitt / Mary Gallagher
Scharf	Henry	Young	08-Aug-1883	22-Jul-1883	William Scharf	Woodward, Alice	Mary Butler
Scharnagl	Charles	G.	15-Aug-1886	07-Aug-1886	Nicolas G. Scharnagl	Foy, Mary Genevieve	Eilena Foy
Scharnagl	Arthur		01-Apr-1888	23-Mar-1888	Nicolas George Scharnagl	Foy, Mary	Agnes Foy
Schaub	Joseph	Anthony	12-Mar-1911	20-Feb-1911	Joseph A. Schaub	Busch, Ann M.	George C. Schaub / Catherine C. Schaub
Schaum	William	Carlton	1-Aug-1909	9-Oct-1908	Louis Albert Schaum	Finnan, Mary Ann	Elizabeth McGinn
Schaus	Margaret	Mary	5-Nov-1911	20-Oct-1911	Ervin Schaus	Bradley, Margaret	Patrick Horan / Catherine Dongan
Scheckel	Gertrude		10-Jul-1904	25-Jun-1904	John Scheckel	Thompson, Maytie	Charles Coyle / Augusta Buttner
Scheckels	Mary	Loretta	21-May-1899	13-May-1899	John Scheckels	Hagerty, Elizabeth	John Wilkening / Ann Wilkening
Schempp	Helen		30-Jan-1898	30-Dec-1897	George Schempp	Calahan, Rose	James Calahan / Ann Kreiger
Schempp	Rhea		20-Oct-1899	29-Aug-1899	George Schempp	Calahan, Rose	Helen Cullerton
Schew	Bernard	Jones	28-Jun-1914	7-Jun-1914	Henry Schew	Smith, Margaret	Bernard McErlain / Bernardine McErlain
Schleck	Julia		11-Sep-1904	8-Aug-1904	James Schleck	Cronin, Julia	Joseph Schleck / Mary Deely
Schleigh	Mary	Florence	19-Feb-1893	24-Jan-1893	William H. Schleigh	Jenkins, Ann M.	Joseph A. Edelman / Barbara Edelman
Schleigh	George	Raymond	21-Mar-1886	29-Nov-1885	William Schleigh	Jenkins, Ann	George Ott / Mary Ott
Schleigh	Samuel	Elmer	17-Feb-1889	17-Aug-1888	William Schleigh	Jenkins, Ann M.	Margaret Long
Schler	Francis		23-Sep-1894	09-Sep-1894	Francis Schler	Cohen, Rachel	Elizabeth Moran
Schloman	Mary	Gertrude	03-Jul-1892	01-Jul-1892	Walter Schloman	Henkle, Margaret	James Casserly / Mary Casserly
Schlung	Ann		08-Oct-1882	02-Oct-1882	Theodore Schlung	Bennett, Elizabeth	Thomas Bennett / Catherine Campbell
Schmidt	Joseph	Theodore	21-Jan-1891	17-Feb-1829	Christian Schmidt	Pisbar, Charlotte	John Paul
Schmidt	Agnes	Margaret	17-Apr-1892	14-Apr-1892	Louis Charles Schmidt	Stinefeldt, Catherine	Charles Schmidt / Agnes Stinefeldt
Schmidt	Bertha	Theresa	29-May-1910	18-May-1910	Michael Schmidt	Saunders, Annabelle	Richard Trageser / Bertha Stemler
Schmidt	Paul	Albert	9-May-1909	10-Apr-1909	Michael Schmidt	Sanders, Annabelle/Isabelle	Paul Albert Thiel / Ann Schmidt
Schmidt	Alma	Mary	07-Aug-1892	12-Jul-1892	William H. Schmidt	Baker, Sara	Mary Hoban
Schmidt	Mary		01-Jun-1890	01-May-1890	William H. Schmidt	Baker, Sara	Mary Warnick
Schmitz	Ann	Teresa	27-Feb-1887	19-Feb-1887	Theodore Schmitz	Cassidy, Mary Agnes	James Nathan / Ann Martin Quinn
Scholtz	John	Henry	31-Jan-1909	4-Jan-1909	James Henry Scholtz	Mason, Dennise	James L. Healy / Mary Tracy
Schramm	Bernard	Charles	06-Sep-1897	03-Jan-1895	Bernard Charles Schramm	Storm, Frances	Mary Schramm / Thomas Leonard
Schramm	Frances		06-Sep-1897	15-Apr-1892	Bernard Charles Schramm	Storm, Frances	Mary Schramm / Thomas Leonard
Schramm	Mary	Elizabeth	26-Jun-1898	18-May-1898	Bernard Schramm	[Blank], Fannie	Mary Schramm
Schroeder	Robert	Cooper	17-Dec-1882	17-Jul-1859	Jacob W. Schroeder	Cooper, Matilda	Greenbury Wilson
Schroeder	Robert	Lyman	17-May-1886	04-Apr-1886	Robert C. Schroeder	Wilson, Martha Rosann	James Wilson / Honora Shilling
Schroeder	Edward		28-Jan-1900	04-Jan-1900	Robert Schroeder	Conway, Ann	John Ward / Catherine Ward
Schroeder	Gertrude	Mary	26-Jul-1896	10-Jul-1896	Robert Schroeder	Conway, Ann	John Ward / Mary Conway
Schroeder	Helen	Mary	04-Mar-1894	20-Feb-1894	Robert Schroeder	Conway, Ann	John A. McGreevey / Catherine Schroen
Schroen	Catherine	Agnes	15-Jul-1894	10-Jul-1894	George Schroen	Myers, Agnes	Peter Schroen / Frances Maythias
Schrufer	Viola	Francis	29-Nov-1885	08-Nov-1885	John S. Schrufer	Pruett, Eleanor M.	Della Schubland
Schubland	George	W.	24-Jul-1898	23-Jun-1895	George Schubland	Michaels, Mary L.	Lauren Sepp / Mary [Blank]
Schuler	Mary	Corinthiam	29-Jan-1910	03-Oct-1870	William Schuler	Hopkinson, Laura	Mary Harkey
Schultz	Mary	Lillian	13-May-1888	22-Dec-1887	August Schultz	Burke, Elizabeth	Catherine Luppi
Schwalenberg	Elizabeth		16-Oct-1883	10-Oct-1883	Francis Aloysius Schwalenberg	Luppi, Elizabeth Josephine	Mary Schwalenberg
Schwalenburg	William	Herman	28-Feb-1886	09-Feb-1886	Francis Schwalenberg	Shepard, Elizabeth	Martin Schwalenberg / Emma Whitney
Schwanebeck	Frederick	William	26-Apr-1907	24-Apr-1907	Frederick Schwanebeck	Whitney, Estelle	Rose Campbell
Schwartz	Vincent		11-May-1902	01-May-1902	Francis Schwartz	Campbell, Catherine	Thomas Campbell / Sarah McNamee
Schwartz	Charles	Louis	5-Nov-1911	22-Oct-1911	Louis Schwartz	[Blank], Catherine	Margaret Sundermyer
Schwartze	Mary	Teresa	09-Oct-1898	03-Oct-1898	Francis E. Schwartze	Campbell, Katherine	Thomas H. Campbell / Elizabeth Schwartze
Schwartze	Joseph	Elmer	29-Mar-1896	28-Mar-1896	Francis Schwartze	Campbell, Catherine	Joseph Campbell / Elizabeth Donnelly
Schwarz	Henry		20-Jan-1895	25-Dec-1894	Henry Schwarz	Donnelly, Mary Joan	John Hynes / Elizabeth Donnelly
Schwarz	John	Charles	08-Oct-1893	25-Sep-1893	Henry Schwarz	Donnelly, Mary J.	Graham Donnelly / Fectrini Mancusa
Sciabarrase	Elizabeth	Joseph	10-Jan-1915	5-Dec-1914	Joseph Scibarrase	Sansone, Mary	Joseph LaGulda / Ann May Steil
Scott	Mary	Richard	8-May-1912	15-May-1911	James M. Scott	Scott, Mary	Mary Ann Schultz
Scott	James		20-Jun-1897	17-Jun-1897	John Byrne Scott	Schuramber, Mary Ann	Adam Schultz / Catherine Driscoll
Scott	John		03-Dec-1882	19-Nov-1882	Peter Scott	Maguire, Mary	Dennis Cronin / Catherine Driscoll
Scott	Thomas		03-Feb-1884	09-Jan-1884	Peter Scott	Maguire, Mary	Timothy Leonard / Catherine Leonard
Scott	Ann		24-Feb-1904	11-Feb-1904	William A. Scott	Bears, Susanna	Elizabeth Scully
Scully	Joseph	James	03-Oct-1886	27-Sep-1886	Peter Scully	Scully, Ann	John Scully / Helen Mary Gammie
Seccombe	John	Samuel	06-Nov-1887	21-Oct-1887	John Henry Clay Seccombe	Patrick, Elizabeth Cecelia	George Bernard Gammie / Mary Taylor
Seebold	Mary		25-Apr-1886	10-Oct-1885	Carl Seebold	Persch, Mary	Elizabeth Hamilton
Seebold	Charles		09-Oct-1892	25-Sep-1892	Robert Seebold	O'Brien, Helen	William J. Buchanon / Alice Armstrong
Seibert	Mary	Christina Alice	23-Sep-1883	06-Sep-1883	Charles Seibert	Armstrong, Mary	Patrick McGuire
Seibert	Mary	Francis	12-Oct-1890	04-Oct-1890	Charles Seibert	McMahon, Lizzie	Lizzie Hoffman / Charles Gosnell

LAST NAME	FIRST NAME	MIDDLE	BAPTISM	BIRTH	Father	Mother	SPONSORS	
Seidenehl	Mary		15-Jun-1890	09-Jun-1890	Charles Seidenehl	Quinn, Ellen		Margaret Dressel
Seifert	Carl	Phillip	16-May-1886	04-May-1886	John Seifert	Lederer, Emily	Carl Seifert	Mary Oliphant
Seifert	Frederick	Mary	13-Sep-1891	04-Sep-1891	John Seifert	Lederer, Amelia	Frederick Sillers	Julia Frances Rochfort
Seifert	Philip	George	08-Jul-1888	03-Jul-1888	John Seifert	Lederer, Amelia	Philip Miller	Minnie Regan
Seigel	Caroline		06-Oct-1895	19-Sep-1895	Frederick Seigel	McAnally, Ann	James McNally	Mary Ryan
Seigel	Margaret		31-Mar-1901	10-Mar-1901	Frederick Seigel	McAnally, Ann	George Smith	
Seitz	Charles	Albert	12-Nov-1893	01-Nov-1893	William Seitz	Gessner, Wilhelmina	Charles Albert Sumwalt	Teresa Francis Sumwalt
Sendeyahl	Laurence	Louis	16-Oct-1898	12-Oct-1898	Charles Sendeyahl	Quinn, Ella	Laurence Huth	Elena Paptistella
Senfh	Elizabeth		07-Feb-1888	01-Feb-1888	Peter Senfh	Maguire, Mary		Mary Morris
Sensum	Maud	Mary	18-Jan-1898	02-Apr-1882	Henry Sansum	Hairs, Louis[sic]	Thomas Leonard	Catherine Montrose
SErin	William		22-Jan-1888	09-Jan-1888	Michael Serin	Donovan, Mary	Michael [Blank]	Rose Serin
Serlove	James	Wilmer	11-Dec-1898	30-Nov-1898	Thomas Serlove	Sadler, Carolina		
Seward	Elizabeth Joan		23-Dec-1883	17-Dec-1883	William Seward	Owens, Margaret	Samuel Joseph Owens	Helen Essender
Sexton	Emma	Mary	19-Nov-1893	29-Sep-1893	Thomas Sexton	Grosh, Emma	Thomas Sexton	Caroline Sexton
Sexton	Thomas	Francis	06-Apr-1902	21-Mar-1902	Thomas Sexton	Carrick, Mary	Ambrose Sexton	Mary [Blank]
Sexton	William		23-May-1891	13-May-1891	Thomas Sexton	Grosh, Emma		Mary Drean
Sexton	Margaret	Mary	25-Jul-1897	02-Jul-1897	William B. Sexton	Rhodes, Florence	Philip Francis Rhodes	Margaret Rhodes
Sexton	Florence	Mary	10-May-1896	25-Apr-1896	William Sexton	Rhodes, Florence	Robert Sebode	Ann Sebode
Seymour	William	Julian	16-Feb-1896	29-Jan-1896	Joseph Seymour	Griffin, Bridget	William Garrity	Elizabeth Kilchenstein
Shabek	Catherine		18-Aug-1907	1-Aug-1907	James Shabeck	Cronin, Julia A.	Timothy Cronin	Mary Wulfert
Shabek	Mary		12-Apr-1903	26-Mar-1903	James Shabek	Cronin, Julia	Daniel Quinn	Mary Cronin
Shaffrey	William	Charles	14-May-1893	18-Apr-1893	Willian Joseph Shaffrey	O'Rourke, Margaret Ignatia	Charles Aloysius Bersick	Teresa O'Rourke
Shanahan	John	Francis Deznnis	11-Jun-1905	4-Jun-1905	John I. Shanahan	Kearney, Ann Louise	Dennis J. Shanahan	Stella Kearney
Shanahan	Ann	Regina	25-Aug-1907	16-Aug-1907	John Shanahan	Kearney, Louise	John Kearney	Margaret Connally
Shanahan	Helen	Angela	12-Jan-1902	04-Jan-1902	John Shanahan	Kearney, Lula	Edward Hogan	Cecelia Kearney
Shanahan	Joseph	L.	11-Sep-1898	28-Aug-1898	John Shanahan	Sheridan, Margaret	John [Blank]	Cecelia Sheridan
Shanahan	John		23-Nov-1891	15-Nov-1891	John T. Shanahan	Miller, Eva	John Miller	Mary Miller
Shanks	Mary	Helen	22-Apr-1897	30-Aug-1888	George Shanks	Shanks, Mary	Thomas Leonard	Mary Shanks
Shanley	Charles		19-Sep-1897	05-Sep-1897	William Shanley	[Blank], Mary C.	Charles Schaefer	Matilda Schaefer
Shanley	Eva	Mary	09-Sep-1900	31-Aug-1900	William Shanley	Brill, Mary	James Lucas	Eula Zink
Shanley	Leo		11-Jun-1899	20-May-1899	William Shanley	Brill, Mary	Leander Johnson	Zana Johnson
Shanley	Mary	Cecelia	27-Aug-1905	18-Aug-1905	William Shanley	Brill, Mary		Janetta Johnson
Sharb	Margaret	Ann	6-Sep-1914	18-Aug-1914	Joseph Sharb	Busch, Ann	Henry Phillips	Margaret Busch
Shaughnessy	Mary	Catherine	24-Sep-1893	15-Sep-1893	John Bernard Shaughnessy	Freeburger, Caroline	William Robert Stevenson	Louise Quinn
Shaum	Viola	Susan	27-Oct-1889	05-Jan-1889	William H. Shaum	Craver, Hester A.		Margaret Kearney
Shaunnesey	Catherine	Elizabeth	10-Feb-1901	26-Jan-1901	John Shaunnesey	Rippenberger, Magdalena	William Flynn	Martha Minnick
Shaw	Catherine	Cecelia	30-Oct-1887	26-Oct-1887	Henry Shaw	Quigley, Catherine		Mary Eleanor Saunders
Shaw	Gertrude	Alice	07-Sep-1902	29-Aug-1902	William A. Shaw	Tierney, Elizabeth	Robert E. Shaw	Alice Tierney
Shea	James		16-Apr-1899	04-Apr-1899	Bart Shea	Kelly, Catherine	John Kelly	Margaret Kelly
Shea	Margaret		05-Apr-1896	22-Mar-1896	Bartholomew Shea	Kelley, Catherine Gertrude	Francis Kelley	Maria Shea
Shea	Mary		24-Mar-1901	09-Mar-1901	Bartholomew Shea	Kelly, Catherine	John McShane	Mary Kelly
Shea	Owen	Donald	26-Jun-1904	17-Jun-1904	Bartholomew Shea	Kelly, Catherine	James Shea	Mary Kelly
Shea	Edward	Teresa	15-Jul-1888	30-Jun-1888	James Shea	McDermott, Mary	James McComb	Susan Sheehan
Shea	Joan	Teresa Isabelle	10-Oct-1886	14-Sep-1886	James Shea	McDermott, Mary	John F. Shea	Ann McCourt
Shea	Mary	Louis	22-Nov-1885	08-Nov-1885	James W. Shea	McDermott, Mary B.	Edward McDermott	Catherine McDermott
Shea	Catherine		15-Nov-1891	06-Nov-1891	James William Shea	McDermott, Mary Isabelle	James Edward McComb	Mary McComb
Shea	Ann	August	27-Dec-1885	14-Dec-1885	John Shea	Treadwell, Catherine	James Shea	Maggie Shea
Shea	James		13-Feb-1887	23-Jan-1887	John Shea	Treadwell, Catherine	Thomas Leonard	Margaret Adams
Shea	Elizabeth	Elmer	15-Jan-1882	22-Dec-1881	Joseph Shea	Conway, Elizabeth		Margaret Shea
Shea	Francis	Edgar	14-Nov-1897	21-Oct-1897	Joseph Shea	Connolly, Elizabeth	A.S. Papka	Agnes Ryan
Shea	Mary	Lillian	02-Oct-1887	24-Sep-1887	Joseph Shea	Conway, Mary E.	James Shea	Mary E. Shea
Shea	Joseph	Neil	22-Dec-1895	10-Dec-1895	Joseph Shea	Conway, Elizabeth	Thomas Kelly	Mary Kelly
Shea	James	Esther	25-Dec-1892	14-Dec-1892	Joseph Shea	Conway, Elizabeth	William Ryan	Catherine Ryan
Shealey	Catherine		15-Jun-1884	07-Jun-1884	William Shea	Byrnes, Elizabeth	Richard Tierney	Helen Lambert
Sheckells	Catherine		21-Apr-1901	07-Apr-1901	Henry Shealey	Kelly, Catherine	John Kelly	Ann Kernan
Sheckells	Mary		28-Apr-1907	12-Apr-1907	John O. Sheckells	Thompson, Martha	John Thompson	Catherine Thompson
Sheckells	John	Elizabeth	30-Apr-1911	18-Apr-1911	John Osborne Sheckells	Thompson, Martha	Joseph Alex. Slaysman	Mary Elizabeth Slaysman
Sheckells	George	Osburn	24-Jan-1897	14-Jan-1897	John Osburn Sheckells	Hagerty, Elizabeth	William Bishop	Mary Hagerty
Sheckells	James	Dennis	7-Mar-1909	22-Feb-1909	John Sheckells	Thompson, Martha	Henry Coyle	Ann Wilkenning
Sheckells	Joseph	H.	04-Jan-1903	19-Dec-1902	John Sheckells	Thompson, Martha	H. Coyle	Mary Battner
Sheckells	John	Osborn	1-Mar-1914	18-Feb-1914	John Sheckells	Conway, Elizabeth	John Sheckells	Loretta McNamera
Sheckells	Laura	Margaret	06-Mar-1898	17-Aug-1870	Otis Sheckells	Miles, Margaret		
Sheehan			1-May-1910	23-Apr-1910	Daniel J. Sheehan	Wetherstine, Laura	Eugene Sheehan	Ann Morris

LAST NAME	FIRST NAME	MIDDLE	BAPTISM	BIRTH	Father	Mother	SPONSORS
Sheehan	William		7-May-1905	28-Apr-1905	Dennis J. Sheehan	Brown, Mary A.	William Donigan	Elizabeth Brown
Sheehan	Robert	Joseph	31-Jul-1892	22-Jul-1892	Dennis Joseph Sheehan	Brown, Mary Agnes	William Edward Brown	Catherine Margaret Downey
Sheehy	Mary		03-Nov-1889	24-Oct-1889	Michael James Sheehy	Bowes, Margaret Teresa		Katherine David
Sheehy	James	Katherine	15-May-1900	13-May-1900	Patrick Sheehy	Burke, Mary		Ella Lowry
Sheeler	James	Lowry	26-Apr-1908	18-Apr-1908	Alexander J. Sheeler	Lowry, Olivia	John J. Klinefelter	A. Yakel
Sheffield	James	Andrew	22-Feb-1914	10-Dec-1813	[Blank]	Sheffield, Margaret	James McCarthy	Margaret Brown
Shehan	Ann		17-Nov-1895	06-Nov-1895	Dennis Shehan	Brown, Mary	William Reiley	Ann Brown
Shehan	Joseph		22-Aug-1897	09-Aug-1897	Dennis Shehan	Brown, Mary A.	Joseph Shehan	Nora Busthison
Sheldon	Hester	Teresa	14-Nov-1886	24-Feb-1863	William W. Sheldon	Gosnell, Amelia		Ann McBridge
Shellcross	Mary	Catherine	17-May-1908	4-May-1908	Joseph Shellcross	Nagle, Mary	Francis Nagle	
Shelley	Rose		27-Jul-1898	[Blank]	[Blank]	[Blank]		
Shelley	James	Ignatius	12-Apr-1903	31-Mar-1903	Edward Shelley	Kuber, Mary	James Kuber	Ella McLaughlin
Sheppard	Ann	Rose	06-Sep-1885	30-Aug-1885	George Sheppard	[Blank], Catherine Elizabeth	John Krener	Barbara Shipper
Sheppard	Joseph	Carroll	05-Aug-1900	23-Jul-1900	William D. Sheppard	Watson, Alice	Joseph Kelly	Ella Watson
Sheridan	Ann		11-Aug-1895	16-Jul-1895	Thomas Sheridan	Welsh, Margaret	James Tauge	Margaret Smith
Sheridan	John		08-Oct-1899	19-Sep-1899	Thomas Sheridan	Welsh, Margaret	Josephh Costello	Winifred Welsh
Sheridan	Mary	Margaret	24-Feb-1901	09-Feb-1901	Thomas Sheridan	Walsh, Margaret	Anthony Walsh	Ann Eliza Larkin
Sherlock	Thomas		12-Jun-1898	30-May-1898	Thomas Sheridan	Walsh, Margaret	John Quinn	Delia Walsh
Sherlock	Nathaniel		21-Mar-1890	12-Jul-1817	William Sherlock	Cook, Nancy	Patrick Stack	
Sherman	William		02-Oct-1887	01-Oct-1887	[Blank] Sherman	Dignan, [Blank]		Catherine Dignan
Sherman	Mary	Regina Linhard	11-Jul-1887	01-Jul-1887	Aloysius J. Sherman	Muldoon, Sara E.	Andrew J. Linhard	Mary Muldoon
Sherman	John	Andrew	23-Dec-1888	15-Dec-1888	John A. Sherman	Cox, Margaret A.	William Schaeffer	Mary Cox
Sherman	Albert	Leo	25-Nov-1894	31-Oct-1894	John Andrew Sherman	Cox, Margaret Ann	Lucas Roddy	Margaret Roddy
Sherman	Ann		18-Jan-1893	15-Jan-1893	John Sherman	Cox, Margaret		Catherine Cox
Sherman	Ann		26-Feb-1893	15-Jan-1893	John Sherman	Cox, Margaret	Thomas Joseph Cox	Margaret Doran
Sherman	John	Andrew	30-Oct-1887	04-Mar-1864	John Sherman	Barringer, Sara Catherine	John O'Callahan	
Sherman	Mary	Laura	25-Jan-1891	11-Jan-1891	John Sherman	Cox, Margaret	Joseph F. Cox	Catherine Cox
Sherman	Regina		02-Jan-1898	10-Dec-1897	John Sherman	Cox, Margaret	Joseph Cox	Bridget Cox
Sherman	Charles	Leo	19-Oct-1890	21-Sep-1890	L. Sherman	Muldoon, Sarah E.		Sarah Muldoon
Sherman	Thomas	Joseph	09-Apr-1882	22-Mar-1882	Louis J. Sherman	Muldoon, Sara Elizabeth	Hieronumus Malden	Amelia C. Gamble
Sherman	Francis	Gamble	17-May-1894	20-Apr-1894	Louis Sherman	Muldoon, Sara E.		Catherine E. Mooney
Shettle	Charles	Perry	22-Aug-1886	06-Aug-1886	Daniel Shettle	Landers, Agnes	George H. Hoen	Mary Nixon
Shettle	Daniel	Joseph	28-Sep-1884	18-Sep-1884	Daniel Shettle	Landers, Agnes Mary Gertrude	John Landers	Mary A. Donohue
Shettle	Florence	Mary	02-Sep-1883	22-Aug-1883	Daniel Shettle	Delavine, Justina	Arthur Delavine	Mary Delavine
Shettle	Howard	Paul	19-Aug-1883	08-Aug-1883	Daniel Shettle	Landers, Agnes	Michael Corcoran	Mary O. Finnan
Shettle	Bernard	Thomas	10-May-1908	30-Apr-1908	Howard B. Shettle	Sinnott, Ella	Charles Shettle	Agnes Shettle
Shields	George		22-Oct-1905	12-Oct-1905	John Shields	Kienan, Catherine	Edward Monaghan	Rose Monaghan
Shipley	Genevieve	Mary	13-Apr-1902	15-Mar-1902	Roger Shipley	Wess, Mary	Edward Wess	E. Wess
Shipper	Mary	Lillian	23-Dec-1888	16-Dec-1888	George M. Shipper	Krener, Catherine E.	John A. Flock	Laura Glady
Shipper	Mary	Agnes	02-Mar-1890	15-Feb-1890	B. Shipper	[Blank], Mary		Julia Mason
Shock	Mary	Agnes	07-Jul-1901	17-Jun-1901	John Shock	Mellen, Mary	George Rooney	Agnes Mullen
Shock	Lillian	Whitcombe	08-Sep-1903	04-Apr-1903	John Whitcombe Shock	Mullen, Mary	Charles A. Koester	Agnes Mullen
Sholl	Catherine		03-May-1903	27-Aug-1889	Henry Sholl	Quigley, Catherine		Mary Helen Landers
Shroeder	Margaret	Genevieve	16-Feb-1909	4-Feb-1909	Lyman Schroeder	Lynch, Margaret	John T. Garvey	Mary Margaret Phillips
Shumack	Elizabeth	Gertrude	18-Feb-1900	08-Feb-1900	William Shumack	Bruder, Dora	John Gessner	Lydia Gessner
Sidenbaugh	Joseph	Henry	24-May-1896	20-May-1896	Charles Sidenbaugh	Quinn, Helen	Edward Goldrick	Catherine Goldrick
Siebert	John	Henry	21-Jun-1885	15-Jun-1885	Caspar Henry Siebert	Burns, Mary Elizabeth	John K. Burns	Ann Burns
Siebert	Joseph	Thomas	29-Jul-1888	20-Jul-1888	Caspar Siebert	Byrnes, Mary	Peter Lally	Ann Lally
Siebert	Mary	Theresa	02-Aug-1891	28-Jul-1891	Caspar Siebert	Byrnes, Mary	James Duffy	Mary Duffy
Siebold	William	Edward	05-Sep-1886	29-Aug-1886	Robert Siebold	Burns, Mary E.	Luke Roddy	
Siebold	Albert	Charles	21-Jan-1883	30-Dec-1882	Robert Siebold	O'Brien, Ellen	Albert Siebold	Mary Genz
Siebold	Michael		07-Feb-1886	18-Jan-1886	Robert Siebold	O'Brien, Ellennor	Murray, Elizabeth	James French
Siebold	Robert		18-May-1884	08-May-1884	Frederick C. Siegle	McNally, Ann	Andrew Wetherstine	Nellie Wetherstine
Siegle	Frederick	Howard	13-May-1908	19-Feb-1908	Frederick C. Siegle	McNally, Ann	James McNally	Ella McNally
Siegle	John	William	10-Apr-1898	26-Mar-1898	C.H. Sigwald	Welby, Catherine	John J. Boland	Susanna Boland
Sigwald	George	Sidney	24-Feb-1895	21-Jan-1895	C.H. Sigwald	Welby, Catherine		Catherine Codire
Silberson	George	Philip	22-Aug-1897	27-Jul-1897	George Silberson	Lerch, Ann	John Lerch	Catherine Lerch
Silk	James	Edward	19-Jul-1895	21-Jul-1894	James Silk	Lewis, Gertrude		Ellen Welch
Silks	John	Henry	15-Jul-1888	21-Jun-1888	John Henry Silks	Thomas, Mary Ann		Mary Dexter
Silver/O'Connor	Nettie	Margaret	4-Oct-1911	20-Dec-1889	Abraham Silver	Silver, Ann		Margaret O'Connor
Simmons	Frederick	Rudolph	11-Apr-1883	09-Feb-1883	John Simmons	Spearman, Helen	Rev. M.F. Foley	
Simmons	Helen	Ann	27-Jan-1885	09-Dec-1884	John Simmons	Spearman, Helen		Mary Butler
Simmons	George	Lane	12-Aug-1887	07-Jul-1888	John T. Simmons	Spearman, Eleanor		Amelia Rudiger

LAST NAME	FIRST NAME	MIDDLE	BAPTISM	BIRTH	Father	Mother	SPONSORS	
Simmons	John	Thomas	17-Feb-1887	06-Jan-1887	John T. Simmons	Spearman, Eleanora	Susan Dawson	
Simms	Mary	Catherine	20-Sep-1914	3-Sep-1914	George F. Simms	Manning, Ellen	Paul Manning	Irene Manning
Simms	George	Francis	13-Dec-1908	21-Nov-1908	George Franklin Simms	Moylan, Joan	Samuel H. Simms	Eleanor Simms
Simms	William	John	01-Jun-1890	12-May-1890	John Thomas Simms	McKevitt, Mary	Michael Jerome Simms	Catherine Simms
Simms	Michael	Joseph	21-May-1882	09-May-1882	Michael H. Simms	Killeen, Catherine	Thomas Killeen	Mary Killan
Simms	Margaret		27-Apr-1890	17-Apr-1890	Michael J. Simms	Killeen, Catherine	Thomas Killeen	Margaret Killeen
Simms	William	John	27-Jan-1895	16-Jan-1895	Michael Jerome Simms	Killeen, Catherine	Thomas Killeen	
Simms	Catherine	Mary	19-Nov-1911	7-Nov-1911	Michael Joseph Simms	Ricketts, Mary	William Simms	Mary Ray
Simms	John	Michael	19-Apr-1914	9-Apr-1914	Michael Joseph Simms	Ricketts, Mary	Michael Jerome Simms	Katherine Simms
Simms	Thomas	Edward	07-Feb-1892	29-Jan-1892	Michael Joseph Simms	Killeen, Catherine	William Hagerty	Mary Simms
Simms	Ann		15-Jul-1888	01-Jul-1888	Michael Simms	Hillen, Catherine	Thomas Simms	Mary Hagerty
Simms	Catherine		18-Apr-1886	06-Apr-1886	Michael Simms	Killeen, Catherine	Patrick Hagerty	Margaret McKenna
Simpson	Mary	Henrietta	16-Sep-1883	01-Sep-1883	John Albert Simpson	Quinn, Mary		Catherine Connelly
Simpson	Mary	Elizabeth	16-Jul-1882	02-Jul-1882	John Simpson	Quinn, Mary		Elizabeth Quinn
Sims	Helen	Albert	17-Aug-1884	05-Aug-1884	Michael Sims	Killeen, Catherine	John Killeen	Julia Killeen
Sims	Leo		20-Jun-1897	08-Jun-1897	Michael Sims	Killeen, Catherine	Patrick Hagerty	Margaret Schafer
Sinclair/Kinsely	Elizabeth		10-Aug-1894	About 1832	Henry Sinclair	Courtney, Elinore		Agnes Ahern
Sindall	James	Howard	16-Dec-1883	06-Dec-1883	James W. Sindall	Smick, Blanch		Dorcas Ann Sindall
Sindall	Joseph	Leon	14-Mar-1886	03-Mar-1886	James Winfield Sindall	Smick, M. Blanche		Elizabeth Smick
Sindall	Mary	Blanche	06-Aug-1882	01-Aug-1882	James Winfield Sindall	Smick, Mary Blanche	Charles Ambrose Medler	Anastasia Medler
Sindall	Ann		05-Jul-1885	25-Jun-1885	John F. Sindall	O'Brien, Sophia		Mary Sindall
Sindall	Mary		28-Dec-1890	20-Dec-1890	John Francis Sindall	O'Brian, Sophia Teresa		Emma Trainor
Sindall	Alphonse		27-Apr-1884	17-Apr-1884	Joseph F. Sindall	O'Brien, Sophia	Dorcus A. Sindall	Alphonse Sindall
Singer	Henry	Walter	09-Jun-1887	09-Nov-1885	John H. Singer	[Blank]		Theresa Brink
Singleton	Joseph		13-Apr-1897	24-Mar-1897	John Singleton	Manly, Agnes	John Minch	Ann Biser
Sinnott	John	Edward	4-Oct-1914	15-Sep-1914	Charles Edmund Sinnott	Toulan, Mary Teresa	Joseph Sinnott	Mary E. Cassidy
Sinnott	Charles	Edmund	22-May-1910	9-May-1910	Charles Sinnott	Toulan, Mary	William P. Collins	Ann Sinnott
Sinnott	Joseph	Francis	7-Feb-1909	28-Jan-1887	Charles Sinnott	Toulan, Mary	Ferdinand Kraus	Ursula Sinnott
Sinnott	Marty	Katherine	15-Mar-1914	28-Feb-1914	Charles Sinnott	Krause, Margaret	John E. Sinnott	Naomi Getz
Sinnott	Robert	Silvester	1-Oct-1911	16-Sep-1911	Charles Sinnott	Toulan, Mary A.	Margaret Keelan	
Sinnott	Francis	Xavier	4-May-1913	21-Apr-1913	Francis Charles Sinnott	Toulan, Mary	Thomas Toulan	Elizabeth Toulan
Sinnott	Catherine	Mary	10-Feb-1907	16-Feb-1907	John D. Sinnott	Probst, Clara S.	John Sinnott	Catherine Umberger
Sinnott	Catherine		31-Oct-1886	25-Oct-1886	John H. Sinnott	Massey, Sarah	James Massey	Ida Massey
Sinnott	Mary	Sarah	18-May-1884	11-May-1884	John Sinnott	Minton, Bridget	Patrick Martin	Mary Hughes
Sinnott	Stephen		3-Dec-1911	25-Nov-1911	John Sinnott	Probst, Sedonna C.	Raymond Conroy	Sada Conroy
Sinnott	Ann		24-Aug-1882	11-Aug-1882	John Sinnott	Minton, Bridget	Stephen Sinnott	Mary Sinnott
Sinnott	Catherine		02-Aug-1891	25-Jul-1891	Laurence Sinnott	Guerin, Mary	Mark Sinnott	Ann McGuire
Sinnott	John	Laurence	18-Jul-1897	09-Jul-1897	Laurence Sinnott	Guerin, Mary Ann	Michael Malloy	Catherine Williams
Sinnott	Laurence	Silvester	09-Oct-1892	26-Sep-1892	Laurence Sinnott	Guerin, Mary Ann	James Byrnes	Ann Lynch
Sinnott	Laurence		6-Jan-1909	13-Dec-1908	Laurence Sinnott	Guerin, Mary A.		Agnes Veronica Clancy
Sinnott	Mary	Joseph	13-Oct-1895	28-Sep-1895	Laurence Sinnott	Guerin, Mary	Richard Guerin	Nora Guerin
Sinnott	Matthew	Edward	09-Apr-1899	01-Apr-1899	Laurence Sinnott	Guerin, Mary	Matthew Guerin	Margaret Guerin
Sinnott	Thomas	N.	23-Nov-1902	3-Nov-1902	Laurence Sinnott	Guerin, Mary	Walter whittey	Margaret Ryan
Sinnott	Lawrence		22-Sep-1900	06-Sep-1900	Lawrence Sinnott	Guerin, Mary	John Byrnes	Mary McShane
Sinnott	Margaret	V.	12-Aug-1894	21-Aug-1906	Lawrence Sinnott	Guerin, Mary	Nicholas McGraw	Matilda Donnelly
Sinnott	Laura	T.	10-Dec-1904	01-Aug-1894	Lawrence Sinnott	Guerin, Mary Ann	Michael Keelan	Mary Keelan
Sinnott	Mark	Ruth	06-Dec-1891	18-Oct-1904	Nicolas Sinnott	O'Rourke, Joan		Nora Connolly
Sinnott	Sara		26-Feb-1893	22-Nov-1891	Nicolas Sinnott	O'Rourke, Joan	Joseph Kehl	Sarah O'Rourke
Siskel	Eleanor	Josephine	28-Oct-1894	13-Feb-1893	Nicolas Sinnott	O'Rourke, Joan	Joseph O'Toole	Catherine Murphy
Slade	Mary		14-Sep-1902	12-Oct-1894	Jefferson Siskel	McLaughlin, Margaret	James Byrne	Helen Kerr
Slaters	John		21-Mar-1897	22-Jul-1902	Elisha Slade	Chase, Catherine	William Burns	Eleanor Wilbert
Slattery	John		21-Jul-1904	10-Feb-1897	John Slaters	Jeffrea, Esther	John Miller	Mary Burns
Slattery	William	Aloysius	16-Jan-1887	17-Feb-1904	Robert A. Slattery	Wyvel, Susan	William John Slattery	Mary Miller
Slaughter	George		01-Jul-1888	21-Dec-1886	Robert Slattery	Ward, Susan	Bernard J. Landers	Sara Wyvel
Slaughter	Francis	John	28-Sep-1884	05-Jun-1888	William John Slattery	McCormick, Helen Teresa	Sebastian McCormick	Ruth Wyvel
Slaysman	Alice		19-Sep-1897	14-Sep-1884	Francis Slaughter	Norton, Catherine	William Burns	Mary McCormick
Slaysman	James		09-Dec-1894	16-Sep-1897	Jerome Slaughter	Marshal, Mary Ann	James Burns	Elizabeth Riley
Slaysman	John	Alexander	07-Feb-1886	20-Sep-1868	Alexander Slaysman	Wilson, Mary J.	John G. Wilson	Alice E. Somerville
Slaysman	John	Alexander	20-Dec-1885	20-Jan-1886	Alexander Slaysman	McCluskey, Mary	Michael McCluskey	Hannah McCluskey
Slaysman	Joseph	A	28-Aug-1887	13-Dec-1885	Alexander Slaysman	Wilson, Mary	John Whalen	Alice Somerville
Slaysman			27-Jul-1892	18-Aug-1887	Alexander Slaysman	Wilson, Mary		Alice Somerville
Slaysman			03-Apr-1898	24-Jul-1892	Alexander Slaysman	Mulligan, Mary	William Curley	Agnes Croghan
Slaysman				19-Mar-1898				

LAST NAME	FIRST NAME	MIDDLE	BAPTISM	BIRTH	Father	Mother	SPONSORS
Slaysman	Mary	Elizabeth	25-Aug-1895	14-Aug-1895	Alexander Slaysman	Muligan, Mary	Charles Leiber	Mary Lieber
Slaysman	Michael		12-Feb-1888	08-Feb-1888	Alexander Slaysman	McCluskey, Mary Ann	Michael McCluskey	Mary Mullholland
Slaysman	Sara	Ida	14-Jul-1889	04-Jul-1889	Alexander Slaysman	Wilson, Mary	John W. Wilson	Mary Wilson
Slaysman	James	Vincent	23-Jul-1911	10-Jul-1911	James H. Slaysman	Daley, Elizabeth	Michael J. Slaysman	Ann Daley
Slaysman	Mary	Elizabeth	21-Sep-1913	9-Sep-1913	James H. Slaysman	Daley, Elizabeth	Vincent Daley	Mary Elizabeth Kornman
Slaysman	Mary	Emma	01-Nov-1886	03-Jul-1886	James Slaysman	Fowler, Eleanor		Agnes Coogan
Slaysman	Timothy	William	27-Jun-1915	12-Jun-1915	James Slaysman	Daley, Elizabeth	William McCrory	Mary McCrory
Slaysman	James	Powers	14-Oct-1906	5-Oct-1906	William A. Slaysman	Powers, Margaret Leona	Michael A. Brady	Rose M. Powers
Slaysman	William	Joseph	10-Jan-1909	30-Dec-1908	William Alexander Slaysman	Powers, Margaret Leona	Joseph J. Gothard	Catherine Gothard
Slaysman/Smith	E.	Mary	28-Jul-1906	14-Jul-1887	Alexander Slaysman	Bell, Carolina		
Small	Peter		7-Jan-1906	4-Jan-1912	John Small	Keane, Elizabeth	James McGraw	Margaret McGraw
Smart	Thomas	Gordon	27-Sep-1907	27-Sep-1907	Thomas F. Smart	Quinn, Eleanor	Edward Gordon	Mary Thompson
Smart	Helen	Alphonsa	14-Oct-1906	29-Sep-1906	Thomas Smart	Quinn, Helen	Henry Ader	Louise Quinn
Smart	Mary Amanda		26-Jun-1910	16-Jun-1910	Thomas Smart	Quinn, Ellen	Louis Ripperbrger	Katherine Gordon
Smick	Maurice	Francis	13-Jun-1897	01-Jun-1897	Joseph Warner Smick	[Blank], Catherine Francis		J. Sindall
Smith	John	Carroll	12-Nov-1882	26-Oct-1882	Aloysius Carroll Smith	Meek, Mary Helen	James McDevitt	Susan E. Smith
Smith	Roman	Neale	20-May-1888	06-May-1888	Aloysius Smith	Meek, Eleanor	William Keagle	Mabel Keagle
Smith	Alice	Teresa	30-Sep-1883	13-Sep-1883	Ambrose Bernard Smith	McKeagney, Catherine	Aloysius Carroll Smith	Margaret Ann Hogan
Smith	Leon		27-Jan-1889	04-Jan-1889	Ambrose Bernard Smith	McKernan, Catherine Elizabeth	John McKernan	Helen McGinity
Smith	Ambrose		15-Feb-1885	05-Feb-1885	AmbSmith, Rose	McKernan, Catherine	J.W. Sullivan	Fannie Wamaling
Smith	Amelia	Florence	26-Mar-1882	11-Mar-1882	Andrew Frederick Smith	O'Donnell, Ann Florence	James O'Donnell	Schneider O'Donnell
Smith	Elizabeth		31-Oct-1886	16-Oct-1886	Bernard A. Smith	McKeagry, Catherine	Aloysius C. Smith	Mary E. Smith
Smith	Mary	Clotilda	28-Apr-1889	16-Apr-1889	Charles A. Smith	Schiekert, Elizabeth A.	Robert R. Smith	Hannah Schiekert
Smith	William	Henry	10-Jul-1892	03-Jul-1892	Charles H. Smith	Condell, Mary E.	William P. Mulligan	Mary Carr
Smith	Katherine		14-Feb-1904	18-Jan-1904	Charles Smith	Condell, Mary		Margaret Mulligan
Smith	Margaret	Edell Smith	20-Oct-1901	03-Oct-1901	Charles Smith	Condell, Mary	Francis Otis	Estelle Otis
Smith	Rhetta	Virginia	11-Aug-1912	4-Aug-1912	Coleman Smith	Fraunholz, Caroline	Charles Finnegan	Mary Finnegan
Smith	Caroline	David	12-Oct-1913	22-Sep-1913	David Smith	Powell, Elizabeth	John Ryan	Margaret Ryan
Smith	Mary	Catherine	10-Feb-1884	09-Jan-1884	E. Ellsworth Smith	McArdle, Sarah Elizabeth		S. Catherine Helen Nolan
Smith	Samuel	Joseph	13-May-1906	12-Apr-1906	E. Smith	Condell, Mary E.		Margaret Mulligan
Smith	Mary	Elsie	3-May-1914	22-Apr-1914	Earl Smith	Gephardt, Margaret	William G. Coyle	Alice Thompson
Smith	Evan		24-Dec-1897	01-Apr-1893	Edward Smith	Criger, Ann	Mary Gershan	
Smith	Jane	Mary	12-Jan-1885	06-Jan-1885	Edward Smith	Farr, Mary		Jane Smith
Smith	Peter		13-Mar-1882	03-Mar-1882	Edward Smith	Farr, Mary		Mary Helen McGeeney
Smith	Frances	Pauline	15-Jan-1885	24-Jul-1867	Eli B. Smith	Smith, Mary A.		Sarah McGraw
Smith	Edna	Irene	14-Apr-1889	04-Apr-1889	Elmer Smith	McCardell, Sara E.		Matilda McCardell
Smith	Georgia	Mary	09-Aug-1887	10-Aug-1876	Francis A. Smith	Miegan, Ann		Helen Essender
Smith	Francis	Amos	09-Aug-1887	21-Nov-1879	Francis Amos Smith	Miegan, Ann		
Smith	Ann	Mary	17-Mar-1901	27-Feb-1901	Francis M. Smith	Brunne, Christina	Adam Myer	Barbara Myer
Smith	Alice	Frances	09-Aug-1887	14-Jun-1882	Francis Smith	Miegan, Ann		Helen Essender
Smith	Helen	Edna	09-Aug-1887	24-Mar-1887	Francis Smith	Miegan, Ann		Ann Hines
Smith	James	Frederick	08-Sep-1901	30-Aug-1901	Francis Smith	Cohees, Ann	Francis Kaufmann	Elizabeth Cotter
Smith	John		05-Nov-1899	27-Oct-1899	Francis Smith	O'Connor, Margaret	Peter Kelly	
Smith	Mary	Elizabeth	10-Apr-1898	30-Mar-1898	Francis Smith	Carter, Ann	James A. Nester	Mary Fallon
Smith	Hederam (Joy)	Teresa	16-Sep-1888	26-Aug-1888	G. Newton Smith	Helmcamp, Teresa	James McClellan Smith	Caroline Birney
Smith	Ann		03-Sep-1900	18-Apr-1887	George Smith	McGarrity, Jane		Rose Monaghan
Smith	G.		28-Dec-1913	15-Dec-1910	George Smith	Lee, Evelyn		
Smith	George		25-Apr-1913	26-Apr-1902	George Smith	Lee, Eva	Walter Connor	Mary J. Fisher
Smith	LeRoy	Alexander	17-Dec-1905	4-Dec-1905	George Smith	Slaysman, Elvina	Daniel Moran	Elizabeth Smith
Smith	Mary	Margaret	22-Nov-1896	08-Nov-1896	Henry A. Smith	Batterden, Margaret G.	Edward Batterden	Mary A. Brown
Smith	Sara	Agnes	17-Oct-1886	30-Sep-1886	Henry M. Smith	McIntyre, Rose	John W. Johnson	Helen McIntyre
Smith	Virginia	Mary	01-Jun-1884	18-May-1884	Henry N. Smith	McIntyre, Rose	Michael McIntyre	Mary Elizabeth McIntyre
Smith	William	Henry	30-Apr-1882	16-Apr-1882	Henry Nicholas Smith	McIntyre, Rose	John Thomas McIntyre	Helen Stolz
Smith	Helen	Genevieve	21-Jan-1900	06-Jan-1900	Henry Smith	Groome, Ida Alay		Mary Schweikert
Smith	Henry		03-Jan-1886	18-Nov-1885	Henry Smith	Schweikert, Elizabeth		Helen Stolz
Smith	Henry		06-Oct-1901	20-Sep-1901	Henry Smith	Groom, Ida		Joan Young
Smith	John	Henry	11-Aug-1912	21-May-1912	Henry Smith	Schelton, Ann		Elizabeth Burns
Smith	Mary	Elizabeth	05-Dec-1886	22-Nov-1886	James Francis Smith	Dorgan, Julia	Louis Burns	Mary Downey
Smith	Eleanor		23-Sep-1888	02-Sep-1888	James Smith	Dorgan, Julia	Thomas Cusick	Margaret Farrell
Smith	Enna	Mary	14-Jun-1914	1-Jun-1914	James Smith	Farrell, James[sic]		Ann Laragy
Smith	Francis	Stuart	13-Mar-1887	20-Feb-1887	James Smith	Laragy, Julia	Joseph Schwinn	Ann Lavery
Smith	George	Edward	09-Sep-1886	01-Aug-1886	James Smith	Lavery, Ann	James Lavery	Frances Gertude Laragy
Smith	Julia	Ethel	24-Jan-1892	12-Jan-1892	Jesse Smith	Laragy, Julia	Julia Largey	

LAST NAME	FIRST NAME	MIDDLE	BAPTISM	BIRTH	Father	Mother	SPONSORS
Smith	Margaret	Elizabeth	11-Aug-1889	31-Jul-1889	Jesse Smith	Laragy, Julia	Margaret Laragy
Smith	Mary		11-Mar-1890	About 1845	Jm. Smith	[Blank]	
Smith	Mary	Cecelia	07-Dec-1890	30-Nov-1890	John C. Smith	O'Connell, Catherine	Cecelia Ellinger
Smith	Charles	Moylan	05-Nov-1882	24-Oct-1882	John Charles Smith	O'Connell, Catherine	Catherine Daly
Smith	Charles	Patrick	26-Mar-1899	17-Mar-1899	John Joseph Smith	Hagan, Mary	J. Francis Daly
Smith	Charles	Patrick	26-Mar-1899	17-Mar-1899	John Joseph Smith	Hagan, Mary	John Thomas Moylan
Smith	John	Joseph	29-Oct-1905	15-Oct-1905	John Joseph Smith	Hagan, Mary	James Hagan
Smith	Mary	Rose	09-Feb-1896	02-Feb-1896	John Joseph Smith	Hagan, Mary	James Hagan
Smith	George	Thomas	16-Jul-1882	04-Jul-1882	John Newton Smith	Boland, Margaret	Cecelia Hagan
Smith	George	Dillon	17-May-1903	13-May-1903	John P. Smith	Evans, Ada M.	Honora Ryan
Smith	Ann	ruth	02-Feb-1902	23-Jan-1902	John Smith	Evans, Adelina	George W. Schanberger
Smith	Charles		22-Jul-1888	09-Jul-1888	John Smith	Connell, Catherine	Catherine Clark
Smith	Earl	John	4-Feb-1909	21-Jan-1909	John Smith	Scott, Sara Ann	Richard Hopkins
Smith	Edwin	John	25-Apr-1915	9-Apr-1915	John Smith	Adler, Sophia	M.W. Gantzhorn
Smith	Frederick		14-Nov-1909	14-Mar-1889	John Smith	Betzold, Margaret	Ann Adler
Smith	Genevieve	Mary	17-Nov-1895	02-Nov-1895	John Smith	Evans, Ada	John Heins
Smith	Helen	Rose	13-Dec-1896	06-Dec-1896	John Smith	Sleinfelt, Catherine	Margaret O'Connor
Smith	James	Francis	18-Aug-1901	11-Aug-1901	John Smith	Egan, Mary	Helen Strassberger
Smith	John	William	07-Feb-1886	25-Jan-1886	John Smith	Connell, Catherine	Katherine Crilly
Smith	John	Joseph	25-Jan-1914	6-Jan-1914	John Smith	Scott, Sara Ann	Catherine Daily
Smith	Lillian	Elizabeth	29-Aug-1915	11-Aug-1915	John Smith	Scott, Sarah Ann	Catherine Coyne
Smith	Mary		28-Oct-1906	22-Sep-1906	John Smith	Scott, Sara A.	Elizabeth Donoghue
Smith	Norman	Clement	11-Jun-1911	27-May-1911	John Smith	Scott, Sara	Mary McLain
Smith	Peter	William	3-Dec-1911	19-Nov-1911	John Smith	Smith, Emma	Elizabeth Smith
Smith	William	Abell	20-Nov-1904	3-Nov-1904	John V. Smith	Wheeler, Margaret	Catherine Smith
Smith	Joseph	Jerome	17-Jul-1910	6-Jul-1910	Joseph C. Smith	Klinefelter, Estelle G.	Richard Callahan
Smith	Albert	Francis	23-Dec-1888	10-Dec-1888	Joseph Smith	Bertrand, Catherine	Mary Smith
Smith	Dorothy	Joan	16-Mar-1913	4-Mar-1913	Joseph Smith	Klinefelter, Stella E.	Teresa Klinefelter
Smith	Joseph	Henry	23-Oct-1887	16-Oct-1887	Joseph Smith	Bertrand, Catherine	Mary Browning
Smith	Ellen	Elizabeth	14-Jul-1909	8-Jul-1909	Martin Smith	Quinn, Elizabeth	Rosalie Klinefelter
Smith	Adele		20-Dec-1900	27-Jul-1900	Mortimer Evans	McDonald, Jane	Catherine Habnick
Smith	Bertha	Latimer	08-Oct-1882	05-Sep-1882	Octavia J. Smith	McWilliams, Ann	Mary McKenna
Smith	Ann	Mary	20-Feb-1887	06-Feb-1887	Patrick Smith	Corcoran, Margaret	Joan King
Smith	Leon	Patrick	01-Feb-1888	28-Jan-1888	Patrick Smith	Corcoran, Margaret	Winifred Corcoran
Smith	Martin		08-Feb-1891	05-Feb-1891	Patrick Smith	Corcoran, Margaret	Ann Bresnan
Smith	Paul	Leo	14-Mar-1897	10-Aug-1894	Paul Smith	Shutt, Mary	Catherine Callaghan
Smith	George	Aloysius	28-Oct-1900	16-Oct-1900	Peter Smith	McGinn, Mary	Frances Hufnagle
Smith	Mary		20-Jul-1902	23-Oct-1882	Richard Groom	Green, Mary	Nelly McGinn
Smith	Robert	Raymond	27-Apr-1902	13-Apr-1902	Robert R. Smith	Smith, Joan	Mrs. Summinbury
Smith	Ann	Teresa	29-Oct-1882	14-Oct-1882	Robert Rudolph Smith	Smith, Mary Joan	Nellie McGahan
Smith	Charles	William	07-Dec-1884	26-Nov-1884	Robert Smith	Smith, Joan	Mary Schweinhert
Smith	Evans	Estelle	12-Jan-1890	24-Dec-1889	Robert Smith	Smith, Mary J.	Helen McGorrigle
Smith	Lillian	May	12-Aug-1894	25-Jul-1894	Robert Smith	Smith, Mary J.	Eva Carey
Smith	Mary	Letta	18-Sep-1887	05-Sep-1887	Robert Smith	Smith, Joan	Mary Dottrich
Smith	Mary		31-Jul-1892	08-Jul-1892	Robert Smith	Smith, Joan	Mary Luby
Smith	Mary	V.	21-Aug-1898	09-Aug-1898	Samuel L. Smith	Kernan, Catherine	Richard Higgins
Smith	Loretta	Genevieve	23-Aug-1896	14-Aug-1896	William A. Smith	Schaefer, Virginia	Charles Mulhare
Smith	Helen		12-Mar-1899	02-Mar-1899	William E. Smith	Smith, Joan A.	[Blank] McCullough
Smith	Mary	Joan	13-Feb-1887	02-Feb-1887	William E. Smith	Smith, Mary E.	Matilda Holtz
Smith	Arthur	Leon	9-Aug-1912	04-Mar-1883	William M. Smith	Smith, Mary J.	Helen Wilhelm
Smith	Agnes	Leona	7-Oct-1906	25-Sep-1906	William Smith	Stimmel, Alice M.	Gertrude McSweeney
Smith	John	Raymond	31-Jul-1892	08-Jul-1892	William Smith	Doyle, Mary	Mary Dixon
Smith	Lillian		6-Jul-1910	8-Feb-1910	William Smith	Smith, Genevieve	Edna Frisby
Smith	William	Edwin	14-Oct-1888	02-Oct-1888	William Smith	Schillinger, Lillian	Susan Strobel
Snack	Joseph	Nelson	10-Jan-1909	14-Dec-1908	Nelson Snack	Smith, Jennie	Mary Lynch
Sneider	John	Donald	15-Sep-1912	2-Sep-1912	John Sneider	Corcoran, Mary	Ann Bracken
Snively	Henry	Leon	7-Dec-1910	20-May-1869	James M. Snively	McNamee, Helen	Margaret McNamee
Snodgrass	Joseph		9-Jul-1911	24-Jun-1911	Charles N. Snodgrass	[Blank]	Catherine Curran
Snowden	Bernard	Richard	1-Jun-1913	24-May-1913	Edward Snowden	Cogar, Mary	Mary Cunningham
Snowden	Francis	Ann	12-Jul-1908	29-Jun-1908	Edward Snowden	Smith, Ellen	Agnes King
Snowden	John	Norman	14-May-1911	5-May-1911	Edward Snowden	Smith, Helen	Frances Smith
Snyder	Mary		28-Feb-1909	19-Feb-1909	Francis P. Snyder	Smith, Helen	Josephine Dillmann
Snyder	Francis	Adam	24-Jun-1888	06-Jun-1888	Francis Snyder	Barrett, Elizabeth G.	Julia Barrett
Snyder	George	Edward	15-Oct-1893	29-Sep-1893	Francis Snyder	Leonard, Catherine	Mary Leonard
						Leonard, Catherine	Alice A. Leonard

LAST NAME	FIRST NAME	MIDDLE	BAPTISM	BIRTH	Father	Mother	SPONSORS
Snyder	James	Leonard	30-Mar-1890	16-Mar-1890	Francis Snyder	Leonard, Catherine	John Joseph Gunning / Susannah Eagan
Snyder	James	Henry	16-Aug-1908	4-Aug-1908	Francis Snyder	Brady, Mary	James Gilhooly / Christina Brady
Snyder	William	Leo	29-Dec-1895	14-Dec-1895	Francis Snyder	Leonard, Catherine	Henry Kline / Mary Deise
Snyder	James	B.	28-Sep-1902	18-Sep-1902	John Snyder	McNamee, Helen	Catherine Snyder
Snyder	John	B.	25-May-1913	8-May-1913	John Snyder	Hammond, Christina	Dennis Noonan / Grace Snyder
Snyder	Loretta	Catherine	4-Oct-1914	2-Sep-1914	John Thomas Snyder	Hammond, Christina	Joseph Brown / Loretta Snyder
Snyder	Helen	Mary	17-May-1891	05-May-1891	Joseph Snyder	Fischer, Elizabeth Philomena	Phillip Strassberger / Helen Strassberger
Snyder	Joseph	George	21-Dec-1902	07-Dec-1902	Josephoh Snyder	Murphy, Bridget	George Olmer / Katherine Olmer
Sofsky	Theodore	Patrick	28-Jul-1901	15-Jul-1901	Francis Sofsky	McGaney, Catherine	Theodore Sofsky / Carrie Giluper
Somerville	James	Winterfield	02-Feb-1882	21-Dec-1881	James Somerville	Butler, Susan	Elizabeth Hawkins
Somerville	John	Charles	22-Jun-1902	25-Mar-1895	John Somerville	Fisher, Helen	Thomas McCaffrey / Lillian McCaffrey
Sommerlock	Florence	Christine	08-Mar-1883	07-Dec-1882	John F. Sommerlock	Cannolles, Theodoshia	Christine Gessner
Sommers	James		24-Jul-1898	15-Jul-1898	James Sommers	[Blank], Mary A.	Michael Conway / Mary McGraw
Sommerville	Mary	Helen	26-Jun-1903	22-Apr-1903	John Sommerville	Ferrell, Helen	Elizabeth McCaffrey
Sourin	Theresa		10-Feb-1901	28-Jan-1901	Edward Sourin	Dyer, Mary	James Dyer / Ann Dyer
Spangler	Charles	Melvin	16-Sep-1906	27-Aug-1906	Charles W. Spangler	Keenan, Edith	Victor Murphy / Catherine O'Brien
Sparman	James	Richard	10-Nov-1895	19-Oct-1895	Michael Sparman	Brown, Emma	James Cather / Mary Conway
Spearman	Elizabeth	Agnes	16-Nov-1890	24-Oct-1890	Michael Spearman	Brown, Emma	Thomas Warren / Bridget Curley
Spearman	Joseph	Michael	13-Jan-1901	25-Dec-1900	Michael Spearman	Brown, Emma	William Hunt / Mary Hardman
Spearman	Julian	Earl	19-Oct-1902	03-Oct-1902	Michael Spearman	[Blank]	Juliam Rudiger / Agnes Mullen
Spearman	Mary	Irene	04-Nov-1888	14-Oct-1888	Michael Spearman	Brown, Emma	William Kirby / Mary Mackin
Spearman	Mary		26-Jun-1898	12-Jun-1898	Michael Spearman	Brown, Emma	Ella Simmons
Spearman	William	Thomas	20-Aug-1893	31-Jul-1893	Michael Spearman	Brown, Emma	Thomas Ryan / Mary A. Conway
Spence	Ann	Genevieve	17-Jun-1900	26-May-1900	William Spence	Quirk, Mary	Thomas Fahey / Mary Evans
Spence	Catherine		06-Jan-1895	22-Dec-1894	William Spence	Quirk, Mary	Thomas Palcidus O'Brien / Mary Quirk
Spence	Margaret	Mary	29-Dec-1889	17-Dec-1889	William Spence	[Blank], Mary	T.J. Burns / Teresa [Blank]
Spence	Mary	Anastasia	04-Oct-1891	24-Sep-1891	William Spence	Quirk, Mary	Mary Parall
Spencer	Sarah	Frances	22-Jan-1888	25-Dec-1867	Daniel Spencer	Bunce, Rachel	Clara Mitchell
Spencer	Mary	Francis	30-Jun-1889	18-Jun-1889	Nicolas Patrick Spencer	Buckley, Ann Elizabeth	George Aloysius Buckley / Agnes Command
Spies	John	Carroll	24-Nov-1889	24-Oct-1889	August Ambrose Spies	Shaney, Amato Josephine	
Spillman	Mary	Margaret	22-Dec-1889	10-Oct-1889	Frederick Spillman	Burns, Ann	Mary Fay
Spiro	Charles		29-Dec-1905	15-Dec-1905	William Spiro	Gould, Mary M.	John F. Gould / Alice Kendall
Spots	John	Franklin	30-Nov-1884	12-Oct-1884	Abram Spots	Woods, Catherine M.	John Delaney / Bridget Dalton
Spots/Gessner	Ann		22-Dec-1892	26-Nov-1861	John Henry Spots	Bain, Ann	Francis Gessner
Spring	Margaret	Mary	28-Jul-1901	14-Jul-1901	Henry Spring	Garvey, Mary	John Garvey / Margaret Garvey
Sprinkle	Nettie	Peare	18-May-1912	29-Nov-1884	Franklin P. Sprinkle	Starks, Catherine V.	Bridget Campbell
Sprouse	Bridget		30-May-1912	16-Jul-1865	Samuel Sprouse	Gibson, Louise	Ann Smith
Squires	James	Michael	20-Jul-1902	17-Jun-1902	Joseph Squires	McMahon, Catherine	Margaret Migan
Squires	John	Michael	14-Oct-1894	03-Oct-1894	Joseph Squires	McMahon, Catherine	Eva Kehln
Squires	Joseph	James	07-Aug-1892	29-Jul-1892	Joseph Squires	McMahon, Catherine	Elizabeth Seibert
Squires	Matthew	Mary	24-Jul-1904	28-Jun-1904	Joseph Squires	McMahon, Catherine	James McMahon / Ann McMahon
Squires	Rose	Helen	05-Mar-1899	05-Feb-1899	Joseph Squires	McMahon, Catherine	Helen Dwyer
St. Leger	Edward	Emmet	02-Mar-1902	28-Feb-1902	Bartholomew St. Leger	Giblin, Mary	Thomas Morrow / Mary McCann
St. Leger	Francis	Daniel	11-Dec-1887	03-Dec-1887	Bartholomew St. Leger	Giblin, Mary	John Kenny / Ann Kenny
St. Leger	George	A.	14-Feb-1897	06-Feb-1897	Bartholomew St. Leger	Giblin, Mary	John Keating / Ann McQuillan
St. Leger	James		20-Sep-1885	04-Sep-1885	Bartholomew St. Leger	Giblin, Mary	Bernard J. Lander / Julia Lander
St. Leger	James	Michael	07-Oct-1894	29-Sep-1894	Bartholomew St. Leger	Giblin, Mary	Patrick Mason / Mary Kelly
St. Leger	Joseph	Aloysius	17-Jul-1892	14-Jul-1892	Joseph Squires	Giblin, Mary	John St. Leger / Mary Moran
St. Leger	Mary	Elizabeth	16-Apr-1899	10-Apr-1899	Bartholomew St. Leger	Giblin, Mary	Martin Reynolds / Elizabeth Mullen
St. Leger	William	Patrick	15-Jul-1883	03-Jul-1883	Bartholomew St. Leger	Giblin, Mary	Michael F. Gaffey / Mary Mason
St. Leger	Ann	Cecelia	09-Aug-1885	27-Jun-1885	William St. Leger	Flaherty, Ann	Teresa McNally
St. Leger	William	Patrick	30-Sep-1883	17-Sep-1883	William St. Leger	Flaherty, Ann	Patrick Dougherty / Mary St. Leger
Stack	Mary	Eleanor	9-Oct-1904	9-Sep-1904	Henry Stack	Beckwith, Mary J.	Charles Beckwith / Helen Beckwith
Stafford	Joseph	Francis	7-May-1911	22-Apr-1911	James P. Stafford	McEvoy, Mary J.	Charles Logue / Margaret Lanahan
Stafford	Mark		06-Dec-1885	25-Nov-1825	James Stafford	Wallace, Catherine	Patrick Crowley / Catherine Wilson
Stafford	Alice		24-Apr-1887	21-Apr-1887	John Stafford	Mullen, Catherine	Michael Wallace / Helen Clooney
Stafford	Ann		4-Jul-1909	26-Jun-1909	Joseph P. Stafford	McEvoy, Mary Joan	P.J. McGreevey / Mary J. Stafford
Stafford	John		10-Nov-1912	28-Oct-1912	Joseph P. Stafford	McAvoy, Mary J.	Thomas Neary / Ann Roach
Stafford	James		23-Jun-1907	18-Jun-1907	Joseph Stafford	McEvoy, Mary	John McEvoy / Alice Stafford
Stafford	Mary		12-Nov-1905	28-Oct-1905	Joseph Stafford	McEvoy, Mary J.	James Stafford / Agnes Stafford
Stafford	Patrick	Francis	4-Apr-1915	15-Mar-1915	Joseph Stafford	McEvoy, Mary Joan	Patrick Conniff / Margaret Ratican
Stallings	Ann	Elizabeth	27-Apr-1884	19-Apr-1884	John E. Stallings	Reinhardt, Wilhemena Mary	Ann Fenne
Stallings	Ferdinand		20-Dec-1887	14-Dec-1887	John Edward Stallings	Reinhardt, Mary	Ferdinand Kerchner / Ann Mary Kerchner

LAST NAME	FIRST NAME	MIDDLE	BAPTISM	BIRTH	Father	Mother	SPONSORS
Stallings	Emil	Charles	12-Jun-1886	05-Jun-1886	John Stallings	Reinhardt, Wilhelmina	Henry Wadefill · Louise Wadefill
Stallings	John	Richard	7-Jan-1906	3-Dec-1905	John Stallings	Kastner, Clara	Charles Kastner · Bridget Donohye
Stallings	Louise		20-May-1885	18-May-1885	John Stallings	Reinhardt, Minnie	Louise Wiedefeld
Stallings	John		12-Nov-1904	14-Sep-1871	Richard Stallings	[Blank], Carolina	Lucas McCusker · Estelle Rider
Stallknecht	John	Harrison	14-Aug-1892	12-Jul-1892	William Stallknicht	Reilly, Ann	Henry John Carle · Clara Fulton
Standiford	William	Albert	15-Feb-1885	17-Jan-1885	James Standiford	McCarthy, Mary Agnes	Henry Carter · Georgia McDaniels
Stanford	Margaret	Regina	14-Oct-1906	5-Oct-1906	Charles R. Stanford	Katzenburger, Margaret R.	Joseph Feeney · Genevieve Starr
Starr	Ann	Francis	30-Jun-1912	20-Jun-1912	Joseph Alphonse Starr	Murray, Elizabeth Ann	Mary Sullivan
Staubs/Mulligan	Florence		23-Apr-1898	17-Mar-1879	Adam Staubs	Roche, Mary	Ida Angel
Staylor	George	Edward Oliver	16-Dec-1882	13-Sep-1882	Francis Staylor	Bunce, Martha Ann	Rose E. Heistermann
Staylor	RoseAnn	Mary	26-Oct-1884	23-Aug-1884	Francis Staylor	Bonce, Martha	Clara T. Dillaway
Staylor	George	Washington J.	25-Jul-1886	12-Jul-1886	George E. Staylor	Dillaway, Mary V.	Phillip J. Staylor · Mary Ann Ratican
Staylor	Joseph	Edward	04-Oct-1885	25-Nov-1825	John Francis Staylor	Staylor, Joan	Mary Ann Dougherty · Ellen Dowd
Steadman	Edward		13-Mar-1910	26-Feb-1910	Edward G. Steadman	Cain, Mary	Edward Carroll · Margaret Manning
Steadman	Catherine	Corine	21-Jun-1887	17-Mar-1887	George Steadman	Reese, Catherine	Mary Ormand
Steadman	Joseph	Charles	31-Mar-1895	19-Mar-1895	John Steadman	Cummings, Sara Joan	Michael Ormand · Rose Cummings
Steadman	Margaret	Catherine	01-Apr-1888	22-Mar-1888	John Steadman	Cummings, Sara Joan	Thomas Connor · Ellen Healey
Steadman	John	Francis	04-Jan-1891	29-Dec-1890	John V. Steadman	Cummings, Genevieve	Francis Louis Healey · Catherine Gammy
Steadman	Mary	Genevieve	30-Apr-1893	20-Apr-1893	John Vincent Steadman	Kain, Mary	James Healy · Mary C. O'Brien
Steedman	Alexander	Ellsworth Joseph	05-Jan-1902	25-Dec-1901	Edward E. Steedman	Ferguson, Mary A.	Michael J. Fallon · Sarah J. Sheehan
Stehley	Alfred	Nichol	03-Feb-1889	13-Nov-1888	Samuel Stehley	Ferguson, Mary A.	Elisa Jones
Stehley	Albert		15-Jun-1886	02-Apr-1886	Samuel Stehley	Lee, Mary	Jane Stevens
Stein	Mary		31-Aug-1902	24-Aug-1902	Albert Stein	Lee, Mary	William Highland · Ann Karrigan
Stein	Mary		13-Dec-1903	04-Dec-1903	Henry W. Stein	Linahan, Mary	Richard Callahan · Sara Steinberg
Steinberg	Ann	Gertrude	13-Apr-1902	25-Mar-1902	William Steinberg	Mooney, Mary R.	Martha Bouik
Steinmeier	Charles	August	17-Aug-1890	27-Jul-1890	George E. Steinmeier	Mooney, Mary R.	John A. Snyder · Martha Brink
Steinmeier	Francis	Eugene	10-Sep-1893	28-Aug-1893	George E. Steinmeier	Mooney, Mary R.	Eugene B. McIntyre · Catherine McIntyre
Steinmeier	Helen	Elizabeth	22-Aug-1897	10-Aug-1897	George E. Steinmeier	Mooney, Mary R.	Thomas Sherman · Catherine Snyder
Steinmeier	Margaret	Agnes	19-Feb-1899	28-Jan-1899	George E. Steinmeier	Mooney, Mary	George Sturgeon · Mary Steinmeierer
Steinmeier	Thomas	Leo	9-Nov-1902	2-Nov-1902	George E. Steinmeier	Mooney, Mary	Emory Mullen · Catherine Mooney
Steinmeier	Angela	Teresa	06-Mar-1892	18-Feb-1892	George Steenmeier	Mooney, Mary R.	James F. Mooney · Margaret Mooney
Steinmeier	Mary	Genevieve	29-Oct-1905	19-Oct-1905	George Steenmeier	Mooney, Mary	James Mooney · Isabelle Jenkins
Steinmeier	Catherine	Gertrude	22-Jan-1888	08-Jan-1888	George Steinmeier	Mooney, Mary	George Sturgeon · Rose Sturgeon
Steinmeyer	Joseph	Milton	29-Sep-1895	11-Sep-1895	George Steinmeyer	Mooney, Mary	William Steinmeyer · Bernard Sturgeon
Steinmyer	George	William	07-Oct-1900	24-Sep-1900	George Steinmyer	Mooney, Mary R.	Rev. J.D. Marr · Mary Mallet
Steling	Mabel	Edith Mary	25-May-1902	21-May-1886	John Stiling	Kastner, Clara	John Kastner · Laura [Blank]
Stephens	Mary		20-May-1905	26-Apr-1902	[Blank]	[Blank]	William Smith
Stergnel	Mary	Elizabeth	18-Sep-1892	About 1878	Charles Edward Stergnel	Dolan, Mary Cecelia	John Thomas Hart · Mary Helen Hanrahan
Stergnel	William	Joseph	10-May-1891	04-Aug-1892	Charles Edward Stergnel	Dolan, Mary	Daniel Dolan · Mary E. Hanrahan
Stevens	Walter	Charles	30-Dec-1888	30-Mar-1891	William Edward Stevens	Buchenkop, Isabelle	Charles Boyle · Margaret Malloy
Stevens	Vincent	Leonard	28-Feb-1909	01-Nov-1888	William Stevens	Stevens, Ann E.	Elizabeth Lowenstein
Stevenson	Norman	Leon	26-Nov-1905	24-Feb-1909	Francis B. Stevenson	[Blank], Mary Blanche	Robert Stevenson · Catherine Snyder
Stevenson	Adalaide	Gertrude	18-May-1913	2-Oct-1905	George N. Stevenson	Elliott, Adalaide	George Bogy · Elizabeth Bogy
Stevenson	George	C.	26-Jun-1910	5-May-1913	George Vincent Stevenson	Elliott, Alice	Willima Bogy · Ann Bogy
Stevenson	Julian	Albert	17-Nov-1902	12-Jun-1910	John Stevenson	Pierce, Juliana	Delia Stevenson
Stevenson	Robert	Richard	06-Dec-1903	16-Nov-1902	Robert R. Stevenson	Fraser, Katherine	William Fraser · Laura Fraser
Stevenson	Francis		26-Sep-1897	9-Nov-1903	Robert Stevenson	Frazier, Catherine	Eugenia Rupp
Stevenson	Mary		19-Mar-1899	04-Sep-1897	Robert Stevenson	Frazier, Catherine	William Frazier · Mary Burke
Stevenson	Margaret	Mary	13-Apr-1884	30-Mar-1899	William Stevenson	Mallon, Margaret	George Bogy · Catherine Bogy
Steverson	Robert	Joseph	19-Feb-1905	03-Mar-1884	Robert D. Steverson	Frazer, Katherine	Frederick Hubert · Katherine Bennett
Steveson	Julian	A.	17-Nov-1902	1-Feb-1905	Westly Pierce	Conner, Margaret	Margaret Steverson
Steveson	Margaret	Elizabeth	02-Dec-1894	16-Jul-1878	William Steveson	Kennedy, Winifred	Mary Steveson
Steward	William		12-Apr-1885	19-Nov-1894	George Steward	McCann, Jane	James Steveson · Louise Feiger
Steward	John	Joseph	9-May-1915	17-Feb-1885	John L. Steward	Ward, Ann	James Breen · Isabelle McCleary
Steward	Catherine	Laura	3-Nov-1912	27-Apr-1915	John Steward	Wilson, Ann	George McCleary · Helen Gentry
Stewart	William	Edward	27-Jan-1909	29-Oct-1894	Andrew Stewart	Ellingsworth, Margaret	Luke Malloy
Stewart	Helen		07-May-1892	25-Aug-1869	George Stewart	Rupp, Susan	Frances Regina Brown
Stewart	Helen	Marie	18-Mar-1883	21-Feb-1863	George W. Stewart	McCann, Sara Joan	Bernard J. McGanty · Sara McCann
Stewart	Margaret		25-Sep-1887	13-Mar-1883	George William Stewart	Stewart, Sara Joan	James Cullen · Ann Cullen
Stewart	Helen	Catherine	2-Aug-1908	15-Sep-1887	William M. Stewart	Powers, Elizabeth Philomena	John T. Roche · Agnes Roche
Stewart	Mary	Bernardine	2-Aug-1908	21-Jul-1908	William M. Stewart	Powers, Elizabeth Philomena	John T. Hogan · Margaret Slaysman
Stewart	Michael	John	20-Sep-1891	21-Jul-1908	William Stewart	Fitzpatrick, Catherine	Michael Fitzpatrick · Margaret Fitzpatrick

ST JOHN'S BAPTISMS 1882-1912

LAST NAME	FIRST NAME	MIDDLE	BAPTISM	BIRTH	Father	Mother	SPONSORS	
Stickler	Sara	Joan	12-Aug-1894	25-Jul-1894	Nicholas Sticker	King, Joan	Michael Noonan	Margaret Noonan
Stickler	George	Andrew	23-Sep-1883	14-Sep-1883	Nicholas Stickler	King, Joan (Jennie)		Mary Emily O'Brien
Stickler	Henry	See	30-Aug-1885	16-Aug-1885	Nicholas Stickler	King, Joan	John Connolly	Ann Smith
Stinchcomb	Francis	Joseph	17-Apr-1892	13-Jun-1867	[Blank] Stinchcomb	[Blank]		Bertha Donahue
Stinebaugh	Agnes		22-Oct-1901	13-Jul-1893	William Stinebaugh	Lowman, Mary A.		Katherine Grace
Stinebaugh	Joseph		22-Oct-1901	13-Jul-1895	William Stinebaugh	Lowman, Mary A.		Katherine Grace
Stober	Margaret		21-Apr-1887	10-May-1850	James Hober	Ehlman, Rebecca	Margaret Seim	Emilia Gamble
Stockman	Mary		24-Sep-1911	12-Feb-1911	Henry Stockman	Finn, Elizabeth	Thomas Finn	Mary Finn
Stockman	Thomas	Joseph	21-Feb-1909	12-Feb-1909	Henry Stockman	Finn, Elizabeth	Joseph Caskey	Ann Caskey
Stolte	Laurence	James	30-Nov-1913	20-Nov-1913	Charles F. Stolte	Klendorf, Agnes	Laurence [Blank]	Bridget Kelly
Story	Raymond	Marr	03-Feb-1889	13-Jan-1889	Edna L. Story	Sturgeon, Laura		Amanda Sturgeon
Story	Lillian	Catherine	08-Mar-1885	17-Feb-1885	Edner L. Story	Sturgeon, Laura V.	John R. Cadigan	Daisy Cadigan
Strab	Valerie	Augusta	15-Mar-1885	20-Feb-1885	Charles Stout	Wingard, Ann		Sara Stout
Strab	William	James	06-Nov-1898	25-Oct-1898	John Strab	Silver, Elizabeth	James W. Bird	Elizabeth Neusel
Straider	August	Henry	12-Aug-1890	15-Jan-1869	August Straider	Gardiner, Mary		
Straney	Joseph	Jerome	27-Feb-1910	19-Jan-1910	Charles J. Straney	Glassner, Matilda	Joseph Sauers	
Strasburg	Reese	Albert	26-Apr-1896	08-Jan-1896	David E. Strasburg	Kite, Emma	Joseph Levelle	
Streb	Agnes		30-Jul-1893	20-Jul-1893	Henry Streb	Lanahan, Ellen	Agnes Yarborough	Mary Smith
Streb	Catherine	Ann	28-Feb-1892	15-Feb-1892	Henry Streb	Lanahan, Ellen	Michael Kearney	Hannah Kearney
Streb	Helen		26-Jan-1896	11-Jan-1896	John Streb	Ellebrock, Elizabeth		Johana Ellebrock
Streckfus	Edward	Ignatius	25-Jul-1886	16-Jul-1886	Leonard Streckfus	Keyhan, Mary Ann	John Zoeller	Catherine Zoeller
Street	Charles	Edward	09-Aug-1885	22-Jul-1885	Henry Street	Fitzpatrick, Mary	Edward Fitzpatrick	Agnes Fitzpatrick
Street	Francis	Elizabeth	11-Jun-1882	22-May-1882	Henry Street	Fitzpatrick, Mary Elizabeth	Peter Kennedy	Cecilia Kennedy
Streets	Samuel	Townsend	09-Oct-1887	01-Oct-1887	George A. Streets	Dietrich, M. Elizabeth	George T. Dietrich	Mary A. Dietrich
Strible	Francis	Elizabeth	27-Sep-1891	31-Aug-1891	John Joseph Strible	Phillips, Mary Beatrice	Henry John McClellan	John Cecelia McGraw
Strible	John		29-Dec-1895	12-Dec-1895	John Joseph Strible	Phillips, Mary	John McGraw	Mary McGraw
Strible	Genevieve		08-Oct-1893	31-Aug-1893	John Strible	Phillips, Mary	George Strible	Ann Wilcox
Strible	Mary		17-Nov-1889	30-Oct-1889	Joseph Strible	Phillips, Mary	H. Phillips	Fanny Phillips
Stricker	Sara	Ann	06-Oct-1901	22-Sep-1901	George Stricker	Teague, Mary	Francis Stricker	Delia Teague
Stricker	Francis	Edward	10-May-1898	13-Apr-1898	John Stricker	[Blank], Mary	Francis Stricker	Delia [Blank]
Stricker	John	Patrick	23-Aug-1896	14-Aug-1896	John Stricker	[Blank], Mary	Thomas L. O'Connor	Margaret O'Donnell
Stricker	William	Thomas	15-Jul-1900	30-Jan-1900	John Stricker	Logue, Mary	Thomas O'Connor	Rose O'Connor
Stricker	Nicolas		09-Oct-1887	26-Sep-1887	Nicholas Stricker		George Galvin	Louise Jamison
Strickler	Catherine		13-Apr-1890	27-Mar-1890	Nicholas Strickler	King, Sara Joan	William Henry King	Ann Smith
Stroble	John	Patrick	01-May-1887	18-Apr-1887	Charles C. Stroble	Smith, Susan	James Kelly	Mary Kelly
Stroebel	Edwin	Bernard	01-Feb-1885	02-Jan-1885	Anthony Stroebel	Smith, Susan	Robert McGeeney	Mary Helen McGeeney
Stromberg	James		15-Jul-1906	4-Jul-1906	Thomas Stromberg	Clarke, Ann	Thomas Clarke	Bridget Clarke
Stropes	Anthony		19-Jun-1910	10-Nov-1909	Joseph Stropes	[Blank]	John Gobben	Blanche [Blank]
Strott	Carl	Joseph	20-Feb-1887	12-Sep-1886	John J. Strott	Roundtree, Mary Elizabeth		Rebecca Roundtree
Strott	Elizabeth		20-Apr-1884	28-Feb-1884	John Strott	Roundtree, Mary E.		Rebecca Roundtree
Strott	Richard	Howard	03-Nov-1889	12-Aug-1889	John Strott	Roundtree, Mary Elizabeth		Helen Riordan
Strout	George	Bennett	06-Dec-1883	16-Nov-1883	George Strout	McCoy, Susan		Mary Egan
Strovel	Mary	Eleanor	20-Jan-1889	01-Jan-1889	Anthony Srovel	Smith, SusAnn		Mary Eleanor Smith
Stuart	George	Berard	12-Jan-1890	28-Dec-1889	George Stuart	McCann, Sara J.	Bernard Rodan	Ann Gottalebein
Stuart	Howard	Patrick	31-Mar-1889	04-Mar-1889	William Stuart	Fitzpatrick, Catherine	Francis P. Kelly	Mary Fitzpatrick
Stuckrath	Emma	Elizabeth	21-Jul-1907	1-Jul-1907	Phillip W. Stuckrath	Warns, Elizabeth		Elizabeth Warns
Sturgeon	George	Fredercik	14-Mar-1886	03-Mar-1886	Geoge L. Sturgeon	Mooney, Rose L.	Edwin Magness	Catherine E. Mooney
Sturgeon	Catherine	Bernadine	29-Apr-1888	12-Apr-1888	George L. Sturgeon	Mooney, Rose L.	Martin Quinn	Catherine Mooney
Sturgeon	Genevieve	Estelle	28-Jan-1894	12-Jan-1894	George L. Sturgeon	Mooney, Rose L.	Alexander J.J. Dennistone	Estelle Dennistone
Sturgeon	Mary	Regiuna	12-Jan-1890	29-Dec-1889	George L. Sturgeon	Mooney, Rose L.	Thomas McNulty	Elizabeth Snyder
Sturgeon	Joseph		14-Sep-1884	27-Aug-1884	George Sturgeon	Mooney, Rose	James Mooney	Amanda Sturgeon
Sturgeon	James	Henry	2-Feb-1913	24-Jan-1913	Henry H. Sturgeon	[Blank], Mary		Margaret Cook
Sturgeon	Elizabeth	Mary	13-Jan-1907	30-Dec-1906	Joseph W. Sturgeon	Rauch, Margaret A.		Elizabeth M. Bancoft
Sturm	Annie	Myrtle	07-Apr-1895	05-Mar-1895	Herman Sturm	Monaghan, Margaret	Henry Rabe	Ann McCabe
Sudsburg	Mary	Viola	12-Feb-1893	17-Jan-1893	Louis Sudsburg	Wurtzer, Margaret	Randolph Sudsburg	Mary Sudsburg
Suerin	James		26-Mar-1904	19-Mar-1904	Edward Suerin	Dyer, Mary		Ann Dyer
Suerin	Edmund		29-May-1898	22-May-1898	Edward Suerin	Dyer, Mary	John Dyer	Ann Dyer
Suit	Mary	Joseph	19-Mar-1893	11-Mar-1893	Edgar M. Suit	Kelly, Cordelia		Catherine M. Freeman
Suit	Ann	Mary	25-Jan-1891	18-Jan-1891	Edgar Suit	Kelly, Bridget	Michael V. Kelly	Catherine Freeman
Sullivan	Ann	L.	16-Apr-1905	4-Apr-1905	Alfred E. Sullivan	Smith, Catherine	James B. Blake	Ann Blake
Sullivan	Bertha	M.	24-Nov-1902	23-Nov-1902	Alfred E. Sullivan	Smith, Catherine	Martin Monaghan	Bertha Smith
Sullivan	William	Howard	17-Jan-1909	6-Jan-1909	Alfred Edward Sullivan	Sullivan, Katherine Sophia	Charles Sullivan	Emma Sullivan
Sullivan	Charles	Francis	30-Sep-1900	10-Sep-1900	Alfred Sullivan	Smith, Katherine		Agnes Barrett

130

LAST NAME	FIRST NAME	MIDDLE	BAPTISM	BIRTH	Father	Mother	SPONSORS		
Sullivan	Elizabeth	Mary	15-Aug-1885	07-Aug-1885	C. Sullivan	Sweeney, Catherine	Timothy Sweeney	Mary Barry	
Sullivan	George	Edward	22-Dec-1889	28-Dec-1889	John H. Sullivan	White, Mary M.	Wenceslaus J. Butta	Mary A. Hoppert	
Sullivan	Laura	Helen	21-Jun-1896	31-May-1896	John H. Sullivan	White, Mary M.		Elizabeth White	
Sullivan	Mary	Elizabeth	10-Mar-1895	16-Feb-1895	John H. Sullivan	White, Mary E.		Elizabeth White	
Sullivan	John	William	08-Mar-1889	18-Feb-1889	John Henry Sullivan	White, Mary Magdalene		Elizabeth Ann White	
Sullivan	Ann	Rebecca	19-Aug-1900	15-Aug-1900	John Sullivan	White, Mary		Elizabeth White	
Sullivan	John	Patrick	11-Apr-1886	17-Mar-1886	Michael Sullivan	Cull, Helen	James Deeley	Mary Deeley	
Sullivan	William		11-May-1884	28-Apr-1884	Michael Sullivan	Cull, Ellen	William Cull	Ellen Daily	
Sullivan	Agnes	Teresa	08-Nov-1885	28-Sep-1885	Timothy Sullivan	Garrity, Mary	John Evans	Jenie Moran	
Sullivan	Mary	susan	14-Oct-1888	06-Oct-1888	Timothy Sullivan	McCarrigle, Eleanor	Patrick McCarrigle	Mary Maguire	
Sullivan	Timothy	Francis	06-Nov-1887	02-Oct-1887	Timothy Sullivan	Garrity, Mary	Timothy James Ryan	Adele Conway	
Sullivan	William	Leon	16-Jul-1911	2-Jul-1911	William P. Sullivan	Manning, Joan C.		Irene Canby	
Sultzer	Walter	Paschal	27-May-1888	17-May-1888	John S. Sultzer	Blessing, Mary	John H. Burroughs	Emma Farrell	
Sultzer	Josephine	Carroll	29-Mar-1885	18-Mar-1885	John Sultzer	Blessing, Mary	Daniel Blessing	Mary Ann Blessing	
Summer	Joseph	Isaac	08-Feb-1885	26-Jan-1885	Joseph Summer	Hess, Emma		Mary Ann Hess	
Sunderland	Bernard		14-Oct-1896	28-Jan-1867	John Sunderland	Banford, Mary	L. Lanaghan		
Sutherland	Sarah	Josephine	07-Mar-1886	20-Feb-1862	Samuel Sutherland	Rison, Martha	Edward G. Graham	Mabel Keagle	
Sutton	Edward	S.	24-Apr-1904	9-Apr-1904	John J. Sutton	Dudy, Mary	Thomas Hennessey	Bessie Daily	
Sutton	Edward		17-May-1891	11-May-1891	John Sutton	O'Connor, Mary	Michael Roche	Catherine Geary	
Sutton	Mary	Margaret	05-Mar-1893	24-Feb-1893	John Sutton	Connor, Mary	John White	Mary Furlong	
Sutton	Michael		11-Mar-1906	9-Feb-1906	John Sutton	Doory, Mary	William L. Molloy	Catherine Fitzgerald	
Swartz	Francis	Edward	01-Jan-1900	31-Dec-1899	Francis Swartz	Campbell, Catherine	Edward Hogan	Margaret Campbell	
Sweeney	Walter	Francis	17-Aug-1892	15-Oct-1891	[Blank]	Sweeney, Catherine		Ellen Reilly	
Sweeney	Helen		24-Sep-1899	17-Sep-1899	George Sweeney	Corrigan, Mary	John McBride	Catherine Sweeney	
Sweeney	Mary	Celeste	25-Nov-1901	17-Nov-1901	George Sweeney	Corrigan, Mary	James McGrory		
Sweeney	Arthur	Francis	12-May-1907	20-Apr-1892	George Washington Sweeney	Jeffreys, Louise Catherine		Helen Grace	
Sweeney	Mary	Louise	6-May-1909	25-Aug-1886	George Washington Sweeney	Jeffers, Louise Catherine			
Sweeney	Edward		29-Dec-1895	29-Nov-1895	John Sweeney	Feehely, Bridget		Margaret Egan	
Sweeney	Elizabeth	Agnes	19-Aug-1888	10-Aug-1888	John Sweeney	Hughes, Elizabeth	Cornelius Sullivan	Catherine Sullivan	
Sweeney	Thomas	Edward	07-Sep-1890	30-Aug-1890	John Sweeney	Cadden, Mary	John Owens	Sarah Dunn	
Sweeney	Joseph		29-May-1887	28-May-1887	Luke A. Sweeney	Gunning, Mary	Patrick Sweeney	Catherine Gunning	
Sweeney	Luke	Andrew	20-Oct-1889	14-Oct-1889	Luke A. Sweeney	Simms, Mary		Mary Arthur	
Sweeney	Thomas	Patrick	18-Oct-1893	11-Oct-1893	Luke August Sweeney	Gunning, Mary Agnes	Thomas Edward Sweeney	Agnes Gertrude Sweeney	
Sweeney	Catherine		09-Mar-1900	07-Mar-1900	Luke Sweeney	Gunning, Mary A.	Joseph Sweeney	Elizabeth Murray	
Sweeney	James		04-Jan-1891	28-Dec-1890	Luke Sweeney	Gunning, Mary A.	James A. Gunning	Margaret Gunning	
Sweeney	John		03-Jul-1892	27-Jun-1892	Luke Sweeney	Gunning, Mary	John Sweeney	Catherine Gilchrist	
Sweeney	Mary		11-Feb-1898	10-Feb-1898	Luke Sweeney	Gunning, Mary Agnes	John Gunning	Catherine Gunning	
Sweeney	Michael	F.	01-Mar-1903	23-Feb-1903	Michael F. Sweeney	Garvey, Helen J.		Delia White	
Sweeney	Mary	Ann	14-Dec-1914	30-Nov-1914	Michael J. Sweeney	Clinton, Ann	Joseph White	Helen White	
Sweeney	John	Thomas	12-Jun-1910	31-May-1910	Michael Sweeney	Clinton, Ann	Thomas Sweeney	Elizabeth Coghlan	
Sweetser	Daniel		12-Sep-1892	04-Aug-1892	Daniel Sweetser	Linzey, Olivia		Teresa Quirk	
Swift	Mary	Margaret	10-Nov-1889	02-Oct-1889	James Henry Swift	Quinlan, Louise	William Ward	Virginia Swift	
Swift	Francis		01-Nov-1896	14-Oct-1896	Luke Swift	Keith, Mary	James Ward	Ella Leonard	
Tabeling	Elizabeth	E.	6-Nov-1910	22-Oct-1910	Stephen B. Tabeling	Dailey, Elizabeth E.	Charles Keith	Catherine I. Tabeling	
Tailer	James	Albert	16-Aug-1908	8-Aug-1908	Samuel Tailer	Morris, Catherine	Bernard Byrnes	Mary Kinmmitt	
Talbot	Thomas	Henry	23-Oct-1892	23-Sep-1892	Thomas Talbot	Sheckles, Mary		Ann Talbot	
Tarlton	George	Leon	01-Dec-1889	20-Nov-1889	Alrico T. Tarlton	Steen, Ann M.	W.A. Seipp	Matilda Dunn	
Tawney	Francis		09-Jan-1898	31-Dec-1894	Francis Tawney	Dotterwich, Ann Rose	Thomas Finn	Teresa Dash	
Taylor	William	Michael	07-Aug-1892	15-Jun-1892	Walter Taylor	McArdle, Agnes		Mary Taylor	
Taylor/Stewart	Janette		19-Jul-1907	About 1836	William Taylor	Taylor, Janette		Frances Fisher	
Taylor	Ann	Margaret	29-Mar-1903	15-Mar-1903	George Taylor	Ryan, Mary	William White	Mary Taylor	
Taylor	Francis	Howard	09-Apr-1899	27-Mar-1899	George Taylor	Ryan, Mary		Margaret McGee	
Taylor	Margaret		13-May-1894	22-Apr-1894	George Taylor	Ryan, Mary	William Ward	Margaret McFee	
Taylor	Mary	Virginia	15-Sep-1895	16-Aug-1895	George Taylor	Ryan, Mary	William White	Joan Ward	
Taylor	George	Thomas	02-May-1897	03-Apr-1897	George Thomas Taylor	Ryan, Mary	James Ward	Mary McKenna	
Taylor	Evelyn	Mary	5-Mar-1911	18-Feb-1911	Samuel Taylor	Myers, Catherine	Robert Gannon	Blanche Gannon	
Taymins	Mary	A.	30-Sep-1906	14-Sep-1906	Joseph P. Taymins	Fox, Delia	E. Grant	Margaret Grant	
Tegeler	Henry	Joseph	22-Oct-1899	04-Oct-1899	William Tegeler	Eckle, Mary	Henry Eckle	Mary Eckle	
Tegeler	Ann		31-Jan-1897	20-Jan-1897	August Tegler	Hutti, Lena	Henry Hutti	Mary Irving	
Tenley	Howard	William	08-Jan-1888	01-Dec-1887	Howard William Tenley	Bavers, Agnes		Emma Bavers	
Tennyson	Albert	Charles	20-May-1894	06-May-1894	Francis Tennyson	O'Connell, Ella	Charles O'Connell	Ann Valee	
Tennyson	James	Edward	26-Aug-1888	10-Aug-1888	Francis Tennyson	O'Connell, Helen	Charles O'Connell	Mary O'Connell	

131

ST JOHN'S BAPTISMS 1882-1912

LAST NAME	FIRST NAME	MIDDLE	BAPTISM	BIRTH	Father	Mother	SPONSORS	
Tennyson	Mary	Elizabeth	11-Aug-1895	18-Jul-1895	Frank Tennyson	Thomas, Ella	Charles O'Connell	Rose Daily
Thalheimer	Mary	August	21-Sep-1913	11-Sep-1913	Francis C. Thalheimer	Cook, Ann V.	John G. Reese	Florence Reese
Thalheimer	Edwin		04-Sep-1898	20-Aug-1898	John Thalheimer	Kuhlmann, Angela	Michael Kulhmann	Mary Thalheimer
Thibou	Bernard	Paul	17-Jan-1915	10-Jan-1915	Edgar Thibou	Kernan, Elizabeth	John H. Kernan	Winifred E. Birthistle
Thiel	John	August	16-Aug-1908	31-Jul-1908	John August Thiel	Tydings, Ella	Paul Thiel	Mary Tydings
Thiel	Camilla	Mary	10-Sep-1905	25-Aug-1905	John Thiel	Tidings, Helen	Anthony Thiel	Agnes Bresner
Thiel	Charles	Francis	26-Nov-1911	13-Nov-1911	John Thiel	Thiel, Helen	Francis Hannon	Mary Tydings
Thomas	Mary	Rebecca	16-Apr-1893	23-Feb-1893	Alfred Thomas	Harris, Rebecca		Alice Thomas
Thomas	Julia		19-Aug-1888	12-Aug-1888	Charles Thomas	Nolan, Ann	Thomas Holton	Julia Holton
Thomas	Ann	Mary	30-Nov-1912	28-Apr-1896	William M. Thomas	Foreman, Rose		Catherine Klostich
Thomas	Rose	Mary	1-Dec-1912	06-May-1894	William M. Thomas	Foreman, Rose		Mary Sprell
Thomason	Catherine	Loretta	26-Jul-1903	10-Jul-1903	Arthur Thomason	Ryan, Ida	Frederick Fahey	Christina Ryan
Thomason	Elizabeth		8-Apr-1906	30-Mar-1906	Arthur Thomason	Ryan, Ida		Margaret Ryan
Thomes	Margaret	Margaret	07-Jul-1901	26-Jun-1901	Francis Thomes	O'Keefe, Nellie	William O'Keefe	Sarah O'Keefe
Thompson	Mary		13-Nov-1904	19-Oct-1904	Charles H. Thompson	Bray, Margaret	Patrick O'Neill	Catherine Bray
Thompson	David	Eaton	10-Nov-1912	12-Oct-1912	David Thompson	Gallagher, Gertrude		Margaret Cook
Thompson	Gertrude	Dora	2-Apr-1911	29-Jan-1911	David Thompson	Gallagher, Gertrude	Thomas P. Harrington	Eunice Byrne
Thompson	J. Henry		15-Jun-1890	02-Jun-1890	Ed. C. Thompson	Minnick, Mary	John Boland	
Thompson	Mary		30-Aug-1891	19-Aug-1891	Edward Batterden	Minnich, Mary	Joseph Canty	Susanna Boland
Thompson	Edward	Regina	05-Feb-1899	27-Feb-1899	Edward Thompson	Minnick, Mary	George Minnick	Catherine Shannssy
Thompson	Martha		07-Sep-1902	28-Aug-1902	Edward Thompson	Minnick, Mary	Louis Ruffinger	Martha Minnick
Thompson	Mary		21-Jul-1884	14-Jun-1884	Edward Thompson	Mobre, Josephine		Mary Parrell
Thompson	William	Joseph	07-Sep-1902	28-Aug-1902	Edward Thompson	Minnick, Mary	Thomas O'Neil	Catherine Gordon
Thompson	Catherine	Gertrude	07-Aug-1883	01-Sep-1866	James Thompson	Blizzard, Virginia	Thomas J. Gaulee	
Thompson	James	Bernard	09-Jan-1883	01-Apr-1880	James Thompson	Blizzard, Virginia		
Thompson	William	Henry	07-Aug-1883	05-Nov-1872	James Thompson	Blizzard, Virginia	Thomas J. Gaule	
Thompson	Ann	Sara	16-Aug-1885	01-Aug-1885	Joseph Thompson	Fitzpatrick, Catherine	Hugh Fitzpatrick	Ann Berterman
Thompson	Carl	Howard	14-Mar-1886	16-Feb-1886	Joseph Thompson	McCrea, Louise		Catherine McCormick
Thompson	Leo	Vincent	08-Jan-1893	18-Dec-1892	Joseph Thompson	Fitzpatrick, Catherine	Caroline Biddle	Ann O'Neill
Thompson	Alice		26-Mar-1899	13-Mar-1899	Robert Thompson	Murphy, Elizabeth	Thomas Deveney	Ann Deveney
Thompson	James		13-Jul-1902	30-Jun-1902	Robert Thompson	Murray, Elizabeth	John Murray	Mary Murphy
Thompson	Sara	Elizabeth	15-Apr-1894	26-Mar-1894	Thomas Thompson	Murphy, Elizabeth	John Kimball	Helen McLaughlin
Thompson	William	Wilson	30-Aug-1885	16-Aug-1885	William O. Thompson	Lynch, Elizabeth		Ann Farridan
Thompson	Henry	Lee	25-May-1902	01-Jul-1879	William Thompson	Johnson, Mary		Mary Murray
Thompson/St. John	Katherine		13-Aug-1900	17-Mar-1837	Alexander Thompson	Roberts, Kaizar		Elizabeth McLaughlin
Thomson	Mary	A.	13-Sep-1896	13-Sep-1896	Robert Thomson	Murphy, Eliza	William McLaughlin	Margaret Curran
Thornberg	Genevieve		04-Oct-1896	22-Sep-1896	William Thornberg	Curran, Mary	M. Thornburg	Genevieve Thornberg
Thornberg	William		01-Jan-1893	17-Dec-1892	William Thornberg	Curran, Mary Helen	John Bisker	Mary Harrison
Thornburg	Helen	Agnes	20-Jan-1895	05-Jan-1895	William Joseph Thornburg	Curran, Mary	William Curran	Ann Winters
Thornburg	Edward	McDevitte	14-Oct-1900	20-Sep-1900	William Thornburg	Curran, Mary	William Curran	Catherine Beran
Thornburg	Elizabeth	Catherine	22-Feb-1891	07-Feb-1891	William Thornburg	Curran, Mary	John Joseph Delaney	Lillian Curran
Thornburg	Rose	Eaton	25-Dec-1898	16-Dec-1898	William Thornburg	Curran, Mary	Thomas Campbell	Ann Curran
Thorne	Carmelita		1-Jan-1905	19-Dec-1904	Francis Thorne	O'Keefe, Mary Elizabeth	Joseph O'Keefe	Beatrice Rogge
Thorne	Francis	Martin	10-May-1903	03-Apr-1903	Francis Thorne	O'Keefe, Mary E.	Marurice Neenan	Gertrude Rodger
Thorpe	Raymond	John	2-Sep-1906	17-Aug-1906	Arthur William Thorpe	Wall, Agnes M.	John Wall	Virginia McKernen
Thorpe	Ruth	Cecelia	28-May-1905	14-May-1905	Arthur William Thorpe	Wall, Agnes	Joseph Burger	Elizabeth Wall
Thorpe	William	Henry	09-Oct-1887	14-Aug-1857	George Thorpe	Hurst, Hannah		Joan T. Lehnser
Thuman	Mary	Catherine	31-Aug-1884	27-Aug-1884	George Thuman	Colton, Mary	Mary Colton	Catherine Woods
Tidings	Helen	Eaton	04-Sep-1887	21-Aug-1887	George Tidings	McDowell, Joan		Laura White
Tidings	Michael		21-May-1882	12-May-1882	John Tidings	Fitzgerald, Catherine		Mary Kennedy
Tiedke	Mary	Elizabeth	14-Jul-1907	22-Jun-1907	Charles Tiedke	Jaffar, Mary	Joseph King	Mary King
Tiernan	Agnes		15-May-1887	29-Apr-1887	Michael Tiernan	Dougherty, Elizabeth	Francis Gilhooly	Bridget Gilhooly
Tierney	James		23-May-1909	11-May-1909	Hugh Tierney	Conlon, Nora		Elizabeth Shaw
Tierney	Margaret		13-Jul-1902	30-Jun-1902	Hugh Tierney	Connelly, Nora	Gustav Shaw	Margaret McIntire
Tierney	Michael	Joseph	12-Aug-1906	22-Jul-1906	Hugh Tierney	Connell, Nora	William Joseph Tierney	Catherine Woods
Tierney	Agnes		13-Jul-1913	19-Jun-1913	Hugo Tierney	O'Connell, Nora		Dorothy Engelmeier
Tierney	Hubert		05-Oct-1884	25-Sep-1884	Hugo Tierney	O'Connell, Nora		Margaret Tierney
Tierney	James		27-Nov-1892	13-Nov-1892	Michael Tierney	Dougherty, Elizabeth	Patrick Dougherty	Elizabeth Dougherty
Tierney	Elizabeth	Agnes	04-Feb-1883	22-Jan-1894	Thomas Tierney	Griffin, Mary	James Tierney	Mary Cawley
Tierney	Elizabeth		17-Aug-1890	04-Aug-1890	Thomas Tierney	Holmes, Nora		Elizabeth Tierney
Tierney	James	Joseph	04-Jul-1897	28-Jun-1897	Thomas Tierney	Griffin, Mary	John Griffin	Mary Cawley
Tierney	John	Francis		28-Jun-1897	Thomas Tierney	Griffin, Mary	Thomas Clark	Mary Kelly
Tierney	Joseph		07-Sep-1902	22-Aug-1902	Thomas Tierney	Griffin, Mary	Patrick Dolan	Bridget Tierney

132

LAST NAME	FIRST NAME	MIDDLE	BAPTISM	BIRTH	Father	Mother	SPONSORS	
Tierney	Margaret		15-Aug-1897	28-Jul-1897	Thomas Tierney	Holmes, Nora	John Homes	Margaret Homes
Tierney	Michael	Thomas	29-Oct-1895	15-Oct-1895	Thomas Tierney	Griffin, Mary	James McMichaels	Mary Hoey
Tighe	Rose		20-Jul-1883	19-Jul-1883	[Blank]	Tighe, Emma		Sara Farley
Tighe	Thomas	Joseph	30-Oct-1904	18-Mar-1904	Thomas Joseph Tighe	Marsteller, Clara	William Marsteller	Agnes Mitchell
Tillman	Eliza		21-Mar-1890	About 1820	Baccho Tillman	Tillman, Phillis	Michael Dorgan	
Tillman	Elizabeth		10-May-1898	About 1880	George V. Tillman	[Blank]	George Watson	Alice Phillips
Tillman	John	Chester	9-Jun-1907	6-Jun-1907	John J. Tillman	Phillips, Alice		
Tilman	Mary		29-Dec-1898	[Blank]	[Blank]	[Blank]		
Timmins	James	Joseph	08-Nov-1891	25-Oct-1891	John Timmins	Reddy, Ann	Thomas Reddy	Alice Timmins
Timmins	John	Thomas	29-Oct-1893	16-Oct-1893	John Timmins	Reddy, Ann	John Whitty	Catherine Whitty
Timmins	Thomas		25-Nov-1900	13-Nov-1900	John Timmins	Reddy, Ann	John Kennedy	Mary Reddy
Timmins	Joseph	L.	18-Sep-1898	02-Sep-1898	John Timmons	Reddy, Ann	Thomas Reddy	Bridget Reddy
Tingle	Mary	Elizabeth	16-Mar-1913	11-Jun-1852	Solomon Tingle	Taylor, Elizabeth		Helen Carr
Tinker	Helen		21-Aug-1910	11-Aug-1910	James Tinker	McKenna, Nellie	Joseph T. Leonard	Ella Tinker
Tinker	Joseph		1-May-1915	27-Apr-1915	Joseph Tinker	McKenna, Nellie	John McKenna	Margaret McKenna
Tinker	Mary	Helen	7-Oct-1906	1-Oct-1906	Joseph Tinker	McKenna, Helen	Patrick Maguire	Mary McKenna
Tinker	Allen	Joseph	22-Apr-1883	07-Mar-1883	William Tinker	Hagerman, Helen		
Tinker	James	Edward	17-Jul-1883	28-Nov-1879	William Tinker	Hagerman, Helen		
Tippett	Charles		08-Sep-1886	03-Jul-1886	John J. Tippett	Wilbach, Julia		Susan Wilbach
Toher	June		30-May-1886	24-May-1886	William Toher	McKewen, Margaret	Bernard Toher	Sara Toher
Toher	Mary		10-Aug-1884	02-Aug-1884	William Toher	McKewen, Margaret	Phillip McKewen	Maria McKewen
Tolly	Amanda	Josephine	23-Oct-1904	12-Sep-1904	John Tolly	Murphy, Ann		Katherine Gallagher
Toner	William	Ignatius	13-Jul-1890	27-Jun-1890	William Toner	Callaghan, Cordelia	James Brown	Susan Toner
Torrence	Grace	Porter	30-Jun-1910	2-Sep-1910	William F. Torrence	Porter, Emma A.		Katherine Touland
Touhey	Martha	Carmelita	30-Sep-1900	02-Sep-1900	James Touhey	Sullivan, Ann	Robert Collins	Mary McDonough
Touhy	Cecelia		01-Dec-1889	22-Nov-1889	James J. Touhy	Sullivan, Ann E.	Michael McGarvey	Cecelia Kelly
Touhy	Honora	A.	19-Nov-1905	6-Nov-1905	James J. Touhy	Sullivan, Ann E.	James Hynes	Honora Sullivan
Touhy	James	Maurice	17-Jun-1894	03-Jun-1894	James J. Touhy	Sullivan, Ann	Peter J. Byrne	Ann McMulhern
Touhy	James	Thomas	16-Dec-1906	17-Nov-1906	James J. Touhy	Sullivan, Ann	Thomas J. McDonough	Mary Casserly
Touhy	John	Leon	16-Dec-1906	17-Nov-1906	James J. Touhy	Sullivan, Ann	Thomas Leo Miller	Mary Casserly
Touhy	Margaret		19-Jul-1896	08-Jul-1896	James J. Touhy	Sullivan, Ann	Joan J. Hynes	Margaret Lynch
Touhy	Margaret	Loretta	3-Jan-1909	13-Nov-1908	James J. Touhy	Sullivan, Ann E.	James F. Miller	Helen McDonald
Touhy	George	Anselman	01-May-1892	21-Apr-1892	James Joseph Touhy	Sullivan, Ann Edith	John Sullivan	Ann Touhy
Touhy	Ann	Virginia	26-Apr-1891	15-Apr-1891	James Touhy	Sullivan, Ann E.	John Leman	Delia McDonough
Touhy	Mary		10-Oct-1897	29-Sep-1897	James Touhy	Sullivan, Ann	John Touhy	Catherine McDonough
Touhy	William	Arbuckel	07-Jul-1895	25-Jun-1895	James Touhy	Sullivan, Annie	Martin Sullivan	Mary Currran
Touhy	Honora		22-Jan-1899	07-Jan-1899	James Touhy	Sullivan, Ann	William Arbuckle	Ann Arbuckle
Touhy	[Blank]	L.	07-Mar-1886	17-Feb-1886	Joan Touhy	McGah, Catherine	James J. Turky	Mary McGah
Touhy	Agnes		05-Dec-1897	22-Nov-1897	John Touhy	McGah, Katherine	James Touhy	Catherine Kesley
Touhy	Gertrude		10-Sep-1899	26-Aug-1899	John Touhy	McGah, Catherine	Patrick Hynes	Mary Clarke
Touhy	Helen		08-Mar-1896	24-Feb-1896	John Touhy	McGaw, Catherine	John McGaw	Mary Boyle
Touhy	James	Patrick	08-Apr-1894	23-Mar-1894	John Touhy	McGah, Catherine	John Dawson	Mary Ann Dougherty
Touhy	John	Blasé	10-Mar-1889	27-Feb-1889	John Touhy	McGann, Catherine	Stephen Elwood	Elizabeth Murphy
Touhy	Sara	Mary	16-Feb-1890	03-Feb-1890	John Touhy	McGann, Catherine	Thomas Moran	Mary Burke
Touhy	Alice		15-May-1892	05-May-1892	John Touhy	McGah, Catherine	William McGah	Mary McGah
Toulan			21-Feb-1886	24-Feb-1885	Thomas Touhy	Landricain, Ann		Catherine Angela Bannon
Toulan	Thomas	Ernest	07-Jan-1883	01-Dec-1882	Thomas Touhy	Landrigan, Ann	James Landrigan	Bridget Daly
Toulan	Daniel		07-Dec-1902	03-Dec-1902	Daniel J. Toulan	McLaughlin, Ann	Patrick T. Toulan	Katherine Byrnes
Toulan	Catherine	Joseph	5-Feb-1905	31-Jan-1905	Daniel Toulan	McLaughlin, Ann	John Gaitley	Elizabeth Toulan
Toulan	Elizabeth	Mary	16-Jun-1901	11-Jun-1901	Daniel Toulan	McLaughlin, Ann	Patrick Toulan	Mary Toulan
Toulan	Mary	Helen	23-Jun-1907	11-Jun-1907	Daniel Toulan	McLaughlin, Ann	James McDonald	Mary McDonald
Toulan	Elizabeth		5-Aug-1906	22-Jul-1906	Michael F. Toulan	McDonald, Mary	Charles J. Murray	Elizabeth Toulan
Toulan	Catherine	Veronica	10-Jul-1910	30-Jun-1910	Michael T. Toulan	McDonald, Mary	Joseph Murray	Helen Casserly
Toulan	Michael	Cecelia	5-Oct-1913	26-Sep-1913	Michael Toulan	McDonald, Mary		Eleanor Neary
Toulan	Patrick	Francis	14-Feb-1909	31-Jan-1909	Michael Toulan	McDonald, Mary	James McDonald	Margaret Emge
Toulan	Ella	Theodore	8-Jul-1906	27-Jun-1906	Patrick Joseph Toulan	Welsh, Ellen	Patrick Burns	Catherine Burns
Toulan	Michael	Theresa	24-Oct-1909	9-Oct-1909	Patrick Toulan	Welsh, Ella	James St. Leger	Elizabeth Donlan
Toulan	Thomas	Francis	9-Feb-1908	1-Feb-1908	Patrick Toulan	Welsh, Ellen	James McDonald	Ann Welsh
Toulan	James	Joseph	21-May-1905	11-May-1905	Patrick Toulan	Walsh, Helen	Thomas Joseph Toulan	Mary Toulan
Toulen	Agnes	Joseph	2-Nov-1907	20-Oct-1907	Michael Toulen	McDonald, Mary	Patrick J. Bierne	Catherine Beirne
Tracey	Gertrude	Edna	08-May-1892	28-Apr-1892	Charles Tracey	Doyle, Mary	William J. Armstrong	Sabina Doyle
Tracey	Myrtle	Helen	17-Oct-1897	03-Oct-1897	Charles Tracey	Doyle, Mary	Dennis Sweeney	Mary Frisby
Tracey		Cecelia	26-Jan-1896	11-Jan-1896	Charles Tracey	Doyle, Mary	Jerome Sweeny	Helen Doyle

133

ST JOHN'S BAPTISMS 1882-1912

LAST NAME	FIRST NAME	MIDDLE	BAPTISM	BIRTH	Father	Mother	SPONSORS
Tracey	Joseph		04-Nov-1882	03-Nov-1882	Dennis O'B Tracey	Carroll, Mary Ann	John Carroll	Margaret Carroll
Tracey	Gertrude	Mary	26-May-1889	12-May-1889	John Tracey	Quinn, Mary Ann	Joseph Dignan	Mary McGuire
Tracey	Ann	Mary	05-Feb-1893	20-Jan-1893	John Vincent Tracey	Quinn, Mary Ann	John Hogan	Mary E. McQuillan
Tracy	Charles	Edward	07-Oct-1894	24-Sep-1894	Charles Edward Tracy	Doyle, Mary Elizabeth	Harry Tucker	Mary Frisby
Tracy	Hazel	Mary	31-Dec-1899	17-Dec-1899	Edward Tracy	Doyle, Mary	Dennis Sweeney	Sabina Sweeney
Tracy	Mary	Rose	10-Aug-1890	31-Jul-1890	Edward Tracy	Doyle, Mary	James Phillip Wise	Elizabeth Gahan
Tracy	Margaret	Josephine	11-May-1913	5-May-1913	Francis Tracy	Adam, Mary	William C. Adam	Margaret Adam
Tracy	Alice	G.	26-Apr-1891	07-Apr-1891	John Tracy	Quinn, Mary A.	Samuel Miles	Emma Coughlin
Tracy	Emma		16-Sep-1883	07-Sep-1883	John Tracy	Quinn, Mary Ann	John McIntyre	Margaret Connelly
Tracy	Hugh		22-Nov-1885	11-Nov-1885	John Tracy	Quinn, Mary Ann	John Delaney	Helen Brannan
Tracy	Agnes		01-May-1887	18-Apr-1887	John Vincent Tracy	Quinn, Mary Ann	James Logue	Helen McIntyre
Tracy	Charles		29-Feb-1888	24-Feb-1888	John Vincent Tracy	Quinn, Mary Ann		Elizabeth Ann White
Trageser	Stella	Mary	27-Jul-1913	9-Jul-1913	Henry Trageser	McBee, Mary C.		Grace Grimes
Trageser	Teresa	Mary	3-Mar-1912	22-Feb-1912	John F. Trageser	Dawson, Ann	Richard Roby	Margaret Roby
Trageser	Josephine	Louise	29-Mar-1914	23-Mar-1914	John Trageser	Dawson, Ann E.	Henry J. McCann	Mary Josephine [Blank]
Tragesser	John	Francis	8-Mar-1908	24-Feb-1908	John F. Tragesser	Dawson, Ann E.	Luke A. Dawson	Teresa Dawson
Tragesser	Margaret	Ann	29-Apr-1906	16-Apr-1906	John F. Tragesser	Dawson, Ann Elizabeth	Alphonse Dawson	Mary Dawson
Trainor	Margaret	Grace	02-Oct-1898	21-Sep-1898	Edward Trainor	Fahey, Mary Helen	James Fahey	Helen McGraw
Trainor	Catherine	Mary	07-Apr-1901	18-Mar-1901	Joseph Aloysius Trainor	Sonnenburg, Louise	John Trageser	Clare Trainor
Traver	Paul	Scott	3-Jan-1909	25-Nov-1908	William Scott Traver	Conelly, Mary	Ann Conelly	Ann Conelly
Traynor	Beatrice	Elizabeth	17-Jun-1900	05-Jun-1900	Edward Joseph Traynor	Fahey, Mary	Thomas Fahey	Mary Fahey
Treadway	Ann		06-Sep-1897	About 1830	Lafayette Treadway	Glazier, Elizabeth		Ann Wright
Trescott	Joseph		11-Mar-1883	05-Mar-1883	Charles H. Trescott	McFlagon, Bessie	Bessie McFlagon	Agnes Carey
Tress	John	Robert	22-Nov-1891	14-Nov-1891	Walter Tress	Freide, Mary	John Freide	Elizabeth Freide
Trimble	R. Lee		5-Jul-1914	22-Apr-1914	Roland Trimble	Smith, Susan		Evelyn Smith
Trimp	Dorothy	Magdalene	8-Aug-1909	18-Jul-1909	Howard J. Trimp	Sweeney, Mary G.	William A. Reilly	Rose M. Reilly
Trimp	Mary	Louise	24-Dec-1911	28-Nov-1911	John H. Trimp	Sweeney, George[sic]		Mary Trimp
Troy	Mary	w.	20-Oct-1895	07-Oct-1895	Patrick Troy	Hines, Catherine	Thomas Howe	Susan Hines
Truelove	Elizabeth		19-Jan-1913	6-Jan-1913	Francis Truelove	Gahan, Catherine	George Truelove	Florina Truelove
Truelove	Mary	Katherine	13-Mar-1910	27-Feb-1910	Francis Truelove	Gahan, Katherine	Michael Vallee	Elizabeth Gahan
Truelove	Francis	William	01-Nov-1885	20-Oct-1885	George R. Truelove	Manning, Mary Joan	Francis Manning	Mary Welch
Truelove	Thomas	Eugene	29-Mar-1891	10-Mar-1891	George R. Truelove	Manning, Mary J.	Patrick Welsh	Mary Scally
Truelove	Mary	Theresa	22-May-1892	11-May-1892	George Robert Truelove	Manning, Mary Joan	Henry Bowers	Mary Cornelius
Truelove	Sara	Veronica	31-Jan-1896	18-Jan-1896	George Robert Truelove	[Blank], Mary Joan		Catherine Biddison
Truelove	Catherine		22-Dec-1883	05-Dec-1883	George Truelove	Manning, Mary	James A. Croghan	Catherine Manning Bennett
Truelove	Charles	Henry	02-Oct-1887	19-Sep-1877	George Truelove	Manning, Mary	Charles J. Kelly	Mary M. Andrews
Truelove	George	Robert Thomas	14-Dec-1900	14-Feb-1856	George Truelove	Johnson, Eliza	Thomas Maskell	
Truelove	John	Albert	27-Oct-1889	10-Oct-1889	George Truelove	Monmonier, Mary		Ann Kenny
Truelove	Mary	Agnes	23-May-1915	9-May-1915	John Albert Truelove	Shanahan, Mary	George Truelove	Mary Joan Truelove
Truelove	Joseph	w.	05-Jun-1898	25-May-1898	Robert Truelove	Mannion, Mary	Thomas Hart	Ella Hart
Tubman	John	Francis	17-Oct-1886	05-Oct-1886	George Tubman	Colton, Mary		Sarah Stout
Tuder	Ellen	Lucy	12-Nov-1899	22-Oct-1899	Howard Tuder	Rooney, Mary	William Dudley	Rose Krieusinger
Tudor	Charles	Elmer	27-Oct-1901	08-Oct-1901	Henry Tudor	Rooney, Mary		Mary Irwin
Tudor	Howard	Joseph	5-May-1907	5-Apr-1907	Howard Tudor	Rooney, Mary	Louis Irving	Grace Hopper
Tulley	Margaret		06-Jul-1890	23-Jun-1890	J. Tulley	Kehoe, Catherine	Thomas Reilly	Maggie Giblin
Tully	Charles	M.	05-May-1895	26-Apr-1895	Charles Tully	Mullen, Elizabeth	Wilbur Mullen	Helen Mullen
Tully	Ann		28-Aug-1887	21-Aug-1887	John J. Tully	Kehoe, Catherine	William Willis	Kelly, Ann
Tully	Helen		28-Aug-1887	21-Aug-1887	John J. Tully	Kehoe, Catherine	Michael Kelly	Amelia Kendall
Tully	Francis	Margaret	16-Aug-1889	14-Sep-1892	John Tully	Kehoe, Catherine	James Tully	Emma Conroy
Tully	Gertrude	Mary	06-Sep-1896	August 1896	John Tully	Kehoe, Catherine	James J. Kelley	Ann Conroy
Tully	Grace	Mary	22-Jul-1894	12-Jul-1894	John Tully	Kehoe, Catherine	Francis Tracy	Margaret O'Connor
Tully	William		08-Nov-1885	20-Oct-1885	John Tully	Kehoe, Catherine	John Kehoe	Alice Giblin
Tully	Lily	Mary	04-Nov-1883	16-Oct-1883	Joseph Tully	McDermott, Elizabeth	Peter Burns	Alice Kelly
Tully	Mary	Josephine	13-Nov-1892	30-Sep-1892	Michael J. Tully	Kelly, Ann M.	James F. Connolly	Mary J. Johnson
Tumbleson	William	Wallace	28-Apr-1895	13-Apr-1895	Andrew Morse Tumbleson	Carpenter, Sara Elizabeth	Francis Aloysius Casey	Virginia Brown Dubel
Tumbleson	Regina		03-Oct-1897	27-Sep-1897	Andrew Tumbleson	Carpenter, Sarah		Mary Hart
Tumbleson	Sara		09-Jan-1900	21-Dec-1899	Andrew Tumbleson	Carpenter, Sara		Sara Hart
Tumbleton	Isabelle	Hart	20-Aug-1893	07-Aug-1893	Andrew M. Tumbleton	Carpenter, Sara		Mary Hart
Tunney	Edmund	Joseph	24-Nov-1900	16-Nov-1900	George Tunney	Corrigan, Mary	Joseph Hanley	Mary Tunney
Tunniecliff	Francis	Margaret	16-Aug-1889	05-Oct-1888	Frederick Tunniecliff	Wiegand, Christina Margaret	Francis Bell	Amanda Sturgeon
Tuony	Catherine		06-Jan-1884	24-Dec-1883	John Tuony	McGann, Catherine	Michael Garrity	Sara McGunn
Turnbaugh	Flora	Mary	17-Apr-1898	23-Mar-1898	James Turnbaugh	Trainor, Agnes	Joseph Trainor	Clara Trainor
Turnbaugh	Francis	T.	6-Aug-1905	1-Jul-1905	James Turnbaugh	Trainor, Agnes		Ann Brown

134

LAST NAME	FIRST NAME	MIDDLE	BAPTISM	BIRTH	Father	Mother	SPONSORS	
Turnbaugh	Gladys	Regina	04-Mar-1900	14-Feb-1900	James Turnbaugh	Trainor, Agnes		Mary Bruder
Turnbaugh	James	Reilly	13-Apr-1902	05-Mar-1902	James Turnbaugh	Trainor, Agnes		Clara Trainor
Turnbaugh	James	Joseph	31-Jan-1909	15-Jan-1909	James Turnbaugh	Trainor, Agnes	Joseph Trainor	Agnes Bradley
Turnbaugh/Trainor	Leda	Ann	14-Nov-1909	23-Aug-1860	James Turnbaugh	Armacost, Sarah	Clara Lambdin	
Turner	Constance		12-Aug-1900	01-Aug-1900	Constantine Turner	Wade, Mary		Bertha Wade
Turner	Katherine		08-Mar-1903	05-Oct-1901	Constantine Turner	Wade, Mary A.		Mary E. Dolan
Turner	Leonard		09-Dec-1900	28-Nov-1900	Lee Eugeme Tyrner	Mooney, Catherine	James Turner	Fannie Bosley
Tydings	Mary	Ellennor	24-Oct-1886	14-Feb-1886	Charles Tydings	Hannan, Marty		Alice Casey
Tydings	Mary	Margaret	06-Aug-1899	27-Jul-1899	Charles Tydings	Hibburd, Ida		Frances Warnick
Tyler	Henry	Robinson	04-May-1884	21-Apr-1884	Samuel Tyler	Lee, Mary	Thomas Reynolds	Delia Gilchrist
Tylie	Ann	Camelia	15-Apr-1883	05-Apr-1883	William C. Tylie	Croghan, Margaret	Patrick Croghan	Mary Timothy
Tyrel	Thomas		08-May-1887	06-May-1887	Thomas Tyrel	Byrnes, Elizabeth	Luke Byrnes	Mary Tyrel
Tyson	Luke		17-Nov-1886	15-Jul-1886	John Tyson	Tyson, Sara		Catherine A. Dudrow
Uhlenberg	Helen	Regina	19-Jan-1890	29-Dec-1889	Henry Uhlenberg	McQuinn, Mary		Lizzie McQuinn
Ulhorn	Mary Irene		22-Nov-1896	09-Nov-1896	John Uhlhorn	Mayer, Emma	John Kearney	Mary Kearney
Ullrich	Edward	Everest	15-Jan-1893	25-Dec-1892	George Francis Ullrich	McCormick, Mary	John McCormick	Athena McCormick
Ulrich	Elsie	Laura	05-Feb-1893	18-Jan-1893	William Ulrich	Wehrle, Philomena	Millard Kohler	Laura Wehrle
Unders	Evelin	Margaret	12-Jan-1904	08-Dec-1903	Pierce Unders	Carbery, Mary E.		Margaret Ackres
Uphoff	Albert		11-Sep-1892	17-Jul-1892	Henry Uphoff	Reilly, Elizabeth		Margaret Reilly
Usher	James	Michael	11-Apr-1886	24-Mar-1886	Richard Usher	Kenny, Mary	William Byrnes	Mary Byrnes
Usher	Richard		20-May-1883	16-May-1883	Richard Usher	Kenny, Mary	John Kavanaugh	Ann Cummings
Vacis	Mary	Letitia	01-Mar-1885	25-Feb-1885	James Bavis	Dunn, Mary	James Cullen	Ann Kerwin
Vallee	Jerome		20-Sep-1903	13-Sep-1903	Michael Vallee	McKee, Jennie	Thomas L. Roche	Mary Vallee
Van Boken	Agnes		17-Oct-1886	01-Oct-1886	Frederick Van Boken	Keene, Hannah	James Gray	Ann Ruane
Van Daniker	James	Howard	2-Apr-1905	1-Nov-1904	George Van Daniker	Brannan, Sara	Edward J. Healy	Mary A. Thorton
Van Holten	James	Millington	06-Mar-1887	10-Feb-1887	William Van Hollen	Flemming, Ella		Margaret Neville
Van Horn	Mary	Josephine	29-Jul-1889	01-Jul-1889	George Van Horn	Parr, Mary		Mary Josephine Moran
Vandaniker	Joseph	B.	15-Nov-1903	1-Nov-1903	George Vandaniker	Deckman, Ann	William Schwarzkoff	
Vansant	Catherine	Annabelle	27-Aug-1893	12-Aug-1893	John W.Vansant	Cavanaugh, Philomena Gert.	James Aloysius Manning	Catherine Cassidy
Vansant	Mary	Jennet	28-Aug-1892	18-Aug-1892	John Webster Vansant	Vansant, Philomena Gertrude	Francis Patrick Kavanaugh	Mary Agnes Jennet
Vanzant	John		20-Dec-1898	24-Dec-1864	John Vanzant	Norris, Mary		
Varsotti	John		12-Jul-1914	1-May-1914	Condo Versotti	Leone, Louise	Vincent Balto	Mary Leone
Vaughan	Philip	James	04-Oct-1903	19-Sep-1903	Patrick Vaughan	McAuliff, Bridget	James McCalliff	Bessie O'Neal
Vaughan	Thomas	Joseph	17-Mar-1907	5-Mar-1907	Patrick Vaughan	McAuliffe, Bridget	John McAuliffe	Catherine Hennessy
Vellaz	Edward	Philip	08-May-1897	18-Jul-1897	Edward Vellaz	Connolly, Mary	Alexander Villard	Helen Saquet
Venburg	Mary	Catherine	19-Feb-1888	04-Feb-1888	Henry Venburg	McGinn, Margaret	James McGinn	Elizabeth Hawkins
Vereker	Joseph	Nicolas	28-Jun-1891	22-Jun-1891	James Denn Vereker	Kelly, Alice	Joseph Kelly	Rose Ann Cummings
Vereker	James	Norman	24-Mar-1901	19-Mar-1901	James Vereker	Kelly, Alice	Norman Dillon	Catherine Kelly
Vereker	John		18-Dec-1892	02-Dec-1892	James Vereker	Kelly, Alice	Joseph C. Dunn	Philomena Young
Vereker	Nicolas	Ferdinand	20-Feb-1896	22-Jan-1896	James Vereker	Kelly, Alice	Michael Rowland	Helen Rowland
Vernaz	James		10-Jun-1906	3-Jun-1906	Ernest Vernaz	Glenn, Winifred		Mary Slaysman
Via	Emma	Mary	3-Oct-1906	16-Nov-1891	Joseph Via	Brame, Addir	Virginia [Blank]	Catherine Smith
Vick	Evelyn		25-Apr-1915	13-Apr-1915	William Vick	Feeney, Julia	Michael Feeney	Julia Feeney
Vick	John	Matthew	18-May-1884	13-Feb-1884	William Vick	Krebs, Mary	John Martin	Cecelia Martin
Vick	Julia	Mary	4-May-1913	24-Apr-1913	William Vick	Vick, Julia	Charles L. Belz	Ida Kehoe
Vick/Bick	Joseph	John	13-Jun-1909	4-Jun-1909	William Vick	Feeney, Julia	Leo Feeney	Mary Feeney
Vincent	Marin	August	18-Jul-1915	20-Jun-1915	Marin Vincent	Guillet, Amelia	Frederick Botta	Rose Villenus
Vincent/Kennedy	Virginia	Elizabeth	13-Feb-1891	15-Sep-1862	Henry Vincent	Love, Margaret		Catherine McLaughlin
Voeglein	James	Fussell	21-Dec-1892	21-Dec-1892	Charles Voeglein	Fussell, Mary Felina		Lydia M. Fussell
Voeglein	Joseph	Francis	12-Sep-1887	05-Sep-1887	Charles Voeglein	Fussell, Mary	John Brickner	Clarissa Brickner
Voglein	Mary	Clarissa	25-Oct-1891	11-Oct-1891	Charles Voeglein	Fussell, Mary Paul	John Schiffer	Joan Rabina Hoggson
Voglein	Charles	Ferdinand	18-May-1890	08-May-1890	Charles Voeglein	Fussell, Mary P.	Joseph A. Hohman	Mary J. Foige
Voglein	Clara	Mary	30-Dec-1894	21-Dec-1894	Charles Voglein	Fussell, Mary	Edward Fussell	Ann McGee
Volkman	Susannah	Lavinia	30-Nov-1890	20-Sep-1890	Henry August Volkman	Westervelt, Susanna Lavinia	Mary Ann Westervelt	
Vondersmith	Dorothy		5-Apr-1908	27-Mar-1908	William F. Vondersmith	Ruckle, Elizabeth	Albert Ward	Edward Ruckle
Vondersmith	Thomas	Lee	12-Jan-1913	2-Jan-1913	William F. Vondersmith	Ruckle, Elizabeth	Thomas Ruckle	Mary Ward
Vondersmith	William	Ward	3-Sep-1911	26-Aug-1911	William F. Vondersmith	Ruckle, Elizabeth	John McGarvey	Ada Ruckle
Vondersmith/Keogh	Ann		21-Jan-1892	13-Jan-1867	Daniel Vondersmith	Umphries, Mary		Mary Gibson
Voss	Richard		26-Apr-1898	10-Dec-1870	Charles Voss	Hobbs, Theresa		Peter Hufnegel
Voss	Edward		16-Sep-1900	15-Sep-1900	Ernest Voss	Graley, Katherine	Patrick Maguire	Mary Graley
Voss	Frederick	Joseph	11-Jan-1903	06-Jan-1903	Frederick Voss	Graley, Catherine	Henry Nooth	Margaret Graley
Voss	Bernard	Agnes	30-Oct-1910	17-Oct-1910	Richard Voss	Graley, Catherine	William Nueth	Mary Graley
Voss	Mary	Teresa	6-Jan-1907	21-Dec-1906	Richard Voss	Graley, Catherine	Leo Clancy	Mary H. Graley

LAST NAME	FIRST NAME	MIDDLE	BAPTISM	BIRTH	Father	Mother	SPONSORS
Voss	William	Charles	24-May-1914	30-Apr-1914	William Voss	Cogewell, Mary	Loretta Lentz
Voyce	Helen	Mary	19-Dec-1914	2-Nov-1914	Henry R. Voyce	Mochman, Ann M.	Catherine Edwards
Wagner	Grace	Hope	24-Sep-1913	17-Aug-1913	[Blank]	Wagner, Ann	Grace Turner
Wagner	Ann	Viola	28-Oct-1894	10-Oct-1894	Henry Wagner	Hinkle, Emma	Catherine Hanly
Wagner	Katherine	Elizabeth	09-May-1897	15-May-1897	William Wagner	Birmingham, Martha	Agnes Birmingham
Wahl	Edward		07-Jul-1895	28-Jun-1895	James Wahl	Malone, Bridget	Ellis Cadogan
							James Murphy
Waldman	Ann	Virginia	25-Sep-1882	09-Feb-1882	William Waldman	Brohue, Julia	Agnes Hanly
							Arthur Hanly
Waldner	Loretta		30-Jan-1898	12-Jan-1898	Francis Waldner	Donohue, Ellen	Mary Driscoll
							John Kelleher
Waldner	Mary	Ann	28-Jan-1900	18-Jan-1900	Francis Waldner	Donohoe, Ella	Mary Byrnes
							John Byrnes
Waldner	Joseph	Anthony	5-Feb-1905	20-Jan-1905	Francis Waldner	Donahue, Helen	Ann G. Bishop
							Patrick G. Donahue
Waldner	Matilda	Estelle	10-Feb-1889	20-Oct-1888	Addison Ealker	Offner, Mary Agnes	Helen Agnes Offner
							Henry Vincent Offner
Walker	Samuel		10-May-1896	11-Apr-1896	Anthony Walker	Hulse, Mary	Ann Farrell
							John Octavia
Walker	Mary	Elizabeth Juliet	23-Aug-1896	11-Aug-1896	Charles W. Walker	Kirby, Mary L.	Ann Kirby
							Charles Kirby
Walker	Elizabeth	Virginia	24-Jul-1886	11-Jul-1886	Hood Walker	Cochlan, Josephine	Elizabeth Roe
Walker	Elizabeth		04-Oct-1903	23-Sep-1903	John H. Walker	Vey, Mary E.	Mary E. Kelly
							James P. Kelly
Walker	John	Thomas	25-Dec-1892	09-Dec-1892	John Walker	Tierney, Mary	Mary Grogan
							Michael James McGann
Walker	Mary	Ann	09-Nov-1890	29-Oct-1890	John Walker	Tierney, Mary	Ella Burns
							Richard Walker
Walker	Helen	Mary	15-Feb-1885	25-Jan-1885	Joseph Walker	Coughlan, Joan	Sadie Baker
							John Coughlan
Walker	Francis		14-Sep-1890	05-Sep-1890	William F. Walker	Herron, Caroline	Mary McGuire
							William Shaffney
Walker/Shaney	William	Ambrose	06-May-1888	16-May-1874	[Blank] Walker	[Blank]	Mary Agnes Shaney
							Alexander Shaney
Wall	Ann		05-Oct-1890	17-Sep-1890	James P. Wall	Malone, Bridget	Ann Malone
							Timothy Murphy
Wall	James		25-Aug-1889	11-Aug-1889	James Wall	Malone, Bridget	Margaret Cahill
							Edward McCormick
Wall	John	Joseph	08-Jul-1888	27-Jun-1888	James Wall	Malone, Bridget	Ann Malone
							William Rowe
Wall	John	Joseph	03-Jul-1892	22-Jun-1892	James Wall	Malone, Bridget	Catherine Murphy
							William Gately
Wall	Mary	Bridget	09-May-1886	25-Apr-1886	James Wall	Malone, Bridget	Eliza Murphy
							John Malone
Wall	Thomas	Patrick	17-Jul-1887	06-Jul-1887	James Wall	Malone, Bridget	Catherine Murphy
							James Cadigan
Wallace	Sara		09-Apr-1882	02-Apr-1882	Patrick Wallace	Donnelly, Mary	Sarah Feely
							Thomas J. Kelly
Walnut	Lillian	Helen	24-Feb-1907	1-Feb-1907	Francis Walnut	Donoghue, Helen	Lillian Guinan
							Vincent Tilly
Walsh	Irene	Elizabeth	19-Jan-1890	13-Jan-1890	Frank P. Walsh	Tennis, Mary	Catherine Ward
							James Ward
Walsh	Ann	Mildred	23-Nov-1913	2-Nov-1913	James F. Walsh	Lundburg, Lillian	Ann Lundberg
							Joseph Kelly
Walsh	Francis	Patrick	24-Mar-1912	9-Mar-1912	John R. Walsh	Hawley, Julia	Mary McHale
							Patrick Flannery
Walsh	Edward		29-Apr-1907	19-Apr-1907	John Walsh	Gaugh, Sarah	Mary J. Walsh
Walsh	John	Thomas	08-Jul-1888	26-Jun-1888	John Walsh	Casserly, Margaret	Bridget A. McGrial
							Thomas Casserly
Walsh	John	Michael	12-Feb-1911	24-Jan-1911	John Walsh	Howley, Julia	Bridget Howley
							James McGovern
Walsh	Margaret		22-Dec-1895	11-Dec-1895	John Walsh	Casserly, Margaret	Margaret Conway
							Thomas Casserly
Walsh	Thomas	Patrick	14-Jan-1894	31-Dec-1893	John Walsh	Casserly, Margaret	Margaret Walsh
							Michael McDermott
Walsh	Thomas	Joseph	27-Jul-1913	15-Jul-1913	John Walsh	Howley, Julia	Margaret Cashen
							Cornelius Cashen
Walsh	James	Dudley	15-Nov-1908	3-Nov-1908	Patrick Joseph Walsh	Conroy, Mary J.	Catherine Conroy
							Patrick K. Hogan
Walsh	Mary	Glydas	04-Oct-1891	29-Sep-1891	Thomas J. Walsh	Baker, Catherine	Mary Garrity
							Thomas Baker
Walsh	Martin	William	25-Jun-1893	13-Jun-1893	Thomas Joseph Walsh	Baker, Catherine	Alice McNally
							Martin Dentes
Walter	Howard	Jefferson	03-Aug-1884	18-Jul-1884	Ambrose Walter	Dietrick, Catherine V.	Wilhemina Linhard
							John F. Feehan
Walter	Thomas		02-Mar-1890	21-Feb-1890	Ambrose Walter	[Blank], Katie Veronica	Katie Mooney
							Thomas McNulty
Walter	William	Ambrose	30-Jan-1887	20-Jan-1887	Ambrose Walter	Dietrick, Catherine	Louis Cecelia Lipp
							Andrew John Linhard
Walter	Martin		23-Sep-1894	29-Aug-1894	Charles P. Walter	Gavin, Honora	Ann Carolan
Walters	Thomas	Josephine	15-Sep-1907	17-Aug-1907	Charles A. Walters	Talbert, Ann F.	Mary A. Freeman
							Henry F. Talbert
Walters	Charles	Patrick	26-Jan-1908	17-Jan-1908	Charles Walters	Gavin, Honora	Mary A. Flaherty
							John M. Murray
Walters	Elizabeth		4-Aug-1906	27-Jul-1906	Charles Walters	Gavin, Ann	Mary O'Neill
Walters	Honora		05-Jul-1897	15-Jun-1897	Charles Walters	Gavin, Ann	Mary Woodward
Walters	John	Patrick	11-Jul-1900	03-Jul-1900	Charles Walters	Gavin, Ann	Mary Gavin
Walters	Laretta	Mary	10-Apr-1892	07-Mar-1892	Charles Walters	Gordon, Nora	Mary Clarke
							John Farley
Walters	Henry	William	30-Nov-1898	23-Nov-1898	Henry Walters	Seufert, Ida	Mary Eingh
Walters	Emma	Mary	3-Oct-1915	23-Sep-1915	Howard J. Walters	Mumma, Edith May	
Walters	John		01-Dec-1891	07-Sep-1891	John Walters	Magnus, Ellen	Ellen Davis
Walters	Josephine	Mary	23-Mar-1903	27-Sep-1902	Louis P. Walters	Harte, Elizabeth	Mary Shiels
Walters	John	Joseph	12-Jul-1890	22-Jun-1890	M. Walter	Magniss, Ellen	Lizzie McCluskey
Walters	Mary	Evelyn	8-Aug-1915	30-Jul-1915	Martin Walker	Lacey, Sara	Agnes Lacey
Walters	William	Lee	22-Nov-1896	13-Nov-1896	Roland Walters	Ruck, Mary A.	Ann Trageser
							John Trageser
Walters	Matilda		22-Nov-1914	10-Nov-1914	William A. Walters	Kohler, Joan M.	Odella [Blank]
							William Kohler
Walters	William	Gerald	23-Oct-1911	16-Oct-1911	William Ambrose Walters	Kohler, Joan Mary	Rose McIntyre
Walton	Florence	Elizabeth	9-Mar-1913	25-Feb-1913	William Walton	Kohler, Joan	Florence M. Kohler
							Francis McIntyre
Walton	Mary	Genevieve	20-Dec-1908	8-Dec-1908	Francis Patrick Walton	Paturzo, Mary	Ann Theresa Croghan
							Anthony Paturzo
Walton	Francis	Salvatore	12-Jun-1910	3-Jun-1910	Francis Walton	Parturzo, Mary	Margaret Parturzo
							Vincent Parturzo
Wambach/McLain	Wilhelmina	Mary	15-Mar-1885	06-Oct-1865	George Wambach	Schultze, Catherine	Mary Catherine Wambach

LAST NAME	FIRST NAME	MIDDLE	BAPTISM	BIRTH	Father	Mother	SPONSORS	
Wanken	Mary	Elizabeth	3-Oct-1909	13-Sep-1909	Louis Wanken	Haskell, Mary E.	George W. Haskell	Mary E. Hamilton
Wanner	Margaret	Loretta	24-Apr-1911	25-Jan-1911	Louis Wanner	Moylan, Virginia		Catherine Moylan
Wanner	Virginia	Mary	4-Oct-1915	5-Sep-1915	Louis Wanner	Moylan, Mary Catherine		Ann Kirwin
Ward	Margaret	Adele	29-Jun-1913	17-Jun-1913	David S. Ward	Murphy, Margaret Ann	John A. Murphy	Margaret Murphy
Ward	David	Sinclair	8-Jan-1911	23-Dec-1910	David Ward	Murphy, Margaret	John A. Murphy	Elizabeth Gees
Ward	Daniel	Charles	17-Jan-1897	08-Jan-1897	Francis P. Ward	[Blank], Mary E.	Daniel Keleher	Gertrude E. Schneider
Ward	Estelle	Ann	09-Aug-1885	30-Jul-1885	Francis P. Ward	Toennies, Mary E.	John Ward	Ann Toennies
Ward	Francis	Joseph	29-Jan-1893	19-Jan-1893	Francis Patrick Ward	Foennix, Mary Elizabeth	Joseph Bernard Finnan	Joan Estelle Ward
Ward	Acerum (Maple)	Mary	07-Oct-1888	01-Oct-1888	Francis Ward	Tennis, Mary	Patrick Healy	Marcella Teresa Finnan
Ward	Ellen	Catherine	13-Mar-1887	11-Mar-1887	Francis Ward	Torni, Mary	Carl Torni	Sara Ward
Ward	John	Thomas	07-Oct-1894	01-Oct-1894	Frank P. Ward	[Blank], Mary E.	John T. Ward	Rose Wilhelm
Ward	Henry		24-Sep-1882	07-Sep-1882	Hugh Ward	Gorman, Bridget	John Ward	Ellen Ward
Ward	Joseph	Bernard	16-Oct-1887	02-Oct-1887	Hugh Ward	Gorman, Bridget	James Gorman	Joan Gibson
Ward	Mary	Estelle	21-Jun-1891	09-Jun-1891	James Joseph Ward	Palmer, Margaret	John Ward	Mary Duvall
Ward	Elizabeth	Blanche	17-Jul-1910	6-Jul-1910	James M. Ward	Ryan, Josephine		Blanche E. Steward
Ward	Ann		23-Jul-1893	11-Jul-1893	James Ward	Ryan, Joan	Edward Ward	Mary Ward
Ward	Gladys	Mary	12-Jun-1898	28-May-1898	James Ward	Ryan, Joan	John Laughlin	Mary Taylor
Ward	James		18-May-1902	05-May-1902	James Ward	Ryan, Josephine	Michael Gahan	Ann Caine
Ward	Julia	Agnes	14-Feb-1904	27-Jan-1904	James Ward	Ryan, Joan		Elizabeth Mei
Ward	Robert		29-Apr-1900	13-Apr-1900	James Ward	Ryan, Johanna	Robert Ryan	Rose Ryan
Ward	Francis	Thomas	2-May-1909	16-Apr-1909	John Joseph Ward	Lamp, Mary	Charles Thomas Gothart	Bertha McCrory
Ward	Howard	Eugene	29-Nov-1903	10-Nov-1903	John Joseph Ward	Lamp, Barbara	Hugh Egan	Eva Waltman
Ward	John	Joseph	16-Apr-1905	5-Apr-1905	John Joseph Ward	Lamp, Mary B.	James McCrory	Elizabeth Daily
Ward	Charles		05-Nov-1893	15-Oct-1893	John T. Ward	Collins, Mary A.	Charles Weanig	Mary Weanig
Ward	William	Cavell	6-Mar-1904	1-Mar-1904	John V. Ward	Kirwan, Margaret	Francis Ward	Ann Kirwan
Ward	Carroll	Patrick	03-May-1891	16-Apr-1891	John Ward	Callaghan, Mary	John Ward	Sara Wood
Ward	Elizabeth		10-Jul-1887	10-Jul-1887	John Ward	Fitzpatrick, Elizabeth	Thomas Fitzpatrick	Bridget Fitzpatrick
Ward	Francisa	Patrick	12-Jan-1890	26-Dec-1889	John Ward	Callahan, Mary	William Delaney	Ella Ward
Ward	Gertrude		21-Mar-1886	02-Mar-1886	John Ward	Callahan, Mary	Elizabeth Ward	Francis Ward
Ward	Helen		03-Mar-1895	12-Feb-1895	John Ward	Callinan, Mary	John Martin Creighton	Helen Callinan
Ward	James	Edmund	24-Jul-1892	22-Jul-1892	John Ward	Fitzpatrick, Elizabeth	Edward Ward	Mary Fitzpatrick
Ward	John	Bernard	08-Jan-1888	24-Dec-1887	John Ward	Callaghan, Mary	James Dempsey	Elizabeth Dempsey
Ward	John	P.	27-Jan-1901	07-Jan-1901	John Ward	Batzer, Mary	William Ward	Margaret Batzer
Ward	Joseph	Allen	01-Mar-1903	18-Feb-1903	John Ward	Kirwan, Margaret A.	Charles Guckart	Agnes Ruckle
Ward	Mary	Catherine	01-Jan-1886	21-Dec-1885	John Ward	Fitzpatrick, Elizabeth	Thomas Fitzpatrick	Agnes Fitzpatrick
Ward	Mary		20-Nov-1910	5-Nov-1910	John Ward	Lamp, Mary	Hugo Ward	Mrs. C. Wehner
Ward	Michael	Matthew	13-Dec-1914	24-Nov-1914	John Ward	Lamp, Mary	Michael Ford	Ann Richards
Ward	Mildred	Elizabeth	13-Oct-1912	20-Sep-1912	John Ward	Lamp, Mary	William Joyce	Mary R. Batterden
Ward	Thomas	Albert	27-Apr-1890	23-Apr-1890	John Ward	Fitzpatrick, Elizabeth	Thomas J. Fitzpatrick	Agnes Fitzpatrick
Ward	Timothy		9-Jun-1907	20-May-1907	John Ward	Lamb, Mary	Timothy Ward	Mary Daly
Ward	Florence	Virginia	15-Jul-1875	15-Jul-1875	Joseph Ward	Georgia Lutz	John Howes	
Ward	Helen	Mary	29-Sep-1895	14-Sep-1895	Michael J. Ward	Smith, Helen	James Carroll	Catherine Smith
Ward	Mary	A.	21-Jan-1906	10-Jan-1906	Michael J. Ward	Ryan, Joan	Corad Baumgardiner	Amelia Barton
Ward	Margaret		12-Apr-1908	27-Mar-1908	Michael James Ward	Ryan, Joan	Joseph M. Gayhardt	Mary Clark
Ward	Mary	Eleanor	22-Sep-1912	5-Sep-1912	Michael James Ward	Regan, Joan Teresa	James Irwin	Margaret Irwin
Ward	Ann	Honora	12-Nov-1882	03-Nov-1882	Michael Ward	Egan, Mary	Hugh Ryan	Catherine Ward
Ward	Edward	B.	10-Oct-1897	24-Sep-1897	Michael Ward	Smith, Ella	James Lynch	Mary Smith
Ward	Edwin	Matthew	16-Jul-1899	05-Jul-1899	Michael Ward	Eagan, Mary	Edward Richard	Bridget Ward
Ward	George	Craig	15-May-1904	30-Apr-1904	Michael Ward	Willingham, Mary	Emil C. Mantz	Mary Mantz
Ward	Hugh	Matthew	27-Nov-1892	10-Nov-1892	Michael Ward	Smith, Helen	Peter Smith	Elizabeth Smith
Ward	Mary	Ellen	31-Dec-1893	17-Dec-1893	Michael Ward	Eagan, Mary	Hugh Henry Eagan	Ann Batterden
Ward	Mary	Teresa	07-Dec-1890	25-Nov-1890	Michael Ward	Eagan, Mary	Michael O'Neill	Delia Ward
Ward	Timothy		22-Jun-1902	20-May-1902	Michael Ward	Willingham, Mary	Henry Ward	Ann Elwood
Ward	Michael	Francis	13-Mar-1887	02-Mar-1887	Michael Ward	Eagan, Mary C.	Michael Kelly	Bridget Eagan
Ward	Michael		26-Aug-1894	13-Aug-1894	Michael Ward	Smith, Helen	Joseph Smith	Helen Smith
Ward	Timothy		26-Oct-1884	11-Oct-1884	Michael Ward	Eagan, Mary	John Hagerty	Fannie Eagan
Ward	John	Gabriel	4-Sep-1910	15-Aug-1910	Thomas J. Ward	Owens, Delia	Patrick Owens	Mary Fitzpatrick
Ward	Thomas	Romanus	4-Apr-1915	25-Mar-1915	Thomas Ward	Owens, Bridget	Thomas Fitzpatrick	Ann Fitzpatrick
Ward	Michael	Leonard	5-May-1912	20-Apr-1912	Timothy Joseph Ward	Lamp, Ida	John Ward	Bertha McCrory
Ward	Adam	Elizabeth	24-Aug-1913	7-Aug-1913	Timothy M. Ward	Lamp, Ida	Thomas Cunningham	Francis Bradley Gallant
Ward	James	Joseph	6-Dec-1908	21-Nov-1908	Timothy Matthew Ward	Lamp, Ida	James Joseph McCrory	Mary Catherine Starkey
Ward	Gertrude	Caroline	7-Mar-1915	21-Feb-1915	Timothy Ward	Lamp, Ida	James M. Shea	Catherine Richards
Ward	Walter	Patrick	23-Oct-1910	[Blank]	Timothy Ward	Lamp, Ida	John Patrick Donovan	Elizabeth E. Donovan

ST JOHN'S BAPTISMS 1882-1912

LAST NAME	FIRST NAME	MIDDLE	BAPTISM	BIRTH	Father	Mother	SPONSORS
Ward	John	Elmer	21-Aug-1904	8-Aug-1904	William P. Ward	Murphy, Margaret C.	George W. Bien	Catherine Bien
Ward	Mary	C.	30-Sep-1906	18-Sep-1906	William P. Ward	Murphy, Margaret	William F. Myers	Ellen Myers
Ward	Margaret		24-Mar-1901	11-Mar-1901	William Ward	Murphy, Margaret	Edward Mulgrew	Catherine Keenan
Ward	Mary		24-Apr-1892	13-Apr-1892	William Ward	Coffay, Mary	Peter Mullen	Margaret Mullen
Ward	William	Joseph	26-Mar-1893	18-Mar-1893	William Ward	Coffay, Mary	James Joseph Coffay	Mary Coffay
Ward	William	Patrick	14-Sep-1902	09-Sep-1902	William Ward	Murphy, Margaret	John McMahon	An Mahoney
Wardbusch	Ann	Mary	11-Nov-1888	01-Nov-1888	Jacob Wardbusch	Dietzwid, Margaret		Ann Mary Stengel
Warner	Mary	Margaret	18-Sep-1887	14-Sep-1887	Charles E. Warner	Breitenbaugh, Margaret E.		Margaret E. Fohner
Warner	Christine	Mary	30-Jun-1891	20-May-1891	Francis A. Warner	Ullrich, Emma		J.D. Martin
Warner	Emma	Mary	12-Apr-1893	03-Apr-1893	Francis A. Warner	Ullrich, Emma	Rev J.D. Marr	Rev. William Bartlett
Warner	Francis		01-Sep-1886	23-Aug-1886	Francis A. Warner	Ullrich, Emma		Katherine Kerr
Warren	Katherine	Virginia	9-Aug-1909	16-Jun-1909	Louis Warner	Moylan, Virginia		Mary A. Kroeber
Warren	Mary	Ann	10-Mar-1904	8-Mar-1904	George Warren	Kroeber, Matilda M.		Ann [Blank]
Washington	Mary	Flegg	11-Nov-1904	02-May-1862	Alfred Flegg	Alger, Mary		Mary Caton
Washington	Ellen	Frances	14-Oct-1890	08-Oct-1890	George W. Washington	Kelley, Mary Catherine	Joseph Carroll	Catherine Carrol
Waterhouse	Margaret	Catherine	17-Jan-1897	24-Dec-1896	Henry Waterhouse	Collins, Regina	P.B. Delaney	Mary Gavin
Waters	Mary		03-Aug-1902	23-Jul-1902	Charles Waters	Gavin, Ann	William J. Rusk	Mary A. Rusk
Waters	Roland	Monrgomery	11-Sep-1895	08-Mar-1895	Richard Waters	Lee, Virginia	Francis Tragesser	Frances Tragesser
Waters	Margaret		06-Aug-1899	30-Jul-1899	Roland Waters	Rusk, Mary	George Stemple	Cerasina Welsh
Watkins	Susannah		28-Oct-1898	About 1885	Isaac Watkins	Watkins, Joan		Mary Matthews
Watson	Edna		04-Dec-1896	[Blank]	Charles Roddney Watson	Smith, Helen	Peter V. Kelly	Catheirne Corcoran
Watson	Regina	Aloysius	2-Jul-1905	20-Jun-1905	George W. Watson	Kelly, Teresa M.	Joseph Kelly	Theresa Fitzpatrick
Watson	L. Sebastian	Joseph	22-Feb-1903	03-Feb-1903	George Watson	Kelly, Theresa	John Tillman	Adalaide Kelly
Watson	Rhetta	Joan Mary	8-Oct-1911	7-Sep-1911	George Watson	Kelly, Teresa	John McWilliams	Mary Smith
Watson	Mary	Mildred	15-Jul-1906	23-Jun-1906	Henry Watson	Corcoran, Mary	Francis Mosler	Catherine Mosler
Watson	Joseph	Edward	15-Nov-1908	6-Nov-1908	Joeph Edward Watson	Lilly, Catherine Elizabeth	Joseph McGuire	Dollie Downs
Watson	Aloysius	Edward	21-Jan-1900	[Blank]	John Watson	McGuire, Agnes	John F. Caton	Margaret Lilly
Watson	John	Edward	30-Jul-1905	20-Jul-1905	Joseph E. Watson	Lilly, Hattie	Henry C. Gafney	Ann Gafney
Watson	Maurice	Michael	24-Aug-1902	12-Aug-1902	Joseph E. Watson	Kilchenstein, Mary		Henrietta Ebert
Watson	Genevieve	Aloysius	25-Jun-1893	03-May-1893	William Henry Watson	Ebert, Grace A.		Julia Ann Gobright
Watson	Helen	Teresa	25-Mar-1883	27-Dec-1882	William Henry Wilson	Corcoran, Mary Ann	Stephen Fitzgerald	Helen Burns
Watts	John	Joseph	7-Jul-1907	26-Jun-1907	Albert H. Watts	Burns, Catherine	Thomas R. Evans	Margaret M. Evans
Watts	Albert		23-Oct-1904	16-Oct-1904	Albert Watts	Barnes, Katherine	P.J. Burns	Margaret Burns
Watts	Catherine		07-Sep-1902	29-Aug-1902	Albert Watts	Burns, Catherine	William McCluskey	Sarah McGuire
Watts	Mary	Ann	23-Jun-1901	13-Jun-1901	James McAllister Watts	O'Connor, Ann	James McDevitt	Sophia Victory
Waugh	Henry	Garfield	08-Oct-1882	25-Oct-1881	William Waugh	Carroll, Rose	Robert Earl Carroll	Emma Carroll
Weatherstine	Robert	Earl	7-Feb-1909	23-Jan-1909	Andrew Weatherstine	Siebold, Helen	James Connelly	Helen Weatherstine
Webb	Mary	Joan	13-May-1885	29-Aug-1885	Arthur Webb	Dougherty, Bridget	John Coffey	Catherine Coffey
Webb	Margaret		15-Apr-1886	11-Apr-1886	Levi Webb	Huyster, Clara		Elizabeth Feelhtig
Webber	Elizabeth		08-Sep-1887	19-Jul-1869	William Webber	Stricker, Catherine A.	John Stricker	Reginald O'Connor
Webber	Edward	William	3-Mar-1912	1-Mar-1912	Joseph Webber	Brink, Catherine		Mary Flynn
Weber	Mary	Agnes	21-Dec-1888	11-Dec-1888	Wade Weber	Riordan, Grace Agnes	Harry J. McClellan	Mary O'Malley
Weber	Wade	Edward	20-Dec-1908	4-Dec-1908	William Weber	Wilkening, Catherine	William Bishop	Mary Wood
Weber/Ebert	Catherine	C.	30-Sep-1899	26-Aug-1899	Laurence Weber	Fresch, Elizabeth		Viola Hall
Weddingfield	August		17-Dec-1904	11-Jun-1877	Henry Charles Weddingfield	Neus, Mary Ann	Walter W. Owens	Ann M. Neus
Weger	Walter		07-Feb-1886	31-Jan-1886	Henry Martin Weger	Hinkley, Lotta	Henry Senft	Laura Senft
Weidman	George	Andrew	09-Dec-1894	30-Nov-1894	Henry Weger	Hagerty, Ann Estelle	John Kelly	Mary A. Loeffler
Weihrauch	Ann	Mary	17-Jul-1898	04-Jul-1898	George Weidman	Bock, Petrina	John Kelly	Joan Callan
Weingierl	Margaret	Mary	1-Aug-1909	21-Jul-1909	Ernest Joseph Weir	Moran, Mary M.	Joseph Moran	Ann Kelly
Weinman	Mary	Olivia	03-Aug-1890	22-Jul-1890	William L. Weihrauch	O'Connor, Margaret	James Lackey	Mary Weingierl
Weinman	James		31-Oct-1897	16-Oct-1897	Charles Weingierl	Butler, Ann	John Griffin	Mary Hagerty
Weinmann	Peter		14-Mar-1886	20-Dec-1886	Albert Weinman	Hagerty, Ann	James Blankford	Eugenia Smith
Weinmann	Margaret	Henrietta	09-Sep-1888	04-Aug-1888	William Weinman	Mallonee, Mildred	Alexander Bonner	Margaret Hagerty
Weir	Alfred	Francis	28-Oct-1883	14-Oct-1883	Alfred Weinmann	McGarry, Nellie	Frederick Bierlein	Ada Moran
Welby	Albert		25-Oct-1882	08-Oct-1882	James Weinmann	Casserly, Margaret	John Edward McGarry	Mary Connolly
Welby	John	Joseph Edward	10-Nov-1907	1-Nov-1907	Ernest Joseph Weir	Needham, Eleanor	John Kelly	Mary O'Keefe
Welby	Margaret	Mary	18-Jul-1915	8-Jul-1915	John Welby	Butler, Ann	Richard Cronan	Nora Connelly
Welby	Mary		22-May-1892	12-May-1892	John Welby	Butler, Ann	James Daily	Agnes Welch
Welby	Thomas		04-Jul-1897	28-Jun-1897	John Welby	Hinkley, Lotta	James King	Ann Sulivan
Welch	Agnes	Mildred	23-May-1915	8-May-1915	Charles Welch	Mallonee, Mildred	John Edward McGarry	Mary Casserly
Welch	John	Edward	12-May-1912	28-Apr-1912	Edward Welch	McGarry, Nellie	Patrick Welch	Mary Murphy
Welch	James	Francis	13-Dec-1891	22-Nov-1891	John Welch	Casserly, Margaret	Patrick Welch	
Welch	Margaret	Eleanor	21-Aug-1887	06-Aug-1887	Patrick Welch	Needham, Eleanor	Michael Kelly	

138

LAST NAME	FIRST NAME	MIDDLE	BAPTISM	BIRTH	Mother	Father	SPONSORS
Welch	Ann	Amelia	17-May-1885	08-Mar-1885	Adelstein, Rose	William J. Welch	Ann A. Hoffman
Welch	Grace	Caroline	16-Jan-1887	08-Dec-1886	Adelstein, Rose	William Joseph Welch	Amelia Hoffman
Welch	Mary	Caroline	15-Dec-1895	04-Nov-1895	Adelstern, Rose	William Welch	Mary Caroline Hoffman
Welch	Sarah	Elizabeth	29-Nov-1891	03-Aug-1891	Adelstein, Rose	William Welch	Sara Elizabeth McGraw
Welden	George	Albert	23-Mar-1890	17-Mar-1890	Lanier, Susan	Peter Weldon	Mary Hamilton
Welden	Rose	Thelma	07-Oct-1894	27-Sep-1894	Lawson, Mary G.	Peter Weldon	Cassie Kerr
Weldner	Eleanor		13-Dec-1908	4-Dec-1908	Donahue, Eleanor	Francis A. Weldner	Henry Kline
Weldon	William	B.	10-Jul-1898	26-Jun-1898	Graham, Eliza Alicia Moran	Michael J. Weldon	Edward Willis
Wellmore	Margaret	Elizabeth	13-Aug-1882	08-Jul-1882	Maher, Josephine	Edward H. Wellmore	Mary Guinan
Wells	Margaret		22-Jan-1905	23-Oct-1904	Wells, Catherine Adalaide	Andrew J. Wells	Mary A. Graham
Wells	John	Joseph	15-Dec-1901	23-Sep-1901	Wamfoot, Mary	Andrew Wells	Mary Mooney
Wells	Catherine		1-Feb-1906	06-Jun-1863	Schultze, Catherine	George Wambach	Maregaret Mulligan
Wells	Joseph		22-Mar-1911	25-Nov-1910	Bluchen, Amelia	John W. Wells	Mary McLain
Wells/Lyle	Mary	Susann Virginia	19-Mar-1891	11-Feb-1833	Smith, Joan	William Wells	Mary McGuire
Welsh	William	Porter	22-Oct-1910	09-Feb-1865	Ballinger, Mary Helen	John Edward Welsh	Bella Boone
Welsh	Mary	Catherine	02-Feb-1890	26-Jan-1890	Casserly, Margaret	John Welsh	Julia Sullivan
Welsh	Michael		16-Apr-1899	21-Feb-1899	Casserly, Margaret	John Welsh	Mary C. Fallenstein
Welsh	Martin	Sylvester	16-Jan-1898	31-Dec-1897	Redmond, Barbara Mary	Martin Welsh	Catherine Murnane
Welsh	Michael	Paul	07-Feb-1897	23-Jan-1897	Redmond, Barbara	Martin Welsh	Joan Kimmett
Welsh	Joan	Elizabeth	03-Jun-1894	21-May-1894	Neethan, Helen	Patrick Welsh	Loretta Hopkins
Welsh	Joseph	Patrick	14-Apr-1889	27-Mar-1889	Needham, Eleanor	Patrick Welsh	Joan Kennedy
Welsh	Louise		28-Jun-1896	12-Jun-1896	Needham, Helen	Patrick Welsh	Elizabeth Jenkins
Welsh/Paston	Elizabeth		10-May-1897	14-Jul-1843	Gardner, Joan	John Paston	Helen Hammell
Wess	Bernard		04-Nov-1888	01-Nov-1888	Burns, Mary	Julia Wess	Helen Welsh
Wess	Mary		01-Oct-1893	21-Sep-1893	Burns, Mary	Julia Wess	Theresa Stengel
Wess	Margaret		23-Sep-1900	01-Sep-1900	Byrne, Mary	Julian Wess	Ann Burns
Wess	Margaret	Collette	14-Sep-1890	11-Sep-1890	Burns, Mary F.	Julio G. Wess	Margaret Boyce
Wess	Henry	Edward	05-Jan-1896	28-Dec-1895	[Blank]	Julio George Wess	Ann Meers
Wess	John		24-Apr-1898	17-Apr-1898	Burns, Mary	Julio Wess	Dora Wess
Wess	Joseph		21-Aug-1910	6-Aug-1910	Doyle, Catherine	Clarence West	Mary Wess
Wess	Paul		21-Sep-1902	30-Aug-1902	Northman, Elizabeth	Eugene P. West	Mary [Blank]
West	Eugene	Luke	20-Jan-1895	07-Jan-1895	Worthman, Amelia Elizabeth	Eugene Phillip West	Ann West
West	Albert	Stuart	20-Jul-1900	18-Jul-1900	Worthman, Amelia	Eugene West	Alice West
West	Raymond	Aloysius	07-Aug-1898	20-Jul-1898	[Blank], Anita	Eugene West	Catherine Steiner
West	William	Edward	13-Dec-1896	01-Dec-1896	Wordman, Amelia	Eugene West	Rebecca West
West	George	Adam	06-Aug-1893	30-Jul-1893	Kober, Margaret	George West	Gertrude West
West	Bernard		24-Sep-1882	16-Sep-1882	Dudley, Mary	Henry West	Mary Kober
West	Helen		02-Dec-1888	17-Nov-1888	Heavey, Mary J.	Isaac West	Helen Stock
Wetherstine	Charles		07-Aug-1887	24-Jul-1887	Siebold, Eileanor	Andrew Wetherstine	Catherine Warrs
Wetherstine	Elizabeth	Helen	08-Jul-1883	23-Jun-1883	Siebold, Helen	Andrew Wetherstine	Mary Meree
Wetherstine	Florence		19-Nov-1893	03-Nov-1893	Seebold, Ellen	Andrew Wetherstine	Caroline Siebold
Wetherstine	laura		06-Oct-1889	23-Sep-1889	Siebold, Eleanor	Andrew Wetherstine	Mary Zellers
Whaite	Constantine		13-Sep-1909	9-Nov-1909	Carraher, Mary	Edward Whaite	Ann Rhodes
Whalen	James	Martin	13-Nov-1892	04-Nov-1892	Gallagher, Mary Ann	Thomas Whalen	Mary Donoghue
Whalen	John	Joseph	24-Apr-1887	05-Apr-1887	Gallagher, Mary Ann	Thomas Whalen	Elizabeth Cassidy
Whalen	Margaret	Joan	14-Oct-1894	04-Oct-1894	Gallagher, Mary Ann	Thomas Whalen	John Gallagher
Whalen	Catherine		12-Jul-1891	01-Jul-1891	Gallagher, Mary Ann	Thomas Whalen	Edward Gallagher
Whalen	Catherine	Mary	08-Nov-1885	02-Nov-1885	Conroy, Nora	James Whalen	Michael Cassidy
Whalen	James	Edward	29-Jun-1884	22-Jun-1884	Conroy, Honora Agnes	James Whalen	James Riordan
Whalen	Howard	Jerome	03-Aug-1890	27-Jul-1890	McKenna, Mary	Joseph H. Whalen	Timothy Riordan
Whalen	Mary		25-Feb-1894	19-Feb-1894	McKenna, Mary Elizabeth	Joseph Henry Whelan	John McKenna
Whalen	Catherine		23-Sep-1900	17-Sep-1900	McKenna, Mary	Joseph Whelan	Francis McKenna
Whalen	Helen		24-Apr-1898	19-Apr-1898	McKenna, Mary	Joseph Whelan	Francis Kelly
Whelan	Margaret	Mary	03-May-1896	01-May-1896	McKenna, Mary	Joseph Whelan	Charles Kelly
Whelan	George		25-Jul-1897	13-Jul-1896	[Blank], Margaret	Patrick Whelan	Francis McKenna
Whelan	Mary		28-Jan-1883	15-Jan-1883	Gallagher, Mary Ann	Thomas Whelan	Louise Kearney
Whelan	Thomas		03-Feb-1889	23-Jan-1889	Gallagher, Mary Ann	Thomas Whelan	Henry Byrne
Whetenburg	Helen	Mary	23-May-1915	6-May-1909	Halfpenny, Ida	John Whetenburg	John Mee
White	William	Murry	14-Dec-1913	1-Dec-1913	Buchanon, Helen	James White	James Dyer
White	John	Joseph	06-Sep-1896	August 1896	Patterson, Bridget	John Joseph White	Albert Harrigan
White	Catherine	E.	11-Jun-1899	25-May-1899	Patterson, Bridget	John White	William Buchanon
White	Laura		13-May-1882	24-Aug-1869	White, Elizabeth	John White	Matthew White
White	Margaret	Gertride	02-Dec-1900	10-Nov-1900	Patterson, Bridget	John White	Edward Bennett
							Catherine Dyer
							Isabelle Kennedy
							Catherine Linaghan
							Mary T. Buchanon
							Mary Patterson
							Ann White
							Catherine M. Morton
							Mary Clarke
							Thomas Cavanaugh

LAST NAME	FIRST NAME	MIDDLE	BIRTH	BAPTISM	Father	Mother	SPONSORS
White	Mary	Ann	30-Dec-1897	16-Jan-1898	John White	Patterson, Bridget	Catherine White
White	Honora	Matilda	1-Jun-1907	16-Jun-1907	Martin J. White	Kavanaugh, Hannah	Matilda Donnelly
White	Thomas	Francis	23-Aug-1901	08-Sep-1901	Martin J. White	Cavanaugh, Nora	Catherine Roddy
White	Martin	Joseph	20-Sep-1902	05-Oct-1902	Martin Joseph White	Kavanaugh, Nora	John White
White	Catherine	Agnes	1-Mar-1904	13-Mar-1904	Martin White	Cavanaugh, Nora	Matthew White
White	Mary	Eugene	06-Oct-1899	22-Oct-1899	Martin White	Garvey, Delia	James McNamara
White	E. Margaret	B.	24-Sep-1905	8-Oct-1905	Martin White	Kavanaugh, Honora	Mayland Garvey
White	Mary		10-Sep-1904	18-Sep-1904	Matthew J. White	Garvey, Delia E.	Michael Garvey
White	Agnes	Lillian	5-Sep-1908	13-Sep-1908	Matthew White	Garvey, Delia	John White
White	Gwendolyn	Bridget	23-Feb-1912	3-Mar-1912	Matthew White	Garvey, Bridget	Francis McNamara
White	Lillian	Ann	10-Sep-1902	21-Sep-1902	Matthew White	Garvey, Delia	Michael Sweeney
White	Margaret	Kathleen	11-Jul-1901	28-Jul-1901	Matthew White	Garvey, Delia	John White
White	Matthew		24-Apr-1906	6-May-1906	Matthew White	Garvey, Delia	Thomas Crocker
White	Thomas	Gordon	13-Nov-1913	30-Nov-1913	Matthew White	Garvey, Bridget	Charles Dolan
White	Eleanor	Elizabeth	18-Oct-1914	1-Nov-1914	Michael White	Murphy, Cecelia	Margaret McCabe
White	Mary		26-Jan-1896	09-Feb-1896	Robert White	Ryan, Helen	Ann White
White	Mary	Eleanor	23-Aug-1886	05-Sep-1886	William H.H. White	McManus, Catherine	Eleanor McManus
White/Labby	Margaret	Elizabeth Ann	28-Mar-1820	27-Feb-1892	John White	Pierce, Elizabeth	Margaret Worthington
Whitman	Bertha	Helen	18-Dec-1888	13-Jan-1889	Charles Edward Whitman	Bacon, Helen Teresa	Mary Agnes Bacon
Whitney	Elizabeth		17-Jun-1883	01-Jul-1883	Francis Whitney	Boone, Margaret	Catherine Woods
Whitney	Estelle		28-Oct-1885	08-Nov-1885	Francis Whitney	Boen, Ann M.	Mary Young
Whitney	Margaret		12-Apr-1882	13-Apr-1882	Francis Whitney	Boone, Margaret	Mary Campbell
Whitney	James	Francis	15-Jan-1888	29-Jan-1888	Francis William Whitney	Bahn, Margaret	Mary Helen Whitney
Whitney	Grace		23-Aug-1892	04-Sep-1892	Henry Whitney	Christ, Margaret	Helen O'Brien
Whitney	Henry	Leon	06-Feb-1890	16-Feb-1890	Henry Whitney	Christ, Margaret	Cormac Finnegan
Whitney	James	Edward	25-Oct-1883	18-Nov-1883	Henry Whitney	Christ, Margaret	Joseph Bernard Whitney
Whitney	John	Lawson	03-Oct-1886	17-Oct-1886	Henry Whitney	Christ, Margaret	Edward C. Lawson
Whitney	William	Wagner	17-Oct-1909	7-Nov-1909	William Whittie	Wagner, Eva	Ellen Elizabeth Whittie
Whittington	Agnes	Estelle	04-Jul-1896	23-Aug-1896	Francis Whittington	Bagwell, Catherine	Regina Connelly
Whittle	Susan	Mary	13-May-1857	25-Jan-1903	John Russell	Russell, Mary	
Whittle	Charles	Leon	12-Jul-1887	7-Feb-1909	Thomas H. Whittle	Russell, Susanna	Andrew O'Brien
Whittle	Helen	J.	18-Sep-1886	17-Oct-1886	Thomas Stockton Whittle	O'Brien, Delia	Patrick J. Donahue
Whitty	Alice	Josephine	20-Mar-1897	11-Apr-1897	John Whitty	O'Neal, Mary	Edward O'Connor
Whitty	Catherine	Josephine	03-Mar-1895	10-Mar-1895	John Whitty	Reddy, Catherine	Joseph Kennedy
Whitty	James	Joseph	26-Apr-1897	09-May-1897	John Whitty	Reddy, Katherine	Thomas Reddy
Whitty	John	Walter	04-Mar-1888	18-Mar-1888	John Whitty	Reddy, Catherine	John Reddy
Whitty	John	Walter	10-Nov-1889	10-Nov-1889	John Whitty	Reddy, Catherine	Mary Mallon
Whitty	John	walter	31-Jul-1882	20-Aug-1882	John Whitty	Ready, Kate	Mary Malloy
Whitty	John		02-Jul-1901	20-Aug-1901	John Whitty	O'Brien, Clara	Katherine O'Neil
Whitty	Mary		31-May-1893	11-Jun-1893	John Whitty	Reddy, Catherine	Agnes Kennedy
Whitty	John		19-Nov-1900	02-Dec-1900	Walter Whitty	Kennedy, Catherine	Walter Whitty
Whitty	Mary	Jilia	08-Dec-1894	23-Dec-1894	Walter Whitty	Kennedy, Catherine	John Whitty
Whitty	Agnes	Virginia	27-Oct-1895	17-Nov-1895	William Whitty	O'Neal, Mary	William Whitty
Whitty	Ann	Laura	21-Aug-1893	03-Sep-1893	William Whitty	O'Neill, Ellen	John O'Neill
Whitty	Catherine	Cecilia	26-Feb-1889	10-Mar-1889	William Whitty	O'Neill, Mary Helen	James McCaffrey
Whitty	Helen		31-Jul-1882	20-Aug-1882	William Whitty	Connor, Marys	Sinnott, Mary
Whitty	John	Edward	24-Feb-1891	15-Mar-1891	William Whitty	O'Neill, Mary	Patrick McCafferty
Whitty	Joseph	Walter	13-Mar-1899	02-Apr-1899	William Whitty	O'Neill, Mary	Edward McGuire
Whitty	Joseph	W.	13-Apr-1899	30-Apr-1899	William Whitty	O'Neill, Mary	Edward McGuire
Whitty	Mary	Julia	27-Feb-1887	13-Mar-1887	William Whitty	O'Neill, Mary	Hugh O'Neill
Whitty	Theresa		25-Dec-1898	08-Jan-1899	William Whitty	Kennedy, Catherine	Thomas Holden
Whitty	William		04-May-1896	17-May-1896	William Whitty	O'Reilly, Mary	Edward Neville
Wicks	Helen	William	10-Dec-1896	27-Dec-1896	Charles Wicks	Reilly, Mary Frances	Robert O'Reilly
Wicks	Charles	William	6-Aug-1904	11-Sep-1904	Charles William Wicks	Reilly, Mary Frances	William E. Reilly
Wicks	Wilbur	Laurence	15-Jun-1894	01-Jul-1894	William Wicks	Reilly, Mary	Samuel Bateman
Widman	Eleanore		24-May-1907	2-Jun-1907	George Widman	Baker, Ann	Martin Baker
Widman	George	William	9-Dec-1905	17-Dec-1905	George Widman	Baker, Ann	Thomas Baker
Wiedefeld	Edward		15-Oct-1896	25-Oct-1896	Francis Wiedefeld	Lannon, Catherine	James Lannan
Wiedefeld	Henry		9-Jan-1904	10-Jan-1904	Francis Wiedefeld	Lannon, Catherine	Mary Rosensteel
Wiedefeld	Mary	Elizabeth	22-Oct-1898	16-Oct-1898	Francis Wiedefeld	Lannon, Katherine	James Wiedefeld
Wiedefeld	Margaret	Theresa	28-Jan-1887	06-Feb-1887	Henry C. Wiedefeld	Burgan, Debora L.	Robecca E. Rosensteel
Wiedefeld	Louis		03-May-1882	07-May-1882	Henry Charles Wiedefeld	Burgan, Debra Louise	John Thomas Broderick
Wiedefeld	Charles		09-Jan-1883	13-Jan-1884	Henry Wiedefeld	Burgan, Louise	William Wiedefeld

LAST NAME	FIRST NAME	MIDDLE	BAPTISM	BIRTH	Father	Mother	SPONSORS
Wiedefeld	Henry	Charles	24-Nov-1898	19-Nov-1898	Henry Wiedefeld	Sullivan, Margaret	George Devine	Helen Wiedefeld
Wiedefeld	Margaret		28-Feb-1900	28-Feb-1900	Henry Wiedefeld	Sullivan, Margaret		Mary Agnes Sullivan
Wiesman	John		08-Feb-1898	20-Jan-1898	John Weisman	[Blank]	P.H. Lanahan	Julia Lyman
Wigard	Frederick	Bascom	02-Aug-1883	12-Jul-1883	Henry M. Wigard	Raborg, Emma Catherine		Alice Raborg
Wigart	Plinia	Earl	06-Oct-1889	16-Nov-1859	Henry Bascom Wigart	Wallace, Mary Catherine	George Edward Adams	
Wigart	Henry	May	04-Mar-1888	11-Dec-1887	Henry Mary Wigart	Rayborg, Emma C.		Alice Rayborg
Wigart	Francis	Earle	02-Jan-1888	28-Dec-1887	Plinio Earle Wigart	Adams, Clara Josephine	George Edward Adams	Mary Berbis
Wigfield	Mary	Elizabeth	4-Nov-1906	18-Oct-1906	E. Wigfield	Powers, Ann		Elizabeth Steward
Wilback (Hall)	Susan	Mary	22-May-1883	28-Mar-1844	Jefferson Hall	Shackleford, Priscilla		Bridget Sinnott
Wilcox	Joseph	Register	26-Jul-1886	05-Jul-1886	Samuel Register Wilcox	Coleman, Ann Teresa		Martha Coleman
Wildon	Charles	Arthur	12-Aug-1888	16-Jul-1888	Peter Wilson	Lawson, Mary G.	Michael Duland	Eleanor Napier
Wilds	Mary	Ethel	14-Mar-1886	08-Mar-1886	Aloysius C. Wild	Strible, Mary A.		Mary A. Strible
Wilds	Louis		22-Oct-1882	28-Sep-1882	Louis Clay Wilds	Stable, Mary Agnes	Thomas C. Bowers	Jeanette S. Stable
Wiley	Mary	Agnes	18-Jun-1882	05-Jun-1882	James B. Wiley	Dignan, Sara	John Griffin	Mary O'Connor
Wiley	James	Wilson	16-Jan-1887	02-Jan-1887	James Benedict Wiley	Kress, Laura Virginia	Albert Gildes Adams	Mary Florence Graham
Wiley	Joseph		23-Feb-1890	05-Feb-1890	Joseph B. Wiley	Kress, Virginia		
Wilhelm	Mary	Genevieve	07-Jun-1896	31-May-1896	Edgar K. Wilhelm	McGeeney, Mary	Margaret McGeeney	Joseph McGeeney
Wilhelm	Joseph	Leo	17-Jul-1898	13-Jul-1898	Edgar Wilhelm	McGinn, Maryey	James W. Hamilton	Julia Baker
Wilkenning	John	Harmon	15-Dec-1894	11-Jul-1850	Christian Gottlieb Wilkenning	Grotte, Catherine		James McDevitt
Williams	Elizabeth	Teresa	7-Sep-1913	22-Aug-1913	George B. Williams	Schucher, Teresa	Francis Taylor	Elizabeth Taylor
Williams	Edward	V.	1-Jan-1905	15-Dec-1904	Henry E. Williams	Kerns, Mona	James J. Kelly	Ann Delaney
Williams	Mary	Ellen	5-Sep-1915	24-Aug-1915	Henry E. Williams	Kern, Honora	John F. Dugan	Ann Delaney
Williams	Charles	Henry	27-Sep-1908	1-Mar-1908	John A. Williams	Williams, Carrie E.	J. Edward Williams	
Williams	Mary	B.	21-Jan-1906	29-Nov-1905	John A. Williams	Garry, Carrie E.		Catherine Mooney
Williams	Catherine		06-Jul-1884	30-Jun-1884	Richard Williams	Sinnott, Mary	Marcus Sinnott	Ann Sinnott
Williams	Richard		25-Dec-1892	19-Dec-1892	Richard Williams	Sinnott, Mary	Matthew Williams	Margaret Sinnott
Williams	William	Victor	08-Sep-1893	21-May-1869	Victor Williams	Corman, Susann	John Silvester McKenna	
Williams	Jesse	Edward	4-Oct-1904	07-Mar-1843	William H. Williams	Durham, Elizabeth	John McShane	
Williams	Margaret		04-Jun-1892	02-Apr-1870	William Williams	Ferguson, Elizabeth		Mary Ratty
Williams	William	Francis	18-Aug-1895	08-Feb-1895	William Williams	Gilley, Ella	Francis Lofsky	Ann Kemmett
Willis	Joseph		22-Mar-1909	24-Feb-1909	Charles Willis	Conway, Mary		Sara Stewart
Willis	Agnes		8-Jul-1909	8-Jul-1909	Edward J. Willis	[Blank] Mary		
Willis	Regina	Mary	14-Dec-1906	7-Dec-1906	Edward John Willis	Friedel, Mary Ann		
Willis	Edward	William	10-Sep-1899	02-Sep-1899	Edward Miller	Friedeal, Mary	Frederick Myers	Mary Hutton
Willis	Charles		10-Nov-1912	9-Oct-1912	Francis Willis	Glossner, Ann C.		Ellen O'Brien
Willis	David		19-Jan-1913	3-Jun-1908	Francis Willis	Glosner, Ann	John Tierney	Elizabeth Quinn
Willis	Emma	Cecelia	5-Jul-1914	5-Jun-1914	Francis Willis	Glosner, Ann	William Young	Frances Auton
Willis	Ferdinand	S.	19-Jan-1913	29-Oct-1907	Hugh Willis	Finn, Ann	Henry Wiedefeld	Rose Price
Willis	Mary	Agnes	29-Dec-1884	14-Dec-1884	William Williams	Finn, Ann		Ann Lally
Willis	Robert		25-Mar-1888	13-Mar-1888	Hugh Willis	Finn, Ann	John Finn	Sara Corrigan
Willis	Agnes		19-Dec-1897	23-Nov-1897	William Willis	Cunningham, Barbara	Michael Kelly	Mary Smith
Willis	Jerome		18-Aug-1901	08-Aug-1901	William Willis	Cunningham, Barbara		Ann Roach
Willis	Michael		18-Oct-1896	02-Oct-1896	William Willis	Cunningham, Barbara	Michael Vallie	Ann [Blank]
Willis	Robert		18-Aug-1901	08-Aug-1901	William Williams	Cunningham, Barbara	Hugh Willis	Mary Willis
Williams/Nelson	Sara		29-May-1891	08-Aug-1803	William Williams	Demby, Amelia		
Wilson	Edward	Neville	10-Feb-1901	26-Jan-1901	Edward Carter Wilson	Murray, Ann	Thomas Murray	Mary Murray
Wilson	Jerome	Emory	22-Jan-1905	4-Jan-1905	Edward Lyman Wilson	Murray, Ann G.	John A. Murray	Lillian M. Wilson
Wilson	Ann	Genevieve	19-Oct-1902	04-Oct-1902	Edward Wilson	Murray, Ann	Edward Murray	Mary Wilson
Wilson	George	Charles	12-Oct-1884	26-Sep-1884	George W. Wilson	Naughton, Mary	George L. Gold	Matilda Clarke
Wilson	Joseph		13-Feb-1898	07-Feb-1898	George W. Wilson	Norton, Mary Elizabeth	John McCarthy	Ann McCarthy
Wilson	Anna		08-Jan-1882	02-Jan-1882	George Wilson	Norton, Mary	John Roddy	Catherine Kearney
Wilson	Henry		25-Feb-1883	17-Feb-1883	George Wilson	Norton, Mary	Joseph Parr	Mary Fannon
Wilson	Walter		14-Apr-1895	08-Apr-1895	George Wilson	Norton, Mary	John James Wright	Mary Clark
Wilson	Cecelia	Violet	23-Sep-1900	06-Sep-1900	Greenbury Wilson	Cullen, Mary	Arthur Mullen	Ann Houck
Wilson	Rose		23-Sep-1900	06-Sep-1900	Greenbury Wilson	Cullen, Mary	Arthur Mullen	Ann Houck
Wilson	Mary	Alice	01-Mar-1891	13-Feb-1891	Grenbury Wilson	Cullen, Mary C.	Joseph G. Hintensoh	Ann A. McGee
Wilson	Mary	G.	19-Mar-1905	3-Mar-1905	Henry M. Wilson	Ruckle, Ann M.	James Wright	Naomi Dunn
Wilson	Catherine	Adalaide	1-Apr-1906	22-Mar-1906	Henry Wilson	Ruckle, Ann	George A. Wilson	Helen Dann
Wilson	Edmund	Francis	11-Nov-1906	20-Oct-1906	Howard L. Wilson	Hies, Carrie E.	Charles Zellers	Margaret Zellers
Wilson	Joan	S.	14-Dec-1902	21-Nov-1902	Howard L. Wilson	Heise, Carrie	John Radivitch	Rolenta Janson
Wilson	M. Genevieve		29-Aug-1897	09-Aug-1897	Howard L. Wilson	Heiss, Clara	James Wilson	Ann Wilson
Wilson	John	Harold	10-Jul-1910	19-Jun-1910	Howard Wilson	Heise, Carolina	John Lurz	Catherine Lurz
Wilson	Charles	Greenbury	26-Jun-1887	12-Jun-1887	James G. Wilson	Cullen, Mary	Charles Cullen	Elizabeth Rupert

ST JOHN'S BAPTISMS 1882-1912

LAST NAME	FIRST NAME	MIDDLE	BAPTISM	BIRTH	Father	Mother	SPONSORS
Wilson	James	William	12-May-1889	29-Apr-1889	James Greenbury Wilson	Cullen, Mary	Francis P. Ragan	Mary Ragan
Wilson	James	Leon	13-Jul-1909	12-Jul-1909	James Leon Wilson	Murray, Margaret	William Kessler	Mary [Blank]
Wilson	Mabel	Regina	28-Jun-1883	07-Jun-1880	James S. Wilson	Gettle, Lena	Henry Wilson	Koan Wilson
Wilson	Ann		28-Feb-1886	11-Feb-1886	John Greenbury Wilson	[Blank]	Robert Schroeder	Ann Dustenhames
Wilson	Mary	Alphonsa	11-Nov-1894	30-Oct-1894	John Greenbury Wilson	Cullen, Mary Catherine		Ann Mary Houck
Wilson	John	James	18-Jun-1882	08-Jun-1882	John James Wilson	Rose, Mary Helen	Laurence Cotter	B. Connor
Wilson	Mary	Bertha	16-Oct-1887	24-Sep-1887	John Oliver Wilson	Burgenstock, Bertha	Martin McManus	Ida Elmore
Wilson	Theresa	Mary	06-Oct-1889	21-Sep-1889	John R. Wilson	Burgenstock, Bertha	James B. Reardon	Mary E. Wilson
Wilson	Faye	Helen	05-Feb-1882	09-Dec-1881	John Ward Wilson	Scott, Florence E.		Adeline Kenny
Wilson	Ann	Joan	27-Feb-1887	10-Feb-1887	John Wilson	Rose, Helen B.	Joseph Bernard Finnan	Mary Ann Donegan
Wilson	John	Samuel	03-Apr-1892	16-Mar-1892	John Wilson	Burgenstock, Bertha	John Kelly	Mary Burns
Wilson	Robert		24-Dec-1899	14-Nov-1899	N. Wilson	Heise, Clara Elizabeth	Charles O'Hara	Jenna Wilson
Wilson	Mary		30-Aug-1891	19-Aug-1891	Thomas Collison	Connor, Delia	William Rowland	Sara Kearney
Wilson	Thomas	Bernard	17-Jul-1898	03-Jul-1898	Thomas Wilson	Mitchell, Emma Perpetua		Clara Mitchell
Wilson	Bridget	Mary	12-Jun-1887	26-May-1887	William Wilson	Porter, Ada	Francis Thomas Lynch	Margaret Fallon
Wilzbacher	Bernard	Martin	17-Mar-1895	13-Feb-1895	Edward Martin Wilzbacher	Sickels, Mary Patricia	William S. Mooney	Helen Wilzbacher
Wilzbacher	Edward	Martin	01-May-1892	11-Apr-1892	Edward Martin Wilzbacher	Sickels, Mary	George Hamilton	Helen Wilzbacher
Wind/Bracken	Ann	Wind	11-Nov-1904	23-Dec-1874	Frederick Wind	Wind, Carolina		Ann Curtis
Wingate	Joseph	Raymond	14-Jun-1896	29-May-1896	William Wingate	Connolly, Catherine	William Bavis	Alice Bavis
Winn	Edward	Cleveland	01-Mar-1885	14-Feb-1885	Patrick Winn	Hanson, Ellen	John Burns	Mary Burns
Winn	Helen	Gertrude	04-Mar-1894	22-Feb-1894	Patrick Winn	Hanson, Ellen	William Cunane	Mary Cunane
Winn	James		13-Nov-1887	31-Oct-1887	Patrick Winn	Hanson, Eleanor		Mary Cunane
Winn	Francis		15-May-1898	30-Apr-1898	Thomas Winn	Detrich, Margaret	Francis Detrich	Teresa Detrich
Winn	Charles	Edward	25-Feb-1906	4-Feb-1906	William H. Winn	Wolseley, Mary		Ann Winn
Winn	Edward		18-Aug-1912	8-Aug-1912	William Winn	Woolsey, Mary	Edward Winn	Grace Russell
Winn	William		27-Nov-1904	30-Oct-1904	William Winn	Wolsey, Mary		Mary Talbert
Winterling	Nadina	Veronica	31-Oct-1915	9-Oct-1915	Frederick Winterling	McGanny, Catherine	John Barry	Mary McGanny
Winters	Mary	L. Stella	08-Jan-1885	10-Jan-1883	Austin Winters	Kenny, Mary	Pete Welden	Caroline Dellone
Wise	Mary	Catherine	15-Mar-1896	10-Mar-1896	August Dellone	Dellone, Ida	William Dellone	Henrietta Dellone
Wise	Regina	Angela	27-Jun-1897	20-Jun-1897	August Wise	Dellone, Ida	William Dellone	Katie Collins
Wise	Catherine	Regina	25-Mar-1884	27-Feb-1884	Jacob P. Wise	Kearns, Mary Ann	Joseph Carroll	Ann Kimmett
Wise	Ida	Cecelia	08-Nov-1891	23-Oct-1891	Phillip Wise	Vergena, Laura		Ellen Kirby
Wiseman	Mary	A.	25-Aug-1895	25-Jul-1895	John V. Wiseman	Wilson, Ann	William Wiseman	Mary Witte
Witte	Helen	Loretta	27-Apr-1902	05-Apr-1902	William Witte	O'Neill, Mary	Francis Witte	Agnes Mitchell
Wittich	James	George	4-Oct-1914	26-Sep-1914	Charles Wittich	Hand, Frances J.	James R. Mitchell	Ann Finerty
Witty	William		05-Mar-1885	27-Feb-1885	William Witty	Conners, Mary		Sadie Riley
Wodeyhand	James	Riley	19-Feb-1911	25-Jan-1911	James Wodyhand	Riley, Evelyn M.	Francis P. Flaherty	Roxe R. Wolf
Wolf	Irene	Rose	17-Dec-1906	8-Dec-1906	Edward J. Wolf	Hubler, Margaret A.	Joseph Wolf	Susan Wolf
Wolf	John	Francis	20-Dec-1891	12-Dec-1891	Ernest Wolf	Engelbach, Mary	Joseph Lacey	
Wolfe	George	A.	28-Oct-1909	07-Nov-1898	[Blank]	[Blank]		Grace Conroy
Wolfe	Mildred	Mary	27-Jun-1901	25-May-1901	Henry Wood	[Blank], Mary		Eleanor Stealy
Wolfe	George	Albert	21-Feb-1915	3-Feb-1915	Edward Wolfe	Hubbel, Margaret	Michael McCabe	Catherine Miller
Wolfe	Joseph	Leonard	9-Apr-1911	26-Mar-1911	George Albert Wolfe	Halpin, Alice	Martin Walters	Mary A. Halpin
Wolff	Emma	Elizabeth	15-Nov-1908	6-Nov-1908	George Albert Wolfe	Halpin, Alice Mary	John E. Rochford	Frances Rockfort
Wolsey	Charles		29-Mar-1912	26-Oct-1911	Charles Wolff	Karle, Amelia	Joseph Sandman	Margaret Wall
Wood	Mary		07-Aug-1887	27-Jul-1887	Charles Wolsey	Dunn, Bridget		Ann Wolsey
Wooden	Ann	Margaret	27-Jun-1901					
Wooden	Eleanor	Catherine	18-Dec-1892	01-Dec-1892	Michael S. Wooden	Walters, Mary Loretta	Michael McCabe	Catherine V. McGarry
Wooden	Joseph	Loretta	14-Jun-1891	24-May-1891	Michael Stephen Wooden	Walters, Mary Loretta	Roger Kenny	Mary McCarthy
Wooden	Michael	Stephen	23-Jul-1889	08-Jul-1889	Michael Stephen Wooden	Kenny, Catherine Mary	Thomas Kenny	Margaret Ward
Wooden	William		30-Dec-1911	26-Dec-1911	Stephen H. Wooden	Brown, Mary C.	John Healy	Catherine Nolan
Wooden	Catherine	Veronica	30-Apr-1892	18-Apr-1892	Stephen H. Wooden	May, Mary Ellen	Michael Malone	Isabelle Quinn
Wooden	Clinton	Gregory	18-Dec-1892	01-Dec-1892	Thomas Cass Wooden	Kenny, Catherine	Thomas Kenny	Mary Thomas
Wooden	Florence	Mary	14-Jun-1891	24-May-1891	Thomas Cass Wooden	Kenny, Catherine		Mary Murray
Wooden	Helen	Gertrude	23-Jul-1889	08-Jul-1889	Thomas Cass Wooden	Kenny, Catherine Mary		Mary Donahue
Wooden	Francis	K.	30-Dec-1911	26-Dec-1911	Thomas L. Wooden	Brown, Mary C.	Thomas Kenny	Catherine Nolan
Wooden	Regina		25-Apr-1886	01-Apr-1886	Thomas Wooden	Kenny, Catherine	James Quinn	Isabelle Quinn
Wooden	Roger	Kenny	30-May-1915	2-May-1915	Thomas Wooden	Brown, Mary	Thomas Kenny	Mary Thomas
Wooden	Thomas	Lee	22-Jan-1899	04-Jan-1899	Thomas Wooden	Kenny, Catherine	Thomas Kenny	Mary McCarthy
Wooden	Virginia	Leon	27-Jan-1884	30-Dec-1883	Thomas Wooden	Kenny, Catherine	William Quinn	Catherine McCarthy
Woods	James	Agnes	19-Jan-1913	31-Dec-1912	Thomas Wooden	Brown, Mary	Thomas Kenny	Mary Elliott
Woods	Mary	Patrick	18-Jan-1914	7-Jan-1914	William Wooden	O'Connor, Rose	Thomas McGraw	Agnes O'Connor
Woods		Agnes	24-Dec-1882	09-Dec-1882	Edward Woods	McGraw, Catherine	Joseph MiSkelly	Sara McGraw
Woods			16-Aug-1885	01-Aug-1885	Edward Woods	McGraw, Catherine	Peter Connelly	Jennie Buntz

142

LAST NAME	FIRST NAME	MIDDLE	BAPTISM	BIRTH	Father	Mother	SPONSORS	
Woods	William	Peter	08-Jun-1884	22-May-1884	Edward Woods	McGraw, Catherine	William J. Kearney	Eliza Rooney
Woods	Annette		24-Apr-1887	18-Apr-1887	Francis Woods	Bolman, Catherine	Andrew Parr	Catherine Flannigan
Woods	Mary	Catherine	25-Apr-1885	18-Apr-1885	Francis Woods	Bolman, Catherine	Michael Curtin	Sophia Parr
Woods	James	Edward	15-May-1904	30-Apr-1904	James P. Woods	Lyons, Katherine	Edward L. Woods	Katherine E. Woods
Woods	Joseph	Scott	22-Jul-1894	11-Jul-1894	James Patrick Woods	Hanley, Ann	William Hanlon	Delia Wright
Woods	Evelyn		13-Oct-1895	27-Sep-1895	James Woods	Hanlon, Ann	Patrick Woods	Catherine Hanlon
Woods	Mildred	Ann	12-Nov-1899	26-Oct-1899	James Woods	Hanlon, Ann	John Hanlon	Mary Moylan
Woods	Rosyln	Mary	22-Sep-1901	11-Sep-1901	James Woods	Hanlon, Ann	Michael Hanlon	Ann Hickey
Woods	William	Francis	23-Jan-1902	10-Jan-1902	James Woods	Lyons, Catherine		Elizabeth Bruning
Woody	John	Joseph	19-Sep-1883	20-Jul-1883	John D. Woody	Davidson, Margaret Ann		Mary Regina Mooney
Woody	Sara	Magdalene	14-Oct-1882	25-Jun-1881	John D. Woody	Davidson, Margaret Ann		Ann Davidson
Woody	William	George	13-Apr-1886	05-Nov-1886	John D. Woody	Davidson, Margaret		Thesa Brink
Woolyhand	John	LeRoy	23-Jun-1912	29-May-1912	James Woolyhand	Riley, Mary	John Fagan	Mary [Blank]
Workman	James	Gordon	17-Jun-1904	17-Jun-1904	George H. Workman	Murray, Ann	George A. Adair	Jessie Doudiken
Wormstick	Henry	August	28-Oct-1898	07-Feb-1827	Zachariah Wormstick	Weis, Mary	George Stemple	
Worthington	James	Louis	11-Aug-1892	05-Aug-1892	Patrick George Worthington	Zink, Mary Antoinette	Louis Zink	Frances Zink
Worthington	Charles	William	11-Oct-1896	29-Sep-1896	Thomas Worthington	Lanahan, Mary	John Keleher	Catherine Murphy
Worthington	Margaret		25-Sep-1887	17-Sep-1887	Thomas Worthington	Lanaghan, Mary	Henry Worthington	Rose Worthington
Wortman	Henry	Leon	11-Nov-1906	30-Oct-1906	Henry Wortman	Murray, Ann	Charles McKenna	Mary Conroy
Wortman	William	Paul	15-Nov-1908	29-Oct-1908	Henry Wortman	Murray, Ann	James McKenna	Emma Raborg
Wright	Clarence	Herbert	06-Jul-1884	27-May-1884	Bradford Henry Wright	Woodburn , Edith		Mary Anthony
Wright	Charles	Louis	20-Feb-1910	26-Jan-1910	Charles Wright	Kane, Ann	Louis Burrier	Mary Sayles
Wright	August	S.	6-Aug-1905	22-Jun-1905	Edward August Wright	Smith, Louise		Sarah Scarboro
Wright	Charles	Edward	15-May-1902	11-Feb-1902	Edward August Wright	Smith, Louise		Elizabeth Scarborough
Wright	Henry		19-Jul-1903	03-Jul-1903	Edward Wright	Smith, Mary		Elizabeth Scarborough
Wright	Catherine	Foster	05-Feb-1888	19-Nov-1887	George H. Wright	Roundtree, Catherine M.		Rebecca Roundtree
Wright	Margaret	Rebecca	18-Oct-1885	03-Sep-1885	George H. Wright	Roundtree, Catherine		Rebecca Roundtree
Wright	Mary	Elizabeth	15-Jul-1883	12-Jun-1883	George H. Wright	Roundtree, Catherine		Rebecca Roundtree
Wright	Robert	Rennert	25-Jan-1891	15-Dec-1890	George H. Wright	Roundtree, Catherine M.		Rebecca Roundtree
Wright	Richard	Leo	30-Sep-1894	10-Sep-1894	George Hynes Wright	Roundtree, Catherine Martha		Rebecca Roundtree
Wright	Margaret	Cecelia	16-Oct-1904	6-Oct-1904	Henry E. Wright	Hogan, Mary	Andrew M. Giblin	Catherine Wright
Wright	Mary	Jane	26-Aug-1906	15-Aug-1906	Henry E. Wright	Hogan, Mary		Isabelle Gill
Wright	Francis	Earl	19-Mar-1911	4-Mar-1911	Henry Edwin Wright	Hogan, Mary Isabelle	Thomas Brockmeyer	Rose Magdalene Reilly
Wright	Charles		19-Jul-1885	02-Jul-1885	Henry Wright	Herron, Caroline (Carrie)	Lee Herron	Mary Brazier
Wright	Helen		08-Jan-1888	28-Dec-1887	Henry Wright	Herron, Caroline	Peter James Jarron	Mary Maguire
Wright	Henry	Frederick	13-Jan-1889	05-Jan-1889	Henry Wright	Herron, Caroline	James Mullen	Arthur Austin
Wright	John	Henry	24-Oct-1909	11-Oct-1909	Henry Wright	Hogan, Mary E.	Bernard J. Cronin	Margaret Dowd
Wright	Genevieve		09-Aug-1903	31-Jul-1903	James Gilbert Wright	Hess, Mary E.	Francis Hess	Genevieve Hess
Wright	Leo	Aloysius	10-Jun-1900	26-May-1900	James Gilbert Wright	Hess, Mary Helen	Leo Aloysius Hess	Bessie Kearney
Wright	James		24-Jul-1898	11-Jul-1895	James Gill Wright	Hess, Mary	William Gilbert	Agnes Hess
Wright	Ann	Mary	4-Aug-1907	26-Jul-1907	John J. Wright	Griffin, Mary T.	William F. Griffin	Teresa B. Griffin
Wright	John	Joseph	22-Nov-1908	15-Nov-1908	John J. Wright	Griffin, Mary	James Anderson	Mary Norton
Wright	Mary	Loretta	19-Jun-1910	6-Jun-1910	John James Wright	Griffin, Mary Theresa	James Wright	Mary McGreevey
Wright	John	Joseph	8-May-1910	16-Apr-1910	John Thomas Wright	Loughran, Elizabeth	Edward Clemsen	Lillian Viola Clemson
Wright	Francis	Xavier	11-May-1913	2-May-1913	John Wright	Griffin, Mary	James Griffin	Edna Anderson
Wright	James	Gibbons	14-Nov-1886	01-Nov-1886	John Wright	Norton, Ann	William Fannon	Matilda Clark
Wright	James	Patrick	17-Dec-1911	21-Nov-1911	John Wright	Laughlin, Bridget	Michael Hanlon	Ann Thomason
Wright	Mary	Elizabeth	10-Mar-1907	21-Feb-1907	John Wright	Loughran, Elizabeth	John Berney	Elizabeth Loughran
Wright	Thomas	Martin	12-Nov-1905	2-Nov-1905	John Wright	Loughran, Elizabeth	William Farrell	Mary Moylan
Wuller	John	Edward	18-Jun-1911	26-May-1911	Julian Wuller	Seigeldorf, Pauline	John Cassidy	Mary Kelly
Wuller	Walter	Albert	9-Nov-1913	26-Oct-1913	Julian Wuller	Seigeldorf, Helen	Adler Seigeldorf	Catherine Seigeldorf
Wyatt	Ann	Florence	13-Sep-1885	20-Aug-1885	Joseph E. Wyatt	Dobbin, Ann E.	James H. Anderson	Agnes Dobbin
Wyatt	Emma	Laura	19-May-1889	24-Apr-1889	Joseph E. Wyatt	Dobbin, Ann Elizabeth		Mary Elizabeth Anderson
Wyatt	Joseph	James	03-Feb-1891	27-Jan-1891	Joseph E. Wyatt	Dobbin, Ann E.		Agnes Dobbin
Wyatt	Francis	Edmund	10-Dec-1882	17-Nov-1882	Joseph Edwin Wyatt	Dobbin, Ann Elizabeth	James McDevitt	Ann Elizabeth Donovan
Wyatt	John	Walter	17-Apr-1892	26-Mar-1892	Joseph Edwin Wyatt	Dobbin, Ann Elizabeth	John Gallagher	Mary Gallagher
Wyatt	Joseph	James	08-Mar-1891	29-Jan-1891	Joseph Wyatt	Dobbin, Ann	James Dobbin	Agnes Dobbin
Wyatt	Mary	Katherine	04-Nov-1894	14-Oct-1894	Joseph Wyatt	Dobbin, Ann E.		Mary Heydrick
Wyman	Ann	Stella	16-Apr-1905	2-Apr-1905	Albert F. Wyman	Goe, Margaret	Robert Boyle	Ann Goe
Wyman	Charles	Alfred	13-Jan-1909	22-May-1909	Albert F. Wyman	Youe, Margaret	Owen P. Kelly	Mary A. Kelly
Wynn	Ann	Mary	07-Oct-1900	02-Sep-1900	James Wynn	Barrett, Delia	William Wynn	Sarah Wynn
Wynn	Ann		28-Sep-1890	12-Sep-1890	Patrick Wynn	Hanson, Helen	John Ward	Mary Snee
Wynn	Theresa	Mary	21-Jan-1900	06-Jan-1900	Thomas Wynn	Goodritch, Margaret	William Wynn	Theresa Goodritch

LAST NAME	FIRST NAME	MIDDLE	BAPTISM	BIRTH	Father	Mother	SPONSORS
Yakel	Edward	Howard	12-Feb-1888	04-Feb-1888	Andrew Yakel	Browning, Mary Isabelle	Margaret Schlase
Yakel	John	Stanley	13-Sep-1914	1-Sep-1914	John Yakel	Spence, Katherine	Mary Quirk
Yakel	Gertrude	Agnes	06-May-1888	12-Apr-1888	Louis Yakel	Kline, Sarah	Joseph Quirk
Yakel	Margaret	Alice	02-Jun-1895	15-May-1895	Louis Yakel	Cline, Sallie	George Kline
Yakel	William	Henry	18-Sep-1892	06-Sep-1892	Louis Yakel	Kline, Sara	Harry Cline
Yeakel	John	Stanley	15-Mar-1891	07-Mar-1891	Andrew Yeakel	Browning, Mary Isabelle	George Morwood
Yeakel	Mary	Isabelle	16-Feb-1896	05-Feb-1896	Andrew Yeakel	Browning, Mary Isabelle	Joseph McCaffrey
Yeakle	Joseph	Albert	07-Nov-1897	25-Oct-1897	Louis Yeakle	Kline, Sarah	Joseph Yeakel
Yeakle	Mary	Emelia	10-Aug-1890	20-Jul-1890	Louis Yeakle	Kline, Sara	Joseph Kelly
Yeakle	Louis	Albert	14-Jun-1900	09-Mar-1862	William Yeakle	Shuck, Louise	Michael Weldon
Yoe	Ann	Mary	07-Jul-1889	24-Jun-1889	Charles Yoe	Callahan, Catherine	Joseph Kelly
Young	Margaret		4-Sep-1904	20-Aug-1904	Albert J. Young	Murray, Catherine	James McAdam
Young	Charles	Rose	23-Jun-1902	20-Jun-1901	Edward Young	Crager, Josephine	Caroline Crager
Young	Henry		01-Feb-1897	About 1896	George William Young	Baer, Genevieve	Mary Mooney
Young	Joseph		8-Nov-1911	05-Jun-1878	George Young	Offenman, Elizabeth	A. Pahka
Young	Mary	Margaret	06-May-1900	January 1900	George Young	Bear, Genevieve	E.L. Devine
Young	James	Joseph	27-Aug-1911	18-Aug-1911	John Joseph Young	Burke, Mary Theresa	Louis Philips
Young	John		05-Jul-1883	04-Jul-1883	John Young	McNamara, Mary	Francis A. Burke
Young	George	Joseph	18-Nov-1900	3-Nov-1900	Joseph Young	Kennedy, Mary	Catherine Whitney
Young	Mary	Elizabeth	10-Aug-1902	18-Jul-1902	Joseph Young	Kennedy, Mary	Joseph Kennedy
Young	Robert	Francis	18-Feb-1892	27-Jan-1892	Samuel R. Young	Hearn, Ellen	Michael Kennedy
Young	Ann		12-Dec-1914	24-Nov-1869	William H. Young	Graham, Margaret	Catherine Hearn
Young	William	Nelson	26-Sep-1899	03-Aug-1898	William Young	Pattison, Clara	Elizabeth Adams
Younghelm	Sarah	Emelia	20-Aug-1893	06-Aug-1893	Frederik Youngheim	McGraw, Mary	John Rutter
Zeller	John	Henry	6-Sep-1914	27-Aug-1914	Henry Zeller	Mooney, Mercede	Sara Donahue
Zellers	Henry	Joseph	08-Oct-1882	02-Oct-1882	Francis Zellers	Harvey, Margaret	Simon Zeller
Zellers	Catherine	Francis	9-Feb-1908	9-Feb-1908	Henry L. Zellers	Kenney, Margaret	Henry Zellers
Zick	William	Conrad	7-Nov-1909	27-Oct-1909	William Conrad Zick	Kennelly, Ann Julia	Francis Zellers
Zimmerman	Charles	Leo	30-Oct-1898	08-Sep-1896	Benjamin Zimmerman	Berger, Ann	Mary J. Kennelly
Zimmerman	Henry	Donald	20-Feb-1896	21-Jan-1896	George F. Zimmerman	Fraser, Ann	Clara Catherine Hagan
Zimmerman	Mary		18-Nov-1898	01-Nov-1898	George Zimmerman	Frazer, Ann	Charles McCourt	Mary Rice
Zimmerman	George	Frederick	12-Dec-1893	10-Jul-1869	William H. Zimmerman	Garth, Mary Elizabeth	Stephen Bonetto

160